Texts and Monographs in Computer Science

Editors

David Gries
Fred B. Schneider

Advisory Board
F.L. Bauer
S.D. Brookes
C.E. Leiserson
M. Sipser

Texts and Monographs in Computer Science

Suad Alagic
Object-Oriented Database Programming
1989. XV, 320 pages, 84 illus.

Suad Alagic
Relational Database Technology
1986. XI, 259 pages, 114 illus.

Suad Alagic and Michael A. Arbib
The Design of Well-Structured and Correct Programs
1978. X, 292 pages, 68 illus.

S. Thomas Alexander
Adaptive Signal Processing: Theory and Applications
1986. IX, 179 pages, 42 illus.

Krzysztof R. Apt and Ernst-Rüdiger Olderog
Verification of Sequential and Concurrent Programs
1991. XVI, 441 pages

Michael A. Arbib, A.J. Kfoury, and Robert N. Moll
A Basis for Theoretical Computer Science
1981. VIII, 220 pages, 49 illus.

Friedrich L. Bauer and Hans Wössner
Algorithmic Language and Program Development
1982. XVI, 497 pages, 109 illus.

W. Bischofberger and G. Pomberger
Prototyping-Oriented Software Development: Concepts and Tools
1992. XI, 215 pages, 89 illus.

Ronald V. Book and Friedrich Otto
String-Rewriting Systems
1993. VII, 200 pages

Kaare Christian
A Guide to Modula-2
1986. XIX, 436 pages, 46 illus.

Edsger W. Dijkstra
Selected Writings on Computing: A Personal Perspective
1982. XVII, 362 pages, 13 illus.

(continued after index)

Algorithmic Algebra

Bhubaneswar Mishra

Springer-Verlag

New York Berlin Heidelberg London Paris
Tokyo Hong Kong Barcelona Budapest

Bhubaneswar Mishra
Courant Institute of Mathematical Sciences
New York University
New York, NY 10012
USA

Series Editors:

David Gries
Department of Computer Science
Cornell University
Upson Hall
Ithaca, NY 14853-7501
USA

Fred B. Schneider
Department of Computer Science
Cornell University
Upson Hall
Ithaca, NY 14853-7501
USA

With 9 Illustrations.

Library of Congress Cataloging-in-Publication Data
Mishra, Bhubaneswar, 1958-
    Algorithmic algebra / Bhubaneswar Mishra.
      p. cm. --(Texts and monographs in computer science)
    Includes bibliographical references and index.
    ISBN 0-387-94090-1.
    1. Algebra--Data processing I. Title. II. Series.
  QC155.7.E4M57 1993
  512'.00285--dc20   92-14094

Printed on acid-free paper.

Production managed by Christin R. Ciresi; manufacturing supervised by Jacqui Ashri.
Photocomposed copy prepared using the author's LaTeX files.
Printed and bound by Hamilton Printing Company, Rensselaer, NY.
Printed in the United States of America.

9 8 7 6 5 4 3 2 1

ISBN 0-387-94090-1 Springer-Verlag New York Berlin Heidelberg
ISBN 3-540-94090-1 Springer-Verlag Berlin Heidelberg New York

To my parents

Purna Chandra & Baidehi Mishra

Preface

In the fall of 1987, I taught a graduate computer science course entitled "Symbolic Computational Algebra" at New York University. A rough set of class-notes grew out of this class and evolved into the following final form at an excruciatingly slow pace over the last five years. This book also benefited from the comments and experience of several people, some of whom used the notes in various computer science and mathematics courses at Carnegie-Mellon, Cornell, Princeton and UC Berkeley.

The book is meant for graduate students with a training in theoretical computer science, who would like to either do research in computational algebra or understand the algorithmic underpinnings of various commercial symbolic computational systems: *Mathematica*, *Maple* or *Axiom*, for instance. Also, it is hoped that other researchers in the robotics, solid modeling, computational geometry and automated theorem proving communities will find it useful as symbolic algebraic techniques have begun to play an important role in these areas.

The main four topics—Gröbner bases, characteristic sets, resultants and semialgebraic sets—were picked to reflect my original motivation. The choice of the topics was partly influenced by the syllabii proposed by the Research Institute for Symbolic Computation in Linz, Austria, and the discussions in Hearn's Report ("Future Directions for Research in Symbolic Computation").

The book is meant to be covered in a one-semester graduate course comprising about fifteen lectures. The book assumes very little background other than what most beginning computer science graduate students have. For these reasons, I have attempted to keep the book self-contained and largely focussed on the very basic materials.

Since 1987, there has been an explosion of new ideas and techniques in all the areas covered here (e.g., better complexity analysis of Gröbner basis algorithms, many new applications, effective Nullstellensatz, multivariate resultants, generalized characteristic polynomial, new stratification algorithms for semialgebraic sets, faster quantifier elimination algorithm for Tarski sentences, etc.). However, none of these new topics could be included here without distracting from my original intention. It is hoped that this book will prepare readers to be able to study these topics on their own.

vii

Also, there have been several new textbooks in the area (by Akritas, Davenport, Siret and Tournier, and Mignotte) and there are a few more on the way (by Eisenbaud, Robbiano, Weispfenning and Becker, Yap, and Zippel). All these books and the current book emphasize different materials, involve different degrees of depth and address different readerships. An instructor, if he or she so desires, may choose to supplement the current book by some of these other books in order to bring in such topics as factorization, number-theoretic or group-theoretic algorithms, integration or differential algebra.

The author is grateful to many of his colleagues at NYU and elsewhere for their support, encouragement, help and advice. Namely, J. Canny, E.M. Clarke, B. Chazelle, M. Davis, H.M. Edwards, A. Frieze, J. Gutierrez, D. Kozen, R. Pollack, D. Scott, J. Spencer and C-K. Yap. I have also benefited from close research collaboration with my colleague C-K. Yap and my graduate students G. Gallo and P. Pedersen. Several students in my class have helped me in transcribing the original notes and in preparing some of the solutions to the exercises: P. Agarwal, G. Gallo, T. Johnson, N. Oliver, P. Pedersen, R. Sundar, M. Teichman and P. Tetali.

I also thank my editors at Springer for their patience and support. During the preparation of this book I had been supported by NSF and ONR and I am gratified by the interest of my program officers: Kamal Abdali and Ralph Wachter.

I would like to express my gratitude to Prof. Bill Wulf for his efforts to perform miracles on my behalf during many of my personal and professional crises. I would also like to thank my colleague Thomas Anantharaman for reminding me of the power of intuition and for his friendship. Thanks are due to Robin Mahapatra for his constant interest.

In the first draft of this manuscript, I had thanked my imaginary wife for keeping my hypothetical sons out of my nonexistent hair. In the interim five years, I have gained a wife Jane and two sons Sam and Tom, necessarily in that order–but, alas, no hair. To them, I owe my deepest gratitude for their understanding.

Last but not least, I thank Dick Aynes without whose unkind help this book would have gone to press some four years ago.

B. Mishra
mishra@nyu.edu.arpa

Contents

Preface   **vii**

1 Introduction   **1**
    1.1   Prologue: Algebra and Algorithms 1
    1.2   Motivations 4
        1.2.1   Constructive Algebra 5
        1.2.2   Algorithmic and Computational Algebra 6
        1.2.3   Symbolic Computation 7
        1.2.4   Applications 9
    1.3   Algorithmic Notations 13
        1.3.1   Data Structures 13
        1.3.2   Control Structures 15
    1.4   Epilogue 18
        Bibliographic Notes 20

2 Algebraic Preliminaries   **23**
    2.1   Introduction to Rings and Ideals 23
        2.1.1   Rings and Ideals 26
        2.1.2   Homomorphism, Contraction and Extension 31
        2.1.3   Ideal Operations 33
    2.2   Polynomial Rings 35
        2.2.1   Dickson's Lemma 36
        2.2.2   Admissible Orderings on Power Products 39
    2.3   Gröbner Bases 44
        2.3.1   Gröbner Bases in $K[x_1, x_2, \ldots, x_n]$ 46
        2.3.2   Hilbert's Basis Theorem 47
        2.3.3   Finite Gröbner Bases 49
    2.4   Modules and Syzygies 49
    2.5 S-Polynomials 55
        Problems 60
        Solutions to Selected Problems 63
        Bibliographic Notes 69

3 Computational Ideal Theory   **71**
  3.1 Introduction 71
  3.2 Strongly Computable Ring 72
     3.2.1 Example: Computable Field 73
     3.2.2 Example: Ring of Integers 76
  3.3 Head Reductions and Gröbner Bases 80
     3.3.1 Algorithm to Compute Head Reduction 83
     3.3.2 Algorithm to Compute Gröbner Bases 84
  3.4 Detachability Computation 87
     3.4.1 Expressing with the Gröbner Basis 88
     3.4.2 Detachability 92
  3.5 Syzygy Computation 93
     3.5.1 Syzygy of a Gröbner Basis: Special Case 93
     3.5.2 Syzygy of a Set: General Case 98
  3.6 Hilbert's Basis Theorem: Revisited 102
  3.7 Applications of Gröbner Bases Algorithms 103
     3.7.1 Membership 103
     3.7.2 Congruence, Subideal and Ideal Equality 103
     3.7.3 Sum and Product 104
     3.7.4 Intersection 105
     3.7.5 Quotient 106
     Problems 108
     Solutions to Selected Problems 118
     Bibliographic Notes 130

4 Solving Systems of Polynomial Equations   **133**
  4.1 Introduction 133
  4.2 Triangular Set 134
  4.3 Some Algebraic Geometry 138
     4.3.1 Dimension of an Ideal 141
     4.3.2 Solvability: Hilbert's Nullstellensatz 142
     4.3.3 Finite Solvability 145
  4.4 Finding the Zeros 149
     Problems 152
     Solutions to Selected Problems 157
     Bibliographic Notes 165

5 Characteristic Sets   **167**
  5.1 Introduction 167
  5.2 Pseudodivision and Successive Pseudodivision 168
  5.3 Characteristic Sets 171
  5.4 Properties of Characteristic Sets 176
  5.5 Wu-Ritt Process 178
  5.6 Computation 181
  5.7 Geometric Theorem Proving 186

Problems 189
Solutions to Selected Problems 192
Bibliographic Notes 196

6 An Algebraic Interlude   199
   6.1 Introduction 199
   6.2 Unique Factorization Domain 199
   6.3 Principal Ideal Domain 207
   6.4 Euclidean Domain 208
   6.5 Gauss Lemma 211
   6.6 Strongly Computable Euclidean Domains 212
        Problems 216
        Solutions to Selected Problems 220
        Bibliographic Notes 223

7 Resultants and Subresultants   225
   7.1 Introduction 225
   7.2 Resultants 227
   7.3 Homomorphisms and Resultants 232
        7.3.1 Evaluation Homomorphism 234
   7.4 Repeated Factors in Polynomials and Discriminants 238
   7.5 Determinant Polynomial 241
        7.5.1 Pseudodivision: Revisited 244
        7.5.2 Homomorphism and Pseudoremainder 246
   7.6 Polynomial Remainder Sequences 247
   7.7 Subresultants 250
        7.7.1 Subresultants and Common Divisors 255
   7.8 Homomorphisms and Subresultants 262
   7.9 Subresultant Chain 265
   7.10 Subresultant Chain Theorem 274
        7.10.1 Habicht's Theorem 274
        7.10.2 Evaluation Homomorphisms 276
        7.10.3 Subresultant Chain Theorem 279
        Problems 283
        Solutions to Selected Problems 291
        Bibliographic Notes 296

8 Real Algebra   297
   8.1 Introduction 297
   8.2 Real Closed Fields 298
   8.3 Bounds on the Roots 306
   8.4 Sturm's Theorem 309
   8.5 Real Algebraic Numbers 315
        8.5.1 Real Algebraic Number Field 316
        8.5.2 Root Separation, Thom's Lemma and Representation 319

8.6 Real Geometry 333
  8.6.1 Real Algebraic Sets 337
  8.6.2 Delineability 339
  8.6.3 Tarski-Seidenberg Theorem 345
  8.6.4 Representation and Decomposition of Semialgebraic
        Sets 347
  8.6.5 Cylindrical Algebraic Decomposition 348
  8.6.6 Tarski Geometry 354
  Problems 361
  Solutions to Selected Problems 372
  Bibliographic Notes 381

Appendix A: Matrix Algebra   **385**
A.1 Matrices 385
A.2 Determinant 386
A.3 Linear Equations 388

Bibliography   **391**

Index   **409**

Chapter 1

Introduction

1.1 Prologue: Algebra and Algorithms

The birth and growth of both algebra and algorithms are strongly intertwined. The origins of both disciplines are usually traced back to Muhammed ibn-Mūsa al-Khwarizmi al-Quturbulli, who was a prominent figure in the court of Caliph Al-Mamun of the Abassid dynasty in Baghdad (813–833 A.D.). Al-Khwarizmi's contribution to Arabic and thus eventually to Western (i.e., modern) mathematics is manifold: his was one of the first efforts to synthesize Greek axiomatic mathematics with the Hindu algorithmic mathematics. The results were the popularization of Hindu numerals, decimal representation, computation with symbols, etc. His tome "al-Jabr wal-Muqabala," which was eventually translated into Latin by the Englishman Robert of Chester under the title "Dicit Algoritmi," gave rise to the terms algebra (a corruption of "al-Jabr") and algorithm (a corruption of the word "al-Khwarizmi").

However, the two subjects developed at a rather different rate, between two different communities. While the discipline of algorithms remained in its suspended infancy for years, the subject of algebra grew at a prodigious rate, and was soon to dominate most of mathematics.

The formulation of geometry in an algebraic setup was facilitated by the introduction of coordinate geometry by the French mathematician Descartes, and algebra caught the attention of the prominent mathematicians of the era. The late nineteenth century saw the function-theoretic and topological approach of Riemann, the more geometric approach of Brill and Noether, and the purely algebraic approach of Kronecker, Dedekind and Weber. The subject grew richer and deeper, with the work of many illustrious algebraists and algebraic geometers: Newton, Tschirnhausen, Euler, Jacobi, Sylvester, Riemann, Cayley, Kronecker, Dedekind, Noether, Cremona, Bertini, Segre, Castelnuovo, Enriques, Severi, Poincaré, Hurwitz, Macaulay, Hilbert, Weil, Zariski, Hodge, Artin, Chevally, Kodaira, van der

1

Waerden, Hironaka, Abhyankar, Serre, Grothendieck, Mumford, Griffiths and many others.

But soon algebra also lost its constructive foundation, so prominent in the work of Newton, Tschirnhausen, Kronecker and Sylvester, and thereby its role as a computational tool. For instance, under Bourbaki's influence, it became fashionable to bring into disrepute the beautiful and constructive *elimination theory*, developed over half a century by Sylvester, Kronecker, Mertens, König, Hurwitz and Macaulay. The revival of the field of constructive algebra is a rather recent phenomenon, and owes a good deal to the work of Tarski, Seidenberg, Ritt, Collins, Hironaka, Buchberger, Bishop, Richman and others. The views of a constructive algebraist are closest to the ones we will take in the book. These views were rather succinctly described by Hensel in the preface to Kronecker's lectures on number theory:

> [Kronecker] believed that one could, and that one must, in these parts of mathematics, frame each definition in such a way that one can test in a finite number of steps whether it applies to any given quantity. In the same way, a proof of the existence of a quantity can only be regarded as fully rigorous when it contains a method by which the quantity whose existence is to be proved can actually be found.

The views of constructive algebraists are far from the accepted dogmas of modern mathematics. As Harold M. Edwards [68] put it: "Kronecker's views are so antithetical to the prevailing views that the natural way for most modern mathematicians to describe them is to use the word 'heresy'."

Now turning to the science of algorithms, we see that although for many centuries there was much interest in mechanizing the computation process, in the absence of a practical computer, there was no incentive to study general-purpose algorithms. In the 1670's, Gottfried Leibnitz invented his so-called "Leibnitz Wheel," which could add, subtract, multiply and divide. On the subject of mechanization of computation, Leibnitz said ([192], pp. 180–181):

> And now that we may give final praise to the machine we may say that it will be desirable to all who are engaged in computations...managers of financial affairs, merchants, surveyors, geographers, navigators, astronomers....But limiting ourselves to scientific uses, the old geometric and astronomic tables could be corrected and new ones constructed....Also, the astronomers surely will not have to continue to exercise the patience which is required for computation....For it is unworthy of excellent men to lose hours like slaves in the labor of computation.

Leibnitz also sought a *characteristica generalis*, a symbolic language, to be used in the translation of mathematical methods and statements into *algorithms* and *formulas*. Many of Leibnitz's other ideas, namely, the binary number system, *calculus ratiocanator* or calculus of reason, and *lingua characteristica*, a universal language for mathematical discourse, were to influence modern-day computers, computation and logical reasoning. The basic notions in *calculus ratiocanator* led to Boolean algebra, which, in turn, formed the foundations for logic design, as developed by C. Shannon.

However, the technology of the time was inadequate for devising a practical computer. The best computational device Leibnitz could foresee was a "learned committee" sitting around a table and saying:

"Lasst uns rechnen!"

In the nineteenth century, Charles Babbage conceived (but never constructed) a powerful calculating machine, which he called an *analytical engine*. The proposed machine was to be an all-purpose automatic device, capable of handling problems in algebra and mathematical analysis; in fact, of its power, Babbage said that "it could do everything but compose country dances." [102]

Except for these developments and a few others of similar nature, the science of computation and algorithms remained mostly neglected in the last century. In this century, essentially two events breathed life into these subjects: One was the study concerning the foundations of mathematics, as established in "Hilbert's program," and this effort resulted in Gödel's incompleteness theorems, various computational models put forth by Church, Turing, Markov and Post, the interrelatedness of these models, the existence of a "universal" machine and the problem of computability (the *Entsheidungsproblem*). The other event was the advent of modern high-speed digital computers in the postwar period. During the Second World War, the feasibility of a large-scale computing machine was demonstrated by Colossus in the U.K. (under M.H.A. Newman) and the ENIAC in the U.S.A. (under von Neumann, Eckert and Mauchly). After the war, a large number of more and more powerful digital computers were developed, starting with the design of EDVAC in the U.S.A. and Pilot ACE and DEDUCE in the U.K.

Initially, the problems handled by these machines were purely numerical in nature, but soon it was realized that these computers could manipulate and compute with purely symbolic objects. It is amusing to observe that this had not escaped one of the earliest "computer scientists," Lady Ada Augusta, Countess Lovelace. She wrote [102], while describing the capabilities of Babbage's analytical engine,

> Many persons who are not conversant with mathematical studies imagine that because the business of [Babbage's analytical engine] is to give its results in numerical notation, the nature of its process must consequently be arithmetical rather than algebraic and analytical. This is an error. The engine can arrange and combine its numerical quantities exactly as if they were letters or any other general symbols; and, in fact, it might bring out its results in algebraic notation were provisions made accordingly.

The next major step was the creation of general-purpose programming languages in various forms: as instructions, introduced by Post; as productions, independently introduced by Chomsky and Backus; and as functions, as introduced by Church in λ-calculus. This was quickly followed by the development of more powerful list processing languages by Newell and Simon of Carnegie-Mellon University, and later the language LISP by McCarthy at M.I.T. The language LISP played a key role in the rapid development of the subjects of artificial intelligence (AI) and symbolic mathematical computation. In 1953, some of the very first symbolic computational systems were developed by Nolan of M.I.T. and Kahrimanian of Temple University.

In parallel, the science of design and complexity analysis of discrete combinatorial algorithms has grown at an unprecedented rate in the last three decades, influenced by the works of Dijkstra, Knuth, Scott, Floyd, Hoare, Minsky, Rabin, Cook, Hopcroft, Karp, Tarjan, Hartmanis, Stern, Davis, Schwartz, Pippenger, Blum, Aho, Ullman, Yao and others. Other areas such as computational geometry, computational number theory, etc. have emerged in recent times, and have enriched the subject of algorithms. The field of computational algebra and algebraic geometry is a relative newcomer, but holds the promise of adding a new dimension to the subject of algorithms.

After a millennium, it appears that the subjects of algorithms and algebra may finally converge and coexist in a fruitful symbiosis. We conclude this section with the following quote from Edwards [68]:

> I believe that Kronecker's best hope of survival comes from a different tendency in the mathematics of our day...., namely, the tendency, fostered by the advent of computers, toward algorithmic thinking.... One has to ask oneself which examples can be tested on a computer, a question which forces one to consider concrete algorithms and to try to make them efficient. Because of this and because algorithms have real-life applications of considerable importance, the development of algorithms has become a respectable topic in its own right.

1.2   Motivations

What happened to Hilbert's man in the street?
—Shreeram S. Abhyankar

There are essentially four groups of people, who have been instrumental in the rapid growth of the subject of "algorithmic algebra." Although, in some sense, all of the four groups are working toward a common goal, namely, that of developing an algorithmic (read, constructive) foundation for various problems in algebra, their motivations differ slightly from one another. The distinction is, however, somewhat artificial, and a considerable overlap among these communities is ultimately unavoidable.

1.2.1   Constructive Algebra

One of the main issues that concerns the constructive algebraists is that of the philosophical foundations of mathematics. We have alluded to this issue in the introductory section, and will refer to this as "the theological issue."

During the last century, the movement of "analysis" toward nonconstructive concepts and methods of proof had a considerable ideological impact on traditionally constructive areas such as algebra and number theory. In this context, there were needs for a revision of what was understood by the "foundations of mathematics." Some mathematicians of the time, most prominently Kronecker, attacked the emergent style of nonconstructivity and defended the traditional views of foundations espoused by their predecessors. However, to most mathematicians of the time, the constraints imposed by constructivity appeared needlessly shackling. It was historically inevitable that the nonconstructivity implied in the Cantorian/Weirstrassian view of the foundation of mathematics would dominate. Indeed, Dedekind, a student of Kronecker and a prominent algebraist on his own, "insisted it was unnecessary—and he implied it was undesirable— to provide an algorithmic description of an ideal, that is, a computation which would allow one to determine whether a given ring element was or was not in the ideal." [67] Kronecker's view, on the other hand, can be surmised from the following excerpts from Edwards' paper on "Kronecker's Views on the Foundations of Mathematics" [67]:

> Kronecker believed God made the natural numbers and all the rest was man's work. We only know of this opinion by hearsay evidence, however, and his paper *Ueber den Zahlbegriff* indicates to me that he thought God made a bit more: *Buchstabenrechnung*, or calculation with letters. In modern terms, Kronecker seems to envisage a cosmic computer which computes not just with natural numbers, but with polynomials with natural number coefficients (in any number of indeterminates). That's the God-given hardware. The man-made software then creates negative numbers, fractions, algebraic irrationals, and goes on from there. Kronecker believed that such a computer, in the hands of an able enough programmer, was adequate for all the purposes of higher mathematics.

A little further on, Edwards summarizes Kronecker's views as follows: "Kronecker believed that a mathematical concept was not well defined until you had shown how, in each specific instance, to decide [algorithmically] whether the definition was fulfilled or not."

Having said this, let us use the following anecdote to illustrate the debates of the time regarding the foundations of mathematics. This concerns the seminal nonconstructive argument of Hilbert (Hilbert's basis theorem) that every ideal in the ring of polynomials in several variables over a field is finitely generated. In applying this theorem to Gordon's problem of finding a finite set of generators for certain rings of invariant forms, Hilbert reduced this problem to that of finding finite sets of generators for certain ideals. As the rings and associated ideals are described in a finite way, Gordon

expected an explicit description of the generators. Gordon had been able
to solve his problems for two variables in a constructive manner, and was
not happy with Hilbert's solution. Gordon dismissed Hilbert's solution as
follows:

> "*Das ist nicht Mathematik. Das ist Theologie.*"

Hilbert was able to return to the original problem to give a satisfactory
construction. We will discuss this particular problem in greater detail.

A more clear and concrete view regarding constructivity appears to have
emerged only very recently. According to this view, the constructive algebra differs significantly from the classical mathematics by its interpretation
of "existence of an object." "In the classical interpretation, an object exists
if its nonexistence is contradictory. There is a clear distinction between this
meaning of existence and the constructive, algorithmic one, under which an
object exists only if we can construct it, at least in principle. As Bishop has
said, such 'meaningful distinctions deserve to be maintained'.[23]" One can
further restrict what one means by the word "construction." According to
G. Hermann, "the assertion that a computation can be carried through in
a finite number of steps shall mean that an upper bound for the number
of operations needed for the computation can be given. Thus, it does not
suffice, for example, to give a procedure for which one can theoretically
verify that it leads to the goal in a finite number of operations, so long as
no upper bound for the number of operations is known."

There are other motivation for studying constructive algebra: it adds
depth and richness to classical algebra. For instance, given the latitude
one has in specifying ideals, Hilbert's proof of the basis theorem had to
be nonconstructive—thus, in a constructive setting, one is led to explore a
much finer structure (such as Noetherianness, coherence) of the underlying
polynomial ring in order to provide a satisfactory answer.

And, of course, this provides a stepping stone for theoretical computer
scientists to study the design and implementation of efficient algorithms.
Once we understand what algebraic objects are amenable to constructive
treatment, we can study how we can improve the associated algorithms
and how these objects can be used to solve important practical problems.

1.2.2   Algorithmic and Computational Algebra

A prominent algebraic geometer advocating the algorithmic view point is
Abhyankar. In his paper "Historical Rambling in Algebraic Geometry,"
Abhyankar [2] categorizes algebraic geometry into three classes (roughly,
in terms of their algorithmic contents): "high school algebra" (Newton,
Tschirnhausen, Euler, Sylvester, Cayley, Kronecker, Macaulay), "college
algebra" (Dedekind, Noether, Krull, Zariski, Chevally, Cohen) and "university algebra" (Serre, Cartan, Eilenberg, Grothendieck, Mumford), and
calls for a return to the algorithmic "high school algebra":

> The method of high-school algebra is powerful, beautiful and acces-
> sible. So let us not be overwhelmed by the groups-rings-fields or the

functorial arrows of [college or university] algebras and thereby lose
sight of the power of the explicit algorithmic processes given to us
by Newton, Tschirnhausen, Kronecker and Sylvester.

The theoretical computer scientists take Abhyankar's viewpoint to the
extreme: they regard the existence of a construction as only a first step
toward a precise classification of the inherent computational complexity of
an algebraic problem. A theoretical computer scientist would be concerned
with questions of the following kinds:

- What are the resource complexities associated with an algebraic problem? Is a certain set of algebraic problems interreducible to one another, thus making it sufficient to look for an efficient solution to any
  one of the problems in the class? That is, are there classes of algebraic problems that are isomorphic to one another in terms of their
  resource requirements? (Note that as algebraic problems, they may
  be addressing rather unrelated questions.)

- Is a particular problem computationally feasible? If not, are there
  restrictive specializations that can be made feasible? Can randomization help?

- How does the problem depend on various models of computation?
  Can the problem be easily parallelized? Can preprocessing, or pre-
  conditioning, help?

- What is the inherent complexity of the problem? Given an algorithm
  for a problem, can we say whether it is the best possible solution in
  terms of a particular resource complexity?

- What are the basic ingredients required to translate these algorithms
  to usable implementations? For instance, how are numbers to be represented: in finite precision, or in infinite precision (algebraic number)? How are algebraic numbers to be stored internally: in terms
  of an algorithm, or by its minimal polynomial and a straddling interval? What kind of data structures are most suitable to a particular
  problem?

1.2.3 Symbolic Computation

In 1953, the first modern computer programs to perform symbolic compu-
tation were realized in two master's theses: one by H.G. Kahrimanian at
Temple University [108] and another by J.F. Nolan at the Massachusetts
Institute of Technology [157]. The differentiation program developed by
Kahrimanian for UNIVAC I took as its input an expression represented
as a linearized binary tree and produced the derivative of the expression.

After the development of the LISP language by McCarthy, the problem of developing symbolic mathematical systems became relatively easy.

James Slagle (a student of Minsky) developed an integration program called SAINT in LISP in 1962. The program was rudimentary and lacked a strong mathematical foundation, but was still able to perform at the level of a freshman calculus student.

During the early sixties, the next important step was the development of general-purpose systems aimed at making computerized mathematical computation accessible to laymen. Notable among such developments: AL-PAK [27] and ALTRAN [25] at Bell Laboratories by a group headed by W.S. Brown, and FORMAC [181] at I.B.M. under the guidance of J.E. Sammet. FORMAC was somewhat limited in scope in comparison to ALPAK and ALTRAN, since it dealt exclusively with polynomial and rational functions.

Around the same time, G. Collins of the University of Wisconsin had been developing PM [48], a polynomial manipulation system, which utilized an efficient canonical recursive representation of polynomials and supported arbitrary precision arithmetic. The PM system was later supplanted by SAC-1 [49], which could perform operations on multivariate polynomials and rational functions with infinite precision coefficients. The algorithms in SAC-1 were based on the decision procedure invented by Tarski, Seidenberg and Cohen for the elementary theory of a real closed field. These algorithms have widespread applications in various areas of computer science and robotics, and will be discussed at length in this book. An improved version of SAC-1, called SAC-2 [36] and written in an algebraic language ALDES, succeeded the older system.

Staring in the late sixties, the focus shifted to the development of symbolic manipulation systems that allowed a more natural interactive usage. The significant systems in this category included: Engleman's MATHLAB-68 developed at M.I.T. [69], Tony Hearn's REDUCE-2 developed at Rand and University of Utah [165], Barton, Bourne and Fitch's CAMAL system (CAMbridge ALgebra system) [71], Moses and Martin's MACSYMA developed under the MAC project at M.I.T. [88], Griesmer and Jenks's SCRATCHPAD system developed at I.B.M. [106] and more recently Jenks and Sutor's AXIOM system that evolved from SCRATCH-PAD[107].

While a detailed comparison of these systems would be fairly hard, we note that they differ from one another in their design goals. MATHLAB-68 is a general-purpose system, designed to perform differentiation, polynomial factorization, indefinite integration, direct and inverse Laplace transforms and the solution of differential equations with symbolic coefficients. REDUCE is a general-purpose software system with built-in algebraic simplification mechanisms, and thus it allows a user to build his own programs to solve "superdifficult" problems [165] with relative ease; this system has been successfully used to solve problems in QED, QCD, celestial mechanics, fluid mechanics, general relativity, plasma physics and various engineering disciplines. CAMAL is a small, fast, powerful and yet general-purpose system consisting of three modules: F-module for Fourier series, E-module for complex exponential series and H-module (the "Hump"), a general-purpose package. In comparison to the above systems, both MACSYMA and SCRATCHPAD systems are "giants" and are designed to incorporate all the state-of-the-art techniques in symbolic algebra and software engineering.

The number of algebraic systems has grown at a tremendous rate in the recent past. An estimate given by Pavelle, Rothstein and Fitch is that in the last thirty years, about sixty systems have been developed for doing some form of computer algebra. The more notable ones among these are SMP, developed by Cole and Wolfram at CalTech and the Institute for Advanced Studies, MAPLE, developed at the University of Waterloo, Bergman's PROLOG-based SYCOPHANTE system, Engeli's SYMBAL system, Rich and Stoutemyr's muMATH system for I.B.M. PC's and Jenks and Sutors's SCRATCHPAD/AXIOM system.

In the last few years, the general-purpose computer algebra system MATHEMATICA [209] developed by Wolfram Research, Inc., and running on several personal computers (including Macintosh II and NeXT computers) has brought symbolic computation to the domain of everyday users. Other notable recent systems with similar interfaces and achievements include MAPLE and SCRATCHPAD/AXIOM. It is hoped these systems will influence, to a substantial degree, the computing, reasoning and teaching of mathematics [186].

The main goal of the researchers in this community has been to develop algorithms that are efficient in practice. Other related issues that concern this group involve developing languages ideal for symbolic computation, easy-to-use user interfaces, graphical display of various algebraic objects (i.e., algebraic curves, surfaces, etc.), and computer architecture best suited for symbolic manipulation.

1.2.4   Applications

The last motivation for the study of computational algebra comes from its wide variety of applications in biology (e.g., secondary structure of RNA), chemistry (e.g., the nature of equilibria in a chemical process), physics (e.g., evaluation of Feynman diagrams), mathematics (e.g., proof of the Macdonald-Morris conjecture), computer science (e.g., design of the IEEE standard arithmetic) and robotics (e.g., inverse kinematic solution of a multilinked robot). Some of the major applications of symbolic computational algebra in various subareas of computer science are summarized as follows:

1. ROBOTICS: Most of the applications of computational algebra in robotics stem from the algebraico-geometric nature of robot kinematics. Important problems in this area include the kinematic modeling

of a robot, the inverse kinematic solution for a robot, the computation
of the workspace and workspace singularities of a robot, the planning
of an obstacle-avoiding motion of a robot in a cluttered environment,
etc.

2. VISION: Most of the applications here involve the representation of
   various surfaces (usually by simpler triangulated surfaces or generalized cones), the classification of various algebraic surfaces, the algebraic or geometric invariants associated with a surface, the effect of
   various affine or projective transformation of a surface, the description of surface boundaries, etc.

3. COMPUTER-AIDED DESIGN (CAD): Almost all applications of CAD
   involve the description of surfaces, the generation of various auxiliary surfaces such as blending surfaces, smoothing surfaces, etc., the
   parametrization of curves and surfaces, various Boolean operations
   such as union and intersection of surfaces, etc.

Other applications include graphical editors, automated (geometric)
theorem proving, computational algebraic number theory, coding theory,
etc.

To give an example of the nature of the solution demanded by various
applications, we will discuss a few representative problems from robotics,
engineering and computer science.

Robot Motion Planning

- GIVEN: The initial and final (desired) configurations of a robot (made
  of rigid subparts) in two- or three-dimensional space.

  The description of stationary obstacles in the space.

  The obstacles and the subparts of the robot are assumed to be represented as the finite union and intersection of algebraic surfaces.

- FIND: Whether there is a continuous motion of the robot from the
  initial configuration to the final configuration.

The solution proceeds in several steps. The first main step involves
translating the problem to a parameter space, called the *C-space*. The
C-space (also called configuration space) is simply the space of all points
corresponding to all possible configurations of the robot.

The C-space is usually a low-dimensional (with the same dimension as
the number of degrees of freedom of the robot) algebraic manifold lying in
a possibly higher-dimensional Euclidean space. The description and computation of the C-space are interesting problems in computational algebra,
and have been intensely studied.

The second step involves classifying the points of the C-space into two
classes:

- *Forbidden Points*: A point of C-space is forbidden if the corresponding configuration of the robot in the physical space would result in the collision of two subparts of the robot and/or a subpart of the robot with an obstacle.

- *Free Points*: A point of C-space that is not forbidden is called a free point. It corresponds to a legal configuration of the robot amidst the obstacles.

The description and computation of the free C-space and its (path) connected components are again important problems in computational algebra, perhaps not dissimilar to the previous problems. Sometimes the free space is represented by a stratification or a decomposition, and we will have to do extra work to determine the connectivity properties.

Since the initial and final configurations correspond to two points in the C-space, in order to solve the motion planning problem, we simply have to test whether they lie in the same connected component of the free space. This involves computing the adjacency relations among various strata of the free space and representing them in a combinatorial structure, appropriate for fast search algorithms in a computer.

Offset Surface Construction in Solid Modeling

- GIVEN: A polynomial $f(x, y, z)$, implicitly describing an algebraic surface in the three-dimensional space. That is, the surface consists of the following set of points:

$$\left\{ p = \langle x, y, z \rangle \in \mathbb{R}^3 \ : \ f(x, y, z) = 0 \right\}.$$

- COMPUTE: The *envelope* of a family of spheres of radius r whose centers lie on the surface f. Such a surface is called a (two-sided) *offset surface* of f, and describes the set of points at a distance r on both sides of f.

First we need to write down a set of equations describing the points on the offset surface. Let $p = \langle x, y, z \rangle$ be a point on the offset surface and $q = \langle u, v, w \rangle$ be a *footprint* of p on f; that is, q is the point at which a normal from p to f meets f. Let $\vec{t_1} = \langle t_{1,1}, t_{1,2}, t_{1,3} \rangle$ and $\vec{t_2} = \langle t_{2,1}, t_{2,2}, t_{2,3} \rangle$ be two linearly independent tangent vectors to f at the point q. Then, we see that the offset surface is given by:

$$\left\{ p - \langle x, y, z \rangle \in \mathbb{R}^3 : \right.$$
$$\left(\exists \langle u, v, w \rangle \in \mathbb{R}^3 \right) \ \left[(x - u)^2 + (y - v)^2 + (z - w)^2 - r^2 = 0 \right.$$
$$\wedge f(u, v, w) = 0$$

$$\wedge\ \langle x - u, y - v, z - w \rangle \cdot \vec{t}_1 = 0$$
$$\wedge\ \langle x - u, y - v, z - w \rangle \cdot \vec{t}_2 = 0 \Big] \Big\}.$$

Thus the system of polynomial equations given below

$$(x - u)^2 + (y - v)^2 + (z - w)^2 - r^2 \ =\ 0, \qquad (1.1)$$
$$f(u, v, w) \ =\ 0, \qquad (1.2)$$
$$(x - u)t_{1,1} + (y - v)t_{1,2} + (z - w)t_{1,3} \ =\ 0, \qquad (1.3)$$
$$(x - u)t_{2,1} + (y - v)t_{2,2} + (z - w)t_{2,3} \ =\ 0, \qquad (1.4)$$

describes a hypersurface in the six-dimensional space with coordinates (x, y, z, u, v, w), which, when projected onto the three-dimensional space with coordinates (x, y, z), gives the offset surface in an implicit form. The offset surface is computed by simply eliminating the variables u, v, w from the preceding set of equations. Note that equation (1.1) states that the point $\langle x, y, z \rangle$ on the offset surface is at a distance r from its footprint $\langle u, v, w \rangle$; the last three equations (1.2), (1.3), (1.4) ensure that $\langle u, v, w \rangle$ is, indeed, a footprint of $\langle x, y, z \rangle$.

The envelope method of computing the offset surface has several problematic features: The method does not deal with self-intersection in a clean way and, sometimes, generates additional points not on the offset surface. For a discussion of these problems, and their causes, see the book by C.M. Hoffmann [99].

Geometric Theorem Proving

- GIVEN: A geometric statement, consisting of a finite set of hypotheses and a conclusion. It is assumed that the geometric predicates in the hypotheses and the conclusion have been translated into an analytic setting, by first assigning symbolic coordinates to the points and then using the polynomial identities (involving only equalities) to describe the geometric relations:

  Hypotheses : $f_1(x_1, \ldots, x_n) = 0, \ldots, f_r(x_1, \ldots, x_n) = 0.$
  Conclusion : $g(x_1, \ldots, x_n) = 0.$

- DECIDE: Whether the conclusion $g = 0$ is a consequence of the hypotheses ($f_1 = 0 \wedge \cdots \wedge f_r = 0$). That is, whether the following universally quantified first-order formula holds:

$$\Big(\forall\, x_1, \ldots, x_n \Big) \Big[\Big(f_1 = 0 \wedge \cdots \wedge f_r = 0 \Big) \Rightarrow g = 0 \Big]. \qquad (1.5)$$

One way to solve the problem is by first translating it into the following form: Decide if the existentially quantified first-order formula, shown below, is unsatisfiable:

$$\left(\exists\, x_1, \ldots, x_n, z \right) \left[f_1 = 0 \wedge \cdots \wedge f_r = 0 \wedge gz - 1 = 0 \right]. \qquad (1.6)$$

The logical equivalence of the formulas (1.5) and (1.6), when the underlying domain is assumed to be a field, is fairly obvious. (Reader, please convince yourself.)

However, the nature of the solutions may rely on different techniques, depending on what we assume about the underlying fields: For instance, if the underlying domain is assumed to be the field of real numbers (a real closed field), then we may simply check whether the following multivariate polynomial (in $x_1, \ldots, x_n, z$) has no real root:

$$f_1^2 + \cdots + f_r^2 + (gz - 1)^2.$$

If, on the other hand, the underlying domain is assumed to be the field of complex numbers (an algebraically closed field), then we need to check if it is possible to express 1 as a linear combination (with polynomial coefficients) of the polynomials $f_1, \ldots, f_r$ and $(gz - 1)$, i.e., whether 1 belongs to the ideal generated by $f_1, \ldots, f_r, (gz - 1)$. Another equivalent formulation of the problem simply asks if g is in the *radical* of the ideal generated by $f_1, \ldots, f_r$. The correctness of these techniques follow via Hilbert's Nullstellensatz.

Later on in the book, we shall discuss, in detail, the algebraic problems arising in both situations. (See Chapters 4 and 8.)

1.3   Algorithmic Notations

As our main goal will be to examine effective algorithms for computing with various algebraic structures, we need a clear and unambiguous language for describing these algorithms. In many cases, a step-by-step description of algorithms in English will be adequate. But we prefer to present these algorithms in a fairly high-level, well-structured computer language that will borrow several concepts from ALGOL [206] and SETL [184]. Occasionally, we will allow ourselves to describe some of the constituent steps, in a language combining English, set theory and mathematical logic.

1.3.1   Data Structures

The primitive objects of our language will consist of simple algebraic objects such as *Booleans*, *groups*, *rings*, *fields*, etc., with their associated algebraic operations. For instance, we may assume that the language provides mechanisms to represent real numbers, and supports operations such as addition, subtraction, multiplication and division. We shall assume that each of these algebraic operations can be performed "effectively," in the sense that the operation produces the correct result in a finite amount of time. We shall also regard an *interval* as a primitive: an *interval* $[j..k]$ is a sequence of integers $j, j+1, \ldots, k$, if $j \leq k$, and an empty sequence otherwise. The notation $i \in [j..k]$ (read, "i belongs to the interval $[j..k]$") means i is an integer such that $j \leq i \leq k$. Occasionally, we shall also use the notation $[j, k..l]$ $(j \neq k)$ to represent the following *arithmetic progression* of integers: $j, j+(k-j), j+2(k-j), \ldots, j+\lfloor (l-j)/(k-j) \rfloor (k-j)$. The notation $i \in [j, k..l]$ (read, "i belongs to the arithmetic progression $[j, k..l]$") means that $i = j + a(k-j)$, for some integer $0 \leq a \leq \lfloor (l-j)/(k-j) \rfloor$.

The main composite objects in the language are *tuples* and *sets*. An ordered n-tuple $T = \langle x_1, x_2, \ldots, x_n \rangle$ is an ordered sequence of n elements (primitive or composite), some of which may be repeated. The size of the tuple T is denoted by $|T|$, and gives the number of elements in T. The *empty tuple* is denoted by $\langle \, \rangle$. The ith element of an n-tuple T $(1 \leq i \leq n)$ is denoted by $T[i]$. A $(j - i + 1)$ subtuple of an n-tuple $T = \langle x_1, x_2, \ldots, x_n \rangle$ $(1 \leq i \leq j \leq n)$, consisting of elements x_i through x_j, is denoted by $T[i, j]$. Note that $T[i, i]$ is a 1-tuple $\langle x_i \rangle$, whereas $T[i]$ is simply the ith element of T, x_i. Given an m-tuple $T_1 = \langle x_{1,1}, x_{1,2}, \ldots, x_{1,m} \rangle$ and an n-tuple $T_2 = \langle x_{2,1}, x_{2,2}, \ldots, x_{2,n} \rangle$, their concatenation, $T_1 \circ T_2$, denotes an $(m + n)$-tuple $\langle x_{1,1}, x_{1,2}, \ldots, x_{1,m}, x_{2,1}, x_{2,2}, \ldots, x_{2,n} \rangle$.

We can also represent arbitrary *insertion* and *deletion* on tuples by combining the primitive operations *subtuples* and *concatenation*. Let T be a tuple and x an arbitrary element. Then

Head(T)	$\equiv$	return $T[1]$
Tail(T)	$\equiv$	return $T[\|T\|]$
Push(x,T)	$\equiv$	return $\langle x \rangle \circ T$
Pop(T)	$\equiv$	return $T[2..\|T\|]$
Inject(x,T)	$\equiv$	return $T \circ \langle x \rangle$
Eject(T)	$\equiv$	return $T[1..\|T\| - 1]$

Using these operations, we can implement *stack* (with head, push and pop), *queue* (with head, inject and pop) or a *deque* (with head, tail, push, pop, inject and eject).

A set $S = \{x_1, x_2, \ldots, x_n\}$ is a finite collection of n distinct elements (primitive or composite). The size of the set S is denoted by $|S|$, and gives the number of elements in S. The *empty set* is denoted by $\emptyset$ (or, sometimes, $\{ \, \}$). The operation Choose(S) returns some arbitrary element of the set S. The main operations on the sets are set-union $\cup$, set-intersection $\cap$ and set-difference $\setminus$: If S_1 and S_2 are two sets, then $S_1 \cup S_2$ yields a set consisting of the elements in S_1 or S_2, $S_1 \cap S_2$ yields a set consisting of the elements in S_1 and S_2, and $S_1 \setminus S_2$ yields a set consisting of the elements in S_1 but not in S_2.

We can also represent arbitrary *insertion* and *deletion* on sets by combining the primitive set operations. Let S be a set and x an arbitrary element. Then

$$\text{Insert}(x,S) \quad \equiv \quad \text{return } S \cup \{x\}$$
$$\text{Delete}(x,S) \quad \equiv \quad \text{return } S \setminus \{x\}$$

1.3.2   Control Structures

A program consists of a sequence of statements, the most basic operation being the assignment. The symbol := denotes the assignment and the symbol ; the sequencer or the statement separator. Thus the assignment statement, $x_i := expression$ first evaluates the *expression* in the right-hand side, then deposits the value of the expression in the location corresponding to the variable x_i in the left-hand side. We also write

$$\langle x_1, \ldots, x_n \rangle := \langle expression_1, \ldots, expression_n \rangle$$

to denote the parallel assignment of the values of the components of the n-tuple of expressions in the right-hand side, in the locations corresponding to the n-tuple of variables $\langle x_1, \ldots, x_n \rangle$ in the left-hand side. Interesting examples of such parallel assignments are the following:

$$\langle x, y \rangle := \langle y, x \rangle$$

swaps the values of the variables x and y;

$$\langle x_1, \ldots, x_{j-i+1} \rangle := \langle expression_1, \ldots, expression_n \rangle [i..j]$$

selects the values of the expressions i through j.

In a program, a Boolean expression corresponds to a propositional statement consisting of atomic predicates, and the connectives **or**, **and** and **not**. We also use the connectives **cor** (conditional or) and **cand** (conditional and) with the following semantics: in "*Boolean condition*$_1$ **cor** *Boolean condition*$_2$," the second Boolean condition is evaluated, only if the first condition evaluates to "false;" and in "*Boolean condition*$_1$ **cand** *Boolean condition*$_2$," the second Boolean condition is evaluated, only if the first condition evaluates to "true."

We use three main control structures:

If-Then-Else:

> if *Boolean condition*$_1$ then
> > *statement*$_1$
>
> elsif *Boolean condition*$_2$ then
> > *statement*$_2$
>
> > $\vdots$
>
> else *statement*$_n$
> end{if }

The effect of this statement is to cause the following execution: First, the Boolean conditions, *Boolean condition*$_1$, *Boolean condition*$_2$, ..., are evaluated sequentially until a "true" Boolean condition is encountered, at which point, the corresponding statement is executed. If all the Boolean conditions evaluate to "false," then the last statement, *statement*$_n$, is executed.

Loop: The loop statements appear in two flavors:

> while *Boolean condition* loop
> > *statement*
>
> end{loop }

The effect of this statement to cause the following execution: First, the Boolean condition is evaluated, and if it evaluates to "true," then the statement is executed. At the end of the statement execution, the control passes back to the beginning of the loop and this process is repeated as long as the Boolean condition continues to evaluate to "true;" if the Boolean condition evaluates to "false," then the control passes to the next statement.

> loop
> > *statement*
>
> until *Boolean condition*
> end{loop }

The effect of this statement to cause the following execution: First, the statement is executed. At the end of the statement execution, the Boolean condition is evaluated. If it evaluates to "false," then the control passes back to the beginning of the loop and the process is repeated; if the Boolean condition evaluates to "true," then the control passes to the next statement.

For-Loop: Generally, the for-loop statements appear in the following form:

> for every *iterator value* loop
> > *statement*
>
> end{loop }

The effect of a for-loop statement is to cause the statement to be evaluated once for each value of the iterator. An iterator may appear in one of the following forms:

1. "$i \in [j..k]$," the statement is evaluated $k - j + 1$ times once for each value of i (in the order, j, $j + 1$, ..., k);

2. "$i \in [j, k..l]$," the statement is evaluated $\lfloor (l-j)/(k-j) \rfloor + 1$ times once for each value of i (in the order j, k, ..., $j + \lfloor (l - j)/(k - j) \rfloor (k - j)$);

3. "$x \in T$," where T is a tuple, the statement is evaluated $|T|$ times once for each value of x in T, according to the order imposed by T; and

4. "$x \in S$," where S is a set, the statement is evaluated $|S|$ times once for each value of x in S, in some arbitrary order.

A program will be organized as a set of named modules. Each module will be presented with its input and output specifications. The modules can call each other in mutual-recursive or self-recursive fashion; a module calls another module or itself by invoking the name of the called module and passing a set of parameters by value. When a called module completes its execution, it either returns a value or simply, passes the control back to the calling module. For each module, we shall need to prove its correctness and termination properties.

As an example of the usage of the notations developed in this section, let us examine the following algorithm of Euclid to compute the GCD (*greatest common divisor*) of two positive integers X and Y. In the program the function Remainder(X, Y) is assumed to produce the remainder, when Y is divided by X.

GCD(X, Y)
Input: Two positive integers X and Y.
Output: The greatest common divisor of X and Y, i.e., a positive integer that divides both X and Y and is divisible by every divisor of both X and Y.

if $X > Y$ then
    $\langle X, Y \rangle := \langle Y, X \rangle$
end{if };

while X does not divide Y loop
    $\langle X, Y \rangle := \langle \text{Remainder}(X, Y), X \rangle$
end{loop };

return X;
end{GCD}   □

Theorem 1.3.1 *The program* GCD *correctly computes the greatest common divisor of two positive integers.*

PROOF.
Let $\langle X_0, Y_0 \rangle$ be the input pair, and $\langle X_1, Y_1 \rangle$, $\langle X_2, Y_2 \rangle$, ..., $\langle X_n, Y_n \rangle$ be the values of X and Y at each invocation of the while-loop. Since $X_0 > X_1 > \cdots X_n$, and since they are all positive integers, the program must terminate.

Furthermore, for all $0 \le i < n$, every divisor of X_i and Y_i is also a divisor X_{i+1}, and every divisor of X_{i+1} and Y_{i+1} is also a divisor of Y_i.

Hence,

$$\text{GCD}(X_0, Y_0) = \text{GCD}(X_1, Y_1) = \cdots = \text{GCD}(X_n, Y_n).$$

But since $\text{GCD}(X_n, Y_n)$ is clearly X_n, the value returned by the program, X_n, is the greatest common divisor of X and Y. $\square$

1.4   Epilogue

We conclude this chapter with the following poem by Abhyankar, which succinctly captures a new spirit of constructiveness in algebra:

Polynomials and Power Series,
May They Forever Rule the World

Shreeram S. Abhyankar

Polynomials and power series.
    May they forever rule the world.

Eliminate, eliminate, eliminate.
    Eliminate the eliminators of elimination theory.

As you must resist the superbourbaki coup,
    so must you fight the little bourbakis too.

Kronecker, Kronecker, Kronecker above all
    Kronecker, Mertens, Macaulay, and Sylvester.

        Not the theology of Hilbert,
        But the constructions of Gordon.

Not the surface of Riemann,
But the algorithm of Jacobi.

Ah! the beauty of the identity of Rogers and Ramanujan!
Can it be surpassed by Dirichlet and his principle?

Germs, viruses, fungi, and functors,
        Stacks and sheaves of the lot
        Fear them not
        We shall be victors.

Come ye forward who dare present a functor,
    We shall eliminate you
    By resultants, discriminants, circulants and alternants.

Given to us by Kronecker, Mertens, Sylvester.

Let not here enter the omologists, homologists,
　　　And their cohorts the cohomologists crystalline
For this ground is sacred.

Onward Soldiers! defend your fortress,
Fight the Tor with a determinant long and tall,
But shun the Ext above all.

Morphic injectives, toxic projectives,
　　　Etal, eclat, devious devisage,
　　　　　Arrows poisonous large and small
　　　　　　May the armor of Tschirnhausen
　　　　　　　Protect us from the scourge of them all.

You cannot conquer us with rings of Chow
　　　And shrieks of Chern
For we, too, are armed with polygons of Newton
　　　And algorithms of Perron.
To arms, to arms, fractions, continued or not,
　　　　Fear not the scheming ghost of Grothendieck
For the power of power series is with you,
　　　May they converge or not
　　　(May they be polynomials or not)
　　　(May they terminate or not).

Can the followers of G by mere "smooth" talk
　　　Ever make the singularity simple?
　　　　Long live Karl Weierstrass!

What need have we for rings Japanese, excellent or bad,
　　　When, in person, Nagata himself is on our side.

What need to tensorize
　　　When you can uniformize,
What need to homologize
　　　When you can desingularize
　　　　(Is Hironaka on our side?)

Alas! Princeton and fair Harvard you, too,
　　　Reduced to satellite in the Bur-Paris zoo.

Bibliographic Notes

For a more detailed history of the development of algebra and algebraic geometry, see the book by Dieudonné [63]. Portions of the first section have been influenced by the views of Abhyankar [1,2].

For the development of digital computers and computer science, the reader may consult the monograph edited by Randell [164] and the books by Cerazzi [44] and Goldstine [84]. A lively account of the connection between the developments in mathematical logic and computer science is given in the paper by M. Davis [59].

For detailed discussions on the impact of nonconstructivity on the foundations of mathematics, and Kronecker's role in the subsequent debate, the reader may consult the works of Edwards [67,68]. The recent interest in constructivity in algebra may be said to have been initiated by the work of Hermann [93] and the works of Seidenberg [187,189]. The results of Ritt [174] and Wu [209-211] on the characteristic sets, the works of Hironaka [96] and Buchberger [33,149,151] on (standard) Gröbner bases, the results by Tarski, Collins, and Bochnak and his colleagues on the real algebraic geometry [21,50,200] and the recent revival of elimination theory, have put the subject of constructive algebra in the forefront of research. For a discussion of the recent renaissance of constructivity in mathematics (in particular in algebra), as espoused by Bishop and Brouwer, the reader may consult the books by Bridges and Richman [23] and by Mines et al. [147]. Glass provides an illuminating discussion on the four categories of existence theorems (mere existence, effective existence, constructive existence and complete solution) with examples from algebra and number theory [83].

For a more detailed account of the history and development of symbolic computational systems, see R. Zippel's notes on "Algebraic Manipulation" [218] and the paper by van Hulzen and Calmet [205]. For a discussion of the research issues in the area of symbolic computational systems, we refer the reader to the 1969 Tobey Report [201], 1986 Caviness Report [43] and 1989 Hearn-Boyle-Caviness Report [22].

For a more detailed discussion of applications of symbolic computational systems in physics, chemistry, mathematics, biology, computer science, robotics and engineering, the reader may consult the papers by Calmet and van Hulzen [37], Grosheva [87], the Hearn-Boyle-Caviness Report [22] and the books by Pavelle [160] and Rand [163].

For a thorough discussion of the algebraic approach employed to solve the robot motion planning problem, the reader is referred to the papers by Reif[166] and Schwartz and Sharir [185]. A somewhat different approach (based on the "road map" techniques) has been developed to solve the same problems by Canny[40], Ó'Dúnlaing, Sharir and Yap [158].

For a discussion of the applications of computational algebra to solid modeling, the reader may consult the book by Hoffmann [99]; the discussion in subsection 1.2.4 on the computation of offset surfaces is adapted from Hoffmann's book. Other useful expository materials in this area include the books by Bartels et al. [14], Farin [70], Mäntylä [138], Mortenson [155], Su and Liu [196], and the survey papers by Requicha and co-worker [171,172].

For additional discussion on the subject of geometric theorem proving and its relation to computational algebra, we refer the readers to the works of Tarski

[200], Chou [46,47], Davis and Cerutti [60], Gelernter et al. [80], Kapur [113], Ko and Hussain [117], Kutzler and Stifter [122], Scott [186] and Wu [209-211].

The poem by Abhyankar in the Epilogue was written in August 1970 during the International Conference in Nice, and was inspired by van der Waerden's historical lecture on the development of algebraic topology.

This book roughly covers the following core courses of the RISC-LINZ computer algebra syllabus developed at the Research Institute for Symbolic Computation at Johannes Kepler University, Linz, Austria (Appendix B, [22]): computer algebra I (algorithms in basic algebraic domain), computer algebra II (advanced topics, e.g., algorithmic polynomial ideal theory) and parts of computational geometry II (algebraic algorithms in geometry). All our algorithms, however, will be presented without any analysis of their computational complexity, although, for each of the algorithms, we shall demonstrate their termination properties. There are quite a few textbooks available in this area, and the reader is urged to supplement this book with the following: the books by Akritas [4], Davenport et al. [58], Lipson [132], Mignotte [145], Sims [191], Stauffer et al. [194], Yap [213], Zimmer [217], Zippel [218] and the mongraph edited by Buchberger et al. [34].

There are several journals devoted to computational algebra and its applications; notable among these are *Journal of Symbolic Computation*, started in 1985, and *Applicable Algebra in Engineering, Communication and Computer Science*, started in 1990. Other important outlets for papers in this area are the *SIAM Journal on Computing* and the *ACM Transactions on Mathematical Software*. There are several professional societies, coordinating the research activities in this area: ACM SIGSAM (*the Association for Computing Machinery Special Interest Group on Symbolic and Algebraic Manipulation*), SAME (*Symbolic and Algebraic Manipulation in Europe*) and ISSAC (*International Symposium on Symbolic and Algebraic Computation*). Other societies, such as AMS (*American Mathematical Society*), AAAS (*American Association for the Advancement of Science*), ACS (*American Chemical Society*), APS (*American Physical Society*) and IEEE (*The Institute of Electrical and Electronics Engineers*), also cover topics in computer algebra.

Chapter 2

Algebraic Preliminaries

2.1 Introduction to Rings and Ideals

In this chapter, we introduce some of the key concepts from commutative algebra. Our focus will be on the concepts of rings, ideals and modules, as they are going to play a very important role in the development of the algebraic algorithms of the later chapters. In particular, we develop the ideas leading to the definition of a basis of an ideal, a proof of Hilbert's basis theorem, and the definition of a Gröbner basis of an ideal in a polynomial ring. Another important concept, to be developed, is that of a syzygy of a finitely generated module.

First, we recall the definition of a group:

Definition 2.1.1 (Group) A *group* G is a nonempty set with a binary operation (*product*, $\cdot$) such that

1. G is closed under the product operation.
$$\left(\forall\, a, b \in G\right) \left[a \cdot b \in G\right].$$

2. The product operation is *associative*. That is,
$$\left(\forall\, a, b, c \in G\right) \left[(a \cdot b) \cdot c = a \cdot (b \cdot c)\right].$$

3. There exists (at least) one element $e \in G$, called the (left) *identity*, so that
$$\left(\forall\, a \in G\right) \left[e \cdot a = a\right].$$

4. Every element of G has a (left) *inverse*:
$$\left(\forall\, a \in G\right) \left(\exists\, a^{-1} \in G\right) \left[a^{-1} \cdot a = e\right].$$

The set G is said to be a *semigroup* if it satisfies only the first two conditions, i.e., it possesses an associative product operation, but does not have
an identity element.

A group is called *Abelian* (or *commutative*) if the product operation
commutes:

$$\left(\forall\, a, b \in G \right) \left[a \cdot b = b \cdot a \right]. \quad \square$$

For instance, the set of bijective transformations of a nonempty set S,
with the product operation as the composite map, and the identity as the
identity map, form the so-called *symmetric group of the set S*, Sym S. In
particular, if $S = \{1, 2, \ldots, n\}$, then Sym $S = S_n$, the *symmetric group of
n letters*; the elements of S_n are the *permutations* of $\{1, 2, \ldots, n\}$. If, on
the other hand, we had considered the set of *all* transformations (not just
the bijective ones) of a nonempty set S, the resulting structure would have
been a semigroup with identity element. (A transformation is invertible if
and only if it is bijective).

Other examples of groups are the following:

1. $(\mathbb{Z}, +, 0)$, the group of integers under addition; the (additive) inverse
   of an integer a is $-a$.

2. $(\mathbb{Q}^*, \cdot, 1)$, the group of nonzero rational numbers under multiplication; the (multiplicative) inverse of a rational p/q is q/p.

3. The set of rotations about the origin in the Euclidean plane under
   the operation of composition of rotations. The rotation through an
   angle θ is represented by the map $\langle x, y \rangle \mapsto \langle x', y' \rangle$, where

   $$x' = x \cos \theta - y \sin \theta, \quad y' = x \sin \theta + y \cos \theta.$$

The following are some of the examples of semigroups:

1. $(\mathbb{N}, +, 0)$, the semigroup of natural numbers under addition. This
   semigroup has zero (0) as its additive identity.

2. $(\mathbb{Z}, \cdot, 1)$, the semigroup of integers under multiplication. This semigroup has one (1) as its multiplicative identity.

Definition 2.1.2 (Subgroup) A *subgroup G'* of a group G is a nonempty
subset of G with the product operation inherited from G, which satisfies the
four group postulates of Definition 2.1.1. Thus, the (left) identity element
$e \in G$ also belongs to G', and the following properties hold for G':

$$\left(\forall\, a, b \in G' \right) \left[a \cdot b \in G' \right]$$

and

$$\left(\forall\, a \in G' \right) \left[a^{-1} \in G' \right].$$

In fact, a subgroup can be characterized much more succinctly: *a nonempty subset G' of a group G is a subgroup, if and only if*

$$\left(\forall\, a, b \in G'\right) \left[a \cdot b^{-1} \in G'\right]. \quad \square$$

If $H \subseteq G$ is a subset of a group G, then the smallest subgroup (with respect to inclusion) of G containing H is said to be the *group generated by H*; this subgroup consists of all the finite products of the elements of H and their inverses.

If H_1 and H_2 are two arbitrary subsets of a group G, then we may define the *product* of the subsets, $H_1 H_2$, to be the subset of G, obtained by the pointwise product of the elements of H_1 with the elements of H_2. That is,

$$H_1 H_2 = \left\{h_1 h_2 : h_1 \in H_1 \text{ and } h_2 \in H_2\right\}.$$

If $H_1 = \{h_1\}$ is a singleton set, then we write $h_1 H_2$ (respectively, $H_2 h_1$) to denote the subset $H_1 H_2$ (respectively, $H_2 H_1$).

We may observe that, if G_1 is a subgroup of G, then the product $G_1 G_1 = G_1$ is also a subgroup of G. In general, however, the product of two subgroups G_1 and G_2 of a group G is not a subgroup of G, except only when the subgroups G_1 and G_2 commute:

$$G_1 G_2 = G_2 G_1.$$

Definition 2.1.3 (Coset) If G' is a subgroup of a group G, and a, an element of G, then the subset aG' is called a *left coset*, and the subset $G'a$ a *right coset* of G' in G. If $a \in G'$, then $aG' = G'a = G'$.

As each element $a \in G$ belongs to *exactly* one (left or right) coset of G' (namely, aG' or $G'a$), the family of (left or right) cosets constitutes a *partition* of the group G. $\quad \square$

All the cosets of a subgroup G' have the same cardinality as G', as can be seen from the one-to-one mapping $G' \to aG'$, taking $g \in G'$ to $ag \in aG'$.

Definition 2.1.4 (Normal Subgroup) A subgroup G' of a group G is called a *normal* (or *self-conjugate*) *subgroup* of G if G' commutes with every element $a \in G$. That is,

$$\left(\forall\, a \in G\right) \left[aG' = G'a\right]. \quad \square$$

Definition 2.1.5 (Quotient Group) If G' is a normal subgroup of G, then the set

$$\overline{G} = \left\{aG' : a \in G\right\}$$

consisting of the cosets of G' forms a group (under the product operation on subsets of G). The coset G' is an identity element of the group $\overline{G}$, since

$$\left(\forall \, aG' \in \overline{G}\right) \left[G' \cdot aG' = aG' \cdot G' = aG'\right].$$

Furthermore,

$$\left(\forall \, aG', bG' \in \overline{G}\right) \left[aG' \cdot bG' = abG'G' = abG' \in \overline{G}\right],$$

$$\left(\forall \, aG', bG', cG' \in \overline{G}\right) \left[(aG' \cdot bG') \cdot cG' = abcG' = aG' \cdot (bG' \cdot cG')\right]$$

and every element aG' has a left inverse $(aG')^{-1} = a^{-1}G'$, since

$$\left(\forall \, aG' \in \overline{G}\right) \left[a^{-1}G' \cdot aG' = a^{-1}aG' = G'\right].$$

The group of cosets of a normal subgroup G' (i.e., $\overline{G}$, in the preceding discussion) is called a *quotient group of G*, with respect to G', and is denoted by G/G'.   □

If the group is Abelian, then every subgroup is a normal subgroup. Let G be an Abelian group under a commutative addition operation $(+)$ and G' a subgroup of G. In this case, the quotient group G/G' consists of the cosets $a + G'$, which are also called the *residue classes of G modulo G'*. Two group elements a and $b \in G$ are said to be *congruent modulo G'*, and denoted

$$a \equiv b \quad \mod (G'),$$

if $a + G' = b + G'$, i.e., $a - b \in G'$.

For example, the multiples of a positive integer m form a subgroup of $(\mathbb{Z}, +, 0)$, and we write

$$a \equiv b \quad \mod (m),$$

if the difference $a - b$ is divisible by m. The residue classes, in this case, are cosets of the form $i + m\mathbb{Z} = \{i + km : k \in \mathbb{Z}\}$, $(0 \le i < m)$, and are called *residue classes of $\mathbb{Z}$ mod m*.

2.1.1   Rings and Ideals

Definition 2.1.6 (Ring) A *ring R* is a set with two binary operations (*addition*, $+$, and *multiplication*, $\cdot$) such that we have the following:

1. R is an Abelian group with respect to addition. That is, R has a zero element 0, and every $x \in R$ has an additive inverse $-x$.

$$\left(\forall \, x \in R\right) \left(\exists \, -x \in R\right) \left[x + (-x) = 0\right].$$

2. R is a semigroup with respect to multiplication. Furthermore, multiplication is distributive over addition:

$$\left(\forall\, x, y, z \in R\right)$$

$$\Big[[x \cdot (y + z) = x \cdot y + x \cdot z] \quad \text{and} \quad [(y + z) \cdot x = y \cdot x + z \cdot x]\Big].$$

We say R has an *identity element* if there is a $1 \in R$ such that

$$\left(\forall\, x \in R\right)\Big[x1 = 1x = x\Big].$$

The ring R is *commutative* if the multiplicative semigroup $(R, \cdot)$ is commutative:

$$\left(\forall\, x, y \in R\right)\Big[xy = yx\Big]. \quad \square$$

The group $(R, +, 0)$ is known as the *additive group* of the ring R.

Some examples of rings are the following: the integers, $\mathbb{Z}$, the rational numbers, $\mathbb{Q}$, the real numbers, $\mathbb{R}$, the complex numbers, $\mathbb{C}$, polynomial functions in n variables over an ambient ring R, $R[x_1, \ldots, x_n]$ and rational functions in n variables over an ambient ring R, $R(x_1, \ldots, x_n)$. The set of even numbers forms a ring without identity.

An interesting example of a finite ring, $\mathbb{Z}_m$, can be constructed by considering the residue classes of $\mathbb{Z}$ mod m. The residue class containing i is

$$[i]_m = i + m\mathbb{Z} = \{i + mk : k \in \mathbb{Z}\}.$$

We can define addition and multiplication operations on the elements of $\mathbb{Z}_m$ as follows:

$$[i]_m + [j]_m = [i + j]_m \quad \text{and} \quad [i]_m \cdot [j]_m = [ij]_m.$$

It can be easily verified that $\mathbb{Z}_m$, as constructed above, is a commutative ring with zero element $[0]_m$ and identity element $[1]_m$; it is called the *ring of residue classes mod m*. $\mathbb{Z}_m$ is a finite ring with m elements: $[0]_m$, $[1]_m$, $\ldots$, $[m-1]_m$. For the sake of convenience, $\mathbb{Z}_m$ is often represented by the *reduced system of residues mod m*, i.e., the set $\{0, 1, \ldots, m-1\}$.

> In what follows we assume that all of our rings are commutative and include an identity element. Any violation of this assumption will be stated explicitly.

A *subring* R' of a ring R is a nonempty subset of R with the addition and multiplication operations inherited from R, which satisfies the ring postulates of Definition 2.1.6.

Definition 2.1.7 (Ideal) A subset $I \subseteq R$ is an *ideal* if it satisfies the following two conditions:

1. I is an additive subgroup of the additive group of R:

$$\left(\forall \, a,b \in I\right) \left[a - b \in I\right].$$

2. $RI \subseteq I$; I is closed under multiplication with ring elements:

$$\left(\forall \, a \in R\right) \left(\forall \, b \in I\right) \left[ab \in I\right].$$

The ideals $\{0\}$ and R are called the *improper ideals* of R; all other ideals are *proper*. □

A subset J of an ideal I in R is a *subideal* of I if J itself is an ideal in R. We make the following observations:

1. If I is an ideal of R, then I is also a *subring* of R.

2. The converse of (1) is not true; that is, not all subrings of R are ideals. For example, the subring $\mathbb{Z} \subset \mathbb{Q}$ is not an ideal of the rationals. (The set of integers is not closed under multiplication by a rational.)

Let $a \in R$. Then the *principal ideal* generated by a, denoted (a), is given by

$$(a) = \{ra : r \in R\}, \quad \text{if } 1 \in R.$$

The principal ideal generated by zero element is $(0) = \{0\}$, and the principal ideal generated by identity element is $(1) = R$. Thus, the improper ideals of the ring R are (0) and (1).

Let $a_1, \ldots, a_k \in R$. Then the *ideal generated by* $a_1, \ldots, a_k$ is

$$(a_1, \ldots, a_k) = \left\{ \sum_{i=1}^{k} r_i a_i \; : \; r_i \in R \right\}.$$

A subset $F \subseteq I$ that generates I is called a *basis* (or, a *system of generators*) of the ideal I.

Definition 2.1.8 (Noetherian Ring) A ring R is called *Noetherian* if any ideal of R has a finite system of generators. □

Definition 2.1.9

An element $x \in R$ is called a *zero divisor* if there exists $y \neq 0$ in R such that $xy = 0$.

An element $x \in R$ is *nilpotent* if $x^n = 0$ for some $n > 0$. A nilpotent element is a zero divisor, but not the converse.

An element $x \in R$ is a *unit* if there exists $y \in R$ such that $xy = 1$. The element y is uniquely determined by x and is written as x^{-1}. The units of R form a multiplicative Abelian group. □

Definition 2.1.10

A ring R is called an *integral domain* if it has no nonzero zero divisor.
A ring R is called *reduced* if it has no nonzero nilpotent element.
A ring R is called a *field* if every nonzero element is a unit.   □

In an integral domain R, $R \setminus \{0\}$ is closed under multiplication, and is denoted by R^*; $(R^*, \cdot)$ is itself a semigroup with respect to multiplication. In a field K, the group of nonzero elements, $(K^*, \cdot, 1)$ is known as the *multiplicative group* of the field.

Some examples of fields are the following: the field of rational numbers, $\mathbb{Q}$, the field of real numbers, $\mathbb{R}$, and the field of complex numbers, $\mathbb{C}$. If p is a prime number, then $\mathbb{Z}_p$ (the ring of residue classes mod p) is a finite field. If $[s]_p \in \mathbb{Z}_p^*$, then the set of elements

$$[s]_p, \ [2s]_p, \ \ldots, \ [(p-1)s]_p$$

are all nonzero and distinct, and thus, for some $s' \in [1..p-1]$, $[s's]_p = [1]_p$; hence, $([s]_p)^{-1} = [s']_p$.

A *subfield* of a field is a subring which itself is a field. If K' is a subfield of K, then we also say K is an *extension field* of K'. Let $a \in K$; then the smallest subfield (under inclusion) of K containing $K' \cup \{a\}$ is called the *extension of K' obtained by adjoining a to K'*, and denoted by $K'(a)$.

The set of rationals, $\mathbb{Q}$, is a subfield of the field of real numbers, $\mathbb{R}$. If we adjoin an algebraic number, such as $\sqrt{2}$, to the field of rationals, $\mathbb{Q}$, then we get an extension field, $\mathbb{Q}(\sqrt{2}) \subseteq \mathbb{R}$.

Definition 2.1.11 A field is said to be a *prime field*, if it does not contain any proper subfield. It can be shown that every field K contains a unique prime field, which is isomorphic to either $\mathbb{Q}$ or $\mathbb{Z}_p$, for some prime number p. We say the following:

1. A field K is of *characteristic* 0 (denoted characteristic $K = 0$) if its prime field is isomorphic to $\mathbb{Q}$.

2. A field K is of *characteristic* $p > 0$ (denoted characteristic $K = p$), if its prime field is isomorphic to $\mathbb{Z}_p$.   □

Proposition 2.1.1 $R \neq \{0\}$ *is a field if and only if* $1 \in R$ *and there are no proper ideals in R.*

PROOF.

($\Rightarrow$) Let R be a field, and $I \subseteq R$ be an ideal of R. Assume that $I \neq (0)$. Hence there exists a nonzero element $a \in I$. Therefore, $1 = aa^{-1} \in I$, i.e., $I = (1) = R$.

($\Leftarrow$) Let $a \in R$ be an arbitrary element of R. If $a \neq 0$, then the principal ideal (a) generated by a must be distinct from the improper ideal (0). Since R has no proper ideal, $(a) = R$. Hence there exists an $x \in R$ such that $xa = 1$, and a has an inverse in R. Thus R is a field.   □

Corollary 2.1.2 *Every field K is a Noetherian ring.*

PROOF.

The ideals of K are simply (0) and (1), each of them generated by a single element. $\square$

Let $R \neq \{0\}$ be a commutative ring with identity, 1 and $S \subseteq R$, a multiplicatively closed subset containing 1 (i.e., if s_1 and $s_2 \in S$, then $s_1 \cdot s_2 \in S$.) Let us consider the following equivalence relation "$\sim$" on $R \times S$:

$$\left(\forall \langle r_1, s_1 \rangle, \langle r_2, s_2 \rangle \in R \times S \right)$$
$$\left[\langle r_1, s_1 \rangle \sim \langle r_2, s_2 \rangle \quad \text{iff} \quad (\exists s_3 \in S) [s_3(s_2 r_1 - r_2 s_1) = 0] \right].$$

Let $R_S = R \times S / \sim$ be the set of equivalence classes on $R \times S$ with respect to the equivalence relation $\sim$. The equivalence class containing $\langle r, s \rangle$ is denoted by r/s. The addition and multiplication on R_S are defined as follows:

$$\frac{r_1}{s_1} + \frac{r_2}{s_2} = \frac{s_2 r_1 + r_2 s_1}{s_1 s_2} \quad \text{and} \quad \frac{r_1}{s_1} \cdot \frac{r_2}{s_2} = \frac{r_1 r_2}{s_1 s_2}.$$

The element $0/1$ is the zero element of R_S and $1/1$ is the identity element of R_S. It is easy to verify that R_S is a commutative ring. The ring R_S is called the *ring of fractions* or *quotient ring of R with denominator set S.*

If S is chosen to be the multiplicatively closed set of all non-zero divisors of R, then R_S is said to be the *full ring of fractions* or *quotient ring of R*, and is denoted by $Q(R)$. In this case, the equivalence relation can be simplified as follows:

$$\left(\forall \langle r_1, s_1 \rangle, \langle r_2, s_2 \rangle \in R \times S \right)$$
$$\left[\langle r_1, s_1 \rangle \sim \langle r_2, s_2 \rangle \quad \text{iff} \quad s_2 r_1 = r_2 s_1 \right].$$

If D is an integral domain and $S = D^*$, then D_S can be shown to be a field; D_S is said to be the *field of fractions* or *quotient field of D*, and is denoted by $QF(D)$. The map

$$i \quad : \quad D \to QF(D)$$
$$: \quad d \mapsto d/1$$

defines an embedding of the integral domain D in the field $QF(D)$; the elements of the form $\frac{d}{1}$ are the "improper fractions" in the field $QF(D)$.

For example, if we choose D to be the integers $\mathbb{Z}$, then $QF(\mathbb{Z})$ is $\mathbb{Q}$, the field of rational numbers.

2.1.2   Homomorphism, Contraction and Extension

Definition 2.1.12 (Ring Homomorphism) The map $\phi: R \to R'$ is called a *ring homomorphism*, if $\phi(1) = 1$ and

$$\left(\forall\, a, b \in R\right) \left[\phi(a + b) = \phi(a) + \phi(b) \text{ and } \phi(a\,b) = \phi(a)\,\phi(b)\right].$$

That is, ϕ respects *identity*, *addition* and *multiplication*.   □

If $\phi: R \to R'$ and $\psi: R' \to R''$ are ring homomorphisms, then so is their composition $\psi \circ \phi$.

The *kernel* of a homomorphism $\phi: R \to R'$ is defined as:

$$\ker \phi = \left\{a \in R \;:\; \phi(a) = 0\right\}.$$

The *image* of a homomorphism $\phi: R \to R'$ is defined as:

$$\operatorname{im} \phi = \left\{a' \in R' \;:\; \left(\exists\, a \in R\right) \left[\phi(a) = a'\right]\right\}.$$

Let I be an ideal of a ring R. The quotient group R/I inherits a uniquely defined multiplication from R which makes it into a ring, called the *quotient ring* (or *residue class ring*) R/I. The elements of R/I are the cosets of I in R, and the mapping

$$\begin{aligned} \phi \;:\; & R \overset{\text{onto}}{\to} R/I \\ :\; & x \mapsto x + I \end{aligned}$$

which maps $x \in R$ to its coset $x + I$ is a surjective ring homomorphism. Thus the multiplication operation on R/I is as follows

$$(x + I)(y + I) = xy + I.$$

This definition is consistent, since, if $y + I = y' + I$, then $y - y' \in I$, i.e., $x(y - y') = xy - xy' \in I$ and $xy + I = xy' + I$.

Proposition 2.1.3

1. *For every ring homomorphism,* ϕ, $\ker \phi$ *is an ideal.*

2. *Conversely, for every ideal* $I \subseteq R$, $I = \ker \phi$ *for some ring homomorphism* ϕ.

3. *For every ring homomorphism,* ϕ, $\operatorname{im} \phi$ *is a subring of* R'.   □

Consider the ring homomorphism

$$\psi \quad : \quad R/\ker\phi \overset{\text{onto}}{\to} \operatorname{im}\phi$$
$$\quad : \quad x + \ker\phi \mapsto \phi(x).$$

ψ is a ring isomorphism, since if $\psi(x + \ker\phi) = \psi(y + \ker\phi)$ (i.e., $\phi(x) = \phi(y)$), then $\phi(x - y) = \phi(x) - \phi(y) = 0$ and $x - y \in \ker\phi$, thus, implying that $x + \ker\phi = y + \ker\phi$. Hence $\phi: R \to R'$ induces a ring isomorphism:

$$R/\ker\phi \cong \operatorname{im}\phi.$$

Proposition 2.1.4 *Let $\phi: R \overset{\text{onto}}{\to} R'$ be a ring homomorphism of R onto R'.*

1. *If $I \subseteq R$ is an ideal of R, then*

$$\phi(I) = \left\{ a' \in R' : \left(\exists\, a \in I\right) \left[\phi(a) = a'\right] \right\}$$

   is an ideal of R'. Similarly, if $I' \subseteq R'$ is an ideal of R', then

$$\phi^{-1}(I') = \left\{ a \in R : \left(\exists\, a' \in I'\right) \left[\phi(a) = a'\right] \right\}$$

   is an ideal of R.

2. *There is a one-to-one inclusions preserving correspondence between the ideals I' of R' and the ideals I of R which contain $\ker\phi$, such that if I and I' correspond, then*

$$\phi(I) = I', \quad \phi^{-1}(I') = I.$$

   When I and I' correspond, ϕ induces a homomorphism of I onto I', and

$$I/\ker\phi \cong I', \quad R/I \cong R'/I'. \quad \square$$

Definition 2.1.13 (Contraction and Extension) Let $\phi: R \to R'$ be a ring homomorphism.

1. If $I' \subseteq R'$ is an ideal of R' then the ideal

$$I'^c = \phi^{-1}(I') = \left\{ a \in R : \left(\exists\, a' \in I'\right) \left[\phi(a) = a'\right] \right\}$$

   in R is called the *contracted* ideal (or, simply, *contraction*) of I'. If the underlying homomorphism ϕ can be inferred from the context, then we also use the notation $I'\{R\}$ for the contracted ideal. In particular, if R is a subring of R', then the ideal $I'\{R\} = R \cap I'$, and it is the largest ideal in R contained in I'.

2. If $I \subseteq R$ is an ideal of R, then the ideal

$$I^e = R'\phi(I) = \left(\left\{ a' \in R' : \left(\exists\, a \in I \right) \left[\phi(a) = a' \right] \right\} \right),$$

i.e., the ideal generated by $\phi(I)$ in R' is called the *extended* ideal[1] (or, simply, *extension*) of I. If the underlying homomorphism ϕ can be inferred from the context, then we also use the notation $I\{R'\}$ for the extended ideal. In particular, if R is a subring of R', then the ideal $I\{R'\} = R'I$, and $R'I$ is the smallest ideal in R' which contains I. $\square$

The following relations are satisfied by the contracted and extended ideals:

1. $I' \subseteq J' \Rightarrow I'^c \subseteq J'^c$, and $I \subseteq J \Rightarrow I^e \subseteq J^e$.

2. $I'^{ce} \subseteq I'$, and $I^{ec} \supseteq I$.

3. $I'^{cec} = I'^c$, and $I^{ece} = I^e$.

The last relation says that *if an ideal in R' is an extended ideal, then it is the extension of its contraction*, and that *if an ideal in R is a contracted ideal, then it is the contraction of its extension*.

Let $\mathcal{C}$ be the set of contracted ideals in R, and let $\mathcal{E}$ be the set of extended ideals in R'. We see that the mapping $I' \mapsto I'^c$ and $I \mapsto I^e$ are one-to-one and are inverse mappings of $\mathcal{C}$ onto $\mathcal{E}$ and of $\mathcal{E}$ onto $\mathcal{C}$, respectively.

2.1.3   Ideal Operations

Let $I, J \subseteq R$ be ideals. Then the following *ideal operations* can be defined:

1. **Sum:** $I + J = \left\{ a + b \,:\, a \in I \text{ and } b \in J \right\}$.
   It is the smallest ideal containing both I and J.

2. **Intersection:** $I \cap J = \left\{ a \,:\, a \in I \text{ and } a \in J \right\}$.
   It is the largest ideal contained in both I and J.

3. **Product:** $IJ = \left\{ \sum_{i=1}^{n} a_i b_i \,:\, a_i \in I, \ b_i \in J \text{ and } n \in \mathbb{N} \right\}$.
   We define the powers I^n $(n \geq 0)$ of an ideal I as follows: conventionally, $I^0 = (1)$, and $I^n = I\,I^{n-1}$. Thus I^n $(n > 0)$ is the ideal generated by all products $x_1\, x_2 \cdots x_n$ in which each factor x_i belongs to I.

---

[1] Note that $\phi(I)$ itself is not an ideal in R' and hence, one needs to extend it sufficiently to obtain the smallest ideal containing $\phi(I)$. Also, the notation $R'\phi(I)$ does not stand for the elementwise product of the sets R' and $\phi(I)$ as such a set is not necessarily an ideal. $R'\phi(I)$ may be interpreted as the ideal product, which will be defined shortly.

4. **Quotient:** $I : J = \left\{ a \in R \ : \ aJ \subseteq I \right\}$.

The quotient $(0) : J$ is called the *annihilator* of J (denoted ann J): it is the set of all $a \in R$ such that $aJ = 0$.

5. **Radical:** $\sqrt{I} = \left\{ a \in R \ : \ \left(\exists\, n \in \mathbb{N} \right) \left[a^n \in I \right] \right\}$.

The following are some interesting properties of the ideal operations:

1. The operations sum, intersection and product are all commutative and associative.

2. **Modular Law:** If $I \supseteq J$, then $I \cap (J + K) = J + (I \cap K)$. This can be also written as follows:

$$[I \supseteq J \text{ or } I \supseteq K] \ \Rightarrow \ [I \cap (J + K) = (I \cap J) + (I \cap K)].$$

3. $I(J + K) = IJ + IK$.
   Hence, $(I + J)(I \cap J) = I(I \cap J) + J(I \cap J) \subseteq IJ$.

4. $IJ \subseteq I \cap J$.
   Two ideals I and J are called *coprime* (or *comaximal*), if $I + J = (1)$. Hence, we have $IJ = I \cap J$ provided that I and J are coprime. [Note that, in this case, $I \cap J = (I + J)(I \cap J) \subseteq IJ$.]

5. (a) $I \subseteq I : J$.

   (b) $(I : J)J \subseteq I$.

   (c) $\left((I : J) : K \right) = (I : JK) = \left((I : K) : J \right)$.

   (d) $\left(\bigcap_i I_i : J \right) = \bigcap_i (I_i : J)$.

   (e) $\left(I : \sum_i J_i \right) = \bigcap_i (I : J_i)$.

6. (a) $\sqrt{I} \supseteq I$.

   (b) $\sqrt{\sqrt{I}} = \sqrt{I}$.

   (c) $\sqrt{IJ} = \sqrt{I \cap J} = \sqrt{I} \cap \sqrt{J}$.

   (d) $\sqrt{I} = (1)$ iff $I = (1)$.

   (e) $\sqrt{I + J} = \sqrt{\sqrt{I} + \sqrt{J}}$.

2.2   Polynomial Rings

Let S be a ring, and x be a new symbol (called a *variable*, or *indeterminate*) not belonging to S. An expression of the form

$$f(x) = \sum_i a_i x^i, \quad \text{where } a_i \in S,$$

in which the sum is taken over a finite number of distinct integers $i \geq 0$, is called a *univariate polynomial* over the ring S. The ring elements a_i's are called the *coefficients* of f. [It is implicitly assumed that $a_i = 0$, if a_i is missing in the expression for $f(x)$.] All powers of x are assumed to commute with the ring elements: $a_i x^i = x^i a_i$.

The operations *addition* and *multiplication* of two polynomials $f(x) = \sum_i a_i x^i$ and $g(x) = \sum_j b_j x^j$ are defined as follows:

$$f(x) + g(x) \quad = \quad \sum_k c_k x^k, \quad \text{where } c_k = a_k + b_k,$$

$$f(x) \cdot g(x) \quad = \quad \sum_k c_k x^k, \quad \text{where } c_k = \sum_{i+j=k} a_i b_j.$$

It can be easily verified that the collection of polynomials with these addition and multiplication rules form a commutative ring with zero element 0 and identity element 1. The *polynomial ring*, thus obtained by *adjoining* the symbol x to S, is denoted by $R = S[x]$.

The *degree* of a nonzero polynomial $f(x)$, (denoted $\deg(f)$), is the highest power of x appearing in f; by convention, $\deg(0) = -\infty$.

Let $x_1, \ldots, x_n$ be n distinct new symbols not belonging to S. Then the ring R obtained by adjoining the variables $x_1, \ldots, x_n$, successively, to S is the *ring of multivariate polynomials* in $x_1, \ldots, x_n$ over the ring S:

$$R = S[x_1] \cdots [x_n] = S[x_1, \ldots, x_n].$$

Thus R consists of the multivariate polynomials of the form:

$$\sum a_{e_1, \ldots, e_n} x_1^{e_1} \cdots x_n^{e_n}.$$

A *power product* (or, a *term*) is an element of R of the form

$$p = x_1^{e_1} \cdots x_n^{e_n}, \quad e_i \geq 0.$$

The *total degree* of the power product p is

$$\deg(p) = \sum_{i=1}^{n} e_i.$$

The degree of p in any variable x_i is $\deg_{x_i}(p) = e_i$. By the expression $PP(x_1, \ldots, x_n)$, we denote the set of all power products involving the variables $x_1, \ldots, x_n$.

A power product $p = x_1^{d_1} \cdots x_n^{d_n}$ is a *multiple* of a power product $q = x_1^{e_1} \cdots x_n^{e_n}$ (denoted $q \mid p$), if

$$\left(\forall\, 1 \leq i \leq n\right) \left[e_i \leq d_i\right].$$

Synonymously, we say p is *divisible* by q. The *least common multiple* (LCM) of two power products $p = x_1^{d_1} \cdots x_n^{d_n}$ and $q = x_1^{e_1} \cdots x_n^{e_n}$ is given by

$$x_1^{\max(d_1, e_1)} \cdots x_n^{\max(d_n, e_n)}.$$

The *greatest common divisor* (GCD) of two power products $p = x_1^{d_1} \cdots x_n^{d_n}$ and $q = x_1^{e_1} \cdots x_n^{e_n}$ is given by

$$x_1^{\min(d_1, e_1)} \cdots x_n^{\min(d_n, e_n)}.$$

A *monomial* is an element of R of the form $m = ap$ where $a \in S$ is its *coefficient* and $p \in PP(x_1, \ldots, x_n)$ is its *power product*. The *total degree* of a monomial is simply the total degree of its power product.

Thus, a *polynomial* is simply a sum of a finite set of monomials. The *length* of a polynomial is the number of nonzero monomials in it. The *total degree* of a polynomial f [denoted $\deg(f)$] is the maximum of the total degrees of the monomials in it; again, by convention, $\deg(0) = -\infty$. Two polynomials are equal, if they contain exactly the same set of monomials (not including the monomials with zero coefficients).

2.2.1   Dickson's Lemma

The following lemma about the power products due to Dickson has many applications:

Lemma 2.2.1 (Dickson's Lemma) *Every set $X \subseteq PP(x_1, \ldots, x_n)$ of power products contains a finite subset $Y \subseteq X$ such that each $p \in X$ is a multiple of some power product in Y.*

PROOF.

We use induction on the number n of variables. If $n = 1$ then we let Y consist of the unique power product in X of minimum degree. So we may assume $n > 1$. Pick any $p_0 \in X$, say

$$p_0 = x_1^{e_1} \cdots x_n^{e_n}.$$

Then every $p \in X$ that is not divisible by p_0 belongs to at least one of $\sum_{i=1}^{n} e_i$ different sets: Let $i = 1, \ldots, n$ and $j = 0, 1, \ldots, e_i - 1$; then the set $X_{i,j}$ consists of those power products p's in X for which $\deg_{x_i}(p) = j$. Let $X'_{i,j}$ denote the set of power products obtained by omitting the factor x_i^j from power products in $X_{i,j}$. By the inductive hypothesis, there exist finite subsets $Y'_{i,j} \subseteq X'_{i,j}$ such that each power product in $X'_{i,j}$ is a multiple of some power product in $Y'_{i,j}$. We define $Y_{i,j}$ as

$$Y_{i,j} = \{p \cdot x_i^j \ : \ p \in Y'_{i,j}\}.$$

It is then clear that every power product in X is a multiple of some power product in the finite set

$$Y = \left(\{p_0\} \ \cup \ \bigcup_{i,j} Y_{i,j}\right) \subseteq X. \qquad \square$$

The proof of Dickson's lemma (Lemma 2.2.1) can be understood pictorially as follows:

Consider the case when $n = 2$; then every power product $x_1^{e_1} x_2^{e_2}$ can be associated with a *representative point* with coordinates (e_1, e_2) in $\mathbb{N}^2$. Note that every power product $x_1^{e'_1} x_2^{e'_2}$ with $e'_1 \geq e_1$ and $e'_2 \geq e_2$ is a multiple of $x_1^{e_1} x_2^{e_2}$; these are the power products whose representative points are above and to the right of the point (e_1, e_2): in Figure 2.1, the shaded region represents all such points.

Thus, given a set $X \subseteq \mathrm{PP}(x_1, x_2)$, we consider their representative points in $\mathbb{N}^2$. We first choose a power product $x_1^{e_1} x_2^{e_2} \in X$. As all the points of X in the shaded region are now "covered" by $x_1^{e_1} x_2^{e_2}$, we only need to choose enough points to cover the remaining points of X, which belong to the region $([0..e_1-1] \times \mathbb{N}) \cup (\mathbb{N} \times [0..e_2-1])$. For every i, $0 \leq i < e_1$, if

$$i' = \min_{x_1^i x_2^k \in X} k,$$

then the power product $x_1^i x_2^{i'}$ covers all the points of X in $i \times \mathbb{N}$. Similarly, for every j, $0 \leq j < e_2$, if

$$j' = \min_{x_1^k x_2^j \in X} k,$$

then the power product $x_1^{j'} x_2^j$ covers all the points of X in $\mathbb{N} \times j$. Thus the finite set

$$\{x_1^{e_1} x_2^{e_2}\} \cup \{x_1^i x_2^{i'} : 0 \leq i < e_1\} \cup \{x_1^{j'} x_2^j : 0 \leq j < e_2\}$$

is the desired set $Y \subseteq X$.

Let $R = S[x_1, \ldots, x_n]$ be a polynomial ring over an ambient ring S. Let $G \subseteq R$ be a (possibly, infinite) set of monomials in R. An ideal $I = (G)$, generated by the elements of G is said to be a *monomial ideal*. Note that if $J \subsetneq I$ is a subideal of I, then there exists a monomial $m \in I \setminus J$.

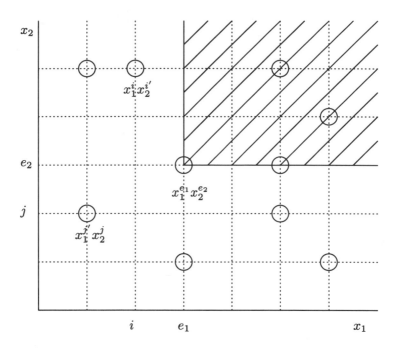

Figure 2.1: A pictorial explanation of Dickson's lemma

Theorem 2.2.2 *Let K be a field, and $I \subseteq K[x_1, \ldots, x_n]$ be a monomial ideal. Then I is finitely generated.*

PROOF.

Let G be a (possibly, infinite) set of monomial generators of I. Let

$$X = \{p \in \mathrm{PP}(x_1, \ldots, x_n) : ap \in G, \text{ for some } a \in K\}.$$

Note that $(X) = (G) = I$.

$$m = ap \in G \;\Rightarrow\; m \in (X), \quad \text{and}$$
$$p \in X \;\Rightarrow\; \left(\exists\, m = ap \in G\right) \left[p = a^{-1}m \in (G)\right].$$

Now, by Dickson's lemma, X contains a finite subset $Y \subseteq X$ such that each $p \in X$ is a multiple of a power product in Y.

Since $Y \subseteq X$, clearly $(Y) \subseteq (X)$. Conversely,

$$p \in X \Rightarrow \left(\exists\, q \in Y\right) \left[\, q \mid p \,\right] \Rightarrow p \in (Y).$$

Thus $(Y) = (X) = I$, and Y is a finite basis of I. $\square$

2.2.2　Admissible Orderings on Power Products

Definition 2.2.1 (Admissible Ordering) A total ordering $\leq_A$ on the set of power products $PP(x_1, \ldots, x_n)$ is said to be *admissible* if for all power products p, p', and $q \in PP(x_1, \ldots, x_n)$,

1. $1 \leq_A p$,　and

2. $p \leq_A p' \;\Rightarrow\; pq \leq_A p'q$.

Any total ordering that satisfies the second condition, but not necessarily the first, is called a *semiadmissible* ordering.

Note that the only semiadmissible orderings on $PP(x)$ are

$$1 <_a x <_a x^2 <_a \cdots <_a x^n <_a \cdots \quad \text{and}$$

$$\cdots <_b x^n <_b \cdots <_b x^2 <_b x <_b 1,$$

of which only the first one is admissible.　□

We also write $p <_A q$ if $p \neq q$ and $p \leq_A q$. Note that if a power product q is a multiple of a power product p, then $p \leq_A q$, under any admissible ordering $\leq_A$:

$$p \mid q \;\Rightarrow\; \left(\exists \text{ a power product, } p'\right) \left[p'p = q\right];$$

but $1 \leq_A p'$, and thus, $p \leq_A p'p = q$.

Lemma 2.2.3 *Every admissible ordering $\leq_A$ on* PP *is a well-ordering.*

PROOF.
This follows from Dickson's lemma: Suppose we have an infinite descending sequence of power products

$$p_1 >_A p_2 >_A \cdots >_A p_i >_A \cdots.$$

Let $X = \{p_1, p_2, \ldots, p_i, \ldots\}$ and let $Y \subseteq X$ be a finite subset such that every $p \in X$ is a multiple of some power product in Y. Let p' be the power product that is smallest in Y under the ordering $\leq_A$:

$$p' = \min_{\leq_A} Y.$$

Since the power products in X constitute an infinite descending sequence,

$$\left(\exists q \in X\right) \left[q <_A p'\right].$$

But, we know that

$$\left(\exists\, p \in Y\right)\left[p \mid q\right].$$

Hence,

$$\left(\exists\, p \in Y\right)\left[p \underset{A}{\leq} q \underset{A}{<} p'\right],$$

contradicting the choice of p'. $\square$

Proposition 2.2.4 *Let* $\underset{X}{\leq}$ *and* $\underset{Y}{\leq}$ *be two semiadmissible orderings on* $\mathrm{PP}(X)$ *and* $\mathrm{PP}(Y)$, *respectively.*

1. *Define* $\underset{L}{\leq}$ *on* $\mathrm{PP}(X,Y)$ *as follows:*

$$pq \underset{L}{\leq} p'q', \quad \textit{where } p, p \in \mathrm{PP}(X) \textit{ and } q, q' \in \mathrm{PP}(Y),$$

if (i) $p \underset{X}{<} p'$, *or (ii)* $p = p'$ *and* $q \underset{Y}{\leq} q'$.

2. *Define* $\underset{R}{\leq}$ *on* $\mathrm{PP}(X,Y)$ *as follows:*

$$pq \underset{R}{\leq} p'q', \quad \textit{where } p, p' \in \mathrm{PP}(X) \textit{ and } q, q' \in \mathrm{PP}(Y),$$

if (i) $q \underset{Y}{<} q'$, *or (ii)* $q = q'$ *and* $p \underset{X}{\leq} p'$.

Then both $\underset{L}{\leq}$ *and* $\underset{R}{\leq}$ *are semiadmissible. Furthermore, if both* $\underset{X}{\leq}$ *and* $\underset{Y}{\leq}$ *are admissible, then so are both* $\underset{L}{\leq}$ *and* $\underset{R}{\leq}$. $\square$

Let $p = x_1^{a_1} x_2^{a_2} \cdots x_n^{a_n}$ and $q = x_1^{b_1} x_2^{b_2} \cdots x_n^{b_n}$ be two power products in $\mathrm{PP}(x_1, x_2, \ldots, x_n)$. We define two semiadmissible orderings, *lexicographic* and *reverse lexicographic* as follows; their semiadmissibility follows from the above proposition.

1. **Lexicographic Ordering:** $(\underset{\mathrm{LEX}}{>})$

   We say $p \underset{\mathrm{LEX}}{>} q$ if $a_i \neq b_i$ for some i, and for the *minimum* such i, $a_i > b_i$, i.e., the first nonzero entry in

$$\langle a_1, \ldots, a_n \rangle - \langle b_1, \ldots, b_n \rangle$$

   is positive. This is easily seen to be also an admissible ordering. Note that, $x_1 \underset{\mathrm{LEX}}{>} x_2 \underset{\mathrm{LEX}}{>} \cdots \underset{\mathrm{LEX}}{>} x_n$. For example, in $\mathrm{PP}(w, x, y, z)$, we have:

$$
\begin{aligned}
1 &\underset{\mathrm{LEX}}{<} z \underset{\mathrm{LEX}}{<} z^2 \underset{\mathrm{LEX}}{<} \cdots \\
&\underset{\mathrm{LEX}}{<} y \underset{\mathrm{LEX}}{<} yz \underset{\mathrm{LEX}}{<} \cdots \underset{\mathrm{LEX}}{<} y^2 \cdots \\
&\underset{\mathrm{LEX}}{<} x \underset{\mathrm{LEX}}{<} xz \underset{\mathrm{LEX}}{<} \cdots \underset{\mathrm{LEX}}{<} xy \underset{\mathrm{LEX}}{<} \cdots \underset{\mathrm{LEX}}{<} x^2 \cdots \\
&\underset{\mathrm{LEX}}{<} w \underset{\mathrm{LEX}}{<} wz \underset{\mathrm{LEX}}{<} \cdots \underset{\mathrm{LEX}}{<} wy \underset{\mathrm{LEX}}{<} \cdots \underset{\mathrm{LEX}}{<} wx \underset{\mathrm{LEX}}{<} \cdots \underset{\mathrm{LEX}}{<} w^2 \cdots
\end{aligned}
$$

2. **Reverse Lexicographic Ordering:** ($\underset{\text{RLEX}}{>}$)

We say $p \underset{\text{RLEX}}{>} q$ if $a_i \neq b_i$ for some i, and for the *maximum* such i, $a_i < b_i$, i.e., the last nonzero entry in

$$\langle a_1, \ldots, a_n \rangle - \langle b_1, \ldots, b_n \rangle$$

is negative. This ordering is semiadmissible, but not admissible. Note that $x_1 \underset{\text{RLEX}}{>} x_2 \underset{\text{RLEX}}{>} \cdots \underset{\text{RLEX}}{>} x_n$. For example, in $\mathrm{PP}(w, x, y, z)$, we have:

$$\cdots \underset{\text{RLEX}}{<} z^2 \underset{\text{RLEX}}{<} \cdots \underset{\text{RLEX}}{<} yz \underset{\text{RLEX}}{<} \cdots \underset{\text{RLEX}}{<} xz \underset{\text{RLEX}}{<} \cdots \underset{\text{RLEX}}{<} wz \underset{\text{RLEX}}{<} z \underset{\text{RLEX}}{<}$$
$$\cdots \underset{\text{RLEX}}{<} y^2 \underset{\text{RLEX}}{<} \cdots \underset{\text{RLEX}}{<} xy \underset{\text{RLEX}}{<} \cdots \underset{\text{RLEX}}{<} wy \underset{\text{RLEX}}{<} y \underset{\text{RLEX}}{<}$$
$$\cdots \underset{\text{RLEX}}{<} x^2 \underset{\text{RLEX}}{<} \cdots \underset{\text{RLEX}}{<} wx \underset{\text{RLEX}}{<} x \underset{\text{RLEX}}{<}$$
$$\cdots \underset{\text{RLEX}}{<} w^2 \underset{\text{RLEX}}{<} w \underset{\text{RLEX}}{<} 1.$$

Let $p = x_1^{a_1} x_2^{a_2} \cdots x_n^{a_n}$ and $q = x_1^{b_1} x_2^{b_2} \cdots x_n^{b_n}$ be two power products in $\mathrm{PP}(x_1, x_2, \ldots, x_n)$. We say $p \underset{\text{TOT}}{\succ} q$, if $\deg(p) > \deg(q)$. The order $\underset{\text{TOT}}{\succ}$ is only a partial ordering, and hence not an admissible ordering. However, we can make it an admissible ordering by refining it via a semiadmissible ordering.

Let $\underset{\text{A}}{>}$ be a semiadmissible ordering. We define a new ordering $\underset{\text{TA}}{>}$ (the total ordering refined via $\underset{\text{A}}{>}$) on $\mathrm{PP}(x_1, \ldots, x_n)$ as follows: We say $p \underset{\text{TA}}{>} q$, if $\deg(p) > \deg(q)$, or if, when $\deg(p) = \deg(q)$, $p \underset{\text{A}}{>} q$. That is, the power products of different degrees are ordered by the degree, and within the same degree the power products are ordered by $\underset{\text{A}}{>}$.

Lemma 2.2.5 *The ordering* $\underset{\text{TA}}{>}$ *is an admissible ordering.*

PROOF.
Since $\underset{\text{TA}}{>}$ is a refinement of the total degree ordering, for all $p \in \mathrm{PP}$, $1 \underset{\text{TA}}{\leq} p$. Now assume that $p \leq p'$. Then if $\deg(p) < \deg(p')$, $\deg(pq) < \deg(p'q)$ and $pq \underset{\text{TA}}{\leq} p'q$. Otherwise $\deg(p) = \deg(p')$ and $p \underset{\text{A}}{\leq} p'$. Hence $\deg(pq) = \deg(p'q)$ and by the semiadmissibility of $\underset{\text{A}}{>}$, $pq \underset{\text{A}}{\leq} p'q$, and $pq \underset{\text{TA}}{\leq} p'q$. $\square$

The next two admissible orderings have important applications in computations involving homogeneous ideals[2]; by the proposition above, both of them are admissible orderings.

---

[2]Roughly, a homogeneous polynomial is one in which every monomial is of the same degree, and a homogeneous ideal is one with a basis consisting of a set of homogeneous polynomials.

1. **Total Lexicographic Ordering:** ($\underset{\text{TLEX}}{>}$)

   We say $p \underset{\text{TLEX}}{>} q$ if

   (a) $\deg(p) > \deg(q)$, or else,

   (b) In case $\deg(p) = \deg(q)$, $a_i \neq b_i$ for some i, and for the *minimum* such i, $a_i > b_i$, i.e., the *first* nonzero entry in

   $$\langle a_1, \ldots, a_n \rangle - \langle b_1, \ldots, b_n \rangle$$

   is *positive*.

   For example, in $\text{PP}(w, x, y, z)$, we have

   $$1 \underset{\text{TLEX}}{<} z \underset{\text{TLEX}}{<} y \underset{\text{TLEX}}{<} x \underset{\text{TLEX}}{<} w \underset{\text{TLEX}}{<} z^2 \underset{\text{TLEX}}{<} yz \underset{\text{TLEX}}{<} y^2 \underset{\text{TLEX}}{<} xz \underset{\text{TLEX}}{<} xy$$

   $$\underset{\text{TLEX}}{<} x^2 \underset{\text{TLEX}}{<} wz \underset{\text{TLEX}}{<} wy \underset{\text{TLEX}}{<} wx \underset{\text{TLEX}}{<} w^2 \cdots$$

2. **Total Reverse Lexicographic Ordering:** ($\underset{\text{TRLEX}}{>}$)

   We say $p \underset{\text{TRLEX}}{>} q$ if

   (a) $\deg(p) > \deg(q)$, or else,

   (b) In case $\deg(p) = \deg(q)$, $a_i \neq b_i$ for some i, and for the *maximum* such i, $a_i < b_i$, i.e., the *last* nonzero entry in

   $$\langle a_1, \ldots, a_n \rangle - \langle b_1, \ldots, b_n \rangle$$

   is *negative*.

   For example, in $\text{PP}(w, x, y, z)$, we have

   $$1 \underset{\text{TRLEX}}{<} z \underset{\text{TRLEX}}{<} y \underset{\text{TRLEX}}{<} x \underset{\text{TRLEX}}{<} w \underset{\text{TRLEX}}{<} z^2 \underset{\text{TRLEX}}{<} yz \underset{\text{TRLEX}}{<} xz \underset{\text{TRLEX}}{<} wz$$

   $$\underset{\text{TRLEX}}{<} y^2 \underset{\text{TRLEX}}{<} xy \underset{\text{TRLEX}}{<} wy \underset{\text{TRLEX}}{<} x^2 \underset{\text{TRLEX}}{<} wx \underset{\text{TRLEX}}{<} w^2 \cdots$$

Henceforth, fix $\underset{A}{\leq}$ to be any admissible ordering. By an abuse of notation, we will say, for any two monomials $m = ap$ and $m' = a'p'$ ($a, a' \in S$ and $p, p' \in \text{PP}$), $m \underset{A}{\leq} m'$, if $p \underset{A}{\leq} p'$. We also assume that every polynomial $f \in R$ is written with its monomials ordered as a descending sequence under $\underset{A}{>}$, i.e., $f = m_1 + m_2 + \cdots + m_k$, where each of m_i's is a monomial of f, and $m_1 \underset{A}{>} m_2 \underset{A}{>} \cdots \underset{A}{>} m_k$.

Definition 2.2.2 (Head Monomial) Let $f \in R$ be a polynomial. The *head monomial* Hmono(f) of f is the monomial in f whose power product is largest relative to $\underset{A}{\leq}$, i.e., if $f = m_1 + m_2 + \cdots + m_k$, then Hmono($f$) = m_1.

We define the *head term* of f (denoted, Hterm(f)) to be the power product of Hmono(f) and the *head coefficient* of f (denoted, Hcoef(f)) to be the coefficient of Hmono(f). Thus

$$\text{Hmono}(f) = \text{Hcoef}(f) \cdot \text{Hterm}(f).$$

By convention, Hcoef(0) = Hmono(0) = 0. We use the notation Tail(f) to stand for $f - \text{Hmono}(f)$.   □

For instance, relative to any admissible total degree ordering, the head monomial of $f = 4xy + y - 5$ is Hmono(f) = $4xy$, when f is considered to be a polynomial in $\mathbb{Z}[x, y]$. Notice that if we consider f to be an element of $(\mathbb{Z}[x])[y]$, then, under any admissible ordering, the head monomial of f is $4xy + y$.

The lexicographic, total lexicographic and total reverse lexicographic (admissible) orderings play certain important roles in various computations involving ideals, the last two of the above three admissible orderings being very crucial in the case of homogeneous ideals. The reasons for their importance are primarily the following:

1. The lexicographic ordering has the property that for each subring $S[x_i, \ldots, x_n] \subseteq R$, and each polynomial $f \in R$, $f \in S[x_i, \ldots, x_n]$ if and only if Hmono(f) $\in S[x_i, \ldots, x_n]$.

2. The total lexicographic ordering has the property that for each subring $S[x_i, \ldots, x_n] \subseteq R$, and each *homogeneous* polynomial $f \in R$, $f \in S[x_i, \ldots, x_n]$ if and only if Hmono(f) $\in S[x_i, \ldots, x_n]$.

3. The total reverse lexicographic ordering has the property that for each *homogeneous* polynomial $f \in S[x_1, \ldots, x_i]$, x_i divides f if and only if x_i divides Hmono(f).

As a result, there is an elimination algorithm (similar to Gaussian elimination for a system of linear equations) such that the elimination using the lexicographic ordering (total lexicographic ordering) produces elements of an ideal (homogeneous ideal) which are free of the first variable, and the elimination using the total reverse lexicographic ordering produces elements of a homogeneous ideal which are divisible by the last variable.

2.3   Gröbner Bases

Definition 2.3.1 (Head Monomial Ideal) Let $G \subseteq R$ be a subset of R. The *head monomial ideal* of G [denoted Head(G)] is the ideal generated by the head monomials of the elements of G, i.e.,

$$\text{Head}(G) = \Big(\{\text{Hmono}(f) : f \in G\} \Big). \quad \square$$

Definition 2.3.2 (Gröbner Basis) A subset G of an ideal $I \subseteq R$ in R is called a *Gröbner basis* of the ideal I if

$$\text{Head}(G) = \text{Head}(I),$$

i.e., if the set of monomials $\{\text{Hmono}(f) : f \in G\}$ is a basis of Head(I).
$\square$

If, in the definitions of head monomial, head monomial ideal and Gröbner basis, the underlying admissible ordering $\underset{\wedge}{>}$ is not readily decipherable, then we explicitly state which ordering is involved by a suitable subscript.

Notice that since $G = I$ satisfies the above condition, every ideal has a Gröbner basis. Also, an ideal can have many distinct Gröbner bases. For instance, if G is a Gröbner basis for I, then so is every G', $G \subseteq G' \subseteq I$. However, since a Gröbner basis need not be finite, as such, it is not computationally very beneficial. Also, in general (for arbitrary ring S), we do not know how to compute a Gröbner basis effectively.

Further, notice that if $G \subseteq I$, then Head(G) $\subseteq$ Head(I). Hence, to demonstrate that G is a Gröbner basis of I, it suffices to show that Head(G) $\supseteq$ Head(I).

The following theorem justifies the term "basis" in a Gröbner basis:

Theorem 2.3.1 *Let $I \subseteq R$ be an ideal of R, and G a subset of I. Then*

$$\text{Head}(G) = \text{Head}(I) \quad \Rightarrow \quad (G) = I.$$

That is, every Gröbner basis of an ideal generates the ideal.
PROOF.
Since $G \subseteq I$, we have $(G) \subseteq I$. If $(G) \neq I$ then we may choose an $f \in I \backslash (G)$ such that Hmono(f) is minimal with respect to the underlying admissible well-ordering, say $\underset{\wedge}{\leq}$, among all such polynomials. Thus, Hmono(f) $\in$ Head(I) = Head(G):

$$\text{Hmono}(f) = \sum_{g_i \in G} t_i \text{Hmono}(g_i), \quad t_i \in R,$$

and
$$f' = \text{Tail}(f) - \sum t_i \text{Tail}(g_i) = f - \sum t_i g_i \in I.$$

Clearly, $f' \in I \backslash (G)$, since, otherwise, $f = f' + \sum t_i g_i$ would be in (G). But, $\text{Hmono}(f') \underset{A}{<} \text{Hmono}(f)$, since every monomial in $\text{Tail}(f)$ as well as every monomial in each of $t_i \text{Tail}(g_i)$ is smaller than $\text{Hmono}(f)$; consequently, we have a contradiction in our choice of f. Hence, $(G) = I$, i.e., every Gröbner basis of an ideal generates the ideal. $\square$

Corollary 2.3.2

1. *Two ideals I and J with the same Gröbner basis G are the same:*
   $I = (G) = J$.

2. *If $J \subseteq I$ are ideal of R, and $\text{Head}(J) = \text{Head}(I)$, then $J = I$.*

PROOF.
(1) is simply a restatement of the previous theorem. (2) follows from (1) since J is a Gröbner basis for both I and J. $\square$

Theorem 2.3.3 *The subset $G \subseteq I$ is a Gröbner basis of an ideal I of R with respect to an admissible ordering $\underset{A}{>}$ if and only if each polynomial $h \in I$ can be expressed as*

$$h = \sum_{g_i \in G} f_i g_i, \quad f_i \in R,$$

such that $\text{Hterm}(f_i) \text{Hterm}(g_i) \underset{A}{\leq} \text{Hterm}(h)$.

PROOF.
($\Rightarrow$) Let $h \in I$. Inductively, assume that the theorem holds for all $h' \underset{A}{<} h$. Since $\text{Hmono}(h) \in \text{Head}(I) = \text{Head}(G)$, it is possible to write

$$\text{Hmono}(h) = \sum_{g_i \in G} a_i p_i \text{Hmono}(g_i), \quad a_i \in S, \ p_i \in \text{PP}(x_1, \ldots, x_n)$$

such that $p_i \text{Hterm}(g_i) = \text{Hterm}(h)$.
Let

$$h' = \text{Tail}(h) - \sum a_i p_i \text{Tail}(g_i) = h - \sum a_i p_i g_i.$$

Since $\text{Hmono}(h') \underset{A}{<} \text{Hmono}(h)$, by the inductive hypothesis, we can write h as

$$h = h' + \sum a_i p_i g_i = \sum f_i' g_i' + \sum a_i p_i g_i,$$

such that $\text{Hterm}(f_i') \text{Hterm}(g_i') \underset{A}{\leq} \text{Hterm}(h') \underset{A}{<} \text{Hterm}(h)$ and $p_i \text{Hterm}(g_i) \underset{A}{\leq} \text{Hterm}(h)$.

($\Leftarrow$) Without loss of generality, we assume that $h \in I$ is expressed as

$$h = a_1 p_1 g_1 + \cdots + a_k p_k g_k, \quad a_i \in S, \ p_i \in \text{PP}(x_1, \ldots, x_n), \ g_i \in G,$$

such that $p_i \operatorname{Hterm}(g_i) \underset{A}{\leq} \operatorname{Hterm}(h)$.

Let L be the set of indices such that

$$L = \Big\{ i \in \{1, \ldots, k\} : \operatorname{Hterm}(h) = p_i \operatorname{Hterm}(g_i) \Big\}.$$

Since $\operatorname{Hterm}(h) \underset{A}{\geq} p_i \operatorname{Hterm}(g_i)$, $L \neq \emptyset$.

Equating terms of equal degree in the previous expression for h, we get $\operatorname{Hcoef}(h) = \sum_{i \in L} a_i \operatorname{Hcoef}(g_i)$. Hence

$$
\begin{aligned}
\operatorname{Hmono}(h) &= \operatorname{Hcoef}(h)\,\operatorname{Hterm}(h) \\
&= \sum_{i \in L} a_i \operatorname{Hcoef}(g_i)\, p_i \, \operatorname{Hterm}(g_i) \\
&= \sum_{i \in L} a_i p_i \operatorname{Hmono}(g_i),
\end{aligned}
$$

i.e., $\operatorname{Head}(G) \supseteq \operatorname{Head}(I)$, and G is a Gröbner basis of I. $\quad\square$

2.3.1   Gröbner Bases in $K[x_1, x_2, \ldots, x_n]$

Let K be any arbitrary field, and $K[x_1, x_2, \ldots, x_n]$ be the polynomial ring over the field K in variables x_1, x_2, $\ldots$, and x_n.

Theorem 2.3.4 *Every ideal I of $K[x_1, x_2, \ldots, x_n]$ has a finite Gröbner basis.*

PROOF.
Let $<$ be an arbitrary but fixed admissible ordering on $\operatorname{PP}(x_1, \ldots, x_n)$.

Let $X = \{\operatorname{Hterm}(f) : f \in I\}$ be a subset of $\operatorname{PP}(x_1, x_2, \ldots, x_n)$. Then by Dickson's lemma, there is a finite subset $Y \subseteq X$ such that every power product of X is divisible by a power product of Y. Define an injective map $\Phi : Y \to I$, as follows: for each power product $p \in Y$ choose a polynomial $g = \Phi(p) \in I$ such that $\operatorname{Hterm}(g) = p$. This map is well defined, since every $p \in Y$ is a head term of some polynomial in I; it is injective, since $p, q \in Y$ and $p \neq q$ implies that $\operatorname{Hterm}(\Phi(p)) \neq \operatorname{Hterm}(\Phi(q))$, and $\Phi(p) \neq \Phi(q)$.

Let $G = \Phi(Y) \subseteq I$. From the finiteness of Y, it trivially follows that G is finite. But, by proceeding as in the proof of Theorem 2.2.2, we see that

$$\operatorname{Head}(G) = (Y) = (X) = \operatorname{Head}(I),$$

and G is a Gröbner basis for I. $\quad\square$

Corollary 2.3.5 *For any field K,*

1. *Every ideal of $K[x_1, x_2, \ldots, x_n]$ has a finite system of generators.*

2. *$K[x_1, x_2, \ldots, x_n]$ is a Noetherian ring.* $\quad\square$

2.3.2　Hilbert's Basis Theorem

Proposition 2.3.6 *Let R be a ring. Then the following three statements are equivalent:*

1. *R is Noetherian.*

2. *The ascending chain condition (ACC) for ideals holds:*
   Any ascending chain of ideals of R

$$I_1 \subseteq I_2 \subseteq \cdots \subseteq I_n \subseteq \cdots$$

   becomes stationary. That is, there exists an n_0 $(1 \leq n_0)$ such that for all $n > n_0$, $I_{n_0} = I_n$.

3. *The maximal condition for ideals holds:*
   Any nonempty set of ideals of R contains a maximal element (with respect to inclusion).

PROOF.

$(1 \Rightarrow 2)$:

For a chain of ideals of R

$$I_1 \subseteq I_2 \subseteq \cdots \subseteq I_n \subseteq \cdots$$

$I = \bigcup_{n=1}^{\infty} I_n$ is also an ideal of R. ($f, g \in I$ implies that for large enough n_0, $f, g \in I_{n_0}$; hence $f - g \in I_{n_0} \subseteq I$. $f \in I$ implies that for large enough n_0, $f \in I_{n_0}$; hence for all $h \in R$, $h \cdot f \in I_{n_0} \subseteq I$.)

By hypothesis, I is finitely generated: $I = (f_1, f_2, \ldots, f_m)$, $f_i \in R$. For sufficiently large n_0 we have $f_i \in I_{n_0}$ $(i = 1, \ldots, m)$. Thus

$$I = (f_1, f_2, \ldots, f_m) \subseteq I_{n_0} \subseteq I_{n_0+1} \subseteq \cdots \subseteq I,$$

and for all $n > n_0$, $I_{n_0} = I_n = I$.

$(2 \Rightarrow 1)$:

Assume to the contrary. Then there is an ideal I of R, which is not finitely generated. If $f_1, f_2, \ldots, f_m \in I$, then $(f_1, f_2, \ldots, f_m) \subsetneq I$. Hence there is an $f_{m+1} \in I$, $f_{m+1} \notin (f_1, f_2, \ldots, f_m)$. Thus

$$(f_1, f_2, \ldots, f_m) \subsetneq (f_1, f_2, \ldots, f_m, f_{m+1}).$$

Thus we can construct an infinite (nonstationary) ascending chain of ideals

$$(f_1) \subsetneq (f_1, f_2) \subsetneq (f_1, f_2, f_3) \subsetneq \cdots,$$

in direct contradiction to our hypothesis.

$(2 \Rightarrow 3)$:

Suppose there is a nonempty set $\mathcal{I}$ of ideals of R without a maximal element.

For each $I_1 \in \mathcal{I}$ there is an $I_2 \in \mathcal{I}$ with $I_1 \subsetneq I_2$. In this way one can construct a nonstationary ascending chain of ideals:

$$I_1 \subsetneq I_2 \subsetneq \cdots \subsetneq I_n \subsetneq \cdots,$$

contradicting the hypothesis.

$(3 \Rightarrow 2)$:

Apply the maximal condition to the set of ideals in a chain of ideals to obtain an I_{n_0}, maximal among the ideals (under inclusion). Thus for all $n > n_0$, $I_{n_0} \not\subset I_n$, i.e., $I_{n_0} = I_n$. $\square$

Theorem 2.3.7 (Hilbert's Basis Theorem) *If R is a Noetherian ring, so is $R[x]$.*

PROOF.

Assume that R is Noetherian, but $R[x]$ is not. We shall derive a contradiction.

Then $R[x]$ must contain an ideal I, which is not finitely generated. Let $f_1 \in I$ be a polynomial of least degree. If f_k $(k \geq 1)$ has already been chosen, choose f_{k+1}, the polynomial of least degree in $I \setminus (f_1, f_2, \ldots, f_k)$. Since I is not finitely generated such a sequence of choices can be carried on.

Let $n_k = \deg(f_k)$ and $a_k \in R$, the leading coefficient of f_k $(k = 1, 2, \ldots)$. Observe that

- $n_1 \leq n_2 \leq \cdots$, simply by the choice of f_k's;

- $(a_1) \subseteq (a_1, a_2) \subseteq \cdots (a_1, a_2, \ldots, a_k) \subseteq (a_1, a_2, \ldots, a_k, a_{k+1}) \subseteq \cdots$ is a chain of ideals that must become stationary, as R is Noetherian. That is, for some k, $(a_1, a_2, \ldots, a_k) = (a_1, a_2, \ldots, a_k, a_{k+1})$, and $a_{k+1} = b_1 a_1 + b_2 a_2 + \cdots b_k a_k$, $b_i \in R$.

Now consider the polynomial

$$g = f_{k+1} - b_1 x^{n_{k+1}-n_1} f_1 - \cdots - b_k x^{n_{k+1}-n_k} f_k.$$

Notice that (1) $\deg g < \deg f_{k+1}$, (2) $g \in I$ and (3) $g \notin (f_1, f_2, \ldots, f_k)$. [Otherwise, it would imply that $f_{k+1} \in (f_1, f_2, \ldots, f_k)$.] But this contradicts our choice of f_{k+1} as a least-degree polynomial in $I \setminus (f_1, f_2, \ldots, f_k)$. $\square$

Corollary 2.3.8

1. If R is a Noetherian ring, so is every polynomial ring $R[x_1, x_2, \ldots, x_n]$.

2. Let R be a Noetherian ring and S an extension ring of R that is finitely generated over R, in the ring sense. (S is a homomorphic image of a polynomial ring $R[x_1, \ldots, x_n]$.) Then S is Noetherian.

3. For any field K, $K[x_1, x_2, \ldots, x_n]$ is a Noetherian ring. $\square$

2.3.3   Finite Gröbner Bases

Theorem 2.3.9 *Let S be a Noetherian ring. Then every ideal of $R = S[x_1, x_2, \ldots, x_n]$ has a finite Gröbner basis.*

PROOF.

Since S is Noetherian, by Hilbert's basis theorem, so is $R = S[x_1, x_2, \ldots, x_n]$. Let $\underset{A}{<}$ be an arbitrary but fixed admissible ordering on $PP(x_1, x_2, \ldots, x_n)$.

Let I be an ideal in R, and $\text{Head}(I)$, the monomial ideal generated by the head monomials of the polynomials in I. Let us choose a polynomial $g_1 \in I$; if $G_1 = \{g_1\} \subseteq I$ is not a Gröbner basis of I, then $\text{Head}(G_1) \subsetneqq \text{Head}(I)$, and there is a polynomial $g_2 \in I$ such that $\text{Hmono}(g_2) \in \text{Head}(I) \setminus \text{Head}(G_1)$. Clearly, $G_2 = \{g_1, g_2\} \subseteq I$ and $\text{Head}(G_1) \subsetneqq \text{Head}(G_2)$.

In the $(k+1)^{\text{th}}$ step, assume that we have chosen a set $G_k = \{g_1, g_2, \ldots, g_k\} \subseteq I$. Now, if G_k is not a Gröbner basis for I, then there is a $g_{k+1} \in I$ such that

$$\text{Hmono}(g_{k+1}) \in \text{Head}(I) \setminus \text{Head}(G_k),$$

and $G_{k+1} = G_k \cup \{g_{k+1}\} \subseteq I$ and $\text{Head}(G_k) \subsetneqq \text{Head}(G_{k+1})$. But, since R is Noetherian, it cannot have a nonstationary ascending chain of ideals

$$\text{Head}(G_1) \subsetneqq \text{Head}(G_2) \subsetneqq \cdots \subsetneqq \text{Head}(G_k) \subsetneqq \cdots,$$

and there is some $n \geq 1$ such that $\text{Head}(G_n) = \text{Head}(I)$. But since $G_n \subseteq I$, we see that $G_n = \{g_1, g_2, \ldots, g_n\}$ is a finite Gröbner basis for I with respect to the admissible ordering $\underset{A}{<}$. $\square$

2.4   Modules and Syzygies

Definition 2.4.1 (Modules) Given a ring S, an Abelian group M, and a mapping

$$
\begin{aligned}
\mu \quad &: \quad S \times M \to M \\
&: \quad \langle s, x \rangle \mapsto sx,
\end{aligned}
$$

we say M is an *S-module* if, for all s, $t \in S$ and x, $y \in M$, the following axioms are satisfied:

$$
\begin{aligned}
s(x + y) &= sx + sy, \\
(s + t)x &= sx + tx, \\
(st)x &= s(tx), \\
1x &= x.
\end{aligned}
$$

Thus, an S-module is an additive Abelian group M on which the ring S acts linearly. $\square$

If S is a field K, then a K-module is said to be a *K-vector space*.

Note that if S is any ring, then any ideal $I \subseteq S$ is an S-module. In particular, S itself is an S-module. Also, every Abelian group $(G, +, 0)$ is a $\mathbb{Z}$-module: here, the mapping $\langle n, x \rangle \mapsto nx$ $(n \in \mathbb{Z}, x \in G)$ has the following outcome:

$$
nx = \begin{cases}
\underbrace{x + x + \cdots + x}_{n} & \text{if } n > 0; \\[2mm]
0 & \text{if } n = 0; \\[2mm]
\underbrace{(-x) + (-x) + \cdots + (-x)}_{n} & \text{if } n < 0.
\end{cases}
$$

Let $S \neq \{0\}$ be a ring, $T \subseteq S$, a multiplicatively closed subset and M, an S-module. Consider the following equivalence relation "$\sim$" on $M \times T$:

$$
\Big(\forall \, \langle x_1, a_1 \rangle, \langle x_2, a_2 \rangle \in M \times T \Big)
$$
$$
\Big[\langle x_1, a_1 \rangle \sim \langle x_2, a_2 \rangle \quad \text{iff} \quad (\exists \, a_3 \in T) \, [a_3(a_2 x_1 - x_2 a_1) = 0] \Big].
$$

Let $M_T = M \times T / \sim$ be the set of equivalence classes on $M \times T$ with respect to the equivalence relation $\sim$. The equivalence class containing $\langle x, a \rangle$ is denoted by x/a. M_T can be made into an S_T-module with the obvious definitions of addition and scalar multiplication. M_T is called the *module of fractions of M with denominator set T*.

Definition 2.4.2 (Module Homomorphisms) Let S be a ring and let M and N be S-modules. Then a mapping

$$
\phi: M \to N
$$

is said to be an *S-module homomorphism* if, for all $s \in S$ and $x, y \in M$,

$$
\phi(x + y) = \phi(x) + \phi(y) \quad \text{and} \quad \phi(sx) = s\phi(x),
$$

i.e., S acts linearly with respect to ϕ.

Let ϕ be an S-module homomorphism as before. We define the *kernel* of ϕ to be

$$
\ker \phi = \{ x \in M \,:\, \phi(x) = 0 \}
$$

and the *image* of ϕ to be

$$
\operatorname{im} \phi = \{ \phi(x) \in N \,:\, x \in M \}.
$$

It can be verified that $\ker \phi$ and $\operatorname{im} \phi$ are both S-modules. $\square$

Definition 2.4.3 (Submodule) Let S be a ring and M an S-module. Then M' is a said to be a *submodule* of M if M' is a subgroup of M and M' is an S-module, i.e., M' is closed under multiplication by the elements of S.   □

Definition 2.4.4 (Quotient Submodule) Given S, M and M' as in the previous definition (Definition 2.4.3), we make the quotient Abelian group M/M' an S-module by allowing it to inherit an S-module structure in a natural manner. In particular, we make the natural definition for multiplication in M/M': for $s \in S$ and $x \in M$,

$$s(x + M') = sx + M'.$$

This definition is consistent, since, if $x + M' = y + M'$, i.e., $x - y \in M'$ then $s(x - y) = sx - sy \in M'$ and $sx + M' = sy + M'$. The axioms for an S-module (as in Definition 2.4.1) follow quite easily.

The S-module M/M' thus defined is called the *quotient submodule of M by M'*, and the mapping

$$\phi \; : \; M \overset{\text{onto}}{\to} M/M'$$
$$: \; x \mapsto x + M',$$

is a surjective S-module homomorphism.   □

Definition 2.4.5 (Module Operations) Let S be a ring, I be an ideal of S, M be an S-module and

$$\mathcal{M} = (M_i)_{i \in I},$$

a family of submodules of M; then:

1. **Sum:**

$$\sum_{i \in I} M_i = \left\{ \sum_{i \in I} x_i : \begin{array}{l} x_i \in M_i, \text{ and all but finitely} \\ \text{many of } x_i\text{'s are zero} \end{array} \right\}$$

   is a submodule of M. Thus $\sum M_i$ consists of all sums formed by taking exactly one element from each submodule in a finite subfamily of $\mathcal{M}$.

2. **Intersection:**

$$\bigcap_{i \in I} M_i,$$

   is a submodule of M.

3. **Product:**

$$IM = \left\{ \sum_{i=1}^{n} a_i x_i : a_i \in I, x_i \in M \text{ and } n \in \mathbb{Z} \right\},$$

is a submodule of M.

4. **Quotient:** Let N and P be two submodules of M:

$$N : P = \left\{ a \in S : aP \subseteq N \right\},$$

is an ideal of S. The quotient $0 : M$ is an ideal and is called the *annihilator* of M (denoted ann M).

An S-module M is *faithful* if ann $M = 0$. $\quad\square$

Definition 2.4.6 (Generators) Let S be a ring and let M be an S-module. Note that, for any $x \in M$,

$$Sx = \{sx : s \in S\}$$

is a submodule of M. Let

$$\mathcal{X} = \{x_i\}_{i \in I}$$

be a (possibly, infinite) subset of M. $\mathcal{X}$ is said to be a *system of generators* of M, if

$$M = \sum_{i \in I} Sx_i.$$

Equivalently, $\mathcal{X}$ is a system of generators of M if every element $x \in M$ can be expressed in the form

$$\sum_{i \in J} s_i x_i,$$

where $J \subseteq I$ is a finite subset of the index set and $s_i \in S$ and $x_i \in \mathcal{X}$. $\quad\square$

If S is a ring and M is an S-module, M is said to be *finitely generated* if M has a finite set of generators, and *cyclic* (or *monogenic*) if it is generated by only one element. A system of generators $u_1, \ldots, u_n$ of an S-module M is a *basis* of M, if

$$\sum a_i u_i = 0 \quad \Rightarrow \quad \left(\forall i \right) \left[a_i = 0 \right],$$

i.e., M has a linearly independent system of generators. M is called *free* (*of rank n*) if it has a *basis* of size n.

If S is a ring, then it is natural to make S^n into an S-module, M, by defining, for any $\langle s_1, \ldots, s_n \rangle$, $\langle t_1, \ldots, t_n \rangle \in S^n$ and any $s \in S$,

$$
\begin{aligned}
\mathbf{0} &= \langle 0, \ldots, 0 \rangle, \\
\langle s_1, \ldots, s_n \rangle + \langle t_1, \ldots, t_n \rangle &= \langle s_1 + t_1, \ldots, s_n + t_n \rangle \quad \text{and} \\
s \langle t_1, \ldots, t_n \rangle &= \langle s t_1, \ldots, s t_n \rangle.
\end{aligned}
$$

It is easy to see that $M = S^n$ is a free S-module of rank n.

Definition 2.4.7 (Noetherian Modules) An S-module M is called *Noetherian* if every submodule N of M is finitely generated. $\quad\square$

Proposition 2.4.1 *If S is a Noetherian ring, then S^n $(n < \infty)$ is a Noetherian S-module.*

PROOF.

Let N be a submodule of S^n. We proceed by induction on n: If $n = 1$, then there is nothing to prove, since, in this case, $N \subseteq S^1 = S$ is a submodule and hence an ideal in S, thus possessing a finite set of generators. If $n > 1$, then let

$$I = \left\{ s \in S : (\exists\, s_2, \ldots, s_n \in S)\, [\langle s, s_2, \ldots, s_n \rangle \in N] \right\}.$$

I is clearly an ideal in S, so I has a finite set of generators $\{s_{1,1}, \ldots, s_{1,k}\}$. Pick $\overline{s_1}, \ldots, \overline{s_k} \in N$ such that for $i = 1, \ldots, k$, $\overline{s_i}$ has as first component $s_{1,i}$. For an arbitrary element $\overline{s} = \langle s_1, s_2, \ldots, s_n \rangle \in N$, we can express s_1 as

$$s_1 = \sum_{i=1}^{k} r_i s_{1,i}, \quad \text{for some } r_1, \ldots, r_k \in S.$$

Now, note that

$$\overline{s}' = \overline{s} - \sum_{i=1}^{k} r_i \overline{s_i}$$

is of the form $\langle 0, s_2^*, \ldots, s_n^* \rangle \in N'$, where N' is the following submodule of S^n:

$$N' = \{\overline{s} = \langle 0, s_2, \ldots, s_n \rangle : \overline{s} \in N\}.$$

But the mapping

$$\phi \;:\; N' \to S^{n-1}$$
$$\;:\; \langle 0, s_2, \ldots, s_n \rangle \mapsto \langle s_2, \ldots, s_n \rangle$$

is a homomorphism with the kernel $(0, 0, \ldots, 0)$. Thus ϕ is an isomorphism of N' into its image $\operatorname{im} \phi \subseteq S^{n-1}$. Hence, by induction, $\operatorname{im} \phi$ a submodule of S^{n-1} has a finite system of generators, and so does N'. Let $\{\overline{t_1}, \ldots, \overline{t_l}\}$ be such a system of generators. Then, since

$$\overline{s}' = \overline{s} - \sum_{i=1}^{k} r_i \overline{s_i} = \sum_{i=1}^{l} q_i \overline{t_i}, \quad \text{where } q_i, r_i \in S$$

and

$$\overline{s} = \sum_{i=1}^{k} r_i \overline{s_i} + \sum_{i=1}^{l} q_i \overline{t_i},$$

$\{\overline{s_1}, \ldots, \overline{s_k}, \overline{t_1}, \ldots, \overline{t_l}\}$ is a finite system of generators of N. $\quad\square$

Definition 2.4.8 (Syzygies) Let S be a ring and let $M = (x_1, \ldots, x_q)$ be a finitely generated S-module. Note that

$$\phi \;:\; S^q \to M$$
$$\;:\; \langle s_1, \ldots, s_q \rangle \mapsto s_1 x_1 + \cdots + s_q x_q$$

is an S-module homomorphism. Thus

$$K = \ker \phi = \{\langle s_1, \ldots, s_q \rangle \in S^q \mid s_1 x_1 + \ldots + s_q x_q = 0\},$$

is a submodule of S^q; K is said to be the (*first module of*) *syzygies* of M [with respect to the system of generators $\{x_1, \ldots, x_q\}$ of M] and is denoted $S(M)$. $\square$

Proposition 2.4.2 *If S is a Noetherian ring and M is a finitely generated S-module, then $S(M)$, the syzygy of M, is finitely generated.*
PROOF.
If $M = (x_1, x_2, \ldots, x_q)$, then $S(M)$ is a submodule of a Noetherian S-module, S^q. Thus, by Proposition 2.4.1, $S(M)$, the syzygy of M is also finitely generated. $\square$

Given S, a Noetherian ring, and $M = (x_1, \ldots, x_q)$, a finitely generated S-module, we have $S(M) = (\overline{s_1}, \ldots, \overline{s_p})$ where

$$\begin{aligned}
\overline{s_1} &= \langle s_{1,1}, s_{1,2}, \ldots, s_{1,q} \rangle \\
\overline{s_2} &= \langle s_{2,1}, s_{2,2}, \ldots, s_{2,q} \rangle \\
&\;\;\vdots \\
\overline{s_p} &= \langle s_{p,1}, s_{p,2}, \ldots, s_{p,q} \rangle
\end{aligned}$$

and, for $i = 1, \ldots, p$

$$s_{i,1} x_1 + \cdots + s_{i,q} x_q = 0.$$

If $u_1 x_1 + u_2 x_2 + \cdots + u_q x_q = 0$, then $\langle u_1, u_2, \ldots, u_q \rangle = \overline{u} \in S(M)$; so there are $v_1, v_2, \ldots, v_p \in S$ such that

$$\overline{u} = v_1 \overline{s_1} + v_2 \overline{s_2} + \cdots + v_p \overline{s_p}.$$

This is equivalent to the following:

$$\begin{aligned}
u_1 &= v_1 s_{1,1} + v_2 s_{2,1} + \cdots + v_p s_{p,1} \\
u_2 &= v_1 s_{1,2} + v_2 s_{2,2} + \cdots + v_p s_{p,2} \\
&\;\;\vdots \\
u_q &= v_1 s_{1,q} + v_2 s_{2,q} + \cdots + v_p s_{p,q}.
\end{aligned}$$

2.5   *S*-Polynomials

Definition 2.5.1 (*S*-Polynomials) Let S be a ring; $R = S[x_1, \ldots, x_n]$ be a ring of polynomials over S; $G \subseteq R$ be a finite subset; and

$$F = \{f_1, \ldots, f_q\} \subseteq G.$$

Set

$$T = \left\{ t_1 = \mathrm{Hcoef}(f_1), \ldots, t_q = \mathrm{Hcoef}(f_q) \right\} \subseteq S$$

and

$$J = (t_1, \ldots, t_q),$$

the ideal in S generated by T. From the previous discussion, we can write the syzygy of J, $S(J) \subseteq S^q$, by its system of generators, $\{\overline{s_1}, \ldots, \overline{s_p}\}$, where $\overline{s_i} \in S^q$, $i = 1, \ldots, p$. That is,

$$S(J) \;=\; \Big(\quad \langle s_{1,1}, s_{1,2}, \ldots, s_{1,q} \rangle,$$

$$\vdots$$

$$\langle s_{p,1}, s_{p,2}, \ldots, s_{p,q} \rangle \; \Big).$$

We define the set of *S-polynomials* of F, which we denote by $SP(F)$, to be the set $\{h_{1,F}, \ldots, h_{p,F}\}$, where, for $i = 1, \ldots, p$,

$$h_{i,F} = s_{i,1} \cdot \frac{m}{\mathrm{Hterm}(f_1)} \cdot f_1 + \cdots + s_{i,q} \cdot \frac{m}{\mathrm{Hterm}(f_q)} \cdot f_q,$$

where $m = LCM(\mathrm{Hterm}(f_1), \ldots, \mathrm{Hterm}(f_q))$.   □

Note that if we simplify the expression for an *S*-polynomial, say $h_{i,F}$, we get

$$
\begin{aligned}
h_{i,F} \;=\;& s_{i,1} t_1 \cdot m + s_{i,1} \cdot \frac{m}{\mathrm{Hterm}(f_1)} \cdot \mathrm{Tail}(f_1) + \cdots \\
& + s_{i,q} t_q \cdot m + s_{i,q} \cdot \frac{m}{\mathrm{Hterm}(f_q)} \cdot \mathrm{Tail}(f_q) \\
\;=\;& (s_{i,1} t_1 + \cdots + s_{i,q} t_q) m \\
& + s_{i,1} \cdot \frac{m}{\mathrm{Hterm}(f_1)} \cdot \mathrm{Tail}(f_1) + \cdots + s_{i,q} \cdot \frac{m}{\mathrm{Hterm}(f_q)} \cdot \mathrm{Tail}(f_q) \\
\;=\;& s_{i,1} \cdot \frac{m}{\mathrm{Hterm}(f_1)} \cdot \mathrm{Tail}(f_1) + \cdots + s_{i,q} \cdot \frac{m}{\mathrm{Hterm}(f_q)} \cdot \mathrm{Tail}(f_q).
\end{aligned}
$$

Thus, $\mathrm{Hterm}(h_{i,F}) \underset{\wedge}{<} m = \mathrm{LCM}\Big(\mathrm{Hterm}(f_i) : f_i \in F\Big)$.

Theorem 2.5.1 *Let* $F = \{f_1, \ldots, f_q\}$ *be as in the previous definition. Assume that for some* $u_1, \ldots, u_q \in S$, $p_1, \ldots, p_q \in \mathrm{PP}(x_1, \ldots, x_n)$,

$$h = \sum_{i=1}^{q} u_i p_i f_i,$$

and that $p_1 \mathrm{Hterm}(f_1) = \cdots = p_q\mathrm{Hterm}(f_q) = M \underset{A}{>} \mathrm{Hterm}(h)$.
   Thus,

$$\sum_{i=1}^{q} u_i p_i \mathrm{Hmono}(f_i) = 0.$$

Then we can express h in terms of the S-polynomialsof the set F as follows:

$$h = \sum_{j=1}^{p} v_{j,F} \, r_F \, h_{j,F},$$

where $v_{j,F} \in S$, $r_F \in \mathrm{PP}(x_1, \ldots, x_n)$ *and* $h_{j,F}$'s *are S-polynomialsof F,* $SP(F)$. *Furthermore,*

$$r_F \mathrm{Hterm}\left(h_{j,F}\right) \underset{A}{\leq} M = p_i \mathrm{Hterm}(f_i).$$

PROOF.
Let
$$t_1 = \mathrm{Hcoef}(f_1), \ldots, t_q = \mathrm{Hcoef}(f_q) \quad \text{and} \quad J = (t_1, \ldots, t_q).$$

Let a system of generators for the syzygy of J, $S(J)$, be given as follows:

$$S(J) \;=\; \Big(\quad \langle s_{1,1}, s_{1,2}, \ldots, s_{1,q} \rangle,$$
$$\vdots$$
$$\langle s_{p,1}, s_{p,2}, \ldots, s_{p,q} \rangle \;\Big).$$

Since
$$\sum_{i=1}^{q} u_i p_i \mathrm{Hmono}(f_i) = M \cdot \sum_{i=1}^{q} u_i t_i = 0,$$

there exist $v_1, \ldots, v_p \in S$ such that

$$u_1 = \sum_{j=1}^{p} v_j s_{j,1}, \quad \ldots, \quad u_q = \sum_{j=1}^{p} v_j s_{j,q}.$$

Now, if we let $m = \mathrm{LCM}\left(\mathrm{Hterm}(f_1), \ldots, \mathrm{Hterm}(f_q)\right)$, then it is clear that

$$m \mid p_i\mathrm{Hterm}(f_i), \qquad \text{for all } i,$$

i.e., there is some power product $r \in \mathrm{PP}(x_1, \ldots, x_n)$ such that

$$m \cdot r = M = p_i \cdot \mathrm{Hterm}(f_i), \qquad \text{for all } i.$$

Thus, we can rewrite h as follows:

$$
\begin{aligned}
h &= \left(\sum_{j=1}^{p} v_j s_{j,1} \right) r \cdot \frac{m}{\mathrm{Hterm}(f_1)} \cdot f_1 + \cdots \\
&\quad + \left(\sum_{j=1}^{p} v_j s_{j,q} \right) r \cdot \frac{m}{\mathrm{Hterm}(f_q)} \cdot f_q \\
&= v_1 r \cdot h_{1,F} + \cdots + v_p r \cdot h_{p,F}.
\end{aligned}
$$

Also, for all i, $\mathrm{Hterm}(r)\,\mathrm{Hterm}(h_{i,F}) \underset{A}{<} r \cdot m = p_i\,\mathrm{Hterm}(f_i)$. □

Definition 2.5.2 (Syzygy Condition for a Finite Set G) Let S be a ring, and let

$$G = \{g_1, g_2, \ldots, g_m\} \subseteq S[x_1, \ldots, x_n],$$

be a finite set of polynomials. We say G satisfies the *syzygy condition* if for every subset $F \subseteq G$ and every *S*-polynomial $h \in SP(F)$, h can be expressed as

$$h = \sum_{i=1}^{m} f_i g_i,$$

where $f_i \subset S[x_1, \ldots, x_n]$ and $\mathrm{Hterm}(h) \underset{A}{\geq} \mathrm{Hterm}(f_i)\,\mathrm{Hterm}(g_i)$. □

Now we are ready to give a new characterization of a Gröbner basis in terms of the syzygy condition:

Theorem 2.5.2 *Let I be an ideal in $R = S[x_1, \ldots, x_n]$, and*

$$G = \{g_1, \ldots, g_m\} \subseteq I,$$

a finite subset of I. Then the following three statements are equivalent:

1. *$\mathrm{Head}(G) = \mathrm{Head}(I)$.*

2. *$\left(\forall \, f \in I \right) \left[f = \sum_{g_i \in G} f_i g_i \right]$, where $f_i \in S[x_1, \ldots, x_n]$ and $\mathrm{Hterm}(f) \underset{A}{\geq} \mathrm{Hterm}(f_i)\,\mathrm{Hterm}(g_i)$, for all i.*

3. *$(G) = I$ and G satisfies the syzygy condition.*

PROOF.

$(1 \Leftrightarrow 2)$:

The equivalence of (1) and (2) is simply Theorem 2.3.3.

$(2 \Rightarrow 3)$:

Note first that (2) establishes G as a Gröbner basis (by Theorem 2.3.3) and that $(G) = I$ (by Theorem 2.3.1). Furthermore, if $F \subseteq G$ and $h \in SP(F)$, then $h \in I$; thus by condition (2) itself,

$$h = \sum_{g_i \in G} f_i g_i,$$

where $f_i \in S[x_1, \ldots, x_n]$ and $\mathrm{Hterm}(h) \underset{A}{\geq} \mathrm{Hterm}(f_i)\,\mathrm{Hterm}(g_i)$. But this is precisely the syzygy condition.

$(3 \Rightarrow 2)$:

We assume to the contrary, i.e., condition (3) holds, but not (2); we shall derive a contradiction.

We first define *height* of a sequence

$$H = \Big\langle h_i : 1 \leq i \leq m, \text{ and } h_i \in R \Big\rangle$$

(with respect to G and the admissible ordering $\underset{A}{<}$) as

$$\mathrm{Height}(H) = \underset{\underset{A}{>}}{\max} \Big\{ \mathrm{Hterm}(h_i)\,\mathrm{Hterm}(g_i) : 1 \leq i \leq m \Big\}.$$

Since by (3), $(G) = I$, every $f \in I$ can be expressed as

$$\sum_{i=1}^{m} f_i g_i, \qquad f_i \in S[x_1, \ldots, x_n].$$

Furthermore, since (2) is assumed to be false, we can choose an $f \in I$ such that

$$\mathrm{Height}\Big(\big\langle f_1, \ldots, f_m \big\rangle\Big) \underset{A}{>} \mathrm{Hterm}(f).$$

We assume that the representation of f is so chosen that it is of a *minimal height*, M. Let

$$F = \Big\{ g_i \in G : \mathrm{Hterm}(f_i)\,\mathrm{Hterm}(g_i) = M \Big\}.$$

Without loss of generality, we may assume that F consists of the first k elements of G. Thus

$$f = \sum_{i=1}^{k} \mathrm{Hmono}(f_i) g_i + \sum_{i=1}^{k} \mathrm{Tail}(f_i) g_i + \sum_{i=k+1}^{m} f_i g_i,$$

where

$$
\begin{aligned}
\mathrm{Hterm}(f_i)\,\mathrm{Hterm}(g_i) &= M, & 1 \le i \le k, \\
\mathrm{Hterm}(\mathrm{Tail}(f_i))\,\mathrm{Hterm}(g_i) &\underset{A}{<} M, & 1 \le i \le k \text{ and} \\
\mathrm{Hterm}(f_i)\,\mathrm{Hterm}(g_i) &\underset{A}{<} M, & k+1 \le i \le m.
\end{aligned}
$$

Since $f \underset{A}{<} M$, we see that

$$
\begin{aligned}
\mathrm{Hterm}(f_1)\,\mathrm{Hterm}(g_1) &= \cdots = \mathrm{Hterm}(f_k)\,\mathrm{Hterm}(g_k) \\
&= M \underset{A}{>} \mathrm{Hterm}\left(\sum_{i=1}^{k} \mathrm{Hmono}(f_i)g_i\right).
\end{aligned}
$$

As noted before (Theorem 2.5.1), we see that the expression $\sum_{i=1}^{k} \mathrm{Hmono}(f_i)g_i$ can be expressed in terms of $SP(F)$, the S-polynomials of F. Thus we may write f as

$$
f = \sum_{j} v_{j,F}\, r_F\, h_{j,F} + \sum_{i=1}^{k} \mathrm{Tail}(f_i)g_i + \sum_{i=k+1}^{m} f_i g_i.
$$

But since $r_F\, \mathrm{Hterm}(h_{j,F}) \underset{A}{<} \mathrm{Hterm}(f_i)\,\mathrm{Hterm}(g_i) = M, \quad 1 \le i \le k$, and since, by the syzygy condition, each

$$
h_{j,F} = \sum_{i} f_{i,j,F}\, g_i
$$

with $\mathrm{Hterm}(h_{j,F}) \underset{A}{\ge} \mathrm{Hterm}(f_{i,j,F})\,\mathrm{Hterm}(g_i)$, we get

$$
f = \sum_{j} \sum_{i} \left(v_{j,F}\, r_F\, f_{i,j,F} \right) g_i + \sum_{i=1}^{k} \mathrm{Tail}(f_i)g_i + \sum_{i=k+1}^{m} f_i g_i.
$$

But, by the previous arguments,

$$
\begin{aligned}
\mathrm{Hterm}\left(v_{j,F}\, r_F\, f_{i,j,F} \right) \mathrm{Hterm}(g_i) &\underset{A}{\le} \mathrm{Hterm}(r_F)\,\mathrm{Hterm}(f_{i,j,F})\,\mathrm{Hterm}(g_i) \\
&\underset{A}{\le} \mathrm{Hterm}(r_F)\,\mathrm{Hterm}(h_{j,F}) \underset{A}{<} M,
\end{aligned}
$$

and hence, we can express f differently as

$$
f = \sum_{i=1}^{m} f_i' g_i,
$$

with $\mathrm{Height}(\langle f_1', \ldots, f_m' \rangle) \underset{A}{<} M$, and thus contradicting our choice of the representation of f relative to G. $\square$

Problems

Problem 2.1

Show the following:

(i) An element $r \in R$ of the ring R is a unit if and only if $(r) = (1)$.

(ii) If r is a unit and x is nilpotent in the ring R, then $r + x$ is again a unit.

Problem 2.2

Prove that if I_1 and I_2, as well as I_1 and I_3 are coprime, then I_1 and $I_2 I_3$ are coprime. Hence, if I_1, I_2, ..., I_n are pairwise coprime, then

$$I_1 I_2 \cdots I_n = I_1 \cap I_2 \cap \cdots \cap I_n.$$

Problem 2.3

Let I_1, $I_2 \subseteq R$ be two ideals with bases B_1 and B_2, respectively. Which of the following statements are true? Justify your answers.

(i) $B_1 \cup B_2$ is a basis for $I_1 + I_2$.

(ii) $\{b_1 \cdot b_2 : b_1 \in B_1 \text{ and } b_2 \in B_2\}$ is a basis for $I_1 I_2$.

(iii) $\{b_{i_1} b_{i_2} \cdots b_{i_n} : b_{i_1}, b_{i_2}, \ldots, b_{i_n} \in B_1\}$ is a basis for I_1^n.

(iv) Let $f \in R$, and C_1, a basis for $I_1 \cap (f)$. Then, every $c_1 \in C_1$ is divisible by f, and $\{c_1/f : c_1 \in C_1\}$ is a basis for $(I_1 : (f))$.

Problem 2.4

Let I, J, K be ideals in a ring R. Prove the following:

(i) *Modular law*: If $I \supseteq J$ or $I \supseteq K$, then $I \cap (J + K) = (I \cap J) + (I \cap K)$.

(ii) $I \subseteq I : J$, and $(I : J)J \subseteq I$.

(iii) $(\bigcap_i I_i : J) = \bigcap_i (I_i : J)$, and $(I : \sum_i J_i) = \bigcap_i (I : J_i)$.

(iv) $\sqrt{I} \supseteq I$, and $\sqrt{\sqrt{I}} = \sqrt{I}$.

Problem 2.5

For each $k = 1, \ldots, n$, we define a function U_k as follows:

$$
\begin{aligned}
U_k \quad &: \quad \mathrm{PP}(x_1, x_2, \ldots, x_n) \to \mathbb{R} \\
&: \quad p = x_1^{a_1} x_2^{a_2} \cdots x_n^{a_n} \mapsto u_{k,1} a_1 + u_{k,2} a_2 + \cdots + u_{k,n} a_n,
\end{aligned}
$$

where each of $u_{k,l}$ ($k = 1, \ldots, n$, $l = 1, \ldots, n$) is a nonnegative real number. Assume that U_k's are so chosen that $\langle U_1(p), \ldots, U_n(p) \rangle = \langle 0, \ldots, 0 \rangle$ if and only if $p = 1$. We define an ordering $\underset{\mathrm{U}}{>}$ on the power products as follows: given two power products p, $q \in \mathrm{PP}(x_1, x_2, \ldots, x_n)$, we say $p \underset{\mathrm{U}}{>} q$, if the first nonzero entry of

$$\langle U_1(p), U_2(p), \ldots, U_n(p) \rangle - \langle U_1(q), U_2(q), \ldots, U_n(q) \rangle$$

is positive.

Show that the ordering $\underset{U}{>}$ is an admissible ordering. Characterize the admissible orderings $\underset{\text{LEX}}{>}$, $\underset{\text{TLEX}}{>}$ and $\underset{\text{TRLEX}}{>}$ in terms of appropriately chosen functions U_k.

Problem 2.6

Let $(x^2 + y^2)$, $(xy) \subseteq \mathbb{Q}[x, y]$ be two ideals with Gröbner bases $\{x^2 + y^2\}$ and $\{xy\}$, respectively, with respect to the $\underset{\text{TRLEX}}{>}$ (with $x \underset{\text{TRLEX}}{>} y$). Is $\{x^2 + y^2, xy\}$ a Gröbner basis for $(x^2 + y^2) + (xy)$ under $\underset{\text{TRLEX}}{>}$?

Problem 2.7

Let $\underset{A}{<}$ be a fixed but arbitrary admissible ordering on $\text{PP}(x_1, \ldots, x_n)$. Consider the following procedure (possibly, nonterminating) to compute a basis for an ideal in the polynomial ring $R = S[x_1, \ldots, x_n]$:

```
G := {0};
while (G) ≠ I loop
        Choose f ∈ I \ (G), such that Hmono(f) is the smallest
            among all such elements with respect to <;
                                                     A
        G := G ∪ {f};
end{loop }
```

Which of the following statements are true? Justify your answers.

(i) The procedure terminates if S is Noetherian.

(ii) The procedure is an effective algorithm.

(iii) Let f_i be the element of I that is added to G in the ith iteration. Then $\text{Hterm}(f_1) \underset{A}{\leq} \text{Hterm}(f_2) \underset{A}{\leq} \cdots \underset{A}{\leq} \text{Hterm}(f_n) \underset{A}{\leq} \cdots$

(iv) The set G at the termination is a Gröbner basis for I.

Problem 2.8

Consider the polynomial ring $R = S[x_1, \ldots, x_n]$, with total reverse lexicographic admissible ordering $\underset{\text{TRLEX}}{>}$ such that $x_1 \underset{\text{TRLEX}}{>} \cdots \underset{\text{TRLEX}}{>} x_n$. The homogeneous part of a polynomial $f \in R$ of degree d (denoted f_d) is simply the sum of all the monomials of degree d in f. An ideal $I \subseteq R$ is said to be homogeneous if the following condition holds: $f \in I$ implies that for all $d \geq 0$, $f_d \in I$

Prove that: If G is a Gröbner basis for a homogeneous ideal I with respect to $\underset{\text{TRLEX}}{>}$ in R, then $G \cup \{x_i, \ldots, x_n\}$ is a Gröbner basis for $(I, x_i, \ldots, x_n)$ $(1 \leq i \leq n)$ with respect to $\underset{\text{TRLEX}}{>}$ in R.

Hint: First show that $(\text{Head}(I), x_i, \ldots, x_n) = \text{Head}(I, x_i, \ldots, x_n)$,

Problem 2.9

Let K be a field and I an ideal in $K[x_1, x_2, \ldots, x_n]$. Let G be a maximal subset of I satisfying the following two conditions:

1. All $f \in G$ are monic, i.e., $\text{Hcoef}(f) = 1$.
2. For all $f \in G$ and $g \in I$, $\text{Hterm}(f) \neq \text{Hterm}(g)$ implies that $\text{Hterm}(g)$ does not divide $\text{Hterm}(f)$.

(i) Show that G is finite.

(ii) Prove that G is a Gröbner basis for I.

(iii) A Gröbner basis $G_{\min}$ for an ideal I is a *minimal Gröbner basis* for I, if no proper subset of $G_{\min}$ is a Gröbner basis for I.

Show that G (defined earlier) is a minimal Gröbner basis for I.

(iv) Let G be a Gröbner basis (not necessarily finite) for an ideal I of $K[x_1, x_2, \ldots, x_n]$. Then there is a finite minimal Gröbner basis $G' \subseteq G$ for I.

Problem 2.10

(i) Given as input $a_0, a_1, \ldots, a_n$ and $b_0, b_1, \ldots, b_n$ integers, write an algorithm that computes all the coefficients of

$$(a_0 + a_1 x + \cdots + a_n x^n)(b_0 + b_1 x + \cdots + b_n x^n).$$

Your algorithm should work in $O(n^2)$ operations.

(ii) Show that given M and v, two positive integers, there is a unique polynomial

$$p(x) = p_0 + p_1 x + \cdots + p_n x^n$$

satisfying the following two conditions:

1. $p_0, p_1, \ldots, p_n$ are all integers in the range $[0, M-1]$, and
2. $p(M) = v$

(iii) Devise an algorithm that on input $a_0, a_1, \ldots, a_n$; M integers evaluates

$$a_0 + a_1 M + \cdots + a_n M^n.$$

Your algorithm should work in $O(n)$ operations.

(iv) Use (ii) and (iii) to develop an algorithm for polynomial multiplication [as in (i)] that uses $O(n)$ arithmetic operations (i.e., additions, multiplications, divisions, etc.).

(v) Comment on your algorithm for (iv). What is the bit-complexity of your algorithm?

Solutions to Selected Problems

Problem 2.3

All but the last statement are true. Since the proofs for the first three assertions are fairly simple, we shall concentrate on the last statement.

(iv) Here is a counterexample (due to Giovanni Gallo of University of Catania):

Let $R = \mathbb{Q}[x, y]/(y^5)$ be a ring, $f = y^2 \in R$ and $I_1 = (xy)$, an ideal in R. Since $xy^2 \in (y^2)$ and $xy^2 \in (xy)$, clearly, $xy^2 \in I \cap (f)$. Conversely, if $a \in I \cap (f)$, then a must be $r \cdot xy^2$ for some $r \in R$. Hence, $a \in (xy^2)$, and $(xy^2) = I \cap (f)$.

On the other hand, as, for all $k \geq 3$,

$$y^k \cdot f \equiv y^{2+k} \equiv 0 \bmod (y^5),$$

$y^k \in I : (f)$. But, for any $k > 0$, $y^k \notin (x)$. Therefore, $\{x\}$ is not a basis for $I : (f)$. In fact, for this example, $\{x, y^3\}$ *is a basis for* $I : (f) = (xy) : (y^2)$, for the following reasons: If $a \in (xy) : (y^2)$, then the following statements are all equivalent.

$$
\begin{aligned}
ay^2 \in (xy) \quad &\Leftrightarrow \quad ay^2 \in (xy) \cap (y^2) = (xy^2) \\
&\Leftrightarrow \quad ay^2 = rxy^2 \bmod (y^5), \qquad r \in R \\
&\Leftrightarrow \quad (a - rx)y^2 = sy^5, \qquad s \in R \\
&\Leftrightarrow \quad a = rx + sy^3, \qquad r, s \in R.
\end{aligned}
$$

However, if $f \in R$ is not a nonzero zero divisor, or if R is an integral domain, then the statement holds. Let $a \neq 0 \in I : (f)$. Then $af \in I$, and $af \neq 0$. Thus, $af = \sum_{c_i \in C} r_i c_i$ and $a = \sum_{c_i \in C} r_i c_i / f$ exists. Hence, $a \in (\{c/f : c \in C\})$. As, for all $c_i \in C$, $c_i/f \in I : (f)$, we see that $\{c/f : c \in C\}$ is a basis for $I : (f)$.

In general, the following holds:

Let $f \in R$, C be a basis for $I \cap (f)$, and D be a basis for ann (f). *Then, every $c \in C$ is divisible by f, and $\{c/f : c \in C\} \cup D$ is a basis for $I : (f)$.*

$$
\begin{aligned}
af \in I \quad &\Leftrightarrow \quad af \in I \cap (f) = (C) \\
&\Leftrightarrow \quad af - \sum_{c_i \in C} r_i c_i = 0, \qquad r_i \in R \\
&\Leftrightarrow \quad \left(a - \sum_{c_i \in C} r_i \frac{c_i}{f}\right) f = 0 \\
&\Leftrightarrow \quad \left(a - \sum_{c_i \in C} r_i \frac{c_i}{f}\right) \in \text{ann}\,(f)
\end{aligned}
$$

$$\Leftrightarrow \quad a = \sum_{c_i \in C} r_i \frac{c_i}{f} + \sum_{d_i \in D} s_i d_i, \qquad r_i, s_i \in R$$

$$\Leftrightarrow \quad a \in \left(\left\{ \frac{c}{f} \mid c \in C \right\} \cup D \right).$$

Thus $\{ c/f : c \in C \} \cup D$ is a basis for $I : (f)$.

Problem 2.7

Let G_i denote $\{ f_1, \ldots, f_i \}$.

(i) True. The termination of the procedure directly follows from the ascending chain condition (ACC) property of the Noetherian ring as

$$(G_1) \subsetneq (G_2) \subsetneq (G_3) \subsetneq \cdots.$$

(ii) False. This algorithm is not effective because it does not say how to find $f \in I \setminus (G)$.

(iii) True. The condition $\text{Hterm}(f_1) \underset{A}{\leq} \text{Hterm}(f_2) \underset{A}{\leq} \cdots$ follows immediately from the fact that, at each step, we choose an f_i such that $\text{Hmono}(f_i)$ is the smallest among all elements of $I \setminus (G_{i-1})$. Indeed, if it were not true, then there would be i and j $(j < i)$ such that

$$\text{Hterm}(f_i) \underset{A}{<} \text{Hterm}(f_j).$$

Assume that among all such elements f_i is the first element which violates the property. But, since $(G_{j-1}) \subset (G_{i-1})$, and since $f_i \in I \setminus (G_{i-1})$, we have $f_i \in I \setminus (G_{j-1})$. Since, $\text{Hterm}(f_i) \underset{A}{<} \text{Hterm}(f_j)$, the algorithm would have chosen f_i in the jth step, instead of f_j, contradicting the hypothesis.

(iv) False. Consider the ideal $I = (xy, x^2 + y^2) \subseteq \mathbb{Q}[x, y]$. Let the first polynomial chosen be $f_1 = xy \in I \setminus (0)$ as $\text{Hmono}(f_1)$ is the smallest among all such elments (with respect to $\underset{\text{TRLEX}}{<}$). Similarly, let the second polynomial chosen be $f_2 = x^2 + y^2 \in I \setminus (xy)$ as $\text{Hmono}(f_2)$ is the smallest among all such elments (with respect to $\underset{\text{TRLEX}}{<}$). As $I = (f_1, f_2)$, the algorithm terminates with $G = \{ f_1, f_2 \}$. Thus $\text{Head}(G) = (xy, x^2)$. Since $y^3 = y(x^2 + y^2) - x(xy) \in I$, we have $y^3 \in \text{Head}(I) \setminus \text{Head}(G)$, and G is not a Gröbner basis of I.

Problem 2.8

Since $G \subseteq I$, we have $(G, x_i, \ldots, x_n) \subseteq (I, x_i, \ldots, x_n)$ and $\text{Head}(G, x_i, \ldots, x_n) \subseteq \text{Head}(I, x_i, \ldots, x_n)$. Hence, we only need to show that $\text{Head}(G, x_i, \ldots, x_n) \supseteq \text{Head}(I, x_i, \ldots, x_n)$.

Following the hint, we proceed as follows: Let $f_d \in (I, x_i, \ldots, x_n)$ be a homogeneous polynomial of degree d. Then, if $\text{Hmono}(f_d) \in (x_i, \ldots, x_n)$, then, plainly, $\text{Hmono}(f_d) \in (\text{Head}(I), x_i, \ldots, x_n)$. Otherwise, $\text{Hmono}(f_d)$ is not divisible by any of the x_j's and f_d can be expressed as follows:

$$f_d = g_d + h_i x_i + \cdots + h_n x_n, \quad g_d \in I, \text{ and } h_i, \ldots, h_n \in S[x_1, \ldots, x_n].$$

Since $\text{Hmono}(f_d) \in \text{PP}(x_1, \ldots, x_n)$, by the choice of our admissible ordering, $\text{Hmono}(f_d) \underset{\text{TRLEX}}{>} \text{Hmono}(h_j x_j)$, and thus

$$\text{Hmono}(f_d) = \text{Hmono}(g_d) \in \text{Head}(I) \subseteq (\text{Head}(I), x_i, \ldots, x_n).$$

This proves that

$$
\begin{aligned}
(\text{Head}(I), x_i, \ldots, x_n) &\supseteq \text{Head}(I, x_i, \ldots, x_n) \\
&\supseteq (\text{Head}(I), x_i, \ldots, x_n).
\end{aligned}
$$

Since $\text{Head}(G, x_i, \ldots, x_n) \supseteq (\text{Head}(G), x_i, \ldots, x_n)$, using the hint, we have

$$
\begin{aligned}
&\text{Head}(G, x_i, \ldots, x_n) \\
&\quad \supseteq (\text{Head}(G), x_i, \ldots, x_n) \\
&\quad = (\text{Head}(I), x_i, \ldots, x_n) \qquad (G \text{ is a Gröbner basis for } I) \\
&\quad \supseteq \text{Head}(I, x_i, \ldots, x_n),
\end{aligned}
$$

as claimed.

Problem 2.9

Since K is a field, for all $a \in K$, $a^{-1} \in K$. Hence,

$$\Big(\forall f \in I\Big) \Big(\exists f' \in I\Big) \Big[\text{Hterm}(f) = \text{Hterm}(f'), \quad \text{but} \quad \text{Hcoef}(f') = 1\Big].$$

Moreover, for all $a \in K$, $af' \in I$.

(i) Let the set of power products, $\widehat{G}$, be the set of head terms of G:

$$\widehat{G} = \{\text{Hterm}(f) : f \in G\}.$$

Let $\text{Hterm}(f)$ and $\text{Hterm}(g)$ be two distinct power products in $\widehat{G}$. Then $f \in G \subseteq I$ and $g \in G \subseteq I$. Thus, by condition (2), $\text{Hterm}(f)$ is not a multiple of $\text{Hterm}(g)$, nor the converse. But, then by Dickson's lemma, $\widehat{G}$ is finite, and so is G, since there is a bijective map between G and $\widehat{G}$.

(ii) We claim that

$$\Big(\forall h \in I\Big) \Big(\exists f \in G\Big) \Big[\text{Hterm}(h) = p \cdot \text{Hterm}(f)\Big],$$

where $p \in \text{PP}(x_1, \ldots, x_n)$.

Indeed if it were not true, then we could choose a "smallest" $h \in I$ [i.e., the Hterm(h) is minimal under the chosen admissible ordering $\underset{A}{\leq}$] violating the above condition. Without loss of generality, we assume that h is monic.

If $g \in I$ is a polynomial with a distinct Hterm from h such that Hterm(g) divides Hterm(h), then Hterm(g) $\underset{A}{<}$ Hterm(h), and by the choice of h, Hterm(g) is a multiple of Hterm(f), for some $f \in G$. But, this contradicts the assumption that Hterm(h) is not divisible by Hterm(f), as $f \in G$.

Thus, for all $g \in I$, Hterm(h) $\neq$ Hterm(g) implies that Hterm(g) does not divide Hterm(h). But, if this is the case, then $G \cup \{h\}$ also satisfies conditions (1) and (2), which contradicts the maximality of G.

Now, we see that if $h \in I$, then

$$\begin{aligned} \text{Hmono}(h) &= \text{Hcoef}(h) \cdot \text{Hterm}(h) = \text{Hcoef}(h) \cdot p\,\text{Hterm}(f), \\ &\qquad\text{where } f \in G,\ p \in \text{PP}(x_1, \ldots, x_n) \\ \Rightarrow\quad &\text{Hmono}(h) \in \text{Head}(G). \end{aligned}$$

Therefore Head(I) $\subseteq$ Head(G); hence G is a Gröbner basis for I.

(iii) Suppose G is not a minimal Gröbner basis for I. Let $G' \subsetneq G$ be a minimal Gröbner basis. Let $f \in G \setminus G'$. By the construction of G, for all $g \in G' \subset I$, Hterm(g) does not divide Hterm(f). Thus Hterm(f) $\in$ Head(G) $\setminus$ Head(G'). This leads us to the conclusion that

$$\text{Head}(G') \neq \text{Head}(G) = \text{Head}(I).$$

Thus G' is not a Gröbner basis, as assumed.

(iv) Let $G' \subseteq G$ be a minimal Gröbner basis for I. Without loss of generality, assume that all the polynomials of G' are monic. Let $f, g \in G'$ with distinct Hterm's. We claim that Hterm(f) does not divide Hterm(g). Since, otherwise,

$$\text{Head}(I) = \text{Head}(G') = \text{Head}\left(G' \setminus \{g\}\right),$$

and, $G' \setminus \{g\} \subsetneq G'$ would be a Gröbner basis for I, contradicting the minimality of G'. Thus, by Dickson's lemma the set of power products,

$$\widehat{G'} = \{\text{Hterm}(g) \mid g \in G'\},$$

is finite and so is G'.

Problem 2.10

  (i) Let $\mathcal{C} = \{c_{2n}, c_{2n-1}, \ldots, c_0\}$ be the coefficients of

$$(a_n x^n + \cdots + a_1 x + a_0) \cdot (b_n x^n + \cdots + b_1 x + b_0).$$

Then

$$\forall_{i,1\leq i\leq 2n}\ c_i = \sum_{j=0}^{i} a_j \cdot b_{i-j}, \quad \text{where } a_i, b_i = 0, \text{ for } i > n.$$

Since c_i is a sum of at most n products, it can be computed using $O(n)$ arithmetic operations. Hence $\mathcal{C}$ can be computed in $O(n^2)$ time assuming that each arithmetic operations takes $O(1)$ time.

(ii) Let

$$p(x) = p_0 + p_1 x + \cdots + p_n x^n.$$

Consider

$$n = \min_{j}\left\{M^j > v\right\} - 1, \text{ and}$$

$$p_i = \text{Quotient}\left(v, M^i\right) \bmod M, \quad 0 \leq i \leq n.$$

It is obvious that $0 \leq p_i < M$ and also

$$\begin{aligned}
p(M) &= \sum_{i=0}^{n} p_i M^i = \sum_{i=0}^{n}\left[\text{Quotient}\left(v, M^i\right) \bmod M\right] \cdot M^i \\
&= \sum_{i=0}^{n}\left[\text{Quotient}\left(v, M^i\right)\right. \\
&\qquad \left. - \text{Quotient}\left(\text{Quotient}\left(v, M^i\right), M\right) \cdot M\right] \cdot M^i \\
&= \sum_{i=0}^{n}\left[\text{Quotient}\left(v, M^i\right) \cdot M^i - \text{Quotient}\left(v, M^{i+1}\right) \cdot M^{i+1}\right] \\
&= \text{Quotient}\left(v, 1\right) - \text{Quotient}\left(v, M^{n+1}\right) \cdot M^{n+1}.
\end{aligned}$$

But $M^{n+1} > v$, therefore $\text{Quotient}(v, M^{n+1}) = 0$ which implies $p(M) = v$.

The uniqueness follows from the fact that $\bar{p} = (p_n, \ldots, p_0)$ gives the unique representation of v in radix M. Since each p_i can be computed using $O(1)$ arithmetic operations (using the fact that $M^i = M^{i-1} \cdot M$), we can find all p_i in $O(n)$ time.

(iii) We can write the polynomial as

$$a_0 + M\left(a_1 + \cdots + M\left(a_{n-1} + M a_n\right)\cdots\right).$$

If we compute the above expression from the innermost level to the outermost, we need only $O(n)$ arithmetic operations and therefore $p(M)$ can be computed using $O(n)$ operations.

(iv) Let

$$\begin{aligned}
A[x] &= a_0 + a_1 x + \cdots + a_n x^n, \\
B[x] &= b_0 + b_1 x + \cdots + b_n x^n, \quad \text{and} \\
C[x] &= A[x] \cdot B[x].
\end{aligned}$$

Assume that

$$\alpha = \max\{a_0, a_1, \ldots, a_n, \ b_0, b_1, \ldots, b_n\};$$

choose $M = (n + 2) \cdot \alpha$. We claim that

$$c_i = \text{Quotient}\left(A[M] \cdot B[M], M^i\right) \bmod M.$$

$c_i = \sum_{j=0}^{i} a_j b_{i-j} < (n+2)\alpha = M$. On the other hand $C[M] = A[M] \cdot B[M]$ and therefore from the previous part it follows that there is a unique decomposition of $C[M]$, such that it can be written as a polynomial whose coefficients are the same as in the above equality. Hence, the above expression correctly gives the coefficients. Moreover $A[M]$ and $B[M]$ can be computed using $O(n)$ arithmetic operations, and once we have $C[M]$, we can obtain all c_i using $O(n)$ arithmetic operations which shows that the total operations required are bounded by $O(n)$.

(v) Since $M = (n + 2)\alpha$, it needs $b = O(\log n + \log \alpha)$ bits. Using Schönhage-Strassen's algorithm, two n-bit integers can be multiplied in $O(n \log n \log \log n)$ time. In our cases the largest number that we multiply is M^n which requires nb bits. Hence the time complexity of one multiplication is $O(nb(\log nb)(\log \log nb))$ and since there are $O(n)$ multiplications, the total bit complexity is bounded by $O(n^2 b(\log nb)(\log \log nb))$.

Note: (*Matrix Multiplication*) Given two $n \times n$ matrices, A and B, we can compute $C = A \cdot B$, using $O(n^2)$ operations as follows: We can represent A as a vector of its rows, i.e., $A = \{a_1, a_2, \ldots, a_n\}$, where $a_i = \{a_{i,1}, a_{i,2}, \ldots, a_{i,n}\}$. Similarly, we can consider B as a vector of columns, each column denoted by $b_j = \{b_{1,j}, b_{2,j}, \ldots, b_{n,j}\}$. If we treat a_i and b_j as polynomials, where

$$\begin{aligned} a_i(x) &= a_{i,1} + a_{i,2}x + \cdots + a_{i,n}x^{n-1}, \quad \text{and} \\ b_j(x) &= b_{1,j}x^{n-1} + \cdots + b_{n-1,j}x + b_{n,j}, \end{aligned}$$

then $c_{i,j} = \sum_{k=1}^{n} a_{i,k} b_{k,j}$ is nothing but the coefficient of x^{n-1} in the polynomial $a_i(x) \cdot b_j(x)$. Now, to compute C, we proceed as follows, choose $M = (n + 2) \max_{1 \le i,j \le n}\{a_{i,j}, \ b_{i,j}\}$, and compute $a_1(M), \ldots, a_n(M)$, $b_1(M), \ldots, b_n(M)$. Then

$$c_{i,j} = \text{Quotient}\left(a_i(M) \cdot b_j(M), M^{n-1}\right) \bmod M.$$

Each of $a_i(M)$'s and $b_j(M)$'s can be computed using $O(n)$ operations, and each $c_{i,j}$ can be computed using $O(1)$ operations. Therefore, the matrix C can be computed using $O(n^2)$ arithmetic operations.

Bibliographic Notes

There are several excellent textbooks on algebra which cover in greater detail most of the topics discussed in this chapter (groups, rings, ideals, modules and syzygies): for example, Atiyah and Macdonald [9], Herstein [94], Jacobson [105], Kostrikin [120], Matsumura [141,142], van der Waerden [204] and Zariski and Samuel [216].

Dickson's lemma for power products first appears in [62]. For homogeneous ideals in $K[x_1, \ldots, x_n]$, the concept of a basis was given by Hilbert [95], and Hilbert's basis theorem (*Hilbert Basissatz*) now appears in all textbooks on algebra, in its dehomogenized version.

The concept and use of admissible orderings (also called *term orderings*) seems to have first appeared in the work of Buchberger [33] and then was further generalized by several authors. First characterization of all possible orderings appeared in the work of Robbiano [175,176], and a more constructive characterization appears in the papers by Dubé et al. [64,65].

In 1965, Bruno Buchberger, in his doctoral dissertation [30], introduced the concept of a Gröbner basis, which Buchberger had named after his teacher, W. Gröbner. During the last two decades, as the significance of Gröbner bases has begun to be widely understood, several survey and expository papers on the topic have appeared: for instance, Barkee [12], Barkee and Ecks [11], Buchberger [33], Mishra and Yap [149], Möller and Mora [151], Mora [154] and Robbiano [177,178]. There have been several generalizations of Buchberger's theory of Gröbner bases to subalgebras [179], rings with valuations or filtrations [197], noncommutative rings [153], free modules over polynomial rings [16], etc.

Problem 2.5 is based on some results due to Dubé et al. [64] and Robbiano [175] and Problem 2.8 is due to Bayer and Stillman [17].

We conclude this note with the following excerpts from the paper by Möller and Mora [151] describing the evolution of the ideas inherent in Gröbner bases.

> For homogeneous ideals in $P := k[x_1, \ldots, x_n]$, the concept of a basis was first given by Hilbert, 1890,....
>
> Macaulay observed, that any set of polynomials obtained by dehomogenization from a basis of a homogeneous ideal is a basis with favourable properties. He denoted such sets therefore H-bases [135]. Macaulay and subsequently Gröbner and Renschuch stressed in their work the significance of H-bases for constructions in Ideal Theory and Algebraic Geometry....
>
> The method of Gröbner bases (G-bases) was introduced in 1965 by Buchberger and starting from 1976, studied in a sequence of articles [33]....
>
> The concept of standard bases , which is strictly related to that one of G-bases was introduced first by Hironaka [96] and studied further among others by Galligo [73,74]. The main difference is that it was given for formal power series rings instead of polynomial ones (the difference can be easily stated saying that "initial" terms for standard bases play the role of the maximal terms for Gröbner bases); the algorithmic problem of constructing such a basis was not undertaken until 1981, when it was solved by [Mora [152]] generalizing and

suitably modifying Buchberger's algorithm for G-bases. The strict interrelation between the two concepts (and algorithms to compute them) is made clear in [Lazard's work[128]].

Chapter 3

Computational Ideal Theory

3.1 Introduction

In the previous chapter, we saw that an ideal in a Noetherian ring admits
a finite Gröbner basis (Theorem 2.3.9). However, in order to develop constructive methods that compute a Gröbner basis of an ideal, we need to
endow the underlying ring with certain additional constructive properties.
Two such properties we consider in detail, are *detachability* and *syzygy-
solvability*. A computable Noetherian ring with such properties will be
referred to as a *strongly computable ring*.

Thus, we will start with the notion of a *strongly computable ring*, and
then provide an algorithm that computes a Gröbner basis for an ideal in
$S[x_1, \ldots, x_n]$, assuming that S is a strongly computable ring. Along the
way, we shall also develop the concept of a *head reduction*[1], which, along
with the notion of S-polynomial, will provide the basic ingredients for the
algorithm.

Next, we will provide a stronger form of Hilbert's basis theorem: namely,
we shall see that *if S is a strongly computable ring, so is $S[x_1, \ldots, x_n]$*.

We will conclude this chapter with a sampling of various applications
of the Gröbner basis algorithm to computational ideal theory. Examples of
such applications include *ideal membership*, *ideal congruence*, *ideal equality*, *syzygy basis construction*, *sum*, *product*, *intersection* and *quotient* operations on ideals.

---

[1]Some authors simply use the term *reduction* for what we call *head reduction* here.
However, we will reserve the term *reduction* for a slightly stronger process that was first
introduced and used by Buchberger.

3.2   Strongly Computable Ring

Definition 3.2.1 (Computable Ring) A ring S is said to be *computable* if for given r, $s \in S$, there are algorithmic procedures to compute $-r$, $r + s$, $r \cdot s$. If, additionally S is a field, then we assume that for a given nonzero field element $r \in S$ $(r \neq 0)$, there is an algorithmic procedure to compute r^{-1}. $\square$

Definition 3.2.2 (Detachable Ring) Let S be a ring, $s \in S$ and $\{s_1, \ldots, s_q\} \subseteq S$. S is said to be *detachable* if there is an algorithm to decide whether $s \in (s_1, \ldots, s_q)$. If so, the algorithm produces a set $\{t_1, \ldots, t_q\} \subseteq S$, such that

$$s = t_1 \, s_1 + \cdots + t_q \, s_q. \quad \square$$

Definition 3.2.3 (Syzygy-Solvable Ring) A ring S is said to be *syzygy-solvable* if for any given $\{s_1, \ldots, s_q\} \subseteq S$, there is an algorithm to compute a (finite) syzygy basis, $\overline{t_1}, \ldots, \overline{t_p}$ for the S-module $S(s_1, \ldots, s_q)$ such that

1. For all $1 \le i \le p$, $\sum_j t_{i,j} \, s_j = 0$.
2. For any $\langle u_1, \ldots, u_q \rangle = \overline{u} \in S^q$, $\sum_j u_j s_j = 0$

$$\Rightarrow \left(\exists \, \overline{v} = \langle v_1, \ldots, v_p \rangle \in S^p \right) \left[\overline{u} = v_1 \, \overline{t_1} + \cdots + v_p \, \overline{t_p} \right]. \quad \square$$

Definition 3.2.4 (Strongly Computable Ring) A ring S is said to be *strongly computable* if it satisfies the following four conditions:

1. S is Noetherian,
2. S is computable,
3. S is detachable, and
4. S is syzygy-solvable. $\square$

Let S be a ring and $R = S[x_1, \ldots, x_n]$ be a ring of polynomials. Let $\underset{A}{\ge}$ be a fixed but arbitrary computable admissible ordering on $\mathrm{PP}(x_1, \ldots, x_n)$. Assume that $G \subseteq R$ and $f \in R$. Then the problems of (1) deciding whether $\mathrm{Hmono}(f) \in \mathrm{Head}(G)$ and (2) computing the S-polynomials of G reduce to simpler *detachability* and *syzygy solvability* problems in the ring S, respectively. The following lemma shows the relationship between the membership problem for the head monomial ideal and detachability.

Lemma 3.2.1 *Let* $G_f = \Big\{ g \in G : \mathrm{Hterm}(g) \mid \mathrm{Hterm}(f) \Big\}$.
Then $\mathrm{Hmono}(f) \in \mathrm{Head}(G)$ *if and only if*

$$\mathrm{Hcoef}(f) \in \Big(\{\mathrm{Hcoef}(g) : g \in G_f\} \Big).$$

PROOF.

($\Rightarrow$) Since $\mathrm{Hmono}(f) \in \mathrm{Head}(G)$, it is possible to write

$$\mathrm{Hmono}(f) = \sum_{g_i \in G} a_i \cdot p_i \cdot \mathrm{Hmono}(g_i), \quad a_i \in S \text{ and } p_i \in \mathrm{PP}(x_1, \ldots, x_n)$$

such that $p_i \cdot \mathrm{Hterm}(g_i) = \mathrm{Hterm}(f)$ (i.e., $g_i \in G_f$). Therefore,

$$\mathrm{Hmono}(f) = \sum_{g_i \in G_f} a_i \cdot \mathrm{Hcoef}(g_i) \cdot \mathrm{Hterm}(f)$$

$$\Rightarrow \quad \mathrm{Hcoef}(f) = \sum_{g_i \in G_f} a_i \cdot \mathrm{Hcoef}(g_i)$$

$$\Rightarrow \quad \mathrm{Hcoef}(f) \in \Big(\{ \mathrm{Hcoef}(g) : g \in G_f \} \Big).$$

($\Leftarrow$) $\mathrm{Hcoef}(f) = \sum_{g_i \in G_f} a_i \cdot \mathrm{Hcoef}(g_i), \qquad a_i \in S$

$$\Rightarrow \quad \mathrm{Hmono}(f) = \mathrm{Hcoef}(f) \cdot \mathrm{Hterm}(f)$$

$$= \sum_{g_i \in G_f} a_i \frac{\mathrm{Hterm}(f)}{\mathrm{Hterm}(g_i)} \cdot \mathrm{Hmono}(g_i) \in \mathrm{Head}(G),$$

$$\text{since } \Big(\forall\, g \in G_f \Big) \left[\frac{\mathrm{Hterm}(f)}{\mathrm{Hterm}(g_i)} \in \mathrm{PP}(x_1, \ldots, x_n) \right]. \quad \square$$

3.2.1   Example: Computable Field

Most of the commonly used rings do satisfy the requirements to be strongly computable. We give two examples in this section: namely, the computable fields (e.g., field of rationals, $\mathbb{Q}$ or field of integer mod a prime, $\mathbb{Z}_p$) and the ring of integers, $\mathbb{Z}$.

Example 3.2.5 (A Computable Field Is Strongly Computable.) Let $S = K$ be a computable field. We show that K is strongly computable.

1. K is Noetherian; recall that a field can have only improper ideals which are obviously finitely generated.

2. K is computable, by assumption.

3. K is detachable. Let $a \in K$ and $\{a_1, \ldots, a_q\} \subseteq K$. If $a \neq 0$ but $a_1 = a_2 = \cdots = a_q = 0$, then $a \notin (a_1, \ldots, a_q)$; otherwise, assume that some $a_i \neq 0$ and has a multiplicative inverse a_i^{-1}. Then

$$a = 0 \cdot a_1 + \cdots + 0 \cdot a_{i-1} + a \cdot a_i^{-1} \cdot a_i + \cdots + 0 \cdot a_q.$$

4. K is syzygy-solvable. Let $\{a_1, \ldots, a_q\} \subseteq K$ (without loss of generality, we may assume that every $a_i \neq 0$). Then the syzygy of $(a_1, \ldots, a_q)$ is a $(q-1)$-dimensional vector space, orthogonal to the vector $\langle a_1, \ldots, a_q \rangle$, with the following basis:

$$
\begin{aligned}
\overline{t_1} &= \langle a_1^{-1}, -a_2^{-1}, 0, \ldots, 0 \rangle \\
\overline{t_2} &= \langle 0, a_2^{-1}, -a_3^{-1}, \ldots, 0 \rangle \\
&\vdots \\
\overline{t_{q-1}} &= \langle 0, 0, \ldots, a_{q-1}^{-1}, -a_q^{-1} \rangle
\end{aligned}
$$

To verify that it is really a syzygy basis, notice that it satisfies both conditions of the definition of syzygy solvability.

The first condition holds, since, for all i, $\sum_{j=1}^{q} t_{i,j} a_j = 0$.

$$
\begin{aligned}
\overline{t_i} \cdot \overline{a} &= 0 \cdot 1 + \cdots + a_i^{-1} \cdot a_i - a_{i+1}^{-1} \cdot a_{i+1} + \cdots + 0 \cdot a_q \\
&= 1 - 1 = 0.
\end{aligned}
$$

Let $\overline{d} = \langle d_1, \ldots, d_q \rangle$ such that $\sum_{j=1}^{q} d_j a_j = 0$. Then, in order to satisfy the second condition, we need to determine a tuple $\overline{v} = \langle v_1, \ldots, v_{q-1} \rangle$ such that

$$
\overline{d} = v_1 \cdot \overline{t_1} + \cdots + v_{q-1} \cdot \overline{t_{q-1}}.
$$

We choose $\overline{v}$ as follows:

$$
\begin{aligned}
v_1 &= a_1 \cdot d_1 \\
v_2 &= a_1 \cdot d_1 + a_2 \cdot d_2 \\
&\vdots \\
v_i &= a_1 \cdot d_1 + a_2 \cdot d_2 + \cdots + a_i \cdot d_i \\
&\vdots \\
v_{q-1} &= a_1 \cdot d_1 + a_2 \cdot d_2 + \cdots + a_{q-1} \cdot d_{q-1}
\end{aligned}
$$

Then the jth component of $v_1 \cdot \overline{t_1} + \cdots + v_{q-1} \cdot \overline{t_{q-1}}$ is computed as follows:

- The first component is $v_1 \cdot a_1^{-1} = a_1 \cdot d_1 \cdot a_1^{-1} = d_1$.
- For $1 < j < q$, the jth component is

$$
\begin{aligned}
v_j \cdot t_{j,j} &+ v_{j-1} \cdot t_{j-1,j} \\
&= (a_1 \cdot d_1 + \cdots + a_j \cdot d_j) \cdot a_j^{-1} \\
&\quad - (a_1 \cdot d_1 + \cdots + a_{j-1} \cdot d_{j-1}) \cdot a_j^{-1} \\
&= a_j \cdot d_j \cdot a_j^{-1} = d_j.
\end{aligned}
$$

- Finally, the qth component is

$$-v_{q-1} \cdot a_q^{-1} \;=\; -(a_1 \cdot d_1 + \cdots + a_{q-1} \cdot d_{q-1}) \cdot a_q^{-1}.$$

But $\sum_{j=1}^{q} d_j a_j = 0$; therefore, $-a_1 \cdot d_1 - \cdots - a_{q-1} \cdot d_{q-1} = a_q \cdot d_q$, and the qth component is simply $a_q \cdot d_q \cdot a_q^{-1} = d_q$. Thus $\overline{t_i}$'s form a basis for the syzygy of $(a_1, \ldots, a_q)$. □

S-Polynomials in $K[x_1, \ldots, x_n]$

Lemma 3.2.2 *Let $G \subseteq K[x_1, \ldots, x_n]$ be a finite set of polynomials over a field K and let*

$$S(g_j, g_k) = \frac{m}{\text{Hmono}(g_j)} \cdot g_j - \frac{m}{\text{Hmono}(g_k)} \cdot g_k$$

where g_j, $g_k \in G$ and $g_j \neq g_k$, $m = LCM(\text{Hterm}(g_j), \text{Hterm}(g_k))$.
Then G satisfies the syzygy condition if and only if every $S(g_j, g_k)$ can be expressed as

$$S(g_j, g_k) = \sum f_i g_i, \quad f_i \in K[x_1, \ldots x_n] \text{ and } g_i \in G,$$

where $\text{Hterm}(S(g_j, g_k)) \underset{A}{\geq} \text{Hterm}(f_i)\,\text{Hterm}(g_i)$.

PROOF.
We need to observe that every $S(g_j, g_k)$ is an S-polynomial for the set $\{g_j, g_k\} \subseteq G$ and every S-polynomial of any subset of G can be expressed as a power-product times some $S(g_j, g_k)$.
Let $\{g_1, \ldots, g_q\} \subseteq G$, and

$$\left\{ a_1 = \text{Hcoef}(g_1), \; \ldots, \; a_q = \text{Hcoef}(g_q) \right\} \subseteq K.$$

In the syzygy basis for $(a_1, \ldots, a_q)$, each $\overline{t_\ell}$ has only two nonzero entries; namely, a_j^{-1} and $-a_k^{-1}$. Hence, each S-polynomial of G has the following form:

$$\text{Hcoef}(g_j)^{-1} \cdot \frac{M}{\text{Hterm}(g_j)} \cdot g_j - \text{Hcoef}(g_k)^{-1} \cdot \frac{M}{\text{Hterm}(g_k)} \cdot g_k,$$

where $M = LCM(\text{Hterm}(g_1), \ldots, \text{Hterm}(g_q)) = p \cdot LCM(\text{Hterm}(g_j), \text{Hterm}(g_k))$, which can be written as

$$p \cdot S(g_j, g_k), \quad p \in PP(x_1, \ldots, x_n). \quad □$$

In view of the above lemma, we shall often refer to $S(g_j, g_k)$'s as S-polynomials while working over a field.

3.2.2   Example: Ring of Integers

Example 3.2.6 (Ring of Integers Is Strongly Computable.) Let $S = \mathbb{Z}$ be the ring of integers. We recall the following useful property of $\mathbb{Z}$: for any $\{a_1, \ldots, a_q\} \subseteq \mathbb{Z}$,

$$\left(\exists\, b \in \mathbb{Z}\right)\left[(b) = (a_1, \ldots, a_q)\right],$$

and

1. $b = \mathrm{GCD}(a_1, \ldots, a_q)$. Let

$$a_1' = \frac{a_1}{b}, \quad a_2' = \frac{a_2}{b}, \quad \ldots, \quad a_q' = \frac{a_q}{b}.$$

2. Since $b \in (a_1, \ldots, a_q)$,

$$\left(\exists\, c_1, \ldots, c_q \in \mathbb{Z}\right)\left[b = c_1 a_1 + \cdots + c_q a_q\right].$$

Note that $b, c_1, \ldots, c_q$ can be computed using Euclid's algorithm; the details of Euclid's algorithm can be found in Knuth [116].

Now, we show that $\mathbb{Z}$ is strongly computable.

1. $\mathbb{Z}$ is Noetherian. This follows from the fact that every ideal in $\mathbb{Z}$ is generated by a single element in $\mathbb{Z}$. (That is, every ideal of $\mathbb{Z}$ is a principal ideal and thus $\mathbb{Z}$ is a principal ideal domain.)

2. $\mathbb{Z}$ is computable. The necessary algorithms are easy to construct.

3. $\mathbb{Z}$ is detachable. Let $a \in \mathbb{Z}$, $\{a_1, \ldots, a_q\} \subseteq \mathbb{Z}$ and $b = \mathrm{GCD}(a_1, \ldots, a_q)$. If $b \nmid a$, then $a \notin (b) = (a_1, \ldots, a_q)$; otherwise, $a \in (b) = (a_1, \ldots, a_q)$. Now, if $a = d \cdot b$, then

$$a = (d \cdot c_1)a_1 + \cdots + (d \cdot c_q)a_q,$$

where $c_1, \ldots, c_q$ are obtained from Euclid's algorithm.

4. $\mathbb{Z}$ is syzygy-solvable. Let $\{a_1, \ldots, a_q\} \subseteq \mathbb{Z}$,

$$b = \mathrm{GCD}(a_1, \ldots, a_q) = c_1 a_1 + \cdots + c_q a_q,$$

and $a_i' = a_i/b$ (for $i = 1, \ldots, q$). Then the syzygy of $(a_1, \ldots, a_q)$ has the following basis:

$$
\begin{aligned}
\overline{t_1} &= \langle (c_2 a_2' + \cdots + c_q a_q'), \ -c_2 a_1', \ \ldots, \ -c_q a_1' \rangle \\
\overline{t_2} &= \langle -c_1 a_2', \ (c_1 a_1' + c_3 a_3' + \cdots + c_q a_q'), \ -c_3 a_2', \ \ldots, \ -c_q a_2' \rangle \\
&\ \vdots \\
\overline{t_q} &= \langle -c_1 a_q', \ \ldots, \ -c_{q-1} a_q', \ (c_1 a_1' + \cdots + c_{q-1} a_{q-1}') \rangle
\end{aligned}
$$

To verify that it is really a syzygy basis, we need to show that it satisfies both conditions of the definition of syzygy solvability. The first condition holds, since, for all i, $\sum_{j=1}^{q} t_{i,j} a_j = 0$.

$$
\begin{aligned}
\sum_{j=1}^{q} t_{i,j} a_j \\
= \quad & -c_1 \, a_i' \, a_1 - \cdots - c_{i-1} \, a_i' \, a_{i-1} \\
& + c_1 \, a_1' \, a_i + \cdots + c_{i-1} \, a_{i-1}' \, a_i + c_{i+1} \, a_{i+1}' \, a_i + \cdots + c_q \, a_q' \, a_i \\
& - c_{i+1} \, a_i' \, a_{i+1} - \cdots - c_q \, a_i' \, a_q \\
= \quad & -c_1 \frac{a_i a_1}{b} - \cdots - c_{i-1} \frac{a_i a_{i-1}}{b} \\
& + c_1 \frac{a_1 a_i}{b} + \cdots + c_{i-1} \frac{a_{i-1} a_i}{b} + c_{i+1} \frac{a_{i+1} a_i}{b} + \cdots + c_q \frac{a_q a_i}{b} \\
& - c_{i+1} \frac{a_i a_{i+1}}{b} - \cdots - c_q \frac{a_i a_q}{b} \\
= \quad & 0.
\end{aligned}
$$

Let $\bar{d} = \langle d_1, \ldots, d_q \rangle$ such that $\sum_{j=1}^{q} d_j a_j = 0$. Then, in order to satisfy the second condition, we need to determine a tuple $\bar{v} = \langle v_1, \ldots, v_{q-1} \rangle$ such that

$$
\bar{d} = v_1 \cdot \overline{t_1} + \cdots + v_{q-1} \cdot \overline{t_{q-1}}.
$$

We show that the choice $\bar{v} = d$ satisfies the condition, that is, the jth component of $d_1 \overline{t_1} + \cdots + d_q \overline{t_q}$ is d_j itself. The jth component is

$$
\begin{aligned}
d_1 \, t_{1,j} &+ d_2 \, t_{2,j} + \cdots + d_q \, t_{q,j} \\
= \quad & -d_1 c_j a_1' - d_2 c_j a_2' - \cdots - d_{j-1} c_j a_{j-1}' \\
& + d_j \left(c_1 a_1' + \cdots + c_{j-1} a_{j-1}' + c_{j+1} a_{j+1}' + \cdots + c_q a_q' \right) \\
& - d_{j+1} c_j a_{j+1}' - \cdots - d_q c_j a_q' \\
= \quad & -c_j \left(\frac{d_1 a_1 + \cdots + d_{j-1} a_{j-1} + d_{j+1} a_{j+1} + \cdots + d_q a_q}{b} \right) \\
& + d_j \left(\frac{c_1 a_1 + \cdots + c_{j-1} a_{j-1} + c_{j+1} a_{j+1} + \cdots + c_q a_q}{b} \right) \\
= \quad & -c_j \left(\frac{-d_j a_j}{b} \right) \\
& + d_j \left(\frac{c_1 a_1 + \cdots + c_{j-1} a_{j-1} + c_{j+1} a_{j+1} + \cdots + c_q a_q}{b} \right) \\
& \qquad \left(\text{Using the fact that } \sum_j d_j a_j = 0 \right) \\
= \quad & d_j \left(\frac{c_1 a_1 + \cdots + c_q a_q}{b} \right)
\end{aligned}
$$

$$= \quad d_j. \qquad \text{(Since } \sum_i c_i a_i = b\text{)}$$

Thus $\overline{t_i}$'s form a basis for the syzygy of $(a_1, \ldots, a_q)$. $\square$

Remark 3.2.7 There is another syzygy basis for $(a_1, \ldots, a_q) \subseteq \mathbb{Z}$ with a somewhat simpler structure. Let $\{a_1, \ldots, a_q\} \subseteq \mathbb{Z}$, $b = \text{GCD}(a_1, \ldots, a_q) = c_1 a_1 + \cdots + c_q a_q$ and $b_{i,j} = \text{GCD}(a_i, a_j)$. Then the syzygy basis for $(a_1, \ldots, a_q)$ can be given as follows:

$$\overline{\tau_{i,j}} = \Big\langle 0, \ldots, 0, \quad \underbrace{\frac{a_j}{b_{i,j}}}_{\text{position } i}, \quad 0, \ldots, 0, \quad \underbrace{-\frac{a_i}{b_{i,j}}}_{\text{position } j}, \quad 0, \ldots, 0 \Big\rangle,$$

for $1 \leq i < j \leq q$.

It now remains to check that both conditions for syzygy-solvability are satisfied.

1. $\displaystyle\sum_j \tau_{i,j} a_j = \frac{a_j \cdot a_i}{b_{i,j}} - \frac{a_i \cdot a_j}{b_{i,j}} = 0.$

2. Since $\overline{t_1}, \ldots, \overline{t_q}$ is a syzygy basis (i.e., any element $\overline{u}$ of syzygy can be written as a linear combination of $\overline{t_i}$'s), it is enough to show that each $\overline{t_i}$ can be written as a linear combination of $\overline{\tau_{i,j}}$. Note that $b \mid b_{i,j}$. Let $b'_{i,j} = b_{i,j}/b$. Then

$$- c_1 b'_{1,i} \overline{\tau_{1,i}} - c_2 b'_{2,i} \overline{\tau_{2,i}} - \cdots - c_{i-1} b'_{i-1,i} \overline{\tau_{i-1,i}}$$
$$+ c_{i+1} b'_{i,i+1} \overline{\tau_{i,i+1}} + \cdots + c_q b'_{i,q} \overline{\tau_{i,q}}$$
$$= \Big\langle -c_1 \frac{a_i}{b}, 0, \ldots, 0, c_1 \frac{a_1}{b}, 0, \ldots, 0 \Big\rangle$$
$$+ \Big\langle 0, -c_2 \frac{a_i}{b}, 0, \ldots, 0, c_2 \frac{a_2}{b}, 0, \ldots, 0 \Big\rangle$$
$$+ \cdots$$
$$+ \Big\langle 0, \ldots, 0, -c_{i-1} \frac{a_i}{b}, c_{i-1} \frac{a_{i-1}}{b}, 0, \ldots, 0 \Big\rangle$$
$$+ \Big\langle 0, \ldots, 0, c_{i+1} \frac{a_{i+1}}{b}, -c_{i+1} \frac{a_i}{b}, 0, \ldots, 0 \Big\rangle$$
$$+ \Big\langle 0, \ldots, 0, c_{i+2} \frac{a_{i+2}}{b}, 0, -c_{i+2} \frac{a_i}{b}, 0, \ldots, 0 \Big\rangle$$
$$+ \cdots$$
$$+ \Big\langle 0, \ldots, 0, c_q \frac{a_q}{b}, 0, \ldots, 0, -c_q \frac{a_i}{b} \Big\rangle$$
$$= \quad \langle -c_1 a'_i, -c_2 a'_i, \ldots, -c_{i-1} a'_i,$$
$$\quad (c_1 a'_1 + \cdots + c_{i-1} a'_{i-1} + c_{i+1} a'_{i+1} + \cdots + c_q a'_q),$$
$$\quad -c_{i+1} a'_i, \ldots, -c_q a'_i \rangle$$
$$= \quad \overline{t_i}. \qquad \square$$

S-Polynomials in $\mathbb{z}[x_1, \ldots, x_n]$

Lemma 3.2.3 *Let $G \subseteq \mathbb{Z}[x_1, \ldots, x_n]$ be a finite set of polynomials over the ring of integers $\mathbb{Z}$ and let*

$$S(g_j, g_k) = \frac{\widehat{m}}{\text{Hmono}(g_j)} \cdot g_j - \frac{\widehat{m}}{\text{Hmono}(g_k)} \cdot g_k$$

where $g_j, g_k \in G$, $g_j \neq g_k$ and $\widehat{m} = LCM(\text{Hmono}(g_j), \text{Hmono}(g_k))$.

Then G satisfies the syzygy condition if and only if every $S(g_j, g_k)$ can be expressed as

$$S(g_j, g_k) = \sum f_i g_i, \quad f_i \in \mathbb{Z}[x_1, \ldots x_n] \quad and \quad g_i \in G,$$

where $\text{Hterm}(S(g_j, g_k)) \underset{A}{\geq} \text{Hterm}(f_i)\, \text{Hterm}(g_i)$.

PROOF.

The proof proceeds in a manner similar to the case for a field K (see Lemma 3.2.2). Let $\{g_1, \ldots, g_q\} \subseteq G$, and

$$\left\{ a_1 = \text{Hcoef}(g_1), \ldots, a_q = \text{Hcoef}(g_q) \right\} \subseteq \mathbb{Z}.$$

We have seen that a basis for the syzygy of $(a_1, \ldots, a_q)$ can be written as follows:

$$\overline{\tau_{j,k}} = \Big\langle 0, \ldots, 0, \underbrace{\frac{a_k}{b_{j,k}}}_{\text{position } j}, 0, \ldots, 0, \underbrace{-\frac{a_j}{b_{j,k}}}_{\text{position } k}, 0, \ldots, 0 \Big\rangle,$$

for $1 \leq j < k \leq q$. Hence, each S-polynomial of G has the following form:

$$\frac{\text{Hcoef}(g_j)}{\text{GCD}(\text{Hcoef}(g_j), \text{Hcoef}(g_k))} \cdot \frac{M}{\text{Hterm}(g_j)} g_j$$

$$- \frac{\text{Hcoef}(g_k)}{\text{GCD}(\text{Hcoef}(g_j), \text{Hcoef}(g_k))} \cdot \frac{M}{\text{Hterm}(g_k)} g_k$$

$$= \frac{\text{LCM}(\text{Hcoef}(g_j), \text{Hcoef}(g_k))M}{\text{Hmono}(g_j)} g_j - \frac{\text{LCM}(\text{Hcoef}(g_j), \text{Hcoef}(g_k))M}{\text{Hmono}(g_k)} g_k$$

$$= p \cdot S(g_j, g_k), \quad \text{where}$$

$$M = \text{LCM}(\text{Hterm}(g_1), \ldots, \text{Hterm}(g_q))$$

$$= p\,\text{LCM}(\text{Hterm}(g_j), \text{Hmono}(g_k)), \text{ and } p \in \text{PP}(x_1, \ldots, x_n). \quad \square$$

In view of the above lemma, we also refer to $S(g_j, g_k)$'s as S-polynomials while working over the integers.

3.3   Head Reductions and Gröbner Bases

In this section, we shall develop an algorithm to compute a Gröbner basis of an ideal in a polynomial ring over an ambient, strongly computable ring. First we need one key ingredient: *head reduction*.

Definition 3.3.1 (Head Reductions) Let S be a ring, let $R = S[x_1, \ldots, x_n]$, let $\underset{A}{\geq}$ be a fixed but arbitrary admissible ordering on $PP(x_1, \ldots, x_n)$, and let $G = \{g_1, g_2, \ldots, g_m\} \subseteq R$ be a finite set of polynomials. We say $f \in R$ is *head-reducible modulo G* if $f \neq 0$ and $Hmono(f) \in Head(G)$.

If f is head-reducible modulo G and, specifically,

$$Hmono(f) = \sum_{i=1}^{m} a_i p_i \, Hmono(g_i), \quad \text{where } a_i \in S, p_i \in PP(x_1, \ldots, x_n)$$

and $p_i Hterm(g_i) = Hterm(f)$, then the polynomial

$$h = f - \sum_{i=1}^{m} a_i p_i \, g_i$$

is said to be a *head-reduct* of f modulo G, and is denoted by

$$f \xrightarrow{G,h} h.$$

We also write $\xrightarrow[*]{G,h}$ for the reflexive and transitive closure of $\xrightarrow{G,h}$; that is,

$$f \xrightarrow[*]{G,h} h,$$

if there is a finite sequence $h_1, h_2, \ldots, h_n$ $(n \geq 1)$ such that $h_1 = f, h_n = h$, and

$$h_i \xrightarrow{G,h} h_{i+1}, \quad \text{for } i = 1, \ldots, n - 1.$$

If f is *not* head-reducible modulo G, or if $f = 0$, we use the (perhaps, unfortunate) notation

$$f \xrightarrow{G,h} f. \quad \square$$

Definition 3.3.2 (Head-Normal Forms) We say h is a *normal form of f modulo G under head-reduction* (briefly, *head-normal form* or simply, *normal form* if there is no confusion) if

$$f \xrightarrow[*]{G,h} h \xrightarrow{G,h} h.$$

We write $NF_G^h(f)$ for the set of head-normal forms of f modulo G. $\quad \square$

Theorem 3.3.1 *If S is a ring, $R = S[x_1, \ldots, x_n]$ and $G = \{g_1, g_2, \ldots, g_m\} \subseteq R$, then*

$$\left(\forall f \in R\right) \left[\mathrm{NF}_G^h(f) \neq \emptyset\right].$$

PROOF.
We proceed by well-founded induction on $\mathrm{Hterm}(f)$ with respect to the well-ordering $\underset{A}{>}$.

Suppose $f = 0$. Then $\mathrm{Hmono}(f) = 0$ and

$$\mathrm{NF}_G^h(f) = \{0\} \neq \emptyset.$$

Henceforth, assume that $f \neq 0$, and thus $\mathrm{Hmono}(f) \neq 0$. To handle the base case, note that if $\mathrm{Hterm}(f) = 1$, then either $\mathrm{Hmono}(f) \notin \mathrm{Head}(G)$, in which case f is already head-reduced modulo G and

$$\mathrm{NF}_G^h(f) = \{f\} \neq \emptyset;$$

or $\mathrm{Hmono}(f) \in \mathrm{Head}(G)$, in which case f head-reduces to 0 modulo G and

$$\mathrm{NF}_G^h(f) = \{0\} \neq \emptyset.$$

To handle the inductive case $(\mathrm{Hterm}(f) \underset{A}{>} 1)$, we assume by the inductive hypothesis that for all $h \in R$

$$\mathrm{Hterm}(h) \underset{A}{<} \mathrm{Hterm}(f) \quad \Rightarrow \quad \mathrm{NF}_G^h(h) \neq \emptyset.$$

As before, either $\mathrm{Hmono}(f) \notin \mathrm{Head}(G)$, in which case f is already head-reduced modulo G and

$$\mathrm{NF}_G^h(f) = \{f\} \neq \emptyset;$$

or $\mathrm{Hmono}(f) \in \mathrm{Head}(G)$, in which case f head-reduces to h modulo G and

$$\mathrm{Hterm}(h) \underset{A}{<} \mathrm{Hterm}(f) \quad \text{and} \quad \mathrm{NF}_G^h(f) \supseteq \mathrm{NF}_G^h(h) \neq \emptyset. \qquad \square$$

Theorem 3.3.2 *Let S be a ring, $R = S[x_1, \ldots, x_n]$, I be an ideal in R, and let $G = \{g_1, g_2, \ldots, g_m\} \subseteq I$ be a finite subset. Then the following three statements are equivalent:*

1. $\mathrm{Head}(G) = \mathrm{Head}(I)$.

2. *Every $f \in I$ head-reduces to 0 modulo G:*

$$\left(\forall f \in I\right) \left[f \xrightarrow[*]{G,h} 0\right].$$

3. $(G) = I$ *and*

$$\left(\forall F \subseteq G\right) \left(\forall h \in SP(F)\right) \left[h \xrightarrow[*]{G,h} 0\right].$$

PROOF.

$[(1) \Rightarrow (2)]$

We proceed by induction on $\mathrm{Hmono}(f)$ with respect to the well-ordering $\underset{A}{>}$.

If $f = 0$ then we are done. Thus we may assume that $f \neq 0$ and $f \in I$, and that, by the inductive hypothesis, for all $h \in I$

$$\mathrm{Hterm}(h) \underset{A}{<} \mathrm{Hterm}(f) \quad \Rightarrow \quad h \xrightarrow[*]{G,h} 0.$$

Since $f \in I$, $\mathrm{Hmono}(f) \in \mathrm{Head}(I) = \mathrm{Head}(G)$ and f head-reduces to some $h \in I$, i.e.,

$$f \xrightarrow{G,h} h, \qquad \mathrm{Hterm}(h) \underset{A}{<} \mathrm{Hterm}(f), \quad \text{and} \quad h \in I.$$

If $h = 0$ then we are done; otherwise, by the inductive hypothesis,

$$f \xrightarrow{G,h} h \xrightarrow[*]{G,h} 0.$$

$[(2) \Rightarrow (1)]$

Note that if $f \xrightarrow[*]{G,h} 0$ then f can be expressed as

$$f = \sum_{i=1}^{m} f_i g_i \qquad \text{where } f_i \in S[x_1, \ldots, x_n], \quad \text{and}$$

$$\mathrm{Hterm}(f) \underset{A}{\geq} \mathrm{Hterm}(f_i)\,\mathrm{Hterm}(g_i), \quad i = 1, \ldots, m.$$

Thus, condition (2) implies that G is a Gröbner basis and $\mathrm{Head}(G) = \mathrm{Head}(I)$.

$[(1) \Rightarrow (3)]$

Since $G \subseteq I$ and $\mathrm{Head}(G) = \mathrm{Head}(I)$, G generates I. Furthermore, every S-polynomial $h \in SP(F)$ $(F \subseteq G)$ is an element of I, and thus

$$\left(\forall\, F \subseteq G \right) \left(\forall\, h \in SP(F) \right) \left[h \xrightarrow[*]{G,h} 0 \right].$$

$[(3) \Rightarrow (1)]$

Note that the condition,

$$\left(\forall\, F \subseteq G \right) \left(\forall\, h \in SP(F) \right) \left[h \xrightarrow[*]{G,h} 0 \right].$$

simply implies that G satisfies the syzygy condition.

Since we also assume that $(G) = I$, by Theorem 2.5.2, we conclude that $\mathrm{Head}(G) = \mathrm{Head}(I)$. $\square$

3.3.1   Algorithm to Compute Head Reduction

In this subsection, we present an algorithm that computes the head reduction and then, using this algorithm, we develop an algorithm for Gröbner basis.

ONEHEADREDUCTION(f, G)
Input: $f \in R$; $G \subseteq R$, G = finite.
Output: h such that $f \xrightarrow{G,h} h$.

> if $f = 0$ or Hcoef(f) $\notin \left(\{\text{Hcoef}(g) \colon g \in G_f\} \right)$ then
>> return f;
>
> else
>
>> Let Hcoef(f) $= \displaystyle\sum_{g_i \in G_f} a_i \cdot \text{Hcoef}(g_i)$, $a_i \in S$;
>>
>> return $f - \displaystyle\sum_{g_i \in G} a_i \cdot \frac{\text{Hterm}(f)}{\text{Hterm}(g_i)} \cdot g_i$;
>
> end{if };
end{ONEHEADREDUCTION}   □

Using the above routine, we can compute the head reduction of a given polynomial f

HEADREDUCTION(f, G)
Input: $f \in R$; $G \subseteq R$, G = finite.
Output: h such that $f \xrightarrow[*]{G,h} h \xrightarrow{G,h} h$.

> $h := f$; $h' := f$;
>
> loop
>> $h := h'$;
>> $h' := \text{ONEHEADREDUCTION}(h, G)$;
>
> until $h = h'$;
>
> return h;
end{HEADREDUCTION}   □

CORRECTNESS AND TERMINATION:

The correctness of the algorithm HEADREDUCTION follows directly from the definition of the head reduction.

In order to prove the termination properties, notice that the until loop satisfies the following loop-invariant at the end of the loop

$$\text{Hterm}(h) \underset{A}{\geq} \text{Hterm}(h'), \quad \text{i.e.,}$$

$$h \neq h' \quad \Rightarrow \quad \text{Hterm}(h) \underset{A}{>} \text{Hterm}(h').$$

Thus, the *head terms* of h' are monotonically decreasing, and since $\underset{A}{>}$ is a well-ordering, we cannot have an infinite sequence of h''s. Thus, the algorithm HEADREDUCTION must eventually terminate.

3.3.2   Algorithm to Compute Gröbner Bases

Now we are in position to give an algorithm that computes the Gröbner basis for a finitely generated ideal.

First, we present a routine which checks if a given basis G is a Gröbner basis for the ideal generated by G and it returns an S-polynomial of G if G is not a Gröbner basis for (G).

> GRÖBNERP(G)
> **Input:** $G \subseteq R,\ G =$ finite.
> **Output:** $S(G) = \bigcup_{\emptyset \neq F \subseteq G} \mathrm{NF}_G^h(SP(F))$,
>
> $=$ head-normal forms of all the S-polynomials.
>
> $S(G) = \{0\},$ if G is Gröbner basis of (G);
> $S(G) \neq \{0\},$ if G is not a Gröbner basis of (G).
>
> $S := \emptyset;$
>
>   for every nonempty subset $F \subseteq G$ loop
>   Compute $S' =$ the S-polynomials of F;
>   for every $h' \in S'$ loop
> $S := S \cup \{\mathrm{HEADREDUCTION}\,(h',\,G)\}$
>   end{loop };
>   end{loop };
>
>   return S;
>   end{GRÖBNERP}   □

CORRECTNESS AND TERMINATION:

The correctness of the algorithm GRÖBNERP is a simple consequence of the characterization of Gröbner bases in terms of the syzygy condition:

$$G = \text{Gröbner basis for } (G)$$

if and only if

$$\left(\forall\, F \subseteq G,\, F \neq \emptyset\right) \left(\forall\, h_F \in SP(F)\right) \left[h_F \xrightarrow[*]{G,h} 0\right].$$

Termination, on the other hand, is a simple consequence of the following obvious conditions:

1. Finiteness of the set of S-polynomials $SP(F)$ of F.

2. Termination of the head reduction.

Now, we give the main algorithm which computes a Gröbner basis for an ideal generated by a given finite basis H:

GRÖBNER(H)
Input: $H \subseteq R$, $H =$ finite.
Output: $G \subseteq R$, $G =$ Gröbner basis for (H).

$G := H$;
$S :=$ GRÖBNERP(G);

while $S \neq \{0\}$ loop
    $G := G \cup S$;
    $S :-$ GRÖBNERP(G);
end{loop };

return G;
end{GRÖBNER}   □

CORRECTNESS AND TERMINATION:
The correctness of the algorithm GRÖBNER follows from the following two facts:

1. Let G_i be the value of G while the loop is executed the ith time. Thus,
$$H = G_0 \subseteq G_1 \subseteq G_2 \subseteq \cdots.$$
The algorithm maintains the following loop invariant:
$$\left(\forall i\right) \left[(G_i) = (H)\right].$$

- $(G_i) \subseteq (H)$. Since, $S \subseteq (G_{i-1}) = (H)$, we have
$$G_i = G_{i-1} \cup S \subseteq (H) \quad \Rightarrow \quad (G_i) \subseteq (H).$$

- Conversely, since $H \subseteq G_i$, we have $(H) \subseteq (G_i)$.

2. At termination, the syzygy condition is satisfied:

$$\left(\forall\, F \subseteq G,\, F \neq \emptyset\right) \left(\forall\, h_F \in SP(F)\right) \left[h_F \xrightarrow[*]{G,h} 0\right]$$

if and only if

$$S = \text{GR\"OBNERP}(G) = 0.$$

Next we show that, as a result of the Noetherianness of R, the terminating condition "$S = \{0\}$" must eventually be satisfied:

$$S = \text{GR\"OBNERP}(G_i) \neq \{0\}$$
$$\Rightarrow\ \left(\exists\, h \in S\right) \left[\text{Hmono}(h) \notin \text{Head}(G_i)\right]$$
$$\Rightarrow\ G_{i+1} = G_i \cup S \quad \text{and} \quad \text{Head}(G_i) \subsetneq \text{Head}(G_{i+1})$$

But, in R, it is impossible to obtain a strictly ascending chain of ideals; that is, eventually,

$$\left(\exists\, \ell\right) \left[S = \text{GR\"OBNERP}(G_\ell) = \{0\}\right].$$

Note that the algorithm given above is a very high-level description. It does not say anything about how to compute it efficiently. There are several issues involved here; for example, how to represent a multivariate polynomial so that all of the operations can be done efficiently, how to find a_i in ONEHEADREDUCTION quickly, how to compute S-polynomials efficiently, etc.

The Gröbner basis algorithm is usually presented somewhat differently. In order to keep the exposition simpler, we have essentially divided the algorithm into two routines: (1) a predicate that decides if a given basis is a Gröbner basis (GRÖBNERP) and (2) a procedure that keeps enlarging a given set until it satisfies the preceding predicate (GRÖBNER). We conclude this section with the presentation of the Gröbner basis algorithm in its more widely used form:

Gröbner(H)
Input: $H \subseteq R$, $H = $ finite.
Output: $G \subseteq R$, $G = $ Gröbner basis for (H).

> $G := H$;
> while there is some nonempty subset $F \subseteq G$
>   such that some S-polynomial $h \in SP(F)$
>   does not head-reduce to 0
> loop
> $h' := $ HeadReduction(h, G);
>   **Comment:** By assumption $h' \neq 0$.
> $G := G \cup \{h'\}$;
> end{loop };
> return G;
> end{Gröbner} $\square$

3.4   Detachability Computation

Let us now consider the detachability property of a polynomial ring $R = S[x_1, \ldots, x_n]$, given that the underlying ring of coefficients S itself is strongly computable. In particular, we will explore the algorithmic constructions for detachability, building up on our Gröbner basis algorithm of the previous section. It is not hard to see that the existence of a finite and computable Gröbner basis in R allows one to solve the problem of ideal membership as follows:

> IdealMembership(f, H)
> **Input:** $H \subseteq R$ and a polynomial $f \in R$; $H = $ finite.
> **Output:**   true , if $f \in (H)$.

To solve this problem, first compute $G = $ the Gröbner basis for H, and output True if HeadReduction $(f, G) = 0$; otherwise, output False. The correctness follows from the fact that $f \in (H)$ if and only if $f \in (G)$, i.e., if and only if $f \xrightarrow[*]{G,h} 0$.

The above algorithm can be easily modified to express the polynomial f as a linear combination of the polynomials in the Gröbner basis G. But in order to solve the detachability problem, we need to do a little more, i.e. express f as a linear combination of the elements of H.

The easiest way to do this is to precompute the expressions for each element of G as linear combinations of the elements of H, and then substitute these expressions in the equation for f, which expresses f as a linear combination of the polynomials of G. We show, in detail, how this can be accomplished with appropriate modifications of the algorithms: ONE-HEADREDUCTION, HEADREDUCTION and GRÖBNER.

3.4.1   Expressing with the Gröbner Basis

Given a finite set of generators $H = \{h_1, \ldots, h_l\} \subseteq R$, and a (finite) Gröbner basis $G = \{g_1, \ldots, g_m\}$, of the ideal (H), there are two matrices:

1. an $l \times m$ matrix $X = \{x_{i,j}\}$ in $R^{l \times m}$, and

2. an $l \times m$ matrix $Y = \{y_{i,j}\}$ in $R^{l \times m}$

such that

$$
\left.
\begin{aligned}
g_1 &= x_{1,1}h_1 + \cdots + x_{l,1}h_l \\
&\;\;\vdots \\
g_m &= x_{1,m}h_1 + \cdots + x_{l,m}h_l
\end{aligned}
\right\}
\quad \text{i.e.,} \quad
\begin{bmatrix} g_1 \\ \vdots \\ g_m \end{bmatrix}
= X^T
\begin{bmatrix} h_1 \\ \vdots \\ h_l \end{bmatrix},
$$

and

$$
\left.
\begin{aligned}
h_1 &= y_{1,1}g_1 + \cdots + y_{1,m}g_m \\
&\;\;\vdots \\
h_l &= y_{l,1}g_1 + \cdots + y_{l,m}g_m
\end{aligned}
\right\}
\quad \text{i.e.,} \quad
\begin{bmatrix} h_1 \\ \vdots \\ h_l \end{bmatrix}
= Y
\begin{bmatrix} g_1 \\ \vdots \\ g_m \end{bmatrix}.
$$

Thus, in order to solve the detachability problem for R, we need to solve the following problem:

> **Input:** $H = \{h_1, \ldots, h_l\} \subseteq R$; $H = $ finite.
> **Output:** $G = \{g_1, \ldots, g_m\}$, a Gröbner basis for (H);
>   Matrix $X = \{x_{i,j}\} \in R^{l \times m}$, and
>   Matrix $Y = \{y_{i,j}\} \in R^{l \times m}$.

Let us begin by modifying ONEHEADREDUCTION and HEADREDUCTION, such that the NEWHEADREDUCTION solves the following problem:

Input: $G = \{g_1, \ldots, g_m\} \subseteq R$, and $f \in R$.
Output: $h =$ HEADREDUCTION(f, G), and express it as
$$f = y_1 g_1 + \cdots + y_m g_m + h.$$

We proceed by making changes to the algorithm ONEHEADREDUCTION as follows:

NEWONEHEADREDUCTION(f, G)
Input: $f \in R$; $G \subseteq R$, $G =$ finite.
Output: h such that $f \xrightarrow{G,h} h$, and
$y_1, \ldots, y_m$ such that $f = y_1 g_1 + \cdots + y_m g_m + h$.

if $f = 0$ or Hcoef$(f) \notin \left(\{\text{Hcoef}(g) : g \in G_f\} \right)$ then

     return $\Big\langle y_1 := 0, \ldots, y_m := 0, h := f \Big\rangle$;

else

     Let Hcoef$(f) = \displaystyle\sum_{g_{i_j} \in G_f} a_{i_j} \cdot \text{Hcoef}(g_{i_j}), \qquad a_{i_j} \in S$

     return $\Big\langle y_1 := 0, \ldots,$

       $y_{i_1} := a_{i_1} \cdot \dfrac{\text{Hterm}(f)}{\text{Hterm}(g_{i_1})}, \ldots, y_{i_k} := a_{i_k} \cdot \dfrac{\text{Hterm}(f)}{\text{Hterm}(g_{i_k})}, \ldots,$

       $y_m := 0,$

       $h := f - \displaystyle\sum_{g_{i_j} \in G_f} a_{i_j} \cdot \dfrac{\text{Hterm}(f)}{\text{Hterm}(g_{i_j})} g_{i_j} \Big\rangle;$

       Comment: $\{i_1, \ldots, i_k\} \subseteq \{1, \ldots, m\}.$

   end{if };
end{NEWONEHEADREDUCTION} $\square$

To see that the algorithm is correct, all we need to observe is the following:

$$
\begin{aligned}
f &= a_{i_1} \cdot \frac{\text{Hterm}(f)}{\text{Hterm}(g_{i_1})} g_{i_1} + \cdots + a_{i_k} \cdot \frac{\text{Hterm}(f)}{\text{Hterm}(g_{i_k})} g_{i_k} + h \\
&= y_{i_1} g_{i_1} + \cdots + y_{i_k} g_{i_k} + h \\
&= y_1 g_1 + \cdots + y_m g_m + h.
\end{aligned}
$$

[Since all the y_i's except y_{i_j}'s are 0.]

Now we can modify the HEADREDUCTION algorithm to keep track of the coefficient polynomials as it repeatedly "calls" NEWONEHEADREDUCTION. The correctness of the algorithm can be shown by an inductive argument over the number of iterations of the main loop.

NEWHEADREDUCTION(f, G)
Input: $f \in R$; $G \subseteq R$, $G = $ finite.
Output: h such that $f \xrightarrow{G,h} h \xrightarrow{G,h} h$, and

$$y_1, \ldots, y_m \text{ such that } f = y_1 g_1 + \cdots + y_m g_m + h.$$

$\langle y_1, \ldots, y_m, h \rangle := \langle 0, \ldots, 0, f \rangle;$
$\langle y_1', \ldots, y_m', h' \rangle := \langle 0, \ldots, 0, f \rangle;$

loop
    $h := h'$

    $\langle y_1, \ldots, y_m \rangle := \langle y_1, \ldots, y_m \rangle + \langle y_1', \ldots, y_m' \rangle;$

    $\langle y_1', \ldots, y_m', h' \rangle := $ NEWONEHEADREDUCTION(h, G)
until $h = h'$;

    return $\langle y_1, \ldots, y_m, h \rangle;$
end{NEWHEADREDUCTION}   □

Now we are ready to modify the algorithm GRÖBNER (on page 87) in such a way that it also produces the X and Y matrices as by-products.

The main idea is to incrementally compute the X matrix (expressing G in terms of H) as the computation of G progresses: Initially, we begin with $G = H$, and the X matrix is simply an identity matrix. At any point in the loop, as we add a new elment g to G, we know how to express the new g in terms of the elements of G computed so far. But, now, using the currently computed matrix, we can also express g in terms of H, and hence the new row of X. Again by an induction on the number of iterations of the main loop, the correctness of the computation of X can be demonstrated.

The computation of the Y matrix is, in fact, relatively easy. Since at the termination G is a Gröbner basis and since each element $h_i \in H$ is in the ideal $(G) = (H)$, $h_i \xrightarrow{G,h} 0$, and the algorithm NEWHEADREDUCTION gives the ith row of Y:

$$h_i = y_{i,1}\, g_1 + y_{i,2}\, g_2 + \cdots + y_{i,m}\, g_m.$$

NEWGRÖBNER(H)
Input: $H \subseteq R$, $H = $ finite.
Output: $G \subseteq R$, $G = $ Gröbner basis for (H), and
               the matrices X and Y, relating G and H.

$g_1 := h_1$;

$\langle x_{1,1}, x_{2,1}, \ldots x_{l,1} \rangle := \langle 1, 0, \ldots, 0 \rangle$;

$g_2 := h_2$;

$\langle x_{1,2}, x_{2,2}, \ldots x_{l,2} \rangle := \langle 0, 1, \ldots, 0 \rangle$;

$\vdots$

$g_l := h_l$;

$\langle x_{1,l}, x_{2,l}, \ldots x_{l,l} \rangle := \langle 0, 0, \ldots, 1 \rangle$;

Comment: $G = H$ and $X = $ the identity matrix.

$k := l$;

while there is some nonempty subset $F \subseteq G$

        such that some S-polynomial $h \in SP(F)$

        does not head-reduce to 0

loop

    Let $h = a_1 g_1 + \cdots + a_k g_k$;

    $\langle y_1, \ldots, y_k, h' \rangle := $ NEWHEADREDUCTION$(h, \{g_1, \ldots, g_k\})$;

    Comment: Note that

$$
\begin{aligned}
h' &= h - y_1 g_1 - \cdots - y_k g_k \\
&= (a_1 - y_1)g_1 + \cdots + (a_k - y_k)g_k \\
&= (a_1 - y_1)(x_{1,1}h_1 + \cdots + x_{l,1}h_l) \\
&\quad + \cdots \\
&\quad + (a_k - y_k)(x_{1,k}h_1 + \cdots + x_{l,k}h_l) \\
&= \big((a_1 - y_1)x_{1,1} + \cdots + (a_k - y_k)x_{1,k}\big)h_1 \\
&\quad + \cdots \\
&\quad + \big((a_1 - y_1)x_{l,1} + \cdots + (a_k - y_k)x_{l,k}\big)h_l
\end{aligned}
$$

    end{**Comment**};

    $g_{k+1} := h'$;

    $\langle x_{1,k+1}, x_{2,k+1}, \ldots x_{l,k+1} \rangle :=$

        $\langle (a_1 - y_1)x_{1,1} + \cdots + (a_k - y_k)x_{1,k},$

        $(a_1 - y_1)x_{2,1} + \cdots + (a_k - y_k)x_{2,k},$

        $\ldots,$

        $(a_1 - y_1)x_{l,1} + \cdots + (a_k - y_k)x_{l,k} \rangle$;

    $G := G \cup \{h'\}$;

    $k := k + 1$;

end{loop };

$\langle y_{1,1}, y_{1,2}, \ldots, y_{1,m} \rangle := $ NEWHEADREDUCTION$(h_1, G)[1..m]$;

$\langle y_{2,1}, y_{2,2}, \ldots, y_{2,m} \rangle := $ NEWHEADREDUCTION$(h_2, G)[1..m]$;

$\vdots$

$\langle y_{l,1}, y_{l,2}, \ldots, y_{l,m} \rangle := $ NEWHEADREDUCTION$(h_2, G)[1..m]$;

return $\langle G, X, Y \rangle$;

end{NEWGRÖBNER} $\square$

3.4.2   Detachability

Using the machinery developed in the previous subsection, we are now ready to solve the detachability problem for the polynomial ring, $R = S[x_1, \ldots, x_n]$.

$\mathrm{DETACH}(f, H)$
Input: $H = \{h_1, \ldots, h_l\} \subseteq R$, $H = $ finite, and an $f \in R$.
Output: Decide whether $f \in (H)$,
            If so, then return $\{x_1, \ldots, x_l\}$
            such that $f = x_1 h_1 + \cdots + x_l h_l$;
            Otherwise, return **False**.

    $\langle G, X, Y \rangle := \mathrm{NEWGR\ddot{O}BNER}(H);$

    Comment: $G = $ Gröbner basis for (H);
                  the matrices X and Y relate G and H.
    end{**Comment**};

    $\langle y_1, \ldots, y_m, h \rangle := \mathrm{NEWHEADREDUCTION}(f, G);$
    if $h = 0$ then

       Comment: $f \in (G) = (H)$, and

$$
\begin{aligned}
f &= y_1 g_1 + \cdots + y_m g_m \\
&= (y_1 x_{1,1} + \cdots + y_m x_{1,m}) h_1 \\
&\quad + \cdots \\
&\quad + (y_1 x_{l,1} + \cdots + y_m x_{l,m}) h_l
\end{aligned}
$$

      end{**Comment**};

      return $\{y_1 x_{1,1} + \cdots + y_m x_{1,m}, \ldots, y_1 x_{l,1} + \cdots + y_m x_{l,m}\};$
   else
      return false ;
    end{if };
  end{DETACH} $\square$

Proving the correctness of the algorithm is now a fairly simple matter. Note that $f \in (H)$ if and only if $f \in (G)$, i.e., if and only if $f \xrightarrow{G, h} 0$. In this case, the algorithm NEWHEADREDUCTION determines the fact that f reduces to zero and that f can be expressed in terms of g_i's as follows

$$f = y_1 g_1 + \cdots + y_m g_m.$$

The rest of the algorithm simply re-expresses g_i's in terms of h_i's using the matrix X.

3.5 Syzygy Computation

Now, we are ready to consider the syzygy solvability property of a polynomial ring $R = S[x_1, \ldots, x_n]$, where we again assume that the underlying ring of coefficients S is strongly computable. As in the previous section, the algorithmic constructions for syzygy solvability will rely on our Gröbner basis algorithm developed earlier. In order to keep our exposition simple, we shall proceed in two stages: First, we will solve the problem for a special case, where we compute the syzygies of a set which is also a Gröbner basis of its ideal. Next, we deal with the general case, where the set is any arbitrary finite subset of R.

3.5.1 Syzygy of a Gröbner Basis: Special Case

We start with the following simple case: Compute the syzygies of the set of polynomials

$$G = \{g_1, \ldots, g_q\} \subseteq R,$$

where G is a Gröbner basis for (G) (under some fixed admissible ordering).

Input: $G = \{g_1, \ldots, g_q\} \subseteq R;\ G =$ finite.
$G =$ a Gröbner basis for (G).

Output: A finite basis, $\{\overline{t_1}, \ldots, t_p\}$ for the R-module $S(G) \subseteq R^q$.

Let T denote the following $p \times q$ matrix over R:

$$T = \begin{bmatrix} \overline{t_1} \\ \vdots \\ \overline{t_p} \end{bmatrix} = \begin{bmatrix} t_{1,1} & \cdots & t_{1,q} \\ \vdots & \ddots & \vdots \\ t_{p,1} & \cdots & t_{p,q} \end{bmatrix}, \quad \text{where } t_{i,j} \in R$$

such that

1. For all $1 \le i \le p$,
$$\sum_j t_{i,j}\, g_j = 0.$$

2. For any $\langle u_1, \ldots, u_q \rangle = \overline{u} \in R^q$

$$\sum_j u_j\, g_j = 0$$

$$\Rightarrow \quad \left(\exists\, \overline{v} = \langle v_1, \ldots, v_p \rangle \in R^p\right) \left[\overline{u} = v_1\, \overline{t_1} + \cdots + v_p\, \overline{t_p}\right].$$

Let $F = \{g_{i_1}, \ldots, g_{i_k}\} \subseteq G$ be a nonempty subset of G. Let

$$\overline{s} = \langle s_{i_1}, \ldots, s_{i_k} \rangle \in S^k$$

be a tuple in the syzygy basis for $\{\mathrm{Hcoef}(g_{i_1}), \ldots, \mathrm{Hcoef}(g_{i_k})\} \subseteq S^k$. In T, we have an entry, $\overline{t}$, for each such F and $\overline{s}$ as explained below:

- Let h be the S-polynomial corresponding to the subset F and the tuple $\overline{s}$. That is,

$$h = s_{i_1} \cdot \frac{m}{\mathrm{Hterm}(g_{i_1})} \cdot g_{i_1} + \cdots + s_{i_k} \cdot \frac{m}{\mathrm{Hterm}(g_{i_k})} \cdot g_{i_k},$$

where $m = LCM(\mathrm{Hterm}(g_{i_1}), \ldots, \mathrm{Hterm}(g_{i_k}))$.

- Since G is a Gröbner basis, we have

$$h \xrightarrow[*]{G,h} 0$$

and h can be expressed as follows (since R is detachable):

$$h = f_1 \cdot g_1 + \cdots + f_q \cdot g_q,$$

where $m \underset{A}{>} \mathrm{Hterm}(h) \underset{A}{\geq} hterm(f_i)\,\mathrm{Hterm}(g_i)$, for all i.

- Let $\overline{t}$, now, be given by the following q-tuple (in R^q).

$$\overline{t} \;=\; \Big\langle \;\; -f_1, \ldots,$$
$$-f_{i_1-1}, \;\; s_{i_1} \cdot \frac{m}{\mathrm{Hterm}(g_{i_1})} - f_{i_1}, \;\; -f_{i_1+1},$$
$$\ldots,$$
$$-f_{i_k-1}, \;\; s_{i_k} \cdot \frac{m}{\mathrm{Hterm}(g_{i_k})} - f_{i_k}, \;\; -f_{i_k+1},$$
$$\ldots, \; -f_q \;\Big\rangle.$$

- From the discussions in the previous section, we know that all of the above steps are computable, since, by assumption, S is strongly computable.

The correctness of the above procedure is a direct consequence of the following observations:

1. Each $\overline{t_j}$ $(1 \leq j \leq p)$ satisfies the following condition:

$$t_{j,1} \cdot g_1 + \cdots + t_{j,q} \cdot g_q$$
$$= \; s_{i_1} \cdot \frac{m}{\text{Hterm}(g_{i_1})} \cdot g_{i_1} + \cdots + s_{i_k} \cdot \frac{m}{\text{Hterm}(g_{i_k})} \cdot g_{i_k}$$
$$-f_1 \cdot g_1 - \cdots - f_q \cdot g_q$$
$$= \; h - h = 0.$$

Thus $\overline{t_j}$ is in the R-module of the syzygies of G.

2. Let $\overline{u} = \langle u_1, \ldots, u_q \rangle$ be an arbitrary element of the R-module $S(G)$. We need to show $\overline{u}$ can be expressed as a linear combination of $\overline{t_j}$'s, i.e., that there are $v_1, \ldots, v_p \in R$ such that

$$\overline{u} = v_1 \, \overline{t_1} + \cdots + v_p \, \overline{t_p}.$$

Given a $\overline{u}$, we define as its *height*, the power-product M, where

$$M = \max_{\underset{A}{>}} \Big\{ \text{Hterm}(u_i) \, \text{Hterm}(g_i) : 1 \leq i \leq q \Big\}.$$

Now, assume to the contrary, i.e., there exists a $\overline{u} \in R^q$ so that we obtain the following:

(a) $\overline{u} \in S(G)$.

(b) $\overline{u} \notin R \, \overline{t_1} + \cdots + R \, \overline{t_p}$.

(c) Every element of R^q satisfying the above two conditions has a *height* no smaller than that of $\overline{u}$. The existence of $\overline{u}$ is guaranteed by our hypothesis and the well-foundedness of the admissible ordering $\underset{A}{<}$.

We shall derive a contradiction!

- M = the height of $\overline{u}$.

  $L = \{i_1, \ldots, i_k\} \subseteq \{1, \ldots, q\}$ such that

$$(1) \quad j \in L \quad \Rightarrow \quad \mathrm{Hterm}(u_j)\,\mathrm{Hterm}(g_j) = M.$$
$$(2) \quad j \notin L \quad \Rightarrow \quad \mathrm{Hterm}(u_j)\,\mathrm{Hterm}(g_j) \underset{\wedge}{<} M.$$

- Since $u_1 \cdot g_1 + \cdots + u_q \cdot g_q = 0$, we see that

$$\mathrm{Hcoef}(u_{i_1}) \cdot \mathrm{Hcoef}(g_{i_1}) + \cdots + \mathrm{Hcoef}(u_{i_k}) \cdot \mathrm{Hcoef}(g_{i_k}) = 0.$$

  Let

$$S = \begin{bmatrix} \overline{s_1} \\ \vdots \\ \overline{s_l} \end{bmatrix} = \begin{bmatrix} s_{1,1} & \cdots & s_{1,k} \\ \vdots & \ddots & \vdots \\ s_{l,1} & \cdots & s_{l,k} \end{bmatrix}, \quad \text{where } s_{i,j} \in S$$

  be a basis for the S-module, $S\Big(\mathrm{Hcoef}(g_{i_1}), \ldots, \mathrm{Hcoef}(g_{i_k})\Big)$.
  Hence there exist $v'_1, \ldots, v'_l \in S$ such that

$$\langle \mathrm{Hcoef}(u_{i_1}), \ldots, \mathrm{Hcoef}(u_{i_k}) \rangle \;=\; v'_1 \cdot \overline{s_1} + \cdots + v'_l \cdot \overline{s_l}.$$

- Let $m = LCM\Big(\mathrm{Hterm}(g_{i_1}), \ldots, \mathrm{Hterm}(g_{i_k})\Big)$, and $Q = \dfrac{M}{m}$. Thus

$$m \cdot Q = M = \mathrm{Hterm}(u_{i_1})\,\mathrm{Hterm}(g_{i_1}) = \cdots = \mathrm{Hterm}(u_{i_k})\,\mathrm{Hterm}(g_{i_k}).$$

- The following key observation is needed in the rest of the proof:

$$\mathrm{Hmono}(u_{i_1}) \cdot g_{i_1} + \cdots + \mathrm{Hmono}(u_{i_k}) \cdot g_{i_k}$$
$$= \left[v'_1 \cdot Q \cdot \left(\frac{s_{1,1}\,m}{\mathrm{Hterm}(g_{i_1})} \right) + \cdots + v'_l \cdot Q \cdot \left(\frac{s_{l,1}\,m}{\mathrm{Hterm}(g_{i_1})} \right) \right] \cdot g_{i_1}$$
$$+ \cdots$$
$$+ \left[v'_1 \cdot Q \cdot \left(\frac{s_{1,k}\,m}{\mathrm{Hterm}(g_{i_k})} \right) + \cdots + v'_l \cdot Q \cdot \left(\frac{s_{l,k}\,m}{\mathrm{Hterm}(g_{i_k})} \right) \right] \cdot g_{i_k}.$$

- Let $\overline{t'_1}, \ldots, \overline{t'_l}$ be the elements of the basis T for $S(G)$, each corresponding to an S-polynomial for a subset $F = \{g_{i_1}, \ldots, g_{i_k}\}$ and an element of $\{\overline{s_1}, \ldots, \overline{s_l}\}$.

  Let

$$\overline{u'} \;=\; \langle u'_1, \ldots, u'_q \rangle \;=\; \overline{u} - v'_1 \cdot Q \cdot \overline{t'_1} - \cdots - v'_l \cdot Q \cdot \overline{t'_l}.$$

By the construction, we see the following:

1. $\overline{u'} \in S(G)$.

2. $\overline{u'} \notin R\,\overline{t_1} + \cdots + R\,\overline{t_p}$, since, otherwise, we can also find $v_1, \ldots, v_p \in R$ such that

$$\overline{u} = v_1 \cdot \overline{t_1} + \cdots + v_p \cdot \overline{t_p}.$$

3. If we now show that the *height* of $\overline{u'}$ is smaller than M under the admissible ordering $\underset{A}{<}$, then we have the desired contradiction.

- Note that the expression $u_1'\, g_1 + \cdots + u_q'\, g_q$ is equal to

$$
\begin{array}{llll}
u_1 g_1 & + \cdots + & \mathrm{Tail}(u_{i_1})g_{i_1} & + \cdots \\
 & + & \mathrm{Tail}(u_{i_k})g_{i_k} & + \cdots + \quad u_q g_q \\
 & + & \mathrm{Hmono}(u_{i_1})g_{i_1} & + \cdots \\
 & + & \mathrm{Hmono}(u_{i_k})g_{i_k} & + \cdots
\end{array}
$$

$$
-v_1'\, Q\left[-f_{1,1}'g_1 \quad - \cdots + \left(s_{1,1}\frac{m}{\mathrm{Hterm}(g_{i_1})} - f_{1,i_1}' \right)g_{i_1} \quad + \cdots \right.
$$
$$
\left. + \left(s_{1,k}\frac{m}{\mathrm{Hterm}(g_{i_k})} - f_{1,i_k}' \right)g_{i_k} \quad + \cdots - \quad f_{1,q}'g_q \right]
$$

$$\vdots$$

$$
-v_l'\, Q\left[-f_{l,1}'g_1 \quad - \cdots + \left(s_{l,1}\frac{m}{\mathrm{Hterm}(g_{i_1})} - f_{l,i_1}' \right)g_{i_1} \quad + \cdots \right.
$$
$$
\left. + \left(s_{l,k}\frac{m}{\mathrm{Hterm}(g_{i_k})} - f_{l,i_k}' \right)g_{i_k} \quad + \cdots - \quad f_{l,q}'g_q \right].
$$

Thus we see that for all j $(1 \le j \le q)$

$$
u_j' = \begin{cases}
\mathrm{Tail}(u_j) + v_1'\, Q\, f_{1,j}' + \cdots + v_l'\, Q\, f_{l,j}', & \text{if } j \in \{i_1, \ldots, i_k\} \\
u_j + v_1'\, Q\, f_{1,j}' + \cdots + v_l'\, Q\, f_{l,j}', & \text{if } j \notin \{i_1, \ldots, i_k\}
\end{cases}
$$

In both cases, $\mathrm{Hterm}(u_j')\,\mathrm{Hterm}(g_j) \underset{A}{<} M$, and $\overline{u'}$ has a *height* smaller than that of $\overline{u}$, contrary to our hypothesis about the minimality of the *height* of the selected $\overline{u}$. Thus

$$S(G) = R\overline{t_1} + \cdots + R\overline{t_p}$$

and T is a basis for the syzygies of G.

Furthermore, our arguments also provide an algorithm that decides if a given $\overline{u} \in R^q$ is in the syzygy of a set G and, additionally, if possible (i.e., if $\overline{u} \in S(G)$), expresses $\overline{u}$ as a linear combination of the syzygy basis computed earlier.

> **Input:** $\overline{u} = \langle u_1, \ldots, u_q \rangle \in R^q$,
> G is a finite Gröbner basis for (G),
> $T = \{\overline{t_1}, \ldots, \overline{t_p}\}$ is a basis for $S(G)$.
>
> **Decide:**   Whether $\overline{u} \in S(G)$. If so, then compute the coefficients
> $v_1, \ldots, v_p \in R$ such that $\overline{u} = v_1 \overline{t_1} + \cdots + v_p \overline{t_p}$.

> if $u_1 g_1 + \cdots + u_q g_q \neq 0$ then
>   return with failure;
>
> $\overline{w} := \overline{u}$;
> $\langle v_1, \ldots, v_p \rangle := \langle 0, \ldots, 0 \rangle$;
> while $\overline{w} \neq \langle 0, \ldots, 0 \rangle$ loop
> $L := \left\{ i_a : \mathrm{Hterm}(w_{i_a} g_{i_a}) = \mathrm{height}(\overline{w}) \right\}$;
>   **Comment:** $L = \{i_1, \ldots, i_k\}$;
>
> $Q := \dfrac{\mathrm{height}(\overline{w})}{LCM(\mathrm{Hterm}(g_{i_1}), \ldots, \mathrm{Hterm}(g_{i_k}))}$;
>   Compute $\overline{s_1}, \ldots, \overline{s_l}$, a basis for
>   the syzygies of $\{\mathrm{Hcoef}(g_{i_1}), \ldots, \mathrm{Hcoef}(g_{i_k})\}$;
> $K := \left\{ j_b : \overline{t_{j_b}} = \text{basis element in } T \text{ for } F \text{ and } \overline{s_b} \right\}$;
>   **Comment:** $K = \{j_1, \ldots, j_l\}$;
>
>   Compute $v_{j_1}, \ldots, v_{j_l} \in S$ such that
> $\langle \mathrm{Hcoef}(u_{i_1}), \ldots, \mathrm{Hcoef}(u_{i_k}) \rangle = v_{j_1} \overline{s_1} + \cdots + v_{j_l} \overline{s_l}$;
> $\langle v_1, \ldots, v_p \rangle := \langle v_1, \ldots, v_p \rangle + \langle 0, \ldots, v_{j_1}, \ldots, v_{j_l}, \ldots, 0 \rangle$;
> $\overline{w} := \overline{w} - Q \left[v_{j_1} \overline{t_{j_1}} + \cdots + v_{j_l} \overline{t_{j_l}} \right]$;
> end{loop };
> return $\langle v_1, \ldots, v_p \rangle$; $\square$

3.5.2   Syzygy of a Set: General Case

Now, we are ready to consider the syzygy computation problem in the most general setting.

> **Input:** $H = \{h_1, \ldots, h_l\} \subseteq R$; $H = $ finite.

> **Output:**   A finite basis $\{\overline{w_1}, \ldots, \overline{w_r}\}$ for the R-module $S(H) \subseteq R^l$.

Let W denote the following $r \times l$ matrix over R:

$$
W = \begin{bmatrix} \overline{w_1} \\ \vdots \\ \overline{w_r} \end{bmatrix} = \begin{bmatrix} w_{1,1} & \cdots & w_{1,l} \\ \vdots & \ddots & \vdots \\ w_{r,1} & \cdots & w_{r,l} \end{bmatrix}, \quad \text{where } w_{i,j} \in R
$$

such that for all $1 \leq i \leq r$,

$$\sum_j w_{i,j} \, h_j = 0$$

and if

$$\sum_j u_j \, h_j = 0, \quad \text{where } u_1, \ldots, u_l \in R$$

then

$$
\begin{aligned}
\overline{u} &= \langle u_1, \ldots, u_l \rangle \\
&= v_1 \, \overline{w_1} + \cdots + v_r \, \overline{w_r}, \quad \text{where } v_1, \ldots, v_r \in R.
\end{aligned}
$$

- Let $G = \{g_1, \ldots, g_m\} = $ a Gröbner basis for (H).
- Let T be given by

$$
T = \begin{bmatrix} \overline{t_1} \\ \vdots \\ \overline{t_p} \end{bmatrix} = \begin{bmatrix} t_{1,1} & \cdots & t_{1,m} \\ \vdots & \ddots & \vdots \\ t_{p,1} & \cdots & t_{p,m} \end{bmatrix}, \quad \text{where } t_{i,j} \in R
$$

be a basis for the R-module $S(G)$. This can be computed using the algorithm of the previous subsection.

- Let Y be an $l \times m$ matrix, $Y = \{y_{i,j}\} \in R^{l \times m}$

$$
Y = \begin{bmatrix} y_{1,1} & \cdots & y_{1,m} \\ \vdots & \ddots & \vdots \\ y_{l,1} & \cdots & y_{l,m} \end{bmatrix}
$$

such that

$$
\left.
\begin{aligned}
h_1 &= y_{1,1} g_1 + \cdots + y_{1,m} g_m \\
&\vdots \\
h_l &= y_{l,1} g_1 + \cdots + y_{l,m} g_m
\end{aligned}
\right\} \quad \text{i.e.,} \quad
\begin{bmatrix} h_1 \\ \vdots \\ h_l \end{bmatrix} = Y \begin{bmatrix} g_1 \\ \vdots \\ g_m \end{bmatrix},
$$

and let X be an $l \times m$ matrix, $X = \{x_{i,j}\} \in R^{l \times m}$

$$
X = \begin{bmatrix} x_{1,1} & \cdots & x_{1,m} \\ \vdots & \ddots & \vdots \\ x_{l,1} & \cdots & x_{l,m} \end{bmatrix},
$$

such that

$$
\left.
\begin{aligned}
g_1 &= x_{1,1} h_1 + \cdots + x_{l,1} h_l \\
&\vdots \\
g_m &= x_{1,m} h_1 + \cdots + x_{l,m} h_l
\end{aligned}
\right\} \quad \text{i.e.,} \quad
\begin{bmatrix} g_1 \\ \vdots \\ g_m \end{bmatrix} = X^T \begin{bmatrix} h_1 \\ \vdots \\ h_l \end{bmatrix}.
$$

Both X and Y can be computed by the modified Gröbner basis algorithm of the previous section.

We now claim that W is given by the following $l \times (l+p)$ matrix:

$$W = \begin{bmatrix} I_l - YX^T \\ TX^T \end{bmatrix} = \begin{bmatrix} \overline{w_1} \\ \vdots \\ \overline{w_l} \\ \overline{w_{l+1}} \\ \vdots \\ \overline{w_{l+p}} \end{bmatrix}.$$

Next we show that $\overline{w_1}, \ldots, \overline{w_l}$, indeed, form a basis for the R-module $S(H)$.

1. Consider first $\overline{w_i}$ $(1 \le i \le l)$

$$w_{i,1}\, h_1 + \cdots + w_{i,i}\, h_i + \cdots + w_{i,l}\, h_l$$
$$= \quad -(y_{i,1}\, x_{1,1} + \cdots + y_{i,m}\, x_{1,m})h_1$$
$$+ \cdots$$
$$+ h_i - (y_{i,1}\, x_{i,1} + \cdots + y_{i,m}\, x_{i,m})h_i$$
$$+ \cdots$$
$$- (y_{i,1}\, x_{l,1} + \cdots + y_{i,m}\, x_{l,m})h_l$$
$$= \quad h_i - y_{i,1}\, g_1 - \cdots - y_{i,m}\, g_m$$
$$= \quad h_i - h_i = 0.$$

2. Next consider $\overline{w_i}$ $(l+1 \le i \le l+p)$

$$w_{i,1}\, h_1 + \cdots + w_{i,i}\, h_i + \cdots + w_{i,l}\, h_l$$
$$= \quad (t_{i,1}\, x_{1,1} + \cdots + t_{i,m}\, x_{1,m})h_1$$
$$+ \cdots$$
$$+ (t_{i,1}\, x_{l,1} + \cdots + t_{i,m}\, x_{l,m})h_l$$
$$= \quad t_{i,1}\, g_1 + \cdots + t_{i,m}\, g_m$$
$$= \quad 0.$$

Thus $S(H) \supseteq R\,\overline{w_1} + \cdots + R\,\overline{w_{l+p}}$.
Conversely, let $\overline{u} = \langle u_1, \ldots, u_l \rangle \in S(H)$, i.e.,

$$u_1\, h_1 + \cdots + u_l\, h_l = 0.$$

Let

$$\widetilde{u_1} = u_1\, y_{1,1} + \cdots + u_l\, y_{l,1}$$
$$\vdots$$
$$\widetilde{u_m} = u_1\, y_{1,m} + \cdots + u_l\, y_{l,m}.$$

Thus

$$\widetilde{u_1}\, g_1 + \cdots + \widetilde{u_m}\, g_m = u_1\, h_1 + \cdots + u_l\, h_l = 0,$$

and there exist $v_1', \ldots, v_p' \in R$ such that

$$\langle \widetilde{u_1}, \ldots, \widetilde{u_m} \rangle = v_1'\, \overline{t_1} + \cdots + v_p'\, \overline{t_p}.$$

We show that

$$
\begin{aligned}
\overline{u} &= \langle u_1, \ldots, u_l \rangle \\
&= u_1\, \overline{w_1} + \cdots + u_l\, \overline{w_l} + v_1'\, \overline{w_{l+1}} + \cdots + v_p'\, \overline{w_{l+p}}.
\end{aligned}
$$

Consider the jth component of the expression on the right-hand side:

$$u_1\, w_{1,j} + \cdots + u_l\, w_{l,j} + v_1'\, w_{l+1,j} + \cdots + v_p'\, w_{l+p,j}$$

$$
\begin{aligned}
&= \; -u_1(y_{1,1}\, x_{j,1} + \cdots + y_{1,m}\, x_{j,m}) \\
&\quad - \cdots \\
&\quad + u_j - u_j(y_{j,1}\, x_{j,1} + \cdots + y_{j,m}\, x_{j,m}) \\
&\quad - \cdots \\
&\quad - u_l(y_{l,1}\, x_{j,1} + \cdots + y_{l,m}\, x_{j,m}) \\
&\quad + v_1'(t_{1,1}\, x_{j,1} + \cdots + t_{1,m}\, x_{j,m}) \\
&\quad + \cdots \\
&\quad + v_p'(t_{p,1}\, x_{j,1} + \cdots + t_{p,m}\, x_{j,m})
\end{aligned}
$$

$$
\begin{aligned}
&= \; u_j \\
&\quad + (-u_1\, y_{1,1} - \cdots - u_l\, y_{l,1} + v_1'\, t_{1,1} + \cdots + v_p'\, t_{p,1})x_{j,1} \\
&\quad + \cdots \\
&\quad + (-u_1\, y_{1,m} - \cdots - u_l\, y_{l,m} + v_1'\, t_{1,m} + \cdots + v_p'\, t_{p,m})x_{j,m}
\end{aligned}
$$

$$
\begin{aligned}
&= \; u_j + (-\widetilde{u_1} + \widetilde{u_1})x_{j,1} + \cdots + (-\widetilde{u_m} + \widetilde{u_m})x_{j,m} \\
&= \; u_j.
\end{aligned}
$$

Thus

$$S(H) \subseteq R\, \overline{w_1} + \cdots + R\, \overline{w_{l+p}} \subseteq S(H),$$

and $\overline{w_1}, \ldots, \overline{w_{l+p}}$ is a basis for $S(H)$.

Using the arguments developed here, we can generalize the algorithm of the previous subsection. That is, we devise an algorithm which decides if a given $\bar{u} \in R^l$ is in the syzygy of an arbitrary subset $H \subseteq R$ and, additionally, when possible (i.e., $\bar{u} \in S(H)$), expresses $\bar{u}$ as a linear combination of the syzygy basis W of H.

Input: $\bar{u} = \langle u_1, \ldots, u_l \rangle \in R^l$,
$\qquad\quad$ $H = \{h_1, \ldots, h_l\} \subseteq R$, $H =$ finite.
$\qquad\quad$ $W = \{\overline{w_1}, \ldots, \overline{w_{l+p}}\}$ is a basis for $S(H)$,
$\qquad\quad$ (as in this section.)

Decide: Whether $\bar{u} \in S(H)$. If so, then compute the coefficients
$\qquad\quad$ $v_1, \ldots, v_{l+p} \in R$ such that $\bar{u} = v_1 \overline{w_1} + \cdots + v_{l+p} \overline{w_{l+p}}$

$\qquad$ if $u_1 h_1 + \cdots + u_l h_l \neq 0$ then
$\qquad\quad$ return with failure;

$\qquad$ Let G, T, X and Y be as defined earlier;
$\qquad$ Let $\widetilde{u_1} = \sum_{j=1}^{l} u_j \, y_{j,1}, \ldots, \widetilde{u_m} = \sum_{j=1}^{l} u_j \, y_{j,m}$;
$\qquad$ Compute $v'_1, \ldots, v'_p \in R$ such that
$\qquad\quad$ $\langle \widetilde{u_1}, \ldots, \widetilde{u_m} \rangle = v'_1 \overline{t_1} + \cdots + v'_p \overline{t_p}$;
$\qquad$ **Comment:** $\langle \widetilde{u_1}, \ldots, \widetilde{u_m} \rangle \in S(G)$.

$\qquad$ return $\langle u_1, \ldots, u_l, v'_1, \ldots, v'_p \rangle$. $\square$

3.6   Hilbert's Basis Theorem: Revisited

We can now summarize the discussions of the earlier sections to provide a stronger version of the classical Hilbert's basis theorem.

Recall that earlier we defined a ring to be *strongly computable* if it is *Noetherian*, *computable* (i.e., it has algorithms for the ring operations), *detachable* (i.e., it has algorithms for the ideal membership problem) and *syzygy-solvable* (i.e., it has algorithms to compute a basis for the module of syzygies). We want to show that a polynomial ring over a strongly computable ring is itself a strongly computable.

Theorem 3.6.1 *If S is a strongly computable ring, then the polynomial ring $R = S[x_1, x_2, \ldots, x_n]$ over S in n variables is also a strongly computable ring.*

PROOF.

Our arguments depend on the existence of an algorithm to compute a Gröbner basis for an ideal in R, with respect to some fixed but arbitrary admissible ordering. In the previous sections we have seen that if the admissible ordering is computable, then this is possible, since S is strongly computable. Assume that the admissible ordering of choice is computable, e.g., purely lexicographic ordering.

1. R is *Noetherian* by Hilbert's basis theorem.

2. R is *computable*, since it is straightforward to develop algorithms to (additively) invert a polynomial as well as to multiply and add two polynomials; these algorithms are based on the algorithms for the ring operations in S.

3. R is *detachable*. See Section 3.4 on detachability computation.

4. R is *syzygy-solvable*. See the Section 3.5 on syzygy computation.   □

3.7 Applications of Gröbner Bases Algorithms

In this section, we consider algorithms for various operations on ideals in a strongly computable ring, R. Thus we assume that all the ideals in this ring are presented in a finitary way, i.e., by their finite bases.

We have already seen how the *ideal membership problem* can be solved using Gröbner basis. It is quite easy to devise algorithms for *ideal congruence*, *subideal* and *ideal equality* problems, simply building on the membership algorithm.

The operations *sum* and *product* are also trivial; the operations *intersection* and *quotient* are somewhat involved and require the algorithm to find a syzygy basis. The operation *radical* requires several concepts, not discussed so far.

3.7.1 Membership

> IDEALMEMBERSHIP(f, H)
> **Input:** $H \subseteq R$ and a polynomial $f \in R$, H — finite.
> **Output:**   TRUE, if $f \in (H)$.

1. Compute G, the Gröbner basis for H.

2. Output TRUE, if HEADREDUCTION(f, G) $= 0$; otherwise FALSE.

The correctness follows from the fact that $f \in (H)$ iff $f \in (G)$ iff $f \xrightarrow[*]{G,h} 0$.

3.7.2 Congruence, Subideal and Ideal Equality

Ideal Congruence

We define, for any ideal $I \subseteq R$, an equivalence relation $\equiv \mod I$ (congruence modulo the ideal I) over R, as follows:

$$\left(\forall f, g \in R \right) \left[f \equiv g \mod I \quad \text{iff} \quad f - g \in I \right].$$

> IDEALCONGRUENCE(f, g, H)
> **Input:** $H \subseteq R$ and polynomials f, $g \in R$; H, finite.
> **Output:**   TRUE, if $f \equiv g \mod (H)$.

Output TRUE, if $f - g \in (H)$ (using membership algorithm); otherwise return FALSE. The correctness of the algorithm follows directly from the definition of congruence.

Subideal

> SUBIDEAL(H_1, H_2)
> **Input:** $H_1, H_2 \subseteq R$; H_1 and H_2, finite.
> **Output:**   TRUE, if $(H_1) \subseteq (H_2)$.

Output TRUE, if $\left(\forall\ h_1 \in H_1 \right) \left[h_1 \in (H_2) \right]$ (use membership algorithm); otherwise return FALSE.

Ideal Equality

> IDEALEQUALITY(H_1, H_2)
> **Input:** $H_1, H_2 \subseteq R$; H_1 and H_2, finite.
> **Output:**   TRUE, if $(H_1) = (H_2)$.

Output TRUE, if $(H_1) \subseteq (H_2)$ and $(H_2) \subseteq (H_1)$; otherwise output FALSE.

3.7.3   Sum and Product

Ideal Sum

> IDEALSUM(H_1, H_2)
> **Input:** $H_1 = \{h_1, \ldots, h_r\}$, $H_2 = \{h_{r+1}, \ldots, h_s\} \subseteq R$; H_1 and H_2, finite.
>
> **Output:**   A finite basis H for the ideal $(H_1) + (H_2)$.

Output simply $H = \left\{ h_1, \ldots, h_r, h_{r+1}, \ldots, h_s \right\}$.

Ideal Product

> IDEALPRODUCT(H_1, H_2)
> **Input:** $H_1 = \{h_1, \ldots, h_r\}$, $H_2 = \{h_{r+1}, \ldots, h_s\} \subseteq R$; H_1 and H_2, finite.
>
> **Output:**   A finite basis H for the ideal $(H_1) \cdot (H_2)$.

Output simply $H = \Big\{ (h_1 \cdot h_{r+1}), \ldots, (h_1 \cdot h_s), \ldots,$
$$(h_r \cdot h_{r+1}), \ldots, (h_r \cdot h_s) \Big\}.$$

3.7.4   Intersection

IDEALINTERSECTION(H_1, H_2)
Input: $H_1 = \{h_1, \ldots, h_r\}$, $H_2 = \{h_{r+1}, \ldots, h_s\} \subseteq R$; H_1 and H_2, finite.

Output: A finite basis for the ideal $(H_1) \cap (H_2)$.

The main idea is to solve the following linear equation

$$u_1 \, h_1 + \cdots + u_r \, h_r = u_{r+1} \, h_{r+1} + \cdots + u_s \, h_s, \qquad (3.1)$$

then the ideal $(H_1) \cap (H_2)$ is equal to the following ideal

$$\left\{ u_1 \, h_1 + \cdots + u_r \, h_r : \right.$$

$$\left. \Big(\exists \, u_{r+1}, \ldots, u_s\Big) \Big[\langle u_1, \ldots, u_s \rangle \text{ is a solution of the equation 3.1}\Big] \right\}.$$

Let W be a syzygy basis for $\{h_1, \ldots, h_r, h_{r+1}, \ldots, h_s\}$:

$$W = \begin{bmatrix} \overline{w_1} \\ \vdots \\ \overline{w_p} \end{bmatrix} = \begin{bmatrix} w_{1,1} & \cdots & w_{1,r} & w_{1,r+1} & \cdots & w_{1,s} \\ \vdots & \ddots & \vdots & \vdots & \ddots & \vdots \\ w_{p,1} & \cdots & w_{p,r} & w_{p,r+1} & \cdots & w_{p,s} \end{bmatrix}.$$

We claim that

$$(\widetilde{h_1}, \ldots, \widetilde{h_p})$$
$$= \Big((w_{1,1} \, h_1 + \cdots + w_{1,r} \, h_r), \ldots, (w_{p,1} \, h_1 + \cdots + w_{p,r} \, h_r)\Big)$$
$$= (H_1) \cap (H_2).$$

PROOF OF THE CLAIM:

($\Rightarrow$)   For all $1 \le i \le p$:
$$\widetilde{h_i} = w_{i,1} \, h_1 + \cdots + w_{i,r} \, h_r \in (H_1),$$
and
$$\widetilde{h_i} = -w_{i,r+1} \, h_{r+1} - \cdots - w_{i,s} \, h_s \in (H_2),$$

and for all i, $\widetilde{h_i} \in (H_1) \cap (H_2)$.
($\Leftarrow$)   Conversely, assume that $h \in (H_1) \cap (H_2)$. Then

$$\begin{aligned} h &= u_1 \, h_1 + \cdots + u_r \, h_r, \quad (\text{since } h \in (H_1)) \\ &= u_{r+1} \, h_{r+1} + \cdots + u_s \, h_s, \quad (\text{since } h \in (H_2)) \end{aligned}$$

Thus

$$u_1 \, h_1 + \cdots + u_r \, h_r - u_{r+1} \, h_{r+1} - \cdots - u_s \, h_s = 0,$$

and

$$\bar{u} = \langle u_1, \ldots, u_r, -u_{r+1}, \ldots, -u_s \rangle \in R\,\overline{w_1} + \cdots + R\,\overline{w_p}.$$

That is, there exist $v_1, \ldots, v_p \in R$ such that

$$\bar{u} = v_1\,\overline{w_1} + \cdots + v_p\,\overline{w_p}.$$

Thus

$$
\begin{aligned}
h &= u_1\,h_1 + \cdots + u_r\,h_r \\
&= \left(v_1\,w_{1,1} + \cdots + v_p\,w_{p,1}\right) h_1 \\
&\quad + \cdots \\
&\quad + \left(v_1\,w_{1,r} + \cdots + v_p\,w_{p,r}\right) h_r \\
&= v_1 \left(w_{1,1}\,h_1 + \cdots + w_{1,r}\,h_r\right) \\
&\quad + \cdots \\
&\quad + v_p \left(w_{p,1}\,h_1 + \cdots + w_{p,r}\,h_r\right) \\
&= v_1\,\widetilde{h_1} + \cdots + v_p\,\widetilde{h_p} \\
&\in \left(\widetilde{h_1}, \ldots, \widetilde{h_p}\right). \qquad \square
\end{aligned}
$$

3.7.5   Quotient

Ideal Quotient, $(H) : (f)$

> IDEALQUOTIENT(f, H)
> **Input:** $f \in R$, $H = \{h_1, \ldots, h_r\} \subseteq R$; H, finite.
>
> **Output:**   A finite basis for the ideal $(H) : (f)$.

As before, the main idea is to solve the following linear equation

$$u_1\,h_1 + \cdots + u_r\,h_r = u_{r+1}\,f. \qquad (3.2)$$

Then the ideal $(H) : (f)$ is equal to the following ideal

$$\left\{ u_{r+1} \colon \left(\exists\, u_1, \ldots, u_r\right) \right.$$

$$\left. \left[\langle u_1, \ldots, u_r, u_{r+1}\rangle \text{ is a solution of the equation 3.2}\right]\right\}.$$

Let W be a syzygy basis for $\{h_1, \ldots, h_r, f\}$:

$$W = \begin{bmatrix} \overline{w_1} \\ \vdots \\ \overline{w_p} \end{bmatrix} = \begin{bmatrix} w_{1,1} & \cdots & w_{1,r} & w_{1,r+1} \\ \vdots & \ddots & \vdots & \vdots \\ w_{p,1} & \cdots & w_{p,r} & w_{p,r+1} \end{bmatrix}.$$

We claim that

$$(w_{1,r+1}, \ldots, w_{p,r+1}) = (H) : (f).$$

PROOF OF THE CLAIM:

($\Rightarrow$)   For all $1 \leq i \leq p$:

$$w_{i,r+1}\, f = -w_{i,1}\, h_1 - \cdots - w_{i,r}\, h_r \in (H).$$

Hence $w_{i,r+1} \in (H) : (f)$.
($\Leftarrow$)   Conversely, assume that $u \in (H) : (f)$, i.e., $u \cdot f \in (H)$. Then

$$u \cdot f = u_1\, h_1 + \cdots + u_r\, h_r,$$

and

$$\overline{u} = \langle u_1, \ldots, u_r, -u \rangle \in R\,\overline{w_1} + \cdots + R\,\overline{w_p}.$$

That is, there exist $v_1, \ldots, v_p \in R$ such that

$$\overline{u} = v_1\,\overline{w_1} + \cdots + v_p\,\overline{w_p}.$$

Thus

$$\begin{aligned} u &= -v_1\, w_{1,r+1} - \cdots - v_p\, w_{p,r+1} \\ &\in (w_{1,r+1}, \ldots, w_{p,r+1}). \quad \square \end{aligned}$$

Ideal Quotient, $(H_1) : (H_2)$

IDEALQUOTIENT(H_1, H_2)
Input: $H_1 = \{h_1, \ldots, h_r\}$, $H_2 = \{h_{r+1}, \ldots, h_s\} \subseteq R$; H_1 and H_2, finite.

Output: A finite basis for the ideal $(H_1) : (H_2)$.

Note that

$$(H_1) : (H_2) = \left((H_1) : \sum_{j=r+1}^{s} (h_j) \right) = \bigcap_{j=r+1}^{s} \big((H_1) : (h_j) \big).$$

One direction follows from the arguments below:

$$u \in (H_1) : (H_2) \quad \Rightarrow \quad u\,(H_2) \subseteq (H_1)$$

$$\Rightarrow \quad \left(\forall\, r+1 \leq j \leq s\right) \left[u \cdot h_j \in (H_1)\right]$$

$$\Rightarrow \quad u \in \bigcap_{j=r+1}^{s} \Big((H_1) : (h_j)\Big).$$

Conversely,

$$u \in \bigcap_{j=r+1}^{s} \Big((H_1) : (h_j)\Big)$$

$$\Rightarrow \quad \left(\forall\, r+1 \leq j \leq s\right) \left[u \cdot h_j \in (H_1)\right]$$

$$\Rightarrow \quad \left(\forall\, f_1, \ldots, f_r \in R\right) \left[u\,(f_1\,h_1 + \cdots + f_r\,h_r) \in (H_1)\right]$$

$$\Rightarrow \quad u\,(H_2) \subseteq (H_1)$$

$$\Rightarrow \quad u \in (H_1) : (H_2).$$

Hence $(H_1) : (H_2)$ can be computed using the algorithm for computing the quotient, $(H) : (f)$, and the algorithm for computing the intersection of two ideals.

Problems

Problem 3.1

Let f_1, f_2, ..., $f_s \in K[x]$ be a set of univariate polynomials with coefficients in a field K. Show that the ideal generated by f_i's has a Gröbner basis with a single element (i.e., $K[x]$ is a principal ideal domain). You may not use any fact other than the properties of the Gröbner basis.

In the case $s = 2$, what is the relation between Buchberger's algorithm to compute a Gröbner basis and Euclid's algorithm to compute the g.c.d. of two univariate polynomials?

Problem 3.2

Prove the following:

(i) Let $G \subseteq I$ be a Gröbner basis of an ideal I of $R = S[x_1, \ldots, x_n]$. Is it true that for every $f \in R$, $|\mathrm{NF}_G^h(f)| = 1$? Is it true that for every $f \in I$, $|\mathrm{NF}_G^h(f)| = 1$?

Hint: Consider a Gröbner basis $\{x^2 + 1, y^3 + 1\}$ for the ideal $(x^2 + 1, y^3 + 1)$ of $\mathbb{Q}[x, y]$ (with respect to $<_{\mathrm{TLEX}}$). Can a polynomial, say $x^6 y^6 +$

$xy^2 + x + 1$, have more than one normal forms (under the head-reduction) with respect to the given Gröbner basis?

(ii) A Gröbner basis $G_{\min}$ for an ideal I is a *minimal Gröbner basis* for I, if no proper subset of $G_{\min}$ is a Gröbner basis for I.

A Gröbner basis G_{shr} for an ideal I is a *self-head-reduced Gröbner basis* for I, if every nonzero $g \in G_{\mathrm{shr}}$ is head-reduced modulo $G_{\mathrm{shr}} \setminus \{g\}$.

Let G be a Gröbner basis for an ideal I of R such that $0 \notin G$. Show that G is a minimal Gröbner basis for I if and only if G is a self-head-reduced Gröbner basis for I.

Problem 3.3

A basis F for an ideal I is said to be a *minimal basis* for I, if no proper subset of F is also a basis for I.

(i) Let F be a self-head-reduced Gröbner basis such that $|F| \leq 2$. Show that F is a minimal basis for (F).

(ii) Consider the following basis F for the ideal $(F) \subseteq \mathbb{R}[x, y]$:

$$F = \{x^2 - y, xy - 1, y^2 - x\},$$

Show that F is a *self-head-reduced, minimal Gröbner basis* for (F) under any admissible total-degree ordering but not a minimal basis for (F).

Hint: $(x^2 - y, xy - 1, y^2 - x) = (xy - 1, y^2 - x)$.

Problem 3.4

Let S be a ring, let $R = S[x_1, \ldots, x_n]$, let $\underset{\mathrm{lex}}{\geq}$ be the fixed admissible ordering of choice on $\mathrm{PP}(x_1, \ldots, x_n)$.

Let $G = \{g_1, g_2, \ldots, g_s\} \subseteq R$ be a finite set of polynomials, and $f \in R$ an arbitrary polynomial such that

$$f \xrightarrow{G,h} f_1 \xrightarrow{G,h} f_2 \xrightarrow{G,h} \cdots \xrightarrow{G,h} f_m \xrightarrow{G,h} f_m.$$

Show that, if the d and D, respectively, bound the degrees (in each variable) of the polynomials in G and of the polynomial f, then

$$m \leq \left(\frac{D}{d} + 1\right)^n (d+1)^{n(n+1)/2}.$$

Hint: If $\pi = x_1^{\alpha_1} x_2^{\alpha_2} \cdots x_n^{\alpha_n}$ is an arbitrary power product, then we assign it a weight as follows:

$$\mathcal{W}_G(\pi) = \alpha_1(d+1)^{n-1} + \alpha_2(d+1)^{n-1} + \cdots + \alpha_n(d+1)^0.$$

Let the weight of a multivariate polynomial be defined to be the biggest of the weights of its power products; that is,

$$\text{if } f = a_1\pi_1 + a_2\pi_2 + \cdots + a_\ell\pi_\ell, \quad \text{then } \mathcal{W}_G(f) = \max_i \mathcal{W}_G(\pi_i).$$

The rest follows from the following two observations:

1. $\mathcal{W}_G(f_m) \leq \mathcal{W}_G(f_{m-1}) \leq \cdots \leq \mathcal{W}_G(f_1) \leq \mathcal{W}_G(f)$.

2. The Hmono(f_i)'s are all distinct.

Problem 3.5

Let $S = $ Noetherian, computable and syzygy-solvable ring. We say S is 1-*detachable* if, given $\{f_1, \ldots, f_r\} \subseteq S$, there is an algorithm to decide whether $1 \in (f_1, \ldots, f_r)$, and if so, to express 1 as

$$1 = h_1 \cdot f_1 + \cdots + h_r \cdot f_r, \quad h_1, \ldots, h_r \in S.$$

Show that S is 1-detachable if and only if S is detachable.

Problem 3.6

Let $S = $ Noetherian, computable and detachable ring.

- We say S is *intersection-solvable* if, given $F_1 = \{f_1, \ldots, f_r\}$ and $F_2 = \{f_{r+1}, \ldots, f_s\}$, $F_1, F_2 \subseteq S$, there is an algorithm to compute a finite basis for $(F_1) \cap (F_2)$.

- We say S is *quotient-solvable* if, given $F_1 = \{f_1, \ldots, f_r\}$ and $F_2 = \{f_{r+1}, \ldots, f_s\}$, $F_1, F_2 \subseteq S$, there is an algorithm to compute a finite basis for $(F_1) : (F_2)$.

- We say S is *annihilator-solvable* if, given $f \in S$, there is an algorithm to compute a finite basis for ann f.

Show that the following three statements are equivalent:

1. S is syzygy-solvable.

2. S is quotient-solvable.

3. S is intersection-solvable and annihilator-solvable.

Problem 3.7

Let S be a Noetherian ring, such that, given a subset $F \subseteq S[t]$, there is an algorithm to compute a finite basis of the contraction of (F) to S, i.e.,

$$(F)\{S[t]\} \cap S.$$

In this case, we say S is *contraction-solvable*.

(i) Show that S is intersection-solvable.

Hint: Show that if I_1 and I_2 are two ideals in S, then

$$I_1 \cap I_2 = (t\, I_1 + (1-t)I_2)\{S[t]\} \cap S.$$

(ii) Show that if S is strongly computable, then S is contraction-solvable.

Problem 3.8

Consider an ideal $\mathcal{M} \subseteq \mathbb{Z}[x_1, x_2, \ldots, x_n]$ generated by a finite set $\mathbf{M} = \{M_1, M_2, \ldots, M_\nu\} \subset \mathbb{Z}[x_1, x_2, \ldots, x_n]$. Let $A \in \mathbb{Z}[x_1, x_2, \ldots, x_n]$ be a multivariate polynomial with integer coefficients, whose terms are ordered according to the lexicographic ordering, with the biggest term occurring first.

If $\mathrm{Hmono}(M_i)$ divides $\mathrm{Hmono}(A)$ and

$$
\begin{aligned}
A' &= A - \frac{\mathrm{Hmono}(A)}{\mathrm{Hmono}(M_i)} M_i \\
&= -\frac{\mathrm{Hmono}(A)}{\mathrm{Hmono}(M_i)} \mathrm{Tail}(M_i) + \mathrm{Tail}(A),
\end{aligned}
$$

then we say that M_i *reduces* A to A' and we denote this by the expression

$$
A \xrightarrow{M_i,h} A'.
$$

Note that, as earlier,

$$
\xrightarrow[*]{\mathbf{M},h}
$$

is the reflexive and transitive closure of $\xrightarrow{M_i,h}$ (for some $M_i \in \mathbf{M}$).

A set of generators $\mathbf{M} = \{M_1, M_2, \ldots, M_\nu\}$ of the ideal $\mathcal{M}$ is an *E-basis* of the ideal if

$$
A \in \mathcal{M} \Leftrightarrow A \xrightarrow[*]{\mathbf{M},h} 0.
$$

Let M_i and M_j be two distinct polynomials in the ideal $\mathcal{M}$. Then we define the *S-polynomial* of M_i and M_j (denoted, $S(M_i, M_j)$) as follows:

$$
S(M_i, M_j) = \frac{\widehat{m}}{\mathrm{Hmono}(M_i)} M_i - \frac{\widehat{m}}{\mathrm{Hmono}(M_j)} M_j,
$$

where $\widehat{m} = \mathrm{LCM}\{\mathrm{Hmono}(M_i), \mathrm{Hmono}(M_j)\}$.

For every nonempty subset $\mathbf{M}' = \{M_{i_1}, \ldots, M_{i_\mu}\} \subseteq \mathbf{M}$, we let

$$
\begin{aligned}
q &= \gcd\left\{\mathrm{Hcoef}(M_{i_1}), \ldots, \mathrm{Hcoef}(M_{i_\mu})\right\} \\
&= a_1 \mathrm{Hcoef}(M_{i_1}) + \cdots + a_\mu \mathrm{Hcoef}(M_{i_\mu}),
\end{aligned}
$$

where $q, a_1, \ldots, a_\mu \in \mathbb{Z}$, and we let,

$$
\pi = \mathrm{LCM}\left\{\mathrm{Hterm}(M_{i_1}), \ldots, \mathrm{Hterm}(M_{i_\mu})\right\}
$$

whence,

$$
q \cdot \pi = a_1 \frac{\pi}{\mathrm{Hterm}(M_{i_1})} \mathrm{Hmono}(M_{i_1}) + \cdots + a_\mu \frac{\pi}{\mathrm{Hterm}(M_{i_\mu})} \mathrm{Hmono}(M_{i_\mu})
$$

and clearly $q \cdot \pi \in \text{Head}(M_1, \ldots, M_\nu)$. Thus, for every such $\mathbf{M}'$ we define

$$\psi(\mathbf{M}') = a_1 \frac{\pi}{\text{Hterm}(M_{i_1})} M_{i_1} + \cdots + a_\mu \frac{\pi}{\text{Hterm}(M_{i_\mu})} M_{i_\mu}.$$

This leads us to define the Ψ expansion of $\mathbf{M}$ to be

$$
\begin{aligned}
\Psi(\mathbf{M}) &= \Psi\Big(\{M_1, \ldots, M_\nu\}\Big) \\
&= \Big\{M_1, \ldots, M_\nu\Big\} \bigcup \Big\{\psi(\mathbf{M}') : \emptyset \subsetneq \mathbf{M}' \subseteq \mathbf{M} \\
&\qquad \wedge (\forall 1 \leq i \leq \nu) \big[\text{Hmono}(M_i) \nmid \text{Hmono}(\psi(\mathbf{M}'))\big]\Big\} \\
&= \{P_1, \ldots, P_\lambda\} = \mathbf{P},
\end{aligned}
$$

where we have removed duplicates or multiples with respect to the head monomials.

Show that the following algorithm computes an E-basis of an ideal $\mathcal{M} \subseteq \mathbb{Z}[x_1, x_2, \ldots, x_n]$ generated by a finite set $\mathbf{M} = \{M_1, M_2, \ldots, M_\nu\}$.

E-Basis Algorithm:

Input: $\mathbf{M} \subseteq \mathbb{Z}[x_1, \ldots, x_n]$,
            $\mathbf{M} = \text{finite}$.
Output: $\mathbf{P} \subseteq \mathbb{Z}[x_1, \ldots, x_n]$,
            $(\mathbf{P}) = (\mathbf{M})$, and $\mathbf{P}$ satisfies the property (E).

    $\mathbf{P} := \mathbf{M}; \quad \mathbf{P} := \Psi(\mathbf{P});$
    $\text{Pairs} := \{\{M_i, M_j\} : M_i, M_j \in \mathbf{P} \text{ and } M_i \neq M_j\};$

    while Pairs $\neq \emptyset$ loop
        Choose $\{M_i, M_j\}$, *any* pair in Pairs;
        $\text{Pairs} := \text{Pairs} \setminus \{\{M_i, M_j\}\};$
        Compute a normal form P of $S(M_i, M_j)$ with respect to *some*
            choice of sequence of reductions modulo $\mathbf{P}$;
        $P = \text{NF}_{\mathbf{P}}^h(S(M_i, M_j));$
        if $P \neq 0$ then
            $\mathbf{P} := \mathbf{P} \cup \{P\}; \quad \mathbf{P} := \Psi(\mathbf{P});$
            $\text{Pairs} := \{\{M_i, M_j\} : M_i, M_j \in \mathbf{P} \text{ and } M_i \neq M_j\};$
        end{if };
    end{loop };
    return $\mathbf{P}$;
end{E-Basis Algorithm}.   □

Problem 3.9

Let $S = K$ be a field and $R = K[x_1, \ldots, x_n]$ be the ring of polynomials in the variables $x_1, \ldots, x_n$ over K.

Given two polynomials $f, g \in R$, we say f is *completely reducible* by g if $\text{Hmono}(g)$ divides *some* monomial m in f. Say $m = a \cdot \text{Hmono}(g)$. Then we say the polynomial $h = f - a \cdot g$ is the *complete-reduct* of f by g and denote the relationship by

$$f \xrightarrow{g,c} h.$$

If G is a set of polynomials, we write $f \xrightarrow{G,c} h$ if $f \xrightarrow{g,c} h$ holds for some $g \in G$. If there is a finite sequence $h_1, \ldots, h_n$ $(n \geq 1)$ such that $h_1 = f, h_n = h$ and $h_i \xrightarrow{G,c} h_{i+1}$ for $i = 1, \ldots, n-1$, then we write

$$f \xrightarrow[*]{G,c} h.$$

If f is not reducible by any $g \in G$, we indicate this by writing $f \xrightarrow{G,c} f$. We say h is a *normal form of f modulo G under complete-reduction* (briefly, *complete-normal form*) if $f \xrightarrow[*]{G,c} h \xrightarrow{G,c} h$, and we write $\mathrm{NF}_G^c(f)$ for the set of all complete-normal forms of f modulo G.

Show that

1. The complete-normal form of f is not unique in general. That is, it is possible that
$$|\mathrm{NF}_G^c(f)| > 1.$$

2. The complete-normal form of f is well-defined. That is, it is *not* possible that
$$|\mathrm{NF}_G^c(f)| = 0,$$

(i.e., the complete-reduction process always terminates).

Problem 3.10

Consider the following set $G = \{g_1, \ldots, g_{n+1}\} \subseteq \mathbb{Q}[x_1, \ldots, x_n]$, a polynomial $f \in \mathbb{Q}[x_1, \ldots, x_n]$ and the admissible ordering $\underset{\mathrm{lex}}{>}$.

$$x_1 \underset{\mathrm{lex}}{>} x_2 \underset{\mathrm{lex}}{>} \cdots \underset{\mathrm{lex}}{>} x_n.$$

Let $d > 0$ and $D > 0$ be two positive integers. Assume that

$$
\begin{aligned}
g_1 &= x_1 - x_2^d x_3^d \cdots x_n^d \\
g_2 &= x_2 - x_3^d \cdots x_n^d \\
&\vdots \\
g_{n-1} &= x_{n-1} - x_n^d \\
g_n &= x_n^2 - x^n \\
g_{n+1} &= x_n - 1
\end{aligned}
$$

and

$$f = x_1^D x_n.$$

Show that there is a complete reduction sequence

$$f \xrightarrow{G,c} f_1 \xrightarrow{G,c} f_2 \xrightarrow{G,c} \cdots \xrightarrow{G,c} f_m,$$

such that

$$m \geq 2^{(d+1)^{n-1}D}.$$

Problem 3.11

Let K be a field and $R = K[x_1, \ldots, x_n]$ be the multivariate polynomial ring, as in Problem 3.9. Let $f, g \in R$; we define the S-polynomial $S(f,g)$ of f and g as follows:

$$S(f,g) = \frac{m}{\text{Hmono}(f)} \cdot f - \frac{m}{\text{Hmono}(g)} \cdot g,$$

where $m = LCM(\text{Hterm}(f), \text{Hterm}(g))$.

Let $I \subseteq R$ be an ideal in R. Show that the following three statements are equivalent:

1. $G \subseteq I$ and $\text{Head}(G) = \text{Head}(I)$.
2. $G \subseteq I$ and for all $f \in I$,

$$f \xrightarrow[*]{G,c} 0.$$

3. $(G) = I$ and for all $f, g \in G$ ($f \neq g$),

$$S(f,g) \xrightarrow[*]{G,c} 0.$$

Problem 3.12

Let K be a field and $R = K[x_1, \ldots, x_n]$ be the multivariate polynomial ring, as in Problem 3.9.

(i) Show that the following two statements are equivalent:

1. G is a Gröbner basis for I.
2. $(G) = I$ and for all $f \in R$, $|\text{NF}_G^c(f)| = 1$.

Hint: You may need to show by induction that

$$f \xleftrightarrow[*]{G,c} g \quad \text{iff} \quad f \equiv g \bmod (G).$$

(ii) Let $(F) \subseteq K[x_1, \ldots, x_n]$ be an ideal and $\equiv \bmod (F)$ the usual congruence relation on $R = K[x_1, \ldots, x_n]$.

A *canonical simplifier* for $\equiv \bmod (F)$ on R is an algorithm C with input and output in R such that for all $f, g \in R$,

$$f \equiv C(f) \bmod (F)$$

and
$$f \equiv g \bmod (F) \quad \Longrightarrow \quad C(f) = C(g).$$

Notice that the function C gives a unique representative in each equivalence class of $T/\sim$. We call $C(f)$ a *canonical form* of f.
Devise a canonical simplifier algorithm.

Problem 3.13

Let K be a field and $R = K[x_1, \ldots, x_n]$ be the multivariate polynomial ring, as in Problem 3.9. A set $G \subseteq R$ is a *minimal Gröbner basis* of the ideal (G), if

$$\left(\forall\, g \in G \right) \left[G \setminus \{g\} \text{ is not a Gröbner basis of } (G) \right].$$

Show that if G and G' are two minimal Gröbner bases for the same ideal, then they have the same cardinality, $|G| = |G'|$.

Hint: Show that (1) the set of head terms in G is equal to the set of head terms in G' and (2) no two polynomials in G (or G') have the same head term.

Problem 3.14

Let K be a field and $R = K[x_1, \ldots, x_n]$ be the multivariate polynomial ring, as in Problem 3.9. A basis $F \subseteq R$ is *self-reduced* if either $F = \{0\}$ or else $0 \notin F$ and

$$\left(\forall\, f \in F \right) \left[f \xrightarrow{\ F\setminus\{f\},c\ } f \right]$$

We call a Gröbner basis $G \subseteq R$ *reduced* if

1. either $G = \{0\}$ or else for all $g \in G$, $\mathrm{Hcoef}(g) = 1$;

2. G is self-reduced.

(i) Devise algorithmic procedures to compute the self-reduced and reduced Gröbner bases of an ideal (F).

(ii) Prove that the reduced Gröbner basis of an ideal in $K[x_1, \ldots, x_n]$ is unique (relative to choice of the admissible ordering).

Note: You may want to use the fact that a reduced Gröbner basis is a minimal Gröbner basis.

Problem 3.15

Consider the ideal $I = (xy+y, xz+1) \subseteq \mathbb{Q}[z, y, x]$. Use the lexicographic ordering, with

$$z \underset{\mathrm{LEX}}{<} y \underset{\mathrm{LEX}}{<} x.$$

(i) Show that the following is a minimal Gröbner basis for I:

$$G = \{xy + y, xz + 1, yz - y\}.$$

(ii) Prove that that G is also a Gröbner basis for I (with respect to degree ordering of x) when it is considered as an ideal in the polynomial ring $(\mathbb{Q}[z,y])[x]$ with variables x and coefficients in $\mathbb{Q}[z,y]$.

(iii) Show that G is not a minimal Gröbner basis for $I\{(\mathbb{Q}[z,y])[x]\}$. Compute a minimal Gröbner basis $G' \subset G$ for $I\{(\mathbb{Q}[z,y])[x]\}$. Is G' also a Gröbner basis for $I\{\mathbb{Q}[z,y,x]\}$?

Hint: Show that

$$
\begin{aligned}
\mathrm{Hmono}_x(xy + y) &= xy \\
&= y(xz) - x(yz - y) \\
&= y\,\mathrm{Hmono}_x(xz + 1) - x\,\mathrm{Hmono}_x(yz - y),
\end{aligned}
$$

where $\mathrm{Hmono}_x(f) = $ head monomial of $f \in (\mathbb{Q}[z,y])[x]$, when f is treated as a univariate polynomial in x. After throwing $(xy + y)$ out of G, you can obtain a minimal Gröbner basis.

Problem 3.16

Consider the polynomial ring $R = S[x_1, \ldots, x_n]$. The homogeneous part of a polynomial $f \in R$ of degree d (denoted f_d) is simply the sum of all the monomials of degree d in f. A polynomial is homogeneous if all of its monomials are of same degree. An ideal $I \subseteq R$ is said to be homogeneous, if the following condition holds: $f \in I$ implies that for all $d \geq 0$, $f_d \in I$

(i) Prove: An ideal $I \subseteq R$ is homogeneous if and only if I has a basis consisting only of homogeneous polynomials.

(ii) Given an effective procedure to test if an element $f \in R$ belongs to an ideal $I \subseteq R$, devise an algorithm to test if I is homogeneous.

(iii) Let $I \subseteq R$ be a homogeneous ideal, and G a Gröbner basis for I (under some admissible ordering $\underset{A}{>}$). Define

$$G'_d = \Big\{ g_d \ : \ g_d \text{ is a homogeneous part of some } g \in G \text{ of degree } d \Big\},$$

and

$$G' = \bigcup_{d=-\infty}^{+\infty} G'_d.$$

Prove that G' is a homogeneous Gröbner basis for I (under $\underset{A}{>}$).

(iii) Let $K = $ field. Show that an ideal $I \subseteq K[x_1, \ldots, x_n]$ is homogeneous if and only if it has a reduced Gröbner basis, each of whose element is homogeneous.

Problem 3.17

Let G be a homogeneous Gröbner basis for I with respect to $\underset{\text{TRLEX}}{>}$, in $S[x_1, \ldots, x_n]$. Define $\widehat{G}^{(d)}$ as follows:

Let $g \in S[x_1, \ldots, x_n]$ be a polynomial, and $d \in \mathbb{N}$ a positive integer. Then

$$\widehat{g}^{(d)} = \begin{cases} \dfrac{g}{x_n^m}, & \text{if } g \text{ is divisible by } x_n^m, \\ & \text{but not by } x_n^{m+1}, \text{ for some } 0 \leq m < d, \\ \dfrac{g}{x_n^d}, & \text{otherwise.} \end{cases}$$

and

$$\widehat{G}^{(d)} = \{\widehat{g}^{(d)} : g \in G\}.$$

Show that $\widehat{G}^{(d)}$ is a homogeneous Gröbner basis for $I : (x_n^d)$ with respect to $\underset{\text{TRLEX}}{>}$.

Problem 3.18

We define a polynomial expression over the ring $\mathbb{Z}$ involving n variables $x_1, x_2, \ldots, x_n$ as follows: $P = 1$, $P = x_i$ ($i \in \{1, \ldots, n\}$) are polynomial expressions; if P and Q are two polynomial expressions, then so are $a_1 \cdot P + a_2 \cdot Q$ and $a_1 \cdot P \cdot Q$ ($a_1, a_2 \in \mathbb{Z}$).

Example: $(x^2 - y^2) - (x + y)(x - y - 1)$.

With each polynomial expression, P, we associate the polynomial obtained by expanding the polynomial into the simplified form and call it $\widehat{P}$—for instance, the polynomial associated with the expression in the example is $x + y$.

Given a polynomial expression P_1, let d_1 be the degree of x_1 in $\widehat{P}_1$, and $\widehat{P}_2 x_1^{d_1}$ be the corresponding term in $\widehat{P}_1$ (considered as a polynomial in x_1 over the ring $\mathbb{Z}[x_2, \ldots, x_n]$); and let d_2 be the degree of x_2 in $\widehat{P}_2$, and so on, up to d_n.

(i) Suppose P is not identically zero. Let $I_i \subseteq \mathbb{Z}$ be an interval in $\mathbb{Z}$ ($i \in \{1, \ldots, n\}$). Show that in the set $I_1 \times I_2 \times \cdots \times I_n \subseteq \mathbb{Z}^n$, P has at most N real zeroes, where

$$N = |I_1 \times I_2 \times \cdots \times I_n| \left(\frac{d_1}{|I_1|} + \frac{d_2}{|I_2|} + \cdots + \frac{d_n}{|I_n|} \right)$$

(ii) Let P be a polynomial expression, not identically zero, and $C > 1$ a constant. Let $I = I_1 = \cdots = I_n$ be intervals in $\mathbb{Z}$ such that $|I| \geq C \cdot \deg \widehat{P}$. Show that the probability that P evaluates to zero at a (uniformly) randomly chosen point in I^n is bounded by C^{-1} from above.

(iii) Devise a probabilistic algorithm to test whether a given polynomial expression is identically zero.

Solutions to Selected Problems

Problem 3.1

Lemma: *Given* $I = (f_1, \ldots, f_s)$ *is an ideal in* $K[x]$, *where* K *is a field, if* $f = x^n + a_1 x^{n-1} + \cdots + a_n$ *is a monic polynomial of minimal degree in* I, *then* $G = \{f\}$ *is a Gröbner basis for* I.

PROOF.

Note first that f has the minimal degree among the polynomials of I, since if there exists an $f' \in I$, $\deg(f') < \deg(f)$, then $f'/\text{Hcoef}(f') \in I$ would contradict our choice of f.

Since $\{f\} \subseteq I$, it is sufficient to show that $\text{Head}(I) \subseteq \text{Head}(\{f\})$. For any $g = b_0 x^m + b_1 x^{m-1} + \cdots + b_m \in I$, $\text{Hmono}(g) = b_0 x^m$, and $n \le m$ by choice. Thus, $\text{Hmono}(f) \mid \text{Hmono}(g)$, and $\text{Hmono}(g) \in \text{Head}(\{f\})$. $\square$

Case s = 2: Both head reductions and S-polynomials do the same thing and correspond to one step of polynomial division. Suppose $f_{i-1} = a_0 x^n + a_1 x^{n-1} + \cdots + a_n$, and $f_i = b_0 x^m + b_1 x^{m-1} + \cdots + b_m$, where $n \le m$; then the following are all equivalent:

$$S(f_i, f_{i-1}) \quad = \quad f_i - \left(\frac{b_0}{a_0}\right) x^{m-n} f_{i-1},$$

$$f_i \quad = \quad \left(\frac{b_0}{a_0}\right) x^{m-n} f_{i-1} + S(f_i, f_{i-1}),$$

$$f_i \xrightarrow{f_{i-1}} S(f_i, f_{i-1}).$$

Because the quotients are restricted to monomials, we get only one step of a complete polynomial division of the type occurring in Euclid's algorithm. We observe that it is never necessary to multiply both f_i and f_{i-1} by a power product to find the LCM of the head monomials.

When we run the Gröbner basis algorithm starting with two univariate polynomials, the S-polynomial computations generate remainders, which then get reduced to normal-forms. The normal-form computations apply head reductions which again compute remainders. The algorithm may be viewed as a "disorganized" Euclidean algorithm, in which remaindering is done in a nondeterministic fashion. As soon as the g.c.d. of the inputs appears (as it must, since we can simulate the Euclidean g.c.d. computation by making the right nondeterministic choices), then all the normal forms of S-polynomials necessarily reduce to zero, and the algorithm terminates. As we are not trying to produce a "reduced" Gröbner basis, it will contain along with the g.c.d. also the input polynomials and all the reduced remainders generated along the way. The g.c.d. can be extracted by simply searching for the lowest-degree polynomial in the basis.

Problem 3.2

(i) In general, for $f \in R$, $\mathrm{NF}_G^h(f)$ is not unique. For instance, if we head-reduce $x^6 y^6 + xy^2 + x + 1$, first using $x^2 + 1$ as long as possible and then using $y^3 + 1$, we get $xy^2 + x$. On the other hand, if we head-reduce the same polynomial, first using $y^3 + 1$ as long as possible and then $x^2 + 1$, we get $xy^2 + x^2 + x + 1$. Thus,

$$\left| \mathrm{NF}_G^h(x^6 y^6 + xy^2 + x + 1) \right| > 1.$$

Let $f \in I$, and $f' \in \mathrm{NF}_G^h(f)$. Thus, $f' \in I$. If $f' \neq 0$ then $\mathrm{Hmono}(f') \in \mathrm{Head}(G)$, and f' is head-reducible. As f' is a normal-form, f' must be 0. Therefore, $\mathrm{NF}_G^h(f) = \{0\}$.

(ii) Let $G_{\min}$ be minimal Gröbner basis, which is not a self-head-reduced Gröbner basis. Then there is a nonzero $g \in G_{\min}$ which is head-reducible modulo $G_{\min} \setminus \{g\}$. Thus, $\mathrm{Hmono}(g) \in \mathrm{Head}(G_{\min} \setminus \{g\})$. Therefore,

$$\mathrm{Head}(I) = \mathrm{Head}(G) = \mathrm{Head}(G_{\min} \setminus \{g\}) + (\mathrm{Hmono}(g)) = \mathrm{Head}(G_{\min} \setminus \{g\}),$$

and $G_{\min} \setminus \{g\} \subsetneqq G_{\min}$ is a Gröbner basis for I, which contradicts the minimality of $G_{\min}$.

Conversely, let G_{shr} be a self-head-reduced Gröbner basis, which is not minimal. Then there is a nonzero $g \in G_{\mathrm{shr}}$ such that $G' = G_{\mathrm{shr}} \setminus \{g\}$ is a Gröbner basis for I. But then

$$\mathrm{Hmono}(g) \in \mathrm{Head}(I) = \mathrm{Head}(G'),$$

and g is head-reducible modulo $G_{\mathrm{shr}} \setminus \{g\}$, which contradicts the self-head-reducibility of G_{shr}.

Problem 3.5

Let S be Noetherian, computable and syzygy-solvable ring. If S is detachable, then obviously it is also 1-detachable, as 1-detachability is a special case of detachability.

CLAIM: *Let $f_1, \ldots, f_r, s \in S$, and let the syzygy-basis for $\{f_1, \ldots, f_r, s\}$, be $\overline{v_1}, \ldots, \overline{v_p}$, where, for $i = 1, \ldots, p$, $\overline{v_i} = \langle w_{i,1}, \ldots, w_{i,r+1} \rangle \in S^{r+1}$. Then*

1. $1 = u_1 \, w_{1,r+1} + \cdots + u_p \, w_{p,r+1}, \quad$ *for some $u_i \in S$*

$$\Rightarrow \quad s = t_1 \, f_1 + \cdots + t_r \, f_r, \quad \text{where } t_i = -\sum_{j=1}^{p} u_j w_{j,i}.$$

2. $1 \in (w_{1,r+1}, \ldots, w_{p,r+1}) \quad \Leftrightarrow \quad s \in (f_1, \ldots, f_r).$

Proof of Claim   The proof is as follows. Let $1 = u_1\, w_{1,r+1} + \cdots + u_p\, w_{p,r+1}$. Since, for all $j = 1, \ldots, p$,

$$w_{j,1}\, f_1 + \cdots + w_{j,r}\, f_r + w_{j,r+1}\, s = 0,$$

we have

$$u_1\left(w_{1,1}\, f_1 + \cdots + w_{1,r}\, f_r + w_{1,r+1}\, s\right) + \cdots$$

$$+ u_p\left(w_{p,1}\, f_1 + \cdots + w_{p,r}\, f_r + w_{p,r+1}\, s\right) = 0$$

$$\Rightarrow \quad \sum_{i=1}^{p} u_i\, w_{i,1}\, f_1 + \cdots + \sum_{i=1}^{p} u_i\, w_{i,r}\, f_r + \sum_{i=1}^{p} u_i\, w_{i,r+1}\, s = 0$$

$$\Rightarrow \quad -t_1\, f_1 - \cdots - t_r\, f_r + s = 0$$

$$\Rightarrow \quad s = t_1\, f_1 + \cdots + t_r\, f_r.$$

Thus

$$1 \in (w_{1,r+1}, \ldots, w_{p,r+1}) \quad \Rightarrow \quad s \in (f_1, \ldots, f_r).$$

Conversely, assume that $s \in (f_1, \ldots, f_r)$. Thus, $s = t_1\, f_1 + \cdots + t_r\, f_r$, and $-t_1\, f_1 - \cdots - t_r\, f_r + s = 0$. Since $\overline{v_1}, \ldots, \overline{v_p}$ is the syzygy-basis, we can find $u_1, \ldots, u_p$ such that

$$\langle -t_1, \ldots, -t_r, 1 \rangle = u_1\, \overline{v_1} + \cdots + u_p\, \overline{v_p}.$$

Thus, $u_1\, w_{1,r+1} + \cdots u_p\, w_{p,r+1} = 1$. Hence, $1 \in (w_{1,r+1}, \ldots, w_{p,r+1})$. (*End of Claim.*)   □

Let us assume that S is 1-detachable. Let $f_1, \ldots, f_r, s \in S$, and let the syzygy-basis for $\{f_1, \ldots, f_r, s\}$, be $\overline{v_1}, \ldots, \overline{v_p}$, as before. (The syzygy-basis can be computed as S is a syzygy-solvable ring.) If $1 \notin (w_{1,r+1}, \ldots, w_{p,r+1})$, then $s \notin (f_1, \ldots, f_r)$. Otherwise, we can express 1 as

$$1 = u_1\, w_{1,r+1} + \cdots + u_p\, w_{p,r+1},$$

using the 1-detachability of S. But by the claim, we see that

$$s = t_1\, f_1 + \cdots + t_r\, f_r,$$

where $t_i = -\sum_{j=1}^{p} u_j w_{j,i}$. Thus S is detachable.

Problem 3.6

(1) $\Rightarrow$ (3):   See the application section (§3.7), in particular the subsections on *intersection* (Subsection 3.7.4, pp. 105) and *quotient* (Subsection 3.7.5, pp. 106).

(3) $\Rightarrow$ (2):   Note that

$$(F_1) : (F_2) = \left((F_1) : \sum_{j=r+1}^{s} (f_j)\right) = \bigcap_{j=r+1}^{s} ((F_1) : (f_j)).$$

Also, for each f_j $(j = r + 1, \ldots, s)$, if C_j is a basis for $(F_1) \cap (f_j)$, and D_j is a basis for $\mathrm{ann}\,(f_j)$, then

$$B_j = \left\{ \frac{c}{f_j} : c \in C_j \right\} \cup D_j$$

is a basis for $(F_1) : (f_j)$. As S is intersection-solvable and annihilator-solvable, all the B_j's can be computed; and as S is intersection-solvable, a basis for $(F_1) : (F_2)$ can also be computed. Thus S is quotient-solvable.

(2) $\Rightarrow$ (1): Let $B^{(s)} = \left\{ b_{s,1}^{(s)}, \ldots, b_{s,p_s}^{(s)} \right\}$ be a basis for the ideal $(0) : (f_s) = \mathrm{ann}\,(f_s)$.

Let $\mathcal{B}^{(s)} \subseteq S^s$ be a set of s-tuples given by

$$\Big\{ \ \big\langle \underbrace{0, \ldots, 0}_{s-1}, b_{s,1}^{(s)} \big\rangle,$$

$$\vdots$$

$$\big\langle \underbrace{0, \ldots, 0}_{s-1}, b_{s,p_s}^{(s)} \big\rangle \ \Big\}.$$

Note that both $B^{(s)}$ and $\mathcal{B}^{(s)}$ are constructible as the ring S is assumed to be quotient-solvable, and for each $\bar{\omega} = \big\langle \underbrace{0, \ldots, 0}_{s-1}, b_{s,j}^{(s)} \big\rangle \in \mathcal{B}^{(s)}$,

$$0\, f_1 + \cdots + 0\, f_{s-1} + b_{s,j}^{(s)}\, f_s = 0.$$

Hence $\bar{\omega} \in S(\{f_1, \ldots, f_s\})$.

Now, for r $(1 \le r < s)$, let $B^{(r)} = \left\{ b_{r,1}^{(r)}, \ldots, b_{r,p_r}^{(r)} \right\}$ be a basis for the ideal $(f_{r+1}, \ldots, f_s) : (f_r)$.

Assume that for each $j \in \{1, \ldots, p_r\}$,

$$b_{r,j}^{(r)}\, f_r = -b_{r+1,j}^{(r)}\, f_{r+1} - \cdots - b_{s,j}^{(r)}\, f_s \in (f_{r+1}, \ldots, f_s),$$

i.e.,

$$b_{r,j}^{(r)}\, f_r + b_{r+1,j}^{(r)}\, f_{r+1} + \cdots + b_{s,j}^{(r)}\, f_s = 0.$$

Let $\mathcal{B}^{(r)} \subseteq S^s$ be a set of s-tuples given by

$$\Big\{ \ \big\langle \underbrace{0, \ldots, 0}_{r-1}, b_{r,1}^{(r)}, b_{r+1,1}^{(r)}, \ldots, b_{s,1}^{(r)} \big\rangle,$$

$$\vdots$$

$$\big\langle \underbrace{0, \ldots, 0}_{r-1}, b_{r,p_r}^{(r)}, b_{r+1,p_r}^{(r)}, \ldots, b_{s,p_r}^{(r)} \big\rangle \ \Big\}.$$

Note that $B^{(r)}$ can be computed as S is quotient-solvable; $b_{r+1,j}^{(r)}, \ldots, b_{s,j}^{(r)}$ $(1 \le j \le p_r)$ can be computed as S is detachable. Thus, finally, the set $B^{(r)}$ is constructible for a Noetherian, computable, detachable and quotient-solvable ring S. Also, for each $\bar\omega = \langle \underbrace{0, \ldots, 0}_{r-1}, b_{r,j}^{(r)}, b_{r+1,j}^{(r)}, \ldots, b_{s,j}^{(r)} \rangle \in B^{(r)}$,

$$0 f_1 + \cdots + 0 f_{r-1} b_{r,j}^{(r)} f_r + b_{r+1,j}^{(r)} f_{r+1} + \cdots + b_{s,j}^{(r)} f_s = 0.$$

Hence $\bar\omega \in S(\{f_1, \ldots, f_s\})$.

Now, we claim that the set $B = B^{(1)} \cup B^{(2)} \cup \cdots \cup B^{(s)}$ is in fact a syzygy basis for $\{f_1, f_2, \ldots, f_s\}$. We have already seen that if $\bar\omega \in B$ then $\bar\omega \in S(\{f_1, \ldots, f_s\})$. Thus, it remains to be checked that every s-tuple $\langle c_1, c_2, \ldots, c_s \rangle \in S^s$ satisfying the condition

$$c_1 f_1 + c_2 f_2 + \cdots + c_s f_s = 0$$

can be expressed as a linear combination of the elements of B. Assume to the contrary. Then there is an s-tuple $\bar\gamma = \langle \underbrace{0, \ldots, 0}_{r-1}, c_r, \ldots, c_s \rangle$ (r possibly 1) in $S(\{f_1, \ldots, f_s\})$, not expressible as a linear combination of the elements of B; assume that $\bar\gamma$ is so chosen that r takes the largest possible value.

We first notice that, since

$$c_r f_r = -c_{r+1} f_{r+1} - \cdots - c_s f_s \in (f_{r+1}, \ldots, f_s),$$

it follows that $c_r \in (f_{r+1}, \ldots, f_s) : (f_r)$. Thus

$$c_r = u_1 b_{r,1}^{(r)} + \cdots + u_{p_r} b_{r,p_r}^{(r)}.$$

Now, consider the s-tuple $\bar\gamma' = \langle \underbrace{0, \ldots, 0}_{r}, c'_{r+1}, \ldots, c'_s \rangle$, where

$$c'_{r+1} = c_{r+1} - \left(u_1 b_{r+1,1}^{(r)} + \cdots + u_{p_r} b_{r+1,p_r}^{(r)} \right),$$

$$\vdots$$

$$c'_s = c_s - \left(u_1 b_{s,1}^{(r)} + \cdots + u_{p_r} b_{s,p_r}^{(r)} \right).$$

But

$$c'_{r+1} f_{r+1} + \cdots + c'_s f_s$$
$$= c_r f_r + c_{r+1} f_{r+1} + \cdots + c_s f_s$$
$$\quad - \sum_{j=1}^{p_r} u_j \left(b_{r,j}^{(r)} f_r + \cdots + b_{s,j}^{(r)} f_s \right)$$
$$= 0.$$

Thus $\bar{\gamma}' \in S(\{f_1, \ldots, f_s\})$. Since $\bar{\gamma}$ is not expressible as a linear combination of the elements of $\mathcal{B}$, and since $(\bar{\gamma} - \bar{\gamma}')$ is a linear combination of the elments of $\mathcal{B}^{(r)} \subseteq \mathcal{B}$, the s-tuple $\bar{\gamma}'$ itself cannot be expressed as a linear combination of the elements of $\mathcal{B}$. But this contradicts the maximality of the initial prefix of 0's in the choice of the s-tuple, $\bar{\gamma}$. Indeed, every element of $S(\{f_1, \ldots, f_s\})$ must be expressible as a linear combination of the elements of $\mathcal{B}$, and $\mathcal{B}$ is a syzygy basis for $\{f_1, \ldots, f_s\}$, as claimed. Thus the ring S is syzygy-solvable.

Problem 3.7

(i) We first prove the statement in the hint:

$$c \in (t\, I_1, (1-t)I_2)\{S[t]\} \cap S$$

$$\Leftrightarrow \quad c = \sum_{i=0}^{k} a_i t^{i+1} + \sum_{i=0}^{k} b_i t^i - \sum_{i=0}^{k} b_i t^{i+1} \in S, \quad a_i \in I_1, b_i \in I_2$$

$$\Leftrightarrow \quad c = (a_k - b_k)t^{k+1} + \sum_{i=1}^{k}(a_{i-1} + b_i - b_{i-1})t^i + b_0 \in S$$

$$\Leftrightarrow \quad a_k - b_k = a_{k-1} + b_k - b_{k-1} = \cdots = a_0 + b_1 - b_0 = 0,$$
$$\text{and } c = b_0 \in S$$

$$\Leftrightarrow \quad b_0 = a_0 + a_1 + \cdots + a_k = c \in S$$

$$\Leftrightarrow \quad c \in I_1 \quad \text{and} \quad c \in I_2$$

$$\Leftrightarrow \quad c \in I_1 \cap I_2.$$

Therefore, contraction-solvability of S implies intersection-solvability of S.

(ii) It was shown in Section 3.3 that the strong-computability of S implies that a Gröbner basis G for $(F) \subseteq S[t]$ can be computed with respect to the admissible ordering $\underset{\text{LEX}}{>}$ (in this case, it is simply the degree ordering). We now claim that $G \cap S$ is a Gröbner basis (also finite) for the contraction of (F), $(F)\{S[t]\} \cap S$ (in S). Thus if S is strongly computable then S is contraction-solvable.

To justify the claim, we make the following observations:

$$\left(\forall\, f \in S[t]\right)\ \left[\text{Hmono}(f) \in S \quad \Leftrightarrow \quad f \in S\right]$$

(i.e., if the highest-order term in f does not involve t, then no term of f involves t, and *vice versa*).

Thus,

$$\text{Head}(G \cap S) = \text{Head}(G) \cap S = \text{Head}(I) \cap S = \text{Head}(I \cap S).$$

Problem 3.9

(i) Let $G = \{x^2 - 1, x^2 - x\}$ and let $f = x^2$, then $\mathrm{NF}_G^c(f) \supseteq \{1, x\}$, showing that $|\mathrm{NF}_G^c(f)| > 1$.

(ii) In this case, we have to simply show that the complete-reduction process always terminates. We start with a definition. Let X be any set with a total ordering $\leq$ and let $S(X)$ be the set of all finite decreasing sequences of elements of X:

$$S(X) = \{\langle x_1, \ldots, x_n \rangle : x_i \in X, x_1 > x_2 > \cdots > x_n\}.$$

Let $S(X)$ have the following induced total-ordering:

$$\langle x_1, \ldots, x_n \rangle \leq' \langle y_1, \ldots, y_m \rangle,$$

if either for some $i < \min(n, m)$, $x_1 = y_1$, ..., $x_i = y_i$ and $x_{i+1} < y_{i+1}$, or else the sequence $\langle x_1, \ldots, x_n \rangle$ is a prefix of the sequence $\langle y_1, \ldots, y_m \rangle$ (thus, $n < m$).

CLAIM: *If X is well-ordered by $\leq$, then $S(X)$ is well-ordered under the induced ordering.*
Proof of Claim   For the sake of contradiction, suppose $\sigma_1 >' \sigma_2 >' \cdots$ is an infinite descending chain in $S(X)$. Let $\sigma_i = (x_{i,1}, \ldots, x_{i,n(i)})$. There are two cases.

(i) The $n(i)$'s are bounded, say $k = \max\{n(i) : i = 1, 2, \cdots\}$. We use induction on k. We get an immediate contradiction for $k = 1$, so assume $k > 1$. If there are infinitely many i's such that $n(i) = 1$, then we get a contradiction from the subsequence consisting of such σ_i's. Hence we may assume that the $n(i)$'s are all greater than 1. Now there is an i_0 such that for all $i \geq i_0$, $x_{i,1} = x_{i+1,1}$. Let $\sigma_i' = (x_{i,2}, \ldots, x_{i,n(i)})$ be obtained from σ_i by omitting the leading item in the sequence. Then the sequence σ_{i_0}', σ_{i_0+1}', $\cdots$ constitutes a strictly decreasing infinite chain with each σ_i' of length $< k$. This contradicts the inductive hypothesis.

(ii) The $n(i)$'s are unbounded. By taking a subsequence if necessary, we may assume that $n(i)$ is strictly increasing in i. Define $m(1)$ to be the largest index such that $x_{m(1),1} = x_{j,1}$ for all $j \geq m(1)$. For each $i > 1$ define $m(i)$ to be the largest index greater than $m(i-1)$ such that $x_{m(i),i} = x_{j,i}$ for all $j \geq m(i)$. Note that the sequence

$$x_{m(1),1}, \; x_{m(2),2}, \; x_{m(3),3}, \; \cdots$$

is strictly decreasing. This contradicts the well-foundedness of X.
(*End of Claim.*) $\square$

Now to see that the complete-reduction process terminates, we proceed as follows: We map a polynomial g to the sequence of monomials $\bar{g} = \langle m_1, \ldots, m_k \rangle$, where m_i's are the monomials occurring in g and

$m_1 \underset{A}{>} m_2 \underset{A}{>} \cdots \underset{A}{>} m_k$. By our claim, the set of $\bar{g}$'s are well-ordered un-

der the induced ordering $\underset{A}{>}'$. It is seen that if $g \xrightarrow{G,c} h$, then $\bar{g} \underset{A}{>}' \bar{h}$. The

termination of the complete-reduction is equivalent to the well-foundedness
of the induced ordering.

Problem 3.11

(1) $\Rightarrow$ (2):

$$G \subseteq I \text{ and } \text{Head}(G) = \text{Head}(I)$$
$$\Rightarrow \left(\forall f \in I \right) \left[f \xrightarrow[*]{G,h} 0 \right]$$
$$\Rightarrow \left(\forall f \in I \right) \left[f \xrightarrow[*]{G,c} 0 \right],$$
$$(\text{since } f \xrightarrow{G,h} g \Rightarrow f \xrightarrow{G,c} g.)$$

(2) $\Rightarrow$ (3): (i)

$$\left(\forall f \in I \right) \left[f \xrightarrow[*]{G,c} 0 \right] \Rightarrow f = \sum_{g_i \in G} f_i g_i \Rightarrow f \in (G),$$

which implies $I \subseteq (G)$ but $G \subseteq I$, therefore $(G) = I$.

(ii)

$$\left(\forall f,g \in C, f \neq g \right) \left[S(f,y) = \frac{m}{\text{Hmono}(f)} \cdot f - \frac{m}{\text{Hmono}(g)} \cdot g \in I \right]$$
$$\Rightarrow \left(\forall f,g \in G, f \neq g \right) \left[S(f,g) \xrightarrow[*]{G,c} 0 \right].$$

(3) $\Rightarrow$ (1): As $(G) = I$, $G \subseteq I$. Let, for each $F \subseteq G$, $SP(F)$ stand for
the set of S-polynomials of F.

$$\left(\forall f,g \in G, f \neq g \right) \left[S(f,g) \xrightarrow[*]{G,c} 0 \right]$$
$$\Rightarrow \left(\forall F \subseteq G \right) \left(\forall h_F \in SP(F) \right) \left[h_F \xrightarrow[*]{G,c} 0 \right]$$
$$\Rightarrow \left(\forall F \subseteq G \right) \left(\forall h_F \subset SP(F) \right) \left[h_F = \sum_{g_i \in G} f_i g_i \right], \text{ such that}$$
$$\text{Hterm}(h_F) \underset{A}{\geq} \text{Hterm}(f_i g_i) \text{ for all } i$$
$$\Rightarrow \quad G \text{ satisfies the syzygy-condition.}$$

It then follows that $\text{Head}(G) = \text{Head}(I)$.

Problem 3.12

(i) (1) $\Rightarrow$ (2): Let $g, g' \in \text{NF}_G^c(f)$. Then $f - g \in I$ and $f - g' \in I$
and therefore $g - g' \in I$. Then by previous part $g - g' \xrightarrow[*]{G,c} 0$. But $g - g'$ is

in normal form with respect to complete-reduction as g, g' are themselves in normal form. Hence $g - g' = 0$, and $g = g'$. Since, for all $f \in R$, $|\mathrm{NF}^c_G(f)| > 0$, we see that $|\mathrm{NF}^c_G(f)| = 1$.

(2) $\Rightarrow$ (1):

We begin by proving the statement in the hint.

CLAIM: *For all $G \subseteq R$, and f, $g \in R$, $f \equiv g \bmod (G)$ if and only if* $f \overset{G,c}{\underset{*}{\longleftrightarrow}} g$.

Proof of Claim

($\Leftarrow$)

This is easily shown by induction on the number of steps between f and g. Let

$$f = g_0 \overset{G,c}{\longleftrightarrow} g_1 \overset{G,c}{\longleftrightarrow} \cdots \overset{G,c}{\longleftrightarrow} g_k = g$$

for some $k \geq 0$. The result is trivial for $k = 0$. Otherwise, by induction, $g_1 - g_k \in (G)$ and it is seen directly from the definition that $g_0 - g_1 \in (G)$. Thus $g_0 \equiv g_k \bmod (G)$.

($\Rightarrow$)

If $f - g \in (G)$, then we can express $f - g$ as $\sum_{i=1}^{m} \alpha_i t_i f_i$, where each $\alpha_i \in K$, and t_i is a power-product and the f_i are members of G. If $m = 0$ the result is trivial. If $m \geq 1$ then we can write $g' = g + \alpha_m f_m$ and $f - g' = \sum_{i=1}^{m-1} \alpha_i t_i f_i$. By induction hypothesis, $f \overset{G,c}{\underset{*}{\longleftrightarrow}} g'$. We also have that $g' - g = \alpha_m t_m f_m \overset{G,c}{\longrightarrow} 0$. Let $t = \mathrm{Hterm}(t_m f_m)$. It is clear that t occurs in g and g' with some (possibly zero) coefficients α and α' (respectively) such that $\alpha_m = \alpha' - \alpha$. Thus $g \overset{G,c}{\underset{*}{\longrightarrow}} (g - \alpha t_m f_m)$, and $g' \overset{G,c}{\underset{*}{\longrightarrow}} (g' - \alpha' t_m f_m)$, i.e., $g \overset{G,c}{\underset{*}{\longleftrightarrow}} g'$. This shows $f \overset{G,c}{\underset{*}{\longleftrightarrow}} g' \overset{G,c}{\underset{*}{\longleftrightarrow}} g$.

(End of Claim.) □

Now, going back to our original problem, we see that since $(G) = I$, $G \subseteq I$. Furthermore,

$$\begin{aligned} f \in I \quad &\Rightarrow \quad f \equiv 0 \bmod (G) \\ &\Rightarrow \quad f \overset{G,c}{\underset{*}{\longleftrightarrow}} 0 \\ &\Rightarrow \quad f = g_0 \overset{G,c}{\longleftrightarrow} g_1 \overset{G,c}{\longleftrightarrow} \cdots \overset{G,c}{\longleftrightarrow} g_k = 0 \\ &\Rightarrow \quad \left(\forall\, 0 \leq i \leq k\right) \left[\mathrm{NF}^c_G(g_i) \cap \mathrm{NF}^c_G(g_{i+1}) \neq \emptyset\right] \\ &\Rightarrow \quad \mathrm{NF}^c_G(f) = \mathrm{NF}^c_G(g_i) = \mathrm{NF}^c_G(g_{i+1}) = \mathrm{NF}^c_G(0) = 0, \\ &\qquad\qquad \text{for all } i, 0 \leq i < k, \\ &\qquad\qquad (\text{since } |\mathrm{NF}^c_G(g_i)| = 1, \text{ for all } i, 0 \leq i < k) \\ &\Rightarrow \quad f \overset{G,c}{\underset{*}{\longrightarrow}} 0. \end{aligned}$$

Hence $G \subseteq I$, and for all $f \in I$, $f \overset{G,c}{\underset{*}{\longrightarrow}} 0$, and G is a Gröbner basis for I.

(ii) Let G be a Gröbner basis for (F). Then use the algorithm that on input of $f \in K[x_1, \ldots, x_n]$ produces its normal-form (under complete reduction) modulo G, i.e., $C(f) = \mathrm{NF}_G^c(f)$. The rest follows from the preceding part and the well-known properties of Gröbner bases.

Problem 3.14

(i) The following two routines terminate correctly with the self-reduced and reduced Gröbner bases of an ideal (F).

SELFREDUCE(F)
Input: F a finite set of polynomials in $K[x_1, \ldots, x_n]$.
Output: R a self-reduced basis for (F).

```
loop
        R := ∅; self-reduced := true
        while F ≠ ∅ loop
                Choose f from F and set F := F \ {f};
                g := NF^c_(R∪F)(f);
                if g ≠ 0  then R := R ∪ {g};
                self-reduced := (g = f) and self-reduced;
        end{while }
        F := R;
    until self-reduced
    end{loop };
    return (R);
end{SELFREDUCE}.    □
```

The routine SELFREDUCE *terminates and is correct.*

In each iteration of the inner while-loop (except for the terminating iteration) there is a selected polynomial f that must be subject to a reducing transformation, i.e., $g \neq \mathrm{NF}_{(R\cup F)}^c(f)$. If $f = f_0, f_1, \ldots$, constitute the successive transformed versions of f, then it is easily seen that the sequence of f_i's is finite. Since this is true for every f in the original F, there can only be a finite number of iterations.

The correctness follows trivially from the definition, once we observe that the ideal $(F \cup R)$ remains invariant over the loops.

Reduce(F)
Input: F a finite set of polynomials in $K[x_1, \ldots, x_n]$.
Output: G a reduced Gröbner basis for (F).

$G := \text{SelfReduce}(F);$

$B := \Big\{ \{f, g\} : f, g \in G, f \neq g \Big\};$

while $B \neq \emptyset$ loop
    Choose $\{f, g\}$ to be any pair in B;
    $B := B \setminus \{\{f, g\}\};$
    $h := S(f, g);$
    $h' := \text{NF}_G^c(h);$
    if $h' \neq 0$ then
        $G := \text{SelfReduce}(G \cup \{h'\});$
        $B := \{\{f, g\} : f, g \in G, f \neq g\};$
    end{if };
end{while };
for every $f \in G$ loop
    $G := (G \setminus \{f\}) \cup \{f/\text{Hcoef}(f)\};$
return (G);
end{Reduce}.   □

The routine Reduce *terminates and is correct.*

The termination and the fact that the output G of the routine is a Gröbner basis of (F) can be proven easily in a manner similar to the proof for the Gröbner basis algorithm. (Use the ascending chain condition and syzygy condition.) When the algorithm terminates, clearly the basis is self-reduced and each element of the basis is monic.

(ii)

Theorem   *The reduced Gröbner basis of an ideal in $K[x_1, \ldots, x_n]$ is unique (relative to the choice of an admissible ordering).*

PROOF.

Let G, G' be two reduced Gröbner bases for the same ideal. We obtain a contradiction by supposing that there is some polynomial g in $G - G'$. By the preceding problem, there is some other polynomial g' in $G' - G$ such that $\text{Hmono}(g) = \text{Hmono}(g')$ [recall that $\text{Hcoef}(g) = 1 = \text{Hcoef}(g')$].

Let $h = g - g'$. Then

$$h \neq 0 \quad \text{and} \quad h \xrightarrow[*]{G, c} 0,$$

since G is a Gröbner basis. So some term t occurring in h can be eliminated by a complete-reduction by some $f \in G$. Now t must occur in g or g'. If t occurs in g, then g is reducible by f, contradicting the assumption that G is reduced. If t occurs in g' then let $f' \in G'$ such that $\text{Hterm}(f') = \text{Hterm}(f)$. Again g' is reducible by f', contradicting the original assumption that G' is reduced.   □

Problem 3.18

(i) We can write $P(x_1, \ldots, x_n)$ as

$$P(X) = P(x_1, \ldots, x_n) = P_{d_1}(x_2, \ldots, x_n)x_1^{d_1} + \cdots + P_0(x_2, \ldots, x_n)$$

If $P(X) \not\equiv 0$, then for a fixed value of X, $P(X)$ can be zero because of two reasons: (a) x_1 is a root of the univariate polynomial $P(X)$ with $P_j(x_2, \ldots, x_n)$ ($0 \le j \le d_1$) as coefficients, or (b) for each j ($0 \le j \le d_1$), $P_j(x_2, \ldots, x_n) = 0$. For a fixed value of $x_2, \ldots, x_n$, there are only d_1 zeroes of $P(X)$ and each x_j can assume only one of the $|I_j|$ values; therefore, there are at most $d_1 \cdot \prod_{j=2}^{n} |I_j|$ zeroes of the first kind. The total number of zeroes of the second kind are obviously bounded by the number of zeroes of $P_{d_1}(x_2, \ldots, x_n)$. Let $\mathcal{Z}[P(X)]$ denote the zeroes of $P(X)$. Then we have the following recurrence:

$$|\mathcal{Z}[P(X)]| \le d_1 \cdot \prod_{j=2}^{n} |I_j| + |\mathcal{Z}(P_{d_1}(x_2, \ldots, x_n))| \cdot |I_1|$$

Therefore,

$$\frac{|\mathcal{Z}(P(X))|}{\prod_{j=1}^{n} |I_j|} \le \frac{|\mathcal{Z}(P_{d_1}(x_2, \ldots, x_n))|}{\prod_{j=2}^{n} |I_j|} + \frac{d_1}{|I_1|}$$

$$< \sum_{j=1}^{n} \frac{d_j}{|I_j|},$$

which gives the required inequality.

(ii) Since there are at most $\prod_{j=1}^{n} |I_j|$ total possible values of P, the probability

$$p = \Pr[P(X) = 0 : P \not\equiv 0] \le \frac{|\mathcal{Z}(P)|}{\prod_{j=1}^{n} |I_j|}.$$

If $|I_j| = |I|$ ($1 \le j \le n$), then the probability is bounded by

$$p = \Pr[P(X) = 0 : P \not\equiv 0] \le \sum_{j=1}^{n} \frac{d_j}{|I|} = \frac{1}{|I|} \sum_{j=1}^{n} d_j = \frac{1}{|I|} \deg(P)$$

Therefore, if $|I| \ge C \cdot \deg(P)$, then $p \le C^{-1}$.

(iii) One possible way to check if $P \equiv 0$ is to choose $x_1, \ldots, x_n$ randomly and evaluate P at this set of values. If $P(X) \ne 0$, then obviously $P \not\equiv 0$; otherwise, return with $P \equiv 0$. If the algorithm returns $P \equiv 0$, then the probability of error is bounded by p. Therefore, if we choose $|I| = \lceil \frac{1}{\varepsilon} \cdot \deg(P) \rceil$, then the algorithm returns the correct answer with probability $\ge 1 - \varepsilon$, for any $0 < \varepsilon < 1$.

However, this algorithm is not very practical because $|I|$ may be very large, in which case all sorts of computational problems arise. One simple solution is to evaluate the polynomial for several sets of values, instead of evaluating it for only one set of values. However, we need to repeat the steps only if $P(X) = 0$. Therefore, the modified algorithm works as follows. Repeat the following steps k (where k is a fixed number) times:

1. Choose randomly $x_1, \ldots, x_n$ in the range $|I|$.

2. Evaluate P at this set of values.

3. If $P \neq 0$, then return with $P \not\equiv 0$.

Now the probability that P evaluates to zero, all of k times, even though $P \not\equiv 0$, is at most C^{-k}, provided that $|I| \geq C \cdot \deg(P)$. By choosing, $C = 2$ and $k = \lceil \log \frac{1}{\varepsilon} \rceil$, we can ensure that the algorithm is correct with the probability at least $1 - \varepsilon$. If P has m terms, then the running time of the algorithm is bounded by $O(kn(m + \deg(P)))$. In order to ensure that the probability of error is $o(1)$, we may choose $k = \Theta(\log n)$; then the running time of the algorithm is $O((m + \deg(P))n \log n)$, and the probability of correctness becomes $1 - \left(\frac{1}{n^{O(1)}}\right)$.

Another way to reduce the range of $|I|$ is to use modular arithmetic. In particular, we can perform all calculations modulo q where q is some prime number.

Bibliographic Notes

The original algorithm for Gröbner bases is due to Bruno Buchberger and appears in his 1965 doctoral dissertation [30]. His algorithm, however, dealt primarily with the ideals in a ring of multivariate polynomials over a field and used many ideas from critical-pair/completion methods, as in term-rewriting systems. There are several excellent survey papers exposing these ideas in depth, for instance, the papers by Buchberger [32,33] and by Mishra and Yap [149].

However, the treatment here, based on the notion of a *strongly computable ring*, has been influenced by the work of Spear[193] and Zacharias [215]. Zacharias credits Richman [173] for the main ideas, as Richman in 1974 had devised a univariate construction for coefficient rings in which ideal membership and syzygies are solvable and showed that ideal membership and syzygies are also solvable in the polynomial ring. The ideas can then be easily extended to multivariate rings by induction, and using the isomorphism

$$S[x_1, \ldots, x_{n-1}, x_n] \equiv (S[x_1, \ldots, x_{n-1}])[x_n].$$

A similar univariate induction approach also appears in Seidenberg [188]. However, note that a (Gröbner) basis constructed inductively in this manner will correspond only to one fixed admissible ordering (namely, lexicographic). For some related developments, also see Ayoub [10], Buchberger [31], Kandri-Rody and Kapur [110], Kapur and Narendran [115], Lankford [126], Pan [159], Schaller [182], Shtokhamer [190], Szekeres [199], Trinks [202] and Watt [207]. Additional related materials can also be found in a special issue on "Computational Aspects of Commutative Algebra" in the *Journal of Symbolic Computation* (Vol. **6**, Nos. 2 & 3, 1988).

The question of degree bounds and computational complexity for the Gröbner basis in various settings is still not completely resolved. However, quite a lot is now known for the case when the underlying ring of polynomials is $K[x_1, \ldots, x_n]$, where $K = $ a field. Let $D(n, d)$, $I(n, d)$ and $S(n, d)$ denote the following:

1. $D(n, d)$ is the minimum integer such that, for any ordering and for any ideal $I \subseteq K[x_1, \ldots, x_n]$ generated by a set of polynomials of degree no larger than d, there exists a Gröbner basis whose elements have degree no larger than $D(n, d)$. $D'(n, d)$ is a similar degree bound for the special case where the ordering is assumed to be degree-compatible.

2. Similarly, $S(n, d)$ is the minimum integer such that, for any set of polynomials $\{g_1, \ldots, g_m\} \subseteq K[x_1, \ldots, x_n]$, all of degree no larger than d, the module of solutions of the following equation:

$$h_1 \, g_1 + \cdots + h_m \, g_m = 0$$

has a basis whose elements have degree no larger than $S(n, d)$.

3. Finally, $I(n, d)$ is the minimum integer such that, for any set of polynomials $\{g_1, \ldots, g_m\} \subseteq K[x_1, \ldots, x_n]$ and a polynomial $f \in (g_1, \ldots, g_m)$, all of degree no larger than d, the following equation

$$h_1 \, g_1 + \cdots + h_m \, g_m = f$$

has a solution of degree no larger than $I(n, d)$.

Following summary is taken from Gallo[76]:

1. Relationship among $D(n, d)$, $D'(n, d)$, $I(n, d)$ and $S(n, d)$:

   (a) $S(n, d) \leq D(n, d)$ (Giusti[82]).

   (b) $S(n, d) \leq I(n, d) \leq S(n, d)^{O(n)}$ (Lazard[129]).

   (c) $D'(n, d) \leq D(n, d)$ (Yap[214]).

2. Upper bounds for $I(n, d)$ and $S(n, d)$:

   (a) $S(n, d) \leq d + 2(md)^{2^{n-1}}$ (Hermann[93] and Seidenberg[187]).

   (b) $I(n, d) \leq 2(2d)^{2^{n-1}}$ (Masser and Wüstholz[140]).

   (c) $S(n, d) \leq d^{2^{(\log 3/ \log 4)n}}$ (Lazard[129]).

   (d) $I(n, d) \leq d^{2^{(\log 3/ \log 4)n + O(\log n)}}$ (Lazard[129]).

3. Upper bounds for $D(n, d)$:

   (a) $D(n, d) = O(d^{2^{O(n)}})$ for homogeneous ideals in generic position (Giusti[82]).

   (b) $D(n, d) \leq h^{2^n}$, where $h = $ the regularity bound is no larger than d^{2^n} (Möller and Mora[150] and Giusti[82]).

(c) $D(n, d) \leq d^{2^n}$ (Dubé[66]).

4. Lower bounds $D(n, d)$, $D'(n, d)$, $I(n, d)$ and $S(n, d)$:

(a) $D(n, d \geq D'(n, d)$ (Yap[214]).

(b) $D'(n, d) \geq \Omega(d^{2^n})$ (Möller and Mora[150] and Huynh[103]).

(c) $I(n, d) \geq d^{2^{n'}}$ and $S(n, d) \geq d^{2^{n'}}$, where $n' \approx n/10$ (Mayr and Meyer[143] and Bayer and Stillman[18]).

(d) $I(n, d) \geq d^{2^{n''}}$ and $S(n, d) \geq d^{2^{n''}}$, where $n'' \approx n/2$ (Yap[214]).

One interesting open question is to close the gap in the following bounds:

$$d^{2^{n/2}} \leq S(n, d) \leq d^{2^{(\log 3/ \log 4)n}}.$$

However, much less is known for the case when the underlying ring of polynomials is over the integers $\mathbb{Z}[x_1, \ldots, x_n]$. Let $D(n, d)$ and $I(n, d)$ denote the degree bounds in this case as earlier. Gallo and Mishra[79] have recently shown that

$$D(n, d) \leq F_{4n+8}(1+\max(n, c, d, m)) \quad \text{and} \quad I(n, d) \leq F_{4n+8}(1+\max(n, c, d, m)),$$

where c and d are the coefficient and degree bounds, respectively, on the input polynomials and F_k is the kth function in the Wainer hierarchy. Note that if n, the number of variables, is assumed to be fixed, then these are primitive recursive bounds.

The set of applications discussed in this chapter are taken from the papers by Buchberger [33], Gianni et al. [81], Spear [193] and some unpublished course notes of Bayer and Stillman.

Problems 3.4 and 3.10 are based on some results in Dubé et al. [64]; Problem 3.7 is taken from Gianni et al. [81]; Problem 3.8 is from Gallo and Mishra [79]; Problems 3.9, 3.11, 3.12 and 3.14 are based on the results of Buchberger [33] (also see Mishra and Yap [149]) and Problem 3.18 is due to Schwartz [183].

In this chapter, what we refer to as a Gröbner basis is sometimes called a "weak Gröbner basis" in order to differentiate it from a stronger form, which has the following two properties (and depends on the associated reduction r):

$G \subseteq R$ *is a "strong Gröbner basis" of* (G), *if*

1. $\left(\forall f \in (G) \right) \left[\text{NF}_G^r(f) = 0 \right]$ *and*

2. $\left(\forall f \in R \right) \left[|\text{NF}_G^r(f)| = 1 \right].$

That is, every element of the ring reduces to a unique normal form, which is 0, if additionally the element is in the ideal. The Gröbner bases defined in this chapter only satisfy the first condition. Existence, construction and properties of strong Gröbner bases have been studied extensively; see Kapur and Narendran [115].

Chapter 4

Solving Systems of Polynomial Equations

4.1 Introduction

The Gröbner basis algorithm can be seen to be a *generalization* of the classical Gaussian elimination algorithm from a set of linear multivariate polynomials to an arbitrary set of multivariate polynomials. The S-polynomial and reduction processes take the place of the *pivoting* step of the Gaussian algorithm. Taking this analogy much further, one can devise a constructive procedure to compute the set of solutions of a system of arbitrary multivariate polynomial equations:

$$
\begin{aligned}
f_1(x_1, \ldots, x_n) &= 0, \\
f_2(x_1, \ldots, x_n) &= 0, \\
&\vdots \\
f_r(x_1, \ldots, x_n) &= 0,
\end{aligned}
$$

i.e., compute the set of points where all the polynomials vanish:

$$
\Big\{ \langle \xi_1, \ldots, \xi_n \rangle \ : \ f_i(\xi_1, \ldots, \xi_n) = 0, \text{ for all } 1 \le i \le r \Big\}.
$$

In this chapter, we shall explore this process in greater details.

Just as the Gaussian algorithm produces a triangular set of linear equations, the Gröbner basis algorithm under the purely lexicographic ordering also produces a *triangular set* of polynomials, where the concept of a triangular set is suitably generalized. Roughly speaking, the constructed basis can be partitioned into classes of polynomial systems, where the last class involves only the last variable, the class before the last involves only the

133

last two variables, etc., and each of these classes also satisfies certain additional algebraic properties in order to guarantee that the set of solutions of the last k classes contain the set of solutions of the last $(k + 1)$ classes. At this point, it is not hard to see how to obtain the set of solutions of the original system of polynomial equations by a simple *back substitution* process: first solve the last class of univariate polynomials; then substitute each of these solutions in the class of polynomials immediately preceding it, thus obtaining a set of univariate polynomials, which can now be easily solved, and so on.

These intuitions have to be clearly formalized. We shall first define the concept of a *triangular set* in the general setting and study how such a triangular set can be computed using the Gröbner basis algorithm of the previous chapter. After a short digression into algebraic geometry, we shall describe the complete algorithms to decide if a system of equations is solvable and to solve the system of equations, in the special case when it has finitely many solutions. A key lemma from algebraic geometry, *Hilbert's Nullstellensatz*, plays an important role here and will be presented in detail.

4.2   Triangular Set

Let $G \subset S[x_1, \ldots, x_n]$ be a finite set of polynomials. Let the set G be partitioned into $(n + 1)$ classes $G_0, G_1, \ldots, G_n$ as follows:

$$
\begin{aligned}
G_0 \;=\;& G \cap S[x_1, x_2, \ldots, x_n] \setminus S[x_2, \ldots, x_n] \\
=\;& \text{the set of polynomials in } G \text{ involving the variable } x_1, \\
& \text{and possibly, the variables } x_2, \ldots, x_n. \\
G_1 \;=\;& G \cap S[x_2, x_3, \ldots, x_n] \setminus S[x_3, \ldots, x_n] \\
=\;& \text{the set of polynomials in } G \text{ involving the variable } x_2, \\
& \text{and possibly, the variables } x_3, \ldots, x_n.
\end{aligned}
$$

$$
\vdots
$$

$$
\begin{aligned}
G_{n-1} \;=\;& G \cap S[x_n] \setminus S \\
=\;& \text{the set of polynomials in } G \text{ involving the variable } x_n. \\
G_n \;=\;& G \cap S \\
=\;& \text{the set of constant polynomials in } G.
\end{aligned}
$$

That is, G_i is the polynomials in G that contain x_{i+1} but do not contain any x_j for $j \leq i$.

Definition 4.2.1 (Triangular Form) The ordered set of polynomials consisting of polynomials in G_0 followed by polynomials in G_1 and so on up to G_n is said to be a *triangular form* of G. □

Definition 4.2.2 (Strongly Triangular Form) Let K be a field, and $G \subset K[x_1, \ldots, x_n]$ a finite subset of $K[x_1, \ldots, x_n]$. We say a triangular form of G is in *strongly triangular form* if

1. $(G_n) = (G \cap K) = (0)$, and

2. For each i $(0 \le i < n)$, there is a $g_i \in G_i$ containing a monomial of the form
$$a\, x_{i+1}^d, \qquad \text{where } a \in K \text{ and } d > 0. □$$

For a given set of polynomials G, if the generators of (G) can be put into a strongly triangular form, then we shall show that there is a finite, nonempty set of common zeros for the system of polynomial equations given by G. While this statement needs to be made formal, first, note that every element in the ideal (G) must vanish at every common zero of G. Therefore we see that any other basis of (G) must have exactly the same set of zeros as G. Intuitively, condition 1 tells us that the set is nonempty as otherwise we have that a (nonzero) constant is equal to zero. Condition 2 tells us that the set has a finite number of common zeros, as the following example shows:

Example 4.2.3 Consider three systems of polynomial equations: G', G'' and $G''' \subseteq \mathbb{C}[x_1, x_2]$, in their triangular forms:

$$
\begin{aligned}
G' &= \{x_1 x_2 - x_2, \ x_2^2 - 1\}, \\
G'' &= \{x_1 x_2 - x_2, \ x_2^2\}, \quad \text{and} \\
G''' &= \{x_1 x_2 - x_2\}.
\end{aligned}
$$

Just by looking at the polynomials in G_0', G_0'' or G_0''', we cannot tell whether the system of equations will have finitely many zeroes or not.

- In the first case, x_2 can take the values $+1$ and -1, since $x_2^2 = 1$. We see that, after substituting $x_2 = +1$ in the equation $x_1 x_2 - x_2$, one of the common zeroes of G' is $(+1, +1)$, and after substituting $x_2 = -1$ in the same equation $x_1 x_2 - x_2$, the other common zero is $(+1, -1)$. Thus G' has finitely many common zeroes. In fact (G') has a basis
$$\{x_1 - 1, \ x_2^2 - 1\},$$
and this basis is in strongly triangular form.

- In the second case, x_2 can take the value 0 (with multiplicity 2), since $x_2^2 = 0$. We see that, when we substitute $x_2 = 0$ in the equation $x_1 x_2 - x_2$, the equation becomes identically zero, thus showing that for all $\xi \in \mathbb{C}$, $(\xi, 0)$ is a common zero. Thus G'' has infinitely many zeroes. In fact, G'' cannot be written in a strongly triangular form.

- In the third case, we see that for all ξ, $\zeta \in \mathbb{C}$, G''' vanishes at $(\xi, 0)$ and $(1, \zeta)$. Again G''' has infinitely many zeroes, and G''' cannot be written in a strongly triangular form. $\square$

Definition 4.2.4 (Elimination Ideal) Let $I \subseteq S[x_1, \ldots, x_n]$ be an ideal in the polynomial ring $S[x_1, \ldots, x_n]$. We define the ith *elimination ideal of I*, I_i, to be:

$$I_i = I \cap S[x_{i+1}, \ldots, x_n], \quad (0 \leq i \leq n).$$

That is,

$$
\begin{aligned}
I_0 &= I \\
I_1 &= I \cap S[x_2, \ldots, x_n] \\
&= \text{the contraction of } I \text{ to the subring } S[x_2, \ldots, x_n]. \\
&\vdots \\
I_{n-1} &= I \cap S[x_n] \\
&= \text{the contraction of } I \text{ to the subring } S[x_n]. \\
I_n &= I \cap S \\
&= \text{the contraction of } I \text{ to the subring } S. \quad \square
\end{aligned}
$$

Now, given a set of polynomial equations $\{f_1 = 0, \ldots, f_r = 0\}$, we would like to generate a new basis $G = \{g_1, \ldots, g_s\}$ for the ideal $I = (f_1, \ldots, f_r)$ such that when we consider the triangular form of G, it has the additional algebraic property that

$$\bigcup_{j=i}^{n} G_j \text{ is a basis for the } i^{\text{th}} \text{ elimination ideal } I_i.$$

Since $I_{i-1} \supseteq I_i$, we shall see that this implies that the set of solutions of the system of polynomials given by $\bigcup_{j=i}^{n} G_j$ contains the set of solutions of $\bigcup_{j=i-1}^{n} G_j$, as desired. As a matter of fact, we shall achieve a somewhat stronger property: our computed basis G will be a Gröbner basis of I and the set $\bigcup_{j=i}^{n} G_j$ will also be a Gröbner basis of I_i with respect to the same lexicographic admissible ordering.

In order to simplify our proofs, we shall use the following generalization of lexicographic ordering.

Definition 4.2.5 (A Generalized Lexicographic Ordering) Consider
the ring $R = S[X, Y] = S[x_1, \ldots, x_n, y_1, \ldots, y_m]$. Let $\underset{X}{>}$, $\underset{Y}{>}$ be two admissible orderings on $PP(X)$ and $PP(Y)$, respectively.

Define the admissible ordering $\underset{L}{>}$ on $PP(X, Y)$ as follows:

$$pq \underset{L}{>} p'q' \quad \begin{cases} \text{if } p \underset{X}{>} p' \text{ or} \\ \text{if } p = p' \text{ and } q \underset{Y}{>} q', \end{cases}$$

where $p, p' \in PP(X)$ and $q, q' \in PP(Y)$. $\quad \square$

Theorem 4.2.1 *If G is a Gröbner basis for I with respect to $\underset{L}{>}$ in $S[X, Y]$,
then $G \cap S[Y]$ is a Gröbner basis for $I \cap S[Y]$ with respect to $\underset{Y}{>}$ in $S[Y]$.*

PROOF.
(1) By the definition of $\underset{L}{>}$, we have, for every $f \in S[X, Y]$,

$$\mathrm{Hmono}_L(f) \in S[Y] \quad \Leftrightarrow \quad f \in S[Y];$$

that is, a polynomial whose head term is in $PP(Y)$ cannot include any
power product involving $x_i \in X$. Hence

$$\begin{aligned}
\mathrm{Head}_Y(G \cap S[Y]) &= \mathrm{Head}_L(G \cap S[Y]) \\
&= \mathrm{Head}_L(G) \cap S[Y] = \mathrm{Head}_L(I) \cap S[Y] \\
&\qquad \text{(Since } G \text{ is a Gröbner basis for } I) \\
&= \mathrm{Head}_L(I \cap S[Y]) = \mathrm{Head}_Y(I \cap S[Y]).
\end{aligned}$$

(2) Since $G \subseteq I$, clearly $G \cap S[Y] \subseteq I \cap S[Y]$.
(3) Thus $G \cap S[Y]$ is also a Gröbner basis for $I\{S[Y]\}$ with respect to
$\underset{Y}{>}$ in $S[Y]$. $\quad \square$

In other words, it is easy to find a basis for a contraction if $\underset{L}{>}$ preserves
the underlying admissible orderings. A useful corollary to the theorem is:

Corollary 4.2.2 *If G is a Gröbner basis of I with respect to $\underset{LEX}{>}$ in $S[x_1,
\ldots, x_n]$ (assuming $x_1 \underset{LEX}{>} \cdots \underset{LEX}{>} x_n$), then for each $i = 0, \ldots, n$,*

1. *$G \cap S[x_{i+1}, \ldots, x_n]$ is a Gröbner basis for $I \cap S[x_{i+1}, \ldots, x_n]$ with
   respect to $\underset{LEX}{>}$ in $S[x_{i+1}, \ldots, x_n]$ (assuming $x_{i+1} \underset{LEX}{>} \cdots \underset{LEX}{>} x_n$).*

2. *Equivalently, $\bigcup_{j=i}^{n} G_j$ is a Gröbner basis for the ith elimination ideal
   I_i with respect to $\underset{LEX}{>}$.* $\quad \square$

As a result of the preceding corollary, we may simply refer to a Gröbner
basis of an ideal with respect to the purely lexicographic admissible ordering
as its *triangular set*.

4.3   Some Algebraic Geometry

From now on, we will only consider polynomial rings $L[x_1, \ldots, x_n]$ where L is an algebraically closed field.

Definition 4.3.1 (Algebraically Closed Field) A field L is called *algebraically closed* if every polynomial in $L[x]$ splits into linear factors, i.e., every nonconstant polynomial in $L[x]$ has a zero in L.   □

Example 4.3.2 (1) $\mathbb{C}$ = Field of complex numbers is algebraically closed.
   (2) $\mathbb{R}$ = Field of reals is not an algebraically closed field, since for example $x^2 + 1 \in \mathbb{R}[x]$ has no real zero.   □

   In general, we could study the geometric properties by considering any arbitrary field K. Then, of course, we would have to answer the question: what do we mean by a solution? That is, where do the solutions live? For instance, we could run into the problem that if we consider the field of rational numbers, $K = \mathbb{Q}$, then an equation of the kind $x^2 + y^2 + z^2 = 1$ has no solution. The usual remedy is to take solutions whose components all lie in an algebraically closed extension of the field K. Sometimes, even more generality is necessary: one considers an extension field Ω which is not only algebraically closed, but has the additional property that the degree of transcendency of Ω over K is infinite. The field Ω is called a *universal domain*. However, we have simply opted to ignore these difficulties by working over a sufficiently general field.
   We shall use the following notations:

$$
\begin{aligned}
A &= L[x_1, \ldots, x_n] = \text{Polynomial ring in } n \text{ variables over } L. \\
\mathbf{A}^n &= \text{Affine } n\text{-space with coordinates in } L, \\
& \quad (n\text{-tuples of elements in } L).
\end{aligned}
$$

Definition 4.3.3 (Zero Set, Zero Map) Let $F \subseteq A$ be a subset of polynomials in A. Then the set

$$
\mathcal{Z}(F) = \left\{ P \in \mathbf{A}^n : \left(\forall f \in F \right) \left[f(P) = 0 \right] \right\},
$$

is the *zero set* of F. The map

$$
\begin{aligned}
\mathcal{Z} &: \{\text{Subsets of } A\} \to \{\text{Subsets of } \mathbf{A}^n\} \\
&: F \mapsto \mathcal{Z}(F)
\end{aligned}
$$

is the *zero map*.   □

   Some authors also refer to a zero set as a variety. In consistence with the accepted terminology, we shall not make any distinction between zero sets and varieties.

Definition 4.3.4 (Ideal, Ideal Map) Let $X \subseteq \mathbf{A}^n$ be a set of points in the affine n-space, $\mathbf{A}^n$. Then the ideal

$$\mathcal{I}(X) \;=\; \left\{ f \in A \,:\, \left(\forall\, P \in X \right) \left[f(P) = 0 \right] \right\},$$

is the *ideal* of X.

$\Big($ Note:

$$\left(\forall\, P \in X \right) \left[f(P) = 0 \;\wedge\; g(P) = 0 \right]$$
$$\Rightarrow \;\; \left(\forall\, P \in X \right) \left[(f - g)(P) = 0 \right],$$

and

$$\left(\forall\, P \in X \right) \left[f(P) = 0 \right]$$
$$\Rightarrow \;\; \left(\forall\, h \in A \right) \left(\forall\, P \in X \right) \left[(hf)(P) = 0 \right],$$

i.e.,

$$\left(\forall\, f, g \in \mathcal{I}(X) \right) \left(\forall\, h \in A \right) \left[f - g \in \mathcal{I}(X) \;\; \text{and} \;\; hf \in \mathcal{I}(X) \right].$$

Thus, $\mathcal{I}(X)$ is in fact an ideal. $\Big)$
    The map

$$\mathcal{I} \;:\; \{\text{Subsets of } \mathbf{A}^n\} \to \{\text{Subsets of } A\}$$
$$:\; X \mapsto \mathcal{I}(X)$$

is the *ideal map*. $\square$

Definition 4.3.5 (Algebraic Set) A set $X \subseteq \mathbf{A}^n$ is said to be an *algebraic set* if X is a zero set of some set of polynomials $F \subseteq A$.

$$X = \mathcal{Z}(F).   \square$$

The following proposition shows that the zero set of a system of polynomials does not change as we augment this set by additional polynomials generated by linear combinations of the original polynomials. In other words, the geometric problem remains unchanged if we replace the system of polynomials by the ideal they generate or if we replace it by another system of generators for their ideal.

Proposition 4.3.1 *Let $F \subseteq A$ be a basis for some ideal $I \subseteq A$, i.e., $(F) = I$. Then the zero set of F and the zero set of I are the same.*

$$\mathcal{Z}(F) = \mathcal{Z}(I).$$

PROOF.
(1) Since $F \subseteq I$, we immediately see that

$$\mathcal{Z}(F) \supseteq \mathcal{Z}(I).$$

That is,

$$P \in \mathcal{Z}(I) \;\Rightarrow\; \left(\forall f \in I\right)\left[f(P) = 0\right]$$
$$\Rightarrow\; \left(\forall f \in F\right)\left[f(P) = 0\right] \;\Rightarrow\; P \in \mathcal{Z}(F).$$

(2) Conversely, let $F = \{f_1, \ldots, f_r\}$.

$$P \in \mathcal{Z}(F) \;\Rightarrow\; f_1(P) = \cdots = f_r(P) = 0$$
$$\Rightarrow\; \left(\forall f = h_1 f_1 + \cdots + h_r f_r\right)\left[f(P) = 0\right]$$
$$\Rightarrow\; \left(\forall f \in I\right)\left[f(P) = 0\right] \;\Rightarrow\; P \in \mathcal{Z}(I). \quad \square$$

Thus, we could have defined an *algebraic set* to be the zero set of some ideal. Note that an empty set $\emptyset$ is an algebraic set as it is the zero set of the improper ideal $A = (1)$ and $\mathbf{A}^n$ is the zero set of the zero ideal (0). Note that it is possible for different ideals to define the same algebraic set. Also algebraic sets are closed under set theoretic operations such as *union* and *intersection*.

Following properties can be demonstrated trivially; we leave the proof as an exercise for the readers:

Proposition 4.3.2 *We have the following:*

1. *If I and J are ideals, then*

$$I \subseteq J \;\Rightarrow\; \mathcal{Z}(I) \supseteq \mathcal{Z}(J).$$

2. *If I and J are ideals, then $\mathcal{Z}(I) \cup \mathcal{Z}(J)$ and $\mathcal{Z}(I) \cap \mathcal{Z}(J)$ are algebraic sets and*

$$\mathcal{Z}(I) \cup \mathcal{Z}(J) \;=\; \mathcal{Z}(I \cap J) = \mathcal{Z}(I \cdot J),$$
$$\mathcal{Z}(I) \cap \mathcal{Z}(J) \;=\; \mathcal{Z}(I + J). \quad \square$$

Proposition 4.3.3 *Let $A = L[x_1, x_2, \ldots, x_n]$ and $B = L[x_2, \ldots, x_n]$ be two polynomial rings. Let Π be a projection map from $\mathbf{A}^n$ to $\mathbf{A}^{n-1}$, defined as follows:*

$$\Pi \ : \ \mathbf{A}^n \rightarrow \mathbf{A}^{n-1}$$
$$: \ \langle \xi_1, \xi_2, \ldots, \xi_n \rangle \mapsto (\xi_2, \ldots, \xi_n).$$

If $I \subseteq A$ is an ideal in A, and $J = I \cap B$ a contraction of I to B, then

$$\Pi(\mathcal{Z}(I)) \subseteq \mathcal{Z}(J). \quad \square$$

Finally,

Proposition 4.3.4 *Let $V \subseteq \mathbf{A}^n$ and $W \subseteq \mathbf{A}^m$ be algebraic sets. Then the product $V \times W \subseteq \mathbf{A}^{n+m}$,*

$$V \times W = \Big\{ \langle \xi_1, \ldots, \xi_n, \zeta_1, \ldots, \zeta_m \rangle \in \mathbf{A}^{n+m} :$$
$$\langle \xi_1, \ldots, \xi_n \rangle \in V \text{ and } \langle \zeta_1, \ldots, \zeta_m \rangle \in W \Big\}$$

is also an algebraic set. Furthermore,

$$\mathcal{I}(V \times W) = IL[x_1, \ldots, x_n, y_1, \ldots, y_m] + JL[x_1, \ldots, x_n, y_1, \ldots, y_m],$$

where I is the ideal of V in $L[x_1, \ldots, x_n]$ and J is the ideal of W in $L[y_1, \ldots, y_m]$. $\square$

4.3.1 Dimension of an Ideal

Definition 4.3.6 (Dimension) Let I be an ideal in the ring $K[x_1, \ldots, x_n]$, where K is an arbitrary field. Assume that the set of variables $x_{\pi(1)} = u_1, \ldots, x_{\pi(l)} = u_l$ forms the largest subset of $\{x_1, \ldots, x_n\}$ such that

$$I \cap K[u_1, \ldots, u_l] = (0),$$

i.e., there is no nontrivial relation among the u_i's.

Then $u_1, \ldots, u_l$ are said to be the *independent variables* with respect to I and the remaining $r = (n - l)$ variables, $x_{\pi(l+1)} = v_1, \ldots, x_{\pi(n)} = v_r$ are the *dependent variables* with respect to I.

Also l is said to be the *dimension* of the ideal I ($\dim I = l$), and $r = (n - l)$, its *codimension*. $\square$

Suppose, now, that the variables $x_1, \ldots, x_n$ are so ordered that the dependent variables $v_1, \ldots, v_r$ appear earlier than the independent variables $u_1, \ldots, u_l$ in the sequence, and that we write the polynomial ring as $K[v_1, \ldots, v_r, u_1, \ldots, u_l] = K[V, U]$. As in our earlier definition, consider the following generalized lexicographic ordering:

Let $\underset{V}{>}$, $\underset{U}{>}$ be two admissible orderings on $PP(V)$ and $PP(U)$, respectively. The admissible ordering $\underset{L}{>}$ on $PP(V,U)$ is derived as follows: For all $p, p' \in PP(V)$ and $q, q' \in PP(U)$,

$$pq \underset{L}{>} p'q' \qquad \text{if } p \underset{V}{>} p' \text{ or if } p = p' \text{ and } q \underset{U}{>} q'.$$

Now by Theorem 4.2.1, we see that if G is a Gröbner basis for I with respect to $\underset{L}{>}$ in $K[V,U]$, then $G \cap K[U]$ is a Gröbner basis for $I \cap K[U] = (0)$ with respect to $\underset{U}{>}$ in $K[U]$. In particular, if G is a reduced Gröbner basis then $G \cap K[U]$ is either an empty set or $\{0\}$.

Thus by considering all possible partitions of the set of variables X into two disjoint subsets V and U, and by computing the Gröbner basis with respect to a lexicographic ordering such that

$$\left(\forall \, v \in V \right) \left(\forall \, u \in U \right) \left[v \underset{\text{LEX}}{>} u \right]$$

one can compute the set of independent variables and hence the dimension of the ideal I.

While the above argument shows that the independent variables and hence the dimension of an ideal can be *effectively* computed, the procedure outlined here is not the most efficient; some of the recent results [61] have improved the computational complexity of the problem significantly, both in sequential and parallel computational domains.

4.3.2   Solvability: Hilbert's Nullstellensatz

Next, we shall develop a key theorem from algebraic geometry: *Hilbert's Nullstellensatz*. Using this theorem, we shall see how Gröbner bases can be advantageously used to settle several important questions about solvability, number of zeros, and, finally, finding the zeros of a system of polynomials F.

Theorem 4.3.5 (Hilbert's Nullstellensatz) *If L is algebraically closed and $I \subset A = L[x_1, \ldots, x_n]$ is an ideal, then*

$$I = L[x_1, \ldots, x_n] \quad \text{if and only if} \quad \mathcal{Z}(I) = \emptyset.$$

PROOF SKETCH.

If $I = A$, then $I = (1)$ and it is easily seen that $\mathcal{Z}(I) = \emptyset$.

We prove the converse by contradiction. Let M be a maximal ideal containing I such that $1 \notin M$:

$$I \subseteq M \subsetneq (1).$$

Since A is Noetherian, such an ideal exists. (Show that this is a consequence of the *ascending chain condition*).

The residue class ring $F = A/M$ has no improper ideal and has a unit; thus, it is a field.

To every polynomial $f(x_1, \ldots, x_n) \in A$ assign an element of the residue class ring $F = A/M$, given by the natural ring homomorphism. Since $M \neq A$, every element a of L will correspond to the distinct element $\bar{a} = a + M$. [Otherwise, if $a \neq b$ ($a, b \in L$) and $\bar{a} = \bar{b}$, then $a - b \in M$; so $1 = (a - b)(a - b)^{-1}$ would be $\in M$.]

Let $\langle \overline{x_1}, \ldots, \overline{x_n} \rangle \in F^n$ be the images of $\langle x_1, \ldots, x_n \rangle$ under the natural ring homomorphism from A into A/M. Since, the ring operations in A/M are naturally induced from the same operations in A, and $a \in L$ maps into itself, we see that, for every $f \in I \subseteq M$, $f(\overline{x_1}, \ldots, \overline{x_n}) = 0$, i.e., I has a zero in F^n.

But F contains the field L (up to an isomorphism) and F arises from L through ring adjunction of the residue classes $\overline{x_i}$ of x_i. Since L is algebraically closed, there is an L-homomorphism

$$\phi: F \to L.$$

Thus

$$\left(\vee f \in I\right) \left[f(\phi(\overline{x_1}), \ldots, \phi(\overline{x_n})) = 0\right].$$

Hence $\langle \phi(x_1), \ldots, \phi(x_n) \rangle \in L^n$ is in $\mathcal{Z}(I)$ and $\mathcal{Z}(I) \neq \emptyset$. ⊔

An immediate corollary of Nullstellensatz is the following:

Corollary 4.3.6 *Let* $F \subseteq L[x_1, \ldots, x_n]$, *where* L *is an algebraically closed field. Then*

$$\mathcal{Z}(F) = \emptyset \quad \text{iff} \quad 1 \in (F)$$

PROOF.

($\Rightarrow$)

$$\begin{aligned}
\mathcal{Z}(F) = \emptyset \quad &\Rightarrow \quad \mathcal{Z}((F)) = \emptyset \\
&\Rightarrow \quad (F) = L[x_1, \ldots, x_n] \\
&\Rightarrow \quad 1 \in (F).
\end{aligned}$$

($\Leftarrow$)

$$\begin{aligned}
1 \in (F) \wedge \mathcal{Z}(F) \neq \emptyset \quad &\Rightarrow \quad \left(\exists P \in \mathcal{Z}(F)\right)\left[1(P) = 1 = 0\right] \\
&\Rightarrow \quad \text{Contradiction, since, in } L, 1 \neq 0. \quad \square
\end{aligned}$$

Definition 4.3.7 (Solvable System of Polynomials) Let $F \subseteq L[x_1, \ldots, x_n]$ be a system of polynomials. F is said to be *solvable* if the system of polynomial equations has a common zero, i.e.,

$$\text{if } \mathcal{Z}(F) \neq \emptyset. \quad \square$$

Corollary 4.3.7 *Let $F \subseteq L[x_1, \ldots, x_n]$ and G be a Gröbner basis for (F). Then F is unsolvable if and only if there is a nonzero $c \in G \cap L$.*

PROOF.

$(\Rightarrow)$

$$\mathcal{Z}(F) = \emptyset \quad \Rightarrow \quad 1 \in (F) \quad \Rightarrow \quad 1 \xrightarrow[*]{G,h} 0$$
$$\Rightarrow \quad \left(\exists\, c \neq 0, c \in L\right) \left[c \in G\right]$$
$$\Rightarrow \quad \left(\exists\, c \neq 0\right) \left[c \in G \cap L\right].$$

$(\Leftarrow)$

$$c \in G \cap L, c \neq 0 \quad \Rightarrow \quad c^{-1}c = 1 \in (G)$$
$$\Rightarrow \quad 1 \in (F) \quad \Rightarrow \quad \mathcal{Z}(F) = \emptyset. \quad \square$$

Another version of Hilbert's Nullstellensatz that we will find useful is as follows:

Theorem 4.3.8 *Let $f \in L[x_1, \ldots, x_n]$, where L is an algebraically closed field. Let $F = \{f_1, \ldots, f_r\} \subseteq L[x_1, \ldots, x_n]$. Then if f vanishes at all common zeros of F, there is some natural number q such that $f^q \in (F)$, i.e., $f \in \sqrt{(F)}$.*

PROOF.

(1) $f = 0$. Then as $0 \in (F)$, there is nothing to prove.

(2) $f \neq 0$. Consider the polynomials $f_1, \ldots, f_r, 1 - zf \in L[x_1, \ldots, x_n, z]$. These do not have a common zero, since if $P = \langle \xi_1, \ldots, \xi_n, \xi \rangle \in \mathbf{A}^{n+1}$ is a common zero of $f_1, \ldots, f_r$, then

$$(1 - zf)(P) = 1 - \xi \cdot f(\xi_1, \ldots, \xi_n) = 1 \neq 0.$$

By the first form of this theorem, we know that

$1 \in (f_1, \ldots, f_r, 1 - zf)$
$\Rightarrow 1 = g_1 f_1 + \cdots + g_r f_r + g(1 - zf)$
where $g_1, \ldots, g_r, g \in L[x_1, \ldots, x_n, z]$

$\Rightarrow$ Substitute $1/f$ for z and the last term disappears:

$$1 = \frac{g_1'}{f^{q_1}} f_1 + \cdots + \frac{g_r'}{f^{q_r}} f_r$$

where $g_1', \ldots, g_r' \in L[x_1, \ldots, x_n]$

$$\Rightarrow f^q = g_1'' f_1 + \cdots + g_r'' f_r$$

where $g_1'', \ldots, g_r'' \in L[x_1, \ldots, x_n]$ and $q = \max\{q_1, \ldots, q_r\}$

$$\Rightarrow f^q \in (F). \quad \square$$

That Theorem 4.3.8 implies Theorem 4.3.5 follows from the following observation:

$$\mathcal{Z}(I) = \emptyset \quad \Leftrightarrow \quad 1 \text{ vanishes at every common zero of } I$$
$$\Leftrightarrow \quad 1 \in I \quad \Leftrightarrow \quad I = (1) = L[x_1, \ldots, x_n].$$

Application: Solvability

> SOLVABILITY(F)
> **Input:** $F = \{f_1, \ldots, f_r\} \subseteq L[x_1, \ldots, x_n]$,
> $L = $ An algebraically closed field.
> **Output:** TRUE, if F has a solution in $\mathbf{A}^n$.

Compute G, the Gröbner basis of (F). Output FALSE, if there is a nonzero c in $G \cap L$; otherwise return TRUE.

4.3.3   Finite Solvability

Definition 4.3.8 (Finite Solvability) Let $F \subset L[x_1, \ldots, x_n]$ be a system of polynomials. F is said to be *finitely solvable* if:

1. F is solvable.

2. The system of polynomial equations has finitely many zeroes. $\square$

We will see that this exactly corresponds to the case when the ideal generated by F is a proper *zero-dimensional* ideal. Also, we will see that this corresponds exactly to the case when we can find a set of generators of (F), expressible in a strongly triangular form.

Theorem 4.3.9 *Let $F \subset L[x_1, \ldots, x_n]$ be a system of polynomial equations. Then the following three statements are equivalent:*

1. *F is finitely solvable;*

2. *(F) is a proper zero-dimensional ideal; and*

3. *If G is a Gröbner basis of (F) with respect to $\underset{\text{LEX}}{>}$, then G can be expressed in strongly triangular form.*

PROOF.

$(1 \Rightarrow 2)$:

As F is solvable, $(F) \neq (1)$, i.e., $(F) \cap L = (0)$. Assume that

$$\langle \xi_{1,1}, \ldots, \xi_{1,n} \rangle$$
$$\vdots$$
$$\langle \xi_{m,1}, \ldots, \xi_{m,n} \rangle$$

are the finite set of common zeros of F. Define

$$f(x_i) = (x_i - \xi_{1,i}) \cdots (x_i - \xi_{m,i}).$$

We see that $f(x_i)$ is a degree m univariate polynomial in x_i that vanishes at all common zeroes of F. Thus

$$\left(\exists\, q > 0 \right) \left[f(x_i)^q \in (F) \right].$$

Thus,

$$(F) \cap L[x_i] \neq (0),$$

and (F) is *zero-dimensional*. Also, since $(0) \subsetneq (F) \subsetneq (1)$, (F) is also proper.

$(2 \Rightarrow 3)$:

Since (F) is a proper zero-dimensional ideal, we have $(F) \cap L = (0)$, and

$$\left(\forall\, x_i \right) \left[(F) \cap L[x_i] \neq (0) \right],$$

i.e.,

$$\left(\forall\, x_i \right) \left(\exists\, f(x_i) \in L[x_i] \right) \left[f(x_i) \in (F) \right].$$

Since G is a Gröbner basis of (F), we see that

$$\mathrm{Hmono}(f(x_i)) = x_i^{D_i} \in \mathrm{Head}(G).$$

Together with the fact that $(G \cap L) = 0$, we get

$$\left(\exists\, g_i \in G \right) \left[\mathrm{Hterm}(g) = x_i^{d_i} \right], \quad d_i \leq D_i.$$

Since we have chosen $\underset{\mathrm{LEX}}{>}$ as our admissible ordering,

$$g_i \in L[x_i, \ldots, x_n] \setminus L[x_i + 1, \ldots, x_n]$$

and it follows that for all i $(0 \leq i < n)$ there exists a $g_{i+1} \in G_i$ such that g_{i+1} has a monomial of the form $a \cdot x_{i+1}^d$ ($a \in L$ and $d > 0$). Thus, G, a Gröbner basis of (F) with respect to $\underset{\mathrm{LEX}}{>}$, can be expressed in strongly triangular form.

$(3 \Rightarrow 1)$:

Let $I = (F) = (G)$, be the ideal generated by F. It follows that

$$\mathcal{Z}(I) = \mathcal{Z}(F) = \mathcal{Z}(G).$$

Thus it suffices to show that I is finitely solvable.

1. Since $(G \cap L) = I \cap L = (0)$, $1 \notin I$, and I is solvable.

2. We will prove by induction on i that for all i $(0 \le i < n)$, the ith elimination ideal, I_i has finitely many zeroes. We recall that by a previous theorem

$$I_i = (\widehat{G}_i)$$

where $\widehat{G}_i = \bigcup_{j=i}^{n} G_j$, and $\widehat{G}_i$ is in strongly triangular form.

- Base Case: $i = n - 1$.

G_{n-1} consists of univariate polynomials in x_n. Since G_{n-1} is strongly triangular, there is some polynomial $p(x_n)$ in G_{n-1} of maximum degree d_n. Thus $p(x_n)$ has finitely many zeros (at most d_n of them). Since we are looking for common zeros of I_{n-1}, and since $p(x_n) \in I_{n-1}$, we see that I_{n-1} has finitely many zeros (not more than d_n).

- Induction Case: $i < n - 1$.

By the inductive hypothesis, the $(i+1)^{\text{th}}$ elimination ideal I_{i+1} has finitely many zeroes, say D_{i+2} of them.

Let Π be the projection map defined as follows:

$$\Pi \;:\; \mathbf{A}^{n-i} \to \mathbf{A}^{n-i-1}$$
$$\;:\; \langle \xi_{i+1}, \xi_{i+2}, \ldots, \xi_n \rangle \mapsto \langle \xi_{i+2}, \ldots, \xi_n \rangle.$$

We partition the zero set of the ith elimination ideal I_i, $\mathcal{Z}(I_i)$ into equivalence classes under the following equivalence relation: $P, Q \in \mathcal{Z}(I_i)$

$$P \sim Q \quad \text{iff} \quad \Pi(P) = \Pi(Q).$$

By Theorem 4.3.3, and the inductive hypothesis, the number of equivalence classes is finite, in fact, less than or equal to D_{i+2}. Let $p(x_{i+1}, x_{i+2}, \ldots, x_n) \in \widehat{G}_i$ be a polynomial containing a monomial of the form $a \cdot x_{i+1}^{d_{i+1}}$ ($a \in L$ and $d_{i+1} > 0$)—assume that d_{i+1} takes the highest possible value. If

$$[P]_\sim = \{Q \colon \Pi(Q) = \langle \xi_{i+2}, \ldots, \xi_n \rangle\}$$

is an equivalence class of P, a common zero of I_i, then ξ (where $Q = \langle \xi, \xi_{i+2}, \ldots, \xi_n \rangle \in [P]_\sim$) is a zero of the univariate polynomial $p(x_{i+1}, \xi_{i+1}, \ldots, \xi_n)$. Thus

$$|[P]_\sim| \le d_{i+1}$$

and I_i has finitely many zeros (not more than $d_{i+1} \cdot D_{i+2}$).

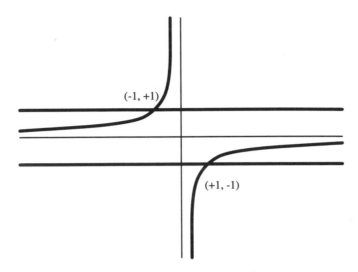

Figure 4.1: The zeros of $x_1x_2 + 1 = 0$ and $x_2^2 - 1 = 0$.

The above argument also provides an upper bound on the number of zeros of the system of polynomials F, which is

$$d_1 \cdot d_2 \cdots d_n$$

where d_i is the highest degree of a term of the form $x_i^{d_i}$ of a polynomial in G_{i-1}. $\square$

Example 4.3.9 Suppose we want to solve the following system of polynomial equations:

$$\{x_1x_2 + 1, \ x_2^2 - 1\} \subseteq \mathbb{C}[x_1, x_2].$$

The zeros of the system are $(-1, +1)$ and $(+1, -1)$, as can be seen from Figure 4.1.

Clearly the system is finitely solvable.

Now if we compute a Gröbner basis of the above system with respect to $\underset{\text{LEX}}{>}$ (with $x_1 \underset{\text{LEX}}{>} x_2$), then the resulting system is strongly triangular, as given below:

$$\{x_1 + x_2, \ x_2^2 - 1\}.$$

We solve for x_2 to get $x_2 = \{+1, -1\}$. After substituting these values for x_2 in the first equation, we get the solutions $(x_1, x_2) = \{(-1, +1), (+1, -1)\}$.

Application: Finite Solvability

FINITESOLVABILITY(F)
Input: $F = \{f_1, \ldots, f_r\} \subset L[x_1, \ldots, x_n]$,
$L = $ An algebraically closed field.
Output: TRUE, if F has finitely many solutions in $\mathbf{A}^n$.

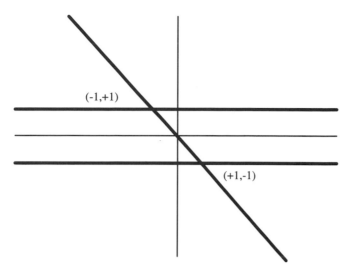

Figure 4.2: The zeros of $x_1 + x_2 = 0$ and $x_2^2 - 1 = 0$.

Compute G, the Gröbner basis of (F) with respect to $\underset{\text{LEX}}{>}$. Output TRUE, if G is solvable, and is in strongly triangular form; FALSE, otherwise.

4.4   Finding the Zeros

Now we are ready to gather all the ideas developed here and devise an algorithm to find the zeros of a system of polynomials. The algorithm works by successively computing the common zeros of the ith elimination ideal and then extending these to the common zeros of the $(i-1)^{\text{th}}$ ideal.

The algorithm involves computing the zeros of a univariate polynomial; while this is a hard problem for large-degree polynomials, the algorithm assumes this can be computed by some *oracle*. An interesting open problem, thus, is to study how this algorithm interfaces with various finite-precision (numeric) and infinite-precision (symbolic) algorithms available for computing the zeros of a univariate polynomial.

However, the main appeal of the following algorithm is that we can turn a multivariate problem into a sequence of univariate problems via the Gröbner basis.

FINDZEROS(F)

Input: $F = \{f_1, \ldots, f_r\} \subset L[x_1, \ldots, x_n]$,
                    $L = $ An algebraically closed field.
Output: The zeros of F in $\mathbf{A}^n$ if F is finitely solvable.

Compute G a Gröbner basis of (F) with respect to $\underset{\text{LEX}}{>}$;

if G is not in strongly triangular form then
        return with failure
end$\{$if $\}$;

$H := \{g \in G_{n-1}\}$;
$p_{n-1} := $ the GCD of the polynomials in H;
$X_{n-1} := \{\langle \xi_n \rangle \, : \, p(\xi_n) = 0\}$;

for $i := n - 1$ down to 1 loop
        $X_{i-1} := \emptyset$;

        for all $\langle \xi_{i+1}, \ldots, \xi_n \rangle \in X_i$ loop
                $H := \{g(x_i, \xi_{i+1}, \ldots, \xi_n) \, : \, g \in G_{i-1}\}$;
                $p_{i-1} := $ the GCD of the polynomials in H;

                if $p_{i-1} \notin L$ then
                        $X_{i-1} := X_{i-1} \cup$
                                $\{\langle \xi_i, \xi_{i+1}, \ldots, \xi_n \rangle \, : \, p_{i-1}(\xi_i) = 0\}$;
                end$\{$if $\}$;
        end$\{$loop $\}$;
end$\{$loop $\}$;

return (X_0);
end$\{$FINDZEROS$\}$ $\square$

Theorem 4.4.1 *Let $F = \{f_1, \ldots, f_r\} \subset L[x_1, \ldots, x_n]$ and L, an algebraically closed field. Assume that there is an effective procedure to compute
the zeros of a univariate polynomial in $L[x]$.*

Then in finite number of steps, the algorithm FINDZEROS *computes the
zeros of F in $\mathbf{A}^n$ if F is finitely solvable.*

PROOF.

The termination of the algorithm easily follows from the fact that there
are effective procedures to compute a Gröbner basis, to check if a system
is in strongly triangular form, to compute the GCD of a set of univariate
polynomials and to compute the zeros of a univariate polynomial.

Assume that F is finitely solvable. We want to show that

$$X_0 = \mathcal{Z}(F).$$

It is easily seen that every element of X_0 is a zero of (G) and thus of the polynomials in F: $X_0 \subseteq \mathcal{Z}(F)$.

To see the converse, we argue by induction on i that for all i $(0 \leq i < n)$,

$$\mathcal{Z}((F)_i) \subseteq X_i,$$

where $(F)_i$ is the ith elimination ideal of F.

- Base Case: $i = n - 1$.

By a previous theorem, we know that $(F)_{n-1} = (G_{n-1} \cup G_n) = (G_n)$, since $(G_n) = (0)$, by assumption. Since $G_{n-1} \subseteq L[x_n]$, a principal ideal domain, $(G_{n-1}) = (p_{n-1})$, where p_{n-1} is a GCD of G_{n-1}. Thus, if $\langle \xi_n \rangle$ is a zero of G_{n-1}, then $\langle \xi_n \rangle$ is also a zero of p_{n-1}, and $\langle \xi_n \rangle \in X_{n-1}$.

- Induction Case: $i < n - 1$.

By the inductive hypothesis, the zeros of $(F)_{i+1}$ are in X_{i+1}. Let Π be the projection map defined as follows:

$$\Pi \; : \; \mathbf{A}^{n-i} \rightarrow \mathbf{A}^{n-i-1}$$
$$: \; \langle \xi_{i+1}, \xi_{i+2}, \dots, \xi_n \rangle \mapsto \langle \xi_{i+2}, \dots, \xi_n \rangle.$$

Let $\langle \xi_{i+1}, \xi_{i+2}, \dots, \xi_n \rangle$ be a zero of $(F)_i$. Then

$$\langle \xi_{i+2}, \dots, \xi_n \rangle = \Pi(\langle \xi_{i+1}, \xi_{i+2}, \dots, \xi_n \rangle) \in \mathcal{Z}((F)_{i+1}) \subseteq X_{i+1}.$$

Since

$$(F)_i = \left(\bigcup_{j=i}^{n} G_j \right),$$

we see that $\langle \xi_{i+1}, \xi_{i+2}, \dots, \xi_n \rangle$ is a zero of G_i, and $\langle \xi_i \rangle$ is a zero of the set

$$H = \{ g(x_{i+1}, \xi_{i+2}, \dots, \xi_n) : g \in G_i \}.$$

But since $H \subseteq L[x_{i+1}]$, a principal ideal domain, we see that $\langle \xi_{i+1} \rangle$ is also a zero of p_i, the GCD of the polynomials in H.

Thus

$$\langle \xi_{i+1}, \xi_{i+2}, \dots, \xi_n \rangle \in X_i,$$

and we see that

$$X_0 \subseteq \mathcal{Z}(F) = \mathcal{Z}((F)_0) \subseteq X_0,$$

and $X_0 = \mathcal{Z}(F)$, as we wanted to show. $\square$

Problems

Problem 4.1

Prove that if I and J are ideals then $\mathcal{Z}(I) \cup \mathcal{Z}(J)$ and $\mathcal{Z}(I) \cap \mathcal{Z}(J)$ are algebraic sets and

$$\begin{aligned} \mathcal{Z}(I) \cup \mathcal{Z}(J) &= \mathcal{Z}(I \cap J) = \mathcal{Z}(I \cdot J), \\ \mathcal{Z}(I) \cap \mathcal{Z}(J) &= \mathcal{Z}(I + J). \end{aligned}$$

Problem 4.2

(i) Let $f_1, \ldots, f_r, g_1, \ldots, g_s \in L[x_1, \ldots, x_n]$ be a finite set of multivariate polynomials over an algebraically closed field L. Devise a procedure to decide if there is a point $p \in L^n$ such that

$$\begin{aligned} f_1(p) &= 0, \ldots, f_r(p) = 0 \quad \text{and} \\ g_1(p) &\neq 0, \ldots, g_s(p) \neq 0. \end{aligned}$$

(ii) Let $f_1, \ldots, f_r, g_1, \ldots, g_s$ and $h \in L[x_1, \ldots, x_n]$ be a finite set of multivariate polynomials over an algebraically closed field L. Devise a procedure to decide if the following statement is true:

$$\left(\forall\, p \in L^n \right)$$
$$\left[\left(f_1(p) = 0 \wedge \cdots \wedge f_r(p) = 0 \wedge g_1(p) \neq 0 \wedge \cdots \wedge g_s(p) \neq 0 \right) \right.$$
$$\left. \Rightarrow h(p) = 0 \right].$$

Problem 4.3

Given $f \in L[x_1, \ldots, x_n]$ and a finite set of polynomials $F = \{f_1, \ldots, f_r\} \subseteq L[x_1, \ldots, x_n]$ (L = an algebraically closed field), devise an algorithm for the *radical ideal membership problem*, i.e., an algorithm that decides if

$$f \in \sqrt{(F)}.$$

If so, express f^q (for an appropriate $q \in \mathbb{N}$) as follows:

$$f^q = h_1\, f_1 + \cdots + h_r\, f_r \qquad \text{where } f_i \in L[x_1, \ldots, x_n].$$

Problem 4.4

Consider the following well-known NP-complete problems:

(i) **Satisfiability:** Let $u_1, \ldots, u_n$ be a set of Boolean variables that can take one of two truth values: *true* and *false*. If u is a variable, then u and $\bar{u}$ are literals with the condition that if u holds true, then $\bar{u}$ holds false and vice versa. A 3-CNF formula is a conjunction of *clauses* where each clause is a disjunction of exactly three literals. For instance:

$$(u_1 \vee \overline{u_3} \vee u_8) \wedge (\overline{u_2} \vee u_3 \vee \overline{u_7}) \wedge (\overline{u_4} \vee \overline{u_5} \vee \overline{u_6}) \wedge (\overline{u_3} \vee u_5 \vee \overline{u_8}).$$

A 3-CNF formula is said to be *satisfiable* if it is possible to assign to each variable a truth value so that the formula evaluates to true (i.e., at least one literal in each clause has the value true).

SATISFIABILITY(C)
Input: A 3-CNF formula C over a set of variables $u_1, \ldots, u_n$.

Output: If C is satisfiable then return True;
Otherwise, return False.

(ii) Graph 3-Colorability: Given an undirected graph $G = (V, E)$, it is said to be *K-colorable*, if there is a mapping $f : V \to [1..K]$ such that every pair of adjacent vertices are assigned distinct colors.

3-COLORABILITY(G)
Input: An undirected graph $G = (V, E)$.

Output: If G is 3-colorable then return True;
Otherwise, return False.

(iii) Hamiltonian Path: For an undirected graph $G = (V, E)$, a *simple path* in G is a sequence of distinct vertices, $\langle v_1, v_2, \ldots, v_k \rangle$, such that $[v_i, v_{i+1}] \in E$ $(1 \leq i < k)$. A *Hamiltonian path* in G from s to t $(s, t \in V$, s and t are distinct) is a simple path from s to t that includes all the vertices of G.

HAMILTONIAN(G, s, t)
Input: An undirected graph G and two distinct vertices s and t.

Output: If G has a Hamiltonian path from s to t then return True;
Otherwise, return False.

Show that in each case, one can find a set of polynomials $f_1, \ldots, f_r \in L[x_1, \ldots, x_m]$ [where m, r, $\max(\deg(f_i))$ are polynomially bounded by the input size of the problem instances] such that the problem has an affirmative answer if and only if the corresponding system of polynomial equations is solvable.

Problem 4.5

One can define inductively a mapping from the class of Boolean formulas over $\{u_1, \ldots, u_n\}$ to the ring $\mathbb{Z}_2[x_1, \ldots, x_n]$ as follows:

$$
\begin{array}{rccl}
\Phi & : & \text{Boolean formulas} & \rightarrow \quad \mathbb{Z}_2[x_1, \ldots, x_n] \\
& : & u_i & \mapsto \quad x_i \\
& : & F \vee G & \mapsto \quad \Phi(F) \cdot \Phi(G) + \Phi(F) + \Phi(G) \\
& : & F \wedge G & \mapsto \quad \Phi(F) \cdot \Phi(G) \\
& : & \neg F & \mapsto \quad \Phi(F) + 1.
\end{array}
$$

This mapping usually follows from the classical Stone isomorphism lemma of logic.

(i.a) Consider a system of polynomials over $\mathbb{Z}_2$:

$$
G = \left\{
\begin{array}{rcl}
x_1^2 + x_1 & = & 0 \\
x_2^2 + x_2 & = & 0 \\
& \vdots & \\
x_n^2 + x_n & = & 0
\end{array}
\right\}
\tag{4.1}
$$

Show that the set of solutions of equation 4.1 in any algebraically closed field containing $\mathbb{Z}_2$ is simply $(\mathbb{Z}_2)^n$.

(i.b) Let $f \in \mathbb{Z}_2[x_1, \ldots, x_n]$ be a polynomial that vanishes at all the points of $(\mathbb{Z}_2)^n$. Show that $f \in (G)$.

(ii.a) Consider a truth assignment

$$
T : \{u_1, \ldots, u_n\} \rightarrow \{\text{true}, \text{false}\}
$$

and a vector $\overline{v_T}$ associated with it:

$$
\overline{v_T} = \langle a_1, \ldots, a_n \rangle \quad \text{where } a_i =
\left\{
\begin{array}{lll}
1 & \text{if } T(u_i) & = \quad \text{true} \\
\\
0 & \text{if } T(u_i) & = \quad \text{false}
\end{array}
\right.
$$

Show that a Boolean formula evaluates to true (respectively, false) under a truth assignment T if and only if $\Phi(F)(\overline{v_T}) = 1$ (respectively, $= 0$).

(ii.b) Show that $F = $ satisfiable if and only if $\Phi(F) \notin (G)$.

(ii.c) Show that $F = $ tautology if and only if $1 + \Phi(F) \in (G)$.

Problem 4.6

We use the same notations as those of the preceding problem. Let

$$
g = \Big(\forall\, u_1, \ldots, u_{n-m} \Big) \Big(\exists\, u_{n-m+1}, \ldots, u_n \Big) \Big[F(u_1, \ldots, u_m) \Big]
$$

be a statement, in which F is a quantifier-free logical formula over the variables $u_1, \ldots, u_n$.

Let

$$\mathrm{NF}_G^c(\Phi(F))$$
$$= f_0(x_1, \ldots, x_{n-m}) + \sum_{i>0} f_i(x_1, \ldots, x_{n-m}) \, p_i(x_{n-m+1}, \ldots, x_n)$$

where $p_i \in \mathrm{PP}(x_{n-m+1}, \ldots, x_n)$. (See Problem 3.9).

Prove that g holds if and only if

$$1 + f_0 \in \left(f_1, f_2, \ldots, x_1^2 + x_1, x_2^2 + x_2, \cdots, x_n^2 + x_n \right).$$

Problem 4.7

If I is a zero-dimensional *prime ideal* in $K[x_1, \ldots, x_n]$, then show that I can be generated by n polynomials: $I = (g_1, \ldots, g_n)$ where $g_i \in K[x_i, \ldots, x_n]$.

Problem 4.8

Consider two planar curves $P(x, y)$ and $Q(x, y)$ in $\mathbb{R}[x, y]$. Let G be a reduced Gröbner basis of the following ideal in $\mathbb{R}[a, b, u, x, y]$:

$$(P(a, b), Q(a, b), u - (a - x)(b - y))$$

computed with respect to a pure lexicographic ordering with $a \underset{\mathrm{LEX}}{>} b \underset{\mathrm{LEX}}{>} u$.

Let $V(u, x, y)$ be the polynomial in $G \cap \mathbb{R}[u, x, y]$.

Assume that $V_p(u) = V(u, x_0, y_0)$ (for some $p = \langle x_0, y_0 \rangle \in \mathbb{R}^2$) is a nonzero square-free polynomial in $\mathbb{R}[u]$.

Show that the number of positive real roots of $V_p(u)$ is exactly equal to the number of real zeros of (P, Q) lying in the top-right and bottom-left orthants centered at p, i.e.,

$$\{\langle a, b \rangle \; : \; (a > x_0, b > y_0) \text{ or } (a < x_0, b < y_0)\}.$$

Problem 4.9

Let $R = K[x_1, \ldots, x_n]$ be a polynomial ring over the field K and I an ideal of R. Then the equivalence relation $\equiv \bmod I$ partitions the ring R into equivalence classes such that $f, g \in R$ belong to the same class if $f \equiv g \bmod I$. The equivalence classes of R are called its *residue classes* modulo I. We use the notation R/I to represent the set of residue classes of R with respect to I.

Let $\overline{f}$ denote the set $\{g : f \equiv g \bmod I\}$. Check that the map $f \mapsto \overline{f}$ is the *natural ring homomorphism* of R onto R/I. We sometimes write $f + I$ for $\overline{f}$. R/I is called the *residue class ring modulo I*.

(i) Prove the following statements:

1. R/I is a vector space over K.

2. Let G be a Gröbner basis, and let

$$B \;=\; \{\overline{p} \;:\; p \in \mathrm{PP}(x_1, \ldots, x_n) \text{ such that } p \text{ is not a multiple}$$
$$\text{of the Hterm of any of the polynomials in } G\}.$$

  Then B is a linearly independent (vector space) basis of $R/(G)$ over K.

  (ii) Devise an algorithm to decide if $R/(F)$ is a finite-dimensional vector space for a given set of polynomials $F \subseteq R$.

  (iii) Devise an algorithm to compute the basis of a residue class ring $R/(F)$, where $F \subseteq R$ and (F) is a zero-dimensional ideal. Also compute the "multiplication table" for the computed basis B; if $\overline{p_i}, \overline{p_j} \in B$, then the $(\overline{p_i}, \overline{p_j})^{\mathrm{th}}$ entry of the multiplication table gives a linear representation of $\overline{p_i} \cdot \overline{p_j}$ in terms of the basis elements in B.

Problem 4.10

  Let K be a computable field and $\underset{A}{<}$ be a fixed but arbitrary computable admissible ordering on $\mathrm{PP}(x_1, \ldots, x_n)$. Assume that $G \subseteq K[x_1, \ldots, x_n]$ is a finite Gröbner basis of (G) with respect to $\underset{A}{<}$. Devise an algorithm to find

$$p \in (G) \cap K[x_1]$$

where p is a univariate polynomial of minimal degree in x_1. Your algorithm must not recompute a new Gröbner basis.

Problem 4.11

  Let $I \subseteq k[x_1, x_2, \ldots, x_n]$ be a zero-dimensional ideal in a ring of multivariate polynomials over an arbitrary field. Let $D_1, D_2, \ldots, D_n$ be a sequence of nonnegative numbers such that

$$\Big(\forall\, 1 \leq i \leq n\Big) \Big(\exists\, f_i \in I \cap k[x_i]\Big) \Big[f_i \neq 0 \text{ and } \deg(f_i) \leq D_i\Big].$$

  Show that I has a Gröbner basis G with respect to total lexicographic ordering such that

$$\Big(\forall\, g \in G\Big) \left[\deg(g) \leq \sum_{i=1}^{n} D_i\right].$$

Problem 4.12

A plane curve C is said to be given by its (*polynomial*) *parametric form* $\langle p(t), q(t) \rangle$, if

$$C = \left\{ \langle \alpha, \beta \rangle \in \mathbb{R}^2 \ : \ \left(\exists \, \tau \in \mathbb{R} \right) \left[\alpha = p(\tau) \text{ and } \beta = q(\tau) \right] \right\}.$$

Similarly, a plane curve C is said to be given by its *implicit form* $f(x, y)$, if

$$C = \{ \langle \alpha, \beta \rangle \in \mathbb{R}^2 \ : \ f(\alpha, \beta) = 0 \}.$$

Give an algorithm that takes as its input a curve in its polynomial parametric form and produces its implicit form.

Solutions to Selected Problems

Problem 4.1

First, we show that $\mathcal{Z}(I) \cup \mathcal{Z}(J) = \mathcal{Z}(IJ) = \mathcal{Z}(I \cap J)$.

(1) $P \in \mathcal{Z}(IJ) \wedge P \notin \mathcal{Z}(I)$

$\Rightarrow \left(\forall \, f \in I \right) \left(\forall \, g \in J \right) \left[fg(P) = 0 \right] \wedge \left(\exists \, f \in I \right) \left[f(P) \neq 0 \right]$

$\Rightarrow \left(\forall \, g \in J \right) \left[g(P) = 0 \right]$

$\Rightarrow P \in \mathcal{Z}(J)$

Hence,

$$\mathcal{Z}(I) \cup \mathcal{Z}(J) \supseteq \mathcal{Z}(IJ).$$

(2) Since $IJ \subseteq I \cap J$, we have

$$\mathcal{Z}(IJ) \supseteq \mathcal{Z}(I \cap J).$$

(3) Lastly, we see that

$(I \cap J \subseteq I) \wedge (I \cap J \subseteq J)$

$\Rightarrow \mathcal{Z}(I \cap J) \supseteq \mathcal{Z}(I) \wedge \mathcal{Z}(I \cap J) \supseteq \mathcal{Z}(J)$

$\Rightarrow \mathcal{Z}(I \cap J) \supseteq \mathcal{Z}(I) \cup \mathcal{Z}(J).$

Hence,

$$\mathcal{Z}(I) \cup \mathcal{Z}(J) \supseteq \mathcal{Z}(IJ) \supseteq \mathcal{Z}(I \cap J) \supseteq \mathcal{Z}(I) \cup \mathcal{Z}(J),$$

thus implying that all of these sets are equal.

Next, we show that $\mathcal{Z}(I) \cap \mathcal{Z}(J) = \mathcal{Z}(I + J)$.

$$P \in \mathcal{Z}(I) \cap \mathcal{Z}(J)$$
$$\Leftrightarrow \left(\forall f \in I\right)\left[f(P) = 0\right] \wedge \left(\forall g \in J\right)\left[g(P) = 0\right]$$
$$\Leftrightarrow \left(\forall h \in I + J\right)\left[h(P) = 0\right]$$
$$\Leftrightarrow P \in \mathcal{Z}(I + J).$$

Problem 4.2

(i) The problem can be reduced to an instance of solvability of a system of *polynomial equations* by means of the following artifice due to A. Rabinowitsch (*Math. Ann.*, **102**:518). Consider the following set of equations in $L[x_1, \ldots, x_n, z]$:

$$
\begin{aligned}
f_1 &= 0 \\
&\vdots \\
f_r &= 0 \\
(1 - g_1 \cdots g_s \cdot z) &= 0.
\end{aligned}
\tag{4.2}
$$

Then, we claim that the following system is solvable if and only if the system in equation 4.2 is solvable:

$$
\begin{aligned}
f_1 &= 0 \\
&\vdots \\
f_r &= 0 \\
g_1 &\neq 0 \\
&\vdots \\
g_s &\neq 0.
\end{aligned}
\tag{4.3}
$$

Assume that $p = \langle \xi_1, \ldots, \xi_n \rangle \in L^n$ is a solution for the system in equation 4.3. Let $\zeta = \left(g_1(p) \cdots g_s(p)\right)^{-1}$. Such a ζ exists, since $g_1(p) \cdots g_s(p) \neq 0$ and we are working in a field L. It is now trivial to see that $p' = \langle \xi_1, \ldots, \xi_n, \zeta \rangle \in L^{n+1}$ is a solution for the system in equation 4.2.

Conversely, if $p' = \langle \xi_1, \ldots, \xi_n, \zeta \rangle \in L^{n+1}$ is a solution for the system in equation 4.3, then $p = \langle \xi_1, \ldots, \xi_n \rangle \in L^n$ is a solution for the system in equation 4.3. Clearly, $f_1(p) = 0, \ldots, f_r(p) = 0$. Additionally, $g_1(p) \cdots g_s(p) \neq 0$, since, otherwise, $(1 - g_1 \cdots g_s \cdot z)(p')$ would have been 1. Since, we are working over a field, it follows that $g_1(p) \neq 0, \ldots, g_s(p) \neq 0$.

Thus it suffices to check that

$$1 \notin \Big(f_1, \ldots, f_r, (1 - g_1 \cdots g_s \cdot z)\Big).$$

(ii) By using a sequence of logical identities, it is easy to show that the formula

$$\Big(\forall\, p \in L^n\Big)$$

$$\Big[\Big(f_1(p) = 0 \wedge \cdots \wedge f_r(p) = 0 \ \wedge \ g_1(p) \neq 0 \wedge \cdots \wedge g_s(p) \neq 0\Big)$$

$$\Rightarrow h(p) = 0 \Big] \tag{4.4}$$

is equivalent to the following:

$$\Big(\neg \exists\, p \in L^n\Big)$$

$$\Big[f_1(p) = 0 \wedge \cdots \wedge f_r(p) = 0 \ \wedge \ g_1(p) \neq 0 \wedge \cdots \wedge g_s(p) \neq 0 \wedge h(p) \neq 0 \Big].$$

Thus formula 4.4 holds true if and only if the following system of equations in $L[x_1, \ldots, x_n, z]$ is unsolvable:

$$
\begin{aligned}
f_1 &= 0 \\
&\;\;\vdots \\
f_r &= 0 \\
(1 - g_1 \cdots g_s \cdot h \cdot z) &= 0
\end{aligned}
$$

is unsolvable, i.e, if

$$1 \in \Big(f_1, \ldots, f_r, (1 - g_1 \cdots g_s \cdot h \cdot z)\Big).$$

Problem 4.4

(i) We shall construct a set of polynomials over $\mathbb{C}[x_{1T}, x_{1F}, \ldots, x_{nT}, x_{nF}, z]$ such that the system of equations has a solution if and only if the given 3-CNF formula is satisfiable. For each variable u_i we introduce two variables, x_{iT} and x_{iF}, and the following set of equations:

$$
\begin{aligned}
x_{iT}^2 - x_{iT} &= 0 \\
x_{iF}^2 - x_{iF} &= 0 \\
x_{iT} + x_{iF} - 1 &= 0
\end{aligned}
\tag{4.5}
$$

These equations guarantee that x_{iT} and x_{iF} only take the values 0 and 1 and that if x_{iT} takes the value 1, then x_{iF} must take the value 0, and vice versa.

Now for each literal we define a mapping T where

$$T(u_i) = x_{iT} \quad \text{and} \quad T(\overline{u_i}) = x_{iF}.$$

Now, extend the mapping T to a clause $C = (u \vee u' \vee u'')$ as follows:

$$T(u \vee u' \vee u'') = T(u) + T(u') + T(u'').$$

Finally, extend the mapping T to a 3-CNF formula $C_1 \wedge \cdots \wedge C_m$:

$$T(C_1 \wedge \cdots \wedge C_m) = 1 - z \prod_{i=1}^{m} T(C_i). \tag{4.6}$$

For instance, the polynomial associated with the 3-CNF example in the problem will be

$$1 - z(x_{1T} + x_{3F} + x_{8T})\,(x_{2F} + x_{3T} + x_{7F})\,(x_{4F} + x_{5F} + x_{6F})\,(x_{3F} + x_{5T} + x_{8F}).$$

Clearly, if the 3-CNF formula is satisfiable, then the system of equations (4.5) and (4.6) have a solution. (If u_i is true then let $x_{iT} = 1$ and $x_{iF} = 0$, etc., and since for each clause C_i evaluates to true, $T(C_i) \neq 0$ and for some value of $z \in \mathbb{C}$ equation 4.6 vanishes.)

Conversely, if the constructed system of equations has a solution then for each such solution, x_{iT} takes a value in $\{0, 1\}$; assign u_i the truth value *true* iff $x_{iT} = 1$. Such a truth assignment obviously satisfies the 3-CNF.

The solution uses $2n + 1$ variables and $3n + 1$ equations each of total degree $\leq (m + 1)$. Note that the equation $T(C_1 \wedge \cdots \wedge C_m)$ can be reduced in polynomial time (using complete-reduction) by the equations $\{x_{iT}^2 - x_{iT}, x_{iF}^2 - x_{iF} : 1 \leq i \leq n\}$ to yield an equation of degree 1 in each variable.

A much simpler solution can be constructed, by considering the following polynomials in $\mathbb{C}[x_1, \ldots, x_n]$. For each Boolean variable u_i, associate a variable x_i. Define a mapping $\widetilde{T}$ over the literals as follows:

$$\widetilde{T}(u_i) = (x_i - 1) \quad \text{and} \quad \widetilde{T}(\overline{u_i}) = x_i.$$

Now, extend the mapping $\widetilde{T}$ to a clause $C = (u \vee u' \vee u'')$ as follows:

$$\widetilde{T}(u \vee u' \vee u'') = \widetilde{T}(u) \cdot \widetilde{T}(u') \cdot \widetilde{T}(u'').$$

For the given 3-CNF formula $C_1 \wedge \cdots \wedge C_m$, construct the following system of equations:

$$\widetilde{T}(C_1) = 0, \ \ldots, \ \widetilde{T}(C_m) = 0.$$

It is easily seen that the system of equations is solvable if and only if the original 3-CNF formula is satisfiable.

For the example 3-CNF formula, the system of equations is the following:

$$
\begin{aligned}
(x_1 - 1)\, x_3\, (x_8 - 1) &= 0 \\
x_2\, (x_3 - 1)\, x_7 &= 0 \\
x_4\, x_5\, x_6 &= 0 \\
x_3\, (x_5 - 1)\, x_8 &= 0.
\end{aligned}
$$

This solution uses n variables and m equations each of total degree 3.

(ii) Again we shall work over the field $\mathbb{C}$ and make use of the three cube roots of unity: 1, ω and ω^2—these three constants will be used to represent the three colors. For each vertex v_i, associate a variable x_i and introduce the following equation into the system:

$$x_i^3 - 1 = 0.$$

This "enforces" that the vertex v_i takes a color in $\{1, \omega, \omega^2\}$. Now the condition that each pair of adjacent vertices $[v_i, v_j] \in E$ are assigned distinct colors can be "enforced" by the following set of equations:

$$x_i^2 + x_i\, x_j + x_j^2 = 0, \quad \text{where } [v_i, v_j] \in E.$$

It is not hard to show that the graph is 3-colorable if and only if the constructed system of equations in $\mathbb{C}[x_1, \ldots, x_n]$ ($n = |V|$) has a solution in $\mathbb{C}^n$.

The solution uses $|V|$ variables and $|V| + |E|$ equations each of total degree at most 3.

(iii) As before, our construction will be over the algebraically closed field, $\mathbb{C}$. Without loss of generality assume that $s = v_1$ and $t = v_n$. It suffices to find a bijective map $f : V \to [1..n]$ such that $f(v_1) = 1$, $f(v_n) = n$ and such that if f maps two vertices to successive values (i.e., k and $k + 1$), then the vertices must be adjacent.

For each vertex v_i, associate a variable x_i and additionally, introduce two auxiliary variable z and z'. The bijectivity of f can be "enforced" by the following sets of equations:

$$
\begin{aligned}
x_1 - 1 = 0, \quad & x_n - n = 0 \\
(x_i - 1)\,(x_i - 2) \cdots (x_i - n) = 0 \qquad & \text{for } 1 < i < k
\end{aligned}
$$

$$1 - z \prod_{1 \le i < j \le n} (x_i - x_j) = 0$$

The last condition (i.e., $(\forall\, [v_i, v_j] \notin E)\ [|f(v_i) - f(v_j)| \ne 1]$) can be "enforced" by the following set of equations:

$$1 + z' - (x_i - x_j)^2\, z' = 0, \quad \text{for all } 1 \le i < j \le n \text{ such that } [v_i, v_j] \notin E.$$

The solution uses $|V| + 2$ variables and $O(|V|^2)$ equations of each of total degree at most $|V|^2$.

Problem 4.5

(**i.a**) Note that G is already in strongly triangular form and one can apply the algorithm in this chapter to find the zeros (finitely many) of G. It is now trivial to see that

$$\mathcal{Z}(G) = \{\xi_1 : \xi_1^2 + \xi_1 = 0\} \times \cdots \times \{\xi_n : \xi_1^n + \xi_n = 0\} = (\mathbb{Z}_2)^n.$$

(**i.b**) Let $h = \mathrm{NF}_G^c(f)$ (see Problem 3.9). Clearly, h vanishes at the common zeroes of G if and only if f vanishes at the common zeroes of G. Also, since the polynomials of G are all univariate and of degree 2, h is of degree ≤ 1 in each variable.

Now we claim that if h vanishes at all $(\mathbb{Z}_2)^n$ points (common zeroes of G), then h must be identically zero. If h is univariate, then this is obvious. In order to prove this inductively, assume that the claim has been proven for all such k-variate polynomials and we want to prove for the case when h is $(k+1)$-variate. Without loss of generality assume that the variable x_1 occurs in h. Thus, we can express h as follows:

$$h = x_1\, h'(x_2, \ldots, x_k) + h''(x_2, \ldots, x_k)$$

If $h \not\equiv 0$, then *not both* h' and h'' are identically zero. Thus for some point

$$\langle \xi_2, \ldots, \xi_k \rangle \in (\mathbb{Z}_2)^k,$$

$h' \neq 0$ or $h'' \neq 0$ (by the inductive argument). Case 1: If $h'' \neq 0$, then h does not vanish at $\langle 0, \xi_2, \ldots, \xi_k \rangle$. Case 2: If $h'' = 0$ and $h' \neq 0$, then h does not vanish at $\langle 1, \xi_2, \ldots, \xi_k \rangle$. In either case, we get a contradiction. Thus we conclude that $h \equiv 0$.

Since G is a Gröbner basis for (G), we conclude that

$$f \text{ vanishes at the common zeroes of } G$$
$$\Rightarrow \quad f \xrightarrow[*]{G,c} h = 0$$
$$\Rightarrow \quad f \in (G).$$

(**ii.a**) The proof follows by a simple structural induction on the Boolean formulas. We omit the details.

(**ii.b**) Clearly f is satisfiable if and only if there is a truth assignment for which f evaluates to true. This is equivalent to saying

$$\left(\exists\, p \in (\mathbb{Z}_2)^n\right)\, \Big[\Phi(F)(p) = 1\Big],$$

i.e., $\Phi(F)$ does not vanish at all the common zeros of G. The rest follows by the results of the preceding parts.

(ii.c)

$$f = \text{tautology}$$
$$\Leftrightarrow \quad \Phi(F)(p) = 1, \quad \text{for all } p \in (\mathbb{Z}_2)^n$$
$$\Leftrightarrow \quad 1 + \Phi(F) \text{ vanishes at all } p \in (\mathbb{Z}_2)^n$$
$$\Leftrightarrow \quad 1 + \Phi(F) \in (G).$$

Problem 4.9

(i) Proof of the statements:

Lemma 4.4.2   1. R/I *is a vector space over* K.

2. *Let* G *be a Gröbner basis, and let*

$$B = \{\overline{p} : p \in \text{PP}(x_1, \ldots, x_n) \text{ such that } p \text{ is not a multiple}$$
$$\text{of the Hterm of any of the polynomials in } G\}. \quad (4.7)$$

Then B *is a linearly independent (vector space) basis of* $R/(G)$ *over* K.

PROOF.
The first statement is trivial; simply check that

$$a(f + g + I) = a f + b g + I,$$
$$(a + b)(f + I) = a f + b f + I,$$
$$(ab)(f + I) = a(b f + I),$$
$$1(f + I) = f + I,$$

where $a, b \in K$ and $f, g \in K[x_1, \ldots, x_n]$.

Let $\overline{f} = f + (G)$ be an element of $R/(G)$ and let

$$\text{NF}_G^c(f) = c_1 \cdot p_1 + \cdots + c_l \cdot p_l,$$

where $c_i \in K$ and $p_i \in \text{PP}(x_1, \ldots, x_n)$. Hence, for all $1 \leq i \leq l$, p_i is not a multiple of the Hterm of any polynomial in G, and $\overline{p_i} \in B$. Since we can write $\overline{f}$ as

$$\overline{f} = c_1 \cdot \overline{p_1} + \cdots + c_l \cdot \overline{p_l},$$

B spans the vector space $R/(G)$.

Furthermore, the elements of B are linearly independent. Assume that for some $\overline{p_1}, \ldots, \overline{p_m} \in B$, we have

$$c_1 \cdot \overline{p_1} + \cdots + c_m \cdot \overline{p_m} = \overline{0}, \quad \text{where } c_i \in K.$$

In other words,

$$f = c_1 \cdot p_1 + \cdots + c_m \cdot p_m \in (G).$$

Hence $\text{NF}_G^c(f) = f = 0$, i.e., $c_1 = \cdots = c_m = 0$. $\square$

(ii) Finite-Dimensionality of a Residue Class Ring

FINITEDIMENSIONALITY(F)

Input: $F \subseteq R$.

Output: TRUE, if $R/(F)$ finite-dimensional.

Compute G, the Gröbner basis of (F). Output true if for all i ($1 \leq i \leq n$), a power product of the form $x_i^{j_i}$ ($j_i \geq 0$) occurs among the Hterms of the polynomials in G; otherwise, false [i.e., (F) is zero-dimensional]. To see that this works, note that if for some i, none of the power products of Hterms in G has the required form, then we get an infinity number of basis elements as x_i, x_i^2, x_i^3, ..., etc., are not reducible. The converse is simple.

(iii) Basis of a Residue Class Ring

BASISCOMPUTATION(F)

Input: $F \subseteq R$.

Assume that $R/(F)$ is a finite-dimensional vector space.

Output: (1) A basis B of the vector space $R/(F)$;

(2) The "multiplication table" for $R/(F)$:

the $(\overline{p_i}, \overline{p_j})^{\text{th}}$ entry of the table gives a linear representation of $\overline{p_i} \cdot \overline{p_j}$ in terms of the basis elements in B.

Compute G, the Gröbner basis of (F). Let the set B be as in equation (4.7). This is easily computed. For each $\overline{p_i}$, $\overline{p_j} \in B$, compute the normal form of $p_i \cdot p_j$:

$$\text{NF}_G^c(p_i \cdot p_j) = c_1 \cdot p_1 + \cdots + c_m \cdot p_m.$$

Then the $(\overline{p_i}, \overline{p_j})^{\text{th}}$ entry of the multiplication table is

$$c_1 \cdot \overline{p_1} + \cdots + c_m \cdot \overline{p_m}.$$

The correctness of the procedure follows immediately from Lemma 4.4.2.

Problem 4.11

We are told that there is a system of nontrivial univariate polynomials

$$f_1(x_1) = a_{1,0}x_1^{d_1} + a_{1,1}x_1^{d_1-1} + \cdots + a_{1,d_1},$$
$$f_2(x_2) = a_{2,0}x_2^{d_2} + a_{2,1}x_2^{d_2-1} + \cdots + a_{2,d_2},$$
$$\vdots$$
$$f_n(x_n) = a_{n,0}x_n^{d_n} + a_{n,1}x_n^{d_n-1} + \cdots + a_{n,d_n}$$

in the ideal $I \subset k[x_1, \ldots, x_n]$, where $(\forall i)$ $[d_i \leq D_i]$, and $D_1, \ldots, D_n$ is a fixed sequence of nonnegative integers.

Let G be a minimal Gröbner basis for I (in the sense of Problem 3.2) with respect to the total lexicographic ordering where $x_1 \underset{\text{LEX}}{>} x_2 \underset{\text{LEX}}{>} \cdots \underset{\text{LEX}}{>} x_n$. We may assume that distinct elements of G have distinct head terms, since if not, throw out one or the other without altering Head(G). Then for all $g \in G$ satisfying the following conditions

$$\begin{aligned}
\text{Hterm}(g) &\neq \text{Hterm}(f_1), \\
\text{Hterm}(g) &\neq \text{Hterm}(f_2), \\
&\vdots \\
\text{Hterm}(g) &\neq \text{Hterm}(f_n),
\end{aligned}$$

we know that Hterm(f_i) $(1 \le i \le n)$ does not divide Hterm(g), since $f_i \in I$. Thus,

$$\left(\forall\, g \in G\right) \left[\deg(\text{Hterm}(g)) \le \max\left(\sum_{i=1}^{n}(D_i - 1), D_1, \ldots, D_n\right) \le \sum_{i=1}^{n} D_i\right].$$

But, since the Gröbner basis is computed with respect to a total lexicographic ordering, each monomial of each $g \in G$ has a total degree smaller than the total degree of the headterm, and

$$\left(\forall\, g \in G\right) \left[\deg(g) \le \sum_{i=1}^{n} D_i\right].$$

Bibliographic Notes

The main algorithm presented in this chapter is due to Bruno Buchberger and has also been discussed and analyzed in many survey papers. The discussion in this chapter is largely based on the survey paper by Mishra and Yap [149]. Also see [16], [32,33]. For some related developments and complexity questions, also consult [38,39,61,123-125,130]

A key to settling many important complexity question in *computational algebraic geometry* has been an *effective version* of Hilbert's Nullstellensatz, due to Brownawell [29] and Kollár [118]. We state this result without proof:

Effective Hilbert's Nullstellensatz.
Let $I = (f_1, \ldots, f_r)$ be an ideal in $K[x_1, \ldots, x_n]$, where K is an arbitrary field, and $\deg(f_i) \le d$, $1 \le i \le r$. Let $h \in K[x_1, \ldots, x_n]$

be a polynomial with $\deg(h) = \delta$. Then h vanishes at the common zeros of I, i.e.,

$$h \in \sqrt{I}$$

if and only if

$$\left(\exists \, b_1, \ldots, b_s \in K[x_1, \ldots, x_n] \right) \left[h^q = \sum_{i=1}^{s} b_i f_i, \right],$$

where $q \leq 2(d+1)^n$ and $\deg(b_i f_i) \leq 2(\delta+1)(d+1)^n, 1 \leq i \leq r$.

There are several textbooks devoted solely to algebraic geometry. The following is a small sample: Artin [7], Hartshorne [89], Kunz [121], Mumford [156], van der Waerden [204] and Zariski and Samuel [216].

Problem 4.4 was influenced by Bayer's dissertation [16]. Problem 4.5 is based on the results of Chazarain et. al. [45] and Kapur & Narendran [114]. Problem 4.8 is based on Milne's work [146]; also, consult Pedersen's dissertation for some related ideas [162]. Problem 4.9 is based on Buchberger's algorithm [33].

Chapter 5

Characteristic Sets

5.1 Introduction

The concept of a characteristic sets was discovered in the late forties by J.F. Ritt (see his now classic book *Differential Algebra* [174]) in an effort to extend some of the constructive algebraic methods to differential algebra. However, the concept languished in near oblivion until the seventies when the Chinese mathematician Wu Wen-Tsün [209–211] realized its power in the case where Ritt's techniques are specialized to commutative algebra. In particular, he exhibited its effectiveness (largely through empirical evidence) as a powerful tool for mechanical geometric theorem proving. This proved to be a turning point; a renewed interest in the subject has contributed to a better understanding of the power of Ritt's techniques in effectively solving many algebraic and algebraico-geometric problems.

For a system of algebraic equations, its characteristic set is a certain effectively constructible triangular set of equations that preserves many of the interesting geometric properties of the original system [47,76–78,173] However, while it shares certain similarities with the triangular forms of the previous chapter, it is smaller in size but fails to retain certain algebraic properties. In particular, *a characteristic set of a system of polynomials* $\{F\}$ *is not a basis of the ideal* (F). But because of their power in geometric settings, characteristic sets do provide an alternative and relatively efficient method for solving problems in algebraic geometry.

Recently, the constructivity of Ritt's characteristic set has been explicitly demonstrated [78]. The original *Wu-Ritt process*, first devised by Ritt [174], subsequently modified by Wu [209-211] and widely implemented [47], computes only an *extended* characteristic set. Furthermore, the *Wu-Ritt process*, as it is, has a worst-case time complexity which can only be expressed as a nonelementary[1] function of the input size and thus, in principle, is infeasible. This difficulty has been alleviated by some of the recent algorithms devised by Gallo and Mishra [76,77].

In this chapter, we begin by discussing the *pseudodivision* process. Next, we shall introduce the concept of a characteristic set, followed by a survey of the original Wu-Ritt process, and its applications in geometric theorem proving. We shall also sketch some of the key ideas that have led to recent efficient algorithms for computing a characteristic set.

5.2   Pseudodivision and Successive Pseudodivision

Let S be a commutative ring. As a convention, we define $\deg(0) = -\infty$.

Theorem 5.2.1 (Pseudodivision) *Let $f(x)$ and $g(x) \neq 0$ be two polynomials in $S[x]$ of respective degrees n and m:*

$$
\begin{aligned}
f(x) &= b_n x^n + \cdots + b_0, \\
g(x) &= a_m x^m + \cdots + a_0.
\end{aligned}
$$

Let $\delta = \max(m - n + 1, 0)$. Then there exist polynomials $q(x)$ and $r(x)$ in $S[x]$ such that

$$
b_n^\delta g(x) = q(x)f(x) + r(x) \qquad \text{and } \deg(r) < \deg(f).
$$

Moreover, if b_n is not a zero divisor in S, then $q(x)$ and $r(x)$ are unique.

PROOF.
We can show the existence of the polynomials $q(x)$ and $r(x)$ by induction on m:
• BASE CASE: $m < n$
Take $q(x) = 0$ and $r(x) = g(x)$.
• INDUCTION CASE: $m \geq n$
The polynomial

$$
\widehat{g}(x) = b_n \cdot g(x) - a_m x^{m-n} \cdot f(x)
$$

has degree at most $(m - 1)$. By the inductive hypothesis, there exist polynomials $\widehat{q}(x)$ and $\widehat{r}(x)$ such that

$$
\begin{aligned}
b_n^{m-n} &\left(b_n \cdot g(x) - a_m x^{m-n} \cdot f(x) \right) \\
&= \widehat{q}(x) \cdot f(x) + \widehat{r}(x) \quad \text{and } \deg(\widehat{r}) < \deg(f).
\end{aligned}
$$

---

[1] For a discussion of the nonelementary computational problems, see pp. 419–423 of the algorithms text by Aho et al. [3]. Roughly, a problem is said to have a nonelementary complexity, if its complexity cannot be bounded by a function that involves only a fixed number of iterations of the exponential function.

Taking $q(x) = a_m b_n^{m-n} x^{m-n} + \widehat{q}(x)$ and $r(x) = \widehat{r}(x)$,

$$b_n^\delta g(x) \quad = \quad q(x) f(x) + r(x) \quad \text{and} \quad \deg(r) < \deg(f).$$

Proof of Uniqueness:
Suppose that b_n is not a zero divisor in S and we have

$$
\begin{aligned}
b_n^\delta g(x) \quad &= \quad q(x) \cdot f(x) + r(x) \quad \text{and} \quad \deg(r) < \deg(f) \\
&= \quad \widehat{q}(x) \cdot f(x) + \widehat{r}(x) \quad \text{and} \quad \deg(\widehat{r}) < \deg(f).
\end{aligned}
$$

If $q(x) - \widehat{q}(x) \neq 0$, then $[q(x) - \widehat{q}(x)]f(x) \neq 0$ and has degree at least n, since b_n is not a zero divisor. However, this is impossible since

$$\deg(r - \widehat{r}) < \deg(f) \quad \text{and} \quad (q(x) - \widehat{q}(x))f(x) = \widehat{r}(x) - r(x).$$

Thus $q(x) - \widehat{q}(x) = 0 = \widehat{r}(x) - r(x)$. $\square$

Definition 5.2.1 (Pseudodivision) For any two polynomials $g(x)$ and $f(x) \neq 0$ in $S[x]$, we shall call polynomials $q(x)$ and $r(x)$ in $S[x]$ the *pseudoquotient* and the *pseudoremainder*, respectively, of $g(x)$ with respect to $f(x)$ [denoted PQuotient(g, f) and PRemainder(g, f)] if

$$b_n^\delta g(x) = q(x) \cdot f(x) + r(x) \quad \text{and} \quad \deg(r) < n,$$

where $m - \deg(g)$, $n - \deg(f)$, $b_n - \text{Hcoef}(f)$ and $\delta - \max(m - n + 1, 0)$. Also, if $g = \text{PRemainder}(g, f)$, then $g(x)$ is said to be *reduced* with respect to $f(x)$. $\square$

Remark 5.2.2 If S is an integral domain, the pseudoquotient and the pseudoremainder of any pair of polynomials in $S[x]$ are unique. $\square$

The above argument leads to a recursive algorithm for pseudodivision:

PSEUDODIVISIONREC$(g(x), f(x))$

Input: $f(x) = b_n x^n + \cdots + b_0 \neq 0 \in S[x]$,
$\qquad\qquad$ $g(x) = a_m x^m + \cdots + a_0 \in S[x]$.

Output: $q(x) = \text{PQuotient}(g, f)$, and $r(x) = \text{PRemainder}(g, f)$.

$\qquad$ if $m < n$ then
$\qquad\qquad \langle q(x), r(x) \rangle := \langle 0, g(x) \rangle$;
$\qquad$ else
$\qquad\qquad \langle q(x), r(x) \rangle :=$
$\qquad\qquad\qquad$ PSEUDODIVISIONREC$(b_n g(x) - a_m x^{m-n} f(x), f(x))$;
$\qquad\qquad q(x) := a_m b_n^{m-n} x^{m-n} + q(x)$
$\qquad$ end{if };
$\qquad$ end{PSEUDODIVISIONREC} $\square$

To derive an iterative algorithm, we introduce an integer variable k and develop a loop that decrements k from m to $(n-1)$, maintaining the following assertion invariant:

$$b_n^\delta g(x) = q(x) \cdot f(x) + b_n^{k-n+1} \cdot r(x).$$

Let us represent $q(x)$ and $r(x)$ by their respective coefficient vectors

$$\langle q_{m-n}, \ldots, q_0 \rangle \quad \text{and} \quad \langle r_m, \ldots, r_0 \rangle.$$

PSEUDODIVISIONIT($g(x)$, $f(x)$)

Input: $f(x) = b_n x^n + \cdots + b_0 \neq 0 \in S[x]$,
$g(x) = a_m x^m + \cdots + a_0 \in S[x]$.

Output: $q(x) = \text{PQuotient}(g, f)$, and $r(x) = \text{PRemainder}(g, f)$.

```
for i := 0 to m − n loop qi := 0;
for i := 0 to m loop ri := ai;
for k := m down to n loop
    q_{k−n} := r_k · b_n^{k−n};
    for j := 1 to n loop
        r_{k−j} := b_n · r_{k−j} − r_k · b_{n−j};
    for j := 0 to k − n − 1 loop
        r_j := b_n · r_j;
end{loop };
end{PSEUDODIVISIONIT}   □
```

The notion of a pseudodivision can be suitably generalized so that given two nonzero polynomials $f(x) \in S[x]$ and $g(x, y_1, \ldots, y_m) \in S[x, y_1, \ldots, y_m]$, we can determine two polynomials $q(x, y_1, \ldots, y_m)$ [pseudoquotient] and $r(x, y_1, \ldots, y_m)$ [pseudoremainder] such that

$$b_n^\delta g(x, \overline{y}) = q(x, \overline{y}) \cdot f(x) + r(x, \overline{y}), \quad \text{and} \quad \deg_x(r) < \deg(f),$$

where $\deg_x$ denotes the maximal degree of x in a polynomial containing the variable x and $b_n = \text{Hcoef}(f)$ and $\delta = \max(\deg_x(g) - \deg_x(f) + 1, 0)$. In order to give prominence to the fact that the pseudodivision was performed with respect to the variable x, we may sometime write

$$q(x, \overline{y}) = \text{PQuotient}(g, f, x) \quad \text{and} \quad r(x, \overline{y}) = \text{PRemainder}(g, f, x).$$

Theorem 5.2.2 (Successive Pseudodivision) *Consider the following triangular form*

$$f_1(u_1, \ldots, u_d, x_1)$$
$$f_2(u_1, \ldots, u_d, x_1, x_2)$$
$$\vdots$$
$$f_r(u_1, \ldots, u_d, x_1, \ldots, x_r)$$

and polynomial $g = g_1(u_1, \ldots, u_d, x_1, \ldots, x_r)$ *all in the ring* $S[u_1, \ldots, u_d, x_1, \ldots, x_r]$. *Let the following sequence of polynomials be obtained by successive pseudodivisions:*

$$
\begin{aligned}
r_r &= g \\
r_{r-1} &= \text{PRemainder}(r_r, f_r, x_r) \\
r_{r-2} &= \text{PRemainder}(r_{r-1}, f_{r-1}, x_{r-1}) \\
&\;\;\vdots \\
r_0 &= \text{PRemainder}(r_1, f_1, x_1).
\end{aligned}
$$

The polynomial $r_0 \in S[u_1, \ldots, u_d, x_1, \ldots, x_r]$ *is said to be the* generalized pseudoremainder *of* g *with respect to* $f_1, \ldots, f_r$ *and denoted*

$$
r_0 = \text{PRemainder}\Big(g, \{f_1, \ldots, f_r\}\Big).
$$

We also say g *is reduced with respect to* $f_1, \ldots, f_r$ *if*

$$
g = \text{PRemainder}\Big(g, \{f_1, \ldots, f_r\}\Big).
$$

Furthermore, there are nonnegative integers $\delta_1, \ldots, \delta_r$ *and polynomials* $q_1, \ldots, q_r$ *such that*

1. $b_r^{\delta_r} \cdots b_1^{\delta_1} g = q_1 \cdot f_1 + \cdots + q_r \cdot f_r + r_0,$

$$
\begin{aligned}
\text{where } b_1 &= \text{Hcoef}(f_1) \in S[u_1, \ldots, u_d], \\
&\;\;\vdots \\
b_r &= \text{Hcoef}(f_r) \in S[u_1, \ldots, u_d, x_1, \ldots, x_{r-1}].
\end{aligned}
$$

2. $\deg_{x_i}(r_0) < \deg_{x_i}(f_i), \quad \text{for } i = 1, \ldots, r.$

PROOF.
The proof is by induction on r and by repeated applications of the pseudodivision theorem given in the beginning of the section. $\square$

5.3   Characteristic Sets

Let $K[x_1, \ldots, x_n]$ denote the ring of polynomials in n variables, with coefficients in a field K. Consider a fixed ordering on the set of variables; without loss of generality, we may assume that the given ordering is the following:

$$
x_1 \prec x_2 \prec \cdots \prec x_n.
$$

Definition 5.3.1 (Class and Class Degree) Let $f \in K[x_1, \ldots, x_n]$ be a multivariate polynomial with coefficients in K. A variable x_j is said to be *effectively present in* f if some monomial in f with nonzero coefficient contains a (strictly) positive power of x_j.

For $1 \leq j \leq n$, *degree of* f *with respect to* x_j, $\deg_{x_j}(f)$, is defined to be the maximum degree of the variable x_j in f.

The *class* and the *class degree* (Cdeg) of a polynomial $f \in K[x_1, \ldots, x_n]$ with respect to a given ordering is defined as follows:

1. If *no variable* x_j *is effectively present in* f, (i.e., $f \in K$), then, by convention,
$$\text{Class}(f) = 0 \quad \text{and} \quad \text{Cdeg}(f) = 0.$$

2. Otherwise, if x_j *is effectively present in* f, *and no* $x_i \succ x_j$ *is effectively present in* f (i.e., $f \in K[x_1, \ldots, x_j] \setminus K[x_1, \ldots, x_{j-1}]$), then
$$\text{Class}(f) = j \text{ and } \text{Cdeg}(f) = \deg_{x_j}(f).$$

Thus, with each polynomial $f \in K[x_1, \ldots, x_n]$, we can associate a pair of integers, its *type*:

$$
\begin{aligned}
\text{Type} \quad &: \quad K[x_1, \ldots, x_n] \to \mathbb{N} \times \mathbb{N} \\
&: \quad f \mapsto \langle \text{Class}(f), \text{Cdeg}(f) \rangle. \quad \square
\end{aligned}
$$

Definition 5.3.2 (Ordering on the Polynomials) Given two polynomials f_1 and $f_2 \in K[x_1, \ldots, x_n]$, we say f_1 is of *lower rank than* f_2,

$$f_1 \prec f_2,$$

if either

1. $\text{Class}(f_1) < \text{Class}(f_2)$, or
2. $\text{Class}(f_1) = \text{Class}(f_2)$ and $\text{Cdeg}(f_1) < \text{Cdeg}(f_2)$.

This is equivalent to saying that the polynomials are ordered according to the lexicographic order on their types:

$$f_1 \prec f_2 \quad \text{iff} \quad \text{Type}(f_1) \underset{\text{LEX}}{<} \text{Type}(f_2).$$

Note that there are distinct polynomials f_1 and f_2 that are not comparable under the preceding order. In this case, $\text{Type}(f_1) = \text{Type}(f_2)$, and f_1 and f_2 are said to be of the *same rank*, $f_1 \sim f_2$. $\square$

Thus, a polynomial f of class j and class degree d can be written as

$$
\begin{aligned}
f = I_d(x_1, \ldots, x_{j-1}) x_j^d \\
+ I_{d-1}(x_1, \ldots, x_{j-1}) x_j^{d-1} + \cdots + I_0(x_1, \ldots, x_{j-1}),
\end{aligned}
\tag{5.1}
$$

where $I_l(x_1, \ldots, x_{j-1}) \in K[x_1, \ldots, x_{j-1}]$ ($l = 0, 1, \ldots, d$).

Definition 5.3.3 (Initial Polynomial) Given a polynomial f of class j and class degree d, its *initial polynomial*, $\text{In}(f)$, is defined to be the polynomial $I_d(x_1, \ldots, x_{j-1})$ as in equation (5.1). $\square$

As a special case of Theorem 5.2.1, we get the following:

Corollary 5.3.1 (Pseudodivision Lemma) *Consider two polynomials f and $g \in K[x_1, \ldots x_n]$, with $\text{Class}(f) = j$. Then using the pseudodivision process, we can write*

$$\text{In}(f)^\alpha g = qf + r, \tag{5.2}$$

where $\deg_{x_j}(r) < \deg_{x_j}(f)$ and $\alpha \leq \deg_{x_j}(g) - \deg_{x_j}(f) + 1$. $\square$

If α is assumed to be the smallest possible power satisfying equation (5.2), then the pseudoquotient and the pseudoremainder are unique. Also, polynomial g is reduced with respect to f if $g = \text{PRemainder}(g, f)$.

Definition 5.3.4 (Ascending Set) A sequence of polynomials $\mathcal{F} = \langle f_1, f_2, \ldots, f_r \rangle \subseteq K[x_1, \ldots, x_n]$ is said to be an *ascending set* (or *chain*), if one of the following two conditions holds:

1. $r = 1$ and f_1 is not identically zero;

2. $r > 1$, and $0 < \text{Class}(f_1) < \text{Class}(f_2) < \cdots < \text{Class}(f_r) \leq n$, and each f_i is reduced with respect to the preceding polynomials, f_j's $(1 \leq j < i)$.

Every ascending set is finite and has at most n elements. The *dimension* of an ascending set $\mathcal{F} = \langle f_1, f_2, \ldots, f_r \rangle$, $\dim \mathcal{F}$, is defined to be $(n - r)$. $\square$

Thus, with each ascending set $\mathcal{F}$ we can associate an $(n+1)$-vector, its *type*,

$$\text{Type: Family of ascending sets} \; \rightarrow \; (\mathbb{N} \cup \{\infty\})^{n+1},$$

where ∞ is assumed to be greater than any integer. For all $0 \leq i \leq n$, the ith component of the vector is

$$\text{Type}\,(\mathcal{F})\,[i] = \begin{cases} \text{Cdeg}(g), & \text{if } \left(\exists g \in \mathcal{F}\right) \left[\text{Class}(g) = i\right]; \\ \\ \infty, & \text{otherwise.} \end{cases}$$

Definition 5.3.5 (Ordering on the Ascending Sets) Given two ascending sets

$$\mathcal{F} = \langle f_1, \ldots, f_r \rangle \quad \text{and} \quad \mathcal{G} = \langle g_1, \ldots, g_s \rangle,$$

we say $\mathcal{F}$ is of *lower rank* than $\mathcal{G}$, $\mathcal{F} \prec \mathcal{G}$, if one of the following two conditions is satisfied,

1. There exists an index $i \leq \min\{r, s\}$ such that

$$\left(\forall\, 1 \leq j < i\right) \left[f_j \sim g_j\right] \text{ and } \left[f_i \prec g_i\right];$$

2. $r > s$ and $\left(\forall\, 1 \leq j \leq s\right) \left[f_j \sim g_j\right]$.

Note that there are distinct ascending sets $\mathcal{F}$ and $\mathcal{G}$ that are not comparable under the preceding order. In this case $r = s$, and $(\forall\, 1 \leq j \leq s)\, [f_j \sim g_j]$, and $\mathcal{F}$ and $\mathcal{G}$ are said to be of the *same rank*, $\mathcal{F} \sim \mathcal{G}$. $\quad\square$

Hence,

$$\mathcal{F} \prec \mathcal{G} \quad \text{iff} \quad \mathrm{Type}\,(\mathcal{F}) \underset{\mathrm{LEX}}{<} \mathrm{Type}\,(\mathcal{G}).$$

Thus the map, *type*, is a partially ordered homomorphism from the family of ascending sets to $(\mathbb{N} \cup \{\infty\})^{n+1}$, where $(\mathbb{N} \cup \{\infty\})^{n+1}$ is ordered by the lexicographic order. Hence, the family of ascending sets endowed with the ordering "$\prec$" is a well-ordered set.

Definition 5.3.6 (Characteristic Set) Let I be an ideal in $K[x_1, \ldots, x_n]$. Consider the family of all ascending sets, each of whose components is in I,

$$\mathbf{S}_I = \left\{ \mathcal{F} = \langle f_1, \ldots, f_r \rangle \; : \; \mathcal{F} \text{ is an ascending set and } f_i \in I, 1 \leq i \leq r \right\}.$$

A minimal element in $\mathbf{S}_I$ (with respect to the $\prec$ order on ascending sets) is said to be a *characteristic set* of the ideal I. $\quad\square$

We remark that if $\mathcal{G}$ is a characteristic set of I, then

$$n \geq |\mathcal{G}| \geq n - \dim I.$$

Since $\mathcal{G}$ is an ascending set, by definition, $n \geq |\mathcal{G}|$. The other inequality can be shown as follows: Consider some arbitrary ordering of variables and assume that $|\mathcal{G}| = k$ and the class variables are $v_k, \ldots, v_1$. Let the remaining variables be called $u_1, \ldots, u_l$. We claim that u's *must all be independent*.

$$I \cap K[u_1, \ldots, u_l] = (0).$$

Then $n - k = l \leq \dim I$ and $|\mathcal{G}| = k \geq n - \dim I$.

The proof of the claim is by contradiction: Suppose that the claim is false, i.e.,

$$\left(\exists\, f(u_1, \ldots, u_l) \neq 0\right) \left[f \in I \cap K[u_1, \ldots, u_l]\right].$$

Assume that $f(u_1, \ldots, u_l)$ is of class u_j. Also, f is reduced with respect to those polynomials of $\mathcal{G}$ with lower ranks. Then one can add f to $\mathcal{G}$ to get an ascending set of lower rank, which is impossible, by the definition of characteristic set.

Also, observe that, for a given ordering of the variables, the characteristic set of an ideal is not necessarily unique. However, any two characteristic sets of an ideal must be of the same rank.

Corollary 5.3.2 (Successive Pseudodivision Lemma) *Consider an ascending set* $\mathcal{F} = \langle f_1, f_2, \ldots, f_r \rangle \subseteq K[x_1, \ldots, x_n]$, *and a polynomial* $g \in K[x_1, \ldots, x_n]$. *Then using the successive pseudodivision (see Theorem 5.2.2), we can find a sequence of polynomials (called a* pseudoremainder chain*),* $g_0, g_1, \ldots, g_r = g$, *such that for each* $1 \leq i \leq r$, *the following equation holds,*

$$\left(\exists \, q_i'\right)\left(\exists \, \alpha_i\right)\left[\operatorname{In}(f_i)^{\alpha_i} g_i = q_i' f_i + g_{i-1}\right]$$

where g_{i-1} *is reduced with respect to* f_i *and* α_i *assumes the smallest possible power, achievable. Thus, the pseudoremainder chain is uniquely determined. Moreover, each* g_{i-1} *is reduced with respect to* $f_i, f_{i+1}, \ldots, f_r$.

$$\operatorname{In}(f_r)^{\alpha_r}\operatorname{In}(f_{r-1})^{\alpha_{r-1}}\cdots\operatorname{In}(f_1)^{\alpha_1} g = \sum_{i=1}^{r} q_i f_i + g_0. \tag{5.3}$$

The polynomial $g_0 \in K[x_1, \ldots, x_n]$ *is said to be the* (generalized) *pseudoremainder of* g *with respect to the ascending set* $\mathcal{F}$,

$$g_0 = \operatorname{PRemainder}(g, \mathcal{F}).$$

By the earlier observations, g_0 *is uniquely determined, and reduced with respect to* $f_1, f_2, \ldots, f_r$. *We say a polynomial* g *is* reduced with respect to an ascending set $\mathcal{F}$ *if* $g = \operatorname{PRemainder}(g, \mathcal{F})$ $\square$

For an ascending set $\mathcal{F}$, we describe the set of all polynomials that are *pseudodivisible* by $\mathcal{F}$, by the following notation:

$$\mathcal{M}(\mathcal{F}) = \left\{g \in K[x_1, \ldots, x_n] \;.\; \operatorname{PRemainder}(g, \mathcal{F}) = 0\right\}.$$

Theorem 5.3.3 *Let* I *be an ideal in* $K[x_1, \ldots, x_n]$. *Then the ascending set* $\mathcal{G} = \langle g_1, \ldots, g_r \rangle$ *is a characteristic set of* I *if and only if*

$$\left(\forall \, f \in I\right)\left[\operatorname{PRemainder}(f, \mathcal{G}) = 0\right].$$

PROOF.
Suppose $\mathcal{G}$ is a characteristic set of I, but that there is a nonzero polynomial $h \in I$ reduced with respect to $\mathcal{G}$, i.e., $\operatorname{PRemainder}(h, \mathcal{G}) = h \neq 0$. If $\operatorname{Class}(h) \leq \operatorname{Class}(g_1)$, then $\langle h \rangle \in S_I$ is an ascending set lower than $\mathcal{G}$, a contradiction. If on the other hand,

$$0 < \operatorname{Class}(g_1) < \cdots < \operatorname{Class}(g_j) < \operatorname{Class}(h)$$

[and $\operatorname{Class}(h) \leq \min(\operatorname{Class}(g_{j+1}), n)$], then $\mathcal{G}' = \langle g_1, \ldots, g_j, h \rangle \in S_I$ is an ascending set lower than $\mathcal{G}$:

1. If $j = r$, then $\mathcal{G}'$ is a longer sequence than $\mathcal{G}$, and $\mathcal{G}$ is a prefix of $\mathcal{G}'$.

2. If $j < r$ and $\text{Class}(h) < \text{Class}(g_{j+1})$, then there is nothing to show.

3. Finally, if $j < r$ and $\text{Class}(h) = \text{Class}(g_{j+1})$, then, since h is reduced, we have $\text{Cdeg}(h) < \text{Cdeg}(g_{j+1})$ thus showing that $\mathcal{F} \prec \mathcal{G}$.

This also contradicts our initial assumption that $\mathcal{G}$ is a characteristic set of I.

Conversely, suppose $\mathcal{G}$ is an ascending set but not a characteristic set of I and that every $h \in I$ reduces with respect to $\mathcal{G}$. By assumption, there is another ascending set $\mathcal{G}' \in S_I$ that is lower than $\mathcal{G}$. Let $g_i' \neq 0$ be the leftmost entry of $\mathcal{G}'$ not occurring in $\mathcal{G}$. By definition, then, $g_i' \in I$ is a polynomial with $\text{PRemainder}(g_i', \mathcal{G}) = g_i' \neq 0$—which leads to the desired contradiction. $\square$

One interesting implication of this theorem is that if $g \in \mathcal{G}$, a characteristic set of I, then $g \in I$ but $\text{In}(g) \notin I$. Simply observe that

$$\text{PRemainder}(\text{In}(g), \mathcal{G}) = \text{In}(g) \neq 0.$$

5.4   Properties of Characteristic Sets

The main properties of characteristic sets are summarized in the next theorem. As in the previous chapter, for any set of polynomials $F = \{f_1, \ldots, f_r\} \subseteq L[x_1, \ldots, x_n]$, ($L = $ and algebraically closed field)[2] we write $\mathcal{Z}(F)$, to denote its *zero set*:

$$\mathcal{Z}(F) = \left\{ \langle \xi_1, \ldots, \xi_n \rangle \in L^n : \left(\forall\, f \in F \right) \left[f(\xi_1, \ldots, \xi_n) = 0 \right] \right\}.$$

By F^∞, we shall denote the set of all *finite products* of

$$\text{In}(f_1), \ldots, \text{In}(f_r),$$

and, for any ideal I in $L[x_1, \ldots, x_n]$, we use the notation $I : F^\infty$ for

$$\left\{ h : \left(\exists\, f \in F^\infty \right) \left[hf \in I \right] \right\}.$$

It is easily seen that $I : F^\infty$ is itself an ideal. Note that, for an ascending set $\mathcal{F} = \langle f_1, \ldots, f_r \rangle$,

$$\text{PRemainder}(h, \mathcal{F}) = 0 \quad \Rightarrow \quad h \in (\mathcal{F}) : \mathcal{F}^\infty,$$

since $\text{PRemainder}(h, \mathcal{F}) = 0$ implies that we can write

$$\text{In}(f_r)^{\alpha_r} \cdots \text{In}(f_1)^{\alpha_1}\, h = q_1\, f_1 + \cdots + q_r\, f_r,$$

---

[2] All the geometric arguments in this chapter do work out, even when we consider a ring of polynomials over an arbitrary field K and consider the zeros over any algebraic extension of K. However, for the sake of simplicity, we shall work over an algebraically closed field.

for some nonnegative integers $\alpha_1, \ldots, \alpha_r$ and polynomials $q_1, \ldots, q_r \in L[x_1, \ldots, x_n]$.

Theorem 5.4.1 *Let I be an ideal in $L[x_1, \ldots, x_n]$ generated by $F = \{f_1, \ldots, f_s\}$. Let $\mathcal{G} = \langle g_1, \ldots, g_r \rangle$ be a characteristic set of I, and let $J = (g_1, \ldots, g_r) \subseteq I$ be the ideal generated by the elements of $\mathcal{G}$. Then*

1. $J \subseteq I \subseteq J : \mathcal{G}^\infty$.

2. $\mathcal{Z}(\mathcal{G}) \setminus \left(\bigcup_{i=1}^r \mathcal{Z}\left(\mathrm{In}(g_i) \right) \right) \subseteq \mathcal{Z}(I) \subseteq \mathcal{Z}(\mathcal{G})$.

3. $I = prime\ ideal \ \Rightarrow \ I \cap \mathcal{G}^\infty = \emptyset$ *and* $I = J : \mathcal{G}^\infty$.

PROOF.
First, make the following two observations:

1. $J = (g_1, \ldots, g_r) \subseteq I$ 　 [because $g_i \in I$ by definition].
2. $\mathrm{In}(g_i) \notin I$ 　 [because $\mathrm{PRemainder}(\mathrm{In}(g_i), \mathcal{G}) = \mathrm{In}(g_i) \neq 0$].

Assertion (1) follows from the first observation and the fact that

$$\left(\forall f \in I \right) \left[\mathrm{PRemainder}(f, \mathcal{G}) = 0 \right];$$

thus, for some element $\mathrm{In}(g_r)^{\alpha_r} \mathrm{In}(g_{r-1})^{\alpha_{r-1}} \cdots \mathrm{In}(g_1)^{\alpha_1} = g \in \mathcal{G}^\infty$,

$$g\,f - \sum_{i=1}^r q_i\, y_i \in J.$$

Assertion (2) follows from the previous assertion and the elementary properties of the zero sets of polynomials. Thus,

$$\mathcal{Z}(I) \subseteq \mathcal{Z}(J) = \mathcal{Z}(\mathcal{G}).$$

Hence, it suffices to prove that

$$\mathcal{Z}(\mathcal{G}) \setminus \left(\bigcup_{i=1}^r \mathcal{Z}\left(\mathrm{In}(g_i) \right) \right) \subseteq \mathcal{Z}(I).$$

Let $P \in L^n$ be a point in the zero set $\mathcal{Z}(\mathcal{G}) \setminus \left(\bigcup_{i=1}^r \mathcal{Z}\left(\mathrm{In}(g_i) \right) \right)$. Let $f \in I$. Then there exists a $g = \prod_{i=1}^r \mathrm{In}(g_i)^{\alpha_i} \in \mathcal{G}^\infty$ such that $gf \in J$. Thus, $g(P)\, f(P) = 0$. But by assumption, $g(P) \neq 0$. Then $f(P) = 0$, as is to be shown.

To see the last assertion, observe that if I is a prime ideal, then we have the following:

- If some $g \in \mathcal{G}^\infty$ belongs to I, then so does one of the factors of g, say $\mathrm{In}(g_i)$. But this contradicts the second observation made in the beginning of this proof.

- Consider an $f \in J : \mathcal{G}^{\infty}$. By definition, there exists a $g \in \mathcal{G}^{\infty}$ such that

$$gf \in J \subseteq I \quad \text{and} \quad g \notin I.$$

From the primality of I, conclude that $f \in I$. That is, $J : \mathcal{G}^{\infty} = I$. □

The inclusions in assertion (2) of Theorem 5.4.1 can be strict. Consider the ideal $I = (x^2 + y^2 - 1, xy)$ and suppose $x \prec y$. A possible characteristic set for I is $\{x^3 - x, \, xy\}$ whose zeroes are a set of higher dimension than the zeroes of I. Removing from it the zeroes of the initial of xy, i.e., the line of equation $y = 0$ one gets only two of the four original points in $\mathcal{Z}(I)$.

One way to interpret the preceding theorem is to say that constructing characteristic sets helps only in answering geometrical questions, but not with general algebraic problems. In particular, we see that characteristic sets are not powerful enough to handle the general *membership problem for an arbitrary ideal*. However, as an immediate consequence of the theorem, we do have the following:

$$\mathrm{PRemainder}(f, \mathcal{G}) = 0 \quad \Leftrightarrow \quad f \in I,$$

provided that I is prime.

5.5   Wu-Ritt Process

Now, let us consider the following triangulation process, due to J.F. Ritt and Wu Wen-Tsün, which computes a so-called *extended characteristic set* of an ideal by repeated applications of the generalized pseudodivision. Historically, this represents the first effort to effectively construct a triangular set corresponding to a system of differential equations. Here, we focus just on the algebraic analog.

Definition 5.5.1 (Ritt's Principle) *Let $F = \{f_1, \ldots, f_s\} \subseteq K[x_1, \ldots, x_n]$ be a finite nonempty set of polynomials, and $I = (F)$ be the ideal generated by F. An ascending set $\mathcal{G}$ satisfying either of the following two properties is called an* extended characteristic set *of F.*

1. $\mathcal{G}$ consists of a polynomial in $K \cap I$, or

2. $\mathcal{G} = \langle g_1, \ldots, g_r \rangle$ with $\mathrm{Class}(g_1) > 0$ and such that

$$
\begin{aligned}
g_i &\in I, &&\text{for all } i = 1, \ldots, r, \\
\mathrm{PRemainder}(f_j, \mathcal{G}) &= 0, &&\text{for all } j = 1, \ldots, s. \quad \Box
\end{aligned}
$$

The following algorithm, the WU-RITT PROCESS, computes an extended characteristic set by repeatedly adding the pseudoremainders R (obtained by successive pseudodivisions by a partially constructed minimum ascending chain) to F and then choosing a minimal ascending set in the enlarged set $R \cup F$.

WU-RITT PROCESS(F)
Input: $F = \{f_1, \ldots, f_s\} \subseteq K[x_1, \ldots, x_n]$.
Output: $\mathcal{G}$, an extended characteristic set of F.

$\mathcal{G} := \emptyset; \quad R := \emptyset;$
loop
     $F := F \cup R; \quad F' := F; \quad R := \emptyset;$
     while $F' \neq \emptyset$ loop
         Choose a polynomial $f \in F'$ of *minimal rank*;
         $F' := F' \setminus \{g \; : \; \mathrm{Class}(g) = \mathrm{Class}(f)$ and
                    g is not reduced with respect to $f\}$;
         $\mathcal{G} := \mathcal{G} \cup \{f\};$
     end{loop };
     for all $f \in F \setminus \mathcal{G}$ loop
         if $r := \mathrm{PRemainder}(f, \mathcal{G}) \neq 0$ then
             $R := R \cup \{r\};$
         end{if };
     end{loop };
until $R = \emptyset$;
return $\mathcal{G}$;
end{WU-RITT PROCESS}. $\square$

It is trivial to see that when the algorithm terminates, it, in fact, returns an ascending set $\mathcal{G}$ that satisfies the conditions given in Definition 5.5.1. The termination follows from the following observations:

Let $F \subseteq K[x_1, \ldots, x_n]$ be a (possibly, infinite) set of polynomials. Consider the family of all ascending sets, each of whose components is in F,

$$\mathbf{S}_F = \left\{ \mathcal{F} - \langle f_1, \ldots, f_r \rangle \; : \; \mathcal{F} \text{ is an ascending set and } f_i \in F, 1 \leq i \leq r \right\}.$$

A minimal element in $\mathbf{S}_F$ (with respect to the $\prec$ order on ascending sets) is denoted as $\mathrm{MinASC}(F)$. The following easy proposition can be shown; the proof is similar to that of Theorem 5.3.3.

Proposition 5.5.1 *Let F be as above. Let g be a polynomial reduced with respect to $\mathrm{MinASC}(F)$. Then*

$$\mathrm{MinASC}(F \cup \{g\}) \prec \mathrm{MinASC}(F).$$

PROOF.
Let $\mathrm{MinASC}(F) = \langle f_1, \ldots, f_r \rangle$. By assumption, g is reduced with respect to F, i.e.,

$$\mathrm{PRemainder}(g, F) = g \neq 0.$$

If $\mathrm{Class}(g) \leq \mathrm{Class}(f_1)$, then $\langle g \rangle$ is an ascending set of $F \cup \{g\}$ lower than $\mathrm{MinASC}(F)$.

If on the other hand,

$$0 < \text{Class}(f_1) < \cdots < \text{Class}(f_j) < \text{Class}(g)$$

[and $\text{Class}(g) \leq \min(\text{Class}(f_{j+1}), n)$], then $\langle g_1, \ldots, g_j, h \rangle$ is an ascending set of $F \cup \{g\}$ lower than $\text{MinASC}(F)$. For more details, see the proof of Theorem 5.3.3. $\square$

Now, let F_i be the set of polynomials obtained at the beginning of the ith iteration of the loop (lines 2–15). Starting from the set F_i, the algorithm constructs the ascending chain $\mathcal{G}_i = \text{MinASC}(F_i)$ in the loop (lines 4–9). Now, if R_i [constructed by the loop (lines 10–14)] is nonempty, then each element of R_i is reduced with respect to $\mathcal{G}_i$. Now, since

$$F_{i+1} = F_i \cup R_i,$$

we observe that

$$\text{MinASC}(F_0) \succ \text{MinASC}(F_1) \succ \cdots \succ \text{MinASC}(F_i) \succ \cdots$$

Since the "$\succ$" is a well-ordering on the ascending sets, the chain above must be finite and the algorithm must terminate. However, it can be shown that the number of steps the algorithm may take in the worst case can be nonelementary in the parameters n (the number of variables) and d (the maximum degree of the polynomials) (see [78]).

In general, an extended characteristic set of an ideal is not a characteristic set of the ideal. However, an extended characteristic set *does* satisfy the following property, in a manner similar to a characteristic set.

Theorem 5.5.2 *Let* $F \subseteq L[x_1, \ldots, x_n]$ *($L =$ an algebraically closed field) be a basis of an ideal I, with an extended characteristic set $\mathcal{G} = \langle g_1, \ldots, g_r \rangle$. Then*

$$\mathcal{Z}(\mathcal{G}) \setminus \left(\bigcup_{i=1}^{r} \mathcal{Z}\big(\text{In}(g_i)\big) \right) \subseteq \mathcal{Z}(I) \subseteq \mathcal{Z}(\mathcal{G}).$$

PROOF.
Let

$$\mathcal{M}(\mathcal{G}) = \Big\{ f \ : \ \text{PRemainder}(f, \mathcal{G}) = 0 \Big\}.$$

denote, as before, the set of all polynomials that are *pseudodivisible* by $\mathcal{G}$. Thus, by the properties of an extended characteristic set,

$$(\mathcal{G}) \subseteq I \subseteq \big(\mathcal{M}(\mathcal{G})\big),$$

since by definition, $F \subseteq \mathcal{M}(\mathcal{G})$. Using the elementary properties of the zero sets of polynomials, we get

$$\mathcal{Z}\big(\mathcal{M}(\mathcal{G})\big) \subseteq \mathcal{Z}(I) \subseteq \mathcal{Z}(\mathcal{G}).$$

Hence, it suffices to prove that

$$\mathcal{Z}(\mathcal{G}) \setminus \left(\bigcup_{i=1}^{r} \mathcal{Z}\Big(\text{In}(g_i)\Big) \right) \subseteq \mathcal{Z}\Big(\mathcal{M}(\mathcal{G})\Big).$$

Let $P \in L^n$ be a point in the zero set $\mathcal{Z}(\mathcal{G}) \setminus \left(\bigcup_{i=1}^{r} \mathcal{Z}\Big(\text{In}(g_i)\Big) \right)$. Let $f \in \mathcal{M}(\mathcal{G})$. Then there exists a $g = \prod_{i=1}^{r} \text{In}(g_i)^{\alpha_i} \in \mathcal{G}^{\infty}$ such that $gf \in J$. Thus, $g(P)\,f(P) = 0$. But by assumption, $g(P) \neq 0$. Then $f(P) = 0$, as is to be shown. $\square$

5.6   Computation

Let $I \subseteq K[x_1, \ldots, x_n]$ be an ideal generated by a set of s generators, f_1, ..., f_s, in the ring of polynomials in n variables over the field K. Further, assume that each of the polynomial f_i in the given set of generators has its "*total*" degree, Tdeg bounded by d:

$$\Big(\forall\, 1 \leq i \leq s\Big) \Big[\text{Tdeg}(f_i) \leq d\Big],$$

where by $\text{Tdeg}(f)$, we denote $\sum_i \deg_{x_i}(f)$. Note that $\deg(f_i) \leq \text{Tdeg}(f_i) \leq n\, \deg(f_i)$.

Let $\mathcal{G} = \langle g_1, \ldots, g_r \rangle$ be a characteristic set of the ideal I with respect to an ordering of the variables that will satisfy certain conditions to be discusses later.

Our approach will be as follows: first, using an effective version of Nullstellensatz[3], we shall derive a degree bound for a characteristic set of a zero-dimensional ideal, and then use a "lifting" procedure to obtain a bound for the more general cases. Equipped with these bounds, we can exhaustively search a bounded portion of the ring for a characteristic set; the search process can be made very efficient by using simple ideas from linear algebra.

Let us begin with the case when our ideal I is zero-dimensional. Note that every zero-dimensional ideal I contains a univariate polynomial $h_j(x_j)$, in each variable x_j, since by definition:

$$I \cap K[x_j] \neq (0), \quad \text{for all } j = 1, \ldots, n.$$

Since the sequence $\langle h_1, \ldots, h_n \rangle$ is clearly an ascending set in $\mathbf{S}_I$, we get a similar bound on the class degrees of the polynomials in a characteristic set of I. Bounds on the total degrees of $\mathcal{G}$ follow.

1. Clearly, $\text{Class}(g_j) = \text{Class}(h_j) = j$.

---

[3]Originally due to Brownawell [29] and later sharpened by Kollár [118]—see the Bibliographic Notes of Chapter 4.

2. $\text{Cdeg}(g_j) \leq \text{Cdeg}(h_j) \leq \deg(h_j)$.

3. For all $1 \leq i < j$, $\deg_{x_i}(g_j) < \deg_{x_i}(g_i)$, as g_j is reduced with respect to the preceding g_i's. Thus

$$\text{Tdeg}(g_j) \leq \left(\sum_{i=1}^{j} \text{Cdeg}(g_i) \right) - j + 1 \leq n \left(\max_i \deg(h_i) \right).$$

By combining bounds obtained by a version of Bezout's inequality[4] with the effective Nullstellensatz, we can show that $\max_i \deg(h_i) \leq 2(d+1)^{2n}$, if $\text{Tdeg}(f_i)$'s are all bounded by d. In fact the following stronger theorem holds:

Theorem 5.6.1 (Zero-Dimensional Upper Bound Theorem) *Let $I = (f_1, \ldots, f_s)$ be a zero-dimensional ideal in $K[x_1, \ldots, x_n]$, where K is an arbitrary field, and $\text{Tdeg}(f_i) \leq d$, $1 \leq i \leq s$. Then I has a characteristic set $\mathcal{G} = \langle g_1, \ldots, g_n \rangle$ with respect to the ordering,*

$$x_1 \prec x_2 \prec \cdots \prec x_n,$$

where for all $1 \leq j \leq n$,

1. $\text{Class}(g_j) = j$.

2. $\text{Tdeg}(g_j) \leq 2n(d+1)^{2n}$.

3.

$$\left(\exists\, a_{j,1}, \ldots, a_{j,s} \in K[x_1, \ldots, x_n] \right) \left[g_j = \sum_{i=1}^{s} a_{j,i} f_i, \right],$$

and $\text{Tdeg}(a_{j,i} f_i) \leq 8n(d+1)^{2n}, 1 \leq i \leq s$. □

The results on the bounds for a characteristic set of a zero-dimensional ideal can be extended to the more general classes of ideals, by a "lifting" process used by Gallo and Mishra [77], leading to the following general result:

Theorem 5.6.2 (General Upper Bound Theorem) *Let $I = (f_1, \ldots, f_s)$ be an ideal in $K[x_1, \ldots, x_n]$, where K is an arbitrary field, and $\text{Tdeg}(f_i) \leq d$, $1 \leq i \leq s$. Assume that $x_1, \ldots, x_l$ are the independent*

---

[4]This effective version of Bezout's inequality is due to Heintz [90] and states the following:

Let I be a zero-dimensional ideal in $L[x_1, \ldots, x_n]$ generated by a set of polynomials of degree no larger than d. Then $|\mathcal{Z}(I)| \leq 2(d+1)^n$.

variables with respect to I. That is, these independent variables form the largest subset of $\{x_1, \ldots, x_n\}$ such that

$$I \cap K[x_1, \ldots, x_l] \neq (0).$$

Let $r = n - \dim I = n - l$. Then I has a characteristic set $\mathcal{G} = \langle g_1, \ldots, g_r \rangle$ with respect to the ordering

$$x_1 \prec x_2 \prec \cdots \prec x_n,$$

where for all $1 \leq j \leq r$,

1. $\mathrm{Class}(g_j) = j + l$.
2. $\mathrm{Tdeg}(g_j) \leq D_1 = 4(s+1)(9r)^{2r}d(d+1)^{4r^2}$.
3.

$$\left(\exists\, a_{j,1}, \ldots, a_{j,s} \in K[x_1, \ldots, x_n]\right) \left[g_j = \sum_{i=1}^{s} a_{j,i} f_i, \right],$$

and $\mathrm{Tdeg}(a_{j,i} f_i) \leq D_2 = 11(s+1)(9r)^{2r}d(d+1)^{4r^2}, 1 \leq i \leq s.$ □

We are now ready to see how one can compute a characteristic set of an ideal, by using the degree bounds of the *general upper bound theorem* and fairly simple ideas from linear algebra. In particular, we shall assume that we have available to us effective algorithms for computing the *rank* and *determinants* of matrices over an arbitrary field.

Let I be an ideal given by a set of generators $\{f_1, \ldots, f_s\} \in K[x_1, \ldots, x_n]$, where K is an arbitrary field, $\mathrm{Tdeg}(f_i) \leq d$. Assume that after some reordering of the variables, the variables $x_1, \ldots, x_n$ are so arranged that the first l of them are *independent* with respect to I, and the remaining $(n - l)$ variables, *dependent*.

$$x_1 \prec x_2 \prec \cdots \prec x_n.$$

See Chapter 4 for further discussion on how dependent and independent variables can be computed.

Assume, inductively, that the first $(j - 1)$ elements $g_1, \ldots, g_{j-1}$, of a characteristic set, $\mathcal{G}$, of I have been computed, and we wish to compute the jth element g_j of $\mathcal{G}$. By Theorem 5.6.2, we know that $\mathrm{Class}(g_1) = (l+1)$, $\ldots$, $\mathrm{Class}(g_{j-1}) = (l+j-1)$ and $\mathrm{Class}(g_j) = (l+j)$. Let

$$\mathrm{Cdeg}(g_1) = d_{l+1}, \ldots, \mathrm{Cdeg}(g_{j-1}) = d_{l+j-1}.$$

Thus, the polynomial g_j sought must be a nonzero polynomial of least degree in x_{l+j}, in $I \cap K[x_1, \ldots, x_{l+j}]$ such that

$$\deg_{x_{l+1}}(g_1) < d_{l+1}, \quad \ldots, \quad \deg_{x_{l+j-1}} < d_{l+j-1}.$$

Furthermore, we know, from the general upper bound theorem, that

$$\left(\exists\, a_{j,1},\ldots,a_{j,s} \in K[x_1,\ldots,x_n]\right)\left[g_j = \sum_{i=1}^{s} a_{j,i}\, f_i,\right], \qquad (5.4)$$

and $\mathrm{Tdeg}(g_j)$, $\mathrm{Tdeg}(a_{j,i}\, f_i) \le D = \max(D_1, D_2)$, $1 \le i \le s$. Thus g_j satisfying all the properties can be determined by solving an appropriate system of linear equations.

Let M_1, M_2, $\ldots$, M_ρ be an enumeration of all the power products in x_1, $\ldots$, x_n [called, $\mathrm{PP}(x_1, \ldots, x_n)$] of degree less than D; thus ρ satisfies the following bound,

$$\rho = \binom{D+n}{n}.$$

The enumeration on the power products is assumed to be so chosen that the indices $\lambda < \mu$ *only if* one of the following three conditions is satisfied:

1. $M_\lambda \in \mathrm{PP}(x_1, \ldots, x_{l+j})$ and $M_\mu \in \mathrm{PP}(x_1, \ldots, x_n) \backslash \mathrm{PP}(x_1, \ldots, x_{l+j})$.

2. M_λ, $M_\mu \in \mathrm{PP}(x_1, \ldots, x_{l+j})$ and

$$\left(\forall\, l < i < l+j\right)\left[\deg_{x_i}(M_\lambda) < d_i\right]$$

and

$$\left(\exists\, l < i < l+j\right)\left[\deg_{x_i}(M_\mu) \ge d_i\right].$$

3. M_λ, $M_\mu \in \mathrm{PP}(x_1, \ldots, x_{l+j})$,

$$\left(\forall\, l < i < l+j\right)\left[\deg_{x_i}(M_\lambda),\ \deg_{x_i}(M_\mu) < d_i\right],$$

and $\deg_{x_{l+j}}(M_\lambda) < \deg_{x_{l+j}}(M_\mu)$.

Let us express $a_{i,j}$ and g_j symbolically as follows:

$$a_{i,j} = \sum_{\lambda=1}^{\rho} \alpha_{(i-1)+\lambda} M_\lambda, \quad 1 \le i \le s,$$

$$g_j = \sum_{\mu=1}^{\rho} \beta_\mu M_\mu.$$

By equating the the terms of the same monomials on both sides of equation (5.4)

$$\left(\exists\, a_{j,1},\ldots,a_{j,s} \in K[x_1,\ldots,x_n]\right)\left[g_j = \sum_{i=1}^{s} a_{j,i}\, f_i,\right],$$

we get at most

$$\binom{d+l+j}{l+j} \cdot \rho \le (d+1)^n \rho$$

equations, in $(s+1)\rho$ unknowns, α's and β's. We represent the homogeneous system as follows:

$$\left[A_1 \cdots A_{s\rho} \vdots B_1 \cdots B_\rho \right] \begin{bmatrix} \alpha_1 \\ \vdots \\ \alpha_{s\rho} \\ \cdots \\ \beta_1 \\ \vdots \\ \beta_\rho \end{bmatrix} = \mathbf{0}.$$

Any solution of this system that minimizes the index of the last nonzero entry of the β's will correspond to the desired g_j. The existence of a solution of the desired nature follows from Theorem 5.6.2, and the rest follows simply from the choice of the ordering on the power products. (The reader may check!)

Let $\lambda_1(=1), \lambda_2, \ldots, \lambda_l$ and m, be a sequence of indices such that, for $1 \le i < l$,

$$\begin{aligned} 0 \quad &< \quad \mathrm{rank}\left[A_1 \cdots A_{\lambda_i} \right] \\ &= \quad \mathrm{rank}\left[A_1 \cdots A_{\lambda_i+1} \right] = \cdots = \mathrm{rank}\left[A_1 \cdots A_{\lambda_{i+1}-1} \right] \\ &< \quad \mathrm{rank}\left[A_1 \cdots A_{\lambda_{i+1}} \right], \end{aligned}$$

and

$$\begin{aligned} \mathrm{rank}\left[A_1 \cdots A_{s\rho} \right] \quad &< \quad \mathrm{rank}\left[A_1 \cdots A_{s\rho} \vdots B_1 \right] \\ &< \quad \cdots < \mathrm{rank}\left[A_1 \cdots A_{s\rho} \vdots B_1 \cdots B_{m-1} \right] \\ &= \quad \mathrm{rank}\left[A_1 \cdots A_{s\rho} B_1 \cdots B_m \right]. \end{aligned}$$

Then, we know that in the desired solution all the α's and β's, not including $\alpha_{\lambda_1}, \ldots, \alpha_{\lambda_l}$ and $\beta_1, \ldots, \beta_m$, must be zero. Thus, we need to solve the following system of linear equations

$$
\begin{bmatrix} A_{\lambda_1} \cdots A_{\lambda_l} \vdots B_1 \cdots B_{m-1} \end{bmatrix}
\begin{bmatrix} \alpha_{\lambda_1} \\ \vdots \\ \alpha_{\lambda_l} \\ \cdots \\ \beta_1 \\ \vdots \\ \beta_{m-1} \end{bmatrix} = B_m.
$$

This linear algebraic problem can be easily solved to derive the element, g_j, a monic polynomial given by:

$$
g_j = M_m - \beta_{m-1} M_{m-1} - \cdots - \beta_1 M_1.
$$

Thus the procedure outlined here is completely effective.

Theorem 5.6.3 *Let $I = (f_1, \ldots, f_s)$ be an ideal in $K[x_1, \ldots, x_n]$, where K is an arbitrary field, and $\mathrm{Tdeg}(f_i) \leq d$, $1 \leq i \leq s$. Then with respect to any ordering on the variables:*

$$
x_1 \prec x_2 \prec \cdots \prec x_n,
$$

where the first $\dim(I)$-many variables are independent, one can effectively compute a characteristic set of I. $\quad \Box$

5.7   Geometric Theorem Proving

Let us consider how the concepts of characteristic sets (or extended characteristic sets) can be used in a simple geometric theorem prover. The first such mechanical theorem prover, devised by Wu Wen-Tsün [209-211] in China, has come to be known as the *China prover* and has been successfully used to prove many classical and some new theorems in plane analytic geometry. Some further improvements in this direction has been achieved by Shang-Ching Chou [47].

Other approaches, based on different constructive methods in computer algebra, have also been proposed for this problem: For instance, Kutzler and Stifter [122], Kapur [111] and Kapur and Narendra [114] have proposed methods based on Gröbner bases; Carrá and Gallo [42] and Gallo [75] have devised a method using the dimension of the underlying algebraic variety; J.W. Hong [101] has introduced a seminumerical algorithm using an interesting gap theorem and "proof-by-example" techniques.

The method based on the Wu-Ritt characteristic sets is not, however, a real theorem prover, in the sense that it does not follow any logical proof-theoretic techniques; it simply takes an algebraic translation of a set of geometric statements and tries to verify its validity in the manner to be made more precise. For most of the geometric statements, however, the translation from geometry to algebra is far from being completely automated. The fundamental principle that the translation method relies on is fairly simple, i.e., the classical coordinate method of Descartes introduced in the 17th century.

Definition 5.7.1 (Elementary Geometry Statement) By an *elementary geometry statement*, we mean a formula of the following kind:

$$\Big(f_1 = 0 \;\wedge\; f_2 = 0 \;\wedge\; \cdots \;\wedge\; f_s = 0 \Big) \quad \Rightarrow \quad \Big(g = 0 \Big), \qquad (5.5)$$

where the f_i's and g are polynomials in $L[x_1, \ldots, x_n]$, the variables x_i's are assumed to be bound by universal quantification and their ranges are assumed to be the field L, the base field of the underlying geometry. We further assume that the base field L is algebraically closed.   □

The conjunct $\bigwedge_i (f_i = 0)$ is called the *premise* of the geometry statement, and will be assumed to be nontrivial, i.e., the set of points in L^n satisfying the premise is nonempty. The statement $g = 0$ is its *conclusion*. *To prove a statement, then, is to show that a geometric formula is valid.*

However, one problem with the above algebraic statement is that it does not mention certain *geometric degeneracies* that are implicitly excluded: For instance, when a geometric statement mentions a *triangle*, it is conventionally assumed to mean those nondegenerate triangles whose vertices are noncollinear. But, on the other hand, spelling out all the conceivable geometric degeneracies makes the process unappealingly cumbersome. Wu's approach permits one to circumvent this problem as it produces these nondegeneracy conditions as a natural by-product. In fact, Wu's approach proves an elementary geometry statement, in the sense that it shows that the *conclusion is true whenever the premises are generically true.*[5] Following Wu, in this case, we will say that the corresponding geometric statement is *generically true.*

The Wu's algorithm is as follows: Assume that the input to the algorithm is an elementary geometry formula which is obtained after the theorem has been translated algebraically.

---

[5] In geometric terms, it shows that the conclusion polynomial vanishes on *some open subset* (under the Zariski topology) of the zero set of the system of polynomials, f_1, f_2, $\ldots$, f_s.

WU'S ALGORITHM(F)
Input: Premises $= F = \{f_1, \ldots, f_s\} \subseteq L[x_1, \ldots, x_n]$,
               Conclusion $= g \in L[x_1, \ldots, x_n]$.
Output: Trivial, if the premises are contradictory;
               True, if the geometry statement is generically true.

Compute $\mathcal{G}$, a characteristic set of (F);
if $\mathcal{G} = \langle 1 \rangle$ then
      return Trivial;
elsif PRemainder$(g, \mathcal{G}) = 0$ then
      return True;
else
      return Unconfirmed;
end{WU'S ALGORITHM}. $\square$

In order to understand Wu's algorithm we need to make the following observations:

- If $\mathcal{G} = \langle 1 \rangle$, then, since every $g_i \in \mathcal{G}$ also belongs to the ideal (F), we see that $(F) = (1)$ and that $\mathcal{Z}(F) = \emptyset$. In this case, the system of premises are inconsistent and the geometry statement is trivially true.

   Also observe that if the ideal $(F) = (1)$, then, by definition, its characteristic set must be $\langle 1 \rangle$. Thus, the algorithm always correctly detects a trivial geometry statement.

- Suppose $\mathcal{G} = \langle g_1, \ldots, g_r \rangle \neq \langle 1 \rangle$. If $r = \text{PRemainder}(g, \mathcal{G}) = 0$, then

$$\text{In}(g_r)^{\alpha_r} \text{In}(g_{r-1})^{\alpha_{r-1}} \cdots \text{In}(g_1)^{\alpha_1} g = \sum_{i=1}^{r} q_i g_i \in (f_1, \ldots, f_s). \quad (5.6)$$

Thus at every point $P \in L^n$, at which f_i's (hence, g_i's) vanish, but not $\text{In}(g_i)$'s, we note that the conclusion polynomial g must also vanish. The clause

$$\text{In}(g_1) = 0 \vee \cdots \vee \text{In}(g_r) = 0$$

has been interpreted by Wu as the associated degeneracy condition for the original geometry statement. Thus, when Wu's algorithm returns the value "true," the following holds:

$$\left(\forall P \in L^n \right) \left[\left(f_1(P) = 0 \wedge \cdots \wedge f_s(P) = 0 \right) \wedge \right.$$
$$\neg \left(\text{In}(g_1)(P) = 0 \vee \cdots \vee \text{In}(g_r)(P) = 0 \right)$$
$$\left. \Rightarrow g(P) = 0 \right]$$

Geometrically, we have

$$\mathcal{Z}(g) \supseteq \mathcal{Z}(f_1, \ldots, f_s) \setminus \bigcup_{i=1}^{r} \mathcal{Z}(\mathrm{In}(g_i)).$$

One problem with Wu's algorithm, as presented here, is that it is not complete, and in fact, it is only the first half of the algorithm developed by Wu. Nevertheless, just this portion of the algorithm has found many applications, as one can argue heuristically that the algorithm succeeds in vast majority of the cases [47].

Wu's algorithm guarantees that whenever the algorithm claims that a statement is generically true, it is indeed so; however, the converse does not hold. In fact, we may have a conclusion g that vanishes on some open set of the zero set of the premises, but Wu's algorithm may fail to detect this without further *decomposition* of the characteristic set.

Even the complete Wu's algorithm has several hard-to-eliminate drawbacks. First, it is unable to work with arbitrary fields (not algebraically closed, e.g., $\mathbb{R}$). If propositions about real geometry are investigated in this way, a false proposition will be rejected (because it is false also in the complex field), but sometimes a true theorem (over real closed field) may unfortunately be rejected. For example, consider the hypothesis $x^2 + y^2 = 0$ and the conclusion $y = 0$. This is of course true in $\mathbb{R}^2$ but false in $\mathbb{C}^2$.

Lastly, the method is unable to handle inequalities. So geometric propositions involving "*internal*," "*external*," or "*between*" are not in the range of such a prover. In this sense, the so called "Wu geometry" is smaller in scope than the more general "Tarski geometry" which includes all the propositions that can be proved by real quantifier elimination algorithms [91]. We shall come back to these questions later in the book.

Problems

Problem 5.1
Show that a characteristic set of an ideal is not necessarily its basis.

Hint: Consider the ideal generated by the set of polynomials $F = \{x^2 + y^2 - 1, xy\} \subset \mathbb{Q}[x, y]$. Show that $\mathcal{G} = \{x^3 - x, xy\}$ is a characteristic set of (F) under the ordering $x \prec y$. However, $(\mathcal{G}) \subsetneq (F)$.

Problem 5.2
True or False:

1. $I = (1)$ if and only if its characteristic set is $\langle 1 \rangle$.
2. $I = (1)$ if and only if its extended characteristic set is $\langle 1 \rangle$.

Problem 5.3
Show that a characteristic set is an extended characteristic set but not the converse.

Problem 5.4
Using the characteristic set algorithm, devise solutions for the following two problems:

(i)

> SOLVABILITY(F)
> **Input:** $F = \{f_1, \ldots, f_r\} \subseteq L[x_1, \ldots, x_n]$,
> $L =$ An algebraically closed field.
> **Output:**   TRUE, if F has a solution in $\mathbf{L}^n$.

(ii)

> FINITESOLVABILITY(F)
> **Input:** $F = \{f_1, \ldots, f_r\} \subset L[x_1, \ldots, x_n]$,
> $L =$ An algebraically closed field.
> **Output:**   TRUE, if F has finitely many solutions in L^n.

Problem 5.5
Let $H = \{h_1, h_2, \ldots, h_n\} \subseteq K[x_1, x_2, \ldots, x_n]$ ($K =$ a field) be a set of univariate monic polynomials, one in each variable:

$$h_j(x_j) \in K[x_j] \setminus K \quad \text{and} \quad \text{In}(h_j) = 1.$$

Then show that $\mathcal{H} = \langle h_1, h_2, \ldots, h_n \rangle$ is a characteristic set of (H) with respect to the following ordering of the variables:

$$x_1 \prec x_2 \prec \cdots \prec x_n.$$

Problem 5.6
Let $F \colon K[x_1, \ldots, x_n] \to K[x_1, \ldots, x_n]$ be a K-endomorphism, where F may be written as $F = (f_1, \ldots, f_n)$ (where $f_i \in K[x_1, \ldots, x_n]$). F is said to be invertible if each variable x_i can be expressed as a polynomial of f_1, $\ldots$, f_n.

Show that that F is invertible with inverse $G = (g_1, \ldots, g_n)$ if and only if

$$G = \{x_1 - g_1(y_1, \ldots, y_n), \ldots, x_n - g_n(y_1, \ldots, y_n)\}$$

is a characteristic set of the ideal

$$I = (y_1 - f_1(x_1, \ldots, x_n), \ldots, y_n - f_n(x_1, \ldots, x_n))$$

of $K[y_1, \ldots, y_n, x_1, \ldots, x_n]$.

Problem 5.7

Let L be an algebraically closed field, and let I be an ideal in $L[x_1, \ldots, x_n]$, generated by the following n polynomials, $F = \{f_1, \ldots, f_n\}$, each of degree d:

$$
\begin{aligned}
f_1 &= x_1 - x_n^d, \\
f_2 &= x_2 - x_1^d, \\
&\vdots \\
f_{n-1} &= x_{n-1} - x_{n-2}^d, \\
f_n &= x_n - x_{n-1}^d.
\end{aligned}
$$

Then show that independent of the ordering on the variables, we have the following:

1. Every characteristic set of F is of degree $D \geq d^n$.

2. Every extended characteristic set of F is of degree $D \geq d^n$.

Problem 5.8

Show that the number of pseudodivision steps, $T(n, d)$ that the Wu-Ritt process may use in the worst case is nonelementary in the parameters n (the number of variables) and d (the maximum degree of the polynomials), independent of the ordering on the variables:

$$
x_1 \prec x_2 \prec \cdots \prec x_n.
$$

In particular, show that

$$
\begin{aligned}
T(0, d) &= 1, \\
T(n, d) &\leq T\left(n - 1, c'(1 + \sqrt{2})^d\right) + d, \quad n \geq 1,
\end{aligned}
$$

leading to

$$
T(n, d) \leq c \cdot \underbrace{d(1 + \sqrt{2})^{d(1+\sqrt{2})^{\cdot^{\cdot^{d(1+\sqrt{2})^d}}}}}_{n} .
$$

Problem 5.9

Consider an ascending set $\mathcal{F} = \langle f_1, \ldots, f_r \rangle \subseteq K[x_1, \ldots, x_n]$ and a polynomial $g \in K[x_1, \ldots x_n]$, where K is an arbitrary field, $\mathrm{Tdeg}(f_i) \leq d$, for all $1 \leq i \leq s$, and $\mathrm{Tdeg}(g) \leq \delta$.

If $g_0 = \mathrm{PRemainder}(g, \mathcal{F})$ is the generalized pseudoremainder of g with respect to $\mathcal{F}$ then show that

$$
\mathrm{Tdeg}(g_0) \leq (d + 1)^r (\delta + 1).
$$

Also, devise an algorithm that can compute the generalized pseudoremainder g_0 using $O(\delta^{O(n)}(d + 1)^{O(nr)})$ arithmetic operations.

Problem 5.10

Consider the following algorithm for geometric theorem proving using the Gröbner basis algorithm:

KAPUR'S ALGORITHM(F)
Input: Premises $= F = \{f_1, \ldots, f_s\} \subseteq L[x_1, \ldots, x_n]$,
              Conclusion $= g \in L[x_1, \ldots, x_n]$.
Output: Trivial, if the premises are contradictory;
              True, if the geometry statement is generically true;
                  Return the nondegeneracy condition $g' = 0$.

Compute $\mathcal{G}_1$, a minimal Gröbner basis of (F);
Compute $\mathcal{G}_2$, a minimal Gröbner basis of $(F \cup \{gz - 1\})$;
Comment: The last computation is done in the ring $L[x_1, \ldots, x_n, z]$;
if $\mathcal{G}_1 = \{1\}$ then
        return Trivial;
elsif $\mathcal{G}_2 = \{1\}$ then
        return True, nondegeneracy condition $g' = 1$;
        Comment: No nondegeneracy condition is necessary;
else for every $g_i \in \mathcal{G}_2 \cap L[x_1, \ldots, x_n]$ loop
      if $g_i \notin (F)$ and $1 \notin (F \cup \{g_i z - 1\})$ then
              return True, nondegeneracy condition $g' = g_i$;
end{if };

return Unconfirmed;
end{KAPUR'S ALGORITHM}.   □

Prove that the above algorithm is correct.

Note that for a given set of premises $F = \{f_1, \ldots, f_s\}$ and a conclusion g we shall say g' represents a nondegeneracy condition if and only if

$$\left(\forall P \in L^n\right) \left[\left(f_1(P) = 0 \wedge \cdots \wedge f_s(P) = 0\right) \wedge \left(g'(P) \neq 0\right) \;\Rightarrow\; g(P) = 0\right],$$

but not the following:

$$\left(\forall P \in L^n\right) \left[\left(f_1(P) = 0 \wedge \cdots \wedge f_s(P) = 0\right) \;\Rightarrow\; g'(P) = 0\right].$$

Solutions to Selected Problems

Problem 5.2

(1) True. Since a characteristic set $\mathcal{G}$ of an ideal I is a subset of I, we have

$$(1) \subseteq (\mathcal{G}) \subseteq I \subseteq (1).$$

The converse is a trivial consequence of the minimality of the characteristic set among the ascending chains.

(2) As earlier, an extended characteristic set $\mathcal{G}'$ is a subset of the ideal I, and $1 \in \mathcal{G}'$ implies that $I = (1)$.

However the converse is not necessarily true. Consider the ideal generated by the polynomials: $F = \{x^2 + 2x + 1, \ xy^2 + y^2 + x\} \subset \mathbb{Q}[x, y]$. It is easily seen (applying the Wu-Ritt process, for instance) that F is an extended characteristic set of (F). However, $(F) = (1)$, while its extended characteristic set does not contain 1. Note that

$$\begin{aligned}
1 &= (y^4 + 2y^2 + 1)(x^2 + 2x + 1) \\
&\quad - (xy^2 + y^2 + x + 2)(xy^2 + y^2 + x) \\
&\in (F).
\end{aligned}$$

Problem 5.5

First, note that $\mathcal{H}$ is an extended characteristic set of H (with respect to the ordering $x_1 \prec x_2 \prec \cdots \prec x_n$); this is easily seen by an application of the Wu-Ritt process to the set H. Thus

$$H \subseteq \mathcal{M}(\mathcal{H}).$$

We claim that the set $\mathcal{M}(\mathcal{H})$ is an ideal. Thus

$$(H) \subseteq \left(\mathcal{M}(\mathcal{H}) \right) = \mathcal{M}(\mathcal{H}),$$

and $\mathcal{H}$ is a characteristic set of (H), since

$$\left(\forall f \in (H) \right) \left[\mathrm{PRemainder}(f, \mathcal{H}) = 0 \right].$$

In order to prove the claim, we make the following simple observations:

1. Since $\mathrm{In}(h_j) = 1$, for all $1 \le j \le n$,

$$\begin{aligned}
&\left[\mathrm{PRemainder}(g', \mathcal{H}) = g_0' \ \wedge \ \mathrm{PRemainder}(g'', \mathcal{H}) = g_0'' \right] \\
&\Rightarrow \quad (A) \ \ \mathrm{PRemainder}(g' + g'', \mathcal{H}) = g_0' + g_0'' \\
&\qquad\ \ (B) \ \ \mathrm{PRemainder}(cg', \mathcal{H}) = cg_0', \quad \left(\forall c \in K \right).
\end{aligned}$$

2. Since $h_j \in K[x_j] \setminus K$, for all $1 \le j \le n$,

$$\left[\mathrm{PRemainder}(g', \mathcal{H}) = 0 \right] \ \Rightarrow \ \mathrm{PRemainder}(x_i g', \mathcal{H}) = 0, \quad \left(\forall x_i \right).$$

Assume that $h_i = x_i^d + c_{d-1} x_i^{d-1} + \cdots + c_0$, and let the following sequence

$$g_0'(= 0), g_1', \ldots, g_{i-1}', \ldots, g_n'(= g')$$

denote the sequence of pseudoremainders, obtained by dividing g' by $\mathcal{H}$. If $\deg_{x_i} g'_{i-1} < (d-1)$, then, clearly,

$$\text{PRemainder}(x_i g', \mathcal{H}) = \text{PRemainder}\left(x_i g', \langle h_{i-1}, \ldots, h_1 \rangle\right) = 0.$$

Otherwise, $\deg_{x_i} g'_{i-1} = (d-1)$, and

$$
\begin{aligned}
x_i g'_{i-1} \;=\;\; & \alpha_d(x_1, \ldots, x_{i-1}, x_{i+1}, \ldots, x_n) x_i^d \\
& + \alpha_{d-1}(x_1, \ldots, x_{i-1}, x_{i+1}, \ldots, x_n) x_i^{d-1} + \cdots \\
& + \alpha_1(x_1, \ldots, x_{i-1}, x_{i+1}, \ldots, x_n) x_i,
\end{aligned}
$$

where $\text{PRemainder}(\alpha_k, \langle h_{i-1}, \ldots, h_1 \rangle) = 0$. But

$$
\begin{aligned}
& \text{PRemainder}(x_i g'_{i-1}, h_i) \\
& = \; (\alpha_{d-1} - c_{d-1}\alpha_d) x_i^{d-1} + \cdots + (\alpha_1 - c_1 \alpha_d) x_i - c_0 \alpha_d,
\end{aligned}
$$

and, by (1), $\text{PRemainder}((\alpha_k - c_k \alpha_d), \langle h_{i-1}, \ldots, h_1 \rangle) = 0$. Hence

$$
\begin{aligned}
& \text{PRemainder}(x_i g', \mathcal{H}) \\
& = \; \text{PRemainder}\left(\text{PRemainder}(x_i g'_{i-1}, h_i), \langle h_{i-1}, \ldots, h_1 \rangle\right) = 0.
\end{aligned}
$$

Thus if g', $g'' \in \mathcal{M}(\mathcal{H})$ and $f \in K[x_1, \ldots, x_n]$, then, by observation (1A), $g' + g'' \in \mathcal{M}(\mathcal{H})$ and, by observations (1) and (2), $fg' \in \mathcal{M}(\mathcal{H})$.

A somewhat indirect proof of the statement may be obtained by first observing that H is a Gröbner basis of the ideal (H) (with respect to any admissible ordering), which immediately implies that

$$\left(\forall\, g \in (H)\right) \left(\forall\, 1 \le j \le n\right) \left[\deg_{x_j}(g) \ge \text{Cdeg}(h_j)\right].$$

Since, $\text{Class}(h_j) = j$, and since it has the minimal possible class degree, indeed, $\mathcal{H}$ is a characteristic set of (H).

Problem 5.7

Let $\pi \in S_n$ be a permutation of $[1..n]$, and the arbitrary but fixed ordering on the variables be the following

$$x_i = x_{\pi(1)} \prec x_{\pi(2)} \prec \cdots \prec x_{\pi(n)}.$$

Note that $I \cap \left(L[x_i] \setminus L\right)$ contains a nonzero polynomial $x_i - x_i^{d^n}$ of *minimal possible degree*, d^n.

1. Let $\mathcal{G} = \langle g_1, \ldots, g_r \rangle$ be a characteristic set of F with respect to the chosen ordering. Since $\dim I = 0$,

$$|\mathcal{G}| = n \quad \text{and} \quad g_1 \in I \cap \left(L[x_i] \setminus L \right).$$

Thus, $D \geq \mathrm{Cdeg}(g_1) = \min\left\{ \deg(f) : f \in I \cap (L[x_i] \setminus L) \right\} = d^n$.

2. Let $\mathcal{G}' = \langle g_1', \ldots, g_r' \rangle$ be an extended characteristic set of F with respect to the chosen ordering. By an examination of the Wu-Ritt process, we see that $\mathrm{In}(g_j') = 1$, for all $1 \leq j \leq r$, and

$$\bigcup \mathcal{Z}\left(\mathrm{In}(g_j') \right) = \emptyset \quad \text{and} \quad \mathcal{Z}(\mathcal{G}') = \mathcal{Z}(I) = \text{a finite set.}$$

Hence

$$|\mathcal{G}'| = n \quad \text{and} \quad g_1 \in I \cap \left(L[x_i] \setminus L \right).$$

Thus, $D \geq \mathrm{Cdeg}(g_1) = \min\left\{ \deg(f) : f \in I \cap (L[x_i] \setminus L) \right\} \geq d^n$.

Problem 5.10

Note that the conditions for g' to represent nondegeneracy are equivalent to the following:

$$g' \notin \sqrt{(F)} \quad \text{and} \quad gg' \in \sqrt{(F)}.$$

Or in geometric terms:

$$\mathcal{Z}(g) \supseteq \mathcal{Z}(F) \setminus \mathcal{Z}(g') \neq \emptyset.$$

We shall need the following two facts:

- Fact 1:

$$g \in \sqrt{(F)} \quad \Leftrightarrow \quad 1 \in (F \cup \{gz - 1\}).$$

See the proof of Theorem 4.3.8.

- Fact 2:

$$g' \in (F \cup \{gz - 1\}) \cap L[x_1, \ldots, x_n] \wedge g' \notin (F)$$
$$\Rightarrow gg' \in \sqrt{(F)}.$$

By assumption, we can express g' as follows:

$$g' = h_1 f_1 + \cdots + h_s f_s + h(gz - 1),$$

where $h \neq 0$. Now after substituting $1/g$ for z and noting that the last term disappears, we see that for some natural number q, we have

$$g' g^q = h_1' f_1 + \cdots + h_s' f_s \in (F).$$

Thus $(gg')^q \in (F)$ and $gg' \in \sqrt{(F)}$.

Thus it is easy to see that if the algorithm outputs "true" with a non-degeneracy condition g', then $g = 0$ in fact follows from $f_1 = 0, \ldots, f_s = 0$, under the assumption that $g' \neq 0$.

Now assume that p is a nondegeneracy condition for the theorem. We wish to show that the algorithm will produce a nondegeneracy condition in this case. By assumption $p \notin \sqrt{(F)}$ but $pg \in \sqrt{(F)}$. Thus,

$$p^m g^m \in (F) \quad \Rightarrow \quad z^m(p^m g^m) - p^m(g^m z^m - 1) = p^m \in (F \cup \{gz - 1\}),$$

but by assumption, $p^m \notin (F)$.

But since $p^m \xrightarrow[*]{G} 0$, $[G = \text{Gröbner}(F \cup \{gz - 1\})]$ there is a $g_i \in (F \cup \{gz - 1\}) \cap L[x_1, \ldots, x_n]$ but $g_i \notin (F)$; and the algorithm will produce such a g_i, since not all such g_i's can be $\sqrt{(F)}$.

Bibliographic Notes

The discussion in this chapter is largely based on the survey paper by Gallo and Mishra [77]. For some recent developments and related applications, also consult [47,76,78,209-211].

The example in the solution to Problem 5.2 is attributed to Narendra (see Kapur[112]). Problem 5.6 is due to Li and Swanson (see [131]) and is closely related to the celebrated Jacobian conjecture [15,203], which states that:

> Let $F : K[x_1, \ldots, x_n] \to K[x_1, \ldots, x_n]$ be a K-endomorphism, where F may be written as $F = (f_1, \ldots, f_n)$ (where $f_i \in K[x_1, \ldots, x_n]$).
> F is invertible, only if
> $$J(F) = \det\left(\frac{\partial f_i}{\partial x_j}\right)$$
> is a nonzero element in the field K.

Problems 5.5, 5.7, and 5.9 are from Gallo and Mishra [77]; Problem 5.8 is from [78]. Problem 5.10 is from Kapur [112].

The following computational complexity result [77] for characteristic sets is now known:

> **Complexity of Characteristic Sets.**
> Let $I = (f_1, \ldots, f_s)$ be an ideal in $K[x_1, \ldots, x_n]$, where K is an arbitrary field, and $\text{Tdeg}(f_i) \leq d$, $1 \leq i \leq s$. Then with respect to any ordering on the indeterminates,
> $$x_1 \prec x_2 \prec \cdots \prec x_n,$$
> where the first $\dim(I)$-many variables are independent, one can compute a characteristic set of I, in $O\left(s^{O(n)}(d+1)^{O(n^3)}\right)$ sequential

time or $O\left(n^7 \log^2(s + d + 1)\right)$ parallel time. The polynomials in the computed characteristic set are of degree $O\left(s(d+1)^{O(n^2)}\right)$.

Although the concept characteristic set has proven to be quite useful in the realm of geometry, several extensions are necessary to improve its power: one such idea is that of an irreducible characteristic set.

Irreducible Characteristic Set.

Let $I = (f_1, \ldots, f_s)$ be an l-dimensional ideal in $K[x_1, \ldots, x_n]$. Further, assume that the first l variables, $x_1, \ldots, x_l$, are the independent variables, the last $r = (n - l)$ variables, $x_{l+1}, \ldots, x_n$, the dependent variables, and the ordering on the variables is the following:

$$x_1 \prec \cdots \prec x_l \prec x_{l+1} \prec \cdots \prec x_n.$$

A characteristic set of I, $\mathcal{G} = \langle g_1, \ldots, g_r \rangle$, is said to be an *irreducible characteristic set* of I, if

$$g_1 = \text{irreducible over } K_1 = K(x_1, \ldots, x_l)$$

$$g_2 = \text{irreducible over } K_2 = QF\left(K_1[x_{l+1}]/(g_1)\right)$$

$$\vdots$$

$$g_j = \text{irreducible over } K_j = QF\left(K_{j-1}[x_{l+j-1}]/(g_{j-1})\right)$$

$$\vdots$$

$$g_r = \text{irreducible over } K_r = QF\left(K_{r-1}[x_{r-1}]/(g_{r-1})\right)$$

where QF denotes the field of fractions over an integral domain.

This definition above is constructive, in the sense that the irreducibility of an ascending set can be tested algorithmically, since there are factorization algorithms over a field and over the successive algebraic extensions of a given field.

The significance of the notion of an irreducible characteristic set becomes clear from the following proposition whose proof, using the concept of a *generic point* of an irreducible variety, can be found in [174] or [211]:

Let I be an ideal, and $\mathcal{G}$ a characteristic set of I. Then

$$\mathcal{G} \text{ is irreducible} \quad \Leftrightarrow \quad I \text{ is prime.}$$

The idea of irreducible characteristic set extends the domain of applicability to a larger class of algebraic problems.

1. **Test for Deciding Primality of an Ideal:** This can be achieved by using the characteristic set algorithm together with the test for irreducibility of a univariate polynomial over an arbitrary field.

2. **Test for Deciding Membership in a Prime Ideal:** Recall that if $I = $ prime and its characteristic set is $\mathcal{G}$, then

$$g \in I \quad \Leftrightarrow \quad \text{PRemainder}(g, \mathcal{G}) = 0.$$

3. For a given ideal I, by using the factorization algorithm, one can construct a sequence of *irreducible characteristic sets* $\mathcal{G}_1, \ldots, \mathcal{G}_k$ such that

$$\mathcal{Z}(I) = \mathcal{Z}(\mathcal{G}_1) \cup \cdots \cup \mathcal{Z}(\mathcal{G}_k).$$

Thus,

$$g \in \sqrt{I} \iff \left(\forall\, i \right) \left[\text{PRemainder}(g, \mathcal{G}_i) = 0 \right].$$

4. Lastly, using above *geometric decomposition*, one can construct a *complete scheme* for geometric theorem proving, where one decides if a formula of the kind

$$\left(\forall\, P \in L^n \right) \left[\left(f_1(P) = 0 \wedge \cdots \wedge f_s(P) = 0 \right) \wedge \right.$$

$$\neg \left(\text{In}(g_1)(P) = 0 \vee \cdots \vee \text{In}(g_r)(P) = 0 \right)$$

$$\left. \Rightarrow g(P) = 0 \right],$$

is "generically true."

Chapter 6

An Algebraic Interlude

6.1 Introduction

Before we move on to the topics of resultants and an algorithmic treatment of real algebra, we shall take a short pause to study in this chapter the unique factorization domain, the principal ideal domain, and the Euclidean domain. Of course, readers familiar with these topics may safely skip this chapter and go directly to the next chapter.

> In what follows we shall let S denote a commutative ring with identity.

ʹ 6.2 Unique Factorization Domain

Divisibility

Definition 6.2.1 (Divisor) In a commutative ring S (with identity), we have the following:

- A ring element s is said to be a *divisor* (or *factor*) of u (denoted $s \mid u$) if

$$\left(\exists\, t \in S\right)\left[u = s \cdot t\right],$$

  that is, $u \in (s)$. If $s \mid u$, we also say u is a *multiple* of s (or u *divisible* by s).

- Let $s_1, \ldots, s_r \in S$ be a set of ring elements. We say s is a *common divisor* of $s_1, \ldots, s_r$ if

$$s \mid s_1, \ldots, s \mid s_r.$$

Thus

$$s_1 \in (s) \wedge \cdots \wedge s_r \in (s) \quad \text{and} \quad (s_1, \ldots, s_r) \subseteq (s).$$

We say s is a *maximal common divisor* of s_1, ..., s_r if s is maximal among all common divisors of s_1, ..., s_r, under the partial ordering $\succ$, defined as $s \succ t$ if $t \mid s$. Thus a maximal common divisor of s_1, ..., s_r is the generator of a minimal principal ideal containing the ideal $(s_1, \ldots, s_r)$.

We say s is a *common multiple* of s_1, ..., s_r if

$$s_1 \mid s, \ldots, s_r \mid s.$$

Thus

$$s \in (s_1) \wedge \cdots \wedge s \in (s_r) \quad \text{and} \quad (s) \subseteq (s_1) \cap \cdots \cap (s_r).$$

We say s is a *minimal common multiple* of s_1, ..., s_r if s is minimal among all common multiples of s_1, ..., s_r, under the partial ordering $\succ$, defined as $s \succ t$ if $t \mid s$. Thus a minimal common multiple of s_1, ..., s_r is the generator of a maximal principal ideal contained in the ideal $(s_1, \ldots, s_r)$.   □

If

$$u = s \cdot t, \qquad u, \, s, \, t \in S,$$

then we say u *admits a factorization into factors* s and t.

If ε is a unit (invertible element) of S, then every ring element u admits a factorization

$$u = u \varepsilon^{-1} \cdot \varepsilon.$$

Such factorizations where one factor is a unit is called a *trivial factorization*; $u\varepsilon^{-1}$ is a *trivial factor* of u.

Definition 6.2.2 (Indecomposable Element) A nonunit ring element u is said to be an *indecomposable element* of S if u admits only trivial factorization of the kind $u = s \cdot t$ where s or t is a unit.   □

Definition 6.2.3 (Prime Element) A nonunit ring element u is said to be a *prime element* of S if for all $s, \, t \in S$

$$u \mid s \cdot t \quad \Rightarrow \quad u \mid s \vee u \mid t.   \square$$

Definition 6.2.4 (Associates) Two ring elements $s, \, t \in S$ are said to be *associates* in S (denoted, $s \approx t$) if $s = t \cdot \varepsilon$ and ε is a unit of S, i.e., if and only if t is a trivial factor of s.

Thus, if $s \approx t$, then $s \mid t$ and $t \mid s$, and they generate the same principal ideal, i.e., $(s) = (t)$. However, the converse is not necessarily true.

Clearly, $\approx$ is an equivalence relation.   □

A ring element s is said to be a *proper divisor* (or *proper factor*) of u (denoted, $s \parallel u$) if s is a factor of u but not a trivial factor of u, i.e.,

$$s \mid u \wedge s \not\approx u.$$

Note that $(u) \subsetneq (s)$ implies that $s \parallel u$, but not necessarily the converse.

Let S be an *integral domain with identity*, i.e., it has no nonzero zero divisor. Then the following propositions hold:

Proposition 6.2.1 *Every pair of domain elements s and t generating the same principal ideal are associates. That is, $(s) = (t)$ implies that $s \approx t$.*
PROOF.
If $(s) = (t) = (0)$, then $s = 0$ and $t = 0$, and there is nothing more to prove. Hence assume that $s \neq 0$ and $t \neq 0$. Since $(s) = (t)$, we have

$$s = t \cdot \varepsilon \quad \text{and} \quad t = s \cdot \varepsilon'.$$

Thus $s = s \cdot \varepsilon' \cdot \varepsilon$. Since S is an integral domain and $s \neq 0$, $\varepsilon \cdot \varepsilon' = 1$, and ε is a unit in S. That is, $s \approx t$. $\square$

Proposition 6.2.2 *Let s and u be two domain elements, such that $s \mid u$ and $u \mid s$. Then $(s) = (u)$, and s and u are associates.* $\square$

Proposition 6.2.3 *A domain element s is a proper divisor of u if $s \mid u$ but $u \nmid s$. Thus $s \parallel u$ if and only if $(u) \subsetneq (s)$.* $\square$

Proposition 6.2.4 *Assume that S is Noetherian. Then, every nonunit of S is a finite product of indecomposable elements.*
PROOF.
Let u be a nonunit of S. If u is indecomposable, there is nothing more to prove. Otherwise, u admits a nontrivial factorization $u = s \cdot t$, where both s and t are nonunits. Continuing this way we see that u admits a factorization into indecomposable elements. The finiteness of this factorization is a consequence of the Noetherianness of S as follows: Since $s \parallel u$ and $t \parallel u$,

$$(u) \subsetneq (s) \quad \text{and} \quad (u) \subsetneq (t).$$

If u admits a factorization into infinitely many indecomposable elements, then so does one of s and t, and we can construct a nonstationary ascending chain of ideals by repeating the above process, which would contradict the Noetherianity of S. $\square$

Proposition 6.2.5 *Every nonzero prime domain element u is indecomposable.*
PROOF.
Assume that u admits a factorization $u = s \cdot t$. Thus $s \mid u$ and $t \mid u$. Furthermore, since u is prime, and $u \mid s \cdot t$, either $u \mid s$ or $u \mid t$ (or both).

Without loss of generality assume that $u \mid s$. Hence $u \approx s$, and $s = u \cdot \varepsilon$.
Thus

$$u = s \cdot t = u \cdot \varepsilon t$$
$$\Rightarrow \quad \varepsilon t = 1 \quad \text{(since } u \neq 0 \text{ and } S \text{ is an integral domain.)}$$
$$\Rightarrow \quad t \text{ is a unit of } S$$
$$\Rightarrow \quad u \text{ admits only trivial factorizations}$$
$$\Rightarrow \quad u \text{ is indecomposable.} \quad \square$$

Unique Factorization Domain

We consider an integral domain S. In the following discussions, the zero
element of S will be excluded from the consideration.

Definition 6.2.5 (Unique Factorization Domain: UFD) Let S be an
integral domain with identity. We say S is a *unique factorization domain*
(or briefly, a *UFD*) if it satisfies the following two conditions:

1. Every nonunit of S is a finite product of indecomposable elements.

2. The factorization, obtained as above, is unique, ignoring order and
   unit factors. $\quad \square$

More explicitly, the second condition in the above definition means the
following: If $a = p_1 \cdots p_m = q_1 \cdots q_m$, where p_i and q_j are indecomposable,
then $m = n$, and on renumbering the indices of q_j's, we have $p_i \approx q_i$, $i = 1$,
..., m.

Theorem 6.2.6 *An integral domain S with identity is a unique factorization domain if and only if we have the following:*

1. *Every nonunit of S is a finite product of indecomposable elements.*

2. *Every indecomposable element of S is a (nonzero) prime element of
   S.*

PROOF.
Since the first condition is the same as the first condition of the definition,
we focus only on the second condition of the statement.

($\Rightarrow$) Let u be an indecomposable element of S. Assume that $u \mid s \cdot t$, i.e.,
$u \cdot v = s \cdot t$. Let

$$s = \prod_i p_i', \quad t = \prod_j p_j'', \quad \text{and} \quad v = \prod_k q_k$$

be factorizations of s, t, and v, respectively, into indecomposable elements. Thus

$$u \cdot \left(\prod_k q_k \right) = \left(\prod_i p'_i \right) \cdot \left(\prod_j p''_j \right),$$

and by the uniqueness of the factorization, we see that u is an associate of either a p'_i or a p''_j. Thus $u \mid s$ or $u \mid t$.

($\Leftarrow$)   Let u be a nonunit element of S which admits a factorization into s indecomposable elements. We shall prove our assertion by induction on the number s.

• Base Case: $s = 1$.
In this case u is indecomposable, and has exactly one obvious factorization.
• Induction Case: $s > 1$.
Assume that u has two factorizations into indecomposable elements one of which involves exactly s factors:

$$u = \prod_{i=1}^{s} p_i = \prod_{j=1}^{t} p'_j.$$

Since p_1 is a nonzero prime element dividing the product $p'_1 \cdots p'_t$, p_1 must divide one of the elements $p'_1, \ldots, p'_t$. Let, say, p_1 divide p'_1. Thus $p'_1 = p_1 \cdot t$, and since p'_1 is indecomposable, $t = \varepsilon$ must be a unit of S, and $p_1 \approx p'_1$. Thus

$$p_1 \cdot \coprod_{i=2}^{s} p_i = p_1 \cdot \varepsilon \prod_{j=2}^{t} p'_j,$$

and since $p_1 \neq 0$ and S is an integral domain, we have

$$\prod_{i=2}^{s} p_i = \varepsilon \prod_{j=2}^{t} p'_j,$$

the left-hand side involving exactly $(s - 1)$ indecomposable factors. Thus by our induction hypothesis, the above two factorizations differ only in the order of the factors and by unit factors. Thus the assertion of the theorem follows. □

Greatest Common Divisor and
Least Common Multiplier

Let S be a unique factorization domain, and $s_1, \ldots, s_r \in S$ be a set of elements in S. Let u be a maximal common divisor and v be a common divisor of $s_1, \ldots, s_r$. If v is a unit of S, then $v \mid u$. Hence assume that v

is a nonunit. Then u must be a nonunit. Let u and v admit factorization into decomposable elements, as follows:

$$u = \prod_i p_i, \quad v = \prod_j p_j'.$$

Then each p_j' is an associate of some indecomposable factor of each of s_1, ..., s_r, and thus an associate of some p_i. Arguing this way we see that $v \mid u$. Thus if u and v are two maximal common divisors of s_1, ..., s_r, then $u \mid v$ and $v \mid u$, and $u \approx v$. Hence s_1, ..., s_r have a maximal common divisor u, unique up to a unit factor; such a maximal common divisor u is said to be a GCD of s_1, ..., s_r:

$$u = \mathrm{GCD}(s_1, \ldots, s_r).$$

Similarly, we can show that s_1, ..., s_r have a minimal common multiplier w, unique up to a unit factor; such a minimal common multiplier w is said to be a LCM of s_1, ..., s_r:

$$w = \mathrm{LCM}(s_1, \ldots, s_r).$$

It is also easy to show that

1. $u = \mathrm{GCD}(s_1, \ldots, s_r) \approx \mathrm{GCD}(\mathrm{GCD}(s_1, \ldots, s_{r-1}), s_r))$.

2. $w = \mathrm{LCM}(s_1, \ldots, s_r) \approx \mathrm{LCM}(\mathrm{LCM}(s_1, \ldots, s_{r-1}), s_r))$.

3. $\mathrm{GCD}(s_1, \ldots, s_r) \cdot \mathrm{LCM}(s_1, \ldots, s_r) \approx s_1 \cdots s_r$.

We can also define GCD and LCM somewhat differently as follows:

Definition 6.2.6 (Greatest Common Divisor) In a unique factorization domain, any set of elements s_1, ..., s_r has a *greatest common divisor* (GCD), that is, an element u which is defined as follows:

1. u is a common divisor of s_1, ..., s_r.

2. If v is a common divisor of s_1, ..., s_r, then v divides u.   □

Definition 6.2.7 (Least Common Multiplier) In a unique factorization domain, any set of elements s_1, ..., s_r has a *least common multiplier* (LCM), that is, an element w which is defined as follows:

1. w is a common multiplier of s_1, ..., s_r.

2. If v is a common multiplier of s_1, ..., s_r, then v is divisible by w.
□

Definition 6.2.8 (Coprimality) Let S be a unique factorization domain with identity. If $GCD(s, t)$ is a unit of S, then s and t are said to be *relatively prime* (or *coprime*).   □

The following are important but straightforward properties of relatively prime elements:

- If s and t are coprime and $t \mid s \cdot u$, then $t \mid u$.

- If s and t are coprime and if $s \mid u$ and $t \mid u$, then $s \cdot t \mid u$.

Primitive Polynomials

Let S be a unique factorization domain, and $S[x]$ be the ring of univariate polynomials over S. Let $f(x) \in S[x]$ be a univariate polynomial of degree $r \geq 0$ with coefficients in S:

$$f(x) = s_r x^r + s_{r-1} x^{r-1} + \cdots + s_0, \qquad s_0, \ldots s_r \in S.$$

The coefficient of the highest-degree monomial of $f(x)$, s_r, is said to be the *head coefficient* of $f(x)$, Hcoef(f).

Lemma 6.2.7 *Every nonunit of $S[x]$ is a finite product of indecomposable elements.*

PROOF.

Since S is an integral domain, so is $S[x]$:

If $f(x) \neq 0$ and $g(x) \neq 0$ but $f(x) \cdot g(x) = 0$, then Hcoef(f) $\neq 0$, Hcoef(g) $\neq 0$ and Hcoef(f) $\cdot$ Hcoef(g) $= 0$.

Furthermore, by Hilbert's basis theorem, since S is Noetherian, so is $S[x]$. Thus $S[x]$ is a Noetherian integral domain and the lemma follows immediately.   □

Definition 6.2.9 Let $f(x) \in S[x]$ be a univariate polynomial of degree $r \geq 0$ with coefficients in S:

$$f(x) = s_r x^r + s_{r-1} x^{r-1} + \cdots + s_0, \qquad s_0, \ldots s_r \in S.$$

If $GCD(s_0, \ldots, s_r)$ is a unit of S, then we say $f(x)$ is a *primitive polynomial*, and if $s_r = $ Hcoef(f) is a unit of S, then we say $f(x)$ is *monic*.

We also call $GCD(s_0, \ldots, s_r)$, the *content* of the polynomial $f(x)$ Content(f). Thus Content(f) is unique up to a unit factor.

Any polynomial $f(x) \in S[x]$ can thus be written as

$$f(x) = s \cdot g(x),$$

where $s = \text{Content}(f)$, and $g(x)$ is a primitive polynomial. Here $g(x)$ is called the *primitive part* of $f(x)$:

$$f(x) = \text{Content}(f) \cdot \text{Primitive}(f).$$

Since the content of f is unique up to a unit factor, and since S is an integral domain, it follows that $\text{Primitive}(f)$ is also unique up to a multiple factor. $\square$

Lemma 6.2.8 *In a unique factorization domain S, the product of two primitive polynomials is a primitive polynomial. Thus if $f(x)$, $g(x) \in S[x]$, then*

$$\begin{aligned}
\text{Content}(f \cdot g) &\approx \text{Content}(f) \cdot \text{Content}(g), \\
\text{Primitive}(f \cdot g) &\approx \text{Primitive}(f) \cdot \text{Primitive}(g).
\end{aligned}$$

PROOF.
Assume that $p(x)$ and $q(x)$ are two primitive polynomials whose product $p(x) \cdot q(x)$ is not primitive:

$$\begin{aligned}
p(x) &= a_n x^n + \cdots + a_r x^r + \cdots + a_1 x + a_0, \\
q(x) &= b_m x^m + \cdots + b_s x^s + \cdots + b_1 x + b_0.
\end{aligned}$$

Since $p(x) \cdot q(x)$ is not primitive, there is a (nonzero) prime element $p' \in S$ that divides the coefficients of $p(x) \cdot q(x)$. Furthermore, since $p(x)$ and $q(x)$ are primitive, we can choose a_r and b_s such that

$$\begin{aligned}
a_r &= \text{the least indexed coefficient of } p(x) \text{ not divisible by } p', \\
b_s &= \text{the least indexed coefficient of } q(x) \text{ not divisible by } p'.
\end{aligned}$$

But the $(r + s)^{\text{th}}$ coefficient of $p(x) \cdot q(x)$ is given by

$$c_{r+s} = a_r \cdot b_s + a_{r+1} \cdot b_{s-1} + \cdots + a_{r-1} \cdot b_{s+1} + a_{r-2} \cdot b_{s+2} + \cdots.$$

Since $p' \mid a_i$ $(0 \le i < r)$, $p' \mid b_j$ $(0 \le j < s)$ and $p' \mid c_{r+s}$, we conclude that $p' \mid a_r \cdot b_s$. Since p' is a prime element, $p' \mid a_r$ or $p' \mid b_s$. In either case, we derive a contradiction to our choice of a_r and b_s.

Let $f(x)$ and $g(x) \in S[x]$. Let $\text{Primitive}(f)\text{Primitive}(g)$ be a primitive polynomial $h(x)$. Then

$$\text{Content}(f \cdot g)\,\text{Primitive}(f \cdot g) = \text{Content}(f) \cdot \text{Content}(g)\ h(x).$$

Thus

$$\begin{aligned}
\text{Content}(f \cdot g) &\approx \text{Content}(f) \cdot \text{Content}(g), \\
\text{Primitive}(f \cdot g) &\approx h(x) = \text{Primitive}(f) \cdot \text{Primitive}(g),
\end{aligned}$$

as was to be shown. $\square$

6.3   Principal Ideal Domain

Definition 6.3.1 (Principal Ideal Domain: PID) Let S be an integral domain with identity. We say S is a *principal ideal domain* (or, briefly, a PID) if every ideal of S is a principal ideal, i.e., generated by a single ring element.   □

Let S be a principal ideal domain with identity. Then the following statements hold.

Proposition 6.3.1 *Every principal ideal domain is Noetherian.*
PROOF.
Since every ideal in a principal ideal domain is finitely generated (actually, generated by one ring element), a principal ideal domain is Noetherian.   □

Proposition 6.3.2 *Every nonunit of S is a finite product of indecomposable elements.*
PROOF.
Follows from Theorem 6.2.4, since every principal ideal domain is a Noetherian integral domain.   □

Proposition 6.3.3 *Let u be an indecomposable element of S. Then (u) is a maximal ideal of S, in the sense that every ideal of S properly containing (u) is the entire ring.*
PROOF.
Let (v) be an ideal of S such that $(u) \subsetneq (v)$. Thus $v \mid u$ and $u \not\approx v$. Hence $u = r \cdot v$, where r is not a unit. Since u admits only trivial factorizations v must be unit of S, and $(v) = S$.   □

Proposition 6.3.4 *Let u be a nonzero prime element of S. Then (u) is a maximal ideal of S.*
PROOF.
Simply note that u is an indecomposable element of S.   □

Proposition 6.3.5 *Let u be an indecomposable element of S. Then u is a nonzero prime element of S.*
PROOF.
Assume that $u \mid s \cdot t$. If $u \mid s$, then there is nothing more to prove. Hence, assume that $u \nmid s$. Hence $(u) \subsetneq (u, s) = (1)$. Thus there exist elements a and b such that

$$1 = a \cdot u + b \cdot s \quad \text{and} \quad t = at \cdot u + b \cdot st.$$

Thus $u \mid t$, and u is a prime element of S.   □

Corollary 6.3.6 *Every principal ideal domain is a unique factorization domain.*   □

Note that

> If S is a principal ideal domain, and if $\{u\}$ is a basis for the principal ideal $(u) = (s_1, \ldots, s_r)$, then
>
> $$u = \text{GCD}(s_1, \ldots, s_r),$$
>
> and if $\{w\}$ is a basis for the principal ideal $(w) = (s_1) \cap \cdots \cap (s_r)$, then
>
> $$w = \text{LCM}(s_1, \ldots, s_r).$$

6.4   Euclidean Domain

Definition 6.4.1 (Euclidean Domain) Let S be a commutative ring (with identity). Let g be a map from $S \setminus \{0\}$ into $\mathbb{N}$, which associates to every nonzero ring element s a nonnegative integer $g(s)$ as follows:

1. (ORDERING ON S)

$$\left(\forall\, s, t \in S,\ s \neq 0,\ t \neq 0\right)\ \left[s \cdot t \neq 0\ \wedge\ g(s \cdot t) \geq g(s)\right].$$

That is, S does not contain a nonzero zero divisor, i.e., S is an integral domain. The map g defines an ordering on the elements of S that preserves multiplication. In particular,

$$\left(\forall\, s \in S,\ s \neq 0\right)\ \left[g(s) = g(1 \cdot s) \geq g(1)\right].$$

2. (DIVISION ALGORITHM)

$$\left(\forall\, s, t \in S,\ s \neq 0\right) \left(\exists\, q, r \in S\right)$$
$$\left[(t = q \cdot s + r)\ \wedge\ \left(r = 0\ \vee\ g(r) < g(s)\right)\right].$$

That is, for any two ring elements s, $t \in S$ ($s \neq 0$), there is an expression

$$t = q \cdot s + r \qquad (q = \text{quotient},\ r = \text{remainder})$$

in which either $r = 0$ or $g(r) < g(s)$.

Such a ring S is said to be a *Euclidean domain*.   □

Remark 6.4.2 For our purpose, we will make further assumption that the map g and the division process are actually computable.   □

Given two elements, s, $s' \in S$, we say $s \trianglelefteq s'$ if $g(s) \le g(s')$. Let I be an ideal in an Euclidean domain. Define $\widehat{m}(I)$ as follows:

$$\widehat{m}(I) = \begin{cases} 0, & \text{if } I = (0); \\ \min_{\triangleleft}(I \setminus \{0\}), & \text{otherwise.} \end{cases}$$

That is, if $I = (0)$, then $\widehat{m}(I) = 0$; otherwise, $\widehat{m}(I)$ is a nonzero $s \in I$ such that for all $s' \in I$ either $s' = 0$ or $g(s') \ge g(s)$.

Clearly, such a map $\widehat{m}$ exists, since the range of g is a subset of the set of nonnegative integers.

Also, if $I \ne (0)$, then define $\widehat{g}(I)$ to be $g(\widehat{m}(I))$.

Proposition 6.4.1 *If $I \subseteq S$ is an ideal in a Euclidean domain S, then I is a principal ideal generated by $\widehat{m}(I)$.*

PROOF.

There are two cases to consider:

- Case 1: $I = (0)$.
  Since I is a principal ideal generated by 0, there is nothing more to prove.

- Case 2: $I \ne (0)$.
  Let $s = \widehat{m}(I)$, and $t \in I$ be an arbitrary element of the ideal I. Since S has a division algorithm, and $s \ne 0$, we can express t as

  $$t = q\,s + r, \qquad q, r \in S,$$

  such that $r = 0$ or $g(r) < g(s)$.
  But $r = t - q\,s \in I$, and thus by our choice of s, $r = 0$ or $g(r) \ge g(s)$.
  Thus we conclude that $r = 0$, and

  $$\left(\forall\, t \in I\right) \left[t = q\,s \in (s)\right].$$

Hence $I \subseteq (s) \subseteq I$, and I is a principal ideal generated by $\widehat{m}(I)$. $\square$

Corollary 6.4.2 *Every Euclidean domain is*

- *Noetherian;*

- *a principal ideal domain;*

- *a unique factorization domain.* $\square$

Proposition 6.4.3 *Let I_1 and I_2 be two ideals in a Euclidean domain, such that $I_1 \ne (0)$, $I_2 \ne (0)$, and $I_1 \subsetneq I_2$. Then $\widehat{g}(I_1) > \widehat{g}(I_2)$.*

PROOF.

Let $s_1 = \widehat{m}(I_1)$ and $s_2 = \widehat{m}(I_2)$. By the hypothesis of the proposition, $s_1 \neq 0$, and $s_2 \neq 0$. Now, by definition,

$$\left(\forall \, s \in (s_2)\right) \left[s = 0 \; \vee \; g(s) \geq g(s_2)\right].$$

By condition 2 of Definition 6.4.1, there exist q_1 and r_1 such that

$$s_2 = q_1 \, s_1 + r_1,$$

where $r_1 = 0$ or $\widehat{g}(I_1) = g(s_1) > g(r_1)$.

Furthermore, since $I_1 \subseteq I_2$, we see that $q_1 \, s_1 \in I_2$, and $r_1 = s_2 - q_1 \, s_1 \in I_2$. Thus $r_1 = 0$ or $g(r_1) \geq g(s_2) = \widehat{g}(I_2)$.

Thus combining the above observations, we see that $r_1 = 0$ or $\widehat{g}(I_1) > g(r_1) \geq \widehat{g}(I_2)$. However, $r_1 = 0$ would imply that $s_2 = q_1 \, s_1 \in I_1$, and $I_2 = (s_2) \subseteq I_1$, contrary to our hypothesis. $\square$

Note the following:

If S is a Euclidean domain, and if $u = \widehat{m}((s_1, \ldots, s_r))$, then

$$u = \mathrm{GCD}(s_1, \ldots, s_r),$$

and if $w = \widehat{m}((s_1) \cap \cdots \cap (s_r))$, then

$$w = \mathrm{LCM}(s_1, \ldots, s_r).$$

Example 6.4.3 (Examples of Euclidean Domains)

1. $S = K$, a field. Let g be the map

$$
\begin{aligned}
g \quad &: \quad K \setminus \{0\} \to \mathbb{N} \\
&: \quad s \mapsto 0.
\end{aligned}
$$

Both the conditions are trivially satisfied. Note that for any two s, $t \in S$ ($s \neq 0$)

$$t = (t \cdot s^{-1}) \cdot s + 0.$$

2. $S = \mathbb{Z}$, the ring of integers. Let g be the map

$$
\begin{aligned}
g \quad &: \quad \mathbb{Z} \setminus \{0\} \to \mathbb{N} \\
&: \quad s \mapsto |s|.
\end{aligned}
$$

3. $S = K[x]$, the ring of univariate polynomials over the field K. Let g be the map

$$g \quad : \quad K[x] \setminus \{0\} \to \mathbb{N}$$
$$: \quad f \mapsto \deg(f). \quad \square$$

Corollary 6.4.4 *Every field is a Euclidean domain* $\square$

6.5   Gauss Lemma

Since S is an integral domain, we can define its *field of fractions* (i.e., quotient field), $\widetilde{S}$ as

$$\widetilde{S} = \left\{ \frac{s}{t} \ : \ s \in S \text{ and } t \in S \setminus \{0\} \right\}$$

with the addition, multiplication, and multiplicative inverse defined, respectively, as below:

$$\frac{s_1}{t_1} + \frac{s_2}{t_2} = \frac{s_1 \cdot t_2 + s_2 \cdot t_1}{t_1 \cdot t_2},$$

$$\frac{s_1}{t_1} \cdot \frac{s_2}{t_2} = \frac{s_1 \cdot s_2}{t_1 \cdot t_2},$$

$$\left(\frac{s_1}{t_1} \right)^{-1} = \frac{t_1}{s_1}, \qquad \text{if } s_1 \neq 0.$$

Since $\widetilde{S}[x]$ is a Euclidean domain, $\widetilde{S}[x]$ is a unique factorization domain. Let

$$\widetilde{f}(x) = \frac{f(x)}{b}, \quad b \in S \setminus \{0\}, \quad \text{and} \quad f(x) \in S[x].$$

Then we associate $f(x)$ with $\widetilde{f}(x)$. Conversely, if $f(x) \in S[x]$, then we associate $\widetilde{f}(x) = f(x) \in \widetilde{S}[x]$ with $f(x)$.

Lemma 6.5.1 *Every indecomposable element of $S[x]$ is a nonzero prime element.*

PROOF.

Assume to the contrary, i.e., for some indecomposable element $p(x) \in S[x]$ there are two polynomials $f(x)$ and $g(x) \in S[x]$ such that

$$p(x) \nmid f(x), \quad p(x) \nmid g(x), \quad \text{but} \quad p(x) \mid f(x)\, g(x).$$

There two cases to consider.

- Case 1: $\deg(p) = 0$, and p is an indecomposable element of S.

  Note that $p \mid h(x)$ if and only if $p \mid \text{Content}(h)$. Thus p is a prime element of S, and

$$p \nmid \text{Content}(f), \quad p \nmid \text{Content}(g), \quad \text{but} \quad p \mid \text{Content}(f)\,\text{Content}(g),$$

which leads to a contradiction.

- Case 2: $\deg(p) > 0$, and $p(x)$ is a primitive indecomposable polynomial of $S[x]$.

  Thus $\widetilde{p}(x)$ is an indecomposable (thus, a prime) element of $\widetilde{S}[x]$: Since if

$$\widetilde{p}(x) = \widetilde{h}(x) \cdot \widetilde{h}'(x) = \frac{h(x)}{b} \cdot \frac{h'(x)}{b'}$$

then $bb'\, p(x) = h(x) \cdot h'(x)$ and

$$p(x) = \text{Primitive}(h) \; \cdot \; \text{Primitive}(h').$$

Also note that $p(x) \mid h(x)$ if and only if $\widetilde{p}(x) \mid \widetilde{h}(x)$. If $h'(x) \cdot p(x) = h(x)$, then $\widetilde{h}'(x) \cdot \widetilde{p}(x) = \widetilde{h}(x)$ and $\widetilde{p}(x) \mid \widetilde{h}(x)$. Conversely, if $\widetilde{p}(x) \mid \widetilde{h}(x)$, then $\widetilde{h}'(x) \cdot \widetilde{p}(x) = \widetilde{h}(x)$. Thus

$$\frac{h'(x)}{b'} \cdot p(x) = \frac{h(x)}{b},$$

and $bh'(x) \cdot p(x) = b'h(x)$. Thus

$$\text{Primitive}(h') \cdot p(x) = \text{Primitive}(h) \quad \text{and} \quad p(x) \mid h(x).$$

Thus $p(x)$ is a prime element of $\widetilde{S}[x]$, and

$$\widetilde{p}(x) \nmid \widetilde{f}(x), \quad \widetilde{p}(x) \nmid \widetilde{g}(x), \quad \text{but} \quad \widetilde{p}(x) \mid \widetilde{f}(x) \cdot \widetilde{g}(x),$$

which leads to a contradiction. □

Theorem 6.5.2 (Gauss Lemma) *If S is a unique factorization domain, then so is $S[x]$.* □

6.6 Strongly Computable Euclidean Domains

Recall that every Euclidean domain is Noetherian. We further assume the following:

1. The Euclidean domain S under consideration is computable, i.e., for all s and $u \in S$ there are effective algorithms to compute

$$-s, \quad s + u, \quad \text{and} \quad s \cdot u.$$

2. For the given Euclidean domain S with the map

$$g: S \setminus \{0\} \to \mathbb{N},$$

there are effective algorithms to compute $g(s)$, for all nonzero $s \in S$ and to compute the quotient $q = q(s, u)$ and the remainder $r = r(s, u)$ of s and $u \in S$, $s \neq 0$:

$$u = q \cdot s + r, \quad \text{such that } r = 0 \ \lor \ g(r) < g(s).$$

In order to show that a Euclidean domain S satisfying the above two computability conditions is in fact strongly computable, we need to demonstrate that S is *detachable* and *syzygy-solvable*.

Detachability: Using Euclid's Algorithm

Let S be a Euclidean domain with the computability properties discussed earlier. We shall present an extended version of Euclid's algorithm, which, given a set of elements $s_1, \ldots, s_r \in S$, computes $s = \text{GCD}(s_1, \ldots, s_r)$, and a set of elements $u_1, \ldots, u_r$ such that

$$s = u_1 \cdot s_1 + \cdots + u_r \cdot s_r.$$

Note that $(s) = (s_1, \ldots, s_r)$, and the detachability of S proceeds as follows:

Let $t \in S$, $\{s_1, \ldots, s_r\} \subseteq S$ and $s = \text{GCD}(s_1, \ldots, s_r)$. If $s \nmid t$, then $t \notin (s) = (s_1, \ldots, s_r)$, otherwise $t \in (s) = (s_1, \ldots, s_r)$ and if $t = v \cdot s$, then

$$t = (v \cdot u_1)s_1 + \cdots + (v \cdot u_r)s_r$$

where s and $u_1, \ldots, u_r$ are obtained from the extended Euclid's algorithm.

Next, we present a generalized extended Euclid's algorithm based on *successive division*:

EXTENDED-EUCLID($s_1, \ldots, s_r$)

Input: $s_1, \ldots, s_r \in S$.
Output: $s = \mathrm{GCD}(s_1, \ldots, s_r) \in S$ and $\langle u_1, \ldots, u_r \rangle \in S^r$ such that
$s = u_1 \cdot s_1 + \cdots + u_r \cdot s_r$.

if $s_1 = \cdots = s_r$ then return $\langle 1, 0, \ldots, 0; s_1 \rangle$;

Assume that $g(s_1) \neq 0, \ldots, g(s_r) \neq 0$, and
$\quad g(s_1) \leq \cdots \leq g(s_r)$;
Insert the following elements into a queue Q
$\quad$ in the ascending order of their g values;
$\langle w_{1,1}, \ldots, w_{1,r}; w_1 \rangle := \langle 1, 0, \ldots, 0; s_1 \rangle$;

$\quad\vdots$

$\langle w_{r,1}, \ldots, w_{r,r}; w_r \rangle := \langle 0, 0, \ldots, 1; s_r \rangle$;

while Q is nonempty loop
$\quad$ if $|Q| = 1$ then
$\quad\quad$ return the queue element $\langle w_{1,1}, \ldots, w_{1,r}; w_1 \rangle$;
$\quad$ end{if };

$\quad$ Dequeue the following first two elements of the queue Q:
$\quad\quad \langle w_{1,1}, \ldots, w_{1,r}; w_1 \rangle$ and $\langle w_{2,1}, \ldots, w_{2,r}; w_2 \rangle$;

$\quad$ Let $w_2 = q \cdot w_1 + r$;
$\quad$ **Comment:** This is computed by an application of the
$\quad\quad$ division algorithm;

$\quad$ Enqueue $\langle w_{1,1}, \ldots, w_{1,r}; w_1 \rangle$ in the queue Q;
$\quad$ if $r \neq 0$ then
$\quad\quad$ Enqueue $\langle w_{2,1}, \ldots, w_{2,r}; w_2 \rangle - q \cdot \langle w_{2,1}, \ldots, w_{2,r}; w_2 \rangle$;
$\quad$ end{if };
end{loop };
end{EXTENDED-EUCLID} $\quad\square$

The correctness and termination of the algorithm follows from the following easily verifiable facts. Assume that at the beginning of each iteration the queue Q contains the following t $(0 \leq t \leq r)$ elements

$$\overline{w_1} = \langle w_{1,1}, \ldots, w_{1,r}; w_1 \rangle,$$

$$\vdots$$

$$\overline{w_t} = \langle w_{t,1}, \ldots, w_{t,r}; w_t \rangle.$$

1. $g(w_1) \leq \cdots \leq g(w_t)$.

2. For all j $(0 \leq j \leq t)$,

$$w_{j,1} \cdot s_1 + \cdots + w_{j,r} \cdot s_r = w_j.$$

3. $(w_1, \ldots, w_t) = (s_1, \ldots, s_r)$.

4. If the queue $Q = [\overline{w_1}, \ldots, \overline{w_t}]$ before the main loop and $Q' = [\overline{w'_1}, \ldots, \overline{w'_{t'}}]$ at the end of the main loop, then

$$g(w_1) \geq g(w'_1) \quad \text{and} \quad t \geq t',$$

with one of the inequalities being strict.

As an immediate consequence of (4), we get the termination with a single tuple

$$\langle w_{1,1}, \ldots, w_{1,r}; w_1 \rangle.$$

Since $(w_1) = (s_1, \ldots, s_r)$ by (3), we have

$$w_1 = \mathrm{GCD}(s_1, \ldots, s_r)$$

at the termination. The rest follows from the condition (2).

Since $\mathrm{GCD}(s_1, \ldots, s_r) = \mathrm{GCD}(\mathrm{GCD}(s_1, \ldots, s_{r-1}), s_r)$, we could have computed the GCD of a set of elements by repeated applications of Euclid's successive division algorithm for pairwise GCD. Note that the pairwise GCD algorithm computes the GCD of a pair of elements s_1 and s_2 with a time complexity of $O(g \cdot C)$, where $g = \min(g(s_1), g(s_2))$ and $C = \mathrm{cost}$ of a division step. The algorithm presented here derives its advantage from computing the pairwise GCD's in an increasing order of the g-values, starting with s_i of the smallest $g(s_i)$, and thus has a time complexity of

$$O\Big((g + r) \cdot C\Big),$$

where $g = \min(g(s_1), \ldots, g(s_r))$.

Syzygy-Solvability

Let $\{s_1, \ldots, s_r\} \subseteq S$. In this subsection, we show that the Euclidean domain S is syzygy-solvable.

$$s = \mathrm{GCD}(s_1, \ldots, s_r) = u_1 \cdot s_1 + \cdots + u_r \cdot s_r$$

and $s'_i = s_i/s$ for $i = 1, \ldots, r$.

Then the syzygy basis for $(s_1, \ldots, s_r)$ is given by

$$
\begin{aligned}
\overline{t_1} &= \langle (u_2 s'_2 + \cdots + u_r s'_r), \ -u_2 s'_1, \ldots, -u_r s'_1 \rangle \\
\overline{t_2} &= \langle -u_1 s'_2, \ (u_1 s'_1 + u_3 s'_3 + \cdots + u_r s'_r), \ -u_3 s'_2, \ldots, -u_r s'_2 \rangle \\
&\ \ \vdots \\
\overline{t_r} &= \langle -u_1 s'_r, \ldots, -u_{r-1} s'_r, \ (u_1 s'_1 + \cdots + u_{r-1} s'_{r-1}) \rangle
\end{aligned}
$$

To see that $\langle \overline{t_1}, \ldots, \overline{t_r} \rangle$ is really a basis for syzygy, we may prove the two required conditions, as in the case of $\mathbb{Z}$.

There is another syzygy basis for $(s_1, \ldots, s_r)$ which has a simpler structure. Let $\{s_1, \ldots, s_r\} \subseteq S$,

$$s = \mathrm{GCD}(s_1, \ldots, s_r) = u_1 \cdot s_1 + \cdots + u_r \cdot s_r,$$

and $s_{i,j} = \mathrm{GCD}(s_i, s_j)$ for all $1 \le i < j \le r$. Then the syzygy basis for $(s_1, \ldots, s_r)$ is given by the following basis:

$$\overline{\tau_{i,j}} = \Big\langle 0, \ldots, 0, \underbrace{\frac{s_j}{s_{i,j}}}_{\text{position } i}, 0, \ldots, 0, \underbrace{-\frac{s_i}{s_{i,j}}}_{\text{position } j}, 0, \ldots, 0 \Big\rangle,$$

for $1 \le i < j \le q$. Again the arguments to prove that it is a basis for the module of syzygies is identical to that given in the case of $\mathbb{Z}$. The proofs are left to the reader.

Problems

Problem 6.1

(i) Show that the extended Euclidean algorithm can compute the GCD of two integers b_1 and b_2 in time $\Theta(\log|b_1| + \log|b_2| + 1)$ time.

(ii) What is the time complexity of the extended Euclidean algorithm for computing the GCD of r integers $b_1, \ldots, b_r$.

(iii) Devise an efficient algorithm to determine if the following linear diophantine equation with rational coefficients has an integral solution:

$$b_1 x_1 + \cdots + b_r x_r = c.$$

Problem 6.2

The complex numbers $\alpha = a + ib$ (a and b are integers) form the ring of *Gaussian integers*: if $\alpha = a + ib$ and $\gamma = c + id$ are two Gaussian integers, then

$$
\begin{aligned}
\alpha + \gamma &= (a+c) + i(b+d), \\
-\alpha &= -a - ib, \\
\alpha \cdot \gamma &= (ac - bd) + i(ad + bc).
\end{aligned}
$$

Let $g(\alpha)$ be defined to be the norm of α, given by $a^2 + b^2$. Show that the ring of Gaussian integers with the above g map forms a Euclidean domain.

Problem 6.3

Prove the following:

Let S be a unique factorization domain. Then every prime element of S generates a prime ideal and every nonprime element of S generates a nonprime ideal.

Problem 6.4

Let S be a Euclidean domain with identity.

(i) Show that if s_1 and s_2 are two nonzero elements in S such that $s_1 \mid s_2$, then $s_1 \parallel s_2$ if and only if $g(s_2) > g(s_1)$.

(ii) Using the above proposition, prove the following:

Let $s \in S$ be a nonunit element. Then s can be expressed as a finite product of indecomposable elements of S.

Problem 6.5

Let S be a unique factorization domain, and $A(x)$ and $B(x) \in S[x]$ two univariate polynomials of respective degrees m and n, $m \geq n$.

(i) Show that

$$\text{Content}(\text{GCD}(A,B)) \approx \text{GCD}(\text{Content}(A), \text{Content}(B)),$$
$$\text{Primitive}(\text{GCD}(A,B)) \approx \text{GCD}(\text{Primitive}(A), \text{Primitive}(B)).$$

(ii) Let $m \geq n > k$. Show that $\deg(\text{GCD}(A,B)) \geq k+1$ if and only if there exist polynomials $T(x)$ and $U(x)$ (not both zero) such that

$$A(x)\, T(x) + B(x)\, U(x) = 0, \qquad \deg(T) \leq n - k - 1,$$
$$\deg(U) \leq m - k - 1.$$

(iii) Let $m \geq n > k$. Suppose that $\deg(\text{GCD}(A,B)) \geq k$. Then for all $T(x)$ and $U(x)$ [not both zero, and $\deg(T) \leq n-k-1$, $\deg(U) \leq m-k-1$], the polynomial $C(x) = A(x)\, T(x) + B(x)\, U(x)$ is either zero or of degree at least k.

Problem 6.6

Consider a Noetherian UFD that, in addition to the ring operations, allows constructive algorithms for

(a) factorization and

(b) 1-detachability for relatively prime elements, i.e.,

$$\text{if} \quad 1 = \text{GCD}(p_1, p_2)$$
$$\text{then} \quad \left(\text{compute } a_1, a_2\right) \left[1 = a_1 p_1 + a_2 p_2\right]$$

Show that such a UFD is a strongly computable ring.

Problem 6.7

Let S be an integral domain and $I_1, \ldots, I_r$, pairwise coprime ideals of S. Prove that there exists a natural isomorphism

$$S/\bigcap_i I_i \cong \prod_i (S/I_i).$$

As an immediate consequence of the above statement, we get the following corollaries *Chinese remainder theorems*:

(i) Let $m_1, \ldots, m_r$ be pairwise coprime integers. Then for any set $a_1, \ldots, a_r$ of integers, the following system of congruences

$$
\begin{aligned}
x &\equiv a_1 \pmod{m_1} \\
x &\equiv a_2 \pmod{m_2} \\
&\;\;\vdots \\
x &\equiv a_r \pmod{m_r}
\end{aligned}
$$

admits an integer solution.

(ii) Let $f_1(x), \ldots, f_r(x) \in K[x]$ be pairwise coprime univariate polynomials over the field K. Then for any set $a_1(x), \ldots, a_r(x)$ of polynomials, the following system of congruences

$$
\begin{aligned}
g(x) &\equiv a_1(x) \;[\mathrm{mod}\; f_1(x)] \\
g(x) &\equiv a_2(x) \;[\mathrm{mod}\; f_2(x)] \\
&\;\;\vdots \\
g(x) &\equiv a_r(x) \;[\mathrm{mod}\; f_r(x)]
\end{aligned}
$$

admits a polynomial solution g.

Finally, devise an algorithm to solve the congruence relations in each case.

Hint: First, show that there is always a solution to the following system of congruences, for each i:

$$
\begin{aligned}
x &\equiv 0 \pmod{I_1} \\
x &\equiv 0 \pmod{I_2} \\
&\;\;\vdots \\
x &\equiv 1 \pmod{I_i} \\
&\;\;\vdots \\
x &\equiv 0 \pmod{I_r}.
\end{aligned}
$$

For each $1 \le j \le r$ ($j \neq i$), we can choose $p_j \in I_i$ and $q_j \in I_j$ such that

$$p_j + q_j = 1.$$

Then the following x is a desired solution to the system of congruences:

$$
\begin{aligned}
x &= q_1 \cdots q_{i-1}\, q_{i+1} \cdots q_r \\
&= (1 - p_1) \cdots (1 - p_{i-1})\,(1 - p_{i+1}) \cdots (1 - p_r)
\end{aligned}
$$

Now it remains to be shown that the solution to a general system of congruences can be obtained as a linear combination of the solutions to such special systems.

Problem 6.8

Let $f(x) \in \mathbb{Z}_p[x]$ ($p = $ a prime) be a square-free polynomial with the following factorization into irreducible polynomials:

$$
f(x) = f_1(x) \cdots f_r(x),
$$

where no factor occurs more than once.

(i) Show that given a set of r distinct elements $a_1, \ldots, a_r \in \mathbb{Z}_p$, there exists a polynomial $g(x)$ $[\deg(g) < \deg(f)]$ such that

$$
f_i(x) \mid g(x) - a_i.
$$

(ii) Show that

$$
g(x)^p - g(x) \equiv g(x)\,(g(x) - 1) \cdots (g(x) - p + 1) \equiv 0 \pmod{f(x)},
$$

for some $g(x) \in \mathbb{Z}_p[x] \setminus \mathbb{Z}_p$, $\deg(g) < \deg(f)$.

Problem 6.9

Let $f(x) \in \mathbb{Z}_p[x]$ ($p = $ a prime). Show the following:

(i) Suppose that there is a polynomial $g \in \mathbb{Z}_p[x]$, $\deg(g) < \deg(f)$, such that

$$
g(x)^p - g(x) \equiv 0 \pmod{f(x)}.
$$

Then, for some $a \in \mathbb{Z}_p$, $\mathrm{GCD}(f, g(x) - a) = $ a polynomial factor of $f(x)$.

(ii) Conclude that

$$
f \in \mathbb{Z}_p[x] \text{ is an irreducible polynomial}
$$

if and only if

$$
g(x)^p - g(x) \equiv 0 \pmod{f(x)}, \quad \deg(g) < \deg(f),
$$

has no polynomial solution.

Problem 6.10

    (i)   Using linear algebra, devise an efficient algorithm to determine a polynomial solution $g(x) \in \mathbb{Z}_p[x]$ ($p =$ a prime) for the following congruence equation

$$g(x)^p - g(x) \equiv 0 \ [\mathrm{mod}\ f(x)], \quad \deg(g) < \deg(f),$$

where $f(x) \in \mathbb{Z}_p[x]$ is given.

    (ii)   Devise an algorithm to factor a square-free polynomial $f(x) \in \mathbb{Z}_p[x]$.

Problem 6.11

    Let $f(x) \in \mathbb{Z}[x]$, and say it factorizes as $f = g\,h$.

    Show that for all $k > 0$, if $f_k \equiv f(\mathrm{mod}\ p^k)$, $g_k \equiv g(\mathrm{mod}\ p^k)$ and $h_k \equiv h(\mathrm{mod}\ p^k)$ then

$$f_k \equiv g_k\,h_k \ (\mathrm{mod}\ p^k).$$

    Devise an algorithm which, given f and a factorization $(\mathrm{mod}\ p^k)$ ($p =$ a prime),

$$f_k \equiv g_k\,h_k \ (\mathrm{mod}\ p^k),$$

can compute a factorization $(\mathrm{mod}\ p^{k+1})$

$$f_{k+1} \equiv g_{k+1}\,h_{k+1} \ (\mathrm{mod}\ p^{k+1}).$$

Solutions to Selected Problems

Problem 6.2

    We will show that ring of Gaussian integers satisfy all three conditions of the Euclidean domain.

    1. $\alpha \cdot \gamma = (ac - bd) + i(ad + bc)$.

        If $\alpha,\ \gamma \neq 0$ but $\alpha \cdot \gamma = 0$, then $ac = bd$, $ad = -bc$ (i.e., $abd^2 = -abc^2$), and therefore $d^2 = -c^2$, which is impossible as $a,\ b,\ c,\ d \in \mathbb{Z}$. Hence

$$\alpha,\ \gamma \neq 0 \ \Rightarrow\ \alpha\gamma \neq 0.$$

    2. $g(\alpha \cdot \gamma) \geq g(\alpha)$ and $g(\alpha \cdot \gamma) \geq g(\gamma)$.

$$\begin{aligned} g(\alpha \cdot \gamma) &= (ac - bd)^2 + (ad + bc)^2 \\ &= (ac)^2 + (bd)^2 + (ad)^2 + (bc)^2 \ \geq\ a^2 + b^2 \ =\ g(\alpha) \end{aligned}$$

3. Let $\overline{\gamma}$ denote the complex conjugate of γ, i.e., $\overline{\gamma} = a - ib$, if $\gamma = a + ib$. Let $\alpha \cdot \overline{\gamma} = p + iq$ and $\overline{\gamma} \cdot \gamma = n$, $n \in \mathbb{Z}$. Let $p = q_1 n + r_1$, $q = q_2 n + r_2$, where $|r_1|$, $|r_2| \leq n/2$. Then obviously

$$\alpha \cdot \overline{\gamma} = \underbrace{(q_1 + iq_2)}_{=q} \cdot n + \underbrace{(r_1 + ir_2)}_{=r} = q\,\gamma \cdot \overline{\gamma} + r,$$

and

$$r_1^2 + r_2^2 \leq \left(\frac{1}{4}\right)(n^2 + n^2) < g(n) = g(\gamma \cdot \overline{\gamma}).$$

Also,

$$g(r) = g(\alpha \cdot \overline{\gamma} - q\gamma \cdot \overline{\gamma}) < g(\gamma \cdot \overline{\gamma})$$

But $g(\alpha \cdot \overline{\gamma} - q\gamma \cdot \overline{\gamma}) = g(\alpha - q\gamma)g(\overline{\gamma})$ and $g(\gamma \overline{\gamma}) = g(\gamma)g(\overline{\gamma})$. Therefore

$$g(\alpha - q\gamma)g(\overline{\gamma}) < g(\gamma)g(\overline{\gamma}).$$

Since $\gamma \neq 0$, $g(\overline{\gamma})$ is a positive integer. Therefore, $g(\alpha - q\gamma) \leq g(\gamma)$. Hence, we can write $\alpha = q\gamma + r'$, where $r' = \alpha - q\gamma$.

Problem 6.4

Let S be a Euclidean domain with identity.

(i) *Let s_1 and s_2 be two elements in S such that $s_1 \mid s_2$. Then $s_1 \parallel s_2$ if and only if $g(s_2) > g(s_1)$.*

PROOF.
Since $s_1 \mid s_2$, $g(s_1) \geq g(s_2)$. But $(s_1) = (s_2)$ implies that $g(s_1) \geq g(s_2) \geq g(s_1)$, and $g(s_1) = g(s_2)$. And $(s_2) \subsetneq (s_1)$ implies that $g(s_2) > g(s_1)$. Hence $(s_2) \subsetneq (s_1)$ if and only if $g(s_2) > g(s_1)$.

The rest follows from the fact that $s_1 \parallel s_2$ if and only if $s_1 \mid s_2$ and $s_1 \not\sim s_2$, that is, if and only if $(s_2) \subsetneq (s_1)$. $\square$

(ii) *Let $s \in S$ be a nonunit element in the Euclidean domain S. Then s can be expressed as a finite product of indecomposable elements of S.*

PROOF.
The proof is by a complete induction on $g(s)$.
• Case 1: $s = $ nonunit indecomposable element.
In this case there is nothing more to prove.
• Case 2: $s = $ nonunit decomposable element.
Assume that s admits a nontrivial factorization $s = t_1 \cdot t_2$, where neither t_1 nor t_2 is a unit. Thus $t_1 \mid s$ and $t_1 \not\sim t_2$, and $t_1 \parallel s$. Similarly $t_2 \parallel s$. Then $g(t_1) < g(s)$ and $g(t_2) < g(s)$. By the induction hypothesis, t_1 and t_2 can be expressed as finite products of indecomposable elements, and so can be s. $\square$

Problem 6.5

   (i)

$$\text{GCD}(A, B) \;\; = \;\; \text{GCD}\Big(\text{Content}(A) \cdot \text{Primitive}(A),$$
$$\text{Content}(B) \cdot \text{Primitive}(B)\Big).$$

Let $g = \text{GCD}(\text{Content}(A), \text{Content}(B))$ and

$$u = \frac{\text{Content}(A)}{g}, \quad v = \frac{\text{Content}(B)}{g},$$

where u and v are relatively prime.

$$\text{GCD}(A, B) \;\; = \;\; \text{GCD}\Big(g\,u\,\text{Primitive}(A), \;\; g\,v\,\text{Primitive}(B)\Big)$$
$$= \;\; g \cdot \text{GCD}\Big(u\,\text{Primitive}(A), \;\; v\,\text{Primitive}(B)\Big).$$

We claim that

$$\text{GCD}\Big(u\,\text{Primitive}(A), \;\; v\,\text{Primitive}(B)\Big)$$
$$\approx \;\; \text{GCD}\Big(\text{Primitive}(A), \;\; \text{Primitive}(B)\Big)$$

It is obvious that

$$\text{GCD}\Big(\text{Primitive}(A), \;\; \text{Primitive}(B)\Big)$$
$$\Big| \;\; \text{GCD}\Big(u\,\text{Primitive}(A), \;\; v\,\text{Primitive}(B)\Big).$$

If they are not associates, then $(\exists\, c \in S[x])$ such that c is not a unit and

$$c \cdot \text{GCD}\Big(\text{Primitive}(A), \;\; \text{Primitive}(B)\Big)$$
$$\Big| \;\; \text{GCD}\Big(u\,\text{Primitive}(A), \;\; v\,\text{Primitive}(B)\Big),$$

but c cannot have degree > 0, therefore $c \in S$ which implies that $c \mid u$ and $c \mid v$, contradicting the fact that u and v are relatively prime. Therefore,

$\text{GCD}(A, B)$

$$= \;\; \text{GCD}\Big(\text{Content}(A), \text{Content}(B)\Big) \cdot \text{GCD}\Big(\text{Primitive}(A), \text{Primitive}(B)\Big).$$

But $\text{Content}(\text{GCD}(\text{Primitive}(A), \text{Primitive}(B)))$ is a unit. Hence,

$$\text{Content}(\text{GCD}(A, B)) \;\; \approx \;\; \text{GCD}(\text{Content}(A), \text{Content}(B)),$$
$$\text{Primitive}(\text{GCD}(A, B)) \;\; \approx \;\; \text{GCD}(\text{Primitive}(A), \text{Primitive}(B)).$$

(ii) Let $G(x) = \text{GCD}(A(x),\ B(x))$ and $A(x) = G(x) \cdot U(x)$, $B(x) = G(x) \cdot T(x)$. Since $\deg(G(x)) \geq k+1$, $\deg(U(x)) \leq m-k-1$ and $\deg(T(x)) \leq n-k-1$,

$$A(x)\,T(x) - B(x)\,U(x) = G(x)\,U(x)\,T(x) - G(x)\,T(x)\,U(x) = 0.$$

Conversely, let

$$A(x)\,T(x) + B(x)\,U(x) \quad = \quad 0, \qquad \deg(T) \leq n-k-1,$$
$$\deg(U) \leq m-k-1.$$

Since $S[x]$ is UFD, we can have unique factorization of $A(x)$, $B(x)$, $T(x)$, $U(x)$. Let

$$G(x) = \text{GCD}\Big(A(x),\ U(x)\Big), \qquad \deg(G) \leq m-k-1.$$

Let $A(x) = G(x) \cdot P(x)$; then $P(x)$ and $U(x)$ are relatively prime, and therefore $P(x) \mid B(x)$. But $\deg(P(x)) = \deg(A(x)) - \deg(G(x)) \geq k+1$. Since $P(x)$ divides $A(x)$ as well as $B(x)$,

$$P(x) \mid \text{GCD}\Big(A(x),\ B(x)\Big).$$

Then $\deg(\text{GCD}(A(x), B(x))) \geq \deg(P(x)) \geq k+1$.

(iii) Let $C(x) = \text{GCD}(A(x), B(x))$,

$$A(x) = G(x)\,P(x) \quad \text{and} \quad B(x) = G(x)\,Q(x).$$

Therefore

$$\begin{aligned}
C(x) \quad &= \quad G(x)P(x)U(x) + G(x)Q(x)T(x) \\
&= \quad G(x) \cdot \Big(P(x)\,U(x) + Q(x)\,T(x)\Big).
\end{aligned}$$

If $P(x)U(x) + Q(x)T(x)$ is not zero, then by the property of Euclidean domain, $\deg(C(x)) \geq \deg(G(x)) \geq k$.

Bibliographic Notes

The topics covered here are standard materials of classical algebra and are dealt with in much greater details in such textbooks as Herstein [94], Jacobson [105], van der Waerden [204] and Zariski and Samuel [216].

Problem 6.7 is the classical *Chinese remainder theorem*; Problems 6.8, 6.9 and 6.10 are inspired by Berlekamp's algorithm for factorization; and Problem 6.11 is the classical *Hensel's lemma*. For more discussions on these topics please consult [58,116,145].

Chapter 7

Resultants and Subresultants

7.1 Introduction

In this chapter we shall study *resultant*, an important and classical idea in constructive algebra, whose development owes considerably to such luminaries as Bezout, Cayley, Euler, Hurwitz, and Sylvester, among others. In recent time, resultant has continued to receive much attention both as the starting point for the *elimination theory* as well as for the computational efficiency of various constructive algebraic algorithms these ideas lead to; fundamental developments in these directions are due to Hermann, Kronecker, Macaulay, and Noether. Some of the close relatives, e.g., *discriminant* and *subresultant*, also enjoy widespread applications. Other applications and generalizations of these ideas occur in *Sturm sequences* and *algebraic cell decomposition*—the subjects of the next chapter.

Burnside and Panton define a resultant as follows [35]:

> Being given a system of n equations, homogeneous between $n-1$ variables, if we combine these equations in such a manner as to eliminate the variables, and obtain an equation $R = 0$ containing only the coefficients of the equations, the quantity R is, when expressed in a rational and integral form, called the *Resultant* or *Eliminant*.

Thus, a resultant is a purely algebraic condition expressed in terms of the coefficients of a given system of polynomials, which is satisfied if and only if the given system of equations has a common solution. There have been historically two ways to view the development of resultant: the first algebraic and the second geometric.

In the first case, one starts from Hilbert's Nullstellensatz, which states,

225

for instance, that given a pair of univariate polynomials f_1 and f_2 (say over a field), they have no common solution exactly when there exist polynomials g_1 and g_2 satisfying the following:

$$f_1 \, g_1 + f_2 \, g_2 = 1.$$

A quick examination would convince the reader that if such polynomials g_1 and g_2 exist then their degrees could be bounded as follows: $\deg(g_1) < \deg(f_2)$, and $\deg(g_2) < \deg(f_1)$; and that their existence can be determined by only examining the coefficients of f_1 and f_2. Thus, at least in principle, an algebraic criterion can be constructed to decide if the polynomials have a common zero. This is essentially Sylvester's *dialytic method of elimination*.

In the second case, one examines the zeroes (in an algebraic extension) of the polynomials. Say the zeros of f_1 are α_1, α_2, ..., and the zeros of f_2, β_1, β_2, ... Then the following is clearly a necessary and sufficient algebraic condition for f_1 and f_2 to have a common solution:

$$C \prod (\alpha_i - \beta_j) = C_{f_1} \prod f_2(\alpha_i) = C_{f_2} \prod f_1(\beta_j) = 0,$$

where C's are nonzero constants. Since these conditions are symmetric in the α's as well as β's, one can express the above conditions in terms of the coefficients of f_1 and f_2 (which are also symmetric polynomials of α's and β's, respectively).

These discussions should make apparent that resultants are also intimately connected to the computation of GCD of two polynomials and the related *Bézout's identity*:

$$f_1 \, g_1 + f_2 \, g_2 = \text{GCD}(f_1, f_2).$$

In an exploration of the extension of the *extended Euclidean algorithm* to the polynomials, we shall also encounter polynomial remainder sequences, the connection between pseudodivision and resultant-like structures (in particular, subresultants), and various efficient computational techniques.

This chapter is organized as follows: Sections 7.2 and 7.3 introduce resultant in a rather general setting and discuss some of their properties. Section 7.4 discusses discriminants—a concept useful in testing whether a polynomial in a unique factorization domain has repeated factors. Next, in Section 7.5, we consider a generalization of the division operation from Euclidean domains to commutative rings by the "pseudodivision" and how it leads to an "extended Euclidean algorithm" for polynomials. We also describe determinant polynomials, a useful tool in proving results about pseudodivision. Section 7.6 touches upon the subject of polynomial remainder sequences, which is then related to the concept of subresultants and subresultant chains. The last two sections explore these connections in greater details.

7.2   Resultants

Let S be a commutative ring with identity. Let $A(x)$ and $B(x) \in S[x]$ be univariate polynomials of respective positive degrees m and n with coefficients in the ring S.

$$
\begin{aligned}
A(x) &= a_m x^m + a_{m-1} x^{m-1} + \cdots + a_0, \quad \deg(A) = m, \quad \text{and} \\
B(x) &= b_n x^n + b_{n-1} x^{n-1} + \cdots + b_0, \quad \deg(B) = n.
\end{aligned}
$$

Definition 7.2.1 (Sylvester Matrix) The *Sylvester matrix* of $A(x)$ and $B(x) \in S[x]$, denoted Sylvester(A, B), is the following $(m + n) \times (m + n)$ matrix over S:

Sylvester(A, B)

$$
= \left[
\begin{array}{ccccccc}
a_m & a_{m-1} & \cdots & a_0 & & & \\
 & a_m & a_{m-1} & \cdots & a_0 & & \\
 & & \ddots & \ddots & \ddots & \ddots & \\
 & & & a_m & a_{m-1} & \cdots & a_0 \\
b_n & b_{n-1} & \cdots & \cdots & b_0 & & \\
 & b_n & b_{n-1} & \cdots & \cdots & b_0 & \\
 & & \ddots & \ddots & \ddots & \ddots & \\
 & & b_n & b_{n-1} & \cdots & \cdots & b_0
\end{array}
\right]
\begin{array}{l}
\left.\begin{array}{l} \\ \\ \\ \\ \end{array}\right\} \begin{array}{l} n \text{ staggered} \\ \text{rows of} \\ \text{coefficients} \\ \text{of } A \end{array} \\
\left.\begin{array}{l} \\ \\ \\ \\ \end{array}\right\} \begin{array}{l} m \text{ staggered} \\ \text{rows of} \\ \text{coefficients} \\ \text{of } B \end{array}
\end{array}
$$

In particular, the first n rows of the Sylvester matrix correspond to the polynomials $x^{n-1}A(x)$, $x^{n-2}A(x)$, ..., $A(x)$, and the last m rows, to $x^{m-1}B(x)$, $x^{m-2}B(x)$, ..., $B(x)$.   □

Definition 7.2.2 (Resultant) The *resultant* of $A(x)$ and $B(x)$, denoted Resultant(A, B), is the determinant of the Sylvester matrix Sylvester(A, B), and thus is an element of S.   □

Since Sylvester(B, A) can be obtained by $m \cdot n$ row transpositions, we see that

$$
\begin{aligned}
\text{Resultant}(B, A) &= \det(\text{Sylvester}(B, A)) \\
&= (-1)^{mn} \det(\text{Sylvester}(A, B)) \\
&= (-1)^{mn} \text{Resultant}(A, B).
\end{aligned}
$$

Properties of Resultant

Lemma 7.2.1 *Let S be a commutative ring with identity, and $A(x)$ and $B(x) \in S[x]$ be univariate polynomials of respective positive degrees m and n with coefficients in the ring S. Then there exist polynomials $T(x)$ and $U(x) \in S[x]$ such that*

$$A(x) \cdot T(x) + B(x) \cdot U(x) = \text{Resultant}(A, B),$$

where $\deg(T) < \deg(B) = n$ and $\deg(U) < \deg(A) = m$.
PROOF.
Consider the Sylvester matrix of A and B:

$$
\text{Sylvester}(A, B)
$$

$$
= \left.\begin{bmatrix}
a_m & a_{m-1} & \cdots & & a_0 & & & & \\
& a_m & a_{m-1} & \cdots & & a_0 & & & \\
& & \ddots & \ddots & & \ddots & \ddots & & \\
& & & & a_m & a_{m-1} & \cdots & a_0 & \\
b_n & b_{n-1} & \cdots & & \cdots & b_0 & & & \\
& b_n & b_{n-1} & \cdots & & \cdots & b_0 & & \\
& & \ddots & \ddots & & \ddots & \ddots & & \\
& & b_n & b_{n-1} & \cdots & & \cdots & b_0 &
\end{bmatrix}\right\}
\begin{array}{l} n \text{ rows} \\ \\ \\ m \text{ rows} \end{array}
$$

Let us create a new matrix M' from M by following *elementary* matrix operations:

1. First, multiply the ith column by x^{m+n-i} and add to the last column of M.

2. All but the last column of M' are same as those of M.

By definition,

$$\text{Resultant}(A, B) = \det(M) = \det(M').$$

We observe that matrix M' is as follows:

$$
\text{Sylvester}(A, B)
$$

$$
= \left.\begin{bmatrix}
a_m & a_{m-1} & \cdots & & a_0 & & \sum_{i=0}^{m} a_i x^{n+i-1} \\
& a_m & a_{m-1} & \cdots & & a_0 & \sum_{i=0}^{m} a_i x^{n+i-2} \\
& & \ddots & \ddots & \ddots & \ddots & \\
& & & a_m & a_{m-1} & \cdots & \sum_{i=0}^{m} a_i x^{i} \\
b_n & b_{n-1} & \cdots & & \cdots & b_0 & \sum_{i=0}^{n} b_i x^{m+i-1} \\
& b_n & b_{n-1} & \cdots & & \cdots\; b_0 & \sum_{i=0}^{n} b_i x^{m+i-2} \\
& & \ddots & \ddots & \ddots & \ddots & \\
& & b_n & b_{n-1} & \cdots & & \sum_{i=0}^{n} b_i x^{i}
\end{bmatrix}\right\}
\begin{array}{l} n \text{ rows} \\ \\ \\ m \text{ rows} \end{array}
$$

$$
= \begin{bmatrix}
a_m & a_{m-1} & \cdots & & a_0 & & & x^{n-1}A(x) \\
& a_m & a_{m-1} & \cdots & & a_0 & & x^{n-2}A(x) \\
& & \ddots & \ddots & \ddots & & \ddots & \vdots \\
& & & a_m & a_{m-1} & \cdots & & A(x) \\
b_n & b_{n-1} & \cdots & & \cdots & b_0 & & x^{m-1}B(x) \\
& b_n & b_{n-1} & \cdots & & \cdots & b_0 & x^{m-2}B(x) \\
& & \ddots & \ddots & \ddots & & \ddots & \vdots \\
& & & b_n & b_{n-1} & \cdots & \cdots & B(x)
\end{bmatrix}
\begin{array}{l} \left. \vphantom{\begin{matrix}a\\a\\a\\a\end{matrix}}\right\} n \text{ rows} \\[2em] \left. \vphantom{\begin{matrix}a\\a\\a\\a\end{matrix}}\right\} m \text{ rows} \end{array}
$$

Note that since the last column of the matrix M' is simply

$$
\left[x^{n-1}A(x), \ \ldots, \ A(x), \ x^{m-1}B(x), \ \ldots, \ B(x) \right]^T,
$$

we can compute the $\det(M')$ explicitly by expanding the determinant with respect to its last column. We then have the following:

$$
\begin{aligned}
\text{Resultant}(A, B) &= \det(M') \\
&= x^{n-1}A(x) \cdot M'_{1,m+n} + \cdots + A(x) \cdot M'_{n,m+n} \\
&\quad + x^{m-1}B(x) \cdot M'_{n+1,m+n} + \cdots + B(x) \cdot M'_{m+n,m+n} \\
&= A(x)\left(M'_{1,m+n}x^{n-1} + \cdots + M'_{n,m+n} \right) \\
&\quad + B(x)\left(M'_{n+1,m+n}x^{m-1} + \cdots + M'_{m+n,m+n} \right) \\
&= A(x) \cdot T(x) + B(x) \cdot U(x).
\end{aligned}
$$

Note that the coefficients of $T(x)$ and $U(x)$ are cofactors of the last column of M', and hence of M, and are ring elements in S.

    Clearly,

$$
\deg(T) \le n - 1 < \deg(B) \quad \text{and} \quad \deg(U) \le m - 1 < \deg(A). \quad \square
$$

Lemma 7.2.2 *Let $A(x)$ and $B(x)$ be univariate polynomials of respective positive degrees m and n, over an integral domain S. Then*

$$
\text{Resultant}(A, B) = 0
$$

if and only if there exist nonzero polynomials $T(x)$ and $U(x)$ over S such that

$$
A(x) \cdot T(x) + B(x) \cdot U(x) = 0,
$$

where $\deg(T) < \deg(B) = n$, *and* $\deg(U) < \deg(A) = m$.

PROOF.

($\Rightarrow$)   By Lemma 7.2.1, Resultant$(A, B) = 0$ implies that there exist univariate polynomials $T(x)$, $U(x) \in S[X]$ such that

$$A(x) \cdot T(x) + B(x) \cdot U(x) = \text{Resultant}(A, B) = 0,$$

where $\deg(T) < \deg(B) = n$ and $\deg(U) < \deg(A) = m$.

Thus we may assume that

$$
\begin{aligned}
T(x) &= t_{n-1}x^{n-1} + t_{n-2}x^{n-2} + \cdots + t_0, \\
U(x) &= u_{m-1}x^{m-1} + u_{m-2}x^{m-2} + \cdots + u_0,
\end{aligned}
$$

where t_i, $u_i \in S$.

We claim that not all t_i's and u_i's are zero. Since

$$A(x) \cdot T(x) + B(x) \cdot U(x) = 0,$$

we have

$$
\begin{aligned}
t_{n-1} \cdot a_m + u_{m-1} \cdot b_n &= 0 \\
t_{n-1} \cdot a_{m-1} + t_{n-2} \cdot a_m + u_{m-1} \cdot b_{n-1} + u_{m-2} \cdot b_n &= 0 \\
&\vdots \\
t_1 \cdot a_0 + t_0 \cdot a_1 + u_1 \cdot b_0 + u_0 \cdot b_1 &= 0 \\
t_0 \cdot a_0 + u_0 \cdot b_0 &= 0,
\end{aligned}
\tag{7.1}
$$

i.e.,

$$
\text{Sylvester}(A, B)^T \cdot
\begin{bmatrix}
t_{n-1} \\
\vdots \\
t_0 \\
u_{m-1} \\
\vdots \\
u_0
\end{bmatrix}
=
\begin{bmatrix}
0 \\
\vdots \\
0 \\
0 \\
\vdots \\
0
\end{bmatrix}.
$$

But since $\det(\text{Sylvester}(A, B)) = \text{Resultant}(A, B) = 0$ by assumption, and since we are working over an integral domain, the system of equations 7.1 has a nontrivial solution. That is, not all t_i's and u_i's are zero, as claimed.

($\Leftarrow$)   Conversely, assume the existence of $T(x)$ and $U(x)$ as in the statement of the lemma:

$$
\begin{aligned}
T(x) &= t_p x^p + t_{p-1}x^{p-1} + \cdots + t_0, \\
U(x) &= u_q x^q + u_{q-1}x^{q-1} + \cdots + u_0,
\end{aligned}
$$

where

$$t_p \neq 0, \; u_q \neq 0, \; p < n, \text{ and } q < m.$$

We may then write $T(x)$ and $U(x)$ as below, while tacitly assuming that

$$t_{n-1} = \cdots = t_{p+1} = 0, \quad t_p \neq 0, \quad u_{m-1} = \cdots = u_{q+1} = 0, \quad \text{and} \quad u_q \neq 0:$$

$$\begin{aligned} T(x) &= t_{n-1}x^{n-1} + t_{n-2}x^{n-2} + \cdots + t_0, \quad t_{n-1} \neq 0, \\ U(x) &= u_{m-1}x^{m-1} + u_{m-2}x^{m-2} + \cdots + u_0, \quad u_{m-1} \neq 0. \end{aligned}$$

Now, expanding the expression $A(x) \cdot T(x) + B(x) \cdot U(x) = 0$, we see that the following linear system

$$\text{Sylvester}(A, B)^T \cdot \begin{bmatrix} t_{n-1} \\ \vdots \\ t_0 \\ u_{m-1} \\ \vdots \\ u_0 \end{bmatrix} = \begin{bmatrix} 0 \\ \vdots \\ 0 \\ 0 \\ \vdots \\ 0 \end{bmatrix},$$

has a nontrivial solution. Since Sylvester(A, B) is over an integral domain S, we have

$$\det(\text{Sylvester}(A, B)) - \text{Resultant}(A, B) = 0. \quad \square$$

Lemma 7.2.3 *Let S be a* unique factorization domain *with identity, and $A(x)$ and $B(x)$ be univariate polynomials of positive degrees with coefficients in S. Then*

$$\text{Resultant}(A, B) = 0$$

if and only if $A(x)$ and $B(x)$ have a common divisor of positive degree.
PROOF.
($\Leftarrow$)   Assume that $A(x)$ and $B(x)$ have a common divisor $C(x)$ of positive degree. Then, since S is an integral domain,

$$\begin{aligned} A(x) &= C(x) \cdot U(x), \quad \deg(U) < \deg(A), \text{ and} \\ B(x) &= C(x) \cdot T(x), \quad \deg(T) < \deg(B). \end{aligned}$$

Therefore,

$$\begin{aligned} &A(x) \cdot T(x) + B(x) \cdot (-U(x)) \\ &= C(x) \cdot T(x) \cdot U(x) - C(x) \cdot T(x) \cdot U(x) = 0. \end{aligned}$$

Thus by Lemma 7.2.2, Resultant$(A, B) = 0$.

($\Rightarrow$) Since Resultant$(A, B) = 0$, we know by Lemma 7.2.2 that there exist two nonzero polynomials $T(x)$ and $U(x) \in S[x]$ such that

$$A(x) \cdot T(x) - B(x) \cdot U(x) = \text{Resultant}(A, B) = 0,$$

where $\deg(T) < \deg(B) = n$, $\deg(U) < \deg(A) = m$, and

$$A(x) \cdot T(x) = B(x) \cdot U(x).$$

By the Gauss lemma, $S[x]$ is also a unique factorization domain. Therefore,

$$\text{Primitive}(A) \cdot \text{Primitive}(T) = \text{Primitive}(B) \cdot \text{Primitive}(U).$$

Thus

$$A_1(x) \cdots A_{m'}(x) \cdot T_1(x) \cdots T_{p'}(x) = B_1(x) \cdots B_{n'}(x) \cdot U_1(x) \cdots U_{q'}(x),$$

where

$$
\begin{array}{ll}
A_1(x) \cdots A_{m'}(x) & \text{is a primitive factorization of } A(x), \\
T_1(x) \cdots T_{p'}(x) & \text{is a primitive factorization of } T(x), \\
B_1(x) \cdots B_{n'}(x) & \text{is a primitive factorization of } B(x), \\
U_1(x) \cdots U_{q'}(x) & \text{is a primitive factorization of } U(x).
\end{array}
$$

By the uniqueness of the factorization, each $A_i(x)$ is an associate of a $B_j(x)$ or an associate of a $U_k(x)$. Since $\deg(A_1 \cdots A_{m'}) > \deg(U_1 \cdots U_{q'})$, there must exist an $A_i(x)$ that is an associate of a $B_j(x)$.

Therefore, $A_i(x)$ is a primitive polynomial of positive degree, and is a divisor of both $A(x)$ and $B(x)$. $\quad\square$

7.3　Homomorphisms and Resultants

Let S and S^* be commutative rings with identities, and

$$\phi : S \to S^*$$

be a ring homomorphism of S into S^*.

Note that ϕ induces a ring homomorphism of $S[x]$ into $S^*[x]$, also denoted by ϕ, as follows:

$$
\begin{array}{rl}
\phi : & S[X] \to S^*[x] \\
: & a_m x^m + a_{m-1} x^{m-1} + \cdots + a_0 \\
\mapsto & \phi(a_m) x^m + \phi(a_{m-1}) x^{m-1} + \cdots + \phi(a_0).
\end{array}
$$

Lemma 7.3.1 *Let $A(x) = \sum_{i=0}^{m} a_i x^i$ and $B(x) = \sum_{i=0}^{n} b_i x^i$ be two univariate polynomials over the ring S with $\deg(A) = m > 0$ and $\deg(B) = n > 0$. If*

$$\deg(\phi(A)) = m \quad and \quad \deg(\phi(B)) = k, \qquad (0 \le k \le n),$$

then

$$\phi(\mathrm{Resultant}(A, B)) = \phi(a_m)^{n-k} \cdot \mathrm{Resultant}\,(\phi(A), \phi(B)).$$

PROOF.

Let

$$
\begin{aligned}
A^* &= \phi(A) = \phi(a_m)x^m + \phi(a_{m-1})x^{m-1} + \cdots + \phi(a_0), \quad \text{and} \\
B^* &= \phi(B) = \phi(b_k)x^k + \phi(b_{k-1})x^{k-1} + \cdots + \phi(b_0).
\end{aligned}
$$

Then, M, the Sylvester matrix of $A(x)$ and $B(x)$, is

$$M = \mathrm{Sylvester}(A, B)$$

$$
= \left[
\begin{array}{cccccccc}
a_m & a_{m-1} & \cdots & & a_0 & & & \\
& a_m & a_{m-1} & \cdots & & a_0 & & \\
& & \ddots & \ddots & & \ddots & \ddots & \\
& & & a_m & a_{m-1} & \cdots & & a_0 \\
b_n & b_{n-1} & \cdots & & b_0 & & & \\
& b_n & b_{n-1} & \cdots & & b_0 & & \\
& & \ddots & \ddots & & \ddots & \ddots & \\
& & b_n & b_{n-1} & \cdots & & & b_0 \\
\end{array}
\right]
\begin{array}{l}
\left.\rule{0pt}{28pt}\right\} n \text{ rows} \\
\left.\rule{0pt}{28pt}\right\} m \text{ rows}
\end{array}
$$

and M^*, the Sylvester matrix of $A^*(x)$ and $B^*(x)$, is

$$M^* = \mathrm{Sylvester}(A^*, B^*) =$$

$$
\left[
\begin{array}{cccccccc}
\phi(a_m) & \phi(a_{m-1}) & \cdots & & \phi(a_0) & & & \\
& \phi(a_m) & \phi(a_{m-1}) & \cdots & & \phi(a_0) & & \\
& & \ddots & \ddots & & \ddots & \ddots & \\
& & & \phi(a_m) & \phi(a_{m-1}) & \cdots & & \phi(a_0) \\
\phi(b_k) & \phi(b_{k-1}) & \cdots & & \phi(b_0) & & & \\
& \phi(b_k) & \phi(b_{k-1}) & \cdots & & \phi(b_0) & & \\
& & \ddots & \ddots & & \ddots & \ddots & \\
& & \phi(b_k) & \phi(b_{k-1}) & \cdots & & & \phi(b_0) \\
\end{array}
\right]
\begin{array}{l}
\left.\rule{0pt}{28pt}\right\} \begin{array}{l}k\\ \text{rows}\end{array} \\
\left.\rule{0pt}{28pt}\right\} \begin{array}{l}m\\ \text{rows}\end{array}
\end{array}
$$

The matrix M^* is obtained from M by the following process:

1. First, the matrix, $\phi(M)$, is computed by replacing the entry a_i by $\phi(a_i)$ (for all $0 \le i \le m$), and by replacing the entry b_j by $\phi(b_j)$ (for all $0 \le j \le n$). By assumption

$$\phi(b_n) = \cdots = \phi(b_{k+1}) = 0.$$

2. Next, from $\phi(M)$, the first $(n - k)$ rows and $(n - k)$ columns are deleted, yielding an $(m + k) \times (m + k)$ matrix equal to M^*.

Thus

$\phi(M)$

$$
= \left[
\begin{array}{ccccccc}
\phi(a_m) & \phi(a_{m-1}) & \cdots & \phi(a_0) & & & \\
 & \ddots & \ddots & \ddots & \ddots & & \\
 & & \phi(a_m) & \phi(a_{m-1}) & \cdots & \phi(a_0) & \\
 & & & & & & \\
 & \mathbf{0} & & M^* & & & \\
\end{array}
\right]
\begin{array}{l}
\left.\vphantom{\begin{array}{c}a\\a\\a\end{array}}\right\}\begin{array}{l}(n-k)\\ \text{rows}\end{array} \\
\left.\vphantom{\begin{array}{c}a\\a\\a\end{array}}\right\}\begin{array}{l}(m+k)\\ \text{rows}\end{array}
\end{array}
$$

Therefore,

$$
\begin{aligned}
\phi(\text{Resultant}(A, B)) &= \phi(\det(\text{Sylvester}(A, B))) \\
&= \det(\phi(M)) = \phi(a_m)^{n-k} \cdot \det(\phi(M^*)) \\
&= \phi(a_m)^{n-k} \cdot \phi(\det(\text{Sylvester}(A^*, B^*))) \\
&= \phi(a_m)^{n-k} \cdot \phi(\text{Resultant}(A^*, B^*)).
\end{aligned}
$$

Therefore,

$$
\phi(\text{Resultant}(A, B)) = \phi(a_m)^{n-k} \cdot \phi(\text{Resultant}(A^*, B^*)). \quad \square
$$

7.3.1 Evaluation Homomorphism

Let S be a commutative ring with an identity, and $\langle \alpha_1, \ldots, \alpha_r \rangle \in S^r$ be an r-tuple. Define a ring homomorphism $\phi_{\alpha_1, \ldots, \alpha_r}$, called the *evaluation homomorphism*, as follows:

$$
\begin{aligned}
\phi_{\alpha_1, \ldots, \alpha_r} \quad &: \quad S[x_1, \ldots, x_r] \to S \\
&: \quad x_1 \mapsto \alpha_1, \\
&\qquad \vdots \\
&: \quad x_r \mapsto \alpha_r.
\end{aligned}
$$

Note that, if $F(x_1, \ldots, x_r) \in S[x_1, \ldots, x_r]$, then we shall write

$$
F(\alpha_1, \ldots, \alpha_r) \quad \text{for} \quad \phi_{\alpha_1, \ldots, \alpha_r}(F).
$$

Definition 7.3.1 Let S be a commutative ring with an identity, and

$$A(x_1, \ldots, x_r) \;=\; \sum_{i=0}^{m} A_i(x_1, \ldots, x_{r-1}) x_r^i \in S[x_1, \ldots, x_r], \quad \text{and}$$

$$B(x_1, \ldots, x_r) \;=\; \sum_{i=0}^{n} B_i(x_1, \ldots, x_{r-1}) x_r^i \in S[x_1, \ldots, x_r].$$

be two polynomials in $S[x_1, \ldots, x_r]$ of respective positive degrees m and n in x_r. Let

$$\text{Resultant}_{x_r}(A, B)$$

$$= \left| \begin{array}{ccccccc}
A_m & A_{m-1} & \cdots & & A_0 & & \\
& A_m & A_{m-1} & \cdots & & A_0 & \\
& & \ddots & \ddots & \ddots & & \ddots \\
& & & A_m & A_{m-1} & \cdots & A_0 \\
B_n & B_{n-1} & \cdots & & \cdots & B_0 & \\
& B_n & B_{n-1} & \cdots & & \cdots & B_0 \\
& & \ddots & \ddots & \ddots & & \ddots \\
& & B_n & B_{n-1} & \cdots & \cdots & B_0
\end{array} \right| \begin{array}{l} \left.\vphantom{\begin{array}{c}a\\a\\a\\a\end{array}}\right\} n \text{ rows} \\[2em] \left.\vphantom{\begin{array}{c}a\\a\\a\\a\end{array}}\right\} m \text{ rows} \end{array}$$

be the *resultant* of two multivariate polynomials $A(x_1, \ldots, x_r)$ and $B(x_1, \ldots, x_r)$, *with respect to* x_r. □

Lemma 7.3.2 *Let L be an algebraically closed field, and let*

$$\text{Resultant}_{x_r}(A, B) = C(x_1, \ldots, x_{r-1})$$

be the resultant of the multivariate polynomials,

$$A(x_1, \ldots, x_r) \;=\; \sum_{i=0}^{m} A_i(x_1, \ldots, x_{r-1}) x_r^i \in L[x_1, \ldots, x_r], \quad \text{and}$$

$$B(x_1, \ldots, x_r) \;=\; \sum_{i=0}^{n} B_i(x_1, \ldots, x_{r-1}) x_r^i \in L[x_1, \ldots, x_r].$$

with respect to x_r. Then

1. *If $\langle \alpha_1, \ldots, \alpha_r \rangle \in L^r$ is a common zero of $A(x_1, \ldots, x_r)$ and $B(x_1, \ldots, x_r)$, then $C(\alpha_1, \ldots, \alpha_{r-1}) = 0$.*
2. *Conversely, if $C(\alpha_1, \ldots, \alpha_{r-1}) = 0$, then at least one of the following four conditions holds:*
   (a) *$A_m(\alpha_1, \ldots, \alpha_{r-1}) = \cdots = A_0(\alpha_1, \ldots, \alpha_{r-1}) = 0$, or*
   (b) *$B_n(\alpha_1, \ldots, \alpha_{r-1}) = \cdots = B_0(\alpha_1, \ldots, \alpha_{r-1}) = 0$, or*
   (c) *$A_m(\alpha_1, \ldots, \alpha_{r-1}) = B_n(\alpha_1, \ldots, \alpha_{r-1}) = 0$, or*

(d) for some $\alpha_r \in L$, $\langle \alpha_1, \ldots, \alpha_r \rangle$ is a common zero of both $A(x_1, \ldots, x_r)$ and $B(x_1, \ldots, x_r)$.

PROOF.
(1) Since there exist T and U in $L[x_1, \ldots, x_{r-1}]$ such that

$$A \cdot T + B \cdot U = C,$$

we have

$$
\begin{aligned}
C(\alpha_1, \ldots, \alpha_{r-1}) \\
= \quad & A(\alpha_1, \ldots, \alpha_r) \cdot T(\alpha_1, \ldots, \alpha_r) + B(\alpha_1, \ldots, \alpha_r) \cdot U(\alpha_1, \ldots, \alpha_r) \\
= \quad & 0,
\end{aligned}
$$

as $A(\alpha_1, \ldots, \alpha_r) = B(\alpha_1, \ldots, \alpha_r) = 0$, by assumption.

(2) Next, assume that $C(\alpha_1, \ldots, \alpha_{r-1}) = 0$, but that conditions (a), (b), and (c) are not satisfied. Then there are two cases to consider:

1. $A_m(\alpha_1, \ldots, \alpha_{r-1}) \neq 0$ and
   for some k $(0 \leq k \leq n)$, $B_k(\alpha_1, \ldots, \alpha_{r-1}) \neq 0$
   (k is assumed to be the largest such index).

2. $B_n(\alpha_1, \ldots, \alpha_{r-1}) \neq 0$ and
   for some k $(0 \leq k \leq m)$, $A_k(\alpha_1, \ldots, \alpha_{r-1}) \neq 0$
   (k is assumed to be the largest such index).

Since Resultant$(B, A) = (-1)^{mn}$Resultant$(A, B) = \pm C$, cases (1) and (2) are symmetric, and without any loss of generality, we may only deal with the first case.

Let $\phi = \phi_{\alpha_1, \ldots, \alpha_{r-1}}$ be the evaluation homomorphism defined earlier. Thus,

$$
\begin{aligned}
0 \quad = \quad & \phi(C) \\
= \quad & \phi(\text{Resultant}(A, B)) \\
= \quad & \phi(A_m)^{n-k} \cdot \text{Resultant}(\phi(A), \phi(B)),
\end{aligned}
$$

and Resultant$(\phi(A), \phi(B)) = 0$, since $\phi(A_m) = A_m(\alpha_1, \ldots, \alpha_{r-1}) \neq 0$.
If $k = 0$, then

$$
\begin{aligned}
\text{Resultant}(\phi(A), \phi(B)) \quad = \quad & \phi(B_0)^m \\
= \quad & B_0(\alpha_1, \ldots, \alpha_{r-1})^m \neq 0 \quad \text{(by assumption)}.
\end{aligned}
$$

Hence $k > 0$ and $\phi(A)$ and $\phi(B)$ are of positive degree and have a common divisor of positive degree, say $D(x_r)$.

Since L is algebraically closed, $D(x_r)$ has at least one zero, say α_r.

Therefore,

$$A(\alpha_1, \ldots, \alpha_{r-1}, x_r) = D(x_r) \cdot \widetilde{A}(x_r), \quad \text{and}$$
$$B(\alpha_1, \ldots, \alpha_{r-1}, x_r) = D(x_r) \cdot \widetilde{B}(x_r),$$

and $\langle \alpha_1, \ldots, \alpha_{r-1}, \alpha_r \rangle$ is a common zero of A and B. $\quad \square$

Now, consider two univariate polynomials

$$A(x) = a_m x^m + a_{m-1} x^{m-1} + \cdots + a_0, \quad \deg(A) = m > 0,$$
$$B(x) = b_n x^n + b_{n-1} x^{n-1} + \cdots + b_0, \quad \deg(B) = n > 0,$$

of positive degrees, with formal (symbolic) coefficients $a_m, a_{m-1}, \ldots, a_0$ and $b_n, b_{n-1}, \ldots, b_0$, respectively.

We consider $A(x)$ and $B(x)$ to be univariate polynomials in the ring

$$\big(\mathbb{Z}[a_m, \ldots, a_0, b_n, \ldots, b_0]\big)[x].$$

Thus, the resultant of $A(x)$ and $B(x)$ with respect to x is a polynomial in the ring

$$\mathbb{Z}[a_m, \ldots, a_0, b_n, \ldots, b_0].$$

Now, if we consider the evaluation homomorphism

$$\phi_{\bar{\alpha}, \bar{\beta}} = \phi_{\alpha_m, \ldots, \alpha_0, \beta_n, \ldots, \beta_0}$$

from $\mathbb{Z}[a_m, \ldots, a_0, b_n, \ldots, b_0]$ into a unique factorization domain S as follows:

$$
\begin{aligned}
\phi_{\bar{\alpha}, \bar{\beta}} \quad &: \quad \mathbb{Z}[a_m, \ldots, a_0, b_n, \ldots, b_0] \to S, \\
&: \quad a_m \mapsto \alpha_m, \\
&\quad \vdots \\
&: \quad a_0 \mapsto \alpha_0, \\
&: \quad b_n \mapsto \beta_0, \\
&\quad \vdots \\
&: \quad b_0 \mapsto \beta_0, \\
&: \quad 0 \mapsto 0, \\
&: \quad n \mapsto \underbrace{1 + \cdots + 1}_{n \text{ times}},
\end{aligned}
$$

then we can show the following:

Lemma 7.3.3 *Let $A(x)$ and $B(x)$ be two univariate polynomials with formal coefficients $a_m, \ldots, a_0$, and $b_n, \ldots, b_0$, respectively. Let $\phi_{\bar{\alpha},\bar{\beta}}$ be any evaluation homomorphism for which $\alpha_m \neq 0$, and $\beta_n \neq 0$.*

Then the necessary and sufficient condition that $\phi_{\bar{\alpha},\bar{\beta}}A(x)$ and $\phi_{\bar{\alpha},\bar{\beta}}B(x)$ have a common divisor of positive degree is:

$\langle \alpha_m, \ldots, \alpha_0, \beta_n, \ldots, \beta_0 \rangle$ *satisfies the equation*

$$\text{Resultant}(A, B) = 0,$$

where $\text{Resultant}(A, B) \in \mathbb{Z}[a_m, \ldots, a_0, b_n, \ldots, b_0]$.

PROOF.
Let $\langle \alpha_m, \ldots, \alpha_0, \beta_n, \ldots, \beta_0 \rangle \in S^{m+n+2}$ be a solution to the equation $\text{Resultant}(A, B) = 0$. Let

$$\begin{aligned} \phi_{\bar{\alpha},\bar{\beta}}(A) &= \alpha_m x^m + \alpha_{m-1} x^{m-1} + \cdots + \alpha_0, \\ \phi_{\bar{\alpha},\bar{\beta}}(B) &= \beta_n x^n + \beta_{n-1} x^{n-1} + \cdots + \beta_0; \end{aligned}$$

then

$$\text{Resultant}\left(\phi_{\bar{\alpha},\bar{\beta}}(A), \phi_{\bar{\alpha},\bar{\beta}}(B)\right) = \phi_{\bar{\alpha},\bar{\beta}}\left(\text{Resultant}(A, B)\right) = 0,$$

and $\phi_{\bar{\alpha},\bar{\beta}}A(x)$ and $\phi_{\bar{\alpha},\bar{\beta}}B(x)$ have a common divisor of positive degree.
    Conversely, let

$$\begin{aligned} \phi_{\bar{\alpha},\bar{\beta}}(A) &= \alpha_m x^m + \alpha_{m-1} x^{m-1} + \cdots + \alpha_0 \quad \text{and} \\ \phi_{\bar{\alpha},\bar{\beta}}(B) &= \beta_n x^n + \beta_{n-1} x^{n-1} + \cdots + \beta_0 \end{aligned}$$

have a common divisor of positive degree. The assertion above implies that

$$\phi_{\bar{\alpha},\bar{\beta}}\left(\text{Resultant}(A, B)\right) = \text{Resultant}\left(\phi_{\bar{\alpha},\bar{\beta}}(A), \phi_{\bar{\alpha},\bar{\beta}}(B)\right) = 0,$$

and so $\langle \alpha_m, \ldots, \alpha_0, \beta_n, \ldots, \beta_0 \rangle \in S^{m+n+2}$ is a solution to the equation $\text{Resultant}(A, B) = 0$. $\square$

7.4   Repeated Factors in Polynomials and Discriminants

Let U be a unique factorization domain of characteristic 0, i.e., satisfying the following condition:

$$n = \underbrace{1 + \cdots + 1}_{n} \neq 0, \qquad \text{for any positive integer } n.$$

Definition 7.4.1 (Differentiation Operator) The formal *differentiation operator* is a map

$$
\begin{aligned}
D : U[x] &\rightarrow U[x] \\
a &\mapsto 0 \\
A(x) = a_m x^m + \cdots + a_0 &\mapsto A'(x) = m a_m x^{m-1} + \cdots + a_1
\end{aligned}
$$

where $a, a_0, \ldots, a_m \in U$ and $m\, a_m = \underbrace{a_m + \cdots + a_m}_{m}$. $\square$

Let $A(x), B(x), A_1(x), \ldots, A_m(x) \in U[x]$. Then

1. If $A(x) \in U$, then $A'(x) = 0$. Otherwise, $\deg(A'(x)) = \deg(A(x)) - 1$.

2. $D(-A(x)) = -D(A(x))$.

3. $D(A(x) + B(x)) = D(A(x)) + D(B(x))$.

4. $D(A(x) \cdot B(x)) = D(A(x)) \cdot B(x) + A(x) \cdot D(B(x))$. [*Chain Rule*]

5. For all i $(1 \le i \le m)$,

$$
\begin{aligned}
D\left(A_1(x) \cdots A_m(x)\right) & \\
= \; A_i(x) \cdot D &\left(\prod_{\substack{j=1 \\ j \neq i}}^{m} A_j(x)\right) + D(A_i(x)) \cdot \left(\prod_{\substack{j=1 \\ j \neq i}}^{m} A_j(x)\right) \\
= \; \sum_{i=1}^{m} D(A_i(x)) \cdot &\left(\prod_{\substack{j=1 \\ j \neq i}}^{m} A_j(x)\right).
\end{aligned}
$$

Definition 7.4.2 (Square-Free Polynomial) Let $A(x) \in U[x]$ be factorized into indecomposable factors as follows :

$$
A(x) = A_1(x) \cdots A_{m'}(x)
$$

$A(x)$ is *square-free* (i.e., has no repeated factor of positive degree) if

$$
\left(\forall\, 1 \le i < j \le m'\right) \left[A_i(x) \not\approx A_j(x) \;\lor\; \deg(A_i) = 0\right].
$$

If

$$
\left(\exists\, 1 \le i < j \le m'\right) \left[A_i(x) \approx A_j(x) \;\land\; \deg(A_i) > 0\right],
$$

then $A_i(x)$ is called a *repeated factor* of $A(x)$. $\square$

Theorem 7.4.1 *A polynomial $A(x) \in U[x]$ of degree at least 2 has a repeated factor if and only if* $\text{Resultant}(A, A') = 0$.

PROOF.

Let

$$A(x) = A_1(x) \cdots A_{m'}(x)$$

$\text{Resultant}(A, A') = 0$

$\Leftrightarrow \quad A(x)$ and $A'(x)$ have a common divisor of positive degree

$\Leftrightarrow \quad \left(\exists\, 1 \le i \le m' \right) \left[A_i(x) \mid A'(x) \;\wedge\; \deg(A_i) > 0 \right]$

$\Leftrightarrow \quad A_i(x) \;\Big|\; \displaystyle\prod_{\substack{j=1 \\ j \ne i}}^{m'} A_j(x) \text{ and } \deg(A_i) > 0$

[Since $A_i(x) \nmid A'_i(x)$ as $\deg(A'_i) < \deg(A_i)$.]

$\Leftrightarrow \quad \left(\exists\, 1 \le i < j \le m' \right) \left[A_i(x) \approx A_j(x) \;\wedge\; \deg(A_i) > 0 \right]$

$\Leftrightarrow \quad A(x)$ has a repeated factor. $\quad \square$

Definition 7.4.3 (Discriminant) The *discriminant* of a polynomial

$$A(x) = a_m x^m + \cdots + a_0, \qquad m \ge 2$$

is

$$\text{Discriminant}(A) \;=\; (-1)^{m(m-1)/2} \times$$

$$
\left|
\begin{array}{ccccccc}
1 & a_{m-1} & \cdots & a_1 & a_0 & & \\
 & a_m & a_{m-1} & \cdots & a_1 & a_0 & \\
 & & \ddots & \ddots & \ddots & \ddots & \\
 & & a_m & a_{m-1} & \cdots & a_1 & a_0 \\
m & (m-1)a_{m-1} & \cdots & a_1 & & & \\
 & ma_m & (m-1)a_{m-1} & \cdots & a_1 & & \\
 & & \ddots & \ddots & \ddots & \ddots & \\
 & & & ma_m & (m-1)a_{m-1} & \cdots & a_1
\end{array}
\right|
\begin{array}{l}
\left.\rule{0pt}{40pt}\right\} \begin{array}{l}(m-1) \\ \text{rows}\end{array} \\[20pt]
\left.\rule{0pt}{40pt}\right\} \begin{array}{l} m \\ \text{rows}\end{array}
\end{array}
$$

i.e., $\text{Resultant}(A, A') = (-1)^{m(m-1)/2}\, a_m\, \text{Discriminant}(A)$. $\quad \square$

Since U is an integral domain, we see the following:

Corollary 7.4.2 *A polynomial $A(x) \in U[x]$ of degree at least 2 has a repeated factor if and only if*

$$\text{Discriminant}(A) = 0. \quad \square$$

Example 7.4.4 The discriminant of the quadratic polynomial

$$A(x) = ax^2 + bx + c$$

is

$$
\text{Discriminant}(A) = (-1)^{2 \cdot \frac{1}{2}} \begin{vmatrix} 1 & b & c \\ 2 & b & 0 \\ 0 & 2a & b \end{vmatrix}
$$

$$
= (-1) \begin{vmatrix} 1 & b & c \\ 0 & -b & -2c \\ 0 & 2a & b \end{vmatrix}
$$

$$
= (-1)(-b^2 + 4ac) = b^2 - 4ac.
$$

Thus $A(x)$ has a repeated factor if and only if $b^2 - 4ac = 0$. $\square$

Thus, we see that discriminant allows us to reduce the problem of testing whether a polynomial has repeated factors to a simple determinant evaluation—a well-studied problem having efficient algorithms even when U is an arbitrary ring with identity.

7.5   Determinant Polynomial

As before, let S be a commutative ring.

Definition 7.5.1 (Determinant Polynomial) Let m and n be two non-negative integers and $M \in S^{m \times n}$ be an $m \times n$ matrix with elements from S. Define $M^{(i)} \in S^{m \times m}$, for $i = m, \ldots, n$ as the $m \times m$ square submatrix of M consisting of the first $(m-1)$ columns of M and the ith column of M, i.e.,

$$
M^{(i)} = \begin{bmatrix} M_{1,1} & \cdots & M_{1,(m-1)} & M_{1,i} \\ M_{2,1} & \cdots & M_{2,(m-1)} & M_{2,i} \\ \vdots & \ddots & \vdots & \vdots \\ M_{m,1} & \cdots & M_{m,(m-1)} & M_{m,i} \end{bmatrix}.
$$

The *determinant polynomial* of M

$$
\text{DetPol}(M) = \sum_{i=m}^{n} \det(M^{(i)}) x^{n-i}.
$$

Note that $\text{DetPol}(M) = 0$ if $n < m$. Otherwise, $\deg(\text{DetPol}(M)) \le n - m$, the equality holds when $\det(M^{(m)}) \ne 0$.

From the definition, it is easy to see that, if $m \leq n$ then

$$\mathrm{DetPol}(M) = \begin{vmatrix} M_{1,1} & \cdots & M_{1,(m-1)} & \sum_{i=m}^{n} M_{1,i} x^{n-i} \\ M_{2,1} & \cdots & M_{2,(m-1)} & \sum_{i=m}^{n} M_{2,i} x^{n-i} \\ \vdots & \ddots & \vdots & \vdots \\ M_{m,1} & \cdots & M_{m,(m-1)} & \sum_{i=m}^{n} M_{m,i} x^{n-i} \end{vmatrix}$$

$$= \begin{vmatrix} M_{1,1} & \cdots & M_{1,(m-1)} & \sum_{i=1}^{n} M_{1,i} x^{n-i} \\ M_{2,1} & \cdots & M_{2,(m-1)} & \sum_{i=1}^{n} M_{2,i} x^{n-i} \\ \vdots & \ddots & \vdots & \vdots \\ M_{m,1} & \cdots & M_{m,(m-1)} & \sum_{i=1}^{n} M_{m,i} x^{n-i} \end{vmatrix}$$

$$= \begin{vmatrix} M_{1,1} & \cdots & M_{1,(m-1)} & \sum_{i=0}^{n-1} M_{1,n-i} x^{i} \\ M_{2,1} & \cdots & M_{2,(m-1)} & \sum_{i=0}^{n-1} M_{2,n-i} x^{i} \\ \vdots & \ddots & \vdots & \vdots \\ M_{m,1} & \cdots & M_{m,(m-1)} & \sum_{i=0}^{n-1} M_{m,n-i} x^{i} \end{vmatrix}$$

$$\in \left(\sum_{i=0}^{n-1} M_{1,n-i} x^{i}, \sum_{i=0}^{n-1} M_{2,n-i} x^{i}, \ldots, \sum_{i=0}^{n-1} M_{m,n-i} x^{i} \right).$$

Let $A_1(x), \ldots, A_m(x)$ be a set of polynomials in $S[x]$ such that

$$n = 1 + \max_{1 \leq i \leq m} \left\{ \deg(A_i) \right\}.$$

The *matrix* of $A_1, \ldots, A_m$, $M = \mathrm{Matrix}(A_1, \ldots, A_m) \in S^{m \times n}$ is defined by:

$$M_{ij} = \text{coefficient of } x^{n-j} \text{ in } A_i(x).$$

Define the *determinant polynomial* of $A_1, \ldots, A_m$ to be

$$\mathrm{DetPol}(A_1, \ldots, A_m) = \mathrm{DetPol}(\mathrm{Matrix}(A_1, \ldots, A_m)).$$

Note that $\mathrm{DetPol}(A_1, \ldots, A_m) = 0$ when $n < m$. $\quad\square$

The determinant polynomial satisfies the following properties:

1. For any polynomial $A(x) = a_m x^m + \cdots + a_0 \in S[x]$,

$$\begin{aligned} \mathrm{Matrix}(A) &= [a_m, \ldots, a_0], \quad \text{a } 1 \times (m+1) \text{ matrix}; \\ \mathrm{DetPol}(A) &= a_m x^m + \cdots + a_0 = A(x). \end{aligned}$$

2. $\mathrm{DetPol}(\ldots, A_i, \ldots, A_j, \ldots) = -\mathrm{DetPol}(\ldots, A_j, \ldots, A_i, \ldots).$

3. For any $a \in S$,

$$\mathrm{DetPol}(\ldots, a \cdot A_i, \ldots) = a \cdot \mathrm{DetPol}(\ldots, A_i, \ldots).$$

4. For any $a_1, \ldots, a_{i-1}, a_{i+1}, \ldots, a_m \in S$,

$$\mathrm{DetPol}\Big(\ldots, A_{i-1}, A_i + \sum_{\substack{j=1 \\ j \neq i}}^{m} a_j A_j, A_{i+1}, \ldots\Big)$$
$$= \mathrm{DetPol}(\ldots, A_{i-1}, A_i, A_{i+1}, \ldots). \quad \square$$

Theorem 7.5.1 *Let $A(x)$ and $B(x) \neq 0$ be polynomials in $S[x]$ with respective degrees k and n. Let m be an integer that is at least k and let*

$$\delta = \max(m - n + 1, 0) \quad and \quad \delta' = \max(k - n + 1, 0).$$

Then

$$\mathrm{DetPol}(x^{m-n}B,\ x^{m-n-1}B,\ \ldots,\ B,\ A)$$
$$= b_n^{\delta - \delta'} \cdot \mathrm{DetPol}(x^{k-n}B,\ x^{k-n-1}B,\ \ldots,\ B,\ A)$$

[**Note:** *If $p < 0$, then $\mathrm{DetPol}(x^p B,\ x^{p-1}B,\ \ldots,\ B,\ A) = \mathrm{DetPol}(A) = A$.*]

PROOF.
There are three cases to consider.

- CASE 1 ($k < n$): That is, $\delta' = 0$: Thus

$$b_n^{\delta - \delta'} \mathrm{DetPol}(x^{k-n}B,\ \ldots,\ B,\ A) = b_n^{\delta} \mathrm{DetPol}(A).$$

  – SUBCASE A ($m < n$): That is, $\delta = 0$: Thus

$$b_n^{\delta} \mathrm{DetPol}(A) = \mathrm{DetPol}(A)$$
$$= \mathrm{DetPol}(x^{m-n}B,\ \ldots,\ B,\ A).$$

  – SUBCASE B ($m \geq n$): That is, $\delta > 0$: Thus

$$b_n^{\delta} \mathrm{DetPol}(A)$$
$$= \mathrm{DetPol} \begin{bmatrix} b_n & \cdots & & b_0 & & & \\ & \ddots & & & \ddots & & \ddots \\ & & b_n & & \cdots & & b_0 \\ 0 & 0 & \cdots & 0 & a_k & \cdots & a_0 \end{bmatrix} \begin{matrix} \Big\} \delta \text{ rows} \\ + \\ \} 1 \text{ row} \end{matrix}$$
$$= \mathrm{DetPol}(x^{m-n}B,\ \ldots,\ B,\ A).$$

- CASE 2 $(k \geq n = 0)$: Thus

$$
\begin{aligned}
\mathrm{DetPol}(x^{m-n}B, \ldots, B, A) &= 0 \\
&= \mathrm{DetPol}(x^{k-n}B, \ldots, B, A) \\
&= b_n^{\delta - \delta'} \mathrm{DetPol}(x^{k-n}B, \ldots, B, A).
\end{aligned}
$$

- CASE 3 $(k \geq n > 0)$: Thus

$$
b_n^{\delta - \delta'} \mathrm{DetPol}(x^{k-n}B, \ldots, B, A)
$$

$$
= b_n^{\delta - \delta'} \mathrm{DetPol}
\left.\begin{bmatrix}
b_n & \cdots & b_0 & & & \\
 & \ddots & \ddots & \ddots & & \\
 & & b_n & \cdots & b_0 & \\
a_k & \cdots & a_n & \cdots & a_0 &
\end{bmatrix}\right.
\begin{matrix}
\left.\vphantom{\begin{matrix}b\\b\\b\end{matrix}}\right\} \delta' \text{ rows} \\
+ \\
\} \, 1 \text{ row}
\end{matrix}
$$

$$
= \mathrm{DetPol}
\left.\begin{bmatrix}
b_n & \cdots & b_0 & & & & \\
 & \ddots & \ddots & \ddots & & & \\
 & & & b_n & \cdots & b_0 & \\
0 & \cdots & \cdots & 0 & a_k & \cdots & a_n & \cdots & a_0
\end{bmatrix}\right.
\begin{matrix}
\left.\vphantom{\begin{matrix}b\\b\\b\end{matrix}}\right\} \delta \text{ rows} \\
+ \\
\} \, 1 \text{ row}
\end{matrix}
$$

$$
= \mathrm{DetPol}(x^{m-n}B, \ldots, B, A). \qquad \square
$$

7.5.1 Pseudodivision: Revisited

Recall the discussion on pseudodivision from Chapter 5. We had shown the following: Let S be a commutative ring.

Theorem 7.5.2 *Let $A(x)$ and $B(x) \neq 0$ be two polynomials in $S[x]$ of respective degrees m and n:*

$$
\begin{aligned}
A(x) &= a_m x^m + a_{m-1} x^{m-1} + \cdots + a_0 \\
B(x) &= b_n x^n + b_{n-1} x^{n-1} + \cdots + b_0
\end{aligned}
$$

Let $\delta = \max(m - n + 1, 0)$. Then there exist polynomials $Q(x)$ and $R(x)$ in $S[x]$ such that

$$
b_n^{\delta} A(x) = Q(x) B(x) + R(x) \quad and \quad \deg(R) < \deg(B).
$$

If b_n is not a zero divisor in S, then $Q(x)$ and $R(x)$ are unique. $\square$

For the given polynomials $A(x)$ and $B(x) \neq 0$ in $S[x]$, we refer to the polynomials $Q(x)$ and $R(x)$ in $S[x]$ the *pseudoquotient* and the *pseudoremainder* of $A(x)$ with respect to $B(x)$ [denoted $\mathrm{PQuotient}(A, B)$ and $\mathrm{PRemainder}(A, B)$], respectively.

Algorithms to compute the *pseudoquotient* and *pseudoremainder* may be found in Chapter 5. Here we shall explore some interesting relations between pseudodivision and determinant polynomial.

Theorem 7.5.3 *Let $A(x)$ and $B(x) \neq 0$ be polynomials in $S[x]$ of respective degrees m and n and $b_n = \mathrm{Hcoef}(B)$. Let $\delta = \max(m - n + 1, 0)$. Then a pseudoremainder of $A(x)$ and $B(x)$ is given by:*

$$b_n^\delta \mathrm{PRemainder}(A, B) = b_n^\delta \mathrm{DetPol}(x^{m-n}B, \ldots, B, A)$$

PROOF.
Let

$$\begin{aligned} \mathrm{PQuotient}(A, B) &= Q(x) = q_{m-n}x^{m-n} + \cdots + q_0 \\ \mathrm{PRemainder}(A, B) &= R(x). \end{aligned}$$

Then

$$\begin{aligned} b_n^\delta \cdot A(x) &= (q_{m-n}x^{m-n} + \cdots + q_0) \cdot B(x) + R(x) \\ &= q_{m-n}x^{m-n}B(x) + \cdots + q_0 B(x) + R(x). \end{aligned}$$

Hence, we see that

$$\begin{aligned} & b_n^\delta \, \mathrm{DetPol}(x^{m-n}B, \ldots, B, A) \\ &= \mathrm{DetPol}(x^{m-n}B, \ldots, B, b_n^\delta A) \\ &= \mathrm{DetPol}(x^{m-n}B, \ldots, B, b_n^\delta A - q_{m-n}x^{m-n}B - \cdots - q_0 B) \\ &= \mathrm{DetPol}(x^{m-n}B, \ldots, B, R) \\ &= b_n^\delta R, \end{aligned}$$

since

$$\mathrm{Matrix}(x^{m-n}B, \ldots, B, R)$$

$$= \begin{bmatrix} b_n & b_{n-1} & \cdots & & b_0 & & \\ & \ddots & \ddots & & & \ddots & \\ & & b_n & b_{n-1} & \cdots & & b_0 \\ & & & r_p & \cdots & & r_0 \end{bmatrix} \begin{array}{l} \left.\vphantom{\begin{matrix}a\\a\\a\end{matrix}}\right\} (m-n+1) \text{ rows} \\ + \\ \left.\vphantom{a}\right\} 1 \text{ row} \end{array}$$

where

$$\begin{aligned} B(x) &= b_n x^n + b_{n-1}x^{n-1} + \cdots + b_0 \\ R(X) &= r_p x^p + r_{p-1}x^{p-1} + \cdots + r_0, \quad \text{and } p < n. \quad \square \end{aligned}$$

Corollary 7.5.4 *If in the above theorem b_n is not a zero divisor, then*

$$\mathrm{PRemainder}(A, B) = \mathrm{DetPol}(x^{m-n}B, x^{m-n-1}B, \ldots, B, A). \quad \square$$

7.5.2 Homomorphism and Pseudoremainder

Let S and S^* be two commutative rings and $\phi \colon S \to S^*$ be a ring homomorphism. Then ϕ induces a homomorphism of $S[x]$ into $S^*[x]$ (also denoted ϕ):

$$
\begin{aligned}
a &\mapsto \phi(a) \\
a_m x^m + \cdots + a_0 &\mapsto \phi(a_m)x^m + \cdots + \phi(a_0),
\end{aligned}
$$

where $a, a_m, \ldots, a_0 \in S$.

For any set of polynomials $A_1, \ldots, A_m \in S[x]$,

$$\phi(\mathrm{DetPol}(A_1, \ldots, A_m)) = \mathrm{DetPol}(\phi(A_1), \ldots, \phi(A_m)).$$

provided $\max(\deg(A_i)) = \max(\deg(\phi(A_i)))$. $\quad\square$

Theorem 7.5.5 *Let $A(x)$ and $B(x) \neq 0$ be two polynomials in $S[x]$ of respective degrees m and n, and $b_n = \mathrm{Hcoef}(B)$. Let*

$$
\begin{aligned}
\delta &= \max(m - n + 1, 0), \\
k &= \deg(\phi(A)) \ \leq \ m, \\
n &= \deg(\phi(B)), \quad and \\
\delta' &= \max(k - n + 1, 0).
\end{aligned}
$$

Then

$$\phi(b_n)^\delta \, \phi(\mathrm{PRemainder}(A, B)) = \phi(b_n)^{2\delta - \delta'} \, \mathrm{PRemainder}(\phi(A), \phi(B)).$$

PROOF.

$$\phi(b_n)^\delta \, \phi(\mathrm{PRemainder}(A, B))$$

$$
\begin{aligned}
&= \ \phi(b_n^\delta \, \mathrm{PRemainder}(A, B)) \\
&= \ \phi(b_n^\delta \, \mathrm{DetPol}(x^{m-n}B, \ldots, B, A)) \\
&= \ \phi(b_n)^\delta \, \mathrm{DetPol}(x^{m-n}\phi(B), \ldots, \phi(B), \phi(A)) \\
&= \ \phi(b_n)^{2\delta - \delta'} \, \mathrm{DetPol}(x^{k-n}\phi(B), \ldots, \phi(B), \phi(A)) \\
&= \ \phi(b_n)^{2\delta - \delta'} \, \mathrm{PRemainder}(\phi(A), \phi(B)). \quad \square
\end{aligned}
$$

Corollary 7.5.6 *If in the above theorem $\phi(b_n)$ is not a zero divisor of S^*, then*

$$\phi(\mathrm{PRemainder}(A, B)) \ = \ \phi(b_n)^{\delta - \delta'} \mathrm{PRemainder}(\phi(A), \phi(B)). \quad \square$$

Theorem 7.5.7 *Let $A(x)$ and $B(x) \neq 0$ be polynomials in $S[x]$ of respective degrees m and n, and $b_n = \mathrm{Hcoef}(B)$. Let $\deg(a\,A) = k$ and $\deg(b\,B) = n$, for some $a, b \in S$. Let*

$$\delta = \max(m - n + 1, 0) \quad and \quad \delta' = \max(k - n + 1, 0).$$

Then

$$b_n^\delta \, a \, b^{\delta+\delta'} \, \text{PRemainder}(A, B) \;=\; b_n^{2\delta-\delta'} \, b^\delta \, \text{PRemainder}(aA, bB).$$

PROOF.
$$b_n^\delta \, a \, b^{\delta+\delta'} \, \text{PRemainder}(A, B)$$

$$= b_n^\delta \, a \, b^{\delta+\delta'} \, \text{DetPol}(x^{m-n}B, \ldots, B, A)$$
$$= b_n^\delta \, b^{\delta+\delta'} \, \text{DetPol}(x^{m-n}B, \ldots, B, aA)$$
$$= b_n^{2\delta-\delta'} \, b^{\delta+\delta'} \, \text{DetPol}(x^{k-n}B, \ldots, B, aA)$$
$$= b_n^{2\delta-\delta'} \, b^\delta \, \text{DetPol}(x^{k-n}bB, \ldots, bB, aA)$$
$$= b_n^{2\delta-\delta'} b^\delta \, \text{PRemainder}(aA, bB). \quad \square$$

Corollary 7.5.8 *In the above theorem:*

1. *If neither b_n nor b is a zero divisor, then*

$$ab^{\delta'}\text{PRemainder}(A, B) = b_n^{\delta-\delta'}\text{PRemainder}(aA, bB).$$

2. *If S is an integral domain and $a \neq 0$, then*

$$\delta \;=\; \delta' \ and$$
$$\text{PRemainder}(aA, bB) \;=\; ab^\delta \text{PRemainder}(A, B). \quad \square$$

7.6   Polynomial Remainder Sequences

Let S be an integral domain.

Definition 7.6.1 (Similar Polynomials) Two polynomials $A(x)$ and $B(x)$ in $S[x]$ are *similar*, denoted

$$A(x) \sim B(x),$$

if there exist $a, b \in S$ such that $aA(x) = bB(x)$. We say a and b are *coefficients of similarity* of $A(x)$ and $B(x)$.

Note that if a and b are units of S, then $A(x)$ and $B(x)$ are associates, $A(x) \approx B(x)$. $\quad \square$

Now we can introduce the concept of a *polynomial remainder sequence* (or, briefly, PRS) as follows:

Definition 7.6.2 (Polynomial Remainder Sequence: PRS) Given S an integral domain, and $F_1(x), F_2(x) \in S[x]$, with $\deg(F_1) \geq \deg(F_2)$, the sequence $F_1, F_2, \ldots, F_k$ of nonzero polynomials is a *polynomial remainder sequence* (or, briefly, PRS) for F_1 and F_2 if we have the following:

1. For all $i = 3, \ldots, k$,

$$F_i \sim \text{PRemainder}(F_{i-2}, F_{i-1}) \neq 0.$$

2. The sequence terminates with $\text{PRemainder}(F_{k-1}, F_k) = 0$.

The following two polynomial remainder sequences are of considerable interest:

- *Euclidean Polynomial Remainder Sequence, EPRS:*
  The polynomial remainder sequence given by the following,

$$
\begin{aligned}
F_i = \text{PRemainder}(F_{i-2}, F_{i-1}) &\neq 0, \quad i = 3, \ldots k, \quad \text{and} \\
\text{PRemainder}(F_{k-1}, F_k) &= 0,
\end{aligned}
$$

  is said to be a *Euclidean polynomial remainder sequence.*

- *Primitive Polynomial Remainder Sequence, PPRS:*
  The polynomial remainder sequence given by the following,

$$
\begin{aligned}
F_i = \text{Primitive}(\text{PRemainder}(F_{i-2}, F_{i-1})) &\neq 0, \quad i = 3, \ldots k, \quad \text{and} \\
\text{PRemainder}(F_{k-1}, F_k) &= 0,
\end{aligned}
$$

  is said to be a *primitive polynomial remainder sequence.* $\square$

From the definition, we see that there must exist nonzero $e_i, f_i \in S$ and $Q_{i-1}(x) \sim \text{PQuotient}(F_{i-2}, F_{i-1})$ such that

$$
\begin{aligned}
e_i F_{i-2} &= Q_{i-1} F_{i-1} + f_i F_i, \quad \text{and} \\
\deg(F_i) &< \deg(F_{i-1}), \qquad \text{for } i = 3, \ldots, k,
\end{aligned}
$$

i.e., $f_i F_i = e_i F_{i-2} - Q_{i-1} F_{i-1}$, for all i.

Also observe that, since pseudodivision is unique, the $\text{PRS}(F_1, F_2)$ is unique up to similarity. Furthermore,

$$\text{GCD}(F_1, F_2) \sim \text{GCD}(F_2, F_3) \sim \cdots \sim \text{GCD}(F_{k-1}, F_k) \sim F_k,$$

so that the PRS essentially computes the GCD of F_1 and F_2 up to similarity.

In defining PPRS, we have reduced the pseudoremainder to its primitive part at each stage of the PRS computation in order to try to limit the growth of polynomial coefficients. However, this incurs a (sometimes) prohibitively high additional cost of computing the contents of each F_i.

Definition 7.6.3 (PRS Based on a Sequence) Let S and (thus) $S[x]$ be UFD's, and $F_1(x), F_2(x) \in S[x]$ be two nonzero univariate polynomials, with $\deg(F_1) \geq \deg(F_2)$. Let $F_1, F_2, \ldots, F_k$ be a PRS such that

$$\beta_i \cdot F_i = \text{PRemainder}(F_{i-2}, F_{i-1}), \qquad i = 3, \ldots, k,$$

where $\beta_i \in S$, and $\beta_i \mid \mathrm{Content}(\mathrm{PRemainder}(F_{i-2}, F_{i-1}))$; then $(F_1, \ldots, F_k)$ is a PRS *"based on the sequence"* $\overline{\beta} = \langle 1, 1, \beta_3, \ldots, \beta_k \rangle$.

Conversely, given a sequence $\overline{\beta} = \langle 1, 1, \beta_3, \ldots, \beta_k \rangle$ (with elements in S), if it is possible to define a PRS bases on $\overline{\beta}$ as follows:

$$F_i = \frac{\mathrm{PRemainder}(F_{i-2}, F_{i-1})}{\beta_i} \neq 0, \qquad i = 3, \ldots k, \quad \text{and}$$

$$\mathrm{PRemainder}(F_{k-1}, F_k) = 0,$$

then we call $\overline{\beta}$ a *well-defined* sequence. Note that not all sequences are well-defined, and thus it is not possible to obtain a polynomial remainder sequence based on an arbitrary sequence. ☐

In particular, the primitive polynomial remainder sequence

$$F_i = \mathrm{Primitive}(\mathrm{PRemainder}(F_{i-2}, F_{i-1})) \neq 0, \qquad i = 3, \ldots k, \quad \text{and}$$

$$\mathrm{PRemainder}(F_{k-1}, F_k) = 0,$$

is based on

$$\overline{\beta} = \Big\langle 1, 1, \mathrm{Content}(\mathrm{PRemainder}(F_1, F_2)), \ldots,$$

$$\mathrm{Content}(\mathrm{PRemainder}(F_{k-2}, F_{k-1})) \Big\rangle.$$

Definition 7.6.4 (Subresultant Polynomial Remainder Sequence: SPRS) Let S be a UFD, and $F_1(x), F_2(x) \in S[x]$ be two nonzero univariate polynomials, with $\deg(F_1) \geq \deg(F_2)$. Let $F_1, F_2, \ldots, F_k$ be a sequence recursively defined with the following initial conditions:

$$\begin{array}{lclcl} \Delta_1 & = & 0, & \Delta_2 & = & \deg(F_1) - \deg(F_2) + 1 \\ b_1 & = & 1, & b_2 & = & \mathrm{Hcoef}(F_2) \\ \psi_1 & = & 1, & \psi_2 & = & (b_2)^{\Delta_2 - 1} \end{array}$$

and

$$\beta_1 = \beta_2 = 1 \quad \text{and} \quad \beta_3 = (-1)^{\Delta_2}$$

and the following recurrences:

- For $i = 3, \ldots, k$,

$$F_i = \frac{\mathrm{PRemainder}(F_{i-2}, F_{i-1})}{\beta_i}$$

$$\Delta_i = \deg(F_{i-1}) - \deg(F_i) + 1$$

$$b_i = \mathrm{Hcoef}(F_i)$$

$$\psi_i = \psi_{i-1} \left(\frac{b_i}{\psi_{i-1}} \right)^{\Delta_i - 1}.$$

- For $i = 3, \ldots, k-1$,

$$\beta_{i+1} = (-1)^{\Delta_i} (\psi_{i-1})^{\Delta_i - 1} b_{i-1}.$$

- PRemainder$(F_{k-1}, F_k) = 0$.

The sequence of polynomials $\langle F_1, F_2, \ldots, F_k \rangle$ is called a *subresultant polynomial remainder sequence* (or briefly, *SPRS*). □

The above definition is somewhat incomplete, since it is not immediately seen that ψ's are in the domain S or, equivalently, that the sequence $\bar{\beta}$ is well-defined. Subsequently, we shall study the well-definedness of $\bar{\beta}$, define the notion of *subresultant*, and show various relations between the SPRS and the *subresultant chain*.

The sequence SPRS occupies a special position in computational algebra, since it allows computation of polynomial remainder sequences without excessive growth in the size of the coefficients, or unduly high inefficiency.

The coefficients of the polynomials involved in EPRS are usually very large. In the computation of PPRS, on the other hand, we have to compute the contents of the polynomials (using the extended Euclidean algorithm), which makes the algorithms highly inefficient. We will see that the subresultant PRS seeks a middle ground between these two extreme cases.

7.7   Subresultants

We now define the notion of *subresultants* and then pursue a detailed motivation for this definition.

Definition 7.7.1 (Subresultant) Let S be a commutative ring with identity and let $A(x)$, $B(x) \in S[x]$ be two univariate polynomials with respective positive degrees m and n:

$$\begin{aligned}
A(x) &= a_m x^m + a_{m-1} x^{m-1} + \cdots + a_0, & \deg(A) = m > 0, \\
B(x) &= b_n x^n + b_{n-1} x^{n-1} + \cdots + b_0, & \deg(B) = n > 0,
\end{aligned}$$

and let

$$\lambda = \min(m, n) \quad \text{and} \quad \mu = \max(m, n) - 1.$$

For all i in the range $(0 \leq i < \lambda)$, the ith *subresultant of A and B is defined as follows:*

1. The 0th subresultant is simply the resultant of the polynomials A and B. Thus

$$\text{SubRes}_0(A, B) = \text{Resultant}(A, B)$$

$$
= \left|
\begin{array}{cccccc}
a_m & \cdots & a_1 & a_0 & & x^{n-1}A(x) \\
 & \ddots & \ddots & \ddots & \ddots & \vdots \\
 & & a_m & \cdots & a_1 \quad a_0 & xA(x) \\
 & & & a_m & \cdots \quad a_1 & A(x) \\
b_n & \cdots & b_1 & b_0 & & x^{m-1}B(x) \\
 & \ddots & \ddots & \ddots & \ddots & \vdots \\
 & & b_m & \cdots & b_1 \quad b_0 & xB(x) \\
 & & & b_m & \cdots \quad b_1 & B(x)
\end{array}
\right|
\begin{array}{l}
\left.\rule{0pt}{40pt}\right\} n \text{ rows} \\[10pt]
\left.\rule{0pt}{40pt}\right\} m \text{ rows}
\end{array}
$$

2. For all i, $(0 < i < \lambda)$, the ith subresultant is:

$$\text{SubRes}_i(A, B)$$

$$
= \left|
\begin{array}{cccccc}
a_m & \cdots & a_1 & a_0 & & x^{n-i-1}A(x) \\
 & \ddots & \ddots & \ddots & \ddots & \vdots \\
 & & a_m & \cdots & a_{i+1} \quad a_i & xA(x) \\
 & & & a_m & \cdots \quad a_{i+1} & A(x) \\
b_n & \cdots & b_1 & b_0 & & x^{m-i-1}B(x) \\
 & \ddots & \ddots & \ddots & \ddots & \vdots \\
 & & b_m & \cdots & b_{i+1} \quad b_i & xB(x) \\
 & & & b_m & \cdots \quad b_{i+1} & B(x)
\end{array}
\right|
\begin{array}{l}
\left.\rule{0pt}{36pt}\right\} (n-i) \text{ rows} \\[8pt]
\left.\rule{0pt}{36pt}\right\} (m-i) \text{ rows}
\end{array}
$$

The matrix in the above definition is obtained from the previous one by removing the top i rows that include the coefficients of A and the top i rows that include the coefficients of B. The first i columns now contain only zeroes, and they are removed. Finally, the i columns preceding the last column are also removed. Thus, in total, $2i$ rows and $2i$ columns are removed to yield a square matrix. $\square$

Using elementary column transforms we also see that

$$\text{SubRes}_i(A, B)$$

$$
= \left|
\begin{array}{cccccc}
a_m & \cdots & a_1 & a_0 & & 0 \\
 & \ddots & \ddots & \ddots & \ddots & \vdots \\
 & & a_m & \cdots & a_{i+1} \quad a_i & \sum_{j=0}^{i-1} x^{j+1} a_j \\
 & & & a_m & \cdots \quad a_{i+1} & \sum_{j=0}^{i} x^{j} a_j \\
b_n & \cdots & b_1 & b_0 & & 0 \\
 & \ddots & \ddots & \ddots & \ddots & \vdots \\
 & & b_m & \cdots & b_{i+1} \quad b_i & \sum_{j=0}^{i-1} x^{j+1} b_j \\
 & & & b_m & \cdots \quad b_{i+1} & \sum_{j=0}^{i} x^{j} b_j
\end{array}
\right|
\begin{array}{l}
\left.\rule{0pt}{40pt}\right\} (n-i) \text{ rows} \\[10pt]
\left.\rule{0pt}{40pt}\right\} (m-i) \text{ rows}
\end{array}
$$

$$= \mathrm{DetPol}\Big(x^{n-i-1}A,\ldots,xA,A,x^{m-i-1}B,\ldots,xB,B\Big).$$

That is, if

$$
M_i \;=\; \left.\left[\begin{array}{ccccccc}
a_m & \cdots & a_0 & & & & \\
 & \ddots & & \ddots & & & \\
 & & a_m & \cdots & a_0 & & \\
b_n & \cdots & b_0 & & & & \\
 & \ddots & & \ddots & & & \\
 & & b_n & \cdots & b_0 & &
\end{array}\right]\right\}
\begin{array}{l}(n-i)\\ \text{rows}\\[1em](m-i)\\ \text{rows}\end{array}
$$

$$\underbrace{}_{m+n-i}$$

i.e., the matrix obtained from the Sylvester matrix of A and B, by *deleting*

1. the first i rows corresponding to A (the upper half),

2. the first i rows corresponding to B (the lower half), and

3. the first i columns, then

$$
\begin{aligned}
\mathrm{SubRes}_i(A,B) \;&=\; \mathrm{DetPol}\,(M_i)\\
&=\; \det\Big(M_i^{(m+n-2i)}\Big)\,x^i + \cdots + \det\Big(M_i^{(m+n-i)}\Big).
\end{aligned}
$$

Thus $\deg(\mathrm{SubRes}_i) \le i$, with equality, if $M_i^{(m+n-2i)}$ is nonsingular. The nominal head coefficient of the SubRes_i, $M_i^{(m+n-2i)}$, will be referred to as the ith *principal subresultant coefficient* (of A and B):

$$
\mathrm{PSC}_i(A,B) \;=\; \mathrm{NHcoef}\Big(\mathrm{SubRes}_i(A,B)\Big) \;=\; \det\Big(M_i^{(m+n-2i)}\Big).
$$

Let S be a commutative ring with identity and let $A(x), B(x) \in S[x]$ be two univariate polynomials with respective positive degrees m and n and let

$$\lambda = \min(m,n) \quad \text{and} \quad \mu = \max(m,n) - 1,$$

as before. We extend the definition of the ith *subresultant of A and B*, for all i $(0 \leq i < \mu)$ as follows:

- Case 1: $(0 \leq i < \lambda)$.

$\text{SubRes}_i(A, B)$

$$
= \begin{vmatrix}
a_m & \cdots & a_1 & a_0 & & & x^{n-i-1}A(x) \\
& \ddots & \ddots & \ddots & \ddots & & \vdots \\
& & a_m & \cdots & a_{i+1} & a_i & xA(x) \\
& & & a_m & \cdots & a_{i+1} & A(x) \\
b_n & \cdots & b_1 & b_0 & & & x^{m-i-1}B(x) \\
& \ddots & \ddots & \ddots & \ddots & & \vdots \\
& & b_n & \cdots & b_{i+1} & b_i & xB(x) \\
& & & b_n & \cdots & b_{i+1} & B(x)
\end{vmatrix}
\begin{aligned}
\left.\vphantom{\begin{matrix}1\\1\\1\\1\end{matrix}}\right\} (n-i) \text{ rows} \\
\left.\vphantom{\begin{matrix}1\\1\\1\\1\end{matrix}}\right\} (m-i) \text{ rows}
\end{aligned}
$$

- Case 2: $(i = \lambda)$.

Since we are assuming that $\lambda < \mu$, then $|m - n| - 1 > 0$, so we have either $m > n + 1$ or $n > m + 1$, with $\lambda = n$ or $\lambda = m$, respectively. The two cases are symmetrical. If $\lambda = n$, then

$\text{SubRes}_\lambda(A, B)$

$$
= \det \begin{bmatrix}
b_n & \cdots & & x^{m-n-1}B(x) \\
& \ddots & & \vdots \\
& & b_n & xB(x) \\
& & & B(x)
\end{bmatrix}
\left.\vphantom{\begin{matrix}1\\1\\1\\1\end{matrix}}\right\} (m-n) \text{ rows}
$$

Hence

$$
\begin{aligned}
\text{SubRes}_\lambda(A, B) &= b_n^{m-n-1} \cdot B(x) \\
&= \text{Hcoef}(B)^{m-n-1} \cdot B.
\end{aligned}
$$

In the other case, if $\lambda = m$, then

$$
\text{SubRes}_\lambda(A, B) = \text{Hcoef}(A)^{n-m-1} \cdot A.
$$

Alternatively, we may write

$$
\text{SubRes}_\lambda(A, B) = \text{Hcoef}(C)^{|m-n|-1} \cdot C,
$$

where

$$
C = \begin{cases}
A, & \text{if } \deg(B) > \deg(A) + 1; \\
B, & \text{if } \deg(A) > \deg(B) + 1; \\
\text{undefined}, & \text{otherwise.}
\end{cases}
$$

- Case 3: $(\lambda < i < \mu)$.

$$
\text{SubRes}_i(A, B) = 0. \quad \square
$$

Note that in all cases where SubRes_i is defined,

$$
\deg(\text{SubRes}_i) \leq i.
$$

Depending on whether the inequality in the above relation is strict, we classify the SubRes$_i$ as defective or regular, respectively. More formally, we have the following:

Definition 7.7.2 (Defective and Regular Subresultants) A subresultant S_i, $(0 \leq i \leq \mu)$ is said to be *defective of degree r* if

$$r = \deg(S_i) \ < \ i;$$

otherwise, S_i is said to be *regular*. $\square$

Sometimes it will be useful to use the following alternative definition of the subresultants in terms of the *determinant polynomials*.

Proposition 7.7.1 *Let S be a commutative ring with identity and let $A(x)$, $B(x) \in S[x]$ be two univariate polynomials with respective positive degrees m and n, and let*

$$\lambda = \min(m,n) \quad and \quad \mu = \max(m,n) - 1,$$

as before. Then the ith subresultant of A and B, for all i $(0 \leq i < \mu)$, is given by:

- CASE 1: $(0 \leq i < \lambda)$.

  $\text{SubRes}_i(A,B) = \text{DetPol}\left(x^{n-i-1}A, \ldots, xA, A, x^{m-i-1}B, \ldots, xB, B\right).$

- CASE 2: $(i = \lambda)$.

  $\text{SubRes}_\lambda(A,B)$

  $$= \begin{cases} \text{DetPol}\left(x^{n-m-1}A, \ldots, xA, A\right) \\ = \text{Hcoef}(A)^{n-m-1} \cdot A, & if \deg(B) > \deg(A) + 1; \\ \\ \text{DetPol}\left(x^{m-n-1}B, \ldots, xB, B\right) \\ = \text{Hcoef}(B)^{m-n-1} \cdot A, & if \deg(A) > \deg(B) + 1. \end{cases}$$

- CASE 3: $(\lambda < i < \mu)$.

  $$\text{SubRes}_i(A,B) = 0. \quad \square$$

Lemma 7.7.2 *Let S be a commutative ring with identity, and $A(x)$ and $B(x)$ be univariate polynomials of respective positive degrees m and n with coefficients in the ring S, and let*

$$\lambda = \min(m,n) \quad and \quad \mu = \max(m,n) - 1,$$

as before. Then for all i, $(0 \leq i < \mu)$

$$\text{SubRes}_i(A,B) \ = \ (-1)^{(m-i)(n-i)}\text{SubRes}_i(B,A).$$

PROOF.
There are three cases to consider:

1. For all $0 \le i < \lambda$

$$\text{Matrix } \left(x^{m-i-1} B, \ldots, xB, B, x^{n-i-1} A, \ldots, xA, A \right)$$

can be obtained from the matrix

$$\text{Matrix } \left(x^{n-i-1} A, \ldots, xA, A, x^{m-i-1} A, \ldots, xB, B \right)$$

by $(m - i)(n - i)$ row transpositions.

2. For $i = \lambda$ then $(m - n)(n - n) = 0$ and

$$\text{SubRes}_i(A, B) = \text{SubRes}_i(B, A).$$

3. Finally, for all $\lambda < i < \mu$,

$$\text{SubRes}_i(A, B) = \text{SubRes}_i(B, A) = 0. \quad \square$$

Lemma 7.7.3 *Let S be a commutative ring with identity, and $A(x)$, $B(x)$ univariate polynomials of respective positive degrees m and n with coefficients in the ring S; $m \ge n > 0$. Let*

$$\lambda = \min(m, n) = n \quad and \quad \delta = m - n + 1.$$

Then

$$
\begin{aligned}
b_n^\delta \, \text{SubRes}_{\lambda-1}(A, B) &= b_n^\delta \, \text{DetPol}(A, x^{m-n} B, x^{m-n-1} B, \ldots, xB, B) \\
&= (-1)^{m-n+1} \, \text{DetPol}(x^{m-n} B, \ldots, xB, B, b_n^\delta A) \\
&= (-1)^\delta \, b_n^\delta \, \text{PRemainder}(A, B).
\end{aligned}
$$

Specifically, if S is an integral domain, then

$$\text{PRemainder}(A, B) = (-1)^{m-n+1} \, \text{SubRes}_{n-1}(A, B). \quad \square$$

7.7.1 Subresultants and Common Divisors

Lemma 7.7.4 *Let S be a commutative ring with identity, and $A(x)$ and $B(x) \in S[x]$ be univariate polynomials of respective positive degrees m and n with coefficients in the ring S. Then there exist polynomials $T_i(x)$ and $U_i(x) \in S[x]$ such that for all $0 \le i < \max(m, n) - 1$*

$$A(x) \cdot T_i(x) + B(x) \cdot U_i(x) = \text{SubRes}_i(A, B),$$

where

$$\deg(T_i) < \deg(B) - i = n - i \quad and \quad \deg(U_i) < \deg(A) - i = m - i.$$

PROOF.

Clearly, the lemma holds trivially for all $\min(m, n) \le i < \max(m, n) - 1$.
Hence, we deal with the case: $0 \le i < \lambda = \min(m, n)$.

Let us expand the following matrix (the ith Sylvester matrix) about the last column:

$$P_i = \begin{bmatrix} a_m & \cdots & a_1 & a_0 & & & & x^{n-i-1}A(x) \\ & \ddots & \ddots & \ddots & \ddots & & & \vdots \\ & & a_m & \cdots & a_{i+1} & a_i & & xA(x) \\ & & & a_m & \cdots & a_{i+1} & & A(x) \\ b_n & \cdots & b_1 & b_0 & & & & x^{m-i-1}B(x) \\ & \ddots & \ddots & \ddots & \ddots & & & \vdots \\ & & b_m & \cdots & b_{i+1} & b_i & & xB(x) \\ & & & b_m & \cdots & b_{i+1} & & B(x) \end{bmatrix} \begin{array}{l} \left.\rule{0pt}{28pt}\right\} (n-i) \text{ rows} \\[20pt] \left.\rule{0pt}{28pt}\right\} (m-i) \text{ rows} \end{array}$$

Thus,

$$\begin{aligned} \text{SubRes}_i(A, B) \\ = \ & x^{n-i-1}A(x) \cdot P_{1,m+n-2i} + \cdots + A(x) \cdot P_{n-i,m+n-2i} \\ & + x^{m-i-1}B(x) \cdot P_{n-i+1,m+n-2i} + \cdots + B(x) \cdot P_{m+n-2i,m+n-2i} \\ = \ & A(x)\left(P_{1,m+n-2i}x^{n-i-1} + \cdots + P_{n-i,m+n-2i}\right) \\ & + B(x)\left(P_{n-i+1,m+n-2i}x^{m-i-1} + \cdots + P_{m+n-2i,m+n-2i}\right) \\ = \ & A(x) \cdot T_i(x) + B(x) \cdot U_i(x); \end{aligned}$$

the coefficients of $T_i(x)$ and $U_i(x)$ are the cofactors of the last column of P_i and (thus) ring elements in S:

$$\deg(T_i) < \deg(B) - i = n - i \quad \text{and} \quad \deg(U_i) < \deg(A) - i = m - i. \quad \square$$

Lemma 7.7.5 *Let $A(x)$ and $B(x)$ be univariate polynomials of respective positive degrees m and n, over an integral domain S. Further assume that there exist polynomials $T_i(x)$ and $U_i(x)$ (not all zero) over S such that for all $0 \le i < \max(m, n) - 1$*

$$A(x) \cdot T_i(x) + B(x) \cdot U_i(x) = 0,$$

with

$$\deg(T_i) < n - i \quad \text{and} \quad \deg(U_i) < m - i.$$

Then

$$\text{SubRes}_i(A, B) = 0.$$

PROOF.

The proof is a simple generalization of the corresponding lemma regarding resultants.

Again, the lemma holds trivially for all $\min(m, n) \le i < \max(m, n) - 1$. Hence, we deal with the case: $0 \le i < \lambda = \min(m, n)$.

Without loss of generality, we may assume the existence of polynomials

$$T_i(x) \quad (\deg(T_i) = n - i - 1) \quad \text{and} \quad U_i(x)(\deg(U_i) < m - i - 1)$$

satisfying the assertion in the statement of the lemma:

$$
\begin{aligned}
T_i(x) &= t_{n-i-1}\, x^{n-i-1} + t_{n-i-2}\, x^{n-i-2} + \cdots + t_0, \\
U_i(x) &= u_{m-i-1}\, x^{m-i-1} + u_{m-i-2}\, x^{m-i-2} + \cdots + u_0,
\end{aligned}
$$

not all t_j's and u_j's zero.

Now, expanding the equation

$$A(x) \cdot T_i(x) + B(x) \cdot U_i(x) = 0,$$

i.e.,

$$
\begin{aligned}
\left(a_m x^m + \cdots + a_0 \right) &\left(t_{n-i-1} x^{n-i-1} + \cdots + t_0 \right) \\
+ \left(b_n x^n + \cdots + b_0 \right) &\left(u_{m-i-1} x^{m-i-1} + \cdots + u_0 \right) = 0
\end{aligned}
$$

and equating the powers of equal degree, we get the following system of $(m + n - i)$ linear equations in $(m + n - 2i)$ variables:

$$
\begin{aligned}
t_{n-i-1} \cdot a_m + u_{m-i-1} \cdot b_n &= 0 \\
t_{n-i-1} \cdot a_{m-1} + t_{n-i-2} \cdot a_m + u_{m-i-1} \cdot b_{n-1} + u_{m-i-2} \cdot b_n &= 0 \\
&\vdots \\
t_{i+1} \cdot a_0 + \cdots + t_0 \cdot a_{i+1} + u_{i+1} \cdot b_0 + \cdots + u_0 \cdot b_{i+1} &= 0 \\
t_i \cdot a_0 + \cdots + t_0 \cdot a_i + u_i \cdot b_0 + \cdots + u_0 \cdot b_i &= 0 \\
t_{i-1} \cdot a_0 + \cdots + t_0 \cdot a_{i-1} + u_{i-1} \cdot b_0 + \cdots + u_0 \cdot b_{i-1} &= 0 \\
&\vdots \\
t_1 \cdot a_0 + t_0 \cdot a_1 + u_1 \cdot b_0 + u_0 \cdot b_1 &= 0 \\
t_0 \cdot a_0 + u_0 \cdot b_0 &= 0.
\end{aligned}
$$

$$(7.2)$$

Next, multiplying the last i equations by x^i, x^{i-1}, ..., x and 1, in that order, and adding them together, we get a new system of $(m+n-2i)$ linear equations in $(m + n - 2i)$ variables (over $S[x]$):

$$t_{n-i-1} \cdot a_m + u_{m-i-1} \cdot b_n = 0$$

$$t_{n-i-1} \cdot a_{m-1} + t_{n-i-2} \cdot a_m + u_{m-i-1} \cdot b_{n-1} + u_{m-i-2} \cdot b_n = 0$$

$$\vdots$$

$$t_{i+1} \cdot a_0 + \cdots + t_0 \cdot a_{i+1} + u_{i+1} \cdot b_0 + \cdots + u_0 \cdot b_{i+1} = 0$$

$$t_i x^i \cdot a_0 + \cdots + t_1 x \cdot \sum_{j=0}^{i-1} x^j a_j + t_0 \cdot \sum_{j=0}^{i} x^j a_j$$

$$+ u_i x^i \cdot b_0 + \cdots + u_1 x \cdot \sum_{j=0}^{i-1} x^j b_j + u_0 \cdot \sum_{j=0}^{i} x^j b_j = 0.$$

But since the above system of equations has a nontrivial solution, we immediately conclude that the corresponding matrix has a determinant equal to zero, i.e.,

$$\det \left(\mathrm{SubRes}_i(A, B) \right) = 0. \quad \square$$

Lemma 7.7.6 *Let $A(x)$ and $B(x)$, as before, be univariate polynomials of respective positive degrees m and n, over an integral domain S. Then, for all $0 \le i < \max(m, n) - 1$, the ith principal subresultant coefficient of A and B vanishes, i.e.,*

$$\mathrm{PSC}_i(A, B) = 0$$

if and only if there exist polynomials $T_i(x)$, $U_i(x)$ and $C_i(x)$ (not all zero) over S such that

$$A(x) \cdot T_i(x) + B(x) \cdot U_i(x) = C_i(x), \tag{7.3}$$

where

$$\deg(T_i) < n - i, \quad \deg(U_i) < m - i, \quad and \quad \deg(C_i) < i.$$

PROOF.
As before, the lemma holds trivially for all

$$\min(m, n) \ \le \ i \ < \ \max(m, n) - 1.$$

($\Leftarrow$)   Note that we can write $T_i(x)$, $U_i(x)$ and $C_i(x)$ symbolically as

$$T_i(x) = t_{n-i-1} x^{n-i-1} + t_{n-i-2} x^{n-i-2} + \cdots + t_0,$$

$$U_i(x) = u_{m-i-1} x^{m-i-1} + u_{m-i-2} x^{m-i-2} + \cdots + u_0,$$

$$C_i(x) = c_{i-1} x^{i-1} + c_{i-2} x^{i-2} + \cdots + c_0,$$

where by assumption not all t_j's, u_j's and c_j's are zero.

Now expanding equation (7.3), we get the following system of $(m+n-i)$ linear equations in $(m+n-i)$ variables:

$$
\begin{aligned}
t_{n-i-1} \cdot a_m + u_{m-i-1} \cdot b_n &= 0 \\
t_{n-i-1} \cdot a_{m-1} + t_{n-i-2} \cdot a_m + u_{m-i-1} \cdot b_{n-1} + u_{m-i-2} \cdot b_n &= 0 \\
&\ \ \vdots \\
t_{i+1} \cdot a_0 + \cdots + t_0 \cdot a_{i+1} + u_{i+1} \cdot b_0 + \cdots + u_0 \cdot b_{i+1} &= 0 \\
t_i \cdot a_0 + \cdots + t_0 \cdot a_i + u_i \cdot b_0 + \cdots + u_0 \cdot b_i &= 0 \qquad (7.4)\\
t_{i-1} \cdot a_0 + \cdots + t_0 \cdot a_{i-1} + u_{i-1} \cdot b_0 + \cdots + u_0 \cdot b_{i-1} - c_{i-1} &= 0 \\
&\ \ \vdots \\
t_1 \cdot a_0 + t_0 \cdot a_1 + u_1 \cdot b_0 + u_0 \cdot b_1 - c_1 &= 0 \\
t_0 \cdot a_0 + u_0 \cdot b_0 - c_0 &= 0.
\end{aligned}
$$

Now consider the matrix M associated with the above set of linear equations:

$$
M^T =
\left[
\begin{array}{ccccccccc}
a_m & a_{m-1} & & \cdots & & a_0 & & & \\
 & a_m & a_{m-1} & & \cdots & & a_0 & & \\
 & & \ddots & \ddots & \ddots & \ddots & \ddots & \ddots & \\
 & & & a_m & a_{m-1} & \cdots & a_{i-1} & \cdots & a_0 \\
b_n & b_{n-1} & & \cdots & & \cdots & b_0 & & \\
 & b_n & b_{n-1} & & \cdots & & \cdots & b_0 & \\
 & & \ddots & \ddots & \ddots & \ddots & \ddots & & \\
 & & b_n & b_{n-1} & & \cdots & b_{i-1} & \cdots & b_0 \\
 & & & & -1 & & & & \\
 & & & & & -1 & & & \\
 & & & & & & \ddots & & \\
 & & & & & & & & -1
\end{array}
\right]
\begin{array}{l}
\left.\rule{0pt}{38pt}\right\} \begin{array}{l}(n-i) \\ \text{rows}\end{array} \\
\left.\rule{0pt}{38pt}\right\} \begin{array}{l}(m-i) \\ \text{rows}\end{array} \\
\left.\rule{0pt}{26pt}\right\} \begin{array}{l}i \\ \text{rows}\end{array}
\end{array}
$$

Since the system of equations (7.4) has a nontrivial solution, we see that $\det(M^T) = 0$. But since the $(m+n-2i) \times (m+n-2i)$ principal submatrix of M is same as $M_i^{(m+n-2i)}$, where

$$
M_i \;=\; \left[\begin{array}{cccc}
a_m & \cdots & a_0 & \\
& \ddots & & \ddots \\
& & a_m & \cdots & a_0 \\
b_n & \cdots & b_0 & \\
& \ddots & & \ddots \\
& & b_n & \cdots & b_0
\end{array}\right]
\begin{array}{l}
\left.\rule{0pt}{20pt}\right\} \begin{array}{l}(n-i) \\ \text{rows}\end{array} \\[10pt]
\left.\rule{0pt}{20pt}\right\} \begin{array}{l}(m-i) \\ \text{rows}\end{array}
\end{array}
\;,
$$

$$\underbrace{}_{m+n-i}$$

we have

$$\det(M^T) = (-1)^i \det\left(M_i^{(m+n-2i)}\right) = (-1)^i \, \mathrm{PSC}_i(A,B) = 0.$$

Here, we have used the fact that:

$$
\begin{aligned}
\mathrm{SubRes}_i(A,B) &= \mathrm{DetPol}\,(M_i) \\
&= \det\left(M_i^{(m+n-2i)}\right) x^i + \cdots + \det\left(M_i^{(m+n-i)}\right).
\end{aligned}
$$

($\Rightarrow$)   In the forward direction, we note that, if $\mathrm{PSC}_i(A,B) = 0$, then

$$\det(M^T) = 0,$$

and that the system of linear equations (7.4) has a nontrivial solution, i.e., condition (7.3) of the lemma holds. $\square$

Lemma 7.7.7 *Let S be a* unique factorization domain *with identity, and $A(x)$ and $B(x)$ be univariate polynomials of positive degrees m and n, respectively, with coefficients in S. Then, for all $0 \le i < \min(m,n)$:*

$$A(x) \cdot T_i(x) + B(x) \cdot U_i(x) \;=\; 0,$$

where $\deg(T_i) < n - i$ and $\deg(U_i) < m - i$, if and only if $A(x)$ and $B(x)$ have a common divisor of degree $> i$.

PROOF.

Let $D(x)$ be a common divisor of $A(x)$ and $B(x)$ and of highest degree among all such. Then $A(x)$ and $B(x)$ can be expressed as follows:

$$A(x) = U'(x)\,D(x) \quad \text{and} \quad B(x) = T'(x)\,D(x),$$

where, by assumption, $U'(x)$ and $T'(x)$ do not have a nonconstant common divisor. Also, note that $\deg(U') = m - \deg(D)$ and $\deg(T') = n - \deg(D)$.

($\Leftarrow$)   If we assume that $\deg(D) > i$, then choose $T_i = T'$ and $U_i = -U'$.
Thus

$$A(x) \cdot T'(x) - B(x) \cdot U'(x) \;=\; 0,$$

where $\deg(T') < n - i$ and $\deg(-U') < m - i$.

($\Rightarrow$)   In the other direction, since

$$A(x) \cdot T_i(x) + B(x) \cdot U_i(x) \;=\; 0,$$

we also have

$$U'(x) \cdot T_i(x) + T'(x) \cdot U_i(x) \;=\; 0 \quad \text{or} \quad U'(x) \cdot T_i(x) = -T'(x) \cdot U_i(x).$$

Now, since $U'(x)$ and $T'(x)$ do not have a nonconstant common divisor, every divisor of $U'(x)$ must be an associate of a divisor of $U_i(x)$, i.e.,

$$\deg(U') \le \deg(U_i) < m - i.$$

In other words,

$$\deg(U') = m - \deg(D) < m - i \quad \Rightarrow \quad \deg(D) > i. \qquad \square$$

Lemma 7.7.8 *Let S be a unique factorization domain with identity, and $A(x)$ and $B(x)$ be univariate polynomials of positive degrees m and n, respectively, with coefficients in S. Then, for all $0 \le i < \min(m, n)$, the following three statements are equivalent:*

1. *$A(x)$ and $B(x)$ have a common divisor of degree $> i$;*

2. *$\left(\forall\, j \le i \right) \left[\mathrm{SubRes}_j(A, B) = 0 \right]$;*

3. *$\left(\forall\, j \le i \right) \left[\mathrm{PSC}_j(A, B) = 0 \right]$.*

PROOF.
$[(1) \Rightarrow (2)]$
Since A and B have a common divisor of degree $> i$, (i.e., A and B have a common divisor of degree $> j$, for all $j \le i$), we have, for all $j \le i$,

$$A(x) \cdot T_j(x) + B(x) \cdot U_j(x) \;=\; 0,$$

where $\deg(T_j) < n - j$ and $\deg(U_j) < m - i$

$$\Rightarrow \left(\forall\, j \le i \right) \left[\mathrm{SubRes}_j(A, B) = 0 \right]. \qquad \text{(Lemma 7.7.5)}$$

$[(2) \Rightarrow (3)]$
This holds trivially.

$[(3) \Rightarrow (1)]$
The proof is by induction on all $j \le i$.

- BASE CASE: Clearly, $\text{PSC}_0(A, B) = 0$ implies that $\text{Resultant}(A, B) = 0$ and that A and B have a common divisor of degree > 0

- INDUCTION CASE: Assume that the inductive hypothesis holds for $j - 1$, and we show the case for $j > 0$:

$\text{PSC}_j(A, B) = 0$
  and A and B have a common zero of degree $> j - 1$
$$\Rightarrow \left(\exists\, C_j(x),\ \deg(C_j) < j\right)\left[A(x) \cdot T_j(x) + B(x) \cdot U_j(x) = C_j(x)\right]$$
$$\deg(T_j) < n - j,\ \deg(U_j) < m - j$$

(But since A and B are both divisible by a polynomial of degree $\geq j$, so is the polynomial C_j; thus, implying that $C_j(x) = 0$.)

$$\Rightarrow A(x) \cdot T_j(x) + B(x) \cdot U_j(x) = 0$$
$$\deg(T_j) < n - j, \deg(U_j) < m - j$$
$$\Rightarrow A \text{ and } B \text{ have a common divisor of degree} > j. \quad \square$$

Corollary 7.7.9 *Let S be a unique factorization domain with identity, and $A(x)$ and $B(x)$ be univariate polynomials of positive degrees m and n, respectively, with coefficients in S. Then, for all $0 < i \leq \min(m, n)$, the following three statements are equivalent:*

1. *$A(x)$ and $B(x)$ have a common divisor of degree $= i$;*

2. *$\left(\forall\, j < i\right)\left[\text{SubRes}_j(A, B) = 0\right] \wedge \text{SubRes}_i(A, B) \neq 0$;*

3. *$\left(\forall\, j < i\right)\left[\text{PSC}_j(A, B) = 0\right] \wedge \text{PSC}_i(A, B) \neq 0.$* $\square$

7.8   Homomorphisms and Subresultants

Let S and S^* be commutative rings with identities, and $\phi: S \to S^*$ be a ring homomorphism of S into S^*. Note that ϕ induces a ring homomorphism of $S[x]$ into $S^*[x]$, also denoted by ϕ, as follows:

$$\phi\ :\ S[X] \to S^*[x]$$
$$:\ a_m x^m + a_{m-1} x^{m-1} + \cdots + a_0$$
$$\mapsto \phi(a_m) x^m + \phi(a_{m-1}) x^{m-1} + \cdots + \phi(a_0).$$

Lemma 7.8.1 *Let S be a commutative ring with identity, and $A(x)$ and $B(x)$ be univariate polynomials of respective positive degrees m and n with coefficients in the ring S, as before.*

$$A(x) \ =\ a_m\, x^m + a_{m-1}\, x^{m-1} + \cdots + a_0, \qquad and$$
$$B(x) \ =\ b_n\, x^n + b_{n-1}\, x^{n-1} \cdots + b_0,$$

where
$$\deg(A) = m > 0 \quad and \quad \deg(B) = n > 0.$$

If
$$\deg(\phi(A)) = m \quad and \quad \deg(\phi(B)) = k, \qquad (0 \le k \le n),$$
then for all $0 \le i < \max(m, k) - 1$
$$\phi(\text{SubRes}_i(A, B)) = \phi(a_m)^{n-k}\text{SubRes}_i(\phi(A), \phi(B)).$$

PROOF.

Let
$$
\begin{aligned}
\mu &= \max(m, n) - 1, &\quad \lambda &= \min(m, n) \\
\mu' &= \max(m, k) - 1, &\quad \lambda' &= \min(m, k).
\end{aligned}
$$

Clearly $\lambda' \le \lambda$.

- CASE A: For i $(0 \le i < \lambda')$, and thus $i < \lambda$.

$$
\begin{aligned}
&\phi(\text{SubRes}_i(A, B)) \\
&= \text{DetPol}\Big(x^{n-i-1}\phi(A), \ldots, x\phi(A), \phi(A), \\
&\qquad\qquad\qquad x^{m-i-1}\phi(B), \ldots, x\phi(B), \phi(B) \Big) \\
&= \phi(a_m)^{n-k} \text{DetPol}\Big(x^{k-i-1}\phi(A), \ldots, x\phi(A), \phi(A), \\
&\qquad\qquad\qquad x^{m-i-1}\phi(B), \ldots, x\phi(B), \phi(B) \Big) \\
&= \phi(a_m)^{n-k} \text{SubRes}_i(\phi(A), \phi(B)).
\end{aligned}
$$

- CASE B: For $i = \lambda'$ there are two cases to consider:
  - (Subcase I) $\lambda' = k$, and thus $\lambda' < \lambda$, and $i < \lambda$.

$$
\begin{aligned}
&\phi(\text{SubRes}_i(A, B)) \\
&= \text{DetPol}\Big(x^{n-k-1}\phi(A), \ldots, x\phi(A), \phi(A), \\
&\qquad\qquad\qquad x^{m-k-1}\phi(B), \ldots, x\phi(B), \phi(B) \Big) \\
&= \phi(a_m)^{n-k} \text{DetPol}\Big(x^{m-k-1}\phi(B), \ldots, x\phi(B), \phi(B) \Big) \\
&= \phi(a_m)^{n-k} \text{SubRes}_i(\phi(A), \phi(B)).
\end{aligned}
$$

Note that $\deg(\phi(A)) > \deg(\phi(B)) + 1$.

— (Subcase II) $\lambda' = m$, and so $\lambda' = \lambda$ and $\deg(A) < \deg(B) + 1$.

$$\phi(\mathrm{SubRes}_i(A, B))$$
$$= \mathrm{DetPol}\Big(x^{n-m-1}\phi(A),\, \ldots,\, x\phi(A),\, \phi(A)\Big)$$
$$= \phi(a_m)^{n-k}\,\mathrm{DetPol}\Big(x^{k-m-1}\phi(A),\, \ldots,\, x\phi(A),\, \phi(A)\Big)$$
$$= \phi(a_m)^{n-k}\,\mathrm{SubRes}_i(\phi(A), \phi(B)).$$

- <u>CASE C</u>: For all i $(\lambda' < i < \mu')$.

$$\phi(\mathrm{SubRes}_i(A, B))$$
$$= \begin{cases} \mathrm{DetPol}\Big(x^{n-i-1}\phi(A),\, \ldots,\, x\phi(A),\, \phi(A), \\ \qquad\qquad x^{m-i-1}\phi(B),\, \ldots,\, x\phi(B),\, \phi(B)\Big), & \text{if } i < \lambda \\[2mm] \mathrm{DetPol}(x^{m-n-1}\phi(B),\, \ldots,\, x\phi(B),\, \phi(B)), & \text{if } i = n = \lambda \\[2mm] \phi(0), & \text{if } \lambda < i < \mu \end{cases}$$
$$= 0$$
$$= \phi(a_m)^{n-k}\,\mathrm{SubRes}_i(\phi(A), \phi(B)). \qquad \square$$

Corollary 7.8.2 *Let S be a commutative ring with identity, and $A(x)$ and $B(x)$ be univariate polynomials of respective positive degrees m and n with coefficients in the ring S, as before.*

$$A(x) = a_m x^m + a_{m-1} x^{m-1} + \cdots + a_0, \qquad \text{and}$$
$$B(x) = b_n x^n + b_{n-1} x^{n-1} + \cdots + b_0.$$

Let

$$\deg(A) = m > 0,$$
$$\deg(B) = n > 0,$$
$$\deg(\phi(A)) = l, \qquad (0 < l \le m) \quad \text{and}$$
$$\deg(\phi(B)) = k, \qquad (0 < k \le n);$$

then for all $0 \le i < \max(l, k) - 1$

1. *if $l = m$ and $k = n$, then*

$$\phi(\mathrm{SubRes}_i(A, B)) = \mathrm{SubRes}_i(\phi(A), \phi(B));$$

2. *if $l < m$ and $k = n$, then*

$$\phi(\mathrm{SubRes}_i(A, B)) = \phi(b_n)^{m-l} \cdot \mathrm{SubRes}_i(\phi(A), \phi(B));$$

3. if $l = m$ and $k < n$, then

$$\phi(\text{SubRes}_i(A, B)) = \phi(a_m)^{n-k} \cdot \text{SubRes}_i(\phi(A), \phi(B));$$

4. if $l < m$ and $k < n$, then

$$\phi(\text{SubRes}_i(A, B)) = 0.$$

PROOF.
We will show case (2). Case (3) is symmetrical, and the other cases are immediate.

$$
\begin{aligned}
\text{SubRes}_i(A, B) &= (-1)^{(m-i)(n-i)} \, \text{SubRes}_i(B, A) \\
\phi(\text{SubRes}_i(B, A)) &= \phi(b_n)^{m-l} \, \text{SubRes}_i(\phi(B), \phi(A)) \\
\text{SubRes}_i(\phi(B), \phi(A)) &= (-1)^{(m-i)(n-i)} \, \text{SubRes}_i(\phi(A), \phi(B))
\end{aligned}
$$

and therefore

$$
\begin{aligned}
\phi(\text{SubRes}_i(A, B)) \\
&= (-1)^{(m-i)(n-i)} \, \phi(b_n)^{m-l} \, (-1)^{(m-i)(n-i)} \, \text{SubRes}_i(\phi(A), \phi(B)) \\
&= \phi(b_n)^{m-l} \, \text{SubRes}_i(\phi(A), \phi(B)). \quad \square
\end{aligned}
$$

7.9 Subresultant Chain

Definition 7.9.1 (Subresultant Chain and PSC Chain) Let S be a commutative ring with identity and let $A(x)$, $B(x) \in S[x]$ be two univariate polynomials with respective positive degrees n_1 and n_2, $n_1 \geq n_2$:

$$
\begin{aligned}
A(x) &= a_{n_1} x^{n_1} + a_{n_1-1} x^{n_1-1} + \cdots + a_0, & \deg(A) = n_1 > 0, & \quad \text{and} \\
B(x) &= b_{n_2} x^{n_2} + b_{n_2-1} x^{n_2-1} + \cdots + b_0, & \deg(B) = n_2 > 0.
\end{aligned}
$$

Let

$$
n = \begin{cases} n_1 - 1, & \text{if } n_1 > n_2, \\ n_2, & \text{otherwise.} \end{cases}
$$

The sequence of univariate polynomials in $S[x]$

$$
\left\langle \begin{aligned}
S_{n+1} &= A, \\
S_n &= B, \\
S_{n-1} &= \text{SubRes}_{n-1}(A, B), \\
&\vdots \\
S_0 &= \text{SubRes}_0(A, B)
\end{aligned} \right\rangle
$$

is said to be the *subresultant chain of A and B*

The sequence of ring elements

$$\left\langle \begin{array}{rcl} \mathrm{PSC}_{n+1} & = & 1, \\[4pt] \mathrm{PSC}_n & = & \mathrm{NHcoef}(S_n), \\[2pt] \mathrm{PSC}_{n-1} & = & \mathrm{NHcoef}(S_{n-1}), \\[2pt] & \vdots & \\[2pt] \mathrm{PSC}_1 & = & \mathrm{NHcoef}(S_1), \\[2pt] \mathrm{PSC}_0 & = & \mathrm{NHcoef}(S_0) \end{array} \right\rangle$$

is said to be the *principal subresultant coefficient chain of A and B.*

By NHcoef, here, we denote the "nominal head coefficient" of a polynomial, i.e., the coefficient associated with the highest possible degree the polynomial may have — the so-called "nominal degree."   □

Definition 7.9.2 (Defective and Regular Subresultant Chain) A subresultant chain is said to be *defective* if any of its members is defective, i.e., for some $(0 \le i \le \mu)$

$$r = \deg(S_i) \; < \; i;$$

otherwise it is *regular.*   □

In order to understand the relation between subresultant chain and PRS's (polynomial remainder sequences), particularly the subresultant PRS, we need to explore the gap structure of a subresultant chain, which occurs when the subresultant chain is defective. This will be formally described by the *subresultant chain theorem* in the next section. However, in this section, we will simply state the theorem, provide simple intuitions behind the theorem and then go on to prove some important results about the relations that exist between subresultant chain and PRS's.

In Figure 7.1, we display the gap structure of a subresultant chain by diagrams in which each rectangle of width $(i + 1)$ denotes a polynomial of degree i. In each case, the top-most rectangle denotes the polynomial A of degree n_1 and the one below it denotes the polynomial B of degree n_2. Loos [134] attributes this pictorial representation to Habicht.

We begin with the following definition of the *block structures* of a subresultant chain:

Definition 7.9.3 (Blocks of a Subresultant Chain) A subresultant chain can be divided into *blocks* of (consecutive) subresultants such that if

$$\left\langle S_i, \; S_{i-1}, \; \ldots, \; S_{j+1}, \; S_j \right\rangle, \qquad n + 1 \ge i \ge j \ge 0,$$

is a block, then, we have the following:

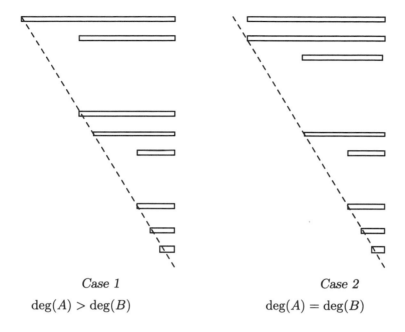

Case 1   Case 2

$\deg(A) > \deg(B)$ $\deg(A) = \deg(B)$

Figure 7.1: Subresultant chains and their gap structures.

1. Either $j = 0$ and $S_i = S_{i-1} = \cdots = S_{j+1} = S_j = 0$,
   (This is the last block in which each subresultant is zero; this is the so-called *zero block*. Note that, in this case, $S_{i-1} \neq 0$. Further, there can only be at most one such block.)

2. Or $S_i \neq 0$, $S_j \neq 0$, $S_i \sim S_j$ and $S_{i-1} = \cdots = S_{j+1} = 0$.
   (This is a so-called *nonzero block*. In this case, S_j is always regular and if $i > j$, then S_i is defective.) □

Thus, every defective subresultant S_i of degree r corresponds to a unique regular subresultant S_j, $j = r$, both belonging to the same nonzero block, and are similar. As an immediate consequence of the *subresultant chain theorem*, we will see that any subresultant chain can be *partitioned* into a sequence of blocks, of which possibly the last one may be a zero block. It then follows that there cannot be two consecutive nonzero defective subresultants.

We write the nonzero blocks of a subresultant chain as follows:

$$\left\langle\ \overline{S_0},\ \overline{S_1},\ \ldots,\ \overline{S_l}\ \right\rangle.$$

The first subresultant in the ith nonzero block will be called the *top* element, $S_{\Uparrow(i)}$ (possibly, defective) and the last subresultant, the *bottom* element, $S_{\Downarrow(i)}$ (always, regular). The PSC, $R_{\Downarrow(i)}$ can be defined, similarly.

Let

$$
\begin{aligned}
d(i) &= \deg(S_{\Psi(i)}) \\
e(i) &= \deg(S_{\Psi(i-1)}) - 1 = d(i-1) - 1 \\
\delta_{i+1} &= \deg(S_{\Psi(i-1)}) - \deg(S_{\Psi(i)}) + 1 \\
&= d(i-1) - d(i) + 1.
\end{aligned}
$$

At this point, it is useful to state the *subresultant chain theorem* and recast it in terms of our notations in the context of the block structures:

Theorem 7.9.1 (Subresultant Chain Theorem) *Let S be an* integral domain *and let*

$$
\left\langle S_{n+1}, \ S_n, \ S_{n-1}, \ \ldots, \ S_0 \right\rangle
$$

be a subresultant chain of S_{n+1} and S_n in $S[x]$ $(\deg(S_{n+1}) \geq \deg(S_n))$.

1. *For $j = 1, \ldots, n$, if S_{j+1} and S_j are both regular, then*

$$
(-R_{j+1})^2 \ S_{j-1} = \mathrm{PRemainder}\,(S_{j+1}, S_j).
$$

2. *For $j = 1, \ldots, n$, if S_{j+1} is regular and S_j is defective of degree r $(r < j)$, then*

$$
\begin{aligned}
S_{j-1} &= S_{j-2} = \cdots = S_{r+1} = 0, \\
(R_{j+1})^{j-r} \ S_r &= \mathrm{Hcoef}\,(S_j)^{j-r} \ S_j, \quad r \geq 0, \\
(-R_{j+1})^{j-r+2} \ S_{r-1} &= \mathrm{PRemainder}\,(S_{j+1}, S_j), \quad r \geq 1. \quad \square
\end{aligned}
$$

The intuition behind this theorem can be seen from the pictorial descriptions of the subresultants given in Figure 7.2.

If we could write S_{j+1} and S_j symbolically as polynomials of degrees $(j + 1)$ and j respectively, then the kth subresultant (symbolically) would be given by the determinant polynomial of a matrix M_k whose top $(j - k)$ rows would come from the coefficients of S_{j+1} and the bottom $(j + 1 - k)$ rows would come from the coefficients of S_j. However, in order to obtain the kth subresultant (numerically) of the polynomials S_{j+1} and S_j, we have to eliminate the last $(j - r)$ rows corresponding to S_{j+1} from the M_k (in the upper half) and force the entries corresponding to $(j - r)$ higher-order coefficients of S_j to vanish in M_k (in the lower half).

1. If $r < k < j$, then $j - r$ exceeds $j - k$ and the matrix M_k would have 0's on the main diagonal, thus making its determinant polynomial equal 0:

$$
S_{j-1} = S_{j-2} = \cdots = S_{r+1} = 0.
$$

2. If $k = r$, then $j - r$ equals $j - k$ and the main diagonal of M_k would have nonzero head coefficients of S_{j+1} and S_j and its determinant polynomial would be a polynomial similar to S_j:

$$S_r \sim S_j.$$

3. If $k = r - 1$, then evaluating the determinant polynomial of M_k, we see that

$$S_{r-1} \quad \sim \quad \text{DetPol}(S_{j+1}, x^{j+1-r} S_j, \ldots, S_j)$$
$$\sim \quad \text{PRemainder}(S_{j+1}, S_j).$$

However, one caveat with the above line of reasoning is that it uses the false premise

$$\phi(\text{SubRes}_k(A, B)) = \text{SubRes}_k(\phi(A), \phi(B)).$$

for an evaluation homomorphism ϕ. The falsity of such a statement has been indicated in Corollary 7.8.2. A more careful and rather technical proof for the subresultant chain theorem is postponed.

Corollary 7.9.2 *Let S be an integral domain and let*

$$\left\langle \, \overline{S_0}, \ \overline{S_1}, \ \ldots, \ \overline{S_l} \, \right\rangle$$

be a sequence of nonzero blocks of a subresultant chain of S_{n+1} and S_n in $S[x]$ ($\deg(S_{n+1}) \geq \deg(S_n)$).
Then

$$\left(R_{\Downarrow(i-1)}\right)^{\delta_{i+1}-2} S_{\Downarrow(i)} \quad = \quad \text{Hcoef}\left(S_{\Uparrow(i)}\right)^{\delta_{i+1}-2} S_{\Uparrow(i)},$$
$$\left(-R_{\Downarrow(i-1)}\right)^{\delta_{i+1}} S_{\Uparrow(i+1)} \quad = \quad \text{PRemainder}\left(S_{\Downarrow(i-1)}, S_{\Uparrow(i)}\right).$$

PROOF.
Simply observe that if we let

$$S_{j+1} = S_{\Downarrow(i-1)} \quad \text{and} \quad S_j = S_{\Uparrow(i)},$$

then

$$S_r = S_{\Downarrow(i)} \quad \text{and} \quad S_{r-1} = S_{\Uparrow(i+1)},$$

and

$$R_{j+1} = R_{\Downarrow(i-1)} \quad \text{and} \quad R_j = 0,$$
$$R_r = R_{\Downarrow(i)} \quad \text{and} \quad R_{r-1} = 0.$$

Also note that

$$j - r = d(i - 1) - d(i) - 1 = \delta_{i+1} - 2. \qquad \square$$

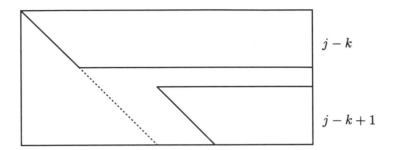

$j - r$ terms of $S_j = 0$

Case 1

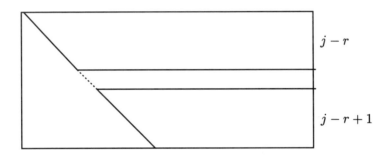

$j - r$ terms of $S_j = 0$

Case 2

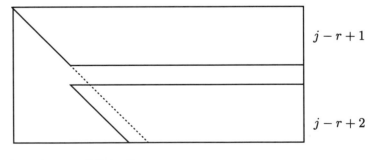

$j - r$ terms of $S_j = 0$

Case 3

Figure 7.2: Intuitive arguments for the subresultant chain theorem.

Hence, we see that

$$S_{\Downarrow(i)} \sim S_{\Uparrow(i)} \quad \text{and}$$
$$S_{\Uparrow(i+1)} \sim \text{PRemainder}\left(S_{\Downarrow(i-1)}, S_{\Uparrow(i)}\right)$$

$$\Rightarrow$$

$$S_{\Downarrow(i+1)} \sim \text{PRemainder}\left(S_{\Downarrow(i-1)}, S_{\Downarrow(i)}\right).$$

The corollary below follows:

Corollary 7.9.3 *Let S be an integral domain, and let $F_1(x), F_2(x) \in S[x]$*
($\deg(F_1) \geq \deg(F_2)$).

Now, consider their polynomial remainder sequence: F_1, F_2, ..., F_k
and their subresultant chain, with the following sequence of nonzero blocks:

$$\left\langle \overline{S_0}, \overline{S_1}, \ldots, \overline{S_l} \right\rangle.$$

Then the elements of the polynomial remainder sequence are similar to
the regular subresultants, in their respective order, i.e.,

1. $k = l + 1$.

2. $S_{\Downarrow(i)} \sim F_{i+1}$. $\square$

In fact, a much stronger result can be shown. Recall the definition of a
subresultant polynomial remainder sequence of two univariate polynomials
F_1 and F_2 ($\deg(F_1) \geq \deg(F_2)$) over a UFD, S:

$$
\begin{array}{lllll}
\Delta_1 &=& 0, & \Delta_2 &=& \deg(F_1) - \deg(F_2) + 1 \\
b_1 &=& 1, & b_2 &=& \text{Hcoef}(F_2) \\
\psi_1 &=& 1, & \psi_2 &=& (b_2)^{\Delta_2 - 1}
\end{array}
$$

and

$$\beta_1 = \beta_2 = 1 \quad \text{and} \quad \beta_3 = (-1)^{\Delta_2}$$

Furthermore,

- For $i = 3, \ldots, k$,

$$
F_i = \frac{\text{PRemainder}(F_{i-2}, F_{i-1})}{\beta_i}
$$

$$
\Delta_i = \deg(F_{i-1}) - \deg(F_i) + 1
$$

$$
b_i = \text{Hcoef}(F_i)
$$

$$
\psi_i = \psi_{i-1}\left(\frac{b_i}{\psi_{i-1}}\right)^{\Delta_i - 1}.
$$

- For $i = 3, \ldots, k - 1$,

$$
\beta_{i+1} = (-1)^{\Delta_i}(\psi_{i-1})^{\Delta_i - 1}\, b_{i-1}.
$$

Theorem 7.9.4 *Let S be a UFD, and let $F_1(x), F_2(x) \in S[x]$ with $\deg(F_1) \geq \deg(F_2)$.*

Now, consider their subresultant polynomial remainder sequence: F_1, F_2, ..., F_k and their subresultant chain, with the following sequence of nonzero blocks:

$$\left\langle \ \overline{S_0}, \ \overline{S_1}, \ ..., \ \overline{S_l} \ \right\rangle.$$

Then

    1. $F_{i+1} = S_{\Uparrow(i)}, \ i = 0, \ ..., \ k-1.$

    2. $\psi_{i+1} = R_{\Downarrow(i)}, \ i = 0, \ ..., \ k-1.$

PROOF.

First, as a consequence of Corollary 7.9.3, we see that

$$\Delta_i = \delta_i, \qquad i = 0, \dots, k.$$

The rest of the proof is by induction.

Claim 1:

(1)   Assume that both (1) and (2) hold for all $j = 0, \ ..., \ i, \ (i \geq 2)$, we shall prove (1) for $i + 1$.

$$
\begin{aligned}
\beta_{i+2} \, & F_{i+2} \\
&= \ \text{PRemainder} \left(F_i, F_{i+1} \right) \\
&= \ \text{PRemainder} \left(S_{\Uparrow(i-1)}, S_{\Uparrow(i)} \right) \\
&= \ \text{PRemainder} \left(\left(\frac{R_{\Downarrow(i-2)}}{\text{Hcoef}(S_{\Uparrow(i-1)})} \right)^{\Delta_i - 2} S_{\Downarrow(i-1)}, \ S_{\Uparrow(i)} \right) \\
&= \ \left(\frac{R_{\Downarrow(i-2)}}{\text{Hcoef}(S_{\Uparrow(i-1)})} \right)^{\Delta_i - 2} \text{PRemainder} \left(S_{\Downarrow(i-1)}, S_{\Uparrow(i)} \right) \\
&= \ \left(\frac{R_{\Downarrow(i-2)}}{\text{Hcoef}(S_{\Uparrow(i-1)})} \right)^{\Delta_i - 2} \left(-R_{\Downarrow(i-1)} \right)^{\Delta_{i+1}} S_{\Uparrow(i+1)} \\
&= \ (-1)^{\Delta_{i+1}} \left(\frac{\psi_{i-1}}{\text{Hcoef}(F_i)} \right)^{\Delta_i - 2} (\psi_i)^{\Delta_{i+1}} S_{\Uparrow(i+1)} \\
&= \ (-1)^{\Delta_{i+1}} \left(\frac{\psi_{i-1}}{b_i} \right)^{\Delta_i - 2} (\psi_i)^{\Delta_{i+1}} S_{\Uparrow(i+1)} \\
&= \ (-1)^{\Delta_{i+1}} (\psi_i)^{\Delta_{i+1}-1} \psi_i \left(\frac{\psi_{i-1}}{b_i} \right)^{\Delta_i - 2} S_{\Uparrow(i+1)} \\
&= \ (-1)^{\Delta_{i+1}} (\psi_i)^{\Delta_{i+1}-1} b_i \, S_{\Uparrow(i+1)} \\
&= \ \beta_{i+2} \, S_{\Uparrow(i+1)}.
\end{aligned}
$$

Since we are working over a UFD, we can clear β_{i+2} from both sides to get

$$F_{i+2} = S_{\Uparrow(i+1)}.$$

Claim 2:

(2)   Assume that (1) holds all $j = 0, \ldots, i$ and (2) holds for all $j = 0, \ldots, i-1$, $(i \geq 1)$, we shall prove (2) for i.

Note that

$$
\begin{aligned}
\psi_{i+1} &= \psi_i \left(\frac{b_{i+1}}{\psi_i}\right)^{\Delta_{i+1}-1} \\
&= \frac{\mathrm{Hcoef}(F_{i+1})^{\Delta_{i+1}-1}}{\psi_i^{\Delta_{i+1}-2}} \\
&= \frac{\mathrm{Hcoef}(S_{\Uparrow(i)})^{\Delta_{i+1}-1}}{R_{\Downarrow(i-1)}^{\Delta_{i+1}-2}}.
\end{aligned}
$$

But since,

$$
\left(R_{\Downarrow(i-1)}\right)^{\Delta_{i+1}-2} S_{\Downarrow(i)} = \mathrm{Hcoef}\left(S_{\Uparrow(i)}\right)^{\Delta_{i+1}-2} S_{\Uparrow(i)},
$$

equating the coefficients, we have

$$
\left(R_{\Downarrow(i-1)}\right)^{\Delta_{i+1}-2} R_{\Downarrow(i)} = \mathrm{Hcoef}\left(S_{\Uparrow(i)}\right)^{\Delta_{i+1}-1}.
$$

Hence

$$
\psi_{i+1} = R_{\Downarrow(i)},
$$

as we are working over a UFD.

In order to complete the proof, we need to take care of the following base cases:

1. $i = 0$:

$$
F_1 = S_{n+1} = S_{\Uparrow(0)} \quad \text{and} \quad \psi_1 = 1 = R_{n+1} = R_{\Downarrow(0)}.
$$

2. $i = 1$:

$$
F_2 = S_n = S_{\Uparrow(1)}.
$$

By claim 1:

$$
\psi_2 = R_{\Downarrow(1)}.
$$

3. $i = 2$:

$$
\begin{aligned}
F_3 &= \frac{\mathrm{PRemainder}(F_1, F_2)}{\beta_3} \\
&= \frac{\mathrm{PRemainder}(F_1, F_2)}{(-1)^{\Delta_2}} \\
&= \frac{\mathrm{PRemainder}(S_{\Uparrow(0)}, S_{\Uparrow(1)})}{(-\psi_1)^{\Delta_2}} \\
&= \frac{\mathrm{PRemainder}(S_{\Downarrow(0)}, S_{\Uparrow(1)})}{(-R_{\Downarrow(0)})^{\Delta_2}} \\
&= S_{\Uparrow(2)}.
\end{aligned}
$$

The rest follows by induction, using the claims (1) and (2) proven earlier. $\square$

7.10   Subresultant Chain Theorem

Here, we shall provide a rigorous proof for the subresultant chain theorem. The proof begins with Habicht's theorem, which considers subresultant chains of two univariate polynomials of degrees $(n+1)$ and n, respectively, and both with symbolic coefficients.

The rest of the proof hinges on a generalization of Habicht's theorem, obtained by applying evaluation homomorphisms. This generalization directly leads to a proof of the subresultant chain theorem.

7.10.1   Habicht's Theorem

Consider two univariate polynomials

$$
\begin{aligned}
A(x) &= a_m x^m + a_{m-1} x^{m-1} + \cdots + a_0, & \deg(A) = m > 0, & \quad \text{and} \\
B(x) &= b_n x^n + b_{n-1} x^{n-1} + \cdots + b_0, & \deg(B) = n > 0,
\end{aligned}
$$

of positive degrees, with formal coefficients a_m, a_{m-1}, ..., a_0 and b_n, b_{n-1}, ..., b_0, respectively.

We shall treat $A(x)$ and $B(x)$ as polynomials in x over the ring

$$
\mathbb{Z}[a_m, \ldots, a_0, b_n, \ldots, b_0].
$$

Thus the subresultants of $A(x)$ and $B(x)$ are in

$$
(\mathbb{Z}[a_m, \ldots, a_0, b_n, \ldots, b_0])\,[x].
$$

In this section, we assume that

$$
\deg(A) = m = n + 1.
$$

Thus the subresultant chain of A and B is

$$
\left\langle
\begin{aligned}
S_{n+1} &= A, \\
S_n &= B, \\
S_{n-1} &= \mathrm{SubRes}_{n-1}(A, B), \\
&\;\;\vdots \\
S_1 &= \mathrm{SubRes}_1(A, B), \\
S_0 &= \mathrm{SubRes}_0(A, B)
\end{aligned}
\right\rangle.
$$

Lemma 7.10.1 *Let $A(x)$ and $B(x)$ be two univariate polynomials of respective degrees $n + 1$ and n, with formal coefficients $a_{n+1}, a_n, \ldots, a_0$ and b_n, b_{n-1}, ..., b_0, respectively. Then*

1. $\mathrm{SubRes}_{n-1}(A, B) = \mathrm{PRemainder}(A, B)$

2. *For* $i = 0, \ldots, n - 2$,

$$b_n^{2(n-i-1)} \, \mathrm{SubRes}_i(A, B) = \mathrm{SubRes}_i(B, \mathrm{PRemainder}(A, B)).$$

PROOF.
First, note that

$$b_n^2 \, \mathrm{SubRes}_{n-1}(A, B)$$
$$= b_n^2 \, \mathrm{DetPol}(A, \, xB, \, B)$$
$$= b_n^2 \, (-1)^2 \, \mathrm{DetPol}(xB, \, B, \, A)$$
$$= b_n^2 \, \mathrm{PRemainder}(A, B)$$

Since there are no nonzero zero divisors in $\mathbb{Z}[a_m, \ldots, a_0, b_n, \ldots, b_0]$, we may clear the b_n^2 from both sides to find

$$\mathrm{SubRes}_{n-1}(A, B) = \mathrm{PRemainder}(A, B).$$

Secondly,

$b_n^{2(n-i)} \, \mathrm{SubRes}_i(A, B)$
$= b_n^{2(n-i)} \, \mathrm{DetPol}(x^{n-i-1}A, \ldots, xA, A, \, x^{n-i}B, \ldots, xB, B)$
$= \mathrm{DetPol}(x^{n-i-1}b_n^2 A, \ldots, xb_n^2 A, b_n^2 A, \, x^{n-i}B, \ldots, xB, B)$

[But $b_n^2 \, A = (q_1 x + q_0) \, B + R$, where $R = \mathrm{PRemainder}(A, B)$ and $\deg(R) = n - 1$.]

$= \mathrm{DetPol}(x^{n-i-1}R, \ldots, xR, R, \, x^{n-i}B, \ldots, xB, B)$
$= (-1)^{(n-i)(n-i+1)} \, \mathrm{DetPol}(x^{n-i}B, \ldots, xB, B, \, x^{n-i-1}R, \ldots, xR, R)$
$= 1 \cdot b_n^2 \, \mathrm{DetPol}(x^{n-i-2}B, \ldots, xB, B, \, x^{n-i-1}R, \ldots, xR, R)$
$= b_n^2 \mathrm{SubRes}_i(B, R).$

Since $b_n \neq 0$ and not a zero divisor in $\mathbb{Z}[a_m, \ldots, a_0, b_n, \ldots, b_0]$, and $R = \mathrm{PRemainder}(A, B)$, we have

$$b_n^{2(n-i-1)}\mathrm{SubRes}_i(A, B) = \mathrm{SubRes}_i(B, \mathrm{PRemainder}(A, B)). \qquad \square$$

Theorem 7.10.2 (Habicht's Theorem) *Let $A(x)$ and $B(x)$ be two univariate polynomials of respective degrees $n+1$ and n, with formal coefficients $a_{n+1}, a_n, \ldots, a_0$ and $b_n, b_{n-1}, \ldots, b_0$, respectively.*

Let $\langle S_{n+1}, S_n, \ldots, S_0 \rangle$ be the subresultant chain of A and B. Let R_j $(0 \leq j \leq n + 1)$ be the jth principal subresultant coefficient of A and B. Then for all $j = 1, \ldots, n$

a) $R_{j+1}^2 S_{j-1} = \mathrm{PRemainder}(S_{j+1}, S_j), \qquad$ *and*

b) $R_{j+1}^{2(j-i)} S_i = \mathrm{SubRes}_i(S_{j+1}, S_j), \qquad$ *for $i = 0, \ldots, j - 1$.*

PROOF.
The proof is by induction on j:

- <u>BASE CASE:</u> $(j = n)$.
  $R_{n+1} = 1$; therefore,

  a) $\begin{aligned} S_{n-1} &= \text{SubRes}_{n-1}(S_{n+1}, S_n) &&\text{(by definition)} \\ &= \text{PRemainder}(S_{n+1}, S_n) &&\text{(by the previous lemma)} \end{aligned}$

  b) $\begin{aligned} S_i &= \text{SubRes}_i(S_{n+1}, S_n) &&\text{(by definition)} \\ &= \text{SubRes}_i(A, B) && i = 0, \ldots, n-1. \end{aligned}$

- <u>INDUCTION CASE:</u> Assume that the inductive hypotheses hold for $n, n-1, \ldots, j+1$ and consider the case when $j < n$.

  b) $R_{j+2}^{2(j-i+1)} \, R_{j+1}^{2(j-i)} \, S_i$

  $$\begin{aligned} &= \ R_{j+1}^{2(j-i)} \, \text{SubRes}_i(S_{j+2}, S_{j+1}) \\ &= \ \text{SubRes}_i(S_{j+1}, \text{PRemainder}(S_{j+2}, S_{j+1})) \quad \text{(by the previous} \\ &\hspace{10cm} \text{lemma)} \\ &= \ \text{SubRes}_i(S_{j+1}, \, R_{j+2}^2 \, S_j) \quad \text{(using part a) inductively)} \\ &= \ \text{DetPol}\Big(x^{j-i-1} S_{j+1}, \ \ldots, \ x S_{j+1}, \ S_{j+1}, \\ &\hspace{3cm} x^{j-i} \, R_{j+2}^2 \, S_j, \ \ldots, \ x R_{j+2}^2 \, S_j, \ R_{j+2}^2 \, S_j \Big) \\ &= \ R_{j+2}^{2(j-i+1)} \, \text{DetPol}\Big(x^{j-i-1} S_{j+1}, \ \ldots, \ x S_{j+1}, \ S_{j+1}, \\ &\hspace{3cm} x^{j-i} S_j, \ \ldots, \ x S_j, \ S_j \Big) \\ &= \ R_{j+2}^{2(j-i+1)} \, \text{SubRes}_i(S_{j+1}, S_j), \end{aligned}$$

  where the $R_{j+2}^{2(j-i+1)}$ terms cancel from both sides to produce

  $$R_{j+1}^{2(j-i)} S_i \ = \ \text{SubRes}_i(S_{j+1}, S_j), \qquad \text{for } i = 0, \ldots, n-1.$$

  a) In particular, for $i = j - 1$ we get

  $$\begin{aligned} R_{j+1}^2 S_{j-1} &= \ \text{SubRes}_{j-1}(S_{j+1}, S_j) \\ &= \ \text{PRemainder}(S_{j+1}, S_j). \quad \square \end{aligned}$$

7.10.2   Evaluation Homomorphisms

Let S^* be a commutative ring with identity, and ϕ an evaluation homomorphism defined as:

$$\phi \ : \ \mathbb{Z}[a_m, \ldots, a_0, b_n, \ldots, b_0] \to S^*,$$

$$: \quad a_i \mapsto a_i^*, \qquad \text{for } i = 0, \ldots, m,$$
$$: \quad b_j \mapsto b_j^*, \qquad \text{for } j = 0, \ldots, n,$$
$$: \quad 1 \mapsto 1, \quad 0 \mapsto 0,$$
$$: \quad k \mapsto \underbrace{1 + \cdots + 1}_{k - \text{times}}.$$

Lemma 7.10.3 *Let $A(x)$ and $B(x)$ be two univariate polynomials of respective positive degrees $n+1$ and n, with formal coefficients $a_{n+1}, a_n, \ldots, a_0$ and $b_n, b_{n-1}, \ldots, b_0$, respectively. Let*

$$\left\langle S_{n+1}, S_n, S_{n-1}, \ldots, S_1, S_0 \right\rangle$$

be the subresultant chain of A and B. Let ϕ be the evaluation homomorphism defined above. If $\phi(S_{j+1})$ is regular and $\phi(S_j)$ is defective of degree r, then

1. $\phi(R_{j+1})^2 \, \phi(S_{j-1}) = \phi(R_{j+1})^4 \, \phi(S_{j-2}) = \cdots$

$$= \phi(R_{j+1})^{2(j-r-1)} \, \phi(S_{r+1}) = 0.$$

2. $\phi(R_{j+1})^{2(j-r)} \, \phi(S_r)$

$$= \left(\text{Hcoef}(\phi(S_{j+1})) \text{Hcoef}(\phi(S_j)) \right)^{j-r} \phi(S_j).$$

3. $\phi(R_{j+1})^{2(j-r+1)} \, \text{Hcoef}(\phi(S_j))^{j-r+2} \, \phi(S_{r-1})$

$$= (-1)^{j-r+2} \text{Hcoef}(\phi(S_{j+1}))^{j-r} \text{Hcoef}(\phi(S_j))^{j-r+2}$$

$$\times \text{PRemainder}(\phi(S_{j+1}), \phi(S_j)).$$

PROOF.
Since

$$\deg(\phi(S_{j+1})) = j + 1, \qquad \deg(\phi(S_j)) = r,$$

and, for all i $(0 \le i < j)$,

$$R_{j+1}^{2(j-i)} S_i = \text{SubRes}_i(S_{j+1}, S_j),$$

we see that

$$\phi(R_{j+1})^{2(j-i)} \phi(S_i) = \phi(\text{SubRes}_i(S_{j+1}, S_j))$$
$$= \phi(\text{Hcoef}(S_{j+1}))^{j-r} \text{SubRes}_i(\phi(S_{j+1}), \phi(S_j))$$
$$= \text{Hcoef}(\phi(S_{j+1}))^{j-r} \text{SubRes}_i(\phi(S_{j+1}), \phi(S_j)).$$

But

$\text{SubRes}_i(\phi(S_{j+1}), \phi(S_j))$

$$= \begin{cases} 0, & \text{if } r < i < j; \\[2mm] \text{Hcoef}(\phi(S_j))^{j-r}\,\phi(S_j), & \text{if } i = r, \text{ and } \deg(\phi(S_j)) + 1 \\ & \qquad\qquad < \deg(\phi(S_{j+1})). \end{cases}$$

For $i = r - 1$,

$\text{Hcoef}(\phi(S_j))^{j-r+2}\ \text{SubRes}_i(\phi(S_{j+1}), \phi(S_j))$
$= (-1)^{j-r+2}\,\text{Hcoef}(\phi(S_j))^{j-r+2}\,\text{PRemainder}(\phi(S_{j+1}), \phi(S_j)).$

Therefore, we have the following:

1. For $i = r + 1, \ldots, j - 1$,

$$\phi(R_{j+1})^{2(j-i)}\phi(S_i) = 0.$$

2. For $i = r$,

$$\phi(R_{j+1})^{2(j-r)}\ \phi(S_r) = \Big(\text{Hcoef}(\phi(S_{j+1}))\text{Hcoef}(\phi(S_j))\Big)^{j-r}\ \phi(S_j).$$

3. For $i = r - 1$,

$$\phi(R_{j+1})^{2(j-r+1)}\,\text{Hcoef}(\phi(S_j))^{j-r+2}\,\phi(S_{r-1})$$
$$= (-1)^{j-r+2}\,\text{Hcoef}(\phi(S_{j+1}))^{j-r}\,\text{Hcoef}(\phi(S_j))^{j-r+2}$$
$$\times\,\text{PRemainder}(\phi(S_{j+1}), \phi(S_j)). \qquad \square$$

Corollary 7.10.4 *Let $A(x)$ and $B(x)$ be two univariate polynomials of respective positive degrees $n+1$ and n, with formal coefficients $a_{n+1}, a_n, \ldots, a_0$ and $b_n, b_{n-1}, \ldots, b_0$, respectively. Let*

$$\Big\langle S_{n+1},\ S_n,\ S_{n-1},\ \ldots,\ S_1,\ S_0 \Big\rangle$$

be the subresultant chain of A and B. Let ϕ be an evaluation homomorphism from $\mathbb{Z}[a_{n+1}, \ldots, a_0, b_n, \ldots, b_0]$ into an integral domain S^*.
If $\phi(S_{j+1})$ is regular and $\phi(S_j)$ is defective of degree r, then

1. $\phi(S_{j-1}) = \phi(S_{j-2}) = \cdots = \phi(S_{r+1}) = 0$.
2. If $j = n$, then

$$\phi(S_r) = \Big(\text{Hcoef}(\phi(S_{n+1}))\text{Hcoef}(\phi(S_n))\Big)^{n-r}\ \phi(S_n).$$

If $j < n$, then

$$\phi(R_{j+1})^{(j-r)}\ \phi(S_r) = \text{Hcoef}(\phi(S_j))^{j-r}\ \phi(S_j),$$

since $\phi(S_{j+1})$ is regular and $\phi(R_{j+1}) = \text{Hcoef}(\phi(S_{j+1}))$.

3. *If $j = n$, then*

$$\phi(S_{r-1}) = \left(-\text{Hcoef}(\phi(S_{n+1}))\right)^{n-r} \text{PRemainder}(\phi(S_{n+1}), \phi(S_n)).$$

If $j < n$, then

$$\phi(-R_{j+1})^{j-r+2} \phi(S_{r-1}) = \text{PRemainder}(\phi(S_{j+1}), \phi(S_j)),$$

since $\phi(S_{j+1})$ is regular and $\phi(R_{j+1}) = \text{Hcoef}(\phi(S_{j+1}))$.   □

7.10.3   Subresultant Chain Theorem

Now we are ready to prove the main theorem of this section, *the subresultant chain theorem.*

Let S^* be an *integral domain*, and $A^*(x)$ and $B^*(x)$ be two univariate polynomials in $S^*[x]$ of respective positive degrees n_1 and n_2 $(n_1 \geq n_2)$:

$$\begin{aligned} A^*(x) &= a^*_{n_1} x^{n_1} + \cdots + a^*_0, \quad \text{and} \\ B^*(x) &= b^*_{n_2} x^{n_2} + \cdots + b^*_0. \end{aligned}$$

If $n_1 > n_2$, then we set $n_1 = n + 1$ and specialize

$$b^*_n = \cdots = b^*_{n_2+1} = 0.$$

If $n_1 = n_2$, then we set $n_2 = n$ and specialize

$$a^*_{n+1} = 0.$$

Therefore,

$$n = \begin{cases} n_1 - 1, & \text{if } n_1 > n_2, \\ n_2, & \text{otherwise.} \end{cases}$$

The next theorem connects the sparsity in the head coefficients of S^*_j with the gap structure of the chain.

Theorem 7.10.5 (Subresultant Chain Theorem) *Let*

$$\left\langle S^*_{n+1}, S^*_n, S^*_{n-1}, \ldots, S^*_0 \right\rangle$$

be a subresultant chain of S^*_{n+1} and S^*_n in $S^*[x]$.

1. *For $j = 1, \ldots, n$, if S^*_{j+1} and S^*_j are both regular, then*

$$\left(-R^*_{j+1}\right)^2 S^*_{j-1} = \text{PRemainder}\left(S^*_{j+1}, S^*_j\right). \tag{7.5}$$

2. *For $j = 1, \ldots, n$, if S^*_{j+1} is regular and S^*_j is defective of degree r $(r < j)$, then*

$$S^*_{j-1} = S^*_{j-2} = \cdots = S^*_{r+1} = 0, \qquad (7.6)$$

$$\left(R^*_{j+1}\right)^{j-r} S^*_r = \text{Hcoef}\left(S^*_j\right)^{j-r} S^*_j, \qquad r \geq 0, \quad (7.7)$$

$$\left(-R^*_{j+1}\right)^{j-r+2} S^*_{r-1} = \text{PRemainder}\left(S^*_{j+1}, S^*_j\right), \quad r \geq 1. \,(7.8)$$

PROOF.
Since the first case is a simple consequence of Habicht's theorem (Corollary 7.10.4), we will focus only on the case when S^*_{j+1} is regular and S^*_j is defective of degree r $(r < j)$. Let

$$\begin{aligned}
A(x) &= a_{n+1} x^{n+1} + \cdots + a_0, \qquad \text{and} \\
B(x) &= b_n x^n + \cdots + b_0,
\end{aligned}$$

be two univariate polynomials with formal coefficients $a_{n+1}, \ldots, a_0$ and $b_n, \ldots, b_0$, respectively. Let

$$\Big\langle S_{n+1}, \ S_n, \ S_{n-1}, \ \ldots, \ S_0 \Big\rangle$$

be a subresultant chain of A and B (in $\mathbb{Z}[a_{n+1}, \ldots, a_0, b_n, \ldots, b_0]$) with the principal subresultant coefficient chain:

$$\Big\langle 1, \ R_n, \ R_{n-1}, \ \ldots, \ R_0 \Big\rangle.$$

We define two evaluation homomorphisms ϕ_1 and ϕ_2, corresponding respectively to the two cases (1) $n_1 > n_2$ (i.e., $n = n_1 - 1$) and (2) $n_1 = n_2$ (i.e., $n = n_2$).

- CASE 1: If $n_1 > n_2$ (i.e., $n = n_1 - 1$), then

$$\begin{aligned}
\phi_1 \ &: \ \mathbb{Z}[a_{n+1}, \ldots, a_0, b_n, \ldots, b_0] \to S^* \\
&: \ a_i \mapsto a^*_i, \qquad \text{for } i = 0, \ldots, n+1, \\
&: \ b_j \mapsto 0, \qquad \text{for } j = n_2 + 1, \ldots, n, \\
&: \ b_j \mapsto b^*_j, \qquad \text{for } j = 0, \ldots, n_2, \\
&: \ 1 \mapsto 1, \quad 0 \mapsto 0.
\end{aligned}$$

- CASE 2: If $n_1 = n_2$ (i.e., $n = n_2$), then

$$\begin{aligned}
\phi_2 \ &: \ \mathbb{Z}[a_{n+1}, \ldots, a_0, b_n, \ldots, b_0] \to S^* \\
&: \ a_{n+1} \mapsto 0, \\
&: \ a_i \mapsto a^*_i, \qquad \text{for } i = 0, \ldots, n, \\
&: \ b_j \mapsto b^*_j, \qquad \text{for } j = 0, \ldots, n, \\
&: \ 1 \mapsto 1, \quad 0 \mapsto 0.
\end{aligned}$$

The following observations are immediate consequences of Corollary 7.8.2:

- In either case (i.e., $k = 1, 2$), for all i ($0 \le i < n$),

$$\phi_k(S_i) = \phi_k(\mathrm{SubRes}_i(A, B))$$

$$= \begin{cases} \phi_1(a_{n+1})^{n-n_2}\mathrm{SubRes}_i(\phi_1(A), \phi_1(B)), & \text{if } k = 1, \\ \phi_2(b_n)^{n+1-n_1}\mathrm{SubRes}_i(\phi_2(A), \phi_2(B)), & \text{if } k = 2, \end{cases}$$

$$= \begin{cases} (a_{n+1}^*)^{n-n_2} S_i^*, & \text{if } k = 1, \\ (b_n^*)^{n-n_1+1} S_i^*, & \text{if } k = 2. \end{cases}$$

- In either case (i.e., $k = 1, 2$), for all i ($0 \le i \le n + 1$),

  1. $\phi_k(S_i)$ is regular if and only if S_i^* is regular, and

  2. $\phi_k(S_i)$ is defective of degree r if and only if S_i^* is defective of degree r.

  Thus, for all $j = 1, \ldots, n$, if S_{j+1}^* is regular and S_j^* is defective of degree r, then for both $k = 1, 2$, $\phi_k(S_{j+1})$ is regular and $\phi_k(S_j)$ is defective of degree r.

- In either case (i.e., $k = 1, 2$), if S_i^* is regular, then for all i ($0 \le i \le n$),

$$\phi_k(R_i) = \phi_k(\mathrm{Hcoef}(S_i)) = \mathrm{Hcoef}(\psi_k(S_i))$$

$$= \begin{cases} (a_{n+1}^*)^{n-n_2} R_i^*, & \text{if } k = 1, \\ (b_n^*)^{n-n_1+1} R_i^*, & \text{if } k = 2. \end{cases}$$

Now, we are ready to prove the lemma. We first consider the special case when $j = n$, and then consider the general case $j < n$.

- **CASE 1** : $j = n$.

That is, S_{n+1}^* is regular and S_n^* is defective of degree $r < n$. Thus

$$\begin{aligned} S_{n+1}^* &= a_{n+1}^* x^{n+1} + \cdots + a_0^*, \\ S_n^* &= b_r^* x^r + \cdots + b_0^*. \end{aligned}$$

Thus $n_1 = n + 1$, and $n_2 = r < n$, and the case 1 (i.e., $n_1 > n_2$) holds. We also see that

$$\lambda^* = \min(n + 1, r) = r.$$

Hence, by the definition of subresultant chains, we get equation (7.6):

$$S_{n-1}^* = S_{n-2}^* = \cdots = S_{r+1}^* = 0;$$

equation (7.7):

$$\left(R_{n+1}^*\right)^{n-r} S_r^* = S_r^* \quad \text{(since } R_{n+1}^* = 1)$$
$$= \text{Hcoef}\left(S_n^*\right)^{n+1-r-1} S_n^*$$
$$= \text{Hcoef}\left(S_n^*\right)^{n-r} S_n^*;$$

and equation (7.8):

$$\left(-R_{n+1}^*\right)^{n-r+2} S_{r-1}^* = (-1)^{n-r+2} S_{r-1}^* \quad \text{(since } R_{n+1}^* = 1)$$
$$= (-1)^{n-r+2} (-1)^{n+1-r+1} \text{PRemainder}\left(S_{n+1}^*, S_n^*\right)$$
$$\text{(using Lemma 7.7.3)}$$
$$= \text{PRemainder}\left(S_{n+1}^*, S_n^*\right).$$

• CASE 2 : $j < n$.

That is, for $k = 1, 2$, $\phi_k(S_{j+1})$ is regular and $\phi_k(S_j)$ is defective of degree $r < j$. By Habicht's theorem (Corollary 7.10.4):

$$\phi_k(S_{j-1}) = \phi_k(S_{j-2}) = \cdots = \phi_k(S_{r+1}) = 0,$$

and

$$\begin{cases} \left(a_{n+1}^*\right)^{n-n_2} S_{j-1}^* = \cdots = \left(a_{n+1}^*\right)^{n-n_2} S_{r+1}^* = 0, & \text{if } k = 1, \\ \left(b_n^*\right)^{n-n_1+1} S_{j-1}^* = \cdots = (b_n^*)^{n-n_1+1} S_{r+1}^* = 0, & \text{if } k = 2. \end{cases}$$

In either case, we get equation (7.6):

$$S_{j-1}^* = S_{j-2}^* = \cdots = S_{r+1}^* = 0.$$

Again by Habicht's theorem (Corollary 7.10.4), we have for $k = 1, 2$,

$$\phi_k(R_{j+1})^{j-r} \phi_k(S_r) = \text{Hcoef}\left(\phi_k(S_j)\right)^{j-r} \phi_k(S_j).$$

Thus

$$\begin{cases} \left(a_{n+1}^*\right)^{(j-r)(n-n_2)} \left(R_{j+1}^*\right)^{j-r} \left(a_{n+1}^*\right)^{n-n_2} S_r^* \\ \quad = \left(\left(a_{n+1}^*\right)^{n-n_2} \text{Hcoef}\left(S_j^*\right)\right)^{j-r} \left(a_{n+1}^*\right)^{n-n_2} S_j^*, & \text{if } k = 1, \\ \\ (b_n^*)^{(j-r)(n-n_1+1)} \left(R_{j+1}^*\right)^{j-r} (b_n^*)^{n-n_1+1} S_r^* \\ \quad = \left((b_n^*)^{n-n_1+1} \text{Hcoef}\left(S_j^*\right)\right)^{j-r} (b_n^*)^{n-n_1+1} S_j^*, & \text{if } k = 2. \end{cases}$$

Thus after cancellation we have equation (7.7):

$$\left(R_{j+1}^*\right)^{j-r} S_r^* = \text{Hcoef}\left(S_j^*\right)^{j-r} S_j^*.$$

Lastly, by another application of Habicht's theorem (Corollary 7.10.4), we have for $k = 1, 2$,

$$\phi_k(-R_{j+1})^{j-r+2} \, \phi_k(S_{r-1}) = \text{PRemainder}\left(\phi_k(S_{j+1}), \phi_k(S_j)\right).$$

Thus

$$\begin{cases} \left(-\left(a_{n+1}^*\right)^{n-n_2} R_{j+1}^*\right)^{j-r+2} \left(a_{n+1}^*\right)^{n-n_2} S_{r-1}^* \\ \quad = \text{PRemainder}\left(\left(a_{n+1}^*\right)^{n-n_2} S_{j+1}^*, \; \left(a_{n+1}^*\right)^{n-n_2} S_j^*\right) \\ \quad = \left(a_{n+1}^*\right)^{n-n_2} \left(a_{n+1}^*\right)^{(n-n_2)(j-r+2)} \\ \qquad \times \text{PRemainder}\left(S_{j+1}^*, S_j^*\right) \qquad \text{if } k = 1, \\[2em] \left(-(b_n^*)^{n-n_1+1} R_{j+1}^*\right)^{j-r+2} (b_n^*)^{n-n_1+1} S_{r-1}^* \\ \quad = \text{PRemainder}\left((b_n^*)^{n-n_1+1} S_{j+1}^*, \; (b_n^*)^{n-n_1+1} S_j^*\right) \\ \quad = (b_n^*)^{n-n_1+1} (b_n^*)^{(n-n_1+1)(j-r+2)} \\ \qquad \times \text{PRemainder}\left(S_{j+1}^*, S_j^*\right) \qquad \text{if } k = 2. \end{cases}$$

Thus after cancellation we have equation (7.8):

$$\left(-R_{j+1}^*\right)^{j-r+2} S_{r-1}^* = \text{PRemainder}\left(S_{j+1}^*, S_j^*\right). \quad \square$$

Problems

Problem 7.1
Devise a simple algorithm to compute the maximal square-free factor of a polynomial $A(x)$ over a field K of characteristic 0.

Problem 7.2
Consider the resultant of two polynomials $A(x)$ and $B(x)$ over a field K:

$$\begin{aligned} A(x) &= a_m x^m + a_{m-1} x^{m-1} + \cdots + a_0, \\ B(x) &= b_n x^n + b_{n-1} x^{n-1} + \cdots + b_0, \end{aligned}$$

of respective degrees $m \geq 0$ and $n \geq 0$, respectively.

Show that the Resultant(A, B) satisfies the following three conditions:

1. Resultant$(A, b_0) = b_0^m$.
2. Resultant$(B, A) = (-1)^{mn}$Resultant(A, B).

3. If $m \leq n$ and $R(x)$ is the remainder of $B(x)$ with respect to $A(x)$ [i.e., $B(x) = Q(x) \cdot A(x) + R(X)$, $\deg(R)$ is minimal], then

$$\text{Resultant}(A, B) = a_m^{n-m} \text{Resultant}(A, R).$$

Show that these three properties define the resultant uniquely.

Hint: Note that the resultant of two polynomials in $K[x]$ can be uniquely computed by using Euclid's algorithm and keeping track of the head coefficients. This algorithm also leads to a uniqueness proof by an induction on $\min(\deg(A), \deg(B))$.

Problem 7.3

Using the results from Problem 7.2, show the following:

Let $A(x)$ and $B(x)$ be two polynomials over an algebraically closed field L:

$$\begin{aligned}
A(x) &= a_m x^m + a_{m-1} x^{m-1} + \cdots + a_0, \\
B(x) &= b_n x^n + b_{n-1} x^{n-1} + \cdots + b_0,
\end{aligned}$$

of respective degrees $m \geq 0$ and $n \geq 0$, respectively. Then

(i) $\text{Resultant}(A, B) = 0$ if and only if A and B have a common zero.

(ii) Let

$$\begin{aligned}
A(x) &= a_m (x - \alpha_1)(x - \alpha_2) \cdots (x - \alpha_m), \\
B(x) &= b_n (x - \beta_1)(x - \beta_2) \cdots (x - \beta_n);
\end{aligned}$$

then

$$\text{Resultant}(A, B) = a_m^n b_n^m \prod_{i=1}^{m} \prod_{j=1}^{n} (\alpha_i - \beta_j).$$

Problem 7.4

Consider a monic polynomial $f(x) \in K[x]$ (K = a field) of degree n and with n zeros $\alpha_1, \alpha_2, \ldots, \alpha_n$ in the field K (or some algebraic extension of K). Let

$$\begin{aligned}
f(x) &= (x - \alpha_1)(x - \alpha_2) \cdots (x - \alpha_n) \\
&= x^n + a_{n-1} x^{n-1} + \cdots + a_k x^k + \cdots + a_0.
\end{aligned}$$

Prove that the following formulas, called *Vieta's formulas*, hold:

$$a_{n-1} = -(\alpha_1 + \alpha_2 + \cdots + \alpha_n),$$

$$\vdots$$

$$a_k = (-1)^{n-k} \sum_{i_1 < i_2 < \cdots < i_{n-k}} \left(\alpha_{i_1} \alpha_{i_2} \cdots \alpha_{i_{n-k}} \right),$$

$$\vdots$$

$$a_0 = (-1)^n \alpha_1 \alpha_2 \cdots \alpha_n.$$

Thus the coefficients of f are symmetric functions of the zeros. Here, symmetric functions are those functions that remain invariant with respect to the permutation of its variables.

Problem 7.5

Consider the following ring automorphism defined over $S[x_1, x_2, \ldots, x_n]$ ($S =$ an integral domain) with respect to a permutation $\pi \in S_n$:

$$\Pi : \quad S[x_1, x_2, \ldots, x_n] \rightarrow S[x_1, x_2, \ldots, x_n]$$
$$: \quad f(x_1, x_2, \ldots, x_n) \mapsto f\left(x_{\pi^{-1}(1)}, x_{\pi^{-1}(2)}, \ldots, x_{\pi^{-1}(n)}\right).$$

The polynomial is *symmetric* if $\Pi(f) = f$ for all $\pi \in S_n$.

Consider the following two classes of symmetric polynomials:

1. *Elementary Symmetric Polynomials*

$$s_k(x_1, x_2, \ldots, x_n) = \sum_{1 \le i_1 < i_2 < \cdots < i_k \le n} x_{i_1} x_{i_2} \cdots x_{i_k}, \qquad k = 1, 2, \ldots, n.$$

2. *Power Sum Symmetric Polynomials*

$$p_k(x_1, x_2, \ldots, x_n) = \sum_{i=1}^{n} x_i^k, \qquad k = 1, 2, \ldots.$$

Prove that the following formulas, called *Newton's formulas*, relate the p_k's to s_k's:

$$p_k - p_{k-1}s_1 + p_{k-2}s_2 + \cdots + (-1)^{k-1}p_1 s_{k-1} + (-1)^k k s_k = 0,$$

for $1 \le k \le n$, and

$$p_k - p_{k-1}s_1 + p_{k-2}s_2 + \cdots + (-1)^{n-1}p_{k-n+1}s_{n-1} + (-1)^n p_{k-n}s_n = 0,$$

for $k > n$.

Problem 7.6

Consider the following matrix, V_n, called a Vandermonde matrix:

$$V_n = \begin{bmatrix} 1 & 1 & \cdots & 1 \\ x_1 & x_2 & \cdots & x_n \\ \vdots & \vdots & \ddots & \vdots \\ x_1^{n-2} & x_2^{n-2} & \cdots & x_n^{n-2} \\ x_1^{n-1} & x_2^{n-1} & \cdots & x_n^{n-1} \end{bmatrix}.$$

Show that the determinant of V_n over a field K is given by

$$\det(V_n) = \prod_{1 \le i < j \le n} (x_j - x_i).$$

Hint: The proof is by induction on n. As $\det(V_n)$ vanishes when x_n in the last column is replaced by x_i ($1 \le i < n$), clearly $(x_n - x_i) \mid \det(V_n)$. After eliminating all such factors, it can be seen that

$$\det(V_n) = \det(V_{n-1}) \prod_{i=1}^{n-1} (x_n - x_i),$$

(consider the coefficients of x_n^{n-1} in the above equation).

Using the above facts show the following: Let $f(x) \in L[x]$ be a univariate polynomial of degree n over an algebraically closed field L and with n roots: $\alpha_1, \alpha_2, \ldots, \alpha_n$. Then

$$\text{Discriminant}(f) = \begin{vmatrix} n & p_1 & p_2 & \cdots & p_{n-1} \\ p_1 & p_2 & p_3 & \cdots & p_n \\ p_2 & p_3 & p_4 & \cdots & p_{n+1} \\ \vdots & \vdots & \vdots & \ddots & \vdots \\ p_{n-1} & p_n & p_{n+1} & \cdots & p_{2n-2} \end{vmatrix},$$

where $p_k = \sum_{i=1}^{n} \alpha_i^k$ ($k = 1, \ldots, 2n - 2$).

Problem 7.7

Prove the following identities: Let $A(x)$, $B(x)$ and $C(x) \in K[x]$ be three univariate polynomials of degrees m, n, and p, respectively.

1. $\text{Resultant}(A(x), x - y) = (-1)^m A(y)$.

2. $\text{Resultant}(AB, C) = \text{Resultant}(A, C) \text{Resultant}(B, C)$.

3. $\text{Discriminant}(AB)$

$$= \text{Discriminant}(A) \text{Discriminant}(B) |\text{Resultant}(A, B)|^2.$$

Problem 7.8

Let K be a field and $A(x) \in K[x]$ be a monic polynomial:

$$A(x) = x^m + a_{m-1} x^{m-1} + \cdots + a_1 x + a_0.$$

The following matrix $C_A \in K^{m \times m}$ is called a *companion matrix* of the polynomial A:

$$C = C_A = \begin{bmatrix} 0 & 1 & 0 & \cdots & 0 & 0 \\ 0 & 0 & 1 & \cdots & 0 & 0 \\ 0 & 0 & 0 & \cdots & 0 & 0 \\ \vdots & \vdots & \vdots & \ddots & \vdots & \vdots \\ 0 & 0 & 0 & \cdots & 0 & 1 \\ -a_0 & -a_1 & -a_2 & \cdots & -a_{m-2} & -a_{m-1} \end{bmatrix}.$$

Prove that the characteristic polynomial of the companion matrix C_A is

$$\chi(C_A) = \det(\lambda I_m - C_A) = A(\lambda).$$

Now, if $B(x) \in K[x]$ is another monic polynomial

$$B(x) = x^n + b_{n-1} x^{n-1} + \cdots + b_1 x + b_0,$$

and if we consider the following $m \times m$ matrix:

$$B(C_A) = C_A^n + b_{n-1} C_A^{n-1} + \cdots + b_1 C_A + b_0 I_m$$

then show that

$$\det(B(C_A)) = \text{Resultant}(A, B).$$

Problem 7.9

Let $A_0(x)$, $A_1(x)$, ..., $A_n(x) \in K[x]$ (K is a field).

Let y be a new indeterminate, and consider the following bivariate polynomial:

$$A(x, y) = A_{n-1}(x) y^{n-1} + \cdots + A_1(x) y + A_0(x),$$

where A is regarded as a polynomial in x with coefficients in $K(y)$.

(i) Show that the GCD of A and A_n (when treated as polynomials in $K(y)[x]$) is the same as the GCD of A_0, A_1, ..., A_n (in $k[x]$).

(ii) Construct the Sylvester matrix M_y of the polynomials A and A_n [with coefficients in $K(y)$] and show that $\det(M_y)$ vanishes identically if and only if the polynomials A_0, A_1, ..., A_n have a nonconstant divisor.

Problem 7.10

Let $A(x, y)$ and $B(x, y) \in K[x, y]$ be two homogeneous polynomials of degrees m and n, respectively:

$$\begin{aligned}
A(x, y) &= a_m x^m + a_{m-1} x^{m-1} y + \cdots + a_0 y^m, \quad \text{and} \\
B(x, y) &= b_n x^n + b_{n-1} x^{n-1} y + \cdots + b_0 y^n.
\end{aligned}$$

Prove that every factor of a homogeneous polynomial is also homogeneous.

Prove the following statement:

A and B have a common factor of degree $\geq k$ if and only if the rank of the following matrix is less than $m + n - 2k + 2$:

$$\left[
\begin{array}{cccccccc}
a_m & a_{m-1} & \cdots & & a_0 & & & \\
 & a_m & a_{m-1} & \cdots & & a_0 & & \\
 & & \ddots & \ddots & \ddots & & \ddots & \\
 & & & a_m & a_{m-1} & \cdots & & a_0 \\
b_n & b_{n-1} & \cdots & & \cdots & b_0 & & \\
 & b_n & b_{n-1} & \cdots & & \cdots & b_0 & \\
 & & \ddots & \ddots & \ddots & & \ddots & \\
 & & & b_n & b_{n-1} & \cdots & & \cdots & b_0
\end{array}
\right]
\begin{array}{l}
\left.\rule{0pt}{28pt}\right\} \begin{array}{l}(n-k+1) \\ \text{rows}\end{array} \\
\left.\rule{0pt}{28pt}\right\} \begin{array}{l}(m-k+1) \\ \text{rows}\end{array}
\end{array}$$

Problem 7.11

Consider r homogeneous polynomials A_1, A_2, ..., A_r in $K[x, y]$ having the same degree n:

$$
\begin{aligned}
A_1(x, y) &= a_{1,n}x^n + a_{1,n-1}x^{n-1}y + \cdots + a_{1,0}y^n, \\
A_2(x, y) &= a_{2,n}x^n + a_{2,n-1}x^{n-1}y + \cdots + a_{2,0}y^n, \\
&\;\;\vdots \\
A_r(x, y) &= a_{r,n}x^n + a_{r,n-1}x^{n-1}y + \cdots + a_{r,0}y^n.
\end{aligned}
$$

Consider the following matrix S_l consisting of r blocks of rows, where each block of rows consists of $l - n + 1$ rows of $a_{i,.}$'s:

$$
S_l = \begin{bmatrix}
a_{1,n} & a_{1,n-1} & \cdots & & a_{1,0} & & & \\
 & a_{1,n} & a_{1,n-1} & \cdots & & a_{1,0} & & \\
 & & \ddots & \ddots & \ddots & & \ddots & \\
 & & & a_{1,n} & a_{1,n-1} & \cdots & a_{1,0} \\
\cdots & \cdots & \cdots & \cdots & \cdots & \cdots & \cdots \\
\cdots & \cdots & \cdots & \cdots & \cdots & \cdots & \cdots \\
a_{r,n} & a_{r,n-1} & \cdots & & a_{r,0} & & & \\
 & a_{r,n} & a_{r,n-1} & \cdots & & a_{r,0} & & \\
 & & \ddots & \ddots & \ddots & & \ddots & \\
 & & & a_{r,n} & a_{r,n-1} & \cdots & a_{r,0}
\end{bmatrix}.
$$

Show that the r polynomials A_1, A_2, ..., A_r have a common divisor of degree $\geq k$ if and only if the matrix S_{2n-k} has rank less than $(2n - k + 1)$.

Generalize this theorem to the case where A_1, A_2, ..., A_r have different degrees: n_1, n_2, ..., n_r.

Hint: Use the fact that in order for a polynomial to be a common divisor of A_1, A_2, ..., A_r, it is necessary and sufficient that it is a common divisor of

$$
A_1u_1 + A_2u_2 + \cdots + A_ru_r \quad \text{and} \quad A_1v_1 + A_2v_2 + \cdots + A_rv_r,
$$

where u's and v's represent $2r$ indeterminates. The resultant of these newly constructed polynomials is related to the so-called Kronecker's U-resultant.

Problem 7.12

Let A_1, A_2, ..., A_r be r polynomials in $K[x, y]$ (K = a field). Show that the number of common zeroes of the A_i's satisfy the following bound:

$$
|\mathcal{Z}(A_1, A_2, \ldots, A_r)| \leq 2 \left(\max_i \deg_x(A_i) \right) \left(\max_i \deg_y(A_i) \right),
$$

where $\deg_x(A)$ and $\deg_y(A)$ are the degrees of A with respect to x and y.

Hint: Use the idea of U-resultant (Problem 7.11) once again. Also, show that there exist polynomials A_1, A_2, ..., $A_r \in K[x, y]$ such that

$$
|\mathcal{Z}(A_1, A_2, \ldots, A_r)| = \left(\max_i \deg_x(A_i) \right) \left(\max_i \deg_y(A_i) \right).
$$

Problem 7.13

Let S be a UFD and let $F_1(x)$ and $F_2(x) \in S[x]$ be two univariate polynomials with

$$\deg(F_1) < \deg(F_2).$$

Let $n = \max(\deg(F_1), \deg(F_2)) = \deg(F_2)$. Define the subresultant chain of F_1 and F_2 as

$$\left\langle \begin{aligned}
S_{n+1} &= F_1, \\
S_n &= F_2, \\
S_{n-1} &= F_1, \\
S_{n-2} &= \mathrm{SubRes}_{n-2}(F_1, F_2), \\
&\vdots \\
S_0 &= \mathrm{SubRes}_0(F_1, F_2)
\end{aligned} \right\rangle$$

and the principal subresultant coefficients as

$$\left\langle \begin{aligned}
\mathrm{PSC}_{n+1} &= 1, \\
\mathrm{PSC}_n &= \mathrm{NHcoef}(S_n), \\
\mathrm{PSC}_{n-1} &= \mathrm{NHcoef}(S_{n-1}), \\
\mathrm{PSC}_{n-2} &= \mathrm{NHcoef}(S_{n-2}), \\
&\vdots, \\
\mathrm{PSC}_1 &= \mathrm{NHcoef}(S_1), \\
\mathrm{PSC}_0 &= \mathrm{NHcoef}(S_0)
\end{aligned} \right\rangle$$

Also modify the definition of subresultant polynomial remainder sequence by redefining Δ_i as

$$\begin{aligned}
\Delta_1 &= 0, \\
\Delta_i &= \max(\deg(F_{i-1}) - \deg(F_i) + 1, 0), \qquad i = 2, 3, \ldots,
\end{aligned}$$

(b_i, ψ_i, β_i and F_i stay just as in the text).

Prove Theorem 7.9.4 for this case:

$$\deg(F_1) < \deg(F_2).$$

Note that you will need to prove the subresultant chain theorem for this case also.

Problem 7.14

Give a direct proof for the following statement (i.e., do not use the identities involving determinant polynomials):

Let S be a unique factorization domain. Let $A(x)$, $B(x) \in S[x]$ be two univariate polynomials of degree m and n, respectively, and α, $\beta \in S$. Then

$$\mathrm{PRemainder}(\alpha A(x),\ \beta B(x))\ =\ \alpha\beta^{\delta}\mathrm{PRemainder}(A(x),\ B(x)),$$

where $\delta = \max\{m - n + 1, 0\}$.

Problem 7.15

Let S be a unique factorization domain, and F_1, F_2, ..., F_k be a Euclidean polynomial remainder sequence $(\deg(F_1) \geq \deg(F_2))$.

(i) Let

$$\Delta_i = \deg(F_{i-1}) - \deg(F_i) + 1, \qquad i = 2, \ldots, k.$$

Let c_1, c_2, ..., c_l, ..., c_k be the sequence of the contents of the polynomials F_i's.

For all $m \geq l$ prove that

$$c_l^{\Delta_l\ \Delta_{l+1}\cdots\Delta_{m-1}}\ \bigm|\ c_m.$$

(ii) Using (i), show that the sizes of the coefficients in an Euclidean polynomial remainder sequence of two polynomials over $\mathbb{Z}$ grow at an exponential rate.

Problem 7.16

(i) Let A be an $n \times n$ matrix over the integers $\mathbb{Z}$. Prove the following inequality, *the Hadamard inequality*,

$$|\det(A)|\ \leq\ \prod_{i=1}^{n}\left(\sum_{j=1}^{n} a_{i,j}^2\right)^{1/2}.$$

Hint: Consider the matrix AA^T.

(ii) Using (i), show that the sizes of the coefficients in a subresultant polynomial remainder sequence of two polynomials over $\mathbb{Z}$ grow at a (small) polynomial rate. That is, show that if F_m is the mth polynomial in the subresultant polynomial remainder sequence of $F_1(x)$ and $F_2(x) \in \mathbb{Z}$, then the sizes of the coefficients of F_m are

$$O\Big((\deg(F_1) + \deg(F_2) - 2\deg(F_m))\ \log(\mathrm{size}(F_1, F_2)(\deg(F_1) + \deg(F_2)))\Big).$$

Problem 7.17

Let S be a unique factorization domain, and F_1, F_2, ..., F_k be a Euclidean polynomial remainder sequence $(\deg(F_1) \geq \deg(F_2))$. Let

$$\Delta_i = \deg(F_{i-1}) - \deg(F_i) + 1, \qquad i = 2, \ldots, k,$$

and
$$c_i = \text{Content}(F_i), \qquad i = 1, \ldots, k.$$

(i) A sequence $\overline{\beta} = \langle \beta_1 = 1, \beta_2 = 1, \beta_3, \ldots, \beta_k \rangle$ is well-defined if and only if

$$\left(\beta_{i-2} \, \beta_{i-1}^{\Delta_{i-1}} \, \beta_i \right) \mid c_i, \qquad i = 3, \ldots, k.$$

(ii) Let $F_1' = F_1$, $F_2' = F_2$,

$$F_i' = \frac{\text{PRemainder}(F_{i-2}', F_{i-1}')}{\beta_i}, \qquad i = 3, \ldots, k.$$

Show that

$$F_i = \left(\alpha_i \beta_{i-2} \, \beta_{i-1}^{\Delta_{i-1}} \, \beta_i \right) F_i', \qquad i = 3, \ldots, k,$$

where $\alpha_1 = \alpha_2 = 1$ and

$$\alpha_i = \alpha_{i-2} \, \alpha_{i-1}^{\Delta_{i-1}} \, \beta_{i-4} \, \beta_{i-3}^{\Delta_{i-3} + \Delta_{i-1}} \, \beta_{i-2}^{(\Delta_{i-2})(\Delta_{i-1})}, \qquad i = 3, \ldots, k.$$

Solutions to Selected Problems

Problem 7.3

(1)   Consider the sequence of polynomials defined by repeated applications of Euclidean divisions:

$$
\begin{aligned}
R_0 &= A \\
R_1 &= B \\
R_2 &= \text{Remainder}(R_0, R_1) \\
&\;\;\vdots \\
R_i &= \text{Remainder}(R_{i-2}, R_{i-1}) \\
&\;\;\vdots \\
R_k &= \text{Remainder}(R_{k-2}, R_{k-1}) = r_0 \in L.
\end{aligned}
$$

where without loss of generality, we have assumed that $\deg(A) \geq \deg(B)$. We have assumed that $R_0, R_1, \ldots, R_{k-1}$ are all nonconstant polynomials over L. By the results of Problem 7.2, we see that

$$\text{Resultant}(A, B) = \text{Resultant}(R_0, R_1) = 0 \quad \text{if and only if} \quad r_0 = 0$$

if and only if A and B have a common nonconstant factor.

(ii) First note that, for any α_i,

$$B(\alpha_i) = b_n \, (\alpha_i - \beta_1)(\alpha_i - \beta_2) \cdots (\alpha_i - \beta_n),$$

and hence

$$\prod_{i=1}^{m} B(\alpha_i) = b_n^m \, \prod_{i=1}^{m} \prod_{j=1}^{n} (\alpha_i - \beta_j).$$

Thus, it suffices to prove that

$$\text{Resultant}(A, B) = a_m^n \, \prod_{i=1}^{m} B(\alpha_i).$$

The proof follows by showing that the right-hand side of the equation above satisfies all three properties of Problem 7.2: Properties (1) and (2) are trivial. To see property (3) note that

If $R(x)$ is the remainder of $B(x)$ with respect to $A(x)$, then

$$B(\alpha_i) = Q(\alpha_i)A(\alpha_i) + R(\alpha_i) = R(\alpha_i).$$

Thus,

$$
\begin{aligned}
\text{Resultant}(A, B) \;&=\; a_m^n \, \prod_{i=1}^{m} B(\alpha_i) \\[2mm]
&=\; (-1)^{mn} \, b_n^m \, \prod_{j=1}^{n} A(\beta_j) \\[2mm]
&=\; a_m^n \, b_n^m \, \prod_{i=1}^{m} \prod_{j=1}^{n} (\alpha_i - \beta_j).
\end{aligned}
$$

Problem 7.8

Note that the characteristic polynomial of C_A can be calculated as follows:

$$
\chi(C_A) = \begin{vmatrix}
\lambda & -1 & 0 & \cdots & 0 & 0 \\
0 & \lambda & -1 & \cdots & 0 & 0 \\
0 & 0 & \lambda & \cdots & 0 & 0 \\
\vdots & \vdots & \vdots & \ddots & \vdots & \vdots \\
0 & 0 & 0 & \cdots & \lambda & -1 \\
a_0 & a_1 & a_2 & \cdots & a_{m-2} & \lambda + a_{m-1}
\end{vmatrix}.
$$

Thus, by using the results of Problem 7.3 (and working over algebraic closure of K), we have:

$$\chi(C_A) \;=\; \text{Resultant}_x \Big(\lambda x - 1,$$

$$a_0 x^{m-1} + a_1 x^{m-2} + \cdots + a_{m-2} x + a_{m-1} + \lambda \Big)$$

$$= \lambda^{m-1} \left(a_0 \left(\frac{1}{\lambda} \right)^{m-1} + a_1 \left(\frac{1}{\lambda} \right)^{m-2} + \cdots \right.$$
$$\left. + a_{m-2} \left(\frac{1}{\lambda} \right) + a_{m-1} + \lambda \right)$$

[since $\text{Resultant}(a(x - \alpha), F(x)) = a^{\deg(F)} \cdot F(\alpha)$.]

$$= \lambda^m + a_{m-1}\lambda^{m-1} + \cdots + a_1\lambda + a_0.$$
$$= A(\lambda).$$

A somewhat direct argument can be given by noting that C_A represents a linear transformation ϕ, over $K[x]/(A(x))$, the residue class ring modulo the ideal generated by $A(x)$:

$$\phi \; : \; K[x]/(A(x)) \to K[x]/(A(x))$$
$$: \; B(x) \mapsto x \cdot B(x) \mod A(x)$$

In particular, if α is a root of $A(x)$, then α is an eigenvalue of C_A with eigenvector

$$(1, \alpha, \alpha^2, \ldots, \alpha^{m-1})^T,$$

since

$$\begin{bmatrix} 0 & 1 & 0 & \cdots & 0 & 0 \\ 0 & 0 & 1 & \cdots & 0 & 0 \\ 0 & 0 & 0 & \cdots & 0 & 0 \\ \vdots & \vdots & \vdots & \ddots & \vdots & \vdots \\ -a_0 & -a_1 & -a_2 & \cdots & -a_{m-2} & -a_{m-1} \end{bmatrix} \cdot \begin{bmatrix} 1 \\ \alpha \\ \alpha^2 \\ \vdots \\ \alpha^{m-1} \end{bmatrix}$$

$$= \begin{bmatrix} \alpha \\ \alpha^2 \\ \alpha^3 \\ \vdots \\ -a_0 - a_1\alpha - \cdots - a_{m-1}\alpha^{m-1} \end{bmatrix}$$

$$= \begin{bmatrix} \alpha \\ \alpha^2 \\ \alpha^3 \\ \vdots \\ \alpha^m - A(\alpha) \end{bmatrix} = \alpha \cdot \begin{bmatrix} 1 \\ \alpha \\ \alpha^2 \\ \vdots \\ \alpha^{m-1} \end{bmatrix}.$$

Now since $\chi(C_A)$ is clearly a monic polynomial of degree m with the same roots as $A(x)$, we have

$$\chi(C_A) = \det(\lambda I_m - C_A) = A(\lambda).$$

The proof for the second part proceeds by showing that the eigenvalues of the matrix $B(C_A)$ are simply $B(\lambda_i)$'s, where λ_i's are respectively the eigenvalues of C_A and hence zeroes of A:

If v_i is an eigenvector of C_A with eigenvalue λ_i, then

$$
\begin{aligned}
B(C_A) \cdot v_i &= C_A^n \cdot v_i + b_{n-1} C_A^{n-1} \cdot v_i + \cdots + b_1 C_A \cdot v_i + b_0 v_i \\
&= \lambda_i^n v_i + b_{n-1} \lambda_i^{n-1} v_i + \cdots + b_1 \lambda_i v_i + b_0 v_i \\
&\quad (\text{since } C_A^k \cdot v_i = C_A^{k-1} \lambda_i v_i = \cdots = \lambda_i^k v_i) \\
&= B(\lambda_i) v_i.
\end{aligned}
$$

Hence, v_i is an eigenvector of $B(C_A)$ with eigenvalue $B(\lambda_i)$, and the determinant of $B(C_A)$ is simply the product of the eigenvalues $B(\lambda_i)$'s.

Now, it follows that

$$
\det(B(C_A)) = \prod_{i=1}^{m} B(\lambda_i) = \text{Resultant}(A, B).
$$

Problem 7.14

Proposition 7.10.6 *Let S be a unique factorization domain. Let $A(x)$, $B(x) \in S[x]$ be two univariate polynomials of degree m and n, respectively, and $\alpha, \beta \in S$. Then*

$$
\text{PRemainder}(\alpha A(x), \beta B(x)) = \alpha \beta^\delta \text{PRemainder}(A(x), B(x)),
$$

where $\delta = \max\{m - n + 1, 0\}$.

PROOF.
Let

$$
\begin{aligned}
R(x) &= \text{PRemainder}(A(x), B(x)) \quad \text{and} \\
R'(x) &= \text{PRemainder}(\alpha A(x), \beta B(x)).
\end{aligned}
$$

Then

$$
b_n^\delta A(x) = Q(x) \cdot B(x) + R(x)
$$

Therefore,

$$
(\beta b_n)^\delta \cdot \alpha A(x) = \alpha \beta^\delta Q(x) \cdot B(x) + \alpha \beta^\delta \cdot R(x).
$$

Since the second term on the right-hand side has degree less than n, $R'(x) = \alpha \beta^\delta R(x)$ as desired. $\square$

Problem 7.15

This is a simple consequence of the preceding problem. Define a sequence $\gamma_1, \gamma_2, \ldots$, as

$$
\begin{aligned}
\gamma_1 &= 1 \\
\gamma_2 &= 1 \\
&\vdots \\
\gamma_{l-1} &= 1 \\
\gamma_l &= c_l \\
&\vdots \\
\gamma_m &= c_l^{\Delta_l \, \Delta_{l+1} \cdots \Delta_{m-1}} \\
&\vdots
\end{aligned}
$$

Clearly $\gamma_i | c_i$, $1 \le l$. We want to prove the statement for $m > l$ assuming that it is true up to $m - 1$.

We may write $F_i = \gamma_i G_i$, for $1 \le i < m$. Then

$$
\begin{aligned}
F_m &= \mathrm{PRemainder}(F_{m-2}, F_{m-1}) \\
&= \mathrm{PRemainder}(\gamma_{m-2} G_{m-2}, \ \gamma_{m-1} G_{m-1}) \\
&= \gamma_{m-2} \, \gamma_{m-1}^{\Delta_{m-1}} \, \mathrm{PRemainder}(G_{m-2}, G_{m-1}).
\end{aligned}
$$

Thus $\gamma_m = c_l^{\Delta_l \, \Delta_{l+1} \cdots \Delta_{m-1}} = \gamma_{m-1}^{\Delta_{m-1}}$ divides the coefficients of F_m and thus $\gamma_m \mid \mathrm{Content}(F_m)$.

The second part is a simple consequence of the above observations: since $\Delta_l \ge 2$ for all $l > 2$,

$$
c_l^{2^{m-l}} | c_m, \qquad m \ge l > 2;
$$

and the size of c_m is of the order $\Omega\left(2^m \, \mathrm{size}(c_l)\right)$.

Problem 7.17

The solution builds on Problem 7.14.

(i)   The "only-if" part is obvious as β_i divides c_i. The "if" part follows from part (ii) of this problem.

(ii)   We will prove that

$$
F_i = \alpha_i \, \beta_{i-2} \, \beta_{i-1}^{\Delta_{i-1}} \, \beta_i \, F_i',
$$

where $\alpha_1 = \alpha_2 = 1$ and

$$
\alpha_i = \alpha_{i-2} \, \alpha_{i-1}^{\Delta_{i-1}} \, \beta_{i-4} \, \beta_{i-3}^{\Delta_{i-3}+\Delta_{i-1}} \, \beta_{i-2}^{(\Delta_{i-2})(\Delta_{i-1})}.
$$

We use induction on i. For $i = 1$, the relation is true by definition itself. Assume it is true for all $i' < i$. Now consider $i' = i$.

$$
\begin{aligned}
F_i &= \text{PRemainder}(F_{i-2}, F_{i-1}) \\
&= \text{PRemainder}\Big(\alpha_{i-2}\,\beta_{i-4}\,\beta_{i-3}^{\Delta_{i-3}}\,\beta_{i-2}\,F'_{i-2}, \\
&\qquad\qquad\quad \alpha_{i-1}\,\beta_{i-3}\,\beta_{i-2}^{\Delta_{i-2}}\,\beta_{i-1}\,F'_{i-1}\Big) \\
&= \alpha_{i-2}\,\beta_{i-4}\,\beta_{i-3}^{\Delta_{i-3}}\left(\alpha_{i-1}\,\beta_{i-3}\,\beta_{i-2}^{\Delta_{i-2}}\right)^{\Delta_{i-1}} \\
&\qquad \beta_{i-2}\,\beta_{i-1}^{\Delta_{i-1}}\,\text{PRemainder}(F'_{i-2}, F'_{i-1}) \\
&= \alpha_i\,\beta_{i-2}\,\beta_{i-1}^{\Delta_{i-1}}\,\text{PRemainder}(F'_{i-2}, F'_{i-1}) \\
&= \alpha_i\,\beta_{i-2}\,\beta_{i-1}^{\Delta_{i-1}}\,\beta_i\,F'_i.
\end{aligned}
$$

Bibliographic Notes

The resultant probably provides the oldest constructive technique to decide if a system of polynomials has a common zero. While it may appear that the resultant simply gives a decision procedure for the existence of a common solution, it can actually be used to compute the common solutions of a system of polynomial equations (see Lazard [127]).

Historically, there seem to have been several attempts at constructing resultants, which turn out to be equivalent. Notable among these are:

1. Euler's method of elimination.

2. Sylvester's dialytic method of elimination.

3. Bezout's method of elimination (the so-called *Bezoutiant*).

For more details, see Burnside and Panton [35]. Our discussion is based on the framework that Sylvester [198] had originally proposed.

The method of the subresultant polynomial remainder sequence is due to George Collins [52]. Our discussion of the subresultants, polynomial remainder sequence, and subresultant chain is based on the following: Brown [24,26], Brown and Traub [28], Collins [51-53], Ho [97], Ho and Yap [98], Knuth [116] and Loos [134]. The proof by Loos [134] of subresultant chain theorem was erroneous and Ho and Yap provided a corrected proof for the case when $\deg(F_1) > \deg(F_2)$, using the notion of a *pseudo prs*. However, the theorem can be seen to hold for all cases [$\deg(F_1) \geq \deg(F_2)$, see §7.10, and $\deg(F_1) < \deg(F_2)$, see Problem 7.13], as originally claimed by Loos.

There have been many interesting developments involving resultants; for some computational issues, see Ierardi and Kozen [104].

Problem 7.8 follows the work of Barnett [13]. Problem 7.9 is due to Ierardi and Kozen [104]. Problems 7.10 and 7.11 are due to Kakié [109].

Chapter 8

Real Algebra

8.1 Introduction

In this chapter, we focus our attention on *real algebra* and *real geometry*. We deal with algebraic problems with a formulation over real numbers, $\mathbb{R}$ (or more generally, over *real closed fields*). The underlying (real) geometry provides a rich set of mechanisms to describe such topological notions as "between," "above/below," "internal/external," since it can use the inherent order relation ($<$) of the real (or, real closed) field. As a result, the subject has found many applications in such practical areas as *computer-aided manufacturing*, *computational geometry*, *computer vision*, *geometric theorem proving*, *robotics*, and *solid modeling*, etc., and thus has generated a renewed interest. We concentrate on the following key ingredients of real algebra: *Sturm theory*, *algebraic numbers*, and *semialgebraic geometry*.

We start our discussions with some preparation for the classical *Sturm's theorem*, which permits us to determine the exact number of real roots of a real polynomial in an interval.

Our starting point is with Artin and Schreier's theory of *formally real fields* developed in the late 20's. In particular, we focus our attention on the *real closed fields*, which are the formally real fields maximal under algebraic extension. Intuitively, real closed fields are "almost algebraically closed" as they are only missing $\sqrt{-1}$, and thus capture some of the most essential properties of the field of real numbers, $\mathbb{R}$. [More formally, if K is a real closed field, then $K(\sqrt{-1})$ is algebraically closed.] With these preparations, we move on to *Sturm theory* in a rather general setting.

Next, we consider a particularly interesting subclass of real numbers, $\mathbb{R}$: the field of real algebraic numbers, $\mathbb{A}$. Both real *algebraic numbers and integers* are useful to computer scientists because they provide an effective way of representing infinite precision numbers that crop up in computations involving an algebraic formulation. In many situations, where it is paramount that the computed answers be *at least* topologically consistent (possibly incorrect)—a weaker requirement, which is nevertheless quite satisfactory in many situations—computing with algebraic numbers provides a practical solution.

Finally, we study how building up on Sturm theory and algebraic number representations one can devise a decision procedure for a wide class of geometric statements: the *Tarski sentences*. Roughly speaking, if such statements have a feasible real model, then they have a model that can be described by algebraic numbers and few auxiliary rational polynomials. Because algebraic numbers can be finitely described, the corresponding finite model can be sought for in a bounded amount of time.

Using these methods, one can consider the geometric objects defined by algebraic equations and inequations (i.e., semialgebraic sets), their decompositions (e.g., cylindrical algebraic decomposition), various topological properties (e.g., connectivity), triangulations, stratifications, etc. We only deal with some of the very basic problems in this field.

8.2   Real Closed Fields

We begin with a few definitions.

Definition 8.2.1 (Ordered Field) An *ordered field* K is a commutative field K together with a subset P, the set of positive elements, of K such that we obtain the following:

1. $0 \notin P$.

2. If $a \in K$, then either $a \in P$, $a = 0$, or $-a \in P$.

3. P is closed under addition and multiplication. If a, $b \in P$, then so are $a + b$ and $a\,b$.   □

Clearly, in a field K with a linear ordering $>$, one can identify P, the set of positive elements, as follows:

- If $a > 0$, we say a is *positive*; $P = \{a \in K \ : \ a > 0\}$.

- If $-a > 0$, we say a is *negative*; $N = \{a \in K \ : \ -a > 0\}$.

Therefore, $K = P \cup \{0\} \cup N$.

We can introduce an ordering in the ordered field K (or more precisely, $\langle K, P \rangle$) by defining

$$a > b \quad \text{if} \quad (a - b) \in P.$$

This ordering relation ">" is a strict linear ordering on the elements of K:

$$\text{(a)} \quad a > b \ \Rightarrow \ \left(\forall\, c \in K\right) \left[a + c > b + c\right]$$

$$\text{(b)} \quad a > b \ \Rightarrow \ \left(\forall\, c \in P\right) \left[a\,c > b\,c\right]$$

$$\text{(c)} \quad a > b, \ a > 0, \ b > 0 \ \Rightarrow \ b^{-1} > a^{-1}$$

Thus, we could have defined an ordered field in terms of a binary transitive relation $>$ as follows:

1. *Trichotomy*: $a = 0$ or $a > 0$ or $-a > 0$.

2. *Closure Under Additions and Multiplications*: $a > 0$ and $b > 0$ $\Rightarrow$ $ab > 0$ and $a + b > 0$.

In an ordered field, we can define various notions of intervals just as on the real line:

- *Closed Interval*:

$$[a, b] = \{x \in K : a \le x \le b\}.$$

- *Open Interval*:

$$(a, b) = \{x \in K : a < x < b\}.$$

- *Half-Open Intervals*:

$$(a, b] = \{x \in K : a < x \le b\} \quad \text{and} \quad [a, b) = \{x \in K : a \le x < b\}.$$

Definition 8.2.2 (Absolute Value) Absolute value of an element $a \in K$ is defined to be

$$|a| = \begin{cases} a, & \text{if } a \ge 0; \\ -a, & \text{if } a < 0. \end{cases}$$

(a) $|a + b| \le |a| + |b|$,
(b) $|a\, b| = |a|\, |b|$. $\square$

Definition 8.2.3 (Sign Function) The sign of an element $a \in K$ is defined to be

$$\operatorname{sgn}(a) = \begin{cases} +1, & \text{if } a > 0; \\ -1, & \text{if } a < 0; \\ 0, & \text{if } a = 0. \end{cases}$$

(a) $a = \operatorname{sgn}(a)\, |a|$ and $|a| = \operatorname{sgn}(a)\, a$.
(b) $\operatorname{sgn}(a\, b) = \operatorname{sgn}(a)\, \operatorname{sgn}(b)$. $\square$

In an ordered field K with 1,

$$-1 < 0 < 1,$$

since if $-1 > 0$ then $(-1) + (-1)^2 = 0 > 0$, which is impossible.
In any ordered field K,

$$a \ne 0 \implies a^2 = (-a)^2 = |a|^2 > 0 > -1.$$

Hence,

1. $\sqrt{-1} \notin K$.

2. If $a_1, a_2, \ldots, a_r$ are $\neq 0$, then $\sum a_i^2 > 0 > -1$, since

$$\sum a_i^2 = \sum |a_i^2| \geq \left| \sum a_i^2 \right| > 0,$$

and the relation $\sum a_i^2 = 0$ has the only solution $a_i = 0$, for all i. Additionally, we see that in an ordered field -1 cannot be expressed as a sum of squares.

The discussion above leads to the following definition:

Definition 8.2.4 (Formally Real Field) A field K is called *formally real* if the only relations in K of the form $\sum_{i=1}^{r} a_i^2 = 0$ are those for which every $a_i = 0$. ☐

From the preceding discussions we conclude that

Corollary 8.2.1

1. *Every ordered field is formally real.*
2. *K is formally real if and only if -1 is not a sum of squares of elements of K.*
3. *A formally real field is necessarily of characteristic zero.*

PROOF.
(1) See the preceding discussion.
(2) First note that if for some b_i's,

$$\sum_{i=1}^{n} b_i^2 = -1,$$

then the relation $(b_1)^2 + \cdots + (b_n)^2 + (1)^2 = 0$ is a nontrivial solution of the equation $\sum_{i=1}^{n+1} a_i^2 = 0$, and K is not a formally real field. Conversely, if K is not a formally real field, then for some set of nonzero $b_i \in K$ ($i = 0, \ldots, n$), we have

$$b_0^2 + b_1^2 + \cdots + b_n^2 = 0,$$

or

$$(b_1/b_0)^2 + \cdots + (b_n/b_0)^2 = -1.$$

Clearly, b_i/b_0 are defined and in K.
(3) Note that in a field of characteristic p, we have

$$\underbrace{1^2 + \cdots + 1^2}_{p\text{-many}} = 0. \quad ☐$$

Definition 8.2.5 (Induced Ordering) If K' is subfield of an ordered field $\langle K, P \rangle$, then K' is ordered relative to $P' = K' \cap P$. We call this the *induced ordering* in K'. $\square$

Definition 8.2.6 (Order Isomorphism) If $\langle K, P \rangle$ and $\langle K', P' \rangle$ are any two ordered fields, then an isomorphism η of K into K' is called an *order isomorphism* if $\eta(P) \subseteq P'$. This implies that $\eta(0) = 0$, $\eta(N) \subseteq N'$ and, if η is surjective, then $\eta(P) = P'$ and $\eta(N) = N'$. $\square$

Definition 8.2.7 (Archimedean Ordered Field) The ordering of a field is called *Archimedean* if for every field element a, there exists a natural number $n > a$, where n stands for

$$\underbrace{1 + \cdots + 1}_{n\text{-many}}. \quad \square$$

In this case there exists also a number $-n < a$ for every a, and a fraction $1/n < a$ for every positive a.

Note that the ordering of the field of rational numbers, $\mathbb{Q}$, is *Archimedean*. As an immediate corollary, we have:

Corollary 8.2.2 *For any two elements $a < b$ in an Archimedean ordered field, K, there are infinitely many points between a and b.*

PROOF.

First note that, in K, there is an infinite strictly increasing sequence of elements in K:

$$1 < n_1 < n_2 < n_3 < \cdots.$$

Let k be the smallest index such that $(b - a) > n_k^{-1}$, then

$$a < (b - n_k^{-1}) < (b - n_{k+1}^{-1}) < (b - n_{k+2}^{-1}) < \cdots$$

and each such element $(b - n_{k+j}^{-1})$ is between a and b. $\square$

Definition 8.2.8 (Real Closed Fields) We call an ordered field $\langle K, P \rangle$ *real closed*, if it has the following properties:

1. Every positive element of K has a square root in K.

2. Every polynomial $f(x) \in K[x]$ of odd degree has a root in K. $\square$

An alternative definition for a real closed field K is the following:

> K *is formally real and no proper algebraic extension of K is formally real.*

We will say more about this later. We state a fundamental result without proof.

Theorem 8.2.3 (Fundamental Theorem of Algebra) *If K is a real closed field, then $K(\sqrt{-1})$ is algebraically closed.* $\square$

An immediate corollary of the *fundamental theorem of algebra* is the following:

Corollary 8.2.4 *The monic irreducible polynomials in $K[x]$ ($K = $ real closed) are either of degree one or two.* $\square$

Furthermore, if K is real closed, then its subfield of elements which are algebraic over $\mathbb{Q}$ ($\subset \mathbb{R}$) is real closed. As before, in a real closed field, we write $b > a$ for $b - a \in P$.

A classical example of a real closed field is, of course, $\mathbb{R}$, the field of real numbers.

Lemma 8.2.5 *A degree two monic polynomial $x^2 + ax + b \in K[x]$ over a real closed field, K, is irreducible if and only if $a^2 < 4b$.*

PROOF.

Write the degree two monic polynomial in the following form:

$$x^2 + ax + b = \left(x + \frac{a}{2}\right)^2 + (4b - a^2).$$

The proof is by following the three possible cases:

Case (1): $4b > a^2$.

$$4b > a^2 \Rightarrow x^2 + ax + b = \left(x + \frac{a}{2}\right)^2 + \left(\frac{c}{2}\right)^2$$

[Note that, by definition, c exists, since $4b - a^2 \in P$ and K is real closed. Also $c^2 = |c|^2 > 0$.]

$$\Rightarrow \left(\forall\, x \in K\right)\left[x^2 + ax + b > 0\right]$$
$$\Rightarrow x^2 + ax + b \ = \ \text{irreducible.}$$

Case (2): $4b = a^2$.

$$4b = a^2 \ \Rightarrow \ x^2 + ax + b = \left(x + \frac{a}{2}\right)^2$$
$$\Rightarrow \ x^2 + ax + b \ = \ \text{reducible.}$$

Case (3): $4b < a^2$.

$$4b < a^2 \ \Rightarrow \ a^2 - 4b \in P$$
$$\Rightarrow \ \left(\exists\, c \in K, c \neq 0\right)[c^2 = a^2 - 4b]$$
$$\Rightarrow \ x^2 + ax + b = \left(x + \frac{a}{2}\right)^2 - \left(\frac{c}{2}\right)^2$$
$$\Rightarrow \ x^2 + ax + b \ = \ \text{reducible.} \quad \square$$

Lemma 8.2.6 *A real closed field has a unique ordering endowing it with the structure of an ordered field. That is, any automorphism of a real closed field is an order isomorphism.*

PROOF.
Consider a real closed field K, and let K^2 be the set of elements consisting of squares of nonzero elements of K. Now, consider $\langle K, P \rangle$, some arbitrary ordered field structure on K.

We know that $K^2 \subseteq P$. Conversely, select an element $b \in P$; by definition, for some $a \in K$, $(a \neq 0)$ $a^2 = b$. Hence, $b \in K^2$, and $K^2 = P$.

The unique ordering is then given by $>$, with $b > a$ if and only if $b - a \in K^2$. $\square$

It is now useful to go back to the alternative definition:

Theorem 8.2.7 *An ordered field K is* real closed *if and only if*

1. *K is formally real, and*

2. *no proper algebraic extension of K is formally real.*

PROOF.
($\Rightarrow$) Since every ordered field is necessarily formally real, the first condition is easily satisfied.

We only need to consider extensions of the kind $K(\sqrt{\gamma})$, where $x^2 - \gamma$ is an irreducible polynomial in K. Thus $0 < -4\gamma$, or $\gamma \notin K^2$, the set of squares of nonzero elements of K. Hence $-\gamma \in K^2$ and $-\gamma = a^2$. But then in $K(\sqrt{\gamma})$,

$$\left(\frac{\sqrt{\gamma}}{a} \right)^2 = -1,$$

thus showing that $K(\sqrt{\gamma})$ is not formally real.

($\Leftarrow$) In the converse direction, first consider the field K with the ordering defined by $P = K^2$ (where K^2, as before, denotes the squares of the nonzero elements in K). There are essentially two objectives: First, to prove that $\langle K, K^2 \rangle$ is an ordered field; second, to show that every polynomial equation of odd degree is solvable. We proceed in order.

The only difficult part is to show that for every $a \in K$ $(a \neq 0)$, either $a \in K^2$ or $-a \in K^2$. Other conditions are trivially satisfied since the sums of squares are squares and the products of squares are obviously squares. Suppose a is not a square, then $x^2 - a$ is irreducible and $K(\sqrt{a})$ is not formally real, i.e.,

$$
\begin{aligned}
-1 &= \sum (\alpha_i + \beta_i \sqrt{a})^2 \\
&= \sum \alpha_i^2 + a \sum \beta_i^2 + 2\sqrt{a} \sum \alpha_i \beta_i.
\end{aligned}
$$

But then the last term should vanish, since otherwise $\sqrt{a}$ would be a zero of the following polynomial in $K[x]$:

$$x^2 \sum \beta_i^2 + 2x \sum \alpha_i \beta_i + \left(1 + \sum \alpha_i^2\right) = 0.$$

Thus

$$-a = \frac{1 + \sum \alpha_i^2}{\sum \beta_i^2} \in K^2,$$

as both numerator and denominator are in K^2.

The second part is shown by contradiction. Consider the smallest odd degree irreducible polynomial $f(x) \in K[x]$. [Clearly, $\deg(f) > 1$.] Let ξ be a root of f; then $K(\xi)$ is not formally real:

$$-1 = \sum g_i(\xi)^2,$$

where $\deg(g_i) < \deg(f)$. Then we see that

$$-1 = \sum g_i(x)^2 + h(x)f(x),$$

by virtue of the isomorphism between $K(\xi)$ and $K[x]/(f(x))$. By examining the above identity, we see that h is of odd degree and $\deg(h) < \deg(f)$. Now substituting a root ξ' of h, in to the above equation, we get

$$-1 = \sum g_i(\xi')^2.$$

We conclude that h is irreducible and that our original choice of f leads to a contradiction. ☐

Theorem 8.2.8 *Let K be a real closed field and $f(x) \in K[x]$. If a, $b \in K$ ($a < b$) and $f(a)\,f(b) < 0$, then there exists a root of $f(x)$ which lies between a and b, i.e.,*

$$\Big(\exists\, c \in (a,b)\Big)\ \Big[f(c) = 0\Big].$$

PROOF.
Assume $f(x)$ is monic. Then $f(x)$ factors in $K[x]$ as

$$f(x) = (x - r_1) \cdots (x - r_m) \cdot g_1(x) \cdots g_s(x),$$

where each $g_i(x) = x^2 + c_i x + d_i$ is, by an earlier corollary, an irreducible monic polynomial of degree 2 and

$$\Big(\forall\, u \in K\Big)\ \Big[g_i(u) > 0\Big],$$

i.e., the quadratic factors are always nonnegative. We know that

$$\Big(\forall\, 1 \le i \le m\Big)\ \Big[a \ne r_i \text{ and } b \ne r_i\Big],$$

since $f(a) f(b) \neq 0$.

Let us now consider the effect of each root r_i on

$$f(a) f(b) = \prod (a - r_i)(b - r_i) \times \text{some nonnegative value,}$$

$$
\begin{array}{lll}
a < r_i \wedge b < r_i & \Rightarrow & (a - r_i)(b - r_i) > 0, \\
a > r_i \wedge b > r_i & \Rightarrow & (a - r_i)(b - r_i) > 0, \\
a < r_i \wedge b > r_i & \Rightarrow & (a - r_i)(b - r_i) < 0.
\end{array}
$$

This implies that if a root lies between a and b, then it contributes a negative sign to $f(a) f(b)$; and if r_i does not lie between a and b, then it does not affect the sign of $f(a) f(b)$.

Hence $f(a) f(b) < 0$ implies that there exist an odd number (and hence at least one) of roots of $f(x)$ between a and b. $\square$

Corollary 8.2.9 *Let K be a real closed field and $f(x) \in K[x]$ such that $f(c) > 0$. Then it is possible to choose an interval $[a, b]$ containing c such that*

$$\Big(\forall\, u \in [a, b] \Big) \Big[f(u) > 0 \Big]. \quad \square$$

Theorem 8.2.10 (Rolle's Theorem) *Let K be a real closed field and $f(x) \in K[x]$. If a, $b \in K$ $(a < b)$ and $f(a) = f(b) = 0$, then*

$$\Big(\exists\, c \in (a, b) \Big) \Big[D(f)(c) = 0 \Big],$$

where D denotes the formal differentiation operator.

PROOF.

Without loss of generality assume that a and b are two consecutive roots of the monic polynomial $f(x)$, of respective multiplicities m and n:

$$f(x) = (x - a)^m (x - b)^n g(x).$$

Now

$$D(f)(x) = (x - a)^{m-1} (x - b)^{n-1} \bar{g}(x),$$

where $\bar{g}(x)$ is given by

$$\bar{g}(x) = [m(x - b) + n(x - a)]g(x) + (x - a)(x - b)D(g)(x).$$

Now, note that

$$\bar{g}(a)\bar{g}(b) = -mn(a - b)^2 g(a)g(b) < 0,$$

as by assumption g does not have a root in (a, b), and $\text{sgn}(g(u))$ is unchanged for all $u \in [a, b]$.

Now by our previous theorem:

$$\Big(\exists\, c \in (a, b) \Big) \Big[\bar{g}(c) = 0 \Big].$$

Hence $D(f)(c) = (c - a)^{m-1}(c - b)^{n-1}\bar{g}(c) = 0$. $\square$

8.3   Bounds on the Roots

Given a polynomial f, we obtain bounds on its roots by showing that every root u must be in an interval $u \in (M_1, M_2)$, or equivalently

$$\Big(\forall \, u \notin (M_1, M_2) \Big) \Big[f(u) \neq 0 \Big].$$

We set out to find such M_1 and M_2 as functions of the *sizes* of the coefficients. Note that then, $|M_1| = |M_2|$, since if u is a zero of $f(x)$, $-u$ is a zero of $\tilde{f}(x) = f(-x)$ and the sizes of f and $\tilde{f}$ are same. Thus, we seek bounds of the kind $|u| < M$ for the roots u of f.

Theorem 8.3.1 *Let K be an ordered field, and*

$$f(x) = x^n + a_{n-1}x^{n-1} + \cdots + a_0,$$

a monic polynomial with coefficients in K. Let M and N denote the followings:

$$\begin{aligned} M = M(f) &= \max(1, |a_{n-1}| + \cdots + |a_0|), \\ N = N(f) &= 1 + \max(|a_{n-1}|, \ldots, |a_0|). \end{aligned}$$

1. If $|u| \geq M$, then $|f(u)| > 0$.

2. If $|u| \geq N$, then $|f(u)| > 0$.

PROOF.

First note that

$$\Big(\forall \, u \Big) \Big[|f(u)| \geq 0 \Big].$$

We may only consider a root u of f, $|u| > 1$. Note that

$$\begin{aligned} f(u) = 0 &\Rightarrow& f(u) = u^n + a_{n-1}u^{n-1} + \cdots + a_0 = 0 \\ &\Rightarrow& |u|^n \leq |a_{n-1}| \cdot |u|^{n-1} + \cdots + |a_0|. \end{aligned}$$

Thus,

(1) $|u|^n \leq |a_{n-1}| \cdot |u|^{n-1} + \cdots + |a_0|$

$\Rightarrow |u|^n < M \cdot |u|^{n-1}$

$\Rightarrow |u| < M.$

(2) $|u|^n \leq |a_{n-1}| \cdot |u|^{n-1} + \cdots + |a_0|$

$\Rightarrow |u|^n \leq (N-1) \cdot (|u|^{n-1} + \cdots + 1) < \dfrac{(N-1) \cdot |u|^n}{|u| - 1}$

$\Rightarrow |u| - 1 < N - 1$

$\Rightarrow |u| < N.$ $\square$

Hence,

$$\Big(\forall \, |u| \geq M, |u| \geq N \Big) \Big[|f(u)| > 0 \Big]. \quad \square$$

The corollary below follows:

Corollary 8.3.2 (Cauchy's Inequality) *Let*

$$f(x) = a_n x^n + a_{n-1} x^{n-1} + \cdots + a_0.$$

be a polynomial over K, an ordered field.
  Then any nonzero root u of f must satisfy the followings:

(1) $\dfrac{|a_0|}{|a_0| + \max(|a_n|, \ldots, |a_1|)} \; < \; |u| \; < \; \dfrac{|a_n| + \max(|a_{n-1}|, \ldots, |a_0|)}{|a_n|}$;

(2) $\dfrac{\min(f)}{\min(f) + \max(f)} \; < \; |u| \; < \; \dfrac{\min(f) + \max(f)}{\min(f)}$,

where

$$\min(f) = \min\{|a_i| : a_i \neq 0\} \quad and \quad \max(f) = \max\{|a_i| : a_i \neq 0\}.$$

PROOF.
This is a direct consequence of the preceding theorem. Assume, without loss of generality, that u is a nonzero root of $f(x)$

$$f(x) = a_n x^n + a_{n-1} x^{n-1} + \cdots + a_m x^m, \qquad a_{m-1} = \cdots = a_0 = 0.$$

Then clearly, u is a root of

$$a_n x^{n-m} + a_{n-1} x^{n-m-1} + \cdots + a_m,$$

and u^{-1} is a root of

$$a_m x^{n-m} + a_{m+1} x^{n-m-1} + \cdots + a_n.$$

Using the preceding theorem:

$$|u| < \frac{|a_n| + \max(|a_{n-1}|, \ldots, |a_m|)}{|a_n|} \leq \frac{\min(f) + \max(f)}{\min(f)},$$

and

$$|u^{-1}| < \frac{|a_m| + \max(|a_{m+1}|, \ldots, |a_n|)}{|a_m|} \leq \frac{\min(f) + \max(f)}{\min(f)}.$$

As a result, we have

$$\frac{|a_m|}{|a_m| + \max(|a_n|, \ldots, |a_{m+1}|)} < |u| < \frac{|a_n| + \max(|a_{n-1}|, \ldots, |a_m|)}{|a_n|},$$

and

$$\frac{\min(f)}{\min(f) + \max(f)} < |u| < \frac{\min(f) + \max(f)}{\min(f)}. \qquad \square$$

Using Cauchy's and Landau's inequalities, we can prove the following useful theorem:

Theorem 8.3.3 *Let $f(x) \in \mathbb{Z}[x]$ be an integral polynomial*

$$f(x) = a_n x^n + a_{n-1} x^{n-1} + \cdots + a_0.$$

Let

$$
\begin{aligned}
\|f\|_1 &= |a_n| + |a_{n-1}| + \cdots + |a_0|, \\
\|f\|_2 &= (a_n^2 + a_{n-1}^2 + \cdots + a_0^2)^{\frac{1}{2}}, \qquad and \\
\|f\|_\infty &= \max(|a_n|, |a_{n-1}|, \ldots, |a_0|).
\end{aligned}
$$

Then all the real roots of f are in the intervals $(-\|f\|_1, \|f\|_1)$, $[-\|f\|_2, \|f\|_2]$ and $(-1 - \|f\|_\infty, 1 + \|f\|_\infty)$.

Also for every nonzero real root u of f,

$$|u| > \frac{1}{1 + \|f\|_\infty}.$$

PROOF.

(1) All the real roots of f are in the intervals $(-\|f\|_1, \|f\|_1)$.
Since $f(x)$ is integral (i.e., if $a_i \neq 0$, then $|a_i| \geq 1$),

$$
\begin{aligned}
\|f\|_1 &= |a_n| + |a_{n-1}| + \cdots + |a_0| \\
&\geq 1 + |a_{n-1}| + \cdots + |a_0| \\
&\geq \max\left(1, \left|\frac{a_{n-1}}{a_n}\right| + \cdots + \left|\frac{a_0}{a_n}\right|\right),
\end{aligned}
$$

which is no other than the M of Theorem 8.3.1.

(2) All the real roots of f are in the intervals $(-1 - \|f\|_\infty, 1 + \|f\|_\infty)$. As before, we use the fact that, if $a_i \neq 0$, then $|a_i| \geq 1$.

$$
\begin{aligned}
1 + \|f\|_\infty &= 1 + \max(|a_n|, |a_{n-1}|, \ldots, |a_0|) \\
&\geq 1 + \max(1, |a_{n-1}|, \ldots, |a_0|) \\
&\geq 1 + \max\left(\left|\frac{a_{n-1}}{a_n}\right|, \ldots, \left|\frac{a_0}{a_n}\right|\right),
\end{aligned}
$$

which equals the N of Theorem 8.3.1.

(3) All the real roots of f are in the intervals $[-\|f\|_2, \|f\|_2]$. This is a direct consequence of *Landau's inequality*, which states that if $\alpha_1, \alpha_2, \ldots, \alpha_k$ are roots of f, then

$$|a_n| \prod \max(1, \alpha_i) \leq \|f\|_2. \qquad \square$$

8.4   Sturm's Theorem

Consider a polynomial $f(x) \in K[x]$ where K is a real closed field. A classical technique due to Sturm shows how to compute the real zeros of $f(x)$ in an interval $[a, b]$. The recipe is as follows:

1. First compute a special sequence of polynomials $\overline{\text{STURM}}(f) = \langle h_0(x) = f(x), h_1(x), \ldots, h_s(x) \rangle$, which will be called a *Sturm sequence*.

2. Next compute the "variations in sign" for the sequences $\overline{\text{STURM}}(f)(a) = \langle h_0(a), h_1(a), \ldots, h_s(a) \rangle$ and $\overline{\text{STURM}}(f)(b) = \langle h_0(b), h_1(b), \ldots, h_s(b) \rangle$—denoted, respectively, by $\text{Var}_a(\overline{\text{STURM}}(f))$ and $\text{Var}_b(\overline{\text{STURM}}(f))$.

3. Then

$$\# \text{ real zeros of } f(x) \text{ in } (a, b) \;=\; \text{Var}_a(\overline{\text{STURM}}(f)) - \text{Var}_b(\overline{\text{STURM}}(f)).$$

However, these notions need to be formalized further. In this section, we shall start with a slightly general version of the statement above: the *Sturm-Tarski theorem*. Later on we shall study some generalizations to higher dimensions.

Definition 8.4.1 (Variations in Sign) If $\bar{c} = \langle c_1, \ldots, c_m \rangle$ is a finite sequence of nonzero elements of a real closed field K, then we define the *number of variations in sign* of $\bar{c}$ to be

$$\left| \left\{ i : 1 \leq i < m \text{ and } c_i \cdot c_{i+1} < 0 \right\} \right|.$$

In general, If $\bar{c} = \langle c_1, \ldots, c_m \rangle$ is an arbitrary sequence of elements of K, then we define the *number of variations in sign* of $\bar{c}$, denoted $\text{Var}(\bar{c})$, to be the number of variations in the sign of the abbreviated sequence $\text{abb}(\bar{c})$, which is obtained by omitting the zeros in $\bar{c}$.

Thus, $\text{Var}(\bar{c})$ is the number of times the entries of $\bar{c}$ change sign when scanned sequentially from left to right. $\square$

For example, $\langle 1, 0, 0, 2, -1, 0, 3, 4, -2 \rangle$ has three variations in sign. Note that for any nonzero $a \in K$

$$\text{Var}(\bar{c}) = \text{Var}(a\,\bar{c}),$$

where $a \langle c_1, \ldots, c_m \rangle = \langle a\,c_1, \ldots, a\,c_m \rangle$. Similarly, if $c_i \cdot c_{i+1} < 0$ then for any $a \in K$

$$\text{Var}(\langle c_1, \ldots, c_i, c_{i+1}, \ldots, c_m \rangle) \;=\; \text{Var}(\langle c_1, \ldots, c_i, a, c_{i+1}, \ldots, c_m \rangle).$$

For a vector of polynomials $\overline{F} = \langle f_1(x), \ldots, f_m(x) \rangle \in K[x]^m$ and a field element $a \in K$, we write $\text{Var}_a(\overline{F})$ for $\text{Var}(\overline{F}(a))$:

$$\text{Var}_a(\overline{F}) \;=\; \text{Var}(\overline{F}(a)) \;=\; \text{Var}(\langle f_1(a), \ldots, f_m(a) \rangle).$$

Definition 8.4.2 (Standard Sturm Sequence) The *standard Sturm sequence* (or, *canonical Sturm sequence*) of a pair of polynomials $f(x)$ and $g(x) \in K[x]$ (K = a field) is

$$\overline{\text{STURM}}(f, g) = \Big\langle h_0(x), h_1(x), \ldots, h_s(x) \Big\rangle,$$

where

$$
\begin{aligned}
h_0(x) &= f(x) \\
h_1(x) &= g(x) \\
h_0(x) &= q_1(x)\, h_1(x) - h_2(x), && \deg(h_2) < \deg(h_1) \\
&\;\;\vdots \\
h_{i-1}(x) &= q_i(x)\, h_i(x) - h_{i+1}(x), && \deg(h_{i+1}) < \deg(h_i) \\
&\;\;\vdots \\
h_{s-1}(x) &= q_s(x)\, h_s(x). && \square
\end{aligned}
$$

Note that the standard sequence is termwise similar to the polynomial remainder sequence, except that we take the negation of the remainder at each step, i.e., it is based on the sequence $\langle 1,\ 1,\ -1,\ -1,\ \ldots \rangle$. Also note that for any $f(x)$ and $g(x)$, the last element in their standard Sturm sequence, $\overline{\text{STURM}}(f, g)$, is in fact their GCD (up to a sign); in particular, $h_s(x) \mid h_i(x)$ ($0 \le i \le s$). In this case, we may consider their *"suppressed"* Sturm sequence,

$$\tilde{h}_i(x) = \frac{h_i(x)}{h_s(x)}.$$

Note, $\tilde{h}_s(x) = 1$. Furthermore, for any $i > 0$, we also have

$$\tilde{h}_{i-1}(x) = q_i(x)\, \tilde{h}_i(x) - \tilde{h}_{i+1}(x).$$

Lemma 8.4.1 *Let $f(x)$ and $g(x) \in K[x]$, K = a real closed field, be a pair of polynomials with a standard Sturm sequence,*

$$\overline{\text{STURM}}(f, g) = H = \Big\langle h_0(x), h_1(x), \ldots, h_s(x) \Big\rangle.$$

Let $[a, b]$ be an interval ($a < b$) not containing a zero of $f(x) = h_0(x)$. Then

$$\text{Var}_a(\overline{\text{STURM}}(f, g)) - \text{Var}_b(\overline{\text{STURM}}(f, g)) = 0.$$

PROOF.
Let us consider an arbitrary subinterval $[a', b'] \subseteq [a, b]$ such that it contains *at most one zero* of the suppressed sequence

$$\widetilde{H} = \langle \tilde{h}_0(x), \tilde{h}_1(x), \ldots, \tilde{h}_s(x) \rangle.$$

It suffices to show that

$$\text{Var}_{a'}(\overline{\text{STURM}}(f, g)) - \text{Var}_{b'}(\overline{\text{STURM}}(f, g)) = 0.$$

Since the interval does not contain a zero of h_0, nor does it contain a zero of $\tilde{h}_0$.

Now, if the interval does not contain a zero of any element of $\tilde{H}$, then $\tilde{h}_i(a') \, \tilde{h}_i(b') > 0$ for all i and

$$\text{Var}_{a'}(\widetilde{H}) - \text{Var}_{b'}(\widetilde{H}) = 0.$$

Alternatively, assume that the interval contains a zero of $\tilde{h}_i \in \tilde{H}$, i.e., for some $c \in [a', b']$, $\tilde{h}_i(c) = 0$ $(i > 0)$. Then

$$\tilde{h}_{i-1}(c) \;=\; q_i(c) \, \tilde{h}_i(c) - \tilde{h}_{i+1}(c) \;=\; -\tilde{h}_{i+1}(c)$$
$$\Rightarrow\; \tilde{h}_{i-1}(c) \, \tilde{h}_{i+1}(c) \;=\; -\tilde{h}_{i+1}^2(c) \;<\; 0.$$

Since $\tilde{h}_{i+1}(c) = 0$ would imply that $\tilde{h}_i(c) = \tilde{h}_{i+1}(c) = \cdots = \tilde{h}_s(c) = 0$, contradicting the fact that $\tilde{h}_s = 1$. Thus,

$$\tilde{h}_{i-1}(c) \cdot \tilde{h}_{i+1}(c) < 0$$
$$\Rightarrow\; \tilde{h}_{i-1}(a') \cdot \tilde{h}_{i+1}(a') < 0 \;\wedge\; \tilde{h}_{i-1}(b') \cdot \tilde{h}_{i+1}(b') < 0,$$

which results in

$$\begin{aligned}
\text{Var}_{a'}(\widetilde{H}) &= \text{Var}(\tilde{h}_0(a'), \ldots, \tilde{h}_{i-1}(a'), \tilde{h}_{i+1}(a'), \ldots, \tilde{h}_s(a')) \\
&= \text{Var}(\tilde{h}_0(b'), \ldots, \tilde{h}_{i-1}(b'), \tilde{h}_{i+1}(b'), \ldots, \tilde{h}_s(b')) \\
&= \text{Var}_{b'}(\widetilde{H}).
\end{aligned}$$

Thus, in either case

$$\text{Var}_{a'}(\widetilde{H}) - \text{Var}_{b'}(\widetilde{H}) = 0.$$

Thus

$$\begin{aligned}
\text{Var}_{a'}&(\overline{\text{STURM}}(f, g)) - \text{Var}_{b'}(\overline{\text{STURM}}(f, g)) \\
&= \text{Var}_{a'}(h_s(a') \, \widetilde{H}) - \text{Var}_{b'}(h_s(b') \, \widetilde{H}) \\
&= \text{Var}_{a'}(\widetilde{H}) - \text{Var}_{b'}(\widetilde{H}) \\
&= 0.
\end{aligned}$$

Clearly, the interval $[a, b]$ can be partitioned into finitely many subintervals such that over each subinterval there is no net change in the variation, thus proving that there is no net change over the entire interval $[a, b]$, either. $\square$

Let $D: K[x] \to K[x]$ be the (formal) derivative map:

$$\begin{aligned}
D \;&:\; x^n \mapsto n \cdot x^{n-1} \\
&:\; a \mapsto 0, \qquad a \in K.
\end{aligned}$$

Assume that $f(x) \in K[x]$ is an arbitrary polynomial over a real closed field K and $f'(x) = D(f(x))$ its *formal derivative* with respect to x.

Lemma 8.4.2 *Let $f(x)$ and $g(x) \in K[x]$, $K = $ a real closed field. Consider a standard Sturm sequence of the polynomials $f(x)$ and $f'(x) g(x)$,*

$$\overline{\text{STURM}}(f, f'g) = H = \Big\langle h_0(x), h_1(x), \dots, h_s(x) \Big\rangle.$$

Let $[a, b]$ be an interval $(a < b)$ containing exactly one zero $c \in (a, b)$ of $f(x) = h_0(x)$. Then

$$\text{Var}_a(\overline{\text{STURM}}(f, f'g)) - \text{Var}_b(\overline{\text{STURM}}(f, f'g)) = \text{sgn}(g(c)).$$

PROOF.

Without loss of generality, we may assume that none of the $h_i(x)$'s vanish in either of the half-open intervals: $[a, c)$ and $(c, b]$.

Let us write $f(x)$ and $g(x)$ as follows:

$$f(x) = (x - c)^r \, \phi(x) \quad \text{and} \quad g(x) = (x - c)^s \, \psi(x), \qquad r > 0, \;\; s \geq 0,$$

where, by assumption, we have $\phi(c) \neq 0$ and $\psi(c) \neq 0$.

Then,

$$f'(x) = (x - c)^{r-1} \left[r\phi(x) + (x - c)\phi'(x) \right].$$

Thus

$$f(x) \, f'(x) g(x) = (x - c)^{2r+s-1} \left[r\phi^2(x)\psi(x) + (x - c)\phi(x)\phi'(x)\psi(x) \right].$$

Now, we are ready to consider each of the cases:

- CASE 1: $s = 0$, i.e., $g(c) \neq 0$.

  In that case,

  $$f(x) \, f'(x) g(x) = (x - c)^{2r-1} \left[r\phi^2(x)\psi(x) + (x - c)\phi(x)\phi'(x)\psi(x) \right],$$

  an *odd function* of x in the neighborhood of $c \in [a, b]$. If $g(c) > 0$, then in the neighborhood of c,

  $$f(x)f'(x)g(x) = (x - c)^{2r-1}[k_+ + \epsilon],$$

  where $k_+ = r\phi^2(c)\psi(c) > 0$. Thus to the left of c, $f(x)$ and $f'(x)g(x)$ have opposite signs and to the right same signs, implying a *loss of sign* as one moves from left to right past c:

  $$\text{Var}_a(\overline{\text{STURM}}(f, f'g)) - \text{Var}_b(\overline{\text{STURM}}(f, f'g)) = +1.$$

  Similarly, if $g(c) < 0$, then in the neighborhood of c,

  $$f(x)f'(x)g(x) = (x - c)^{2r-1}[k_- + \epsilon],$$

  where $k_- = r\phi^2(c)\psi(c) < 0$. Thus to the left of c $f(x)$ and $f'(x)g(x)$ have same signs and to the right opposite signs, implying a *gain of sign*:

  $$\text{Var}_a(\overline{\text{STURM}}(f, f'g)) - \text{Var}_b(\overline{\text{STURM}}(f, f'g)) = -1.$$

- CASE 2: $s > 0$, i.e., $g(c) = 0$.

  1. SUBCASE 2A: $s = 1$.
     In this case

     $$h_0(x) = f(x) \quad = \quad (x - c)^r \, \phi(x), \quad \text{and}$$
     $$h_1(x) = f'(x)g(x) \quad = \quad (x - c)^r \, [r\phi(x)\psi(x) + (x - c)\phi'(x)\psi(x)].$$

     Thus

     $$\tilde{h}_0(x) \quad = \quad \frac{h_0(x)}{(x - c)^r} \quad = \quad \phi(x),$$
     $$\tilde{h}_1(x) \quad = \quad \frac{h_1(x)}{(x - c)^r} \quad = \quad r\phi(x)\psi(x) + (x - c)\phi'(x)\psi(x).$$

     Hence the suppressed sequence has no zero in the interval $[a, b]$, and thus the suppressed sequence undergoes no net variation of signs. Arguing as in the previous lemma, we have:

     $$\text{Var}_a(\overline{\text{STURM}}(f, f'g)) - \text{Var}_b(\overline{\text{STURM}}(f, f'g)) = 0.$$

  2. SUBCASE 2B: $s > 1$.
     In this case $\deg(h_0) = \deg(f) < \deg(f'g) = \deg(h_1)$; thus,

     $$h_2(x) = h_0(x),$$

     i.e., the first and third entry in the sequence have exactly the opposite signs. Again considering the suppressed sequence, we see that the suppressed sequence (and hence the original sequence) suffers zero net variation of signs. Hence:

     $$\text{Var}_a(\overline{\text{STURM}}(f, f'g)) - \text{Var}_b(\overline{\text{STURM}}(f, f'g)) = 0. \quad \square$$

Theorem 8.4.3 (General Sturm-Tarski Theorem) *Let $f(x)$ and $g(x)$ be two polynomials with coefficients in a real closed field K and let*

$$\overline{\text{STURM}}(f, f'g) \quad = \Big\langle \quad \begin{aligned} &h_0(x) = f(x), \\ &h_1(x) = f'(x)g(x), \\ &h_2(x), \\ &\vdots \\ &h_s(x) \end{aligned} \Big\rangle,$$

where h_i's are related by the following relations $(i > 0)$:

$$h_{i-1}(x) = q_i(x)\, h_i(x) - h_{i+1}(x), \qquad \deg(h_{i+1}) < \deg(h_i).$$

Then for any interval $[a, b] \subseteq K$ $(a < b)$:

$$\mathrm{Var}\left[\overline{\mathrm{STURM}}(f, f'g)\right]_a^b \;=\; c_f\left[g > 0\right]_a^b - c_f\left[g < 0\right]_a^b,$$

where

$$\mathrm{Var}\left[\overline{\mathrm{STURM}}(f, f'g)\right]_a^b \;\triangleq\; \mathrm{Var}_a(\overline{\mathrm{STURM}}(f, f'g)) - \mathrm{Var}_b(\overline{\mathrm{STURM}}(f, f'g)).$$

and $c_f[P]_a^b$ counts the number of distinct roots ($\in K$, and without counting multiplicity) of f in the interval $(a, b) \subseteq K$ at which the predicate P holds.

PROOF.
Take all the roots of all the polynomials $h_j(x)$'s in the Sturm sequence, and decompose the interval $[a, b]$ into finitely many subintervals each containing at most one of these roots.

The rest follows from the preceding two lemmas, since

$$\mathrm{Var}\left[\overline{\mathrm{STURM}}(f, f'g)\right]_a^b \;=\; \sum_{c \in (a,b),\; f(c)=0} \mathrm{sgn}(g(c)). \qquad \square$$

Corollary 8.4.4 *Let $f(x)$ be a polynomial with coefficients in a real closed field K.*

$$f(x) = a_n x^n + a_{n-1} x^{n-1} + \cdots + a_0.$$

Then

1. For any interval $[a, b] \subseteq K$ $(a < b)$:

$$\mathrm{Var}\left[\overline{\mathrm{STURM}}(f, f')\right]_a^b$$
$$= \quad \#\textit{distinct roots} \in K \textit{ of } f \textit{ in the interval } (a, b).$$

2. Let $L \in K$ be such that all the roots of $f(x)$ are in the interval $(-L, +L)$; e.g.,

$$L = \frac{|a_n| + \max(|a_{n-1}|, \ldots, |a_0|)}{|a_n|}.$$

Then the total number of distinct roots of f in K is given by

$$\mathrm{Var}\left[\overline{\mathrm{STURM}}(f, f')\right]_{-L}^{+L} = \mathrm{Var}_{-L}(\overline{\mathrm{STURM}}(f, f')) - \mathrm{Var}_{+L}(\overline{\mathrm{STURM}}(f, f')).$$

PROOF.
(1) The first part is a corollary of the preceding theorem, with g taken to be the constant positive function 1.

(2) The second part follows from the first, once we observe that all the roots of f lie in the interval $[-L, +L]$. $\square$

Corollary 8.4.5 *Let $f(x)$ and $g(x)$ be two polynomials with coefficients in a real closed field K, and assume that*

$$f(x) \text{ and } f'(x)g(x) \text{ are relatively prime.}$$

Then

$$\mathrm{Var}\left[\overline{\mathrm{STURM}}(f,g)\right]_a^b = c_f\left[(f'g) > 0\right]_a^b - c_f\left[(f'g) < 0\right]_a^b. \quad \square$$

Corollary 8.4.6 *Let $f(x)$ and $g(x)$ be two polynomials with coefficients in a real closed field K. For any interval $[a,b] \subseteq K$ $(a < b)$, we have*

$$c_f\left[g = 0\right]_a^b + c_f\left[g > 0\right]_a^b + c_f\left[g < 0\right]_a^b = \mathrm{Var}\left[\overline{\mathrm{STURM}}(f,f')\right]_a^b,$$

$$c_f\left[g > 0\right]_a^b - c_f\left[g < 0\right]_a^b = \mathrm{Var}\left[\overline{\mathrm{STURM}}(f,f'g)\right]_a^b,$$

$$c_f\left[g > 0\right]_a^b + c_f\left[g < 0\right]_a^b = \mathrm{Var}\left[\overline{\mathrm{STURM}}(f,f'g^2)\right]_a^b. \quad \square$$

Thus the previous corollary can be expressed as follows,

$$\begin{bmatrix} 1 & 1 & 1 \\ 0 & 1 & -1 \\ 0 & 1 & 1 \end{bmatrix} \begin{bmatrix} c_f\left[g = 0\right]_a^b \\ c_f\left[g > 0\right]_a^b \\ c_f\left[g < 0\right]_a^b \end{bmatrix} = \begin{bmatrix} \mathrm{Var}\left[\overline{\mathrm{STURM}}(f,f')\right]_a^b \\ \mathrm{Var}\left[\overline{\mathrm{STURM}}(f,f'g)\right]_a^b \\ \mathrm{Var}\left[\overline{\mathrm{STURM}}(f,f'g^2)\right]_a^b \end{bmatrix},$$

or equivalently:

$$\begin{bmatrix} 1 & 0 & -1 \\ 0 & \frac{1}{2} & \frac{1}{2} \\ 0 & -\frac{1}{2} & \frac{1}{2} \end{bmatrix} \begin{bmatrix} \mathrm{Var}\left[\overline{\mathrm{STURM}}(f,f')\right]_a^b \\ \mathrm{Var}\left[\overline{\mathrm{STURM}}(f,f'g)\right]_a^b \\ \mathrm{Var}\left[\overline{\mathrm{STURM}}(f,f'g^2)\right]_a^b \end{bmatrix} = \begin{bmatrix} c_f\left[g = 0\right]_a^b \\ c_f\left[g > 0\right]_a^b \\ c_f\left[g < 0\right]_a^b \end{bmatrix}.$$

8.5   Real Algebraic Numbers

In this section, we study how real algebraic numbers may be described and manipulated. We shall introduce some machinery for this purpose, i.e., root separation and Thom's lemma.

8.5.1　Real Algebraic Number Field

Consider a field E. Let F be subfield in E. An element $u \in E$ is said to be *algebraic* over F if for some nonzero polynomial $f(x) \in F[x]$, $f(u) = 0$; otherwise, it is *transcendental* over F.

Similarly, let S be a subring of E. An element $u \in E$ is said to be *integral* over S if for some monic polynomial $f(x) \in S[x]$, $f(u) = 0$.

For example, if we take $E = \mathbb{C}$, and $F = \mathbb{Q}$, then the elements of $\mathbb{C}$ that are algebraic over $\mathbb{Q}$ are the *algebraic numbers*; they are simply the algebraic closure of $\mathbb{Q}$: $\overline{\mathbb{Q}}$. Similarly, if we take $S = \mathbb{Z}$, then the elements of $\mathbb{C}$ that are integral over $\mathbb{Z}$ are the *algebraic integers*.

Other useful examples are obtained by taking $E = \mathbb{R}$, $F = \mathbb{Q}$ and $S = \mathbb{Z}$; they give rise to the *real algebraic numbers* and *real algebraic integers*— topics of this section; they are in a very real sense a significant fragment of "*computable numbers*" and thus very important.

Definition 8.5.1 (Real Algebraic Number) A real number is said to be a *real algebraic number* if it is a root of a univariate polynomial $f(x) \in \mathbb{Z}[x]$ with integer coefficients.　□

Example 8.5.2 Some examples of real algebraic numbers:

1. All integers:
$$n \in \mathbb{Z} \text{ is a root of } x - n = 0.$$

2. All rational numbers:
$$\alpha = \frac{p}{q} \in \mathbb{Q} \ (q \neq 0) \text{ is a root of } qx - p = 0.$$

3. All real radicals of rational numbers:
$$\beta = \sqrt[n]{p/q} \in \mathbb{R} \ (p \geq 0, \ q > 0) \text{ is a root of } qx^n - p = 0.　□$$

Definition 8.5.3 (Real Algebraic Integer) A real number is said to be a *real algebraic integer* if it is a root of a univariate monic polynomial $f(x) \in \mathbb{Z}[x]$ with integer coefficients.　□

Example 8.5.4 The golden ratio,
$$\xi = \frac{1 + \sqrt{5}}{2},$$
is an algebraic integer, since ξ is a root of the monic polynomial
$$x^2 - x - 1.　□$$

Lemma 8.5.1 *Every real algebraic number can be expressed as a real algebraic integer divided by an integer.*

(This is a corollary of the following general theorem; the proof given here is the same as the general proof, *mutatis mutandis. Every algebraic number is a ratio of an algebraic integer and an integer.*)

PROOF.
Consider a real algebraic number ξ. By definition,

$$\xi = \text{a real algebraic number}$$
$$\Leftrightarrow \quad \xi = \text{real root of a polynomial}$$
$$f(x) = a_n x^n + a_{n-1} x^{n-1} + \cdots + a_0 \in \mathbb{Z}[x], \qquad a_n \neq 0.$$

Now, if we multiply $f(x)$ by a_n^{n-1}, we have

$$a_n^{n-1} f(x)$$
$$= \quad a_n^{n-1} a_n \, x^n + a_n^{n-1} a_{n-1} \, x^{n-1} + \cdots + a_n^{n-1} a_0$$
$$= \quad (a_n x)^n + a_{n-1} (a_n x)^{n-1} + \cdots + a_0 a_n^{n-1}.$$

Clearly, $a_n \xi$ is a real root of the polynomial

$$g(y) = y^n + a_{n-1} y^{n-1} + \cdots + a_0 a_n^{n-1} \in \mathbb{Z}[y],$$

as $g(a_n \xi) = a_n^{n-1} f(\xi) = 0$. Thus $a_n \xi$ a real algebraic integer, for some $a_n \in \mathbb{Z} \setminus \{0\}$. $\square$

Lemma 8.5.2

1. *If α, β are real algebraic numbers, then so are $-\alpha$, α^{-1} ($\alpha \neq 0$), $\alpha + \beta$, and $\alpha \cdot \beta$.*

2. *If α, β are real algebraic integers, then so are $-\alpha$, $\alpha + \beta$, and $\alpha \cdot \beta$.*

PROOF.

1. (a) If α is a real algebraic number (defined as a real root of $f(x) \in \mathbb{Z}[x]$), then $-\alpha$ is also a real algebraic number.

   $$\alpha = \text{a real root of } f(x) = a_n x^n + a_{n-1} x^{n-1} + \cdots + a_0$$
   $$\Leftrightarrow \quad -\alpha = \text{a real root of } a_n(-x)^n + a_{n-1}(-x)^{n-1} + \cdots + a_0$$
   $$\Leftrightarrow \quad -\alpha = \text{a real root of}$$
   $$(-1)^n a_n x^n + (-1)^{n-1} a_{n-1}(-x)^{n-1} + \cdots + a_0 \in \mathbb{Z}[x].$$

   (b) If α is a real algebraic integer, then $-\alpha$ is also a real algebraic integer.

2. If α is a nonzero real algebraic number (defined as a real root of $f(x) \in \mathbb{Z}[x]$), then $1/\alpha$ is also a real algebraic number.

$\alpha = $ a real root of $f(x) = a_n x^n + a_{n-1} x^{n-1} + \cdots + a_0$

$\Leftrightarrow \quad 1/\alpha = $ a real root of

$$x^n a_n \left(\frac{1}{x}\right)^n + x^n a_{n-1} \left(\frac{1}{x}\right)^{n-1} + \cdots + x^n a_0$$

$\Leftrightarrow \quad 1/\alpha = $ a real root of $a_0 x^n + a_1 x^{n-1} + \cdots + a_n \in \mathbb{Z}[x]$.

Note that, if α is a nonzero real algebraic integer, then $1/\alpha$ is a real algebraic number, but not necessarily a real algebraic integer.

3. (a) If α and β are real algebraic numbers (defined as real roots of $f(x)$ and $g(x) \in \mathbb{Z}[x]$, respectively), then $\alpha + \beta$ is also a real algebraic number, defined as a real root of

$$\text{Resultant}_y(f(x - y),\ g(y)).$$

$\alpha = $ a real root of $f(x)$ and $\beta = $ a real root of $g(x)$

$\Leftrightarrow \quad x - \alpha = $ a real root of $f(x - y) \in (\mathbb{Z}[x])[y]$,

$\qquad \beta = $ a real root of $g(y) \in (\mathbb{Z}[x])[y]$ and

$\qquad x - \alpha = \beta = $ a common real root of $f(x - y)$ and $g(y)$

$\Leftrightarrow \quad x = \alpha + \beta = $ a real root of

$\qquad \text{Resultant}_y(f(x - y), g(y)) \in \mathbb{Z}[x]$.

(b) If α and β are real algebraic integers, then $\alpha + \beta$ is also a real algebraic integer.

4. (a) If α and β are real algebraic numbers (defined as real roots of $f(x)$ and $g(x) \in \mathbb{Z}[x]$, respectively), then $\alpha\beta$ is also a real algebraic number, defined as a real root of

$$\text{Resultant}_y \left(y^m f\left(\frac{x}{y}\right),\ g(y) \right), \qquad \text{where } m = \deg(f).$$

$\alpha = $ a real root of $f(x)$ and $\beta = $ a real root of $g(x)$

$\Leftrightarrow \quad \dfrac{x}{\alpha} = $ a real root of $y^m f\left(\dfrac{x}{y}\right) \in (\mathbb{Z}[x])[y]$,

$\qquad \beta = $ a real root of $g(y) \in (\mathbb{Z}[x])[y]$ and

$\qquad \dfrac{x}{\alpha} = \beta = $ a common real root of $y^m f\left(\dfrac{x}{y}\right)$ and $g(y)$

$\Leftrightarrow \quad x = \alpha\beta = $ a real root of

$\qquad \text{Resultant}_y \left(y^m f\left(\dfrac{x}{y}\right),\ g(y) \right) \in \mathbb{Z}[x]$.

(b) If α and β are real algebraic integers, then $\alpha\beta$ is also a real algebraic integer. $\square$

Corollary 8.5.3

1. *The real algebraic integers form a ring.*

2. *The real algebraic numbers form a field, denoted by $\mathbb{A}$.* $\square$

Since an algebraic number α, by definition, is a root of a nonzero polynomial $f(x)$ over $\mathbb{Z}$, we may say that f is α's *polynomial*. Additionally, if f is of minimal degree among all such polynomials, then we say that it is α's *minimal polynomial*. The *degree* of a nonzero algebraic number is the degree of its minimal polynomial; and by convention, the *degree* of 0 is $-\infty$. It is not hard to see that an algebraic number has a unique minimal polynomial modulo *associativity*; that is, if $f(x)$ and $g(x)$ are two minimal polynomials of an algebraic number α, then $f(x) \approx g(x)$.

If we further assume that α is a real algebraic number, then we can talk about its *minimal polynomial* and *degree* just as before.

Theorem 8.5.4 *The field of real algebraic numbers, $\mathbb{A}$, is an Archimedean real closed field.*

PROOF.
Since $\mathbb{A} \subset \mathbb{R}$ and since $\mathbb{R}$ itself is an ordered field, the induced ordering on $\mathbb{A}$ defines the unique ordering.

$\mathbb{A}$ is Archimedean: Consider a real algebraic number α, defined by its minimal polynomial $f(x) \in \mathbb{Z}[x]$:

$$f(x) = a_n x^n + a_{n-1} x^{n-1} + \cdots + a_0,$$

and let $N = 1 + \max(|a_{n-1}|, \ldots, |a_0|) \in \mathbb{Z}$. Then $\alpha < N$.

$\mathbb{A}$ is real closed: Clearly every positive real algebraic number α (defined by its minimal polynomial $f(x) \in \mathbb{Z}[x]$) has a square root $\sqrt{\alpha} \in \mathbb{A}$ defined by a polynomial $f(x^2) \in \mathbb{Z}[x]$. Also if $f(x) \in \mathbb{A}[x]$ is a polynomial of odd degree, then as its complex roots appear in pair, it must have at least one real root; it is clear that this root is in $\mathbb{A}$. $\square$

8.5.2 Root Separation, Thom's Lemma and Representation

Given a real algebraic number α, we will see that it can be finitely represented by its *polynomial* and some additional information that identifies the root, if α's polynomial has more than one real root.

If we want a succinct representation, then we must represent α by its *minimal polynomial* or simply a polynomial of sufficiently small degree (e.g., by asking that its polynomial is square-free). In many cases, if we require that even the intermediate computations be performed with succinct representations, then the cost of the computation may become prohibitive, as we will need to perform polynomial factorization over $\mathbb{Z}$ at each step. Thus the prudent choice seems to be to represent the inputs and outputs succinctly, while adopting a more flexible representation for intermediate computation.

Now coming back to the component of the representation that identifies the root, we have essentially three choices: *order* (where we assume the real roots are indexed from left to right), *sign* (by a vector of signs) and *interval* (an interval $[a, b] \subset \mathbb{R}$ that contains exactly one root). Again the choice may be predicated by the succinctness, the model of computation, and the application.

Before we go into the details, we shall discuss some of the necessary technical background: namely, *root separation*, *Fourier sequence* and *Thom's lemma*.

Root Separation

In this section, we shall study the distribution of the real roots of an integral polynomial $f(x) \in \mathbb{Z}[x]$. In particular, we need to determine how small the distance between a pair of distinct real roots may be as some function of the *size* of their polynomial. Using these bounds, we will be able to construct an interval $[a, b]$ ($a, b \in \mathbb{Q}$) containing exactly one real root of an integral polynomial $f(x)$, i.e., an interval that can *isolate* a real root of $f(x)$.

We keep our treatment general by taking $f(x)$ to be an arbitrary polynomial (not just square-free polynomials). Other bounds in the literature include cases (1) where $f(x)$ may be a rational complex polynomial or a Gaussian polynomial; (2) where $f(x)$ is square-free or irreducible; or (3) when we consider complex roots of $f(x)$. For our purpose, it is sufficient to deal with the separation among the real roots of an integral polynomial.

Definition 8.5.5 (Real Root Separation) If the distinct real roots of $f(x) \in \mathbb{Z}[x]$ are $\alpha_1, \ldots, \alpha_l$ ($l \geq 2$),

$$\alpha_1 < \alpha_2 < \cdots < \alpha_l,$$

then define the *separation*[1] of f to be

$$\text{Separation}(f) = \min_{1 \leq i < j \leq l} (\alpha_j - \alpha_i).$$

If f has less than two distinct roots, then $\text{Separation}(f) = \infty$. □

The following bound is due to S.M. Rump:

---

[1] Or more exactly, *real separation*.

Theorem 8.5.5 (Rump's Bound) *Let $f(x) \in \mathbb{Z}[x]$ be an integral polynomial as follows:*

$$f(x) = a_n x^n + a_{n-1} x^{n-1} + \cdots + a_0, \qquad a_i \in \mathbb{Z}.$$

Then[2]

$$\text{Separation}(f) > \frac{1}{n^{n+1}(1 + \|f\|_1)^{2n}}.$$

PROOF.

Let $h \in \mathbb{R}$ be such that, for any arbitrary real root, α, of f, the polynomial f remains nonzero through out the interval $(\alpha, \alpha + h)$. Then, clearly,

$$\text{Separation}(f) > h.$$

Using the intermediate value theorem (see Problem 8.2), we have

$$f(\alpha + h) = f(\alpha) + h f'(\mu), \qquad \text{for some } \mu \in (\alpha, \alpha + h).$$

Since $f(\alpha) = 0$, we have

$$h = \frac{|f(\alpha + h)|}{|f'(\mu)|}.$$

Thus we can obtain our bounds by choosing h such that $|f(\alpha + h)|$ is "fairly large" and $|f'(\mu)|$, "fairly small," for all $\mu \in (\alpha, \alpha + h)$. Thus the polynomial needs enough space to go from a "fairly large" value to 0 at a "fairly small" rate.

Let β be a real root of $f(x)$ such that β is immediately to the right of α. Then there are following two cases to consider:

- CASE 1:　$|\alpha| < 1 < |\beta|$.
  We consider the situation $-1 < \alpha < 1 < \beta$, as we can always achieve this, by replacing $f(x)$ by $f(-x)$, if necessary. Take $\alpha + h = 1$. Then

  1. $|f(\alpha + h)| \geq 1$, since $f(1) \neq 0$.
  2. Since $\mu \leq 1$, we have

  $$|f'(\mu)| \leq |n a_n| + |(n-1)a_{n-1}| + \cdots + |a_1| \leq n\|f\|_1.$$

Thus

$$\text{Separation}(f) > h \geq \frac{1}{n\|f\|_1} > \frac{1}{n^{n+1}(1 + \|f\|_1)^{2n}}.$$

---

[2]Note: A tighter bound is also given by Rump:

$$\text{Separation}(f) > \frac{2\sqrt{2}}{n^{n/2+1}(1 + \|f\|_1)^n}.$$

For the next case, we need the following technical lemma:

Lemma 8.5.6 *Let $f(x) \in \mathbb{Z}[x]$ be an integral polynomial as in the theorem. If γ satisfies*

$$f'(\gamma) = 0, \quad \text{but} \quad f(\gamma) \neq 0,$$

then

$$|f(\gamma)| > \frac{1}{n^n(1 + \|f\|_1)^{2n-1}}.$$

PROOF.
Consider the polynomials $f'(x)$ and $\tilde{f}(x,y) = f(x) - y$. Since γ is a zero of $f'(x)$ and $\langle \gamma, f(\gamma) \rangle$ is a zero of $\tilde{f}(x,y)$, we see that $f(\gamma) \neq 0$ is a root of

$$R(y) = \text{Resultant}_x(f'(x), \tilde{f}(x,y)).$$

Using the Hadamard-Collins-Horowitz inequality theorem (with 1-norm) (see Problem 8.11), we get

$$\|R\|_\infty \leq (\|f\|_1 + 1)^{n-1} (n\|f\|_1)^n,$$

and

$$1 + \|R\|_\infty < n^n(1 + \|f\|_1)^{2n-1}.$$

Since $f(\gamma)$ is a nonzero root of the integral polynomial $R(y)$, we have

$$|f(\gamma)| > \frac{1}{1 + \|R\|_\infty} > \frac{1}{n^n(1 + \|f\|_1)^{2n-1}}. \qquad \square$$

(End of Lemma)

- CASE 2: $|\alpha|, |\beta| \leq 1$.
  By Rolle's theorem there is a $\gamma \in (\alpha, \beta)$, where $f'(\gamma) = 0$. Take $\alpha + h = \gamma$. Then

  1. By Lemma 8.5.6,

  $$|f(\alpha + h)| = |f(\gamma)| > \frac{1}{n^n(1 + \|f\|_1)^{2n-1}}.$$

  2. As before, since $\mu \leq 1$, we have

  $$|f'(\mu)| \leq n\|f\|_1.$$

  Thus

  $$\begin{aligned}
  \text{Separation}(f) \quad & > \quad h \\
  & > \quad \frac{1}{n^n(1 + \|f\|_1)^{2n-1})(n\|f\|_1)} \\
  & > \quad \frac{1}{n^{n+1}(1 + \|f\|_1)^{2n}}.
  \end{aligned}$$

Note: The remaining case $|\alpha|, |\beta| \geq 1$, requires no further justification as the following argument shows: Consider the polynomial $x^n f(1/x)$. Then α^{-1} and β^{-1} are two consecutive roots of the new polynomial of same "size" as $f(x)$; $|\alpha^{-1}|, |\beta^{-1}| \leq 1$; and

$$\beta - \alpha \geq \frac{\beta - \alpha}{\alpha\,\beta} = \alpha^{-1} - \beta^{-1}.$$

But using case 2, we get

$$\text{Separation}(f) > \beta - \alpha > \frac{1}{n^{n+1}(1 + \|f\|_1)^{2n}}. \quad \square$$

Let $r = p/q \in \mathbb{Q}$ be a rational number $(p, q \in \mathbb{Z})$. We define *size* of r as

$$\text{size}(r) = |p| + |q|.$$

Theorem 8.5.7 *Let $f(x) \in \mathbb{Z}[x]$ be an integral polynomial of degree n. Then between any two real roots of $f(x)$ there is a rational number r of size*

$$\text{size}(r) < 2 \cdot n^{n+1}(1 + \|f\|_1)^{2n+1}.$$

PROOF.
Consider two consecutive roots of $f(x)$: $\alpha < \beta$. Let $Q \in \mathbb{Z}$ be

$$Q = n^{n+1}(1 + \|f\|_1)^{2n}.$$

Consider all the rational numbers with Q in the denominator:

$$\ldots, -\frac{i}{Q}, -\frac{i-1}{Q}, \ldots, -\frac{2}{Q}, -\frac{1}{Q}, 0, \frac{1}{Q}, \frac{2}{Q}, \ldots, \frac{i-1}{Q}, \frac{i}{Q}, \ldots$$

Since

$$\beta - \alpha > 1/Q,$$

for some P,

$$\alpha < \frac{P}{Q} < \beta < \|f\|_1,$$

since β is a root of f.
    Hence

$$|P| < n^{n+1}(1 + \|f\|_1)^{2n+1}.$$

Thus the size of $r = P/Q$ is

$$\text{size}(r) < 2 \cdot n^{n+1}(1 + \|f\|_1)^{2n+1}. \quad \square$$

Definition 8.5.6 (Isolating Interval) An *isolating interval* for an integral polynomial $f(x) \in \mathbb{Z}[x]$ is an interval $[a, b]$ $(a, b \in \mathbb{Q})$, in which there is precisely one real root of the polynomial. $\square$

By the preceding theorem, we see that for every real root of an integral polynomial, we can find an isolating interval. Furthermore,

Corollary 8.5.8 *Every isolating interval of a degree n integral polynomial $f(x) \in \mathbb{Z}[x]$ is of the form $[a, b]$, $(a, b \in \mathbb{Q})$ and $\text{size}(a)$ and $\text{size}(b)$ are no larger than*

$$2 \cdot n^{n+1}(1 + \|f\|_1)^{2n+1}. \quad \square$$

Hence every isolating interval can be represented with $O(n(\lg n + \beta(f)))$ bits, where $\beta(f) = O(\lg \|f\|_1)$ is the bit-complexity of the polynomial $f(x)$ in any reasonable binary encoding. An important related computational problem is the so-called *root isolation problem*, where we are asked to compute an isolating interval of an integral polynomial $f(x)$.

RootIsolation($f(x)$)

Input: $f(x) \in \mathbb{Z}[x]\}$; $\deg(f) = n$.

Output: An isolating interval $[a, b]$ $(a, b \in \mathbb{Q})$,
       containing a real root of $f(x)$.

Let $\overline{S} = \overline{\text{STURM}}(f, f')$, be a Sturm sequence;
$a := -\|f\|_1$; $b := \|f\|_1$;

if $\text{Var}_a(\overline{S}) = \text{Var}_b(\overline{S})$ then return failure;

while $\text{Var}_a(\overline{S}) - \text{Var}_b(\overline{S}) > 1$ loop
    $c := (a + b)/2$;
    if $\text{Var}_a(\overline{S}) > \text{Var}_c(\overline{S})$ then $b := c$ else $a := c$
    end{if };
end{loop };

return $[a, b]$;
end{RootIsolation} $\square$

Note that each polynomial of the Sturm sequence can be evaluated by $O(n)$ arithmetic operations, and since there are at most n polynomials in the sequence, each successive refinement of the interval $[a, b]$ (by binary division) takes $O(n^2)$ time. Thus the time complexity of root isolation is

$$O(n^2) \cdot O\left(\lg\left(\frac{2\|f\|_1}{\text{Separation}(f)}\right)\right),$$

which is simplified to

$$O\left(n^2 \, \lg\left(\frac{2\|f\|_1}{n^{-n-1}(1 + \|f\|_1)^{-2n}}\right)\right)$$
$$= \ O\left(n^2 \, \lg\left(2n^{n+1}(1 + \|f\|_1)^{2n+1}\right)\right)$$
$$= \ O(n^3(\lg n + \beta(f))),$$

where $\beta(f)$, as before, is the bit-complexity of the polynomial $f(x)$.

Fourier Sequence and Thom's Lemma

Definition 8.5.7 (Fourier Sequence) Let $f(x) \in \mathbb{R}[x]$ be a real univariate polynomial of degree n. Its *Fourier sequence* is defined to be the following sequence of polynomials:

$$\overline{\mathrm{FOURIER}}(f) \;=\; \Big\langle \quad f^{(0)}(x) = f(x),$$
$$f^{(1)}(x) = f'(x),$$
$$f^{(2)}(x),$$
$$\vdots$$
$$f^{(n)}(x) \quad \Big\rangle,$$

where $f^{(i)}$ denotes the ith derivative of f with respect to x. $\quad\square$

Note that $\overline{\mathrm{FOURIER}}(f')$ is a suffix of $\overline{\mathrm{FOURIER}}(f)$ of length n; in general, $\overline{\mathrm{FOURIER}}(f^{(i)})$ is a suffix of $\overline{\mathrm{FOURIER}}(f)$ of length $n - i + 1$.

Lemma 8.5.9 (Little Thom's Lemma) *Let $f(x) \in \mathbb{R}[x]$ be a real univariate polynomial of degree n. Given a sign sequence $\bar{s}$:*

$$\bar{s} = \langle s_0, s_1, s_2, \ldots, s_n \rangle,$$

we define the sign-invariant region of $\mathbb{R}$ determined by $\bar{s}$ with respect to $\overline{\mathrm{FOURIER}}(f)$ *as follows:*

$$R(\bar{s}) = \Big\{ \xi \in \mathbb{R} : \mathrm{sgn}(f^{(i)}(\xi)) = s_i, \text{ for all } i = 0, \ldots, n \Big\}.$$

Then every nonempty $R(\bar{s})$ must be connected, i.e., consist of a single interval.

PROOF.
The proof is by induction on n. The base case (when $n = 0$) is trivial, since, in this case, either $R(\bar{s}) = \mathbb{R}$ (if $\mathrm{sgn}(f(x)) = s_0$) or $R(\bar{s}) = \emptyset$ (if $\mathrm{sgn}(f(x)) \neq s_0$).

Consider the induction case when $n > 0$. By the inductive hypothesis, we know that the sign-invariant region determined by $\bar{s}'$,

$$\bar{s}' = \langle s_1, s_2, \ldots, s_n \rangle,$$

with respect to $\overline{\mathrm{FOURIER}}(f')$ is either $\emptyset$ or a single interval. If it is empty, then there is nothing to prove. Thus we may assume that

$$R(\bar{s}') \neq \emptyset.$$

Now, let us enumerate the distinct real roots of $f(x)$:

$$\xi_1 < \xi_2 < \cdots < \xi_m.$$

Note that if $R(\bar{s}')$ consists of more than one interval, then a subsequence of real roots

$$\xi_i < \xi_{i+1} < \cdots < \xi_j, \qquad j - i > i$$

must lie in the interval $R(\bar{s}')$. Now, since there are at least two roots ξ_i and $\xi_{i+1} \in R(\bar{s}')$, then, by Rolle's theorem, for some $\xi' \in R(\bar{s}')$ ($\xi_i < \xi' < \xi_{i+1}$), $f'(\xi') = 0$. Thus,

$$\left(\forall\, x \in R(\bar{s}') \right) \left[f'(x) = 0 \right] \quad \Rightarrow \quad f'(x) \equiv 0 \quad \Rightarrow \quad \deg(f) = 0,$$

a contradiction. $\square$

Corollary 8.5.10 *Consider two real roots ξ and ζ of a real univariate polynomial $f(x) \in \mathbb{R}[x]$ of positive degree $n > 0$. Then $\xi = \zeta$, if, for some $0 \leq m < n$, the following conditions hold:*

$$
\begin{aligned}
f^{(m)}(\xi) &= f^{(m)}(\zeta) = 0,, \\
\mathrm{sgn}(f^{(m+1)}(\xi)) &= \mathrm{sgn}(f^{(m+1)}(\zeta)), \\
&\vdots \\
\mathrm{sgn}(f^{(n)}(\xi)) &= \mathrm{sgn}(f^{(n)}(\zeta)).
\end{aligned}
$$

PROOF.
Let

$$\bar{s}'' = \langle 0, \mathrm{sgn}(f^{(m+1)}(\xi)), \ldots, \mathrm{sgn}(f^{(n)}(\xi)) \rangle,$$

and $R(\bar{s}'')$ be the sign-invariant region determined by $\bar{s}''$ with respect to $\overline{\mathrm{FOURIER}}(f^{(m)})$. Since ξ and $\zeta \in R(\bar{s}'')$, we see that $R(\bar{s}'')$ is a nonempty interval, over which $f^{(m)}$ vanishes. Hence $f^{(m)}$ is identically zero. But this would contradict the fact that $\deg(f) = n > m \geq 0$. $\square$

Let us define $\mathrm{sgn}_\xi(\overline{\mathrm{FOURIER}}(f))$ to be the sign sequence obtained by evaluating the polynomials of $\overline{\mathrm{FOURIER}}(f)$ at ξ:

$$
\begin{aligned}
&\mathrm{sgn}_\xi(\overline{\mathrm{FOURIER}}(f)) \\
&= \Big\langle \mathrm{sgn}(f(\xi)),\ \mathrm{sgn}(f'(\xi)),\ \mathrm{sgn}(f^{(2)}(\xi)),\ \ldots, \mathrm{sgn}(f^{(n)}(\xi)) \Big\rangle.
\end{aligned}
$$

As an immediate corollary of Thom's lemma, we have:

Corollary 8.5.11 *Let ξ and ζ be two real roots of a real univariate polynomial $f(x) \in \mathbb{R}[x]$ of positive degree $n > 0$. Then $\xi = \zeta$, if the following condition holds:*

$$\mathrm{sgn}_\xi(\overline{\mathrm{FOURIER}}(f')) = \mathrm{sgn}_\zeta(\overline{\mathrm{FOURIER}}(f')). \qquad \square$$

Representation of Real Algebraic Numbers

A real algebraic number $\alpha \in \mathbb{A}$ can be represented by its polynomial $f(x) \in \mathbb{Z}[x]$, an integral polynomial with α as a root, and additional information identifying this particular root. Let

$$f(x) = a_n \, x^n + a_{n-1} \, x^{n-1} + \cdots + a_0, \qquad \deg(f) = n,$$

and assume that the distinct real roots of $f(x)$ have been enumerated as follows:

$$\alpha_1 < \alpha_2 < \cdots < \alpha_{j-1} < \alpha_j = \alpha \; < \alpha_{j+1} < \cdots < \alpha_l,$$

where $l \leq n = \deg(f)$.

While in certain cases (i.e., for input and output), we may require $f(x)$ to be a minimal polynomial α, in general, we relax this condition.

The Following is a list of possible representations of α:

1. **Order Representation:**   The algebraic number α is represented as a pair consisting of its polynomial, f, and its index, j, in the sequence enumerating the real roots of f:

$$\langle \alpha \rangle_o = \langle f, j \rangle.$$

Clearly, this representation requires only $O(n \lg \|f\|_1 + \log n)$ bits.

2. **Sign Representation:**   The algebraic number α is represented as a pair consisting of its polynomial, f, and a sign sequence, $\overline{s}$, representing the signs of the Fourier sequence of f' evaluated at the root α:

$$\langle \alpha \rangle_s = \langle f, \overline{s} = \mathrm{sgn}_\alpha (\overline{\mathrm{FOURIER}}(f')) \rangle.$$

The validity of this representation follows easily from the Little Thom's theorem. The sign representation requires only $O(n \lg \|f\|_1 + n)$ bits.

3. **Interval Representation:**   The algebraic number α is represented as a triple consisting of its polynomial, f, and the two end points of an isolating interval, (l, r) $(l, r \in \mathbb{Q}, l < r)$ containing only α:

$$\langle \alpha \rangle_i = \langle f, l, r \rangle.$$

By definition,

$$\max(\alpha_{j-1}, -1 - \|f\|_\infty) < l < \alpha_j = \alpha < r < \min(\alpha_{j+1}, 1 + \|f\|_\infty),$$

using our bounds for the real root separation, we see that the interval representation requires only $O(n \lg \|f\|_1 + n \lg n)$ bits.

Additionally, we require that the representation be *normalized* in the sense that if $\alpha \neq 0$ then $0 \notin (l, r)$, i.e., l and r have the same sign. We will provide a simple algorithm to normalize any arbitrary interval representation.

Example 8.5.8 Consider the representations of the following two algebraic numbers $-\sqrt{2} + \sqrt{3}$ and $\sqrt{2} + \sqrt{3}$:

$$\langle -\sqrt{2} + \sqrt{3} \rangle_o = \langle x^4 - 10x^2 + 1, \; 3 \rangle,$$
$$\langle \sqrt{2} + \sqrt{3} \rangle_o = \langle x^4 - 10x^2 + 1, \; 4 \rangle,$$

$$\langle -\sqrt{2} + \sqrt{3} \rangle_s = \langle x^4 - 10x^2 + 1, \; (-1, -1, +1) \rangle,$$
$$\langle \sqrt{2} + \sqrt{3} \rangle_s = \langle x^4 - 10x^2 + 1, \; (+1, +1, +1) \rangle,$$

$$\langle -\sqrt{2} + \sqrt{3} \rangle_i = \langle x^4 - 10x^2 + 1, \; 1/11, \; 1/2 \rangle,$$
$$\langle \sqrt{2} + \sqrt{3} \rangle_i = \langle x^4 - 10x^2 + 1, \; 3, \; 7/2 \rangle. \quad \square$$

Here, we shall concentrate only on the interval representation, as it appears to be the best representation for a wide class of models of computation. While some recent research indicates that the sign representation leads to certain efficient parallel algebraic algorithms, it has yet to find widespread usage. Moreover, many of the key algebraic ideas are easier to explain for interval representation than the others. Henceforth, unless explicitly stated, we shall assume that the real algebraic numbers are given in the interval representation and are written without a subscript:

$$\langle \alpha \rangle = \langle f, l, r \rangle.$$

The following interval arithmetic operations simplify our later exposition:

Let $I_1 = (l_1, r_1) = \{x \; : \; l_1 < x < r_1\}$ and $I_2 = (l_2, r_2) = \{x \; : \; l_2 < x < r_2\}$ be two real intervals; then

$$I_1 + I_2 = (l_1 + l_2, r_1 + r_2)$$
$$= \{x + y \; : \; l_1 < x < r_1 \text{ and } l_2 < x < r_2\},$$

$$I_1 - I_2 = (l_1 - r_2, r_1 - l_2)$$
$$= \{x - y \; : \; l_1 < x < r_1 \text{ and } l_2 < x < r_2\},$$

$$I_1 \cdot I_2 = (\min(l_1 l_2, l_1 r_2, r_1 l_2, r_1 r_2), \max(l_1 l_2, l_1 r_2, r_1 l_2, r_1 r_2))$$
$$= \{xy \; : \; l_1 < x < r_1 \text{ and } l_2 < x < r_2\}.$$

We begin by describing algorithms for *normalization, refinement* and *sign evaluation.*

Normalization

NORMALIZE(α)

Input: A real algebraic number $\alpha = \langle f, l, r \rangle \in \mathbb{A}$.

Output: A representation of $\alpha = \langle f, l', r' \rangle$ such that $0 \notin (l', r')$.

$p := 1/(1 + \|f\|_\infty)$;

if $\mathrm{Var}_l(\overline{S}) > \mathrm{Var}_{-p}(\overline{S})$ then
       return $\alpha = \langle f,\ l,\ -p \rangle$
elsif $\mathrm{Var}_{-p}(\overline{S}) > \mathrm{Var}_p(\overline{S})$ then
       return $\alpha = 0$
else
       return $\alpha = \langle f,\ p,\ r \rangle$
end{if };
end{NORMALIZE} $\square$

The correctness of the theorem is a straightforward consequence of Sturm's theorem and bounds on the nonzero zeros of f. It is easily seen that the algorithm requires $O(n^2)$ arithmetic operations.

Refinement

REFINE(α)

Input: A real algebraic number $\alpha = \langle f, l, r \rangle \in \mathbb{A}$.

Output: A finer representation of $\alpha = \langle f, l', r' \rangle$ such that
            $2(r' - l') \le (r - l)$.

Let $\overline{S} = \overline{\mathrm{STURM}}(f, f')$ be a Sturm sequence;

$m := (l + r)/2$;
if $\mathrm{Var}_l(\overline{S}) > \mathrm{Var}_m(\overline{S})$ then
       return $\langle f,\ l,\ m \rangle$
else
       return $\langle f,\ m,\ r \rangle$
end{if };
end{REFINE} $\square$

Again the correctness of the algorithm follows from the Sturm's theorem and its time complexity is $O(n^2)$.

Sign Evaluation

SIGN(α, g)
Input: A real algebraic number $\alpha = \langle f, l, r \rangle \in \mathbb{A}$, and
           a univariate rational polynomial $g(x) \in \mathbb{Q}[x]$.

Output: $\text{sgn}(g(\alpha)) = $ sign of g at α.

   Let $\overline{S_g} = \overline{\text{STURM}}(f, f'g)$, be a Sturm sequence;

      return $\text{Var}_l(\overline{S_g}) - \text{Var}_r(\overline{S_g})$;
   end{SIGN} $\square$

   The correctness of the algorithm follows from Sturm-Tarski theorem,
since

$$\text{Var}_l(\overline{\text{STURM}}(f, f'g)) - \text{Var}_r(\overline{\text{STURM}}(f, f'g))$$

$$= \quad c_f \Big[g > 0 \Big]_l^r - c_f \Big[g < 0 \Big]_l^r$$

$$= \quad \begin{cases} +1, & \text{if } g(\alpha) > 0; \\ 0, & \text{if } g(\alpha) = 0; \\ -1, & \text{if } g(\alpha) < 0; \end{cases}$$

and since f has only one root α in the interval (l, r). The algorithm has
a time complexity of $O(n^2)$. This algorithm has several applications: for
instance, one can compare an algebraic number α with a rational number
p/q by evaluating the sign of the polynomial $qx - p$ at α; one can compute
the multiplicity of a root α of a polynomial f by computing the signs of
the polynomials f', $f^{(2)}$, $f^{(3)}$, etc., at α.

Conversion Among Representations

Interval representation to order representation:

INTERVALTOORDER(α)
Input: A real algebraic number $\langle \alpha \rangle_i = \langle f, l, r \rangle \in \mathbb{A}$.

Output: Its order representation $\langle \alpha \rangle_o = \langle f, j \rangle$.

   Let $\overline{S} = \overline{\text{STURM}}(f, f')$ be a Sturm sequence;

      return $\langle f, \text{Var}_{(-1-\|f\|_\infty)}(\overline{S}) - \text{Var}_r(\overline{S}) \rangle$;
   end{INTERVALTOORDER} $\square$

Interval representation to sign representation:

> INTERVALTOSIGN(α)
> **Input:**　　A real algebraic number $\langle \alpha \rangle_i = \langle f, l, r \rangle \in \mathbb{A}$.
>
> **Output:**　Its sign representation $\langle \alpha \rangle_s = \langle f, \bar{s} \rangle$.
>
> Let $\langle f', f^{(2)}, \ldots, f^{(n)} \rangle = \overline{\text{FOURIER}}(f')$;
>
> $\bar{s} := \Big\langle$　$\text{SIGN}(\alpha, f')$,
>
> 　　　　$\text{SIGN}(\alpha, f^{(2)})$,
>
> 　　　　$\vdots$
>
> 　　　　$\text{SIGN}(\alpha, f^{(n)})$ $\Big\rangle$;
> 　　　return $\langle f, \bar{s} \rangle$;
> end{INTERVALTOORDER}　　$\square$

Again, the correctness of these algorithms follow from Sturm-Tarski theorem. The algorithms INTERVALTOORDER has a time complexity of $O(n^2)$, and INTERVALTOSIGN has a complexity of $O(n^3)$.

Arithmetic Operations

Additive inverse:

> ADDITIVEINVERSE(α)
> **Input:**　　A real algebraic number $\langle \alpha \rangle = \langle f, l, r \rangle \in \mathbb{A}$.
>
> **Output:**　$-\alpha$ in its interval representation.
>
> 　　　return $\langle f(-x),\ -r,\ -l \rangle$;
> end{ADDITIVEINVERSE}　　$\square$

The correctness follows from the fact that if α is a root of $f(x)$, then $-\alpha$ is a root of $f(-x)$. Clearly, the algorithm has a linear time complexity.

Multiplicative inverse:

> MULTIPLICATIVEINVERSE(α)
> **Input:**　　A nonzero real algebraic number $\langle \alpha \rangle = \langle f, l, r \rangle \in \mathbb{A}$.
>
> **Output:**　$1/\alpha$ in its interval representation.
>
> 　　　return $\left\langle x^{\deg(f)} f\left(\dfrac{1}{x}\right),\ \dfrac{1}{r},\ \dfrac{1}{l} \right\rangle$;
> end{MULTIPLICATIVEINVERSE}　　$\square$

The correctness follows from the fact that if α is a root of $f(x)$, then $1/\alpha$ is a root of $x^{\deg(f)} f(1/x)$. Again, the algorithm has a linear time complexity.

Addition:

ADDITION(α_1, α_2)
Input: Two real algebraic numbers
            $\langle \alpha_1 \rangle = \langle f_1, l_1, r_1 \rangle$ and $\langle \alpha_2 \rangle = \langle f_2, l_2, r_2 \rangle \in \mathbb{A}$.

Output: $\alpha_1 + \alpha_2 = \alpha_3 = \langle f_3, l_3, r_3 \rangle$ in its interval representation.

   $f_3 := \text{Resultant}_y(f_1(x - y),\ f_2(y))$;

   $\overline{S} := \overline{\text{STURM}}(f_3, f_3')$;

   $l_3 := l_1 + l_2$;
   $r_3 := r_1 + r_2$;

   while $\text{Var}_{l_3}(\overline{S}) - \text{Var}_{r_3}(\overline{S}) > 1$ loop

      $\langle f_1, l_1, r_1 \rangle := \text{REFINE}(\langle f_1, l_1, r_1 \rangle)$;
      $\langle f_2, l_2, r_2 \rangle := \text{REFINE}(\langle f_2, l_2, r_2 \rangle)$;

      $l_3 := l_1 + l_2$;
      $r_3 := r_1 + r_2$;
   end{loop };

   return $\langle f_3, l_3, r_3 \rangle$;
end{ADDITION}   □

The correctness of the algorithm follows from the main properties of the resultant and the repeated refinement process yielding an isolating interval. The resulting polynomial f_3 in this algorithm has the following size complexities:

$$\deg(f_3) \ \leq \ n_1\, n_2,$$

$$\|f_3\|_1 \ \leq \ 2^{O(n_1 n_2)} \|f_1\|_1^{n_2} \|f_2\|_1^{n_1},$$

where $\deg(f_1) = n_1$ and $\deg(f_2) = n_2$. It can now be shown that the complexity of the algorithm is $O(n_1^3 n_2^4 \lg \|f_1\|_1 + n_1^4 n_2^3 \lg \|f_2\|_1)$.

Multiplication:

MULTIPLICATION(α_1, α_2)
Input: Two real algebraic numbers
               $\langle\alpha_1\rangle = \langle f_1, l_1, r_1\rangle$ and $\langle\alpha_2\rangle = \langle f_2, l_2, r_2\rangle \in \mathbb{A}$.

Output: $\alpha_1 \cdot \alpha_2 = \alpha_3 = \langle f_3, l_3, r_3\rangle$ in its interval representation.

$$f_3 := \mathrm{Resultant}_y\left(y^{\deg(f_1)} f_1\left(\frac{x}{y}\right), f_2(y)\right);$$

$$\overline{S} := \overline{\mathrm{STURM}}(f_3, f_3');$$

$$l_3 := \min(l_1 l_2, l_1 r_2, r_1 l_2, r_1 r_2);$$
$$r_3 := \max(l_1 l_2, l_1 r_2, r_1 l_2, r_1 r_2);$$

while $\mathrm{Var}_{l_3}(\overline{S}) - \mathrm{Var}_{r_3}(\overline{S}) > 1$ loop

$$\langle f_1, l_1, r_1\rangle := \mathrm{REFINE}(\langle f_1, l_1, r_1\rangle);$$
$$\langle f_2, l_2, r_2\rangle := \mathrm{REFINE}(\langle f_2, l_2, r_2\rangle);$$

$$l_3 := \min(l_1 l_2, l_1 r_2, r_1 l_2, r_1 r_2);$$
$$r_3 := \max(l_1 l_2, l_1 r_2, r_1 l_2, r_1 r_2);$$
end{loop };

return $\langle f_3, l_3, r_3\rangle$;
end{MULTIPLICATION} $\square$

The correctness of the multiplication algorithm can be proven as before. The size complexities of the polynomial f_3 are:

$$\deg(f_3) \leq n_1 n_2,$$
$$\|f_3\|_1 \leq n_1 n_2 \|f_1\|_1^{n_2} \|f_2\|_1^{n_1},$$

where $\deg(f_1) = n_1$ and $\deg(f_2) = n_2$. Thus, the complexity of the algorithm is $O(n_1^3 n_2^4 \lg \|f_1\|_1 + n_1^4 n_2^3 \lg \|f_2\|_1)$.

8.6   Real Geometry

Definition 8.6.1 (Semialgebraic Sets) A subset $S \subseteq \mathbb{R}^n$ is a said to be a *semialgebraic set* if it can be determined by a set-theoretic expression of the following form:

$$S = \bigcup_{i=1}^{m} \bigcap_{j=1}^{l_i} \left\{ \langle\xi_1, \ldots, \xi_n\rangle \in \mathbb{R}^n : \mathrm{sgn}(f_{i,j}(\xi_1, \ldots, \xi_n)) = s_{i,j} \right\},$$

where $f_{i,j}$'s are multivariate polynomials in $\mathbb{R}[x_1, \ldots, x_n]$:

$$f_{i,j}(x_1, \ldots, x_n) \in \mathbb{R}[x_1, \ldots, x_n], \qquad i = 1, \ldots, m, \;\; j = 1, \ldots, l_i,$$

and $s_{i,j}$'s are corresponding set of signs in $\{-1, 0, +1\}$.   □

Such sets arise naturally in solid modeling (as constructive solid geometric models), in robotics (as kinematic constraint relations on the possible configurations of a rigid mechanical system) and in computational algebraic geometry (as classical loci describing convolutes, evolutes and envelopes).

Note that the semialgebraic sets correspond to the minimal class of subsets of $\mathbb{R}^n$ of the following forms:

1. Subsets defined by an algebraic *inequality*:

$$S = \left\{ \langle \xi_1, \ldots, \xi_n \rangle \in \mathbb{R}^n \; : \; f(\xi_1, \ldots, \xi_n) > 0 \right\},$$

where $f(x_1, \ldots, x_n) \in \mathbb{R}[x_1, \ldots, x_n]$.

2. Subsets closed under following set-theoretic operations, *complementation*, *union* and *intersection*. That is, if S_1 and S_2 are two semialgebraic sets, then so are

$$S_1^c \;\; = \;\; \left\{ p = \langle \xi_1, \ldots, \xi_n \rangle \in \mathbb{R}^n \; : \; p \notin S_1 \right\},$$

$$S_1 \cup S_2 \;\; = \;\; \left\{ p = \langle \xi_1, \ldots, \xi_n \rangle \in \mathbb{R}^n \; : \; p \in S_1 \text{ or } p \in S_2 \right\},$$

$$S_1 \cap S_2 \;\; = \;\; \left\{ p = \langle \xi_1, \ldots, \xi_n \rangle \in \mathbb{R}^n \; : \; p \in S_1 \text{ and } p \in S_2 \right\}.$$

After certain simplifications, we can also formulate a *semialgebraic set* in the following equivalent manner: it is a finite union of sets of the form shown below:

$$\begin{aligned} S \;\; = \;\; \Big\{ \langle \xi_1, \ldots, \xi_n \rangle \; : \; & \\ & g_1(\xi_1, \ldots, \xi_n) = \cdots = g_r(\xi_1, \ldots, \xi_n) = 0, \\ & g_{r+1}(\xi_1, \ldots, \xi_n) > 0, \;\; \ldots, \;\; g_s(\xi_1, \ldots, \xi_n) > 0 \; \Big\}, \end{aligned}$$

where the $g_i(x_1, \ldots, x_n) \in \mathbb{R}[x_1, \ldots, x_n]$ $(i = 1, \ldots, s)$.

It is also not hard to see that every propositional algebraic sentence composed of algebraic inequalities and Boolean connectives defines a semialgebraic set. In such sentences,

1. A constant is a real number;

2. An algebraic variable assumes a real number as its value; there are finitely many such algebraic variables: $x_1, x_2, \ldots, x_n$.

3. An algebraic expression is a constant, or a variable, or an expression combining two algebraic expressions by an arithmetic operator: "+" (addition), "−" (subtraction), "·" (multiplication) and "/" (division).

4. An atomic Boolean predicate is an expression comparing two arithmetic expressions by a binary relational operator: "=" (equation), "≠" (inequation), ">" (strictly greater), "<" (strictly less), "≥" (greater than or equal to) and "≤" (less than or equal to).

5. A propositional sentence is an atomic Boolean predicate, a negation of a propositional sentence given by the unary Boolean connective: "¬" (negation), or a sentence combining two propositional sentences by a binary Boolean connective: "⇒" (implication), "∧" (conjunction) and "∨" (disjunction).

Thus another definition of semialgebraic sets can be given in terms of a propositional algebraic sentence $\psi(x_1, \ldots, x_n)$ involving n algebraic variables: This is a subset $S \subseteq \mathbb{R}^n$ determined by ψ as follows:

$$S = \left\{ \langle \xi_1, \ldots, \xi_n \rangle \in \mathbb{R}^n \ : \ \psi(\xi_1, \ldots, \xi_n) = \mathsf{True} \right\}.$$

It turns out that if we enlarge our propositional sentences to include first-order universal and existential quantifiers (the so-called *Tarski sentences*), then the set determined by such sentences (*Tarski sets*) are also semialgebraic sets. That is, quantifiers do not add any additional power! This result follows from Tarski's famous quantifier elimination theorem, which states that any set S determined by a quantified sentence is also determined by a quantifier-free sentence ψ', or

Proposition 8.6.1 *Every Tarski set has a* quantifier-free *defining sentence.*   □

Later on in this section, we shall come back to a more detailed discussion of Tarski sentences and some results on an effective procedure to decide if a given Tarski sentence is true—geometric theorem proving problem.

Example 8.6.2 Some examples of such propositional algebraic sentences include the following:

1.
$$\phi_1(x_1, x_2, \ldots, x_n) \ = \ x_1^2 + x_2^2 + \cdots + x_n^2 < 0.$$

The semialgebraic set defined by ϕ_1 is the empty set.

2.
$$(x^4 - 10x^2 + 1 = 0) \ \wedge \ (2x < 7) \ \wedge \ (x > 3)$$

defines the only root of the polynomial $x^4 - 10x^2 + 1$ in the isolating interval $[3, 7/2]$—namely, the real algebraic number $\sqrt{2} + \sqrt{3}$.

3.

$$(x^2 + bx + c = 0) \; \wedge \; (y^2 + by + c = 0) \; \wedge \; (x \neq y),$$

which has a real solution $\langle x, y \rangle$ if and only if $b^2 > 4c$, i.e., when the quadratic polynomial $x^2 + bx + c$ has two distinct real roots. $\square$

The following properties of semialgebraic sets are noteworthy:

- A semialgebraic set S is *semialgebraically connected*, if it is not the union of two disjoint nonempty semialgebraic sets.

  A semialgebraic set S is *semialgebraically path connected* if for every pair of points $p, q \in S$ there is a semialgebraic path connecting p and q (one-dimensional semialgebraic set containing p and q) that lies in S.

- A semialgebraic set is semialgebraically connected if and only if it is semialgebraically path connected. Working over the real numbers, it can be seen that a semialgebraic set is semialgebraically path connected if and only if it is *path connected*. Thus, we may say a semialgebraic set is connected when we mean any of the preceding notions of connectedness.

- A *connected component* (semialgebraically connected component) of a semialgebraic set S is a maximal (semialgebraically) connected subset of S.

- Every semialgebraic set has a finite number of connected components.

- If S is a semialgebraic set, then its *interior*, $\text{int}(S)$, *closure*, $\overline{S}$, and *boundary* $\partial(S) = \overline{S} \setminus \text{int}(S)$ are all semialgebraic.

- For any semialgebraic subset $S \subseteq \mathbb{R}^n$, a *semialgebraic decomposition* of S is a finite collection $\mathcal{K}$ of disjoint connected semialgebraic subsets of S whose union is S. Every semialgebraic set admits a semialgebraic decomposition.

  Let $\mathcal{F} = \{f_{i,j} : i = 1, \ldots, m, \; j = 1, \ldots, l_i\} \subseteq \mathbb{R}[x_1, \ldots, x_n]$ be a set of real multivariate polynomials in n variables. Any point $p = \langle \xi_1, \ldots, \xi_n \rangle \in \mathbb{R}^n$ has a *sign assignment* with respect to $\mathcal{F}$ as follows:

$$\text{sgn}_{\mathcal{F}}(p) = \Big\langle \text{sgn}(f_{i,j}(\xi_1, \ldots, \xi_n)) : i = 1, \ldots, m, \; j = 1, \ldots, l_i \Big\rangle.$$

  Using sign assignments, we can define the following equivalence relation: Given two points $p, q \in \mathbb{R}^n$, we say

$$p \sim_{\mathcal{F}} q, \quad \text{if and only if} \quad \text{sgn}_{\mathcal{F}}(p) = \text{sgn}_{\mathcal{F}}(q).$$

Now consider the partition of $\mathbb{R}^n$ defined by the equivalence relation $\sim_{\mathcal{F}}$; each equivalence class is a semialgebraic set comprising finitely many connected semialgebraic components. Each such equivalence class is called a *sign class* of $\mathcal{F}$.

Clearly, the collection of semialgebraic components of all the sign classes, $\mathcal{K}$, provides a semialgebraic decomposition of $\mathbb{R}^n$. Furthermore, if $S \subseteq \mathbb{R}^n$ is a semialgebraic set defined by some subset of $\mathcal{F}$, then it is easily seen that

$$\Big\{ C \in \mathcal{K} \; : \; C \cap S \neq \emptyset \Big\},$$

defines a semialgebraic decomposition of the semialgebraic set S.

- A *semialgebraic cell-complex* (*cellular decomposition*) for $\mathcal{F}$ is a semialgebraic decomposition of $\mathbb{R}^n$ into finitely many disjoint semialgebraic subsets, $\{C_i\}$, called *cells* such that we have the following:

     1. Each cell C_i is homeomorphic to $\mathbb{R}^{\delta(i)}$, $0 \leq \delta(i) \leq n$. $\delta(i)$ is called the *dimension of the cell* C_i, and C_i is called a $\delta(i)$-*cell*.

     2. Closure of each cell C_i, $\overline{C_i}$, is a union of some cells C_j's:

$$\overline{C_i} = \bigcup_j C_j.$$

     3. Each C_i is contained in some semialgebraic sign class of $\mathcal{F}$—that is, the sign of each $f_{i,j} \in \mathcal{F}$ is *invariant* in each C_i.

Subsequently, we shall study a particularly "nice" semialgebraic cell-complex that is obtained by Collin's *cylindrical algebraic decomposition* or CAD.

8.6.1   Real Algebraic Sets

A special class of semialgebraic sets are the *real algebraic sets* determined by a conjunction of algebraic equalities.

Definition 8.6.3 (Real Algebraic Sets) A subset $Z \subseteq \mathbb{R}^n$ is a said to be a *real algebraic set*, if it can be determined by a system of algebraic equations as follows:

$$Z = \Big\{ \langle \xi_1, \ldots, \xi_n \rangle \in \mathbb{R}^n \; : \; f_1(\xi_1, \ldots, \xi_n) = \cdots = f_m(\xi_1, \ldots, \xi_n) = 0 \Big\},$$

where f_i's are multivariate polynomials in $\mathbb{R}[x_1, \ldots, x_n]$. $\square$

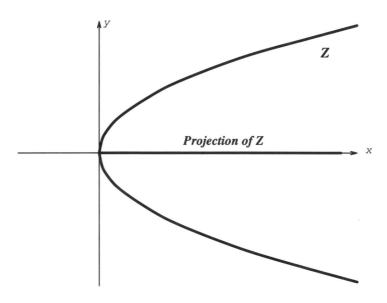

Figure 8.1: Projection of a real algebraic set Z.

Note that a real algebraic set Z could have been defined by a single algebraic equation as follows:

$$Z = \left\{ \langle \xi_1, \ldots, \xi_n \rangle \in \mathbb{R}^n \ : \ f_1^2(\xi_1, \ldots, \xi_n) + \cdots + f_m^2(\xi_1, \ldots, \xi_n) = 0 \right\},$$

as we are working over the field of reals, $\mathbb{R}$.

While real algebraic sets are quite interesting for the same reasons as complex algebraic varieties, they lack certain "nice" geometric properties and hence, are somewhat unwieldy. For instance, *real algebraic sets are not closed under projection onto a subspace*.

Consider the following simple real algebraic set defining a parabola:

$$Z = \left\{ \langle x, y \rangle \in \mathbb{R}^2 \ : \ x = y^2 \right\}.$$

If π_x is a projection map defined as follows:

$$\pi \ : \ \mathbb{R}^2 \to \mathbb{R}$$
$$: \ \langle x, y \rangle \mapsto x,$$

then

$$\pi(Z) = \{ x \in \mathbb{R} \ : \ x \geq 0 \}.$$

See Figure 8.1.

Clearly, $\pi(Z)$ is not algebraic, since only algebraic sets in $\mathbb{R}$ are finite or entire $\mathbb{R}$. However, it is semialgebraic. Additionally, we shall see that semialgebraic sets are closed under projection as well as various other set-theoretic operations. In fact, semialgebraic sets are the smallest class of subsets of $\mathbb{R}^n$ containing real algebraic sets and closed under projection. In the next two subsection, we shall develop some machinery that among other things shows that semialgebraic sets are closed under projection.

8.6.2 Delineability

Let $f_i(x_1, \ldots, x_{n-1}, x_n) \in \mathbb{R}[x_1, \ldots, x_{n-1}, x_n]$ be a polynomial in n variables:

$$\begin{aligned}
f_i(x_1, \ldots, x_{n-1}, x_n) &= f_i^{d_i}(x_1, \ldots, x_{n-1}) \, x_n^{d_i} \\
&\quad + \cdots + f_i^0(x_1, \ldots, x_{n-1}),
\end{aligned}$$

where f_i^j's are in $\mathbb{R}[x_1, \ldots, x_{n-1}]$. Let $p' = \langle \xi_1, \ldots, \xi_{n-1} \rangle \in \mathbb{R}^{n-1}$. Then we write

$$f_{i,p'}(x_n) = f_i^{d_i}(p') \, x_n^{d_i} + \cdots + f_i^0(p'),$$

for the univariate polynomial obtained by substituting p' for the first $(n-1)$ variables.

Definition 8.6.4 (Delineable Sets) Let

$$\mathcal{F} = \left\{ \begin{array}{l}
f_1(x_1, \ldots, x_n), \\
f_2(x_1, \ldots, x_n), \\
\vdots \\
f_s(x_1, \ldots, x_n)
\end{array} \right\} \subseteq \mathbb{R}[x_1, \ldots, x_n]$$

be a set of s n-variate real polynomials. Let $C \subseteq \mathbb{R}^{n-1}$ be a nonempty set homeomorphic to $\mathbb{R}^\delta$ $(0 \leq \delta \leq n - 1)$.

We say $\mathcal{F}$ is *delineable* on C (or, C is $\mathcal{F}$-*delineable*), if it satisfies the following invariant properties:

1. For every $1 \leq i \leq s$, the *total number of complex roots* of $f_{i,p'}$ (counting multiplicity) remains invariant as p' varies over C.

2. For every $1 \leq i \leq s$, the *number of distinct complex roots* of $f_{i,p'}$ (not counting multiplicity) remains invariant as p' varies over C.

3. For every $1 \leq i < j \leq s$, the *total number of common complex roots* of $f_{i,p'}$ and $f_{j,p'}$ (counting multiplicity) remains invariant as p' varies over C. □

Theorem 8.6.2 *Let $\mathcal{F} \subseteq \mathbb{R}[x_1, \ldots, x_n]$ be a set of polynomials as in the preceding definition, and let $C \subseteq \mathbb{R}^{n-1}$ be a connected maximal $\mathcal{F}$-delineable set. Then C is semialgebraic.*

PROOF.

We show that all the three invariant properties of the definition for delineability have semialgebraic characterizations.

(1) The first condition states that

$$\left(\forall\, i\right) \left(\forall\, p' \in C\right) \left[|\mathcal{Z}(f_{i,p'})| = \text{invariant}\right],$$

where $\mathcal{Z}(f)$ denotes the complex roots of f. This condition is simply equivalent to saying that "$\deg(f_{i,p'})$ is invariant (say, k_i)." A straightforward semialgebraic characterization is as follows:

$$\left(\forall\, 1 \le i \le s\right) \left(\exists\, 0 \le k_i \le d_i\right)$$

$$\left[(\forall\, k > k_i)\, [f_i^k(x_1, \ldots, x_{n-1}) = 0] \,\wedge\, f_i^{k_i}(x_1, \ldots, x_{n-1}) \ne 0\right]$$

holds for all $p' \in C$.

(2) The second condition, in view of the first condition, can be restated as follows:

$$\left(\forall\, i\right) \left(\forall\, p' \in C\right) \left[|\mathcal{C}\mathcal{Z}(f_{i,p'}, D_{x_n}(f_{i,p'}))| = \text{invariant}\right],$$

where D_{x_n} denotes the formal derivative operator with respect to the variable x_n and $\mathcal{C}\mathcal{Z}(f,g)$ denotes the common complex roots of f and g. Using principal subresultant coefficients, we can provide the following semialgebraic characterization:

$$\left(\forall\, 1 \le i \le s\right) \left(\exists\, 0 \le l_i \le d_i - 1\right)$$

$$\left[(\forall\, l < l_i)\, [\text{PSC}_l^{x_n}(f_i(x_1, \ldots, x_n), D_{x_n}(f_i(x_1, \ldots, x_n))) = 0]\right.$$

$$\left.\wedge\, \text{PSC}_{l_i}^{x_n}(f_i(x_1, \ldots, x_n), D_{x_n}(f_i(x_1, \ldots, x_n))) \ne 0\right]$$

holds for all $p' \in C$; here $\text{PSC}_l^{x_n}$ denotes the lth principal subresultant coefficient with respect to x_n.

(3) Finally, the last condition can be restated as follows:

$$\left(\forall\, i \ne j\right) \left(\forall\, p' \in C\right) \left[|\mathcal{C}\mathcal{Z}(f_{i,p'}, f_{j,p'})| = \text{invariant}\right].$$

Using principal subresultant coefficients, we can provide the following semialgebraic characterization:

$$\left(\forall\, 1 \le i < j \le s\right) \left(\exists\, 0 \le m_{ij} \le \min(d_i, d_j)\right)$$

$$\left[(\forall\, m < m_{ij})\, [\text{PSC}_m^{x_n}(f_i(x_1, \ldots, x_n), f_j(x_1, \ldots, x_n)) = 0]\right.$$

$$\left.\wedge\, \text{PSC}_{m_{ij}}^{x_n}(f_i(x_1, \ldots, x_n), f_j(x_1, \ldots, x_n)) \ne 0\right],$$

holds for all $p' \in C$; here $\text{PSC}_m^{x_n}$ denotes the mth principal subresultant coefficient with respect to x_n. $\square$

In summary, given a set of polynomials, $\mathcal{F} \in \mathbb{R}[x_1, \ldots, x_n]$, as shown below, we can compute another set of $(n-1)$-variate polynomials, $\Phi(\mathcal{F}) \in \mathbb{R}[x_1, \ldots, x_{n-1}]$, which precisely characterizes the connected maximal $\mathcal{F}$-delineable subsets of $\mathbb{R}^{n-1}$. Let

$$\mathcal{F} = \Big\{ f_1, \ f_2, \ \ldots, \ f_s \Big\};$$

then

$$
\begin{aligned}
\Phi(\mathcal{F}) \ = \ & \Big\{ f_i^k(x_1, \ldots, x_{n-1}) \ : \ 1 \le i \le s, \ 0 \le k \le d_i \Big\} \\
& \cup \Big\{ \mathrm{PSC}_l^{x_n}(f_i(x_1, \ldots, x_n), D_{x_n}(f_i(x_1, \ldots, x_n))) \ : \\
& \qquad\qquad 1 \le i \le s, \ 0 \le l \le d_i - 1 \Big\} \\
& \cup \Big\{ \mathrm{PSC}_m^{x_n}(f_i(x_1, \ldots, x_n), f_j(x_1, \ldots, x_n)) \ : \\
& \qquad\qquad 1 \le i < j \le s, \ 0 \le m \le \min(d_i, d_j) \Big\}.
\end{aligned}
$$

Now, we come to the next important property that *delineability* provides. Clearly, by definition, *the total number of distinct complex roots of the set of polynomials $\mathcal{F}$ is invariant over the connected set $C \subseteq \mathbb{R}^{n-1}$.* But it is also true that *the total number of distinct real roots of $\mathcal{F}$ is invariant over the set C.*

Consider an arbitrary polynomial $f_i \in \mathcal{F}$; since it has real coefficients, its complex roots must occur in conjugate pairs. Thus as $f_{i,p'}$ varies to $f_{i,q'}$ such that some pair of complex conjugate roots (which are necessarily distinct) coalesce into a real root (of multiplicity two), somewhere along a path from p' to q' the total number of distinct roots of f must have dropped. Thus a transition from a nonreal root to a real root is impossible over C. Similar arguments also show that a transition from a real root to a nonreal is impossible as it would imply a splitting of a real root into a pair of distinct complex conjugate roots.

More formally, we argue as follows:

Lemma 8.6.3 *Let $\mathcal{F} \subseteq \mathbb{R}[x_1, \ldots, x_n]$ be a set of polynomials as before, and let $C \subseteq \mathbb{R}^{n-1}$ be a connected $\mathcal{F}$-delineable set. Then the total number of distinct real roots of $\mathcal{F}$ is locally invariant over the set C.*

PROOF.
Consider a polynomial $f_i \in \mathcal{F}$. Let p' and q' be two points in C such that $\|p' - q'\| < \epsilon$ and assume that every root of $f_{i,p'}$ differs from some root of $f_{i,q'}$ by no more that

$$\delta < \left(\frac{1}{2}\right) \mathrm{Separation}(f_{i,p'}),$$

where Separation denotes the complex root separation of $f_{i,p'}$.

Now, let z_j be a complex root of $f_{i,p'}$ such that a disc of radius δ centered around z_j in the complex plane contains a real root y_j of $f_{i,q'}$. But then it can also be shown that y_j is also in a disc of radius δ about $\overline{z_j}$, the complex conjugate of z_j. But then z_j and $\overline{z_j}$ would be closer to each other than Separation$(f_{i,p'})$, contradicting our choice of δ. Thus the total number of distinct complex roots as well as the total number of distinct real roots of f_i remains invariant in any small neighborhood of a point $p' \in C$. $\square$

Lemma 8.6.4 *Let $\mathcal{F} \subseteq \mathbb{R}[x_1, \ldots, x_n]$ and $C \subseteq \mathbb{R}^{n-1}$ be a connected $\mathcal{F}$-delineable set, as in the previous lemma. Then the total number of distinct real roots of $\mathcal{F}$ is invariant over the set C.*

PROOF.

Let p' and q' be two arbitrary points in C connected by a path $\gamma : [0, 1] \to C$ such that $\gamma(0) = p'$ and $\gamma(1) = q'$. Since γ can be chosen to be continuous (even semialgebraic) the image of the compact set $[0, 1]$ under γ, $\Gamma = \gamma([0, 1])$ is also compact. At every point $r' \in \Gamma$ there is a small neighborhood $N(r')$ over which the total number of distinct real roots of $\mathcal{F}$ remains invariant. Now, since the path Γ has a finite cover of such neighborhoods $N(r_1'), N(r_2'), \ldots, N(r_k')$ over each of which the total number of distinct real roots remain invariant, this number also remains invariant over the entire path Γ. Hence, as C is path connected, the lemma follows immediately. $\square$

As an immediate corollary of the preceding lemmas we have the following:

Corollary 8.6.5 *Let $\mathcal{F} \subseteq \mathbb{R}[x_1, \ldots, x_n]$ be a set of polynomials, delineable on a connected set $C \subseteq \mathbb{R}^{n-1}$.*

1. *The complex roots of $\mathcal{F}$ vary continuously over C.*

2. *The real roots of $\mathcal{F}$ vary continuously over C, while maintaining their order; i.e., the jth smallest real root of $\mathcal{F}$ varies continuously over C.* $\square$

Using this corollary, we can describe how the real roots are structured above C. Consider the cylinder over C obtained by taking the direct product of C with the two-point compactification of the reals, $\mathbb{R} \cup \{\pm\infty\}$. Note that the two-point compactification makes it possible to deal with vertical asymptotes of the real hypersurfaces defined by $\mathcal{F}$.

The cylinder $C \times (\mathbb{R} \cup \{\pm\infty\})$ can be partitioned as follows:

Definition 8.6.5 (Sections and Sectors) Suppose $\mathcal{F} \subseteq \mathbb{R}[x_1, \ldots, x_n]$ is delineable on a connected set $C \subseteq \mathbb{R}^{n-1}$. Assume that $\mathcal{F}$ has finitely many distinct real roots over C, given by m continuous functions

$$r_1(p'), r_2(p'), \ldots, r_m(p'),$$

where r_j denotes the jth smallest root of $\mathcal{F}$. (See Figure 8.2). Then we have the following:

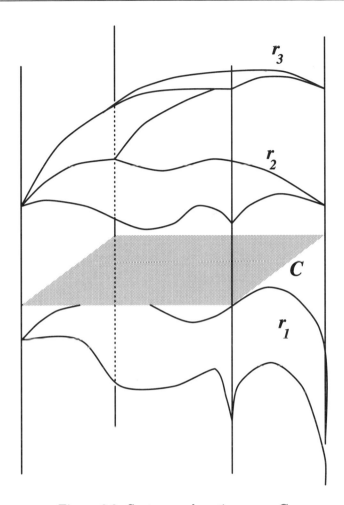

Figure 8.2: Sectors and sections over C.

1. The jth *$\mathcal{F}$-section* over C is

$$\Big\{ \langle p', x_n \rangle \;\; : \;\; p' \in C, \; x_n = r_j(p') \Big\}.$$

2. The jth $(0 < j < n)$ *intermediate $\mathcal{F}$-sector* over C is

$$\Big\{ \langle p', x_n \rangle \;\; : \;\; p' \in C, \; r_j(p') < x_n < r_{j+1}(p') \Big\}.$$

The *lower semiinfinite $\mathcal{F}$-sector* over C is

$$\Big\{ \langle p', x_n \rangle \;\; : \;\; p' \in C, \; x_n < r_1(p') \Big\}.$$

The *upper semiinfinite $\mathcal{F}$-sector* over C is

$$\Big\{ \langle p', x_n \rangle \;\; : \;\; p' \in C, \; x_n > r_m(p') \Big\}. \quad \square$$

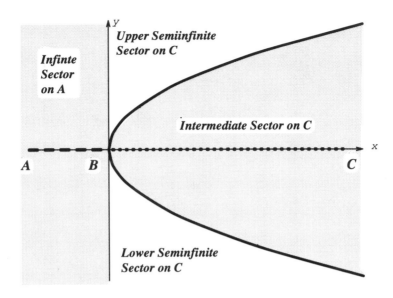

Figure 8.3: Sectors and sections for the parabola example.

Example 8.6.6 Consider the real polynomial $f(x, y) = y^2 - x \in \mathbb{R}[x, y]$ defining a parabola in the plane (see Figure 8.3). Note that

$$f(x, y) = y^2 \, (1) + y^1 \, (0) + y^0 \, (-x),$$

and thus

$$f^2(x) = 1, \quad f^1(x) = 0, \quad \text{and} \quad f^0(x) = -x.$$

Since the subresultant chain of $f = y^2 - x$ and $f' = D_y(f) = 2y$ are given by

$$\begin{aligned}
\text{SubRes}_2(f, f') &= y^2 - x \\
\text{SubRes}_1(f, f') &= 2y \\
\text{SubRes}_0(f, f') &= -4x,
\end{aligned}$$

the principal subresultant coefficients are

$$\text{PSC}_2(x) = 1, \quad \text{PSC}_1 = 2, \quad \text{and} \quad \text{PSC}_0 = -4x.$$

Thus

$$\Phi(\{f\}) = \{1, x\},$$

and the maximal connected f-delineable sets are $A = [-\infty, 0)$, $B = [0, 0]$ and $C = (0, +\infty]$. There is only one infinite sector over A, as for every $x \in A$, $y^2 - x$ has no real zero. There are two semiinfinite sectors and one section over B, as $y^2 - x$ has one zero (of multiplicity two) at $y = 0$.

Finally, there are three sectors and two sections over C, as for every $x \in C$, $y^2 - x$ has two distinct real zeros (each of multiplicity one).

Note that as we traverse along the x-axis from $-\infty$ to $+\infty$, we see that $y^2 - x$ has two distinct complex zeros for all $x < 0$, which coalesce into one real zero at $x = 0$ and then split into two distinct real zeros for $x > 0$.   □

Observe that the $\mathcal{F}$-sections and sectors are uniquely defined by the distinct real root functions of $\mathcal{F}$:

$$r_1(p'), \ r_2(p'), \ \ldots, \ r_m(p'),$$

where it is implicitly assumed that not all $f_{i,p'} \equiv 0$ ($f_i \in \mathcal{F}$). It is sometimes easier to use a single multivariate polynomial $g = \Pi(\mathcal{F})(x_1, \ldots, x_n)$ with

$$g'_p(x_n) = g(p', x_n)$$

vanishing precisely at the distinct roots $r_1(p'), \ r_2(p'), \ \ldots, \ r_m(p')$.

$$\Pi(\mathcal{F})(x_1, \ldots, x_n) = \prod_{f_i \in \mathcal{F}, f_{i,p'} \not\equiv 0} f_i(x_1, \ldots, x_n),$$

where $p' \in C$, a connected $\mathcal{F}$-delineable set. By convention, we shall have $\Pi(\mathcal{F}) = 1$, if all $f_{i,p'} \equiv 0$ ($f_i \in \mathcal{F}$). Also, when $\Pi(\mathcal{F}) = $ constant, the cylinder over C will have exactly one *infinite $\mathcal{F}$-sector*: $C \times \{\mathbb{R} \cup \{\pm\infty\}\}$.

8.6.3   Tarski-Seidenberg Theorem

As an immediate consequence of the preceding discussions, we are now ready to show that *semialgebraic sets are closed under projection*. A more general result in this direction is the famous *Tarski-Seidenberg theorem*.

Definition 8.6.7 (Semialgebraic Map) A map $\psi : S \to T$, from a semialgebraic set $S \subseteq \mathbb{R}^m$ to a semialgebraic set $T \subseteq \mathbb{R}^n$ is said to be a *semialgebraic map*, if its graph

$$\left\{ \langle s, \psi(s) \rangle \in \mathbb{R}^{m+n} : s \in S \right\}$$

is a semialgebraic set in $\mathbb{R}^{m+n}$.   □

Theorem 8.6.6 (Tarski-Seidenberg Theorem) *Let S be a semialgebraic set in $\mathbb{R}^m$ and*

$$\psi : \mathbb{R}^m \to \mathbb{R}^n$$

be a semialgebraic map; then $\psi(S)$ is semialgebraic in $\mathbb{R}^n$.
PROOF.
The proof is by induction on m. We start by considering the base case $m = 1$. Then the graph of ψ, say V, is a semialgebraic set in $\mathbb{R}^{n+1}$ and

the image of S, $\psi(S)$, is a subset of $\mathbb{R}^n$. After suitable renaming of the coordinates, we can so arrange that V is defined by a set of polynomials $\mathcal{F} \subseteq \mathbb{R}[x_1, \ldots, x_{n+1}]$ and $\psi(S) = \pi(V)$ is the projection of V onto the first n coordinates:

$$\pi \; : \; \mathbb{R}^{n+1} \to \mathbb{R}^n$$
$$: \; \langle \xi_1, \ldots, \xi_n, \xi_{n+1} \rangle \mapsto \langle \xi_1, \ldots, \xi_n \rangle.$$

Corresponding to the set $\mathcal{F}$, we can define the set of polynomials $\Phi(\mathcal{F})$ as earlier. Now, note that if C is a cell of a sign-invariant cell decomposition, $\mathcal{K}$ of $\mathbb{R}^n$, defined by $\Phi(\mathcal{F})$, then C is a maximal connected $\mathcal{F}$-delineable set.

Next, we claim that for every $C \in \mathcal{K}$,

$$C \cap \pi(V) \neq \emptyset \;\Rightarrow\; C \subseteq \pi(V).$$

To see this, note that since $C \cap \pi(V) \neq \emptyset$, there is a point $p \in V$, such that $p' = \pi(p) \in C$. Thus p belongs to some $\mathcal{F}$-section or sector defined by some real functions $r_i(p')$ and $r_{i+1}(p')$. Now consider an arbitrary point $q' \in C$; since C is path connected, there is a path $\gamma' : [0,1] \to C$ such that $\gamma'(0) = p'$ and $\gamma'(1) = q'$. This path can be lifted to a path in V, by defining $\gamma : [0,1] \to V$ as follows:

$$\gamma(t) \;=\; \frac{r_{i+1}(\gamma'(t))[p - r_i(p')] - r_i(\gamma'(t))[p - r_{i+1}(p')]}{r_{i+1}(p') - r_i(p')},$$

where $t \in [0,1]$.

Clearly, the path $\gamma([0,1]) \in V$; $\pi(\gamma(t)) = \gamma'(t)$, and $q' \in \pi(V)$, as required. Hence $\psi(S) = \pi(V)$ can be expressed as a union of finitely many semialgebraic cells of the decomposition $\mathcal{K}$, since

$$\pi(V) \;\subseteq\; \bigcup \left\{ C \;:\; C \cap \pi(V) \neq \emptyset \right\} \;\subseteq\; \pi(V).$$

Hence, $\psi(S)$ is semialgebraic in $\mathbb{R}^n$.

For $m > 1$, the proof proceeds by induction, as any projection from $\Pi : \mathbb{R}^m \times \mathbb{R}^n \to \mathbb{R}^n$ can be expressed as a composition of the following two projection maps: $\Pi' : \mathbb{R}^{m-1} \times \mathbb{R}^{n+1} \to \mathbb{R}^{n+1}$ and $\pi' : \mathbb{R}^{n+1} \to \mathbb{R}^n$. $\square$

Corollary 8.6.7 *Let S be a semialgebraic set in $\mathbb{R}^m$ and*

$$\psi : \mathbb{R}^m \to \mathbb{R}^n$$

be a polynomial map; then $\psi(S)$ is semialgebraic in $\mathbb{R}^n$.

PROOF.

Let ψ be given by the following sequence of polynomials

$$g_k(x_1, \ldots, x_m) \in \mathbb{R}[x_1, \ldots, x_m], \qquad k = 1, \ldots, n.$$

Then the graph of the map is defined by

$$(S \times \mathbb{R}^n) \cap T,$$

where

$$T = \Big\{ \langle \xi_1, \ldots, \xi_m, \zeta_1, \ldots, \zeta_n \rangle \in \mathbb{R}^{m+n} :$$

$$g_k(\xi_1, \ldots, \xi_m) - \zeta_k = 0, \quad \text{for all } k = 1, \ldots, n \Big\}.$$

Thus ψ is a semialgebraic map and the rest follows from the Tarski-Seidenberg theorem. $\square$

8.6.4   Representation and Decomposition of Semialgebraic Sets

Using the ideas developed in this chapter (i.e., Sturm's theory and real algebraic numbers), we can already see how semialgebraic sets in $\mathbb{R} \cup \{\pm\infty\}$ can be represented and manipulated easily. In this one-dimensional case, the semialgebraic sets can be represented as a union of finitely many intervals whose endpoints are real algebraic numbers. For instance, given a set of univariate defining polynomials:

$$\mathcal{F} = \Big\{ f_{i,j}(x) \in \mathbb{Q}[x] \ : \ i = 1, \ldots, m, \ j = 1, \ldots, l_i \Big\},$$

we may enumerate all the real roots of the $f_{i,j}$'s (i.e., the real roots of the single polynomial $F = \prod_{i,j} f_{i,j}$) as

$$-\infty < \xi_1 < \xi_2 < \cdots < \xi_{i-1} < \xi_i < \xi_{i+1} < \cdots < \xi_s < +\infty,$$

and consider the following finite set $\mathcal{K}$ of elementary intervals defined by these roots:

$$[-\infty, \xi_1), \ [\xi_1, \xi_1], \ (\xi_1, \xi_2), \ \ldots,$$

$$(\xi_{i-1}, \xi_i), \ [\xi_i, \xi_i], \ (\xi_i, \xi_{i+1}), \ \ldots, \ [\xi_s, \xi_s], \ (\xi_s, +\infty].$$

Note that, these intervals are defined by real algebraic numbers with defining polynomial

$$\Pi(\mathcal{F}) = \prod_{f_{i,j} \not\equiv 0 \in \mathcal{F}} f_{i,j}(x).$$

Now, any semialgebraic set in $S \subseteq \mathbb{R} \cup \{\pm\infty\}$ defined by $\mathcal{F}$:

$$S = \bigcup_{i=1}^{m} \bigcap_{j=1}^{l_i} \Big\{ \xi \in \mathbb{R} \cup \{\pm\infty\} \ : \ \mathrm{sgn}(f_{i,j}(\xi)) = s_{i,j} \Big\},$$

where $s_{i,j} \in \{-1, 0, +1\}$, can be seen to be the union of a subset of elementary intervals in $\mathcal{K}$. Furthermore, this subset can be identified as follows: if, for every interval $C \in \mathcal{K}$, we have a sample point $\alpha_C \in C$, then C belongs to S if and only if

$$\left(\forall \, i, j \right) \left[\operatorname{sgn}(f_{i,j}(\alpha)) = s_{i,j} \right].$$

For each interval $C \in \mathcal{K}$, we can compute a sample point (an algebraic number) α_C as follows:

$$\alpha_C = \begin{cases} \xi_1 - 1, & \text{if } C = [-\infty, \xi_1); \\ \xi_i, & \text{if } C = [\xi_i, \xi_i]; \\ (\xi_i + \xi_{i+1})/2, & \text{if } C = (\xi_i, \xi_{i+1}); \\ \xi_s + 1, & \text{if } C = (\xi_s, +\infty]. \end{cases}$$

Note that the computation of the sample points in the intervals, their representations, and the evaluation of other polynomials at these points can all be performed by the Sturm theory developed earlier.

A generalization of the above representation to higher dimensions can be provided by using the machinery developed for delineability. In order to represent a semialgebraic set $S \subseteq \mathbb{R}^n$, we may assume recursively that we can represent its projection $\pi(S) \subseteq \mathbb{R}^{n-1}$ (also a semialgebraic set), and then represent S as a union of the sectors and sections in the cylinders above each cell of a semialgebraic decomposition of $\pi(S)$. This also leads to a semialgebraic decomposition of S.

We can further assign an algebraic sample point in each cell of the decomposition of S recursively as follows: Assume that the (algebraic) sample points for each cell of $\pi(S)$ have already been computed recursively. Note that a vertical line passing through a sample point of $\pi(S)$ intersects the sections above the corresponding cell at algebraic points. From these algebraic points, we can derive the algebraic sample points for the cells of S, in a manner similar to the one-dimensional case.

If $\mathcal{F}$ is a defining set for $S \subseteq \mathbb{R}^n$, then for no additional cost, we may in fact compute a sign invariant semialgebraic decomposition of $\mathbb{R}^n$ for all the sign classes of $\mathcal{F}$, using the procedure described above. Such a decomposition leads to a semialgebraic cell-complex, called *cylindrical algebraic decomposition* (CAD). This notion will be made more precise below. Note that since we have an algebraic sample point for each cell, we can compute the sign assignment with respect to $\mathcal{F}$ of each cell of the decomposition and hence determine exactly those cells whose union constitutes S.

8.6.5   Cylindrical Algebraic Decomposition

Definition 8.6.8 [Cylindrical Algebraic Decomposition (CAD)] A *cylindrical algebraic decomposition* (CAD) of $\mathbb{R}^n$ is defined inductively as follows:

- BASE CASE: $n = 1$.

  A partition of $\mathbb{R}^1$ into a finite set of algebraic numbers, and into the finite and infinite open intervals bounded by these numbers.

- INDUCTIVE CASE: $n > 1$.

  Assume inductively that we have a CAD $\mathcal{K}'$ of $\mathbb{R}^{n-1}$. Define a CAD $\mathcal{K}$ of $\mathbb{R}^n$ via an *auxiliary polynomial*

$$g_{C'}(\overline{x}, x_n) = g_{C'}(x_1, \ldots, x_{n-1}, x_n) \in \mathbb{Q}[x_1, \ldots, x_n],$$

one per each $C' \in \mathcal{K}'$. The cells of $\mathcal{K}$ are of two kinds:

1. For each $C' \in \mathcal{K}'$,

$$C' \times (\mathbb{R} \cup \{\pm\infty\}) = \textit{cylindrical over } C.$$

2. For each cell $C' \in \mathcal{K}'$, the polynomial $g_{C'}(p', x_n)$ has m distinct real roots for each $p' \in C'$:

$$r_1(p'), r_2(p'), \ldots, r_m(p'),$$

each r_i being a continuous function of p'. The following sectors and sections are cylindrical over C':

$$
\begin{aligned}
C_0^* &= \left\{ \langle p', x_n \rangle \ : \ x_n \in [-\infty, r_1(p')) \right\}, \\
C_1 &= \left\{ \langle p', x_n \rangle \ : \ x_n \in [r_1(p'), r_1(p')] \right\}, \\
C_1^* &= \left\{ \langle p', x_n \rangle \ : \ x_n \in (r_1(p'), r_2(p')) \right\}, \\
C_2 &= \left\{ \langle p', x_n \rangle \ : \ x_n \in [r_2(p'), r_2(p')] \right\}, \\
&\ \ \vdots \\
C_m &= \left\{ \langle p', x_n \rangle \ : \ x_n \in [r_m(p'), r_m(p')] \right\}, \\
C_m^* &= \left\{ \langle p', x_n \rangle \ : \ x_n \in (r_m(p'), +\infty] \right\}.
\end{aligned}
$$

See Figure 8.4 for an example of a cylindrical algebraic decomposition of $\mathbb{R}^2$. $\quad\square$

Let

$$\mathcal{F} = \left\{ f_{i,j}(x_1, \ldots, x_n) \in \mathbb{Q}[x_1, \ldots, x_n] \ : \ i = 1, \ldots, m, \ \ j = 1, \ldots, l_i \right\}.$$

In order to compute a cylindrical algebraic decomposition of $\mathbb{R}^n$, which is $\mathcal{F}$-sign-invariant, we follow the following three steps:

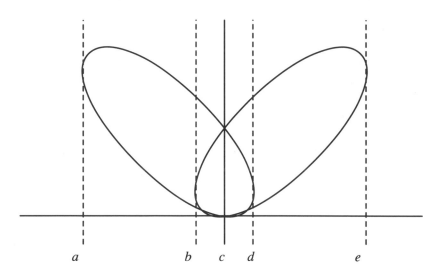

Figure 8.4: Cylindrical algebraic decomposition.

1. **Project**: Compute the $(n-1)$-variate polynomials $\Phi(\mathcal{F})$. Note that if $|\mathcal{F}|$ is the number of polynomials in $\mathcal{F}$ and d is the maximum degree of any polynomial in $\mathcal{F}$, then

$$|\Phi(\mathcal{F})| = O(d\,|\mathcal{F}|^2) \quad \text{and} \quad \deg(\Phi(\mathcal{F})) = O(d^2).$$

2. **Recur**: Apply the algorithm recursively to compute a CAD of $\mathbb{R}^{n-1}$ which is $\Phi(\mathcal{F})$-sign-invariant.

3. **Lift**: Lift the $\Phi(\mathcal{F})$-sign-invariant CAD of $\mathbb{R}^{n-1}$ up to a $\mathcal{F}$-sign-invariant CAD of $\mathbb{R}^n$ using the auxiliary polynomial $\Pi(\mathcal{F})$ of degree no larger than $d\,|\mathcal{F}|$.

It is easy to see how to modify the above procedure in order that we also have a sample point (with algebraic number coordinates) for each cell of the final cell decomposition. The complete algorithm is as follows:

CAD($\mathcal{F}$)
Input: $\mathcal{F} \subseteq \mathbb{Q}[x_1, \ldots, x_n]$.

Output: A $\mathcal{F}$-sign-invariant CAD of $\mathbb{R}^n$.

     if $n = 1$ then
         Decompose $\mathbb{R} \cup \{\pm\infty\}$ by the set of real roots of the polynomials of $\mathcal{F}$; Compute the sample points to be these real roots and their midpoints;

elsif $n > 1$ then
    Construct $\Phi(\mathcal{F}) \subseteq \mathbb{Q}[x_1, \ldots, x_{n-1}]$;

$\mathcal{K}' := \text{CAD}(\Phi(\mathcal{F}))$;
Comment: $\mathcal{K}'$ is a $\Phi(\mathcal{F})$-sign-invariant CAD of $\mathbb{R}^{n-1}$.

for each $C' \in \mathcal{K}'$ loop
    Construct $\Pi(\mathcal{F})$, the product of those polynomials of $\mathcal{F}$ that do not vanish at some sample point $\alpha_{C'} \in C'$; Decompose $\mathbb{R} \cup \{\pm\infty\}$ by the roots of $\Pi(\mathcal{F})$ into sections and sectors;
    Comment: The decomposition leads to a decomposition $\mathcal{K}_{C'}$ of $C' \times (\mathbb{R} \cup \{\pm\infty\})$;

The sample points above C':

$$\langle \alpha_{C'}, \; r_1(\alpha_{C'}) - 1 \rangle,$$
$$\langle \alpha_{C'}, \; r_1(\alpha_{C'}) \rangle,$$
$$\langle \alpha_{C'}, \; (r_1(\alpha_{C'}), r_2(\alpha_{C'}))/2 \rangle,$$
$$\langle \alpha_{C'}, \; r_2(\alpha_{C'}) \rangle,$$
$$\vdots$$
$$\langle \alpha_{C'}, \; r_m(\alpha_{C'}) \rangle,$$
$$\langle \alpha_{C'}, \; r_m(\alpha_{C'}) + 1 \rangle,$$

where r_i's are the real root functions for $\Pi(\mathcal{F})$;

Each cell of the $\mathcal{K}_{C'}$ has a propositional defining sentence involving sign sequences for $\Phi(\mathcal{F})$ and $\mathcal{F}$;
end{loop };

$\mathcal{K} := \bigcup_{C' \in \mathcal{K}'} \mathcal{K}_{C'}$;
end{if };

return $\mathcal{K}$;
end{CAD} $\square$

Complexity

If we assume that the dimension n is a fixed constant, then the algorithm CAD is polynomial in $|\mathcal{F}|$ and $\deg(\mathcal{F})$. However, the algorithm can be easily seen to be double exponential in n as the number of polynomials produced at the lowest dimension is

$$\left(|\mathcal{F}| \; \deg(\mathcal{F}) \right)^{2^{O(n)}},$$

each of degree no larger than $d^{2^{O(n)}}$. Also, the number of cells produced by the algorithm is given by the *double exponential* function

$$\left(|\mathcal{F}| \deg(\mathcal{F})\right)^{2^{O(n)}},$$

while it is known that the total number of $\mathcal{F}$-sign-invariant connected components are bounded by the following *single-exponential* function:

$$\left(\frac{O(|\mathcal{F}| \deg(\mathcal{F}))}{n}\right)^n.$$

In summary, we have the following:

Theorem 8.6.8 (Collin's Theorem) *Given a finite set of multivariate polynomials*

$$\mathcal{F} \subseteq \mathbb{Q}[x_1, \ldots, x_n],$$

we can effectively construct the followings:

- *An $\mathcal{F}$-sign-invariant cylindrical algebraic decomposition of $\mathcal{K}$ of $\mathbb{R}^n$ into semialgebraic connected cells. Each cell $C \in \mathcal{K}$ is homeomorphic to $\mathbb{R}^\delta$, for some $0 \le \delta \le n$.*

- *A sample algebraic point p_C in each cell $C \in \mathcal{K}$ and defining polynomials for each sample point p_C.*

- *Quantifier-free defining sentences for each cell $C \in \mathcal{K}$.*   □

Furthermore, the cylindrical algebraic decomposition produced by the CAD algorithm is a *cell complex*, if the set of defining polynomials

$$\mathcal{F} \subseteq \mathbb{Q}[x_1, \ldots, x_n],$$

is *well-based* in $\mathbb{R}^n$ in the sense that the following nondegeneracy conditions hold:

1. For all $p' \in \mathbb{R}^{n-1}$,

$$\left(\forall f_i \in \mathcal{F}\right) \left[f_i(p', x_n) \not\equiv 0\right].$$

2. $\Phi(\mathcal{F})$ is *well-based* in $\mathbb{R}^{n-1}$. That is, For all $p'' \in \mathbb{R}^{n-2}$,

$$\left(\forall g_j \in \Phi(\mathcal{F})\right) \left[g_j(p'', x_{n-1}) \not\equiv 0\right],$$

and so on.

The resulting CAD is said to be *well-based*. Also note that, given an $\mathcal{F}$, there is always a linear change of coordinates that results in a well-based system of polynomials. As a matter of fact, any random change of coordinates will result in a well-based system *almost surely*.

Theorem 8.6.9 *If the cellular decomposition $\mathcal{K}$ produced by the* CAD *algorithm is well-based, then $\mathcal{K}$ is a* semialgebraic cell complex.

PROOF.

As a result of Collin's theorem, we only need to show that

Closure of each cell $C_i \in \mathcal{K}$, $\overline{C_i}$ is a union of some cells C_j's:

$$\overline{C_i} = \bigcup_j C_j.$$

The proof proceeds by induction on the dimension, n. When $n = 1$, it is easy to see that the decomposition is a cell complex as the decomposition consists of zero-dimensional closed cells (points) or one-dimensional open cells (open intervals) whose limit points (endpoints of the interval) are included in the decomposition.

Let $C_i \in \mathcal{K}$ be a cell in $\mathbb{R}^n$, which is cylindrical over some cell $C'_k \in \mathcal{K}'$, a CAD of $\mathbb{R}^{n-1}$. By the inductive hypothesis, we may assume that $\mathcal{K}'$ is a cell complex and

$$\overline{C'_k} = C'_k \cup C'_{k_1} \cup C'_{k_2} \cup \cdots \cup C'_{k_l},$$

where C'_{k_i}'s are in $\mathcal{K}'$.

We show that

1. If C_i is a *section*, then $\overline{C_i}$ consists of

   (a) C_i itself.

   (b) Limit points of C_i. These are comprised of sections cylindrical over cells in $\partial C'_k$.

2. If C_i is a *sector*, then $\overline{C_i}$ consists of:

   (a) C_i itself.

   (b) Limit points of C_i. These are comprised of upper and lower bounding sections for C_i, cylindrical over C'_K, and sectors and sections cylindrical over cells in $\partial C'_k$.

The key idea is to show that, since sections are given by some continuous real root function $r_j(p')$, the closure of a particular section C_i is simply the image of a real root function over some cell $C'_{k_m} \subseteq \partial C'_k$ *which extends* $r_j(p')$.

The proof is by contradiction: consider a sequence of points p'_1, p'_2, p'_3, ..., in C'_k, which converges to some point $p'^* \in C'_{k_1} \subseteq \partial C'_k$, say. This sequence of points can be lifted to a sequence of points in the section C_i by the real root function r_j:

$$p_1 = \langle p'_1, r_j(p'_1) \rangle, \quad p_2 = \langle p'_2, r_j(p'_2) \rangle, \quad p_3 = \langle p'_3, r_j(p'_3) \rangle, \ldots.$$

For every neighborhood N containing p'^*, consider its image under the map r_j. The intersection of all such neighborhoods must be a connected interval of $J \subseteq p'^* \times \mathbb{R}$. Also, all the defining polynomials $\mathcal{F}$ must vanish over J. But as a direct consequence of the well-basedness assumption, we find that J must be a point contained in the image of a real root function over $C'_{k_1} \subseteq \partial C'_k$. The rest follows from a direct examination of the geometry of a cylindrical algebraic decomposition. $\square$

The resulting cell complex is usually represented by a labeled directed graph $G = \langle V, E, \delta, \sigma \rangle$, where

$$V \quad = \quad \text{vertices representing the cells}$$

$$E \quad = \quad \text{edges representing the incidence relation among the cells}$$

$$uEv \quad \Leftrightarrow \quad C_u \subseteq \overline{C_v}$$

$$\delta \quad : \quad V \to \mathbb{N} \quad = \quad \text{dimension of the cells}$$

$$\sigma \quad : \quad V \to \{-1, 0, +1\} \quad = \quad \text{sign assignment to the cells}$$

Such a graph allows one to study the connectivity structures of the cylindrical decomposition, and has important applications to robotics path planning. G is said to be a *connectivity graph of a cell complex*.

8.6.6 Tarski Geometry

Tarski sentences are semantic clauses in a first-order language (defined by Tarski in 1930) of equalities, inequalities, and inequations of algebraic functions over the real. Such sentences may be constructed by introducing the following quantifiers, "$\forall$" (universal quantifier) and "$\exists$" (existential quantifier), to the propositional algebraic sentences. The quantifiers are assumed to range over the real numbers.

Let $\mathcal{Q}$ stand for a quantifier (either universal $\forall$ or existential $\exists$). If $\phi(y_1, \ldots, y_r)$ is a propositional algebraic sentence, then it is also a first-order algebraic sentence. All The variables y's are *free* in ϕ. Let $\Phi(y_1, \ldots, y_r)$ and $\Psi(z_1, \ldots, z_s)$ be two first-order algebraic sentences (with free variables y's and z's, respectively); then a sentence combining Φ and Ψ by a Boolean connective is a first-order algebraic sentence with free variables $\{y_i\} \cup \{z_i\}$. Lastly, let $\Phi(y_1, \ldots, y_r, x)$ be a first-order algebraic sentence (with free variables x and y), then

$$\left(\mathcal{Q}\, x \right) \left[\Phi(y_1, \ldots, y_r, x) \right]$$

is a first-order algebraic sentence with only y's as the free variables. The variable x is *bound* in $(\mathcal{Q}\, x)[\Phi]$.

A Tarski sentence $\Phi(y_1, \ldots, y_r)$ with free variable y's is said to be true, if for all $\langle \zeta_1, \ldots, \zeta_r \rangle \in \mathbb{R}^r$

$$\Phi(\zeta_1, \ldots, \zeta_r) = \mathsf{True}.$$

Example 8.6.9   1. Let $f(x) \in \mathbb{Z}[x]$ have the following real roots:

$$\alpha_1 < \cdots < \alpha_{j-1} < \alpha_j < \cdots .$$

Then the algebraic number α_j can be expressed as

$$f(y) = 0 \quad \wedge \quad \left(\exists\, x_1, \ldots, x_{j-1} \right)$$
$$\Big[(x_2 - x_1 > 0) \wedge \cdots \wedge (x_{j-1} - x_{j-2} > 0)$$
$$\wedge\, (f(x_1) = 0) \wedge \cdots \wedge (f(x_{j-1}) = 0)$$
$$\wedge\, (\forall\, z)\, [(f(z) = 0 \wedge y - z > 0)$$
$$\Rightarrow\, ((z - x_1 = 0) \vee \cdots \vee (z - x_{j-1} = 0))] \;\Big].$$

If (l, r) is an isolating interval for α_j, we could also express the real root α_j by the following Tarski sentence:

$$(f(y) = 0) \wedge (y - l > 0) \wedge (r - y > 0)$$
$$\wedge\, \left(\forall\, x \right) \Big[((x - y \neq 0) \wedge (x - l > 0) \wedge (r - x > 0)) \;\Rightarrow\; f(x) \neq 0 \Big].$$

2. Consider the following Tarski sentence:

$$\left(\exists\, x \right) \left(\forall\, y \right) \Big[(y^2 - x > 0) \Big].$$

The sentence can be seen to be true, since if we choose a strictly negative number as a value for x, then for all y, the difference of y^2 and x is always strictly positive.

Next, consider the following Tarski sentence:

$$\left(\exists\, x \right) \left(\forall\, y \right) \Big[(y^2 - x < 0) \Big].$$

The sentence can be seen to be false.

3. Let $S \subseteq \mathbb{R}^n$ be a semialgebraic set; then its closure $\overline{S}$ can be defined by the following Tarski sentence:

$$\Psi(\bar{x}) = \left(\forall\, \epsilon \right) \Big[(\epsilon > 0) \;\Rightarrow\; (\exists\, \bar{y})\, [\Phi_S(\bar{y}) \wedge \|\bar{x} - \bar{y}\|_2 < \epsilon] \Big],$$

where Φ_S is a defining formula for S. $\overline{S} = \{\bar{x} : \Psi(\bar{x})\}$.

4. Let C_1 and C_2 be two cells of a cylindrical algebraic decomposition of $\mathbb{R}^n$, with defining formulas Φ_{C_1} and Φ_{C_2}, respectively. C_1 and C_2 are *adjacent* if and only if

$$C_1 \cap \overline{C_2} \neq \emptyset \quad \text{or} \quad \overline{C_1} \cap C_2 \neq \emptyset.$$

The following Tarski sentence characterizes the adjacency relation:

$$\left(\exists \, \bar{x}\right)\left(\forall \, \epsilon\right)\left(\exists \, \bar{y}\right)$$
$$\Big[(((\epsilon > 0) \wedge \Phi_{C_1}(\bar{x})) \Rightarrow (\Phi_{C_2}(\bar{y}) \wedge (\|\bar{x} - \bar{y}\|_2 < \epsilon)))$$
$$\vee \, (((\epsilon > 0) \wedge \Phi_{C_2}(\bar{x})) \Rightarrow (\Phi_{C_2}(\bar{y}) \wedge (\|\bar{x} - \bar{y}\|_2 < \epsilon)))\Big].$$

Since we shall produce an effective decision procedure for Tarski sentences, we see that one can construct the connectivity graph of a cell complex effectively, provided that we have the defining formulas for the cells of the cell complex. $\square$

A Tarski sentence is said to be *prenex* if it has the form

$$\left(\mathcal{Q} \, x_1\right)\left(\mathcal{Q} \, x_2\right) \cdots \left(\mathcal{Q} \, x_n\right) \Big[\phi(y_1, y_2, \ldots, y_r, x_1, \ldots, x_n)\Big],$$

where ϕ is quantifier-free. The string of quantifiers $(\mathcal{Q} \, x_1)(\mathcal{Q} \, x_2) \cdots (\mathcal{Q} \, x_n)$ is called the *prefix* and ϕ is called the *matrix*. Given a Tarski sentence Ψ, a prenex Tarski sentence logically equivalent to Ψ is called its *prenex form*.

The following procedure shows that for every Tarski sentence, one can find its prenex form:

1. STEP 1: Eliminate redundant quantifiers. Replace a subformula $(\mathcal{Q} \, x)[\Phi]$ by Φ, if x does not occur in Φ.

2. STEP 2: Rename variables such that the same variable does not occur as free and bound. If there are two subformulas $\Psi(x)$ and $(\mathcal{Q} \, x)[\Phi(x)]$ at the same level, replace the latter by $(\mathcal{Q} \, x_{\text{new}})[\Phi(x_{\text{new}})]$, where x_{new} is a new variable not occurring before.

3. STEP 3: Move negations ($\neg$) inward.

$$
\begin{array}{rcl}
\neg(\forall \, x)[\Phi(x)] & \rightarrow & (\exists \, x)[\neg\Phi(x)] \\
\neg(\exists \, x)[\Phi(x)] & \rightarrow & (\forall \, x)[\neg\Phi(x)] \\
\neg(\Phi \vee \Psi) & \rightarrow & (\neg\Phi \wedge \neg\Psi) \\
\neg(\Phi \wedge \Psi) & \rightarrow & (\neg\Phi \vee \neg\Psi) \\
\neg\neg\Phi & \rightarrow & \Phi
\end{array}
$$

4. STEP 4: Push quantifiers to the left.

$$
\begin{array}{rcl}
(\mathcal{Q} \, x)[\Phi(x)] \wedge \Psi & \rightarrow & (\mathcal{Q} \, x)[\Phi(x) \wedge \Psi] \\
(\mathcal{Q} \, x)[\Phi(x)] \vee \Psi & \rightarrow & (\mathcal{Q} \, x)[\Phi(x) \vee \Psi] \\
\Psi \wedge (\mathcal{Q} \, x)[\Phi(x)] & \rightarrow & (\mathcal{Q} \, x)[\Psi \wedge \Phi(x)] \\
\Psi \vee (\mathcal{Q} \, x)[\Phi(x)] & \rightarrow & (\mathcal{Q} \, x)[\Psi \vee \Phi(x)]
\end{array}
$$

Example 8.6.10 Consider the following Tarski sentence:

$$\Big(\forall\, x\Big)\ \Big[((\forall\, y)\ [f(x) = 0] \vee (\forall\, z)\ [g(z,y) > 0]) \ \Rightarrow\ \neg(\forall\, y)\ [h(x,y) \le 0]\Big].$$

After eliminating redundant quantifiers and renaming variables,

$$\Big(\forall\, x\Big)\ \Big[(([f(x) = 0] \vee (\forall\, z)\ [g(z,y) > 0]) \ \Rightarrow\ \neg(\forall\, w)\ [h(x,w) \le 0]\Big].$$

After simplification, we have

$$\Big(\forall\, x\Big)\ \Big[(([f(x) \ne 0] \wedge \neg(\forall\, z)\ [g(z,y) > 0]) \ \vee\ \neg(\forall\, w)\ [h(x,w) \le 0]\Big].$$

After moving negations inward,

$$\Big(\forall\, x\Big)\ \Big[(([f(x) \ne 0] \wedge (\exists\, z)\ [g(z,y) \le 0]) \ \vee\ (\exists\, w)\ [h(x,w) > 0]\Big].$$

After pushing the quantifiers outward,

$$\Big(\forall\, x\Big)\ \Big(\exists\, z\Big)\ \Big(\exists\, w\Big)\ \Big[((f(x) \ne 0) \wedge (g(z,y) \le 0)) \ \vee\ (h(x,w) > 0)\Big]. \qquad \square$$

Finally, we are ready to consider an effective procedure to decide whether a given Tarski sentence $\Psi(x_1, \ldots, x_r)$ is true. Here $x_1, \ldots, x_r$ are assumed to be its free variables, and the polynomials occurring in Ψ are assumed to have rational coefficients.

As a result of our earlier discussion, we may assume that our Tarski sentence is presented in its prenex form and that it is universally closed with respect to its free variables.

$$(\forall\, x_1) \ \cdots\ (\forall\, x_r)\ \Psi(x_1, \ldots, x_r)$$
$$= \ (\forall\, x_1)\ \cdots\ (\forall\, x_r)\ (\mathcal{Q}x_{r+1})\ \cdots\ (\mathcal{Q}x_n)\ [\psi(x_1, \ldots, x_r, x_{r+1}, \ldots, x_n)],$$

ψ is a quantifier-free matrix. Thus from now on we deal only with prenex Tarski sentences with no free variable and where the variables are so ordered that in the prefix the n variables appear in the order

$$x_1, x_2, \ldots, x_n.$$

One can describe the decision procedure for such a Tarski sentence in terms of a Player-Adversary game. We start with the following illustrations:

Example 8.6.11   1. The game for the following Tarski sentence proceeds as shown below:

$$\Big(\exists\, x\Big)\ \Big(\forall\, y\Big)\ \Big[(y^2 - x > 0)\Big].$$

The first quantifier is $\exists$ and the first move is Player's. Player chooses a strictly negative number for x, say -1. The second quantifier is a $\forall$ and the next move is Adversary's. Now independent of what Adversary chooses for y, we see that

$$y^2 - (-1) = y^2 + 1 > 0.$$

The matrix is true, and hence Player *wins* and the Tarski sentence is true.

2. Next consider the game for the following Tarski sentence:

$$\left(\exists\, x\right) \left(\forall\, y\right) \left[(y^2 - x < 0)\right].$$

Again the first quantifier is $\exists$ and the first move is Player's. Let Player choose $x = a$. The second quantifier is a $\forall$ and the next move is Adversary's. Adversary chooses $y = a + (1/2)$, and we have

$$y^2 - x \; = \; (a + 1/2)^2 - a \; = \; a^2 + 1/4 \; > \; 0.$$

The matrix is false, and hence Adversary *wins* and the Tarski sentence is false.

Thus given a Tarski sentence

$$(\mathcal{Q}_1 x_1) \; \cdots \; (\mathcal{Q}_n x_n) \, [\psi(x_1, \ldots, x_n)],$$

the ith $(i = 1, \ldots, n)$ move is as follows: Assume the values selected up to this point are

$$\zeta_1, \; \zeta_2, \; \ldots, \; \zeta_{i-1}$$

- If the ith quantifier $\mathcal{Q}_i$ is $\exists$, then it is Player's move; otherwise, if $\mathcal{Q}_i$ is $\forall$, then it is Adversary's move.

- If it is Player's move, he selects $x_i = \zeta_i$ in order to force a win for himself, i.e., he tries to make the following hold:

$$(\mathcal{Q}_{i+1} x_{i+1}) \; \cdots \; (\mathcal{Q}_n x_n) \, [\psi(\zeta_1, \ldots, \zeta_i, x_{i+1}, \ldots, x_n)] = \mathsf{True}.$$

If it is Adversary's move, he selects $x_i = \zeta_i$ in order to force a win for himself, i.e., he tries to make the following hold:

$$(\mathcal{Q}_{i+1} x_{i+1}) \; \cdots \; (\mathcal{Q}_n x_n) \, [\psi(\zeta_1, \ldots, \zeta_i, x_{i+1}, \ldots, x_n)] = \mathsf{False}.$$

After all ζ_i's have been chosen, we evaluate

$$\psi(\zeta_1, \ldots, \zeta_n);$$

If it is true, then Player wins (i.e., the Tarski sentence is true); otherwise, Adversary wins (i.e., the Tarski sentence is false). Thus, the sequence of choices in this game results in a point

$$p = \langle \zeta_1, \ldots, \zeta_n \rangle \in \mathbb{R}^n,$$

and the final outcome depends on this point p.

Let $\mathcal{F} \subseteq \mathbb{Q}[x_1, \ldots, x_n]$ be the set of polynomials appearing in the matrix ψ. Now consider a cylindrical algebraic decomposition $\mathcal{K}$ of $\mathbb{R}^n$ for $\mathcal{F}$. Let $C_p \in \mathcal{K}$ be the cell containing p. If $q \in C_p$ is a sample point in the cell C_p

$$q = \langle \alpha_1, \ldots, \alpha_n \rangle \in \mathbb{R}^n,$$

then the α_i's constitute a winning strategy for Player (respectively, Adversary) if and only if ζ_i's also constitute a winning strategy for Player (respectively, Adversary). Thus, *the search could have been conducted only over the coordinates of the sample points in the cylindrical algebraic decomposition*. This leads to an effective procedure, once a cylindrical algebraic decomposition for $\mathcal{F}$, endowed with the sample points, have been computed.

Since the cylindrical algebraic decomposition produces a sequence of decompositions:

$$\mathcal{K}_1 \text{ of } \mathbb{R}^1, \quad \mathcal{K}_2 \text{ of } \mathbb{R}^2, \quad \ldots, \quad \mathcal{K}_n \text{ of } \mathbb{R}^n,$$

such that the each cell $C_{i-1,j}$ of $\mathcal{K}_i$ is cylindrical over some cell C_{i-1} of $\mathcal{K}_{i-1}$, the search progresses by first finding cells C_1 of $\mathcal{K}_1$ such that

$$(\mathcal{Q}_2 x_2) \cdots (\mathcal{Q}_n x_n) [\psi(\alpha_{C_1}, x_2, \ldots, x_n)] = \mathsf{True}.$$

For each C_1, the search continues over cells C_{12} of $\mathcal{K}_2$ cylindrical over C_1 such that

$$(\mathcal{Q}_3 x_3) \cdots (\mathcal{Q}_n x_n) [\psi(\alpha_{C_1}, \alpha_{C_{12}}, x_3, \ldots, x_n)] = \mathsf{True},$$

etc. Finally, at the bottom level the truth properties of the matrix ψ are evaluated at all the sample points.

This produces a tree structure, where each node at the $(i-1)^{\text{th}}$ level corresponds to a cell $C_{i-1} \in \mathcal{K}_{i-1}$ and its children correspond to the cells $C_{i-1,j} \in \mathcal{K}_i$ that are cylindrical over C_{i-1}. The leaves of the tree correspond to the cells of the final decomposition $\mathcal{K} = \mathcal{K}_n$. Using the game-theoretic nature of the problem discussed earlier we can further label every node at the $(i-1)^{\text{th}}$ level "AND" (respectively, "OR") if $\mathcal{Q}_i$ is a universal quantifier $\forall$ (respectively, $\exists$). Such a tree is a so-called AND-OR tree.

The tree may be evaluated as follows: First label the leaves true or false, depending on whether the matrix ψ evaluates to true or false in the corresponding cell. Note that the truth value of ψ depends only on the sign assignment of the cell. Inductively, assuming all the nodes up to level $(i - 1)$ have been labeled, an ith level node is labeled true if it is an AND (respectively, OR) node and all (respectively, some) of its children are labeled true. Finally, the Tarski sentence is true if and only if the root of the tree is labeled true. This constitutes a decision procedure for the Tarski sentences.

Consider a sample point

$$p = \langle \alpha_1, \alpha_2, \ldots, \alpha_n \rangle,$$

in some cell $C \in \mathcal{K}$. Assume that the algebraic number α_i has an interval representation $\langle f_i, l_i, r_i \rangle$. The truth value at a leaf corresponding to C, (i.e., $\psi(\alpha_1, \ldots, \alpha_n)$) can be expressed by the following logically equivalent quantifier-free sentences involving only polynomials with rational coefficients:

$$(f_1(z_1) = f_2(z_2) = \cdots = f_n(z_n) = 0)$$
$$\wedge (l_1 < z_1 < r_1) \wedge \cdots \wedge (l_n < z_n < r_n)$$
$$\wedge \psi(z_1, z_2, \ldots, z_n).$$

Thus each leaf of the AND-OR tree can be expressed as a quantifier-free sentence as above. Now, the tree itself can be expressed as a quantifier-free sentence involving conjunctions and disjunctions for the AND and OR nodes, respectively. Clearly, all the polynomials involved are over $\mathbb{Q}$.

For examples, consider the sentences

$$\left(\exists \, x \right) \left(\forall \, y \right) \left[(y^2 - x > 0) \right]$$

and

$$\left(\exists \, x \right) \left(\forall \, y \right) \left[(y^2 - x < 0) \right].$$

The sample points for a CAD of $y^2 - x$ are as follows:

$$(-1, 0), \quad \left\{ \begin{array}{c} (0, 1) \\ (0, 0) \\ (0, -1) \end{array} \right\}, \quad \left\{ \begin{array}{c} (1, 2) \\ (1, 1) \\ (1, 1/2) \\ (1, 0) \\ (1, -1/2) \\ (1, -1) \\ (1, -2) \end{array} \right\}$$

The equivalent quantifier-free sentences are

$$(0 > -1)$$
$$\vee \quad (1 > 0) \wedge (0 > 0) \wedge (1 > 0)$$
$$\vee \quad (4 > 1) \wedge (1 > 1) \wedge (1/4 > 1) \wedge (0 > 1) \wedge (1/4 > 1) \wedge (1 > 1) \wedge (4 > 1),$$

and

$$(0 < -1)$$
$$\vee \quad (1 < 0) \wedge (0 < 0) \wedge (1 < 0)$$
$$\vee \quad (4 < 1) \wedge (1 < 1) \wedge (1/4 < 1) \wedge (0 < 1) \wedge (1/4 < 1) \wedge (1 < 1) \wedge (4 < 1).$$

By a simple examination we see that the first sentence is true, while the second is false.

In summary, we have the following:

Theorem 8.6.10 *Let Φ be a Tarski sentence involving polynomials with rational coefficients. Then we have the following:*

- *There is an effective decision procedure for Φ.*

- *There is a quantifier-free propositional sentence ϕ logically equivalent to Φ. The sentence ϕ involves only polynomials with rational coefficients.* □

Corollary 8.6.11 *Tarski sets (subsets of $\mathbb{R}^n$ defined by a Tarski sentence) are exactly the semialgebraic sets.* □

Problems

Problem 8.1

In an ordered field K, we define $|x|$ for all $x \in K$ as follows:

$$|x| = \begin{cases} x, & \text{if } x \geq 0; \\ -x, & \text{if } x < 0. \end{cases}$$

Prove that for all $x, y \in K$,
(i) $|x + y| \leq |x| + |y|$.
(ii) $|x\,y| = |x|\,|y|$.

Problem 8.2

Give a proof for the following:

Let K be a real closed field and $f(x) \in K[x]$. If $a, b \in K$, $a < b$, then

$$\Big(\exists\, c \in (a, b)\Big) \Big[f(b) - f(a) = (b - a)D(f)(c)\Big].$$

This is the so-called *intermediate value theorem*.

Problem 8.3

Is it true that every integral polynomial $f(x) \in \mathbb{Z}[x]$ has all its real roots in the closed interval $[-\|f\|_\infty, \|f\|_\infty]$?

Hint: Consider the polynomial $x^2 - x - 1$.

Problem 8.4

Show that an algebraic number has a unique minimal polynomial up to *associativity*.

Problem 8.5

Consider a real univariate polynomial

$$f(x) = x^n + a_{n-1}x^{n-1} + \cdots + a_m x^m + a_1 x + a_0 \in \mathbb{R}[x],$$

and u a real root of f.

(i) *Lagrange-Maclaurin's Inequality.* Let

$$a_{n-1} \geq 0, \ldots, a_{m-1} \geq 0, \quad \text{and} \quad a_m < 0.$$

Prove that

$$u < 1 + \left(\min(a_i) \right)^{1/(n-m)}.$$

Hint: Assume that $u > 1$ and

$$
\begin{aligned}
0 = f(u) &= u^n + a_{n-1}u^{n-1} + \cdots + a_m u^m + a_1 u + a_0 \\
&> u^n - \min(a_i)(u^m + u^{m-1} + \cdots + u + 1) \\
&= u^n - \min(a_i)\left(\frac{u^{m+1} - 1}{u - 1} \right).
\end{aligned}
$$

(ii) *Cauchy's Inequality.* Let

$$a_{m_1} < 0, \ a_{m_2} < 0, \ldots, a_{m_k} < 0, \qquad (m_1 > m_2 > \cdots > m_k),$$

be the only negative coefficients of f. Prove that

$$u \leq \max_j \left((k \, |a_{m_j}|)^{1/(n-m_j)} \right).$$

Hint: Assume that $u > 1$ and

$$
\begin{aligned}
0 = f(u) &= u^n + a_{n-1}u^{n-1} + \cdots + a_m u^m + a_1 u + a_0 \\
&> u^n - a_{m_1}u^{m_1} - \cdots - a_{m_k}u^{m_k} \\
&\geq u^n - k \max_j(|a_{m_j}|u^{m_j}).
\end{aligned}
$$

Problem 8.6

Let $f(x) \in \mathbb{R}[x]$ be a univariate real polynomial of positive degree $n > 0$.

(i) Consider f's Fourier sequence:

$$\overline{\text{FOURIER}}(f) \;=\; \Big\langle \;\; f^{(0)}(x) = f(x),$$
$$f^{(1)}(x) = f'(x),$$
$$f^{(2)}(x),$$
$$\vdots$$
$$f^{(n)}(x) \;\Big\rangle,$$

where $f^{(i)}$ denotes the ith derivative of f with respect to x. Prove the following:

Budan-Fourier Theorem.

> Let $f(x) \in \mathbb{R}[x]$ and a and $b \in \mathbb{R}$ be two real numbers with $a < b$. Then
>
> # real roots of f (counted with multiplicity) in (a, b)
> $$\begin{cases} \leq & \text{Var}_a(\overline{\text{FOURIER}}(f)) - \text{Var}_b(\overline{\text{FOURIER}}(f)), \quad \text{and} \\[2mm] \equiv & \text{Var}_a(\overline{\text{FOURIER}}(f)) - \text{Var}_b(\overline{\text{FOURIER}}(f)) \pmod 2. \end{cases}$$

(ii) Using the Budan-Fourier theorem, present a proof for the following:

Descartes' Theorem.

> Let $f(x) \in \mathbb{R}[x]$ be as follows:
>
> $$f(x) = a_n x^n + a_{n-1} x^{n-1} + \cdots + a_0,$$
>
> and
> $$V(f) = \text{Var}(\langle a_n, a_{n-1}, \ldots, a_0 \rangle).$$
>
> Then the number of strictly positive real roots of f (counted with multiplicity) does not exceed $V(f)$ and is congruent to $V(f) \pmod 2$.

Problem 8.7

Let $\langle h_0, h_1, \ldots, h_s \rangle$ be a Sturm sequence of f and f'.

Let V be the number of sign variations in the sequence

$$\overline{v} = \langle \text{Hcoef}(h_0), \; \text{Hcoef}(h_1), \; \ldots, \; \text{Hcoef}(h_s) \rangle,$$

and W be the number of sign variations in the sequence

$$\overline{w} = \langle \text{SHcoef}(h_0), \text{SHcoef}(h_1), \ldots, \text{SHcoef}(h_s) \rangle,$$

where $\text{Hcoef}(h)$ is the leading coefficient of h and

$$\text{SHcoef}(h) = (-1)^{\deg(h)}\text{Hcoef}(h)$$

is the "*sign-adjusted*" leading coefficient of h.

Show that the number of distinct real roots of f is $W - V$.

Compute $\overline{v}$ and $\overline{w}$ for a quadratic polynomial $x^2 + bx + c$. What is $W - V$ as a function of b and c? Can you derive an algebraic criterion for the number of real zeros of $x^2 + bx + c$?

Problem 8.8

Let f, g_1 and g_2 be a *simple set of polynomials* in $K[x]$ ($K = $ a real closed field), in the sense that all their roots are distinct, i.e., they are all square-free and pairwise relatively prime.

(i) For any interval $[a, b] \subseteq K$ $(a < b)$, show that

$$
\begin{bmatrix}
1 & 1 & 1 & 1 \\
1 & -1 & 1 & -1 \\
1 & 1 & -1 & -1 \\
1 & -1 & -1 & 1
\end{bmatrix}
\begin{bmatrix}
c_f \left[g_1 > 0, g_2 > 0 \right]_a^b \\
c_f \left[g_1 > 0, g_2 < 0 \right]_a^b \\
c_f \left[g_1 < 0, g_2 > 0 \right]_a^b \\
c_f \left[g_1 < 0, g_2 < 0 \right]_a^b
\end{bmatrix}
$$

$$
=
\begin{bmatrix}
\text{Var}\left[\overline{\text{STURM}}(f, f') \right]_a^b \\
\text{Var}\left[\overline{\text{STURM}}(f, f'g_1) \right]_a^b \\
\text{Var}\left[\overline{\text{STURM}}(f, f'g_2) \right]_a^b \\
\text{Var}\left[\overline{\text{STURM}}(f, f'g_1g_2) \right]_a^b
\end{bmatrix}.
$$

(ii) Show how the preceding formulation can be generalized to the case when f, g_1 and g_2 are *not simple*.

(iii) Show how to obtain a further generalization of this formulation when there are more than two g's: f, g_1, g_2, ..., g_n.

(iv) Suppose you are given a system of polynomial inequalities, involving polynomials g_1, g_2, ..., g_n in $\mathbb{R}[x]$, as follows:

$$
\begin{aligned}
g_1(x) &\lesseqgtr 0, \\
g_2(x) &\lesseqgtr 0, \\
&\;\;\vdots \\
g_n(x) &\lesseqgtr 0,
\end{aligned}
$$

where the notation "$g_i(x) \lesseqgtr 0$" represents one of the following three relations: $g_i(x) < 0$, $g_i(x) = 0$ or $g_i(x) > 0$. Using the formulation (iii) and linear algebra, devise a process to determine if there is a solution x at which all the inequalities are satisfied.

Hint: Construct a sequence f, g_1, g_2, ..., g_n as in (iii), where f is such that, for any sign assignment to g_i's, the interval corresponding to this assignment, f has a zero:

$$
\begin{aligned}
G(x) &= g_1(x)\, g_2(x) \cdots g_n(x), \\
\widetilde{G}(x) &= \frac{G(x)}{\mathrm{GCD}(G(x), G'(x))}.
\end{aligned}
$$

Let

$$
f(x) = \widetilde{G}(x)\, \widetilde{G}'(x)(x - N)(x + N),
$$

where

$$
N = 1 + \max \left| \frac{a_i}{a_k} \right|,
$$

the a_i's are coefficients of $\widetilde{G}(x)$, and $a_k = \mathrm{Hcoef}(\widetilde{G}(x))$.

Problem 8.9

Let $f(x)$ and $g(x) \in \mathbb{Z}[x]$ be two arbitrary integral polynomials of positive degrees $m = \deg(f)$ and $n = \deg(g)$, respectively. Show that

$$
\Big(\forall\, \alpha,\ \text{s.t. } g(\alpha) = 0 \Big) \left[f(\alpha) = 0 \quad \text{or} \quad |f(\alpha)| > \frac{1}{1 + \|g\|_1^m (1 + \|f\|_1)^n} \right].
$$

Hint: Consider the zeros of the resultant, $\mathrm{Resultant}_x(g(x), f(x) - y)$.

Problem 8.10

Consider the following monic irreducible integral polynomial $f(x)$,

$$
f(x) = x^n - 2(ax - 1)^2, \qquad n \geq 3, a \geq 3, a \in \mathbb{Z}.
$$

Show that

$$\text{Separation}(f) < 2 \frac{1}{(\|f\|_1/4)^{n+2/4}}.$$

Hint: Show that $f(1/a) > 0$ and $f(1/a \pm h) < 0$, for $h = a^{-(n+2)/2}$.

Problem 8.11 *(Hadamard-Collins-Horowitz Inequality.)*
   If S is a commutative ring, a *seminorm* for S is a function

$$\nu: S \to \{r \geq 0 : r \in \mathbb{R}\}$$

satisfying the following three conditions: For all $a, b \in S$,

$$
\begin{align}
\nu(a) &= 0 \iff a = 0, \tag{8.1}\\
\nu(a+b) &\leq \nu(a) + \nu(b), \tag{8.2}\\
\nu(a\,b) &\leq \nu(a)\,\nu(b). \tag{8.3}
\end{align}
$$

(i) Show that $\|a\|_1 = |a|$ is a seminorm for the integers $\mathbb{Z}$.
(ii) Show the following:

1. If ν is a seminorm over S, then its extension to $S[x]$ defined below

$$\nu(a_n x^n + a_{n-1}x^{n-1} + \cdots + a_0) = \nu(a_n) + \nu(a_{n-1}) + \cdots + \nu(a_0)$$

   is also a seminorm over $S[x]$.

2. If ν is a seminorm over S, then its extension to an arbitrary matrix $M \in S^{m \times n}$

$$\nu(M) = \sum_{i=1}^{m} \sum_{j=1}^{n} \nu(M_{i,j})$$

   satisfies the conditions (8.1), (8.2) and (8.3), whenever the operations are defined.

   (iii) If M is a square matrix over a commutative ring S with a seminorm ν, then show that the following generalization of Hadamard's inequality holds:

$$\nu(\det M) \leq \prod_i \nu(M_i),$$

where M_i is the ith row of M and $\det M$ is the determinant of M.

Problem 8.12
   Consider an $n \times n$ polynomial matrix with integral polynomial entries

$$M(x) = \begin{bmatrix} A_{1,1}(x) & A_{1,2}(x) & \cdots & A_{1,n}(x) \\ A_{2,1}(x) & A_{2,2}(x) & \cdots & A_{2,n}(x) \\ \vdots & \vdots & \ddots & \vdots \\ A_{n,1}(x) & A_{n,2}(x) & \cdots & A_{n,n}(x) \end{bmatrix}.$$

Prove that

$$\det(M(x)) \equiv 0 \quad \Leftrightarrow \quad \det\left(M\left(\frac{1}{2(adn)^n}\right)\right) = 0,$$

where

$$a = \max_{i,j} \|A_{i,j}\|_\infty \quad \text{and} \quad d = \max_{i,j} \deg(A_{i,j}).$$

Problem 8.13

Consider two real algebraic numbers α and β defined by two polynomials $f(x)$ and $g(x)$ of respective positive degrees m and n. Prove that if $\alpha \neq \beta$ then

$$\Delta = |\alpha - \beta| > \frac{1}{2^{(n+1)(m+1)} \|f\|_1^n \|g\|_1^m}.$$

Problem 8.14

Let $f(x) \in \mathbb{C}[x]$ be an arbitrary polynomial:

$$f(x) = c_n x^n + c_{n-1} x^{n-1} + \cdots + c_0.$$

Consider the usual norm for complex numbers:

$$|a + ib| = (a^2 + b^2)^{1/2}.$$

The 1-norm of f can now defined to be

$$\|f\|_1 = |c_n| + |c_{n-1}| + \cdots + |c_0|.$$

Let the zeros of f be enumerateed as

$$|\xi_1| \leq |\xi_2| \leq \cdots |\xi_m| \leq 1 < |\xi_{m+1}| \leq \cdots \leq |\xi_n|,$$

counting each zero as many times as its multiplicity.

Let $\mathcal{M}(f)$ be defined as

$$\mathcal{M}(f) = \left| c_n \prod_{i=1}^{n} \max(1, \xi_i) \right| = |c_n| \prod_{i=1}^{n} \max(1, |\xi_i|).$$

First we want to derive the following relations:

$$\mathcal{M}(f) \leq \|f\|_1 \leq 2^n \mathcal{M}(f).$$

(i) Prove that

$$\|f\|_1 = \sum |c_n \xi_{i_1} \xi_{i_2} \cdots \xi_{i_l}| \leq 2^n \mathcal{M}(f).$$

(ii) Next show that

$$\log \mathcal{M}(f) = \frac{1}{2\pi} \int_0^{2\pi} \log |f(e^{it})|\, dt \leq \max_{1 \leq t \leq 2\pi} \log |f(e^{it})| \leq \log \|f\|_1,$$

Thus, concluding that

$$\mathcal{M}(f) \leq \|f\|_1.$$

Hint: Use Jensen's integral formula:

$$\frac{1}{2\pi} \int_0^{2\pi} \log |F(\rho e^{it})|\, dt = \log |F(0)| + \sum_{i=1}^m \log \frac{\rho}{|\xi_i|}, \qquad F(0) \neq 0,$$

where $F(x)$ is a function of the complex variable, regular on the circle of radius ρ. The zeros of F in $|x| \leq \rho$ are given as $\xi_1, \ldots, \xi_m$.

(iii) Using these inequalities show that, if f is factorized as follows

$$f(x) = f_1(x)\ f_2(x) \cdots f_s(x),$$

then

$$\|f_1\|_1\ \|f_2\|_1 \cdots \|f_s\|_1 \leq 2^{\deg(f)}\ \|f\|_1.$$

Problem 8.15

Let $f(x)$ be a polynomial with zeros in $\mathbb{C}$. Then we denote its complex root separation by $\Delta(f)$:

$$\Delta(f) = \min\{|\alpha - \beta| : \alpha \neq \beta \in \mathbb{C} \ \wedge\ f(\alpha) = f(\beta) = 0\}.$$

Let $f(x)$ be an integral polynomial:

$$f(x) = a_n x^n + a_{n-1} x^{n-1} + \cdots + a_0.$$

Prove the following:

(i) If $f(x)$ is square-free, then

$$\Delta(f) > \sqrt{3}\, n^{-(n+2)/2}\, \|f\|_1^{-(n-1)}.$$

(ii) In general,

$$\Delta(f) > \sqrt{3}\, 2^{-n(n-1)}\, n^{-(n+2)/2}\, \|f\|_1^{-(n-1)}.$$

Problem 8.16

(i) Devise a simple and efficient $(O(n^3 \lg n)$-time)algorithm to convert a real algebraic number from its order representation to its interval representation.

(ii) Prove the following corollary of Thom's lemma:

Consider two real roots ξ and ζ of a real univariate polynomial $f(x) \in \mathbb{R}[x]$ of positive degree $n > 0$. Then

$$\xi > \zeta$$

if and only if, for some $0 \leq m < n$, the following conditions hold:

$$\mathrm{sgn}(f^{(m)}(\xi)) \neq \mathrm{sgn}(f^{(m)}(\zeta))$$
$$\mathrm{sgn}(f^{(m+1)}(\xi)) = \mathrm{sgn}(f^{(m+1)}(\zeta)),$$
$$\vdots$$
$$\mathrm{sgn}(f^{(n)}(\xi)) = \mathrm{sgn}(f^{(n)}(\zeta)).$$

and

1. either $\mathrm{sgn}(f^{(m+1)}) = +1$ and $f^{(m)}(\xi) > f^{(m)}(\zeta)$,
2. or $\mathrm{sgn}(f^{(m+1)}) = -1$ and $f^{(m)}(\xi) < f^{(m)}(\zeta)$.

(iii) Using the corollary above, devise an efficient $(O(n^3 \lg^2 n)$-time) algorithm to convert a real algebraic number from its sign representation to its interval representation.

Problem 8.17

Prove that if S is a semialgebraic set then its interior, $\mathrm{int}(S)$, closure $\overline{S}$, and boundary $\partial(S) - S \setminus \mathrm{int}(S)$ are all semialgebraic.

Problem 8.18

Show that every semialgebraic set is locally connected.

Problem 8.19

Let $S \subseteq \mathbb{R}^n$ be a semialgebraic set. Prove that for some $m \in \mathbb{N}$, there is a *real algebraic set* $T \subseteq \mathbb{R}^{n+m}$ such that

$$\pi(T) = S,$$

where
$$\pi : \mathbb{R}^{n+m} \to \mathbb{R}^n$$
$$: \langle \xi_1, \ldots, \xi_n, \xi_{n+1}, \ldots, \xi_{n+m} \rangle \mapsto \langle \xi_1, \ldots, \xi_n \rangle$$
is a natural projection map.

Thus, show that semialgebraic sets constitute the smallest class of subsets of $\mathbb{R}^n$ closed under projection and containing real algebraic sets.

Hint: Let $S \subseteq \mathbb{R}^n$ be defined as follows:

$$S = \left\{ \langle x_1, \ldots, x_n \rangle \in \mathbb{R}^n : \mathrm{sgn}(f_i(x_1, \ldots, x_n)) = s_i \right\},$$

where $i = 1, \ldots, m$. Let us now define T as follows:

$$T = \Big\{ \langle x_1, \ldots, x_n, x_{n+1}, \ldots, x_{n+m} \rangle \in \mathbb{R}^n \ : $$

$$\sum_{j;s_j<0} (x_{n+j}^2 f_j + 1)^2 + \sum_{j;s_j=0} f_j^2 + \sum_{j;s_j>0} (x_{n+j}^2 f_j - 1)^2 = 0 \Big\}.$$

Verify that $S = \pi(T)$.

Problem 8.20

A *robotic system* $\mathcal{R}$ is defined to be a finite collection of rigid compact subparts

$$\Big\{ B_1, \ B_2, \ \ldots, \ B_m \Big\},$$

where each subpart is assumed to be defined by a piecewise algebraic surface.

A configuration is an n-tuple of parameters that describes the positions and the orientations of the subparts uniquely; the corresponding space of parameters $\mathbb{R}^n$ is called a *configuration space*.

Additionally, we may assume that between every pair of subparts B_i and B_j at most one of the following *holonomic kinematic constraints* may exist:

- REVOLUTE JOINT: There is a fixed axis L through a pair of points $p_i \in B_i$ and $p_j \in B_j$ such that B_i and B_j are only allowed to rotate about L.

- PRISMATIC JOINT: There is a fixed axis L through a pair of points $p_i \in B_i$ and $p_j \in B_j$ such that B_i and B_j are only allowed to translate about L.

(i) B_i's are assumed to be able to take any configuration subject to the kinematic constraints such that no two subpart occupies the same space.

A point of the configuration space corresponding to such a configuration is said to be *free*. Otherwise, it is called *forbidden*. The collection of points of configuration space that are free are said to constitute the *free space*, and its complement *forbidden space*.

Show that the *free* and *forbidden spaces* are semialgebraic subsets of $\mathbb{R}^n$.

(ii) Given an *initial* and a desired *final* configurations of the *robotic system*, $\mathcal{R}$, the *motion planning problem* is to decide whether there is a continuous motion of the subparts from the initial to the final configuration that avoids collision and respects the kinematic constraints.

Devise an algorithm to solve the motion planning problem.

Hint: First compute the connectivity graph for the polynomials defining the free space, and show that there is a continuous motion from one configuration in a free cell to another configuration in a free cell, if there is a path between the vertices corresponding to the respective free cells.

Problem 8.21

Consider the following set of $N = 2^{2^n}$ complex numbers corresponding to the Nth roots of unity:

$$\left\{ \alpha_i + i\beta_i \ : \ i = 1, \dots, N \right\} \ \subseteq \ \mathbb{C}.$$

Define

$$S_n = \left\{ \langle \alpha_i, \beta_i \rangle \ : \ i = 1, \dots, N \right\} \ \subseteq \ \mathbb{R}^2.$$

Show that there is a Tarski sentence $\Psi_n(x, y)$ with two free variables (x and y) and $O(n)$ quantifiers, $O(n)$ variables, $O(n)$ real linear polynomials, and $O(1)$ real quadratic polynomial such that

$$\left\{ \langle \alpha, \beta \rangle \ : \ \Psi_n(\alpha, \beta) = \text{TRUE} \right\} \ = \ S_n.$$

Problem 8.22

(i.a) Let $g_i(x, y)$ and $g_j(x, y) \in \mathbb{R}[x, y]$. Define

$$
\begin{aligned}
D(g_i) &= \text{isolated points of } g_i = 0; \\
D(g_i, g_j) &= \text{isolated points of } g_i = 0 \text{ and } g_j = 0 \\
&\qquad \setminus (D(g_i) \cup D(g_j)).
\end{aligned}
$$

If $g_i(x, y)$ and $g_j(x, y)$ are irreducible polynomials, show that

$$|D(g_i)| \leq (\deg(g_i))^2 \quad \text{and} \quad |D(g_i, g_j)| \leq 2 \deg(g_i) \deg(g_j).$$

(i.b) Given a quantifier-free sentence in two variables x and y, involving polynomials

$$\mathcal{F} \ = \ \left\{ f_1(x, y), \ f_2(x, y), \ \dots, \ f_m(x, y) \right\} \ \subseteq \ \mathbb{R}[x, y],$$

show that every isolated point is either in some $D(g_i)$ or some $D(g_i, g_j)$, where g_i's and g_j's are irreducible factors of f_i's.

(i.c) Show that the total number of isolated points of a quantifier-free sentence defined by $\mathcal{F}$ is bounded from above by

$$\left(\sum_{i=1}^{m} \deg(f_i) \right)^2.$$

Problem 8.23

As direct consequences of the preceding two problems, show the following:

(i) For every $n \in \mathbb{N}$, there exists a quantified Tarski sentence Ψ_n with n quantifiers, of length $O(n)$, and degree $O(1)$ such that any quantifier-free sentence ψ_n logically equivalent to Ψ_n must involve polynomials of

$$\text{degree} = 2^{2^{\Omega(n)}} \quad \text{and} \quad \text{length} = 2^{2^{\Omega(n)}}.$$

(ii) For every $n \in \mathbb{N}$, there exists a quantified Tarski sentence Ψ_n with n quantifiers, of length $O(n)$, and degree $O(1)$ such that Ψ_n induces a cylindrical decomposition, $\mathcal{K}_n$, of $\mathbb{R}^m$ $(m = O(n))$ with

$$|\mathcal{K}_n| = 2^{2^{\Omega(n)}} \quad \text{cells.}$$

(iii) Thus, argue that both *quantifier elimination problem* and *cylindrical algebraic decomposition problem* have double exponential lower bounds for their time complexity as a function of the input size.

Solutions to Selected Problems

Problem 8.2

First, we choose a linear function $\bar{f}(x)$ such that

$$\tilde{f}(x) = f(x) - \bar{f}(x),$$

vanishes at the points a and b. Hence,

$$\bar{f}(a) = f(a) \quad \text{and} \quad \bar{f}(b) = f(b).$$

Thus,

$$D(\bar{f}) = \frac{f(b) - f(a)}{b - a},$$

and

$$\bar{f}(x) = \frac{f(b) - f(a)}{b - a} x + \frac{bf(a)}{b - a} - \frac{af(b)}{b - a}.$$

Now we can apply Rolle's theorem to $\tilde{f}(x)$ as $\tilde{f}(a) = \tilde{f}(b) = 0$:

$$\left(\exists c \in (a, b) \right) \left[D(\tilde{f})(c) = D(f)(c) - D(\bar{f})(c) = 0 \right].$$

But since, $D(\bar{f}) = (f(b) - f(a))/(b - a)$, we have the necessary conclusion. We may rewrite the formula above in the following form:

$$f(b) = f(a) + f'(c)(b - a), \qquad \text{for some } c \in (a, b).$$

Problem 8.4

Consider an algebraic number α. Let $f(x)$ and $g(x) \in \mathbb{Z}[x]$ be two nonzero minimal polynomials of α. Clearly $f(x)$ and $g(x)$ have the same degree. Thus, if we consider the following polynomial

$$r(x) = \mathrm{Hcoef}(g)\ f(x) - \mathrm{Hcoef}(f)\ g(x) \in \mathbb{Z}[x],$$

then $\deg(r) < \deg(f) = \deg(g)$ and $r(\alpha) = \mathrm{Hcoef}(g)\ f(\alpha) - \mathrm{Hcoef}(f)\ g(\alpha) = 0$. Thus $r(x)$ must be identically zero as, otherwise, it would contradict our assumption that $f(x)$ and $g(x)$ were two minimal polynomials of α. Thus

$$\mathrm{Hcoef}(g)\ f(x) = \mathrm{Hcoef}(f)\ g(x) \quad \text{and} \quad f(x) \approx g(x).$$

Problem 8.6

(i) Using Taylor's expansion theorem, we may express the values of the Fourier sequence in a neighborhood of a real number c as follows:

$$
\begin{aligned}
f(c+\epsilon) &= f(c) + \epsilon f^{(1)}(c) + \frac{\epsilon^2}{2!} f^{(2)}(c) + \cdots + \frac{\epsilon^m}{m!} f^{(m)}(c) \\
&\quad + \cdots + \frac{\epsilon^n}{n!} f^{(n)}(c), \\
f^{(1)}(c+\epsilon) &= f^{(1)}(c) + \epsilon f^{(2)}(c) + \frac{\epsilon^2}{2!} f^{(3)}(c) + \cdots + \frac{\epsilon^{m-1}}{(m+1)!} f^{(m)}(c) \\
&\quad + \cdots + \frac{\epsilon^{n-1}}{(n-1)!} f^{(n)}(c), \\
&\vdots \\
f^{(m)}(c+\epsilon) &= f^{(m)}(c) + \epsilon f^{(m+1)}(c) + \cdots + \frac{\epsilon^{n-m}}{(n-m)!} f^{(n)}(c), \\
&\vdots \\
f^{(n)}(c+\epsilon) &= f^{(n)}(c).
\end{aligned}
$$

Let us now consider an interval $[a, b]$ containing *exactly one real root* c of f with multiplicity m. Note that it suffices to consider the sign variations in some interval $(c - \epsilon, c + \epsilon) \subseteq [a, b]$. Clearly:

$$f^{(0)}(c) = f^{(1)}(c) = \cdots = f^{(m-1)}(c) = 0 \quad \text{and} \quad f^{(m)}(c) \neq 0.$$

Let $s = \text{sgn}(f^{(m)}(c))$. Hence

$$
\begin{aligned}
\text{sgn}(f(c-\epsilon)) &= (-1)^m s, & s &= \text{sgn}(f(c+\epsilon)), \\
\text{sgn}(f^{(1)}(c-\epsilon)) &= (-1)^{m-1} s, & s &= \text{sgn}(f^{(1)}(c+\epsilon)), \\
&\vdots & &\vdots
\end{aligned}
$$

$$
\begin{aligned}
\text{sgn}(f^{(m)}(c-\epsilon)) &= s & &= \text{sgn}(f^{(m)}(c+\epsilon)), \\
\text{sgn}(f^{(m+1)}(c-\epsilon)) &= \text{sgn}(f^{(m+1)}(c)) & &= \text{sgn}(f^{(m+1)}(c+\epsilon)), \\
&\vdots & &\vdots
\end{aligned}
$$

$$
\text{sgn}(f^{(n)}(c-\epsilon)) = \text{sgn}(f^{(n)}(c)) = \text{sgn}(f^{(n)}(c+\epsilon)).
$$

Thus it is easily seen that the sequence at the left has exactly m more sign variations than the sequence at the right. Hence, in this case,

$$
\begin{aligned}
\# \text{ real roots of } f \text{ (counted with multiplicity) in } (a,b) & \\
= \text{Var}_a(\overline{\text{FOURIER}}(f)) - \text{Var}_b(\overline{\text{FOURIER}}(f)), &
\end{aligned}
$$

Next let us consider an interval $[a, b]$ containing *exactly one real root* c of $f^{(k)}$ ($k > 0$) with multiplicity l. Let $m = k + l$. As before, it suffices to consider the sign variations in some interval $(c - \epsilon, c + \epsilon) \subseteq [a, b]$. Clearly:

$$
f^{(k)}(c) = f^{(k+1)}(c) = \cdots = f^{(m-1)}(c) = 0 \quad \text{and} \quad f^{(m)}(c) \neq 0.
$$

Let $s = \text{sgn}(f^{(m)}(c))$. Hence

$$
\begin{aligned}
\text{sgn}(f(c-\epsilon)) &= \text{sgn}(f(c)) &&= \text{sgn}(f(c+\epsilon)), \\
&\vdots && \vdots
\end{aligned}
$$

$$
\begin{aligned}
\text{sgn}(f^{(k-1)}(c-\epsilon)) &= \text{sgn}(f^{(k-1)}(c)) &&= \text{sgn}(f^{(1)}(c+\epsilon)), \\
\text{sgn}(f^{(k)}(c-\epsilon)) &= (-1)^l s, & s &= \text{sgn}(f^{(k)}(c+\epsilon)), \\
\text{sgn}(f^{(k+1)}(c-\epsilon)) &= (-1)^{l-1} s, & s &= \text{sgn}(f^{(k+1)}(c+\epsilon)), \\
&\vdots && \vdots
\end{aligned}
$$

$$
\begin{aligned}
\text{sgn}(f^{(m)}(c-\epsilon)) &= s &&= \text{sgn}(f^{(m)}(c+\epsilon)), \\
\text{sgn}(f^{(m+1)}(c-\epsilon)) &= \text{sgn}(f^{(m+1)}(c)) &&= \text{sgn}(f^{(m+1)}(c+\epsilon)), \\
&\vdots && \vdots
\end{aligned}
$$

$$
\text{sgn}(f^{(n)}(c-\epsilon)) = \text{sgn}(f^{(n)}(c)) = \text{sgn}(f^{(n)}(c+\epsilon)).
$$

We only need to consider the sign variations form $c - \epsilon$ to $c + \epsilon$ for the following subsequence:

$$
\langle f^{(k-1)}, f^{(k)}, \ldots, f^{(m)}, f^{(m+1)} \rangle.
$$

There are two cases to consider:

1. $\text{sgn}(f^{(k-1)}(c)) = \text{sgn}(f^{(m+1)}(c))$, in which case the subsequence has *even* number of sign variations both at $c - \epsilon$ and $c + \epsilon$, and

2. $\text{sgn}(f^{(k-1)}(c)) \neq \text{sgn}(f^{(m+1)}(c))$, in which case the subsequence has *odd* number of sign variations both at $c - \epsilon$ and $c + \epsilon$;

and in either case the subsequence at the left has more sign variations than the subsequence at the right. Thus,

$$0 \begin{cases} \leq & \text{Var}_a(\overline{\text{FOURIER}}(f)) - \text{Var}_b(\overline{\text{FOURIER}}(f)) \quad \text{and} \\ \equiv & \text{Var}_a(\overline{\text{FOURIER}}(f)) - \text{Var}_b(\overline{\text{FOURIER}}(f)) \quad (\text{mod}\,2). \end{cases}$$

(ii) Using Budan-Fourier theorem, we have

\# strictly positive real roots of f (counted with multiplicity)

$$\begin{cases} \leq & \text{Var}_0(\overline{\text{FOURIER}}(f)) - \text{Var}_\infty(\overline{\text{FOURIER}}(f)) \quad \text{and} \\ \equiv & \text{Var}_0(\overline{\text{FOURIER}}(f)) - \text{Var}_\infty(\overline{\text{FOURIER}}(f)) \quad (\text{mod}\,2). \end{cases}$$

Thus Descartes' theorem follows, once we show that

$$\text{Var}_0(\overline{\text{FOURIER}}(f)) = V(f) \quad \text{and} \quad \text{Var}_\infty(\overline{\text{FOURIER}}(f)) = 0.$$

This is obvious as

$$\text{sgn}_0(\overline{\text{FOURIER}}(f)) = \text{sgn}(\langle a_0, a_1, 2a_2, \dots, m!a_m, \dots, n!a_n \rangle),$$

and

$$\text{sgn}_\infty(\overline{\text{FOURIER}}(f)) = \text{sgn}(\langle a_n, a_n, a_n, \dots, a_n, \dots, a_n \rangle).$$

Problem 8.10
First note that

$$\|f\|_1 = 2a^2 + 4a + 3 \leq (2 + 4/3 + 1/3)a^2, \qquad \text{for all } a \geq 3.$$

Hence $a \geq \sqrt{\|f\|_1/2}$ and it suffices to show that

$$\text{Separation}(f) < 2h = 2a^{-(n+2)/2}.$$

Next observe that since

$$\begin{aligned} f(x) &= x^n - 2a^2x^2 + 4ax - 2, \quad \text{and} \\ f(-x) &= (-1)^n x^n - 2a^2 x^2 - 4ax - 2, \end{aligned}$$

by Descartes' rule, f has at most two positive real roots and at most one negative real root.

Clearly,
$$f(1/a) = (1/a)^n > 0.$$

Now, notice that
$$f(1/a \pm h) = (1/a \pm h)^n - 2(a(1/a \pm h) - 1)^2 = (1/a \pm h)^n - 2a^2h^2.$$

Thus, choosing $h = a^{-(n+2)/2}$, we have
$$(1/a \pm h)^n \leq (a^{-1} + a^{-(n+2)/2})^n = (1 + a^{-n/2})^n a^{-n} < \left(\frac{413}{243}\right)a^{-n},$$

and
$$f(1/a \pm h) < \left(\frac{413}{243}\right)a^{-n} - 2a^2 a^{-(n+2)} < 0.$$

Thus, f has two positive real roots in the open interval $(1/a - h,\ 1/a + h)$ and
$$\text{Separation}(f) < \min(1/a - h, 2h) = 2h = 2a^{-(n+2)/2}.$$

Problem 8.11

(i) and (ii) are tedious but straightforward.

(iii) The proof is by induction on the order of the matrix n. The case $n = 1$ is trivial. Consider an $n \times n$ matrix M, $n > 1$. Let $M_{i,j}$ denote the $(i,j)^{\text{th}}$ entry of M and let $M'_{i,j}$ denote the $(i,j)^{\text{th}}$ minor of M (i.e., the submatrix of M obtained by deleting the ith row and j^{th} column). Since

$$\nu(\det(M)) \leq \sum_{j=1}^{n} \nu(M_{1,j})\nu(\det(M'_{1,j}))$$

(by Laplace expansion formula for determinants)

$$\leq \sum_{j=1}^{n} \left(\nu(M_{1,j}) \prod_{i=2}^{n} \nu(M_i)\right)$$

(since every row of $M'_{1,j}$ is a subrow of some M_i, $i \geq 2$)

$$= \prod_{i=2}^{n} \nu(M_i) \left(\sum_{j=1}^{n} \nu(M_{1,j})\right)$$

$$\leq \prod_{i=1}^{n} \nu(M_i).$$

Problem 8.13

Let $\delta = \alpha - \beta$. Then $\langle \delta,\ \beta \rangle$ is a zero of $\tilde{f}(x,y) = f(x+y)$ and β is a zero of $g(y)$. Thus δ is a nonzero root of the polynomial

$$R(y) = \text{Resultant}_y(\tilde{f}(x,y),\ g(y)),$$

and

$$\Delta = |\delta| > \frac{1}{1 + \|R\|_\infty}.$$

Now,

$$\|R\|_\infty \le \|R\|_1 \le \|\tilde{f}(x, y)\|_1^n \|g(y)\|_1^m.$$

Observe that the 1-norm of $\tilde{f}(x, y)$ is taken over $\mathbb{Z}[x, y]$. Now writing

$$f(x) = a^m x^m + a_{m-1} x^{m-1} + \cdots + a_0$$

we have

$$
\begin{aligned}
\tilde{f}(x, y) &= f(x + y) = a^m(x + y)^m + a_{m-1}(x + y)^{m-1} + \cdots + a_0 \\
&= \sum_{i=0}^{m} a_i \sum_{j=0}^{i} \binom{i}{j} x^{i-j} y^j \\
&= \sum_{j=0}^{m} \left(\sum_{i=j}^{m} a_i \binom{i}{j} x^{i-j} \right) y^j \\
&= \sum_{j=0}^{m} A_j(x) y^j.
\end{aligned}
$$

Thus

$$
\begin{aligned}
\|\tilde{f}(x, y)\|_1 &= \|A_m(x)\|_1 + \cdots + \|A_0(x)\|_1 \\
&\le \sum_{j=0}^{m} \|f\|_\infty \sum_{i=j}^{m} \binom{i}{j} \\
&\le \|f\|_\infty \sum_{i=0}^{m} \sum_{j=0}^{i} \binom{i}{j} \\
&\le \|f\|_1 \sum_{i=0}^{m} 2^i < \|f\|_1 2^{m+1}.
\end{aligned}
$$

Thus

$$\|R\|_\infty < 2^{n(m+1)} \|f\|_1^n \|g\|_1^m,$$

and

$$\Delta > \frac{1}{1 + \|R\|_\infty} > 2^{-(n+1)(m+1)} \|f\|_1^{-n} \|g\|_1^{-m}.$$

Problem 8.15

(i) Let the roots of f be enumerated as $\xi_1, \xi_2, \ldots, \xi_n$. Now consider the determinant of the following Vandermonde matrix:

$$
V_n = \begin{bmatrix}
1 & 1 & \cdots & 1 \\
\xi_1 & \xi_2 & \cdots & \xi_n \\
\vdots & \vdots & \ddots & \vdots \\
\xi_1^{n-2} & \xi_2^{n-2} & \cdots & \xi_n^{n-2} \\
\xi_1^{n-1} & \xi_2^{n-1} & \cdots & \xi_n^{n-1}
\end{bmatrix}.
$$

Since $\det(V_n V_n^T) = \text{Discriminant}(f) \neq 0$ (f is square-free) and since f is integral, we have

$$
|\det V_n| \geq 1.
$$

Now if we subtract the jth column of V_n from its ith column, then this elementary matrix operation does not change $\det V_n$, and we have

$$
\det V_n = \begin{vmatrix}
1 & 1 & \cdots & 0 & \cdots & 1 \\
\xi_1 & \xi_2 & \cdots & \xi_i - \xi_j & \cdots & \xi_n \\
\vdots & \vdots & \ddots & \vdots & \ddots & \vdots \\
\xi_1^d & \xi_2^d & \cdots & \xi_i^d - \xi_j^d & \cdots & \xi_n^d \\
\vdots & \vdots & \ddots & \vdots & \ddots & \vdots \\
\xi_1^{n-2} & \xi_2^{n-2} & \cdots & \xi_i^{n-2} - \xi_j^{n-2} & \cdots & \xi_n^{n-2} \\
\xi_1^{n-1} & \xi_2^{n-1} & \cdots & \xi_i^{n-1} - \xi_j^{n-1} & \cdots & \xi_n^{n-1}
\end{vmatrix}.
$$

Using the Hadamard inequality, we have

$$
1 \leq |\det V_n|
$$

$$
\leq \left(\sum_{d=1}^{n-1} |\xi_i^d - \xi_j^d|^2 \right)^{1/2} \prod_{k \neq i} \left(\sum_{d=0}^{n-1} |\xi_k|^{2d} \right)^{1/2}.
$$

Now

$$
\begin{aligned}
|\xi_i^d - \xi_j^d| &= |\xi_i - \xi_j| \, |\xi_i^{d-1} + \xi_i^{d-2}\xi_j + \cdots + \xi_j^{d-1}| \\
&\leq d|\xi_i - \xi_j| \, |\xi_i|^{d-1},
\end{aligned}
$$

assuming $|\xi_i| \geq |\xi_j|$.

Hence,

$$
\sum_{d=1}^{n-1} |\xi_i^d - \xi_j^d|^2 < \left(\frac{n^3}{3} \right) |\xi_i - \xi_j|^2 \, \max(1, |\xi_i|)^{2n-2}.
$$

Similarly,

$$
\sum_{d=0}^{n-1} |\xi_k|^{2d} < n \, \max(1, |\xi_k|)^{2n-2}.
$$

Thus, combining these inequalities, we get

$$1 < |\xi_i - \xi_j| \left(n^{n-1} \left(\frac{n^3}{3}\right)\right)^{1/2} \prod_{k=1}^{n} \max(1, |\xi_k|)^{n-1}.$$

and

$$|\xi_i - \xi_j| > \frac{\sqrt{3}}{n^{(n+2)/2} \, \mathcal{M}(f)^{n-1}}.$$

Thus since $\mathcal{M}(f) \leq \|f\|_1$, we have the result

$$\Delta(f) > \frac{\sqrt{3}}{n^{(n+2)/2} \, \|f\|_1^{n-1}}.$$

(ii) Assume that $f(x)$ is not square-free. Then its square-free factor $g(x)$ is given by

$$g(x) = \frac{f(x)}{\mathrm{GCD}(f(x), f'(x))}, \quad \text{and} \quad \|g\|_1 \leq 2^n \|f\|_1.$$

Then writing $m = \deg(g)$,

$$\Delta(f) = \Delta(g)$$
$$> \frac{\sqrt{3}}{m^{(m+2)/2} \, \|g\|_1^{m-1}}$$
$$> \frac{\sqrt{3}}{m^{(m+2)/2} \, (2^n \|f\|_1)^{m-1}}$$
$$> \frac{\sqrt{3}}{2^{n(n-1)} \, n^{(n+2)/2} \, \|f\|_1^{n-1}}.$$

Problem 8.18

Let $S \subseteq \mathbb{R}^n$ be a semialgebraic set. Let $p \in S$ be an arbitrary point of S and consider a small open neighborhood of p defined as follows:

$$N_{S,\epsilon}(p) \;=\; S \cap \{q : \|p - q\|_2 < \epsilon\},$$

for some $\epsilon > 0$. Clearly, $N_{S,\epsilon}$ is a semialgebraic set defined by a set of polynomials $\mathcal{F}_\epsilon$. Now consider a cylindrical algebraic decomposition $\mathcal{K}_\epsilon$ of $\mathbb{R}^n$ defined by $\mathcal{F}_\epsilon$. Note that $\mathcal{K}_\epsilon$ has finitely many cells and that for every ϵ there is an open connected cell $C_\epsilon \subseteq N_{S,\epsilon}(p)$ such that

$$p \in C_\epsilon \subseteq S.$$

Thus S is locally connected.

Problem 8.21

The proof is in two steps: First, we shall construct a sequence of complex quantified sentences Φ_k's each equivalent to a single polynomial as follows:

$$\Phi_k(z_0, z_k) \; : \quad z_k^{2^{2^k}} = z_0.$$

In the second step, we shall obtain a sequence of real quantified sentences Ψ_k's each being an equivalent real version of Φ_k.

$$\Psi_k(\Re(z_0), \Im(z_0), \Re(z_k), \Im(z_k)) \; :$$
$$\left(\Re\left([\Re(z_k) + i\Im(z_k)]^{2^{2^k}} \right) = \Re(z_0) \right)$$
$$\wedge \; \left(\Im\left([\Re(z_k) + i\Im(z_k)]^{2^{2^k}} \right) = \Im(z_0) \right),$$

where $\Re(z)$ and $\Im(z)$ stand, respectively, for the real and imaginary parts of z. Now renaming $x = \Re(z_k)$ and $y = \Im(z_k)$ and letting $z_0 = 1$ (i.e., $\Re(z_0) = 1$ and $\Im(z_0) = 0$), we get the final Tarski sentence.

BASE CASE: $k = 0$, $N = 2^{2^0} = 2$:

$$\Phi_0(z_0, z_1) \; : \quad z_1^2 = z_0.$$

Thus Ψ_0 is

$$\Psi_0(\Re(z_0), \Im(z_0), \Re(z_1), \Im(z_1)) \; :$$
$$(\Re(z_1)^2 - \Im(z_1)^2 = \Re(z_0)) \;\wedge\; (2\Re(z_1)\,\Im(z_1) = \Im(z_0)),$$

or, after renaming

$$\Psi_0(x, y) \;\equiv\; \Psi_0(1, 0, x, y) \;\equiv\; (x^2 - y^2 - 1 = 0) \;\wedge\; (xy = 0).$$

INDUCTION CASE: $k > 0$, $N = 2^{2^k}$:
We would like to define

$$\Phi_k(z_0, z_k) \;\equiv\; \left(\exists\, w \right) \left[(\Phi_{k-1}(w, z_k)) \;\wedge\; (\Phi_{k-1}(z_0, w)) \right].$$

Thus Φ_k is equivalent to saying

$$\left(z_k^{2^{2^{k-1}}} = w \right) \wedge \left(w^{2^{2^{k-1}}} = z_0 \right) \;\equiv\; z_k^{2^{2^k}} = z_0.$$

However, in this case the formula size becomes "exponentially large"! We avoid the exponential growth by making sure that only one copy of Φ_{k-1}

appears in the definition of Φ_k as follows:

$$\Phi_k(z_0, z_k) \equiv \left(\exists \, w\right)\left(\forall \, z', z''\right)$$
$$\left[[(z' = z_k) \wedge (z'' = w)] \vee [(z' = w) \wedge (z'' = z_0)]\right.$$
$$\left. \Rightarrow (\Phi_{k-1}(z', z''))\right].$$

Thus

$$\Psi_k(\Re(z_0), \Im(z_0), \Re(z_k), \Im(z_k))$$
$$\equiv \left(\exists \, u, v\right)\left(\forall \, x', y', x'', y''\right)$$
$$\left[\; [[(x' \neq \Re(z_k)) \vee (y' \neq \Im(z_k)) \vee (x'' \neq u) \vee (y'' \neq v)]\right.$$
$$\wedge [(x' \neq u) \vee (y' \neq v) \vee (x'' \neq \Re(z_0)) \vee (y'' \neq \Im(Z_0))]]$$
$$\left. \vee \; \; \Psi_{k-1}(x', y', x'', y'')\right].$$

Finally, after renaming, we have

$$\Psi_k(x, y) \equiv \Psi_k(1, 0, x, y).$$

Bibliographic Notes

The study of *real closed field* was initiated by Artin and Schreier in the late twenties in order to understand certain *nonalgebraic properties* (such as positiveness, reality, etc.) of the numbers in an algebraic number field. (See [8].) These topics are also discussed extensively in the standard algebra textbooks. See, for instance: Jacobson [105] and van der Waerden [204].

Fourier is usually credited with the idea of solving an algebraic equation (for a real solution) in two steps: a *root isolation* step followed by an *approximation* step. These ideas lead to what has come to be known *Sturm's theory*. During the period between 1796 and 1820, Budan (1807) and Fourier (1796 and 1820) achieved initial success in devising an algorithm to determine an *upper bound* on the number of real roots of a real polynomial in any given interval. (Also, see Problem 8.6.) In 1835, Sturm [195], building on his own earlier work, finally presented an algorithm that determines the *exact* number of real roots of a real polynomial in a given interval. Some later generalizations are credited to Tarski.

Our discussion of the *Sturm-Tarski theorem* is based on the exposition given in Mishra and Pedersen [148]. The formulation of Corollary 8.4.6 is due to Ben-Or et al. [19]. (Also, see Mishra and Pedersen [148].) Our discussion of the bounds on the roots and root separation are based on the papers by Collins and

Horowitz [54], Mignotte [144], and Rump [180]. Also, consult the classic book of
Marden on the "geometry of the zeros of a polynomial" [139].

For a discussion of the representation and applications of real algebraic numbers, consult the papers by Loos [133] and Coste and Roy [55]. Our complexity
analysis of various operations on the real algebraic numbers uses fast implementations of the Sturm sequence and resultant computation, first given by Schwartz
and Sharir [185].

A generalization of Sturm's theorem to the multivariate case, embodying a
decision procedure for the *first-order theory of real closed fields*, was devised by
Tarski [200] in the early thirties, but published in 1948, after the Second World
War. However, the original algorithm of Tarski has a nonelementary complexity
and the computational infeasibility of the algorithm made it only of theoretical interest. In 1973, Collins [50] discovered the algorithm, discussed here, and
demonstrated that it has a polynomial complexity, if the number of variables is
kept constant. Many of the key ideas in Collins' work had, however, appeared in
the work of Koopman and Brown [119]. Because of its wide range of applicability, Collins' work has been surveyed for various groups of readership, as in the
papers by Arnon [5], Davenport [56], Hong [100], Pedersen [161] and Schwartz
and Sharir [185]. For an extended bibliography in the area, see Arnon [6].

In the last five years or so, certain significant improvements have been achieved
in the time complexity (both sequential and parallel) of the decision problem for
first-order theory of real closed fields. Some of the influential works in this area
are due to: Ben-Or et al. [19], Canny [40,41], Davenport and Heintz [57], Fitchas
at al. [72], Grigor'ev [85], Grigor'ev and Vorbjov [86], Heintz et al. [92], Renegar
[166-169] and Weispfenning [208].

Assume that the given Tarski sentence involves the multivariate polynomials
$\mathcal{F}$ in n variables and has ω alternating quantifiers

$$\mathcal{Q}_1, \ldots, \mathcal{Q}_\omega, \qquad \mathcal{Q}_i \neq \mathcal{Q}_{i+1},$$

with the ith quantifier involving n_i variables.

The time complexity of the currently best sequential algorithm is

$$\left(|\mathcal{F}| \ \deg(\mathcal{F}) \right)^{\prod O(n_i)},$$

and the time complexity of the currently best parallel algorithm is

$$\left[\prod O(n_i) \ \left(|\mathcal{F}| \ \deg(\mathcal{F}) \right) \right]^{O(1)}.$$

For more details, see the survey paper by Renegar [170].

On the general subject of *real algebra*, the reader may consult the following
books by Bochnak et al. [21] and Benedetti and Risler [20]. Also, consult the
special issue of *J. Symbolic Computation* entitled "Algorithms in Real Algebraic
Geometry" (Volume 5, Nos. 1 & 2, February/April 1988).

Problem 8.8 is based on the work of Ben-Or et al. [19]. Problem 8.9 is
taken from Rump's paper (lemma 2) [180]. Problem 8.10 is due to Mignotte
[144]. The inequality of Problem 8.11 was derived by Collins and Horowitz [54].
Problem 8.13 is motivated by [54], though Collins and Horowitz's techniques

will produce a somewhat sharper bound. Problems 8.14 and 8.15 are due to Mahler [136,137]. Problem 8.16 (ii) is from [55]. A solution to *robot motion planning problem* (Problem 8.20) was given by Reif [166] and Schwartz and Sharir [185]. A more efficient solution is due to Canny [40] and uses a stratification to study connectivity of semialgebraic sets. Problems 8.21, 8.22 and 8.23 are due to Davenport and Heintz [57].

Appendix A:
Matrix Algebra

A.1 Matrices

Let S be a commutative ring. We write $M_{m \times n}(S) \in S^{m \times n}$ to denote the class of matrices with m rows and n columns and with entries in S. Consider $A \in M_{m \times n}(S)$:

$$A = (a_{i,j}) = \begin{bmatrix} a_{1,1} & a_{1,2} & \cdots & a_{1,n} \\ a_{2,1} & a_{2,2} & \cdots & a_{2,n} \\ \vdots & \vdots & \ddots & \vdots \\ a_{m,1} & a_{m,2} & \cdots & a_{m,n} \end{bmatrix}$$

We write $A_{.,i}$ to denote the ith column of A and $A_{i,.}$ to denote the ith row. We also write $A_{i,j}$ to denote the submatrix of A obtained from A by deleting the ith row and the jth column.

The *transpose* of a matrix A is the matrix A^T obtained by exchanging the rows and columns of A:

$$A^T = (a_{j,i}).$$

The class of $n \times n$ square matrices with entries in S is denoted by $M_n(S)$. The set of such matrices form a ring, with matrix addition and matrix multiplication, defined as follows.

Assume A and $B \in M_n(S)$. Then

$$C = A + B \quad \Rightarrow \quad c_{i,j} = a_{i,j} + b_{i,j}, \qquad i = 1, \dots, n, \ j = 1, \dots, n,$$

and

$$C = A \cdot B \quad \Rightarrow \quad c_{i,j} = \sum_{k=1}^{n} a_{i,k}\, b_{k,j}, \qquad i = 1, \dots, n, \ j = 1, \dots, n.$$

The additive identity is the zero matrix 0_n and the multiplicative identity is the "identity" matrix I_n:

$$0_n = \begin{bmatrix} 0 & 0 & \cdots & 0 \\ 0 & 0 & \cdots & 0 \\ \vdots & \vdots & \ddots & \vdots \\ 0 & 0 & \cdots & 0 \end{bmatrix}, \qquad I_n = \begin{bmatrix} 1 & 0 & \cdots & 0 \\ 0 & 1 & \cdots & 0 \\ \vdots & \vdots & \ddots & \vdots \\ 0 & 0 & \cdots & 1 \end{bmatrix}.$$

A.2   Determinant

Definition A.2.1 (Determinant) The *determinant* of an $n \times n$ square matrix $A = (a_{i,j})$ is defined by the following *Laplace expansion* formula:

$$\det(A) = \begin{cases} a_{1,1}, & \text{if } n = 1; \\ \sum_{i=1}^{n}(-1)^{i+1} a_{i,1} \det(A_{i,1}), & \text{if } n > 1. \quad \square \end{cases}$$

We also write $|A|$ to mean $\det(A)$. Let us define $A'_{i,j}$ the $(i, j)^{\text{th}}$ *cofactor* of A as

$$A'_{i,j} = (-1)^{i+j} \det(A_{i,j}),$$

where, as before, $A_{i,j}$ is the submatrix of A obtained from A by deleting the ith row and the jth column.

The $n \times n$ matrix $\operatorname{adj}(A) = (A'_{i,j})^T \in M_n(S)$, whose $(i, j)^{\text{th}}$ entry is the $(j, i)^{\text{th}}$ *cofactor* of A, is called the *adjoint* of A.

The Laplace expansion formula can be generalized as follows:

Expansion with respect to the ith row:

$$\det(A) = \sum_{j=1}^{n} a_{i,j} A'_{i,j},$$

where $A'_{i,j}$ are the cofactors of A.

Expansion with respect to the jth column:

$$\det(A) = \sum_{i=1}^{n} a_{i,j} A'_{i,j},$$

where $A'_{i,j}$ are again the cofactors of A.

Thus,

$$A \cdot \operatorname{adj}(A) = \operatorname{adj}(A) \cdot A = \det(A) \cdot I.$$

Let $\pi \in S_n$ be a permutation of $[1, n] \subset \mathbb{Z}$. Define the *sign* of a permutation π as follows:

$$\begin{aligned}
\mathrm{sgn}(i) &= +1, & i &= \text{identity permutation} \\
\mathrm{sgn}(\tau) &= -1, & \tau &= \text{transposition permutation} \\
\mathrm{sgn}(\pi_1 \pi_2) &= \mathrm{sgn}(\pi_1)\,\mathrm{sgn}(\pi_2),
\end{aligned}$$

where π_1 and π_2 are arbitrary permutations. Then

$$\det(A) = \sum_{\pi \in S_n} \mathrm{sgn}(\pi) \prod_{i=1}^{n} a_{i,\pi(i)}.$$

The following properties of determinant can be easily demonstrated:

1.

$$\det(A^T) = \det(A), \qquad \text{where } A \in M_n(S).$$

2.

$$\det(A\,B) = \det(A)\,\det(B), \qquad \text{where } A, B \in M_n(S).$$

3. If $A_{.,i} = A_{.,j}\ (i \neq j)$, then

$$\det(A) = 0.$$

4. Let A, B, and $C \in M_n(S)$ be three $n \times n$ square matrices whose columns are all identical except the ith column.

$$A_{.,j} = B_{.,j} = C_{.,j}, \qquad \text{for all } j \neq i,$$

$$A_{.,i} = \xi\,B_{.,i} + \zeta\,C_{.,i},$$

where $\xi, \zeta \in S$. Then

$$\det(A) = \xi\,\det(B) + \zeta\,\det(C).$$

5. If $\widehat{A}$ is obtained by replacing its ith column by a linear combination of all the column vectors as follows:

$$\widehat{A}_{.,i} = \xi_1\,A_{.,1} + \cdots + \xi_i\,A_{.,i} + \cdots + \xi_n\,A_{.,n},$$

then

$$\det(\widehat{A}) = \xi_i\,\det(A).$$

A.3   Linear Equations

Next, we consider a system of n linear equations in n variables over a commutative ring S:

$$
\begin{aligned}
a_{1,1}\,x_1 + a_{1,2}\,x_2 + \cdots + a_{1,n}\,x_n &= 0 \\
a_{2,1}\,x_1 + a_{2,2}\,x_2 + \cdots + a_{2,n}\,x_n &= 0 \\
&\;\;\vdots \\
a_{n,1}\,x_1 + a_{n,2}\,x_2 + \cdots + a_{n,n}\,x_n &= 0.
\end{aligned}
\tag{A.4}
$$

The system of equation (A.4) is said to have a *nontrivial* solution, if it is satisfied by some assignment $x_1 = \xi_1, \ldots, x_n = \xi_n$, $\xi_i \in S$ and *not all ξ_i zero*.

The matrix associated with the above system of equations is denoted by A:

$$
A = \begin{bmatrix}
a_{1,1} & a_{1,2} & \cdots & a_{1,n} \\
a_{2,1} & a_{2,2} & \cdots & a_{2,n} \\
\vdots & \vdots & \ddots & \vdots \\
a_{n,1} & a_{n,2} & \cdots & a_{n,n}
\end{bmatrix}
\tag{A.5}
$$

Theorem A.3.1 *If the system of linear equations (A.4) has a nontrivial solution, then the determinant of its associated matrix A, $\det(A)$ is a zero divisor in S.*

Specifically, if $S =$ an integral domain and equation (A.4) has a nontrivial solution, then $\det(A) = 0$.

PROOF.
Suppose that $\langle \xi_1, \xi_2, \ldots, \xi_n \rangle$ is a nontrivial solution of (A.4). Assume without loss of generality that $\xi_1 \neq 0$. Let $\widehat{A}$ be obtained by replacing the first column of A by

$$
\xi_1 A_{.,1} + \xi_2 A_{.,2} + \cdots + \xi_n A_{.,n} = 0.
$$

Then,

$$
\det(\widehat{A}) = \xi_1 \det(A) = 0. \quad \square
$$

Lemma A.3.2 *Let S be a commutative ring. Consider the following two systems of linear equations:*

$$a_{1,1}\, x_1 + a_{1,2}\, x_2 + \cdots + a_{1,n}\, x_n \;=\; 0$$

$$\vdots$$

$$a_{i,1}\, x_1 + a_{i,2}\, x_2 + \cdots + a_{i,n}\, x_n \;=\; 0$$

$$\vdots \qquad\qquad (\text{A.6})$$

$$a_{j,1}\, x_1 + a_{j,2}\, x_2 + \cdots + a_{j,n}\, x_n \;=\; 0$$

$$\vdots$$

$$a_{n,1}\, x_1 + a_{n,2}\, x_2 + \cdots + a_{n,n}\, x_n \;=\; 0,$$

and

$$a_{1,1}\, x_1 + a_{1,2}\, x_2 + \cdots + a_{1,n}\, x_n \;=\; 0$$

$$\vdots$$

$$\widehat{a_{i,1}}\, x_1 + \widehat{a_{i,2}}\, x_2 + \cdots + \widehat{a_{i,n}}\, x_n \;=\; 0$$

$$\vdots \qquad\qquad (\text{A 7})$$

$$a_{j,1}\, x_1 + a_{j,2}\, x_2 + \cdots + a_{j,n}\, x_n \;=\; 0$$

$$\vdots \quad .$$

$$a_{n,1}\, x_1 + a_{n,2}\, x_2 + \cdots + a_{n,n}\, x_n \;=\; 0,$$

where either

1.

$$\widehat{a_{i,1}} = \mu\, a_{i,1},\ldots,\widehat{a_{i,n}} = \mu\, a_{i,n}, \qquad \mu \neq \text{ zero divisor } \in S, \qquad or\,,$$

2.

$$\widehat{a_{i,1}} = a_{i,1} + a_{j,1},\ldots,\widehat{a_{i,n}} = a_{i,n} + a_{j,n}.$$

If the system of equations (A.7) has a nontrivial solution, then so does the system of equations (A.6), and vice versa.

PROOF.

Let $\langle \xi_1, \xi_2, \ldots, \xi_n \rangle$ be a nontrivial solution of the system (A.7).

Then, in the first case (where $\widehat{a_{i,k}} = \mu\, a_{i,k}$), $\langle \mu\, \xi_1, \mu\, \xi_2, \ldots, \mu\, \xi_n \rangle$ is a solution of (A.6), and since μ is not a zero divisor, this is also a nontrivial solution.

Similarly, in the second case (where $\widehat{a_{i,k}} = a_{i,k} + a_{j,k}$), $\langle \xi_1, \xi_2, \ldots, \xi_n \rangle$ is clearly a nontrivial solution of (A.6). $\square$

Theorem A.3.3 *Consider a system of equations over an* integral domain *S as in (A.4) with the associated matrix A as shown in (A.5).*

Then the system of equations (A.4) has a nontrivial solution if and only if $\det(A) = 0$.

PROOF.

($\Rightarrow$)   The forward direction is simply Theorem A.3.1.

($\Leftarrow$)   The converse can be shown by induction on the size n of the matrix A. If $n = 1$, the proof is trivial. Hence, assume that $n > 1$.

Starting with the original system of equations modify all but the first equation such that the last $(n-1)$ equations only involve the last $(n-1)$ variables: x_2, ..., x_n.

Without loss of generality, assume that $a_{1,1} \neq 0$.

The ith equation is modified by subtracting an $a_{i,1}$ multiple of the first equation from an $a_{1,1}$ multiple of the ith equation. This has the effect of eliminating the first variable from all but the first equation. The resulting system may be written as

$$
\begin{array}{ccccccc}
a_{1,1}\, x_1 & + & a_{1,2}\, x_2 & + & \cdots & + & a_{1,n}\, x_n & = & 0 \\
 & & \widehat{a_{2,2}}\, x_2 & + & \cdots & + & \widehat{a_{2,n}}\, x_n & = & 0 \\
 & & & & & & & \vdots & \\
 & & \widehat{a_{n,2}}\, x_2 & + & \cdots & + & \widehat{a_{n,n}}\, x_n & = & 0,
\end{array}
$$

and by the preceding lemma, has a nontrivial solution if and only if (A.4) does.

The associated matrix is given by:

$$
\widehat{A} =
\begin{bmatrix}
a_{1,1} & a_{1,2} & \cdots & a_{1,n} \\
0 & \widehat{a_{2,2}} & \cdots & \widehat{a_{2,n}} \\
\vdots & \vdots & \ddots & \vdots \\
0 & \widehat{a_{n,2}} & \cdots & \widehat{a_{n,n}}
\end{bmatrix}
=
\begin{bmatrix}
a_{1,1} & a_{1,2} & \cdots & a_{1,n} \\
0 & & & \\
\vdots & & \widehat{A_{1,1}} & \\
0 & & &
\end{bmatrix}
$$

Since $\det(A) = \det(\widehat{A}) = a_{1,1}\det(\widehat{A_{1,1}}) = 0$, and since $a_{1,1} \neq 0$, $\det(\widehat{A_{1,1}}) = 0$. Thus by the inductive hypothesis, the following system:

$$
\begin{array}{ccccc}
\widehat{a_{2,2}}\, x_2 & + & \cdots & + & \widehat{a_{2,n}}\, x_n & = & 0 \\
 & & & & & \vdots & \\
\widehat{a_{n,2}}\, x_2 & + & \cdots & + & \widehat{a_{n,n}}\, x_n & = & 0.
\end{array}
$$

has a nontrivial solution, say $\langle \xi_2, \ldots, \xi_n \rangle$. Then,

$$
\left\langle -(a_{1,2}\xi_2 + \cdots + a_{1,n}\xi_n),\ a_{1,1}\xi_2,\ \cdots,\ a_{1,1}\xi_n \right\rangle,
$$

is a nontrivial solution of the original system of equation (A.4). $\square$

Bibliography

[1] S.S. Abhyankar. *A Glimpse of Algebraic Geometry*. Lokamanya Tilak Memorial Lectures, University of Poona, Poona, India, 1969.

[2] S.S. Abhyankar. Historical Rambling in Algebraic Geometry. *American Mathematical Monthly*, 83(6):409–448, 1976.

[3] A.V. Aho, J.E. Hopcroft, and J.D. Ullman. *The Design and Analysis of Computer Algorithms*. Addison-Wesley Publishing Company, Reading, Massachusetts, 1974.

[4] A.G. Akritas. *Elements of Computer Algebra with Applications*. John Wiley & Sons, Inc., Publishers, New York, 1989.

[5] D.S. Arnon. *Algorithms for the Geometry of Semi-Algebraic Sets*. Ph.D. thesis, University of Wisconsin, Madison, 1981. (Technical Report No. 436.)

[6] D.S. Arnon. A Bibliography of Quantifier Elimination for Real Closed Fields. *J. Symbolic Computation*, 5(1-2):267–274, 1988.

[7] E. Artin. *Elements of Algebraic Geometry*. Courant Institute of Mathematical Sciences, New York University, New York, 1955.

[8] E. Artin and O. Schreier. Algebraische Konstruktion Reeller Körper. *Abh. Math. Sam. Hamburg*, 5:83–115, 1926.

[9] M.F. Atiyah and I.G. Macdonald. *Notes on Commutative Algebra*. Mathematical Institute, Oxford, July 1966.

[10] C.W. Ayoub. On Constructing Bases for Ideals in Polynomial Rings over the Integers. *J. of Number Theory*, 17:204–225, 1983.

[11] B. Barkee and J. Ecks. *Buchberger Theory: Techniques with Polynomials for Computer and Mathematical Applications*. Unpublished manuscript, 1989.

[12] B. Barkee. *Groebner Bases: The Ancient Secret Mystic Power of the Algu Compubraicus: A Reveletion Whose Simplicity Will Make Ladies Swoon and Grown Men Cry*. Report No. 88–87, Mathematical Science Institute, Cornell University, Ithaca, 1988.

[13] S. Barnett. Greatest Common Divisors from Generalized Sylvester Resultant Matrices. *Linear and Multilinear Algebra*, 8:271–279, 1980.

[14] R. Bartels, J.Beatty, and R. Barsky. *An Introduction to Splines for Use in Computer Graphics and Geometric Modeling*. Morgan Kaufmann Publishers, Inc., Los Altos, California, 1987.

[15] H. Bass, E. Connell, and D. Wright. The Jacobian Conjecture: Reduction of Degree and Formal Expression of the Inverse. *Bull. Amer. Math. Soc.*, 7:287–300, 1982.

[16] D. Bayer. *The Division Algorithm and the Hilbert Scheme*. Ph.D. thesis, Harvard University, Cambridge, Massachusetts, 1982.

[17] D. Bayer and M. Stillman. A Criterion for Detecting m-Regularity. *Inventiones Mathematicae*, 87:1–11, 1987.

[18] D. Bayer and M. Stillman. On the Complexity of Computing Syzygies. *Journal of Symbolic Computation*, 6:135–147, 1988.

[19] M. Ben-Or, D. Kozen, and J. Reif. The Complexity of Elementary Algebra and Geometry. *Journal of Computer and Systems Sciences*, 32:251–264, 1986.

[20] R. Benedetti and J.-J. Risler. *Real Algebraic and Semi-Algebraic Sets*. Actualités Mathématiques. Hermann, Éditeurs des Sciences et des Arts, 1990.

[21] J. Bochnak, M. Coste, and M.-F. Roy. *Geométrie Algébarique Réelle*. Ergebnisse der Mathematik, Springer-Verlag, Berlin, 1987.

[22] A. Boyle and B.F. Caviness, editors. *Symbolic Computation: Directions for Future Research. SIAM Reports on Issues in Mathematical Sciences*. Society for Industrial and Applied Mathematics, Philadelphia, 1990.

[23] D. Bridges and F. Richman. *Varieties of Constructive Mathematics*. Cambridge University Press, Cambridge, 1987.

[24] W.S. Brown. On Euclid's Algorithm and the Computation for Polynomial Greatest Common Divisors. *Journal of Associate for Computing Machinery*, 18:476–504, 1971.

[25] W.S. Brown. *ALTRAN User's Manual*. Bell Laboratories, Murray Hill, New Jersey, 1977.

[26] W.S. Brown. The Subresultant PRS Algorithm. *ACM Transactions on Mathematical Software*, 4:237–249, 1978.

[27] W.S. Brown, B.A. Tague, and J.P. Hyde. The ALPAK System for Numerical Algebra on a Digital Computer. *Bell Sys. Tech. Jour.*, 43:1547–1562, 1964.

[28] W.S. Brown and J.F. Traub. On Euclid's Algorithm and the Theory of Subresultants. *Journal of Associate for Computing Machinery*, 18:505–514, 1971.

[29] D. Brownawell. Bounds for the Degree in the Nullstellensatz. *Annals of Mathematics, Second Series*, 126(3):577–591, 1987.

[30] B. Buchberger. *Ein Algorithmus zum Auffinden der Basiselemente des Restklassenringes nach einem nulldimensionalen Polynomideal.* Ph.D. thesis, University of Innsbruck, Austria, 1965.

[31] B. Buchberger. A Critical-Pair/Completion Algorithm in Reduction Rings. In *Proceedings in Logic and Machines: Decision Problems and Complexity*, (edited by E. Börger, G. Hasenjaeger and D. Rödding), pp. 137–161, *Lecture Notes in Computer Science*, 171, Springer-Verlag, New York, 1984.

[32] B. Buchberger. Basic Features and Developments of the Critical-pair/Completion Procedure. In *Rewriting Techniques and Applications* (edited by J.P. Jounnaud), pp. 1–45, *Lecture Notes in Computer Science*, 202, Springer-Verlag, Berlin, 1985.

[33] B. Buchberger. Gröbner Bases: An Algorithmic Method in Polynomial Ideal Theory. In *Recent Trends in Multidimensional System Theory* (edited by N.K. Bose), chapter 6, pp. 184–232, D. Reidel, Dordrecht, 1985.

[34] B. Buchberger, G.E. Collins, and R. Loos, editors. *Computer Algebra: Symbolic and Algebraic Computation.* Springer-Verlag, New York, 1983.

[35] W.S. Burnside and A.W. Panton. *The Theory of Equations: with an Introduction to the Theory of Binary Algebraic Forms*, Volume 2. Dover Publications, Inc., New York, 1928.

[36] J. Calmet. User's Presentation of SAC-2/ALDES. In *CALSYF-Bulletin*, (edited by M. Bergman and J. Calmet), Volume 1, 1981.

[37] J. Calmet and J.A. van Hulzen. Computer Algebra Applications. In *Computer Algebra: Symbolic and Algebraic Computation* (edited by B. Buchberger, G.E. Collins and R. Loos), pp. 245–258, Springer-Verlag, New York, 1982.

[38] L. Caniglia, A. Galligo, and J. Heintz. Borne Simple Exponentielle pour les Degrés dans le Théorème des Zéros sur un Corps de Caractéristique Quelconque. *C.R. Academic Science, Série I*, 307:255–258, 1988.

[39] L. Caniglia, A. Galligo, and J. Heintz. Some New Effectivity Bounds in Computational Geometry, In *Applied Algebra, Algebraic Algorithms, and Error-Correcting Codes (AAECC-6)*, (edited by F. Mora), pp. 131–151. *Lecture Notes in Computer Science*, 357, Springer-Verlag, New York, 1989.

[40] J.F. Canny. *The Complexity of Robot Motion Planning*. Ph.D. thesis, Massachusetts Institute of Technology, Cambridge, Massachusetts, 1988.

[41] J.F. Canny. Generalized Characteristic Polynomials. *Journal of Symbolic Computation*, 9:241–250, 1990.

[42] G. Carrá and G. Gallo. A Procedure to Prove Geometrical Statements. In *Lecture Notes in Computer Science*, 365, pp. 141–150, 1986.

[43] B.F. Caviness. Computer Algebra: Past and Future. *Journal of Symbolic Computation*, 2(3):217–236, 1986.

[44] P.E. Cerazzi. *Reckoners: The Prehistory of the Digital Computer, From Relays to the Stored Program Concept, 1933–1945*. Greenwood Press, Westport, Connecticut, 1983.

[45] J. Chazarain, A. Riscos, J.A. Alonso, and E. Briales. Multivalued Logic and Gröbner Bases with Applications to Modal Logic. *Journal of Symbolic Computation*, 11:181–194, 1991.

[46] S.C. Chou. *Proving and Discovering Theorems in Elementary Geometries Using Wu's Method*. Ph.D. thesis, University of Texas, Austin, 1985.

[47] S.C. Chou. *Mechanical Geometry Theorem Proving*. D. Reidel, Dordrecht, 1988.

[48] G. Collins. PM, a System for Polynomial Manipulation. *Communications of the ACM*, 9:578–589, 1966.

[49] G. Collins. The SAC-1 System: An Introduction and Survey. In *Proceedings of the ACM Symposium on Symbolic and Algebraic Manipulation*, Los Angeles, pp. 144–152, ACM Press, 1971.

[50] G. Collins. Quantifier Elimination for Real Closed Fields by Cylindrical Algebraic Decomposition, Volume 33 of *Second GI Conference on Automata Theory and Formal Languages, Lecture Notes in Computer Science*, pp. 134–183. Springer-Verlag, Berlin, 1975.

[51] G.E. Collins. Polynomial Remainder Sequences and Determinants. *American Mathematical Monthly*, 73:708–712, 1966.

[52] G.E. Collins. Subresultants and Reduced Polynomial Remainder Sequences. *Journal of Association for Computing Machinery*, 14:128–142, 1967.

[53] G.E. Collins. The Calculation of Multivariate Polynomial Resultants. *Journal of Association for Computing Machinery*, 19:515–532, 1971.

[54] G.E. Collins and E. Horowitz. The Minimum Root Separation of a Polynomial. *Mathematics of Computation*, 28(126):589–597, April 1974.

[55] M. Coste and M.F. Roy. Thom's Lemma, the Coding of Real Algebraic Numbers and the Computation of the Topology of Semialgebraic Sets. *J. Symbolic Computation*, 5(1-2):121–129, 1988.

[56] J.H. Davenport. Computer Algebra for Cylindrical Algebraic Decomposition. Technical Report S-100 44, The Royal Institute of Technology, Stockholm, Sweden, 1985.

[57] J.H. Davenport and J. Heintz. Real Quantifier Elimination Is Doubly Exponential. *J. Symbolic Computation*, 5(1-2):29–35, 1988.

[58] J.H. Davenport, Y. Siret, and E. Tournier. *Computer Algebra: Systems and Algorithms for Algebraic Computation*. Academic Press, San Diego, California, 1988.

[59] M. Davis. Relationship Between Mathematical Logic and Computer Science. Courant Institute of Mathematical Sciences, New York University, New York, 1987.

[60] P.J. Davis and E. Cerutti. FORMAC Meets Pappus. *The American Mathematical Monthly*, 76:895–905, 1969.

[61] A. Dickenstein, N. Fitchas, M. Giusti, and C. Sessa. The Membership Problem for Unmixed Polynomial Ideals Is Solvable in Subexponential Time. In *Proceedings of Applied Algebra, Algebraic Algorithms, and Error-Correcting Codes-7*, Toulouse, 1989.

[62] L.E. Dickson. Finiteness of the Odd Perfect and Primitive Abundant Numbers with n Distinct Prime Factors. *American Journal of Mathematics*, 35:413–426, 1913.

[63] J. Dieudonné. *History of Algebraic Geometry.* Wadsworth Advanced Books and Software, A Division of Wadsworth, Inc., Monterey, California, 1985. Translated from French by Judith D. Sally.

[64] T. Dubé, B. Mishra, and C. K. Yap. *Admissible Orderings and Bounds for Gröbner Bases Normal Form Algorithm.* Technical Report No. 88, Courant Institute of Mathematical Sciences, New York University, New York, 1986.

[65] T. Dubé, B. Mishra, and C. K. Yap. Complexity of Buchberger's Algorithm for Gröbner Bases. Extended Abstract, New York University, New York, 1986.

[66] T.W. Dubé. *Quantitative Analysis Problems in Computer Algebra: Gröbner Bases and the Nullstellensatz.* Ph.D. thesis, Courant Institute of Mathematical Sciences, New York University, New York, 1989.

[67] H.M. Edwards. *Kronecker's Views on the Foundations of Mathematics.* Courant Institute of Mathematical Sciences, New York University, New York, 1989.

[68] H.M. Edwards. An Appreciation of Kronecker. *Mathematical Intelligencer,* 9(1):28–35, 1987.

[69] C. Engelman. MATHLAB-68. In *Proceedings of IFIP 68,* pp. 462–467, North-Holland, Amsterdam, 1969.

[70] G. Farin. *Curves and Surfaces for Computer-Aided Geometric Design.* Academic Press, Boston, Massachusetts, 1988.

[71] J.P. Fitch. The Cambridge Algebra System—An Overview. In *Proceedings of SHARE European Association Anniversary Meeting,* Dublin, 1975.

[72] N. Fitchas, A. Galligo, and J. Morgenstern. Algorithmes Rapides en Sequentiel et en Parallel pour l'Élimination de Quantificateurs en Geométrie Élémentaire. Séminaire Structures Ordonnées, U.E.R. de Math. Univ. Paris VII, 1987.

[73] A. Galligo. A Propos du Théorème de Préparation de Wieierstrass, In *Fonctiones de Plusieurs Variables Complexes,* pp. 543–579, *Lecture Notes in Mathematics,* 409, Springer-Verlag, New York, 1973.

[74] A. Galligo. Théorème de division et stabilité en géométrie analytique locale. *Ann. Inst. Fourier,* 29:107–184, 1979.

[75] G. Gallo. *La Dimostrazione Automatica in Geometria e Questioni di Complessita' Correlate.* Tesi di Dottorato, University of Catania, Italy, 1989.

[76] G. Gallo. *Complexity Issues in Computational Algebra*. Ph.D. thesis, Courant Institute of Mathematical Sciences, New York University, New York, 1992.

[77] G. Gallo and B. Mishra. *Efficient Algorithms and Bounds for Wu-Ritt Characteristic Sets*, Volume 94 of *Progress in Mathematics, Effective Methods in Algebraic Geometry*, (edited by F. Mora and C. Traverso), pp. 119–142. Birkhäuser, Boston, 1991.

[78] G. Gallo and B. Mishra. *Wu-Ritt Characteristic Sets and Their Complexity*, Volume 6 of *Discrete and Computational Geometry: Papers from the DIMACS (Discrete Mathematics and Computer Science) Special Year*, (edited by J.E. Goodman, R. Pollack and W. Steiger), pp. 111–136. American Mathematical Society and Association of Computing Machinery, 1991.

[79] G. Gallo and B. Mishra. *A Solution to Kronecker's Problem*. Technical Report No. 600, Courant Institute of Mathematical Sciences, New York University, New York, 1992.

[80] H. Gelernter, J.R. Hanson, and D.W. Loveland. Empirical Exploration of the Geometry Theorem Proving Machine. In *Proceedings West. Joint Computer Conference*, pp. 143–147, 1960.

[81] P. Gianni, B. Trager, and G. Zacharias. Gröbner Bases and Primary Decomposition of Polynomial Ideals. (Special Issue on Computational Aspects of Commutative Algebra), *J. Symbolic Computation*, 6(2-3):149–168, 1988.

[82] M. Giusti. Some Effectivity Problems in Polynomial Ideal Theory, In *Proceedings of International Symposium on Symbolic and Algebraic Computation, EUROSAM '84*, (edited by J. Fitch), pp. 159–171. *Lecture Notes in Computer Science*, 174. Springer-Verlag, New York, 1984.

[83] A.M.W. Glass. Existence Theorems in Mathematics. *Mathematical Intelligencer*, 11(1):56–62, 1989.

[84] H.H. Goldstine. *The Computer from Pascal to von Neumann*. Princeton University Press, Princeton, New Jersey, 1972.

[85] D.Yu. Grigor'ev. The Complexity of Deciding Tarski Algebra. *Journal of Symbolic Computation*, 5:65–108, 1988.

[86] D.Yu. Grigor'ev and N.N. Vorobjov. Solving System of Polynomial Inequalities. *Journal of Symbolic Computation*, 5:37–64, 1988.

[87] M.V. Grosheva. Computer Algebra Systems on Computers (Analytical Packages of Application Programs). Technical Report No. 1, Keldysh Inst. Appl. Math., USSR Academy of Sciences, 1983.

[88] Mathlab Group. *MACSYMA Reference Manual.* Laboratory for Computer Science, Massachusetts Institute of Technology, Cambridge, Massachusetts, 1977.

[89] R. Hartshorne. *Algebraic Geometry.* Springer-Verlag, New York, 1977.

[90] J. Heintz. Definability and Fast Quantifier Elimination over Algebraically Closed Fields. *Theoretical Computer Science*, 24:239–277, 1983.

[91] J. Heintz, T. Recio, and M.-F. Roy. *Algorithms in Real Algebraic Geometry and Applications to Computational Geometry*, Volume 6 of *Discrete and Computational Geometry: Papers from the DIMACS (Discrete Mathematics and Computer Science) Special Year*, (edited by J.E. Goodman, R. Pollack and W. Steiger), pp. 137–164. American Mathematical Society and Association of Computing Machinery, 1991.

[92] J. Heintz, M.-F. Roy, and P. Solernó. Sur la Complexite du Principe de Tarski-Seidenberg. *Bull. Soc. Math. France*, 118:101–126, 1990.

[93] G. Hermann. Die Frage der Endlichen Vielen Schritte in der Theorie der Polynomeideale. *Math. Ann.*, 95:736–788, 1926.

[94] I.N. Herstein. *Topics in Algebra.* John Wiley & Sons, Publishers, New York, 1975. Second Edition.

[95] D. Hilbert. Über die Theorie der algebraischen Formen. *Math. Ann.*, 36:473–534, 1890.

[96] H. Hironaka. Resolution of Singularities of an Algebraic Variety over a Field of Characteristic 0. *Ann. of Math.*, 79:109–326, 1964.

[97] C.J. Ho. *Algorithms for Decomposing Radical Ideals.* Ph.D. thesis, Courant Institute of Mathematical Sciences, New York University, New York, 1989.

[98] C.J. Ho and C.K. Yap. *Polynomial Remainder Sequences and Theory of Subresultants.* Technical Report No. 319, Courant Institute of Mathematical Sciences, New York University, New York, 1987.

[99] C.M. Hoffmann. *Geometric and Solid Modeling.* Morgan Kaufmann Publishers, Inc., San Mateo, California, 1989.

[100] H. Hong. *Improvement in CAD-Based Quantifier Elimination.* Ph.D. thesis, The Ohio State University, Columbus, Ohio, 1990.

[101] J.W. Hong. Proving by Example and Gap Theorem. In *27th Annual Symposium on Foundations of Computer Science*, Toronto, Ontario, pp. 107–116. IEEE Computer Society Press, 1986.

[102] V.R. Huskey and H.D. Huskey. Lady Lovelace and Charles Babbage. *Annals of the History of Computing*, 2:229–329, 1980.

[103] D.T. Huynh. A Superexponential Lower Bound for Gröbner Bases and Church-Rosser Commutative Thue Systems. *Information and Control*, 86:196–206, 1986.

[104] D. Ierardi and D. Kozen. *Parallel Resultant Computation*. Technical Report No. TR 90-1087, Department of Computer Science, Cornell University, Ithaca, New York, 1990.

[105] N. Jacobson. *Basic Algebra, Volumes 1 & 2*. W.H. Freeman and Company, San Francisco, California, 1974.

[106] R.D. Jenks. The SCRATCHPAD-Language. *SIGSAM Bull.*, 8(2):16–26, 1974.

[107] R.D. Jenks and R.S. Sutor. *AXIOM: The Scientific Computation System*. The Numerical Algorithms Group Limited and Springer-Verlag, New York, 1992.

[108] H.G. Kahrimanian. Analytic Differentiation by a Digital Computer. Master's thesis, Temple University, Philadelphia, Pennsylvania, 1953.

[109] K. Kakié. The Resultant of Several Homogeneous Polynomials in Two Indeterminates. *Proceedings of American Math. Society*, 54:1–7, 1976.

[110] A. Kandri-Rody and D. Kapur. Algorithms for Computing the Gröbner Bases of Polynomial Ideals over Various Euclidean Rings. In *Proceedings of EUROSAM '84, Lecture Notes in Computer Science*, 174, (edited by J. Fitch), pp. 195–206, Springer-Verlag, Berlin, 1984.

[111] D. Kapur. Geometry Theorem Proving Using Gröbner Bases. *Journal of Symbolic Computation*, 2:399–412, 1986.

[112] D. Kapur. Geometry Theorem Proving Using Hilbert's Nullstellensatz. In *Proceedings of SYMSAC '86*, Waterloo, Canada, July 1986.

[113] D. Kapur. Geometry Theorem Proving Using Hilbert's Nullstellensatz. In *Proceedings of the 1986 Symposium on Symbolic and Algebraic Computation*, pp. 202–208, 1986.

[114] D. Kapur and P. Narendran. *An Equational Approach to Theorem Proving in First-Order Predicate Calculus.* Corporate Research and Development Report Report No. 84CRD322, General Electric Company, Schenectady, New York, September 1985.

[115] D. Kapur and P. Narendran. Existence and Construction of a Gröbner Basis for a Polynomial Ideal. Presented at the workshop: Combinatorial Algorithms in Algebraic Structures, Otzenhausen, Germany, September 1985.

[116] D.E. Knuth. *The Art of Computer Programming, Volume 2.* Addison-Wesley, Reading, Massachusetts, Second Edition, 1981.

[117] H.P. Ko and M.A. Hussain. *ALGE-Prover—An Algebraic Geometry Theorem Proving Software.* Technical Report No. 85CRD139, General Electric Company, Schenectady, New York, 1985.

[118] J. Kollár. Sharp Effective Nullstellensatz. *J. American Mathematical Society*, 1:963–975, 1988

[119] B.O. Koopman and A.B. Brown. On the Covering of Analytic Loci by Complexes. *Trans. Amer. Math.*, 34:231–251, 1932.

[120] A.I. Kostrikin. *Introduction to Algebra.* Springer-Verlag, New York, 1982.

[121] E. Kunz. *Introduction to Commutative Algebra and Algebraic Geometry.* Birkhüser, Boston, 1978.

[122] B. Kutzler and S. Stifter. Automated Geometry Theorem Proving Using Buchberger's Algorithm. In *Proceedings of the 1986 Symposium on Symbolic and Algebraic Computation*, pp. 209–214, 1986.

[123] Y.N. Lakshman. On the Complexity of Computing a Gröbner Basis for the Radical of a Zero-Dimensional Ideal. In *Proceedings of the Twenty Second Symposium on Theory of Computing*, Baltimore, Maryland, pp. 555–563. ACM Press, 1990.

[124] Y.N. Lakshman. *A Single Exponential Bound on the Complexity of Computing Gröbner Bases of Zero-Dimensional Ideals*, Volume 94 of *Progress in Mathematics, Effective Methods in Algebraic Geometry*, (edited by F. Mora and C. Traverso), pp. 227–234. Birkhäuser, Boston, 1991.

[125] Y.N. Lakshman and D. Lazard. *On the Complexity of Zero Dimensional Algebraic Systems*, Volume 94 of *Progress in Mathematics, Effective Methods in Algebraic Geometry*, (edited by F. Mora and C. Traverso), pp. 217–225. Birkhäuser, Boston, 1991.

[126] D. Lankford. Generalized Grobner Bases: Theory and Applications. In *Rewriting Techniques and Applications, Lecture Notes in Computer Science*, 355, (edited by N. Dershowitz), pp. 203-221, Springer-Verlag, New York, 1989.

[127] D. Lazard. Résolution des Systems d'Équations Algèbraiques. *Theoretical Computer Science*, 15:77–110, 1981.

[128] D. Lazard. Gröbner Bases, Gaussian Elimination and Resolution of Systems of Algebraic Equations. In *Proceedings for EUROCAL '83, Lecture Notes in Computer Science*, 162, pp. 146–156, 1983.

[129] D. Lazard. A Note on Upper Bounds for Ideal Theoretic Problems. *Journal of Symbolic Computation*, 13(3):231–233, 1992.

[130] D. Lazard. Solving Zero-Dimensional Algebraic Systems. *Journal of Symbolic Computation*, 13(2):117–131, 1992.

[131] W. Li and S. Swanson. *A Wu-Ritt Characteristic Set Criterion for the Invertibility of Polynomial Maps*. Unpublished manuscript, 1991.

[132] J.D. Lipson. *Elements of Algebra and Algebraic Computing*. The Benjamin/Cummings Publishing Company, Inc., Menlo Park, California, 1981.

[133] R. Loos. Computing in Algebraic Extensions, In *Computer Algebra: Symbolic and Algebraic Computation*, (edited by B. Buchberger, G.E. Collins and R. Loos), pp. 173–188, Springer-Verlag, New York, 1982.

[134] R. Loos. Generalized Polynomial Remainder Sequences, In *Computer Algebra: Symbolic and Algebraic Computation*, (edited by B. Buchberger, G.E. Collins and R. Loos), pp. 115–137, Springer-Verlag, New York, 1982.

[135] F.S. Macaulay. Algebraic Theory of Modular Systems. *Cambridge Tracts in Math. and Math. Phys.*, Volume 19, 1916.

[136] K. Mahler. An Application of Jensen's Formula to Polynomials. *Mathematika*, 7:98–100, 1960.

[137] K. Mahler. An Inequality for the Discriminant of a Polynomial. *Michigan Math. Journal*, 11:257–262, 1964.

[138] M. Mäntylä. *An Introduction to Solid Modeling*. Computer Science Press, Rockville, Maryland, 1988.

[139] M. Marden. *The Geometry of the Zeroes of a Polynomial in a Complex Variable*, Volume 3 of *Math. Surveys*. American Mathematical Society, Providence, Rhode Island, 1949.

[140] D.W. Masser and G. Wüstholz. Fields of Large Transcendence Degree Generated by Values of Elliptic Functions. *Inventiones Math.*, 72:407–464, 1983.

[141] H. Matsumura. *Commutative Algebra.* W.A. Benjamin, Inc., New York, 1970.

[142] H. Matsumura. *Commutative Ring Theory.* Cambridge University Press, Cambridge, 1986.

[143] E.W. Mayr and A.R. Meyer. The Complexity of the Word Problems for Commutative Semigroups and Polynomial Ideals. *Advances in Mathematics*, 46:305–329, 1982.

[144] M. Mignotte. *Some Useful Bounds*, In *Computer Algebra: Symbolic and Algebraic Computation* (edited by B. Buchberger, G.E. Collins and R. Loos), pp. 259–263, Springer-Verlag, New York, 1982.

[145] M. Mignotte. *Mathematics for Computer Algebra.* Springer-Verlag, New York, 1992.

[146] P. Milne. On the Solutions of a Set of Polynomial Equations. University of Bath, England, June 1990.

[147] R. Mines, F. Richman, and W. Ruitenburg. *A Course in Constructive Algebra.* Springer-Verlag, New York, 1988.

[148] B. Mishra and P. Pedersen. Computation with Sign Representations of Real Algebraic Numbers. In *ISSAC '90: Proceedings of the International Symposium on Symbolic and Algebraic Computation*, pp. 120–126, Tokyo, Japan, August 1990.

[149] B. Mishra and C. Yap. Notes on Gröbner Bases. *Information Sciences*, 48:219–252, 1989.

[150] H.M. Möller and F. Mora. Upper and Lower Bounds for the Degree of Gröbner Bases, pp. 172–183. *Lecture Notes in Computer Science*, 174. Springer-Verlag, 1984.

[151] H.M. Möller and F. Mora. New Constructive Methods in Classical Ideal Theory. *Journal of Algebra*, 100:138–178, 1986.

[152] F. Mora. An Algorithm to Compute the Equations of Tangent Cones. In *Proceedings for EUROCAM '82, Lecture Notes in Computer Science*, 144, pp. 158–165, 1982.

[153] F. Mora. Groebner Bases for Non Commutative Polynomial Rings. In *Proceedings for the AAECC, Lecture Notes in Computer Science*, 229, pp. 353–362, 1986.

[154] F. Mora. Seven Variations on Standard Bases. Report No. 45, University of Genoa, Italy, March 1988.

[155] M. Mortenson. *Geometric Modeling.* John Wiley & Sons, Publishers, New York, 1985.

[156] D. Mumford. *Algebraic Geometry I: Complex Projective Varieties.* Springer-Verlag, New York, 1976.

[157] J.F. Nolan. Analytic Differentiation on a Digital Computer. Master's thesis, Massachusetts Institute of Technology, Cambridge, Massachusetts, 1953.

[158] C. Ó'Dúnlaing, M. Sharir, and C. Yap. Retraction: A New Approach to Motion Planning. In *Proceedings of the Symposium on the Theory of Computing*, pp. 207–220, Boston, ACM Press, 1983.

[159] L. Pan. *Applications of Rewriting Techniques.* Ph.D. thesis, University of California, Santa Barbara, 1985.

[160] R. Pavelle, editor. *Applications of Computer Algebra.* Kluwer Academic Publishers, Boston, 1985.

[161] P. Pedersen. *Computational Semialgebraic Geometry.* Technical Report No. 212, Courant Institute of Mathematical Sciences, New York University, New York, 1989.

[162] P. Pedersen. *Counting Real Zeroes.* Ph.D. thesis, Courant Institute of Mathematical Sciences, New York University, New York, 1991.

[163] R.H. Rand. *Computer Algebra in Applied Mathematics: An Introduction to MACSYMA.* Pitman Publishing, Inc., Marsfield, Massachusetts, 1984.

[164] B. Randell, editor. *The Origins of Digital Computers: Selected Papers.* Springer-Verlag, New York, 1973.

[165] G. Rayna. *REDUCE: Software for Algebraic Computation.* Springer-Verlag, New York, 1987.

[166] J. Reif. Complexity of the Mover's Problem and Generalizations. In *Proceedings of the Twentieth Symposium on the Foundations of Computer Science*, pp. 421–427, 1979.

[167] J. Renegar. *On the Computational Complexity and Geometry of the First-Order Theory of the Reals: Part I.* Report No. 853, School of Operations Research and Industrial Engineering, Cornell University, Ithaca, July 1989.

[168] J. Renegar. *On the Computational Complexity and Geometry of the First-Order Theory of the Reals: Part II*. Report No. 854, School of Operations Research and Industrial Engineering, Cornell University, Ithaca, July 1989.

[169] J. Renegar. *On the Computational Complexity and Geometry of the First-Order Theory of the Reals: Part III*. Report No. 856, School of Operations Research and Industrial Engineering, Cornell University, Ithaca, July 1989.

[170] J. Renegar. *Recent Progress on the Complexity of the Decision Problem for the Reals*, Volume 6 of *Discrete and Computational Geometry: Papers from the DIMACS (Discrete Mathematics and Computer Science) Special Year*, (edited by J.E. Goodman, R. Pollack and W. Steiger), pp. 287–308. American Mathematical Society and Association of Computing Machinery, 1991.

[171] A.A.G. Requicha. Solid Modeling—A 1988 Update. In *CAD-Based Programming for Sensory Robots*, (edited by B. Ravani), pp. 3–22. Springer-Verlag, New York, 1988. (Recent update of [172].).

[172] A.A.G. Requicha and H.B. Voelcker. Solid Modeling: Current Status and Research Directions. *IEEE Computer Graphics and Applications*, pp. 25–37, 1983.

[173] F. Richman. Constructive Aspects of Noetherian Rings. *Proceedings of Amer. Math. Soc.*, 44:436–441, 1974.

[174] J.F. Ritt. *Differential Algebra*. American Mathematical Society, New York, 1950.

[175] L. Robbiano. *Term Orderings on the Polynomial Ring*, In *Proceedings of EUROCAL '85, Lecture Notes in Computer Science*, 204, pp. 513–517. Springer-Verlag, New York, 1985.

[176] L. Robbiano. On the Theory of Graded Structures. *Journal of Symbolic Computation*, 2:139–170, 1986.

[177] L. Robbiano. Computer and Commutative Algebra. In *Proceedings of Applied Algebra, Algebraic Algorithms, and Error Correcting Codes (AAECC 8)*, (edited by F. Mora), pp. 31–44, *Lecture Notes in Computer Science*, 357, Springer-Verlag, New York, 1988.

[178] L. Robbiano. *Introduction to the Theory of Gröbner Bases*. Queen's Papers in Pure and Applied Mathematics, Volume V, Number 80, 1988.

[179] L. Robbiano and M. Sweedler. *Subalgebra Bases*. Unpublished manuscript, 1990.

[180] S.M. Rump. Polynomial Minimum Root Separation. *Mathematics of Computation*, 33(145):327–336, 1979.

[181] J.E. Sammet and E. Bond. Introduction to FORMAC. *IEEE Trans. Electronic Computers*, EC-13(4):386–394, 1964.

[182] S. Schaller. *Algorithmic Aspects of Polynomial Residue Class Rings*. Ph.D. thesis, University of Wisconsin, Madison, 1979. Computer Science Technical Report No. 370.

[183] J.T. Schwartz. Fast Probabilistic Algorithms for Verification of Polynomial Identities. *Journal of Association for Computing Machinery*, 27:701–717, 1980.

[184] J.T. Schwartz, R.B.K. Dewar, E. Dubinsky, and E. Schonberg. *Programming with Sets: An Introduction to SETL*. Springer-Verlag, New York, 1986.

[185] J.T. Schwartz and M. Sharir. On the Piano Movers' Problem: II. General Techniques for Computing Topological Properties of Real Algebraic Manifolds. *Advances in Appl. Math.*, 4:298–351, 1983.

[186] D.S. Scott. *Implementing Projective Geometry via Symbolic Computation*. School of Computer Science, Carnegie-Mellon University, Pittsburgh, Pennsylvania, 1989.

[187] A. Seidenberg. Constructions in Algebra. *Transactions of American Mathematical Society*, 197:273–313, 1974.

[188] A. Seidenberg. What Is Noetherian? *Rend. Sem. Mat. Fis. Milano*, 44:55–61, 1974.

[189] A. Seidenberg. Survey of Constructions in Noetherian Rings. *Proceedings of Symp. Pure Mathematics*, 42:377–385, 1985.

[190] R. Shtokhamer. Lifting Canonical Algorithms from a Ring R to the Ring $R[x]$. Department of Computer and Information Sciences, University of Delaware, Newark, Delaware, 1986.

[191] C. Sims. *Abstract Algebra: A Computational Approach*. John Wiley & Sons, Publishers, 1984.

[192] D.E. Smith. *A Source Book of Mathematics*. McGraw-Hill, 1929.

[193] D. Spear. A Constructive Approach to Commutative Ring Theory. In *Proceedings of 1977 MACSYMA User's Conference*, pp. 369–376. NASA CP-2012, 1977.

[194] D. Stauffer, F.W. Hehl, V. Winkelmann, and J.G. Zabolitzky. *Computer Simulation and Computer Algebra: Lectures for Beginners*. Springer-Verlag, New York, 1988.

[195] C. Sturm. Mémoire sur la Résolution des Équations Numériques. *Mémoire des Savants Etrangers*, 6:271–318, 1835.

[196] B-Q. Su and D-Y. Liu. *Computational Geometry: Curve and Surface Modeling*. Academic Press, Inc., Boston, Massachusetts, 1989.

[197] Moss Sweedler. *Ideal Bases and Valuation Rings*. Unpublished Manuscript, 1987.

[198] J.J. Sylvester. On a Theory of the Syzygetic Relations of Two Rational Integral Functions, Comprising an Application to the Theory of Sturm's Functions, and That of the Greatest Algebraic Common Measure. *Philosophical Transactions*, 143:407–548, 1853.

[199] G. Szekeres. A Canonical Basis for the Ideals of a Polynomial Domain. *American Mathematical Monthly*, 59(6):379–386, 1952.

[200] A. Tarski. *A Decision Method for Elementary Algebra and Geometry*. University of California Press, Berkeley, California, 1951.

[201] R.G. Tobey. Significant Problems in Symbolic Mathematics. In *Proceedings of the 1968 Summer Institute on Symbolic Mathematical Computation*, IBM Boston Programming Center, Cambridge, Massachusetts, 1969.

[202] W. Trinks. Ueber B. Buchbergers verfahren systeme algebraischer gleichungen zu loesen. *J. of Number Theory*, 10:475–488, 1978.

[203] A. van den Essen. A Criterion to Determine if a Polynomial Map Is Invertible and to Compute the Inverse. *Comm. Algebra*, 18:3183–3186, 1990.

[204] B.L. van der Waerden. *Algebra, Volumes 1 & 2*. Frederick Ungar Publishing Co., New York, 1970.

[205] J.A. van Hulzen and J. Calmet. Computer Algebra Systems, In *Computer Algebra: Symbolic and Algebraic Computation*, (edited by B. Buchberger, G.E. Collins and R. Loos), pp. 221–244, Springer-Verlag, New York, 1982.

[206] A. van Wijngaarden, B.J. Mailloux, J.E.L. Peck, C.H.A. Koster, M.Sintzoff, L.G.L.T. Meertens C.H. Lindsey, and R.G. Fisker. *Revised Report on the Algorithmic Language ALGOL 68*. Springer-Verlag, New York, 1976.

[207] S.M. Watt. *Bounded Parallelism in Computer Algebra*. Ph.D. thesis, Department of Mathematics, University of Waterloo, Ontario, 1986.

[208] V. Weispfenning. The Complexity of Linear Problems in Fields. *Journal of Symbolic Computation*, 5:3–27, 1988.

[209] S. Wolfram. *Mathematica: A System for Doing Mathematics by Computer*. Addison-Wesley, Reading, Massachusetts, 1988.

[210] W-T. Wu. On the Decision Problem and the Mechanization of Theorem Proving in Elementary Geometry. *Scientia Sinica*, 21:157–179, 1978.

[211] W-T. Wu. Basic Principles of Mechanical Theorem Proving in Geometries. *Journal of Sys. Sci. and Math. Sci.*, 4(3):207–235, 1984. Also in *Journal of Automated Reasoning*, 2(4):221–252, 1986.

[212] W-T. Wu. *Some Recent Advances in Mechanical Theorem Proving of Geometries*, Volume 29 of *Automated Theorem Proving: After 25 Years, Contemporary Mathematics*, pp. 235–242. American Mathematical Society, Providence, Rhode Island, 1984.

[213] C.K. Yap. *A Course on Solving Systems of Polynomial Equations*. Courant Institute of Mathematical Sciences, New York University, New York, 1989.

[214] C.K. Yap. A Double-Exponential Lower Bound for Degree-Compatible Gröbner Bases. *Journal of Symbolic Computation*, 12:1–27, 1991.

[215] G. Zacharias. Generalized Gröbner Bases in Commutative Polynomial Rings. Master's thesis, Massachusetts Institute of Technology, Cambridge, Massachusetts, 1978.

[216] O. Zariski and P. Samuel. *Commutative Algebra, Volumes 1 & 2*. Springer-Verlag, New York, 1960.

[217] H.G. Zimmer. *Computational Problems, Methods, and Results in Algebraic Number Theory*, Volume 268 of *Lecture Notes in Mathematics*. Springer-Verlag, New York, 1972.

[218] R. Zippel. *Algebraic Manipulation*. Massachusetts Institute of Technology, Cambridge, Massachusetts, 1987.

Index

λ-calculus, 4

AAAS, American Association for the Advancement of Science, 21
AAECC, Applicable Algebra in Engineering, Communication and Computer Science, 21
Abelian group,
    congruence, 26
    residue class, 26
ACM SIGSAM, Association for Computing Machinery, Special Interest Group on Symbolic and Algebraic Manipulation, 21
ACS, American Chemical Society, 21
ADDITION algorithm for algebraic numbers, 332
ADDITIVEINVERSE algorithm for algebraic numbers, 331
adjoint, 386
admissible ordering, 39, 69
    examples, 40
    lexicographic, 40
    total lexicographic, 42
    total reverse lexicographic, 42
ALDES, 8
algebraic cell decomposition, 225
algebraic element, 316
algebraic integer, 298, 316
algebraic number, 298, 316
    degree, 319
    minimal polynomial, 319
    polynomial, 319
algebraic set, 139–140
    product, 141
    properties, 140–141
algebraically closed field, 138
ALGOL, 13

ALPAK, 8
ALTRAN, 8
AMS, American Mathematical Society, 21
analytical engine, 3
AND-OR tree, 359
APS, American Physical Society, 21
ascending chain, 173
ascending set, 173
    ordering, 174
    type, 173–174
assignment statement, 15
associate, 201
AXIOM, 8, 9

back substitution, 134
Bézout,
    identity, 226
    inequality, 182
    method of elimination, 296
Boolean, 14
bound variables, 354

CAD algorithm, 351
calculus ratiocanator, 3
CAMAL, 8, 9
Cantorian/Weirstrassian view, 5
cell complex, 352
    connectivity graph, 354
cellular decomposition, 337
characteristic set, 20, 167–168, 174
    algorithm, 181, 186
    complexity, 197
    extended, 168, 178
    general upper bound, 183
    geometric properties, 176
    geometric theorem proving, 186

irreducible, 197–198
  zero-dimensional upper bound,
      182
characteristica generalis, 3
Chinese remainder theorem, 223
class, 172
  degree, 172
coding theory, 10
cofactor, 386
coherence, 6
Collin's theorem, 352
Colossus, 3
combinatorial algorithms, 4
computable field, 73
computable ring, 72
computational geometry, 4, 297–298,
      334
computational number theory, 4, 10
computer-aided design (CAD), 10,
      298
  blending surfaces, 10
  smoothing surfaces, 10
computer-aided manufacturing (CAM),
      10, 297
computer vision, 10, 297
  generalized cones, 10
conditional and, 15
conditional or, 15
configuration space, 10
  forbidden points, 11
  free points, 11
congruence, 26
connected component, 336
connectivity, 298
  path connected, 336
  semialgebraically connected, 336
  semialgebraically path connected,
      336
content, 205
coprime, 205
coset, 25
cyclic submodule, 52
cylindrical algebraic decomposition,
      CAD, 298, 337, 348, 359

data structures, 7
decomposition, 298
DEDUCE, 3

delineability, 339
dependent variables, 141
deque, 14
DETACH algorithm, 92
detachability, 71–72, 87–92, 213
  correctness, 92
  detachable ring, 72
  in Euclidean domain, 213
determinant, 386
determinant polynomial, 241–242
Dickson's lemma, 36–37, 69
differentiation, 239
dimension, 186
discriminant, 225, 240
divisors, 199
  common, 200
  maximal common, 200
  proper, 201

EDVAC, 3
effective Hilbert's Nullstellensatz, 166
eliminant, 225
elimination ideal, 136–137
elimination theory, 2, 20, 225
ENIAC, 3
Entsheidungsproblem, 3
Euclid's algorithm, 213, 226
Euclidean domain, 199, 208
Euclidean polynomial remainder se-
      quence, EPRS, 248
Euler's method of elimination, 296
extended characteristic set, 168, 178–
      179
  geometric properties, 180
EXTENDED-EUCLID algorithm, 214
extension field, 29

factor, 199
  proper factor, 201
factorization, 200, 223
field, 14, 29
  algebraically closed, 138
  characteristic, 29
  examples, 29
  extension field, 29
  multiplicative group of the field,
      29

prime field, 29
quotient field, 30
residue classes mod p, $\mathbb{Z}_p$, 29
subfield, 29
field of fractions, 30, 197
field of residue classes mod p, $\mathbb{Z}_p$, 29
filtration, 69
FINDZEROS algorithm, 150
finite solvability, 145, 149, 190
FINITESOLVABILITY algorithm, 149
first module of syzygies, 54
for-loop statement, 17
FORMAC, 8
formal derivative, 311
formal power series ring, 70
formally real field, 297, 300
Fourier sequence, 320, 325
free module, 52, 69
free variables, 354
full quotient ring, 30
full ring of fractions, 30
fundamental theorem of algebra, 302

G-bases, 70
gap theorem, 186
Gauss lemma, 211–212
Gaussian elimination, 133
Gaussian polynomial, 320
generalized pseudoremainder, 171, 175
generic point, 197
generically true, 187
geometric decomposition, 198
geometric theorem proving, 10, 198, 297
geometry statement, 187
  degeneracies, 187
  elementary, 187
greatest common divisor, GCD, 17–18, 36, 204
  polynomials, 226
groups, 14, 24, 69
  Abelian, 24
  coset, 25
  examples, 24
  left coset, 25
  product of subsets, 25
  quotient, 26
  right coset, 25

subgroup, 25
symmetric, 24
GRÖBNER algorithm, 85
GRÖBNER algorithm, modified, 88, 90
GRÖBNERP algorithm, 84
Gröbner basis, 20, 23, 44, 69, 79, 84–85
  algorithm, 80, 85
  applications, 71, 103–108
  complexity, 131–132

H-bases, 70
Habicht's theorem, 274–275
head coefficient, 43, 205
head monomial, 43
  examples, 43
  head coefficient, 43, 205
  head term, 43
head monomial ideal, 44
head reducible, 80
head reduct, 80
head reduction, 71, 80
HEADREDUCTION algorithm, 83
HEADREDUCTION algorithm, modified, 88–90
Hensel's lemma, 223
Hilbert Basissatz, 69
Hilbert's basis theorem, 6, 23, 48, 69, 71
  stronger form, 102–103
Hilbert's Nullstellensatz, 13, 134, 142–143, 182, 226
Hilbert's program, 3
homomorphism, 31
  image, 31
  kernel, 31
  module, 50

ideal, 23, 28, 69, 139
  annihilator, 34
  basis, 23, 28
  codimension, 141
  comaximal, 34
  contraction, 32
  coprime, 34
  dimension, 141

extension, 33
generated by, 28
Gröbner basis, 23
Hilbert's basis theorem, 23
ideal operations, 33
improper, 28
intersection, 33
modular law, 34
monomial ideal, 37
power, 33
principal, 28
product, 33, 71, 103–104
properties of ideal operations,
    34
proper, 28
quotient, 34, 103, 106–107
radical, 34
subideal, 28
sum, 33, 103–104
system of generators, 28
zero-dimensional, 145
ideal congruence, 71
ideal congruence problem, 103
ideal equality, 71
ideal equality problem, 103–104
ideal intersection, 103, 105
ideal map, 139
ideal membership, 71
ideal membership problem, 87, 103,
    178
    prime ideal, 178, 197
    using characteristic sets, 178
ideal operations, 33, 103–107
IEEE, The Institute of Electrical and
    Electronics Engineers, 21
if-then-else statement, 16
indecomposable element, 200
independent variables, 141
indeterminate, 35
initial polynomial, 173
integral domain, 29
integral element, 316
intersection of ideals, 71
interval, 14, 299
    closed, 299
    half-open, 299
    open, 299
interval representation, 327

INTERVALTOORDER conversion algo-
    rithm for algebraic num-
    bers, 330–331
isolating interval, 324
ISSAC, International Symposium on
    Symbolic and Algebraic Com-
    putation, 21

KAPUR'S ALGORITHM, 192

Jacobian conjecture, 196
Journal of Symbolic Computation, JSC,
    21

Laplace expansion formula, 386
least common multiple, LCM, 36, 204
Leibnitz wheel, 3
lexicographic ordering, 40, 136
    generalization, 137, 142
lingua characteristica, 3
LISP, 4
loop statement,
    until, 16
    while, 16

Macdonald-Morris conjecture, 9
MACSYMA, 8, 9
Maple, 9
Mathematica, 9
MATHLAB-68, 8, 9
matrix, 385
    addition, 385
    adjoint, 386
    cofactor, 386
    determinant, 386
    identity matrix, 386
    multiplication, 385
    submatrix, 385
matrix of a polynomial, 242
maximal common divisor, 204
mechanical theorem proving, 167
minimal ascending set, 179–180
minimal common multiplier, 204
minimal polynomial, 319
modular law, 34

module, 23, 50, 69
    basis, 52
    examples, 50
    free, 52
    homomorphism, 50
    module of fractions, 50
    Noetherian, 53
    quotient submodule, 51
    submodule, 51
    syzygy, 23, 54
module homomorphism, 50
module of fractions, 50
monic polynomial, 205
monogenic submodule, 52
monomial, 36
    degree, 36
    head monomial, 43
monomial ideal, 37
    head monomial ideal, 44
multiple, 199
    common multiple, 200
    minimal common multiple, 200
MULTIPLICATION algorithm for alge-
        braic numbers, 333
MULTIPLICATIVEINVERSE algorithm
        for algebraic numbers, 331
muMATH, 9

NEWGRÖBNER algorithm, 90
NEWHEADREDUCTION algorithm, 88,
        90
NEWONEHEADREDUCTION algorithm,
        88
nilpotent, 29
Noetherianness, 6
noncommutative ring, 69
normal form, 80
NORMALIZE algorithm for algebraic
        numbers, 329
Nullstellensatz, 13, 134, 142–143, 182,
        226

offset surface, 11
ONEHEADREDUCTION algorithm, 83
ONEHEADREDUCTION algorithm, mod-
        ified, 88
order isomorphism, 301

order representation, 327
ordered field, 298
    Archimedean, 301
    induced ordering, 301
ordering, ≺, 171

parallelization, 7
path connected, 336
Pilot ACE, 3
pivoting, 133
PM, 8
polynomial, 35, 36
    degree, 35, 36
    length, 36
    multivariate, 35
    ordering, 172
    rank, 172
    repeated factor, 239
    ring, 35
    similarity, 247
    square-free, 239
    univariate, 35
polynomial remainder sequence, PRS,
        226, 247–249, 266, 271
    Euclidean polynomial remain-
        der sequence, EPRS, 248
    primitive polynomial remainder
        sequence, PPRS, 248
power product, 36
    admissible ordering, 39
    divisibility, 36
    greatest common divisor, 36
    least common multiple, 36
    multiple, 36
    semiadmissible ordering, 39
    total degree, 36
prenex form, 356
    matrix, 356
    prefix, 356
primality testing, 197
prime element, 200
    relatively prime, 205
prime field, 29
primitive polynomial, 205–206
primitive polynomial remainder se-
        quence, PPRS, 248
principal ideal domain, PID, 199, 207,
        209

principal subresultant coefficient, PSC, 252, 266
    principal subresultant coefficient chain, 266
product of ideals, 71
PROLOG, 9
proof by example, 186
propositional algebraic sentences, 335
pseudodivision, 168, 169, 173, 226, 244
    quotient, 169
    reduced, 169
    remainder, 169
pseudoquotient, 169, 245
pseudoremainder, 169, 245
    homomorphism, 246
pseudoremainder chain, 175
PSEUDODIVISIONIT algorithm, 170
PSEUDODIVISIONREC algorithm, 170

quantifier elimination, 335
queue, 14
quotient,
    field, 30
    group, 26
    of ideals, 71
    ring, 30–31
    submodule, 51

randomization, 7
real algebra, 301
real algebraic geometry, 20
real algebraic integer, 298, 316
real algebraic number, 298, 316, 347
    addition, 332
    additive inverse, 331
    arithmetic operations, 331
    conversion, 330
    degree, 319
    interval representation, 320, 327
    minimal polynomial, 319–320
    multiplication, 333
    multiplicative inverse, 331
    normalization, 328–329
    order representation, 320, 327
    polynomial, 319
    refinement, 328–329
    representation, 327
    sign evaluation, 328, 330
    sign representation, 320, 327
real algebraic sets, 337–338
    projection, 339
real closed field, 189, 297, 301
real geometry, 297, 334
real root separation, 320
    Rump's bound, 321
REDUCE, 8, 9
REFINE algorithm, 329
reduction, 71, 133
repeated factor, 239
representation, 7
residue class, 26
    ring, 31
    of $\mathbb{Z}$ mod m, 26
resultant, 225, 227, 235, 296
    common divisor, 261–262
    evaluation homomorphism, 234
    homomorphism, 232
    properties, 228, 230–231, 260–262
reverse lexicographic ordering, 40–41
ring, 14, 23, 27, 69
    addition, 27
    additive group of the ring, 27
    commutative, 27
    computable, 72
    detachable, 72
    examples, 27
    of fractions, 30
    full quotient ring, 30
    homomorphism, 31
    multiplication, 27
    Noetherian, 28
    polynomial ring, 35
    quotient ring, 30–31
    reduced, 29
    residue class ring, 31
    residue classes mod m, $\mathbb{Z}_m$, 27
    strongly computable, 71–72, 102
    subring, 27–28
    syzygy-solvable, 72

RISC-LINZ, Research Institute for Symbolic Computation at the Johannes Kepler University, Linz, Austria, 21
Ritt's principle, 178
robotics, 9–10, 297–298, 334
Rolle's theorem, 305
root separation, 315, 320
RootIsolation algorithm, 324
Rump's bound, 321

S-polynomials, 55, 71, 75, 79, 133
SAC-1, 8
SAINT, 8
SAME, Symbolic and Algebraic Manipulation in Europe, 21
sample point, 348
SCRATCHPAD, 8, 9
sections, 343
sectors, 343
    intermediate, 343
    lower semiinfinite, 343
    upper semiinfinite, 343
semiadmissible ordering, 39
    examples, 40
    lexicographic, 40
    reverse lexicographic, 40, 41
semialgebraic cell-complex, 337
semialgebraic decomposition, 336
semialgebraic map, 345
semialgebraic set, 298, 334–335
semialgebraically connected, 336
semialgebraically path connected, 336
semigroup, 24
set, 14
    choose, 14
    deletion, 15
    difference, 14
    empty set, 14
    insertion, 15
    intersection, 14
    union, 14
SETL, 13
Sign algorithm for algebraic numbers, 330
sign,
    assignment, 337
    class, 337

invariance, 327
representation, 327
variation, 309
similar polynomials, 247
SMP, 9
solid modeling, 297–298, 334
solvability, 142, 145, 190
    finite, 145, 149
Solvability algorithm, 145
solving a system of polynomial equations, 133, 144
square-free polynomial, 239
stack, 14
standard bases, 70
statement separator, 15
Stone isomorphism lemma, 154
stratification, 298
strongly computable ring, 71–72, 102
    Euclidean domain, 213
    example, 73, 76
strongly triangular form, 135–136
Sturm sequence, 225
    canonical, 310
    standard, 310
    suppressed, 310
Sturm's theorem, 297, 309, 347
Sturm-Tarski theorem, 309, 314, 330
subalgebra, 69
subfield, 29
    examples, 29
subgroup, 25
    generated by a subset, 25
    normal, 25
    self-conjugate, 25
subideal, 103–104
submatrix, 385
submodule, 51
    annihilator, 52
    cyclic, 52
    finitely generated, 52
    monogenic, 52
    product, 52
    quotient, 52
    sum, 52
    system of generators, 52
subresultant, 225–226, 250
    defective, 254
    evaluation homomorphism, 277, 279

homomorphism, 262–263, 265
properties, 256, 258
regular, 254
relation with determinant polynomial, 254
subresultant chain, 266, 271–272
block structures, 266–267
defective, 266
nonzero block, 267
regular, 266
zero block, 267
subresultant chain theorem, 266, 268–269, 274, 279, 296
subresultant polynomial remainder sequence, SPRS, 249, 271–272, 296
subring, 27
successive division, 213
successive pseudodivision, 171
successive pseudodivision lemma, 175
Sycophante, 9
Sylvester matrix, 227
Sylvester's dialytic method of elimination, 226, 296
Symbal, 9
symmetric group, 24
symmetric polynomial, 226
system of linear equations, 388
nontrivial solution, 388
syzygy, 23, 54, 69
  S-polynomials, 55, 71, 75, 79, 133
  condition, 57
syzygy basis, 71
syzygy computation, 93–102
syzygy condition, 57
syzygy solvability, 71–72, 93–102, 213, 215
  Euclidean domain, 215

Tarski geometry, 189, 354
Tarski sentence, 298, 335, 354
Tarski set, 335
Tarski-Seidenberg theorem, 345
term ordering, 69

Thom's lemma, 315, 320, 325
total degree, Tdeg, 181
total lexicographic ordering, 42
total reverse lexicographic ordering, 42
transcendental element, 316
triangular form, 135–136, 167
  strong, 135
triangular set, 134, 137
triangulation, 298
tuple, 14
  concatenation, 14
  deletion, 14
  eject, 14
  empty, 14
  head, 14
  inject, 14
  insertion, 14
  pop, 14
  push, 14
  subtuple, 14
  tail, 14

unique factorization domain, UFD, 199, 202, 209
unit, 29
universal domain, 138

valuation, 69
variable, 35
variety, 138
vector space, 50

well-based polynomials, 352
Wu geometry, 189
WU'S ALGORITHM, 188
Wu-Ritt process, 168, 179

zero divisor, 29
zero map, 138
zero set, 138, 176
zeros of a system of polynomials, 149–150

Texts and Monographs in Computer Science

(continued from page ii)

Edsger W. Dijkstra and Carel S. Scholten
Predicate Calculus and Program Semantics
1990. XII, 220 pages

W.H.J. Feijen, A.J.M. van Gasteren, D. Gries, and J. Misra, Eds.
Beauty Is Our Business: A Birthday Salute to Edsger W. Dijkstra
1990. XX, 453 pages, 21 illus.

P.A. Fejer and D.A. Simovici
Mathematical Foundations of Computer Science, Volume I:
Sets, Relations, and Induction
1990. X, 425 pages, 36 illus.

Melvin Fitting
First-Order Logic and Automated Theorem Proving
1990. XIV, 242 pages, 26 illus.

Nissim Francez
Fairness
1986. XIII, 295 pages, 147 illus.

R.T. Gregory and E.V. Krishnamurthy
Methods and Applications of Error-Free Computation
1984. XII. 194 pages. 1 illus.

David Gries, Ed.
Programming Methodology: A Collection of Articles by Members of IFIP WG2.3
1978. XIV, 437 pages, 68 illus.

David Gries
The Science of Programming
1981. XV, 366 pages

John V. Guttag and James J. Horning
Larch: Languages and Tools for Formal Specification
1993. XIII, 250 pages, 76 illus.

Eric C.R. Hehner
A Practical Theory of Programming
1993. IV, 248 pages, 10 illus.

Micha Hofri
Probabilistic Analysis of Algorithms
1987. XV, 240 pages, 14 illus.

Texts and Monographs in Computer Science

(continued)

A.J. Kfoury, Robert N. Moll, and Michael A. Arbib
A Programming Approach to Computability
1982. VIII, 251 pages, 36 illus.

Dexter C. Kozen
The Design and Analysis of Algorithms
1992. X, 320 pages, 72 illus.

E.V. Krishnamurthy
Error-Free Polynomial Matrix Computations
1985. XV, 154 pages

Ming Li and Paul Vitányi
An Introduction to Kolmogorov Complexity and Its Applications
1993. XXII, 517 pages, 33 illus.

David Luckham
Programming with Specifications: An Introduction to ANNA, A Language for Specifying Ada Programs
1990. XVI, 418 pages, 20 illus.

Ernest G. Manes and Michael A. Arbib
Algebraic Approaches to Program Semantics
1986. XIII, 351 pages

Bhubaneswar Mishra
Algorithmic Algebra
1993. XIV, 425 pages, 9 illus.

Robert N. Moll, Michael A. Arbib, and A.J. Kfoury
An Introduction to Formal Language Theory
1988. X, 203 pages, 61 illus.

Helmut A. Partsch
Specification and Transformation of Programs
1990. XIII, 493 pages, 44 illus.

Franco P. Preparata and Michael Ian Shamos
Computational Geometry: An Introduction
1988. XII, 390 pages, 231 illus.

Brian Randell, Ed.
The Origins of Digital Computers: Selected Papers, 3rd Edition
1982. XVI, 580 pages, 126 illus.

Texts and Monographs in Computer Science

(continued)

Thomas W. Reps and Tim Teitelbaum
The Synthesizer Generator: A System for Constructing Language-Based Editors
1989. XIII, 317 pages, 75 illus.

Thomas W. Reps and Tim Teitelbaum
The Synthesizer Generator Reference Manual, 3rd Edition
1989. XI, 171 pages, 79 illus.

Arto Salomaa and Matti Soittola
Automata-Theoretic Aspects of Formal Power Series
1978. X, 171 pages

J.T. Schwartz, R.B.K. Dewar, E. Dubinsky, and E. Schonberg
Programming with Sets: An Introduction to SETL
1986. XV, 493 pages, 31 illus.

Alan T. Sherman
VLSI Placement and Routing: The PI Project
1989. XII, 189 pages, 47 illus.

Santosh K. Shrivastava, Ed.
Reliable Computer Systems
1985. XII, 580 pages, 215 illus.

Jan L.A. van de Snepscheut
What Computing Is All About
1993. XII, 478 pages, 78 illus.

William M. Waite and Gerhard Goos
Compiler Construction
1984. XIV, 446 pages, 196 illus.

Niklaus Wirth
Programming in Modula-2, 4th Edition
1988. II, 182 pages

Study Edition

Edward Cohen
Programming in the 1990s: An Introduction to the Calculation of Programs
1990. XV, 265 pages